CRITICAL COMPANION TO

Mary Shelley

A Literary Reference to Her Life and Work

CRITICAL COMPANION TO

Mary Shelley

A Literary Reference to Her Life and Work

VIRGINIA BRACKETT

Critical Companion to Mary Shelley

Copyright © 2012 Virginia Brackett

All rights reserved. No part of this book may be reproduced or utilized in any form or by any means, electronic or mechanical, including photocopying, recording, or by any information storage or retrieval systems, without permission in writing from the publisher. For information contact:

Facts On File, Inc.
An imprint of Infobase Learning
132 West 31st Street
New York NY 10001

Library of Congress Cataloging-in-Publication Data

Brackett, Virginia.
Critical companion to Mary Shelley / Virginia Brackett.
    p. cm.
Includes bibliographical references and index.
ISBN 978-0-8160-8123-3 (alk. paper)
1. Shelley, Mary Wollstonecraft, 1797–1851.—Criticism and interpretation.
2. Women and literature—England—History—19th century. I. Title.
   PR5398.C73 2011
   823.7—dc22   2011011882

Facts On File books are available at special discounts when purchased in bulk quantities for businesses, associations, institutions, or sales promotions. Please call our Special Sales Department in New York at (212) 967-8800 or (800) 322-8755.

You can find Facts On File on the World Wide Web at http://www.infobaselearning.com

Excerpts included herewith have been reprinted by permission of the copyright holders; the author has made every effort to contact copyright holders. The publishers will be glad to rectify, in future editions, any errors or omissions brought to their notice.

Text design by Erika K. Arroyo
Composition by Hermitage Publishing Services
Cover printed by Yurchak Printing, Inc., Landisville, Pa.
Book printed and bound by Yurchak Printing, Inc., Landisville, Pa.
Date printed: February 2012
Printed in the United States of America

10 9 8 7 6 5 4 3 2 1

This book is printed on acid-free paper.

Contents

Introduction	v
Part I: Biography	1
Part II: Works A to Z	23
"The Bride of Modern Italy"	25
"The Dream"	31
"The Evil Eye"	37
Falkner	44
"The False Rhyme"	67
The Fortunes of Perkin Warbeck	72
Frankenstein	102
History of a Six Weeks' Tour	167
journals and letters	170
The Last Man	173
Lodore	196
Mathilda	235
"The Mortal Immortal"	254
Proserpine and *Midas*	259
"Roger Dodsworth: the Reanimated Englishman"	264
"Transformation"	267
Valperga, or the Life and Adventures of Castruccio, Prince of Lucca	275

Part III: Related People and Topics	291
Byron, George Gordon	293
Byronic hero	298
feminist criticism	300
Godwin, William	302
gothic fiction	308
hero's journey	309
The Keepsake	311
Paradise Lost	312
Polidori, John William	320
Prometheus	321
psychoanalytic criticism	322
romanticism	324
science fiction	326
Shelley, Percy Bysshe	327
Trelawny, Edward John	333
Wollstonecraft, Mary	336
Part IV: Appendixes	343
Mary Shelley Chronology	345
Bibliography of Works by Mary Shelley	355
Selected Bibliography of Secondary Sources	357

INTRODUCTION

Some may look at the title of this companion and wonder: Does the world truly need another book about Mary Shelley? In the case of this book, the question should more properly be, Does the world truly need another book about Mary Shelley's writing? Distinguishing between those two questions remains crucial. The former question focuses on Mary Shelley's life, while the latter addresses her writing, or art. As with any artist, Mary Shelley's life and her art are inseparable. However, in Shelley's case, the record of her life has too often overshadowed, or even substituted for, that of her art. Such substitution proves understandable, as the facts of few authors' lives are as fascinating as Mary Shelley's. One may go so far as to state that her biography is filled with more of the elements of compelling fiction—including forbidden romance, birth, death, tragedy, and triumph—than are many novels. However, Shelley's life and her art are not the same, nor would she want her readers to believe that to be true. This literary companion makes that point perfectly clear, and it does so in part by introducing a number of writings by Shelley unfamiliar to most readers.

In the case of this book, then, one may answer the question, Does the world truly need another book about Mary Shelley's writing?, with a resounding "yes!"

Casual readers tend to reduce Mary Shelley's work to a single novel—*Frankenstein: or, the Modern Prometheus* (1818)—unwittingly overlooking a rich body of work. This hardly surprises, as Victor Frankenstein's monster has become an enduring icon in popular culture worldwide. We encounter him everywhere (often in the form of "Frankenstein," the name commonly, and incorrectly, given him), from A-grade movies to cheap thrillers; from cereal boxes to lunch boxes; from a name for a kayak (the Wave Sport Frankenstein) to a nickname for a basketball player turned movie grip (6'7", 249 pound Olympic gold medal winner Frank Lubin), to a common term for genetically altered food ("Frankenfood"). The monster and his creator have so captured our imagination that both are continually reimagined in the fiction of others, including a full series by the popular author Dean Koontz. Of course, Shelley's novel is much more than a phenomenon of popular culture. *Frankenstein* has achieved formal recognition in academia, being one of the relatively few novels by a woman author included in the approved literary canon even prior to the expansion of the canon by cultural and feminist critics of the 1980s. Today, the novel appears with astonishing frequency in high school and undergraduate college literary courses.

Nonetheless, *Frankenstein* does not accurately or adequately represent Shelley's entire body of work, much of which would probably surprise even many of her devoted fans. That body of work has gained increasing attention in recent decades from scholars. It includes five additional novels, a novella, poetry, short stories, literary reviews, and essays written and published either by herself or by others. Also crucial are her various letters and journals, recently made more widely available to readers through edited collections. In fact, most of Shelley's works are now easily accessible to any interested reader. At the time of the writing of this literary companion, one could purchase and download to a personal computer a digitized version of all of Shelley's long fiction and much of her short fiction for less than $2. This is a stunning and revolutionary development for those who would like to read more works written by Mary Shelley.

Thus, this companion takes its place as a natural component of the revolution that continues to bring us materials previously out of reach of the non-specialist reader. Now that Shelley's entire body of work is available to any reader, it makes sense to provide plot synopses and commentaries for all of her novels, her novella, and her important short fiction. This book also examines a myriad of political, social, and cultural ideas and events informing Shelley's writing and its reception, in order to spark the imaginations and ideas of students and general readers alike.

How to Use This Book

This volume is organized like the other volumes in Facts On File's Critical Companion series. Part I of this volume contains an overview of Mary Shelley's life. Part II provides detailed synopses and analyses of her major works, including her seven novels, her two verse dramas (treated together, as they have been published in one volume), her best short stories, and her most famous nonfictional work, *History of a Six Weeks' Tour*. Her letters and journals are treated together in one entry. Minor works, such as her handful of poems and a number of her tales and nonfictional works, are not discussed in their own entries, as they are rarely read by nonspecialists. Part III contains separate entries devoted to important related subjects, such as her husband, Percy Bysshe Shelley, and the works of literature that affected her, such as John Milton's *Paradise Lost*, as well as other topics. Throughout the text, terms that are listed as entries in Part III are displayed in SMALL CAPITAL LETTERS, to indicate a cross-reference. Part IV contains appendixes, including a bibliography of Mary Shelley's works, a bibliography of secondary sources, and a time line that also offers quotations from Shelley's personal writings to help elucidate and contextualize the amazing events of her life.

I must express gratitude to my colleagues and students in the English Department at Park University who patiently listened to my ruminations about Shelley and helped sustain my excitement and delight as I became engaged with many of her works for the first time. My greatest hope for the companion is that my enthusiasm will prove contagious and extend to readers. I also offer special thanks to the students who helped manage the logistics necessary to the writing of any book, Rachel Dryden and Rebekah Purvis. I am most especially grateful to that devoted proofreader and interrogator, Claire Petersen, for her continual assistance over the many months required to produce this book. Finally, I extend my gratitude to my husband, Edmund for his endurance and fortitude.

FURTHER READING

Grant, Gordon. "The River Intimate." *Outside Magazine* (June 1996). Available online. URL: http://away.com/outside/magazine/0696/9606rev.html. Accessed August 22, 2010.

Lustig, Andrew. "The lessons of Frankenstein: nature, nurture, & what lies between." *Commonweal* (August 13, 2004). Available online. URL: http://findarticles.com/p/articles/mi_m1252/is_14_131/ai_n9505377/. Accessed August 22, 2010.

PART I

Biography

Mary Wollstonecraft Shelley
(1797–1845)

Mary Wollstonecraft Shelley was destined to live the life less ordinary. Both of her parents were influential writers and social reformers. Her mother, MARY WOLLSTONECRAFT, distinguished herself as one of the earliest feminist radicals. Author of essays, poetry, and fiction, Wollstonecraft held political and social views that gained both great respect and criticism. Her writing drew attention from those who shared her support of the French Revolution and its promise of universal equality, as well as from conservative critics. Mary's father, WILLIAM GODWIN, was a well-known rational philosopher and novelist who attempted to adopt and apply Wollstonecraft's political views to their brief life together. The couple would find their ideology far easier to write about than to live, as their culture was not yet ready for their reformist attitudes toward sociopolitical issues. Both openly expressed their opinions during a time of tremendous change for Britain, which was shifting focus from farming to industry and technology. Not only would Mary Shelley serve what the critics Betty T. Bennett and Charles E. Robinson refer to as "an eager and learned discipleship" with her parents, she would also be strongly influenced by her husband, PERCY BYSSHE SHELLEY, a disciple of her father and radical poet in his own right. Her flight from London with, and later marriage to, the celebrated poet brought Mary Shelley together with one of the most sensational and provocative group of writers of all times.

Traditional scholarship on Mary Shelley tended to focus on her as a "one hit wonder," in light of the consistent popularity of her novel *Frankenstein* from the time of its first publication in 1818. Some readers believed that Percy Shelley actually wrote that novel. That idea was supported by the original assumption on the part of Sir Walter Scott and others that the anonymously authored work must have been written by a male. However, recent scholarship focusing on Mary Shelley's voluminous writings has made clear her complex and wide-ranging imagination in application to 19th-century political and religious views. Her letters and journal entries

Portrait of Mary Shelley from 1840 *(Painting by Richard Rothwell)*

were finally published in the 1980s, showing her to be far different from the dependent and compromising woman previously imagined. Not only did she act as a commentator and critic on both civil and social revolutions, she also supported the replacement of the traditional power-based cultural and political systems with a humanist credo supporting universal love. In a letter written in 1830, she stated, "You see what a John or rather Joan Bull I am so full of politics." While never the radical that her parents were, due to her more retiring personality, she worked tirelessly in her fiction to focus on issues of family stability and openly supported a number of political causes.

Her collected novels and selected works were at last published by Pickering and Chatto Press in 1996 and were republished almost immediately by Johns Hopkins University Press. In addition to her enduring novel *Frankenstein*, Shelley wrote five novels, a novella, two books about her travels, two dramas, five volumes of biographical lives, a myriad of short stories and essays, poems, and editions of Percy Shelley's work. Added to her journals and correspondence, her work fills many volumes.

One of Shelley's strongest influences was her mother. Mary Wollstonecraft lived a brief life that served as a study in contradictions. She rejected the patriarchal view of women as passive creatures and of marriage as a worthy institution, yet she allowed herself to be manipulated by an uncaring lover and eventually pressured by societal mores and civic law to marry. She advocated universal equality and freedom, made obvious through her essays, fiction, travel writing, and political and education tracts, yet she departed from what E. J. Clery refers to as "enlightenment rationalism" advocacy to emotional excess in her personal relationships.

Wollstonecraft had to work to support herself and her family from an early age, due to her father's profligate lifestyle. She supported herself through writing, a pursuit unheard-of for an 18th-century female. She also participated in public debate regarding politics in an arena that involved few female voices. One month after Sir Edmund Burke (1729–92) published his 1790 treatise *Reflections on the Revolution in France*, Wollstonecraft published the anonymous response *A Vindication of the Rights of Man*. She followed in 1792 with a widely discussed work titled *A Vindication of the Rights of Woman*, regarded later as a document that clearly looked forward to the women's rights movement; it would be studied by academicians and students far into the future. Her treatise supported civil rights and career choices for females, but most of all, it stressed the importance of an education for all women. She adopted a skillful rhetorical approach, declaring that unless women gained such freedoms, a moral democratic society could never exist.

William Godwin also responded to Burke with his most famous work, *An Inquiry Concerning the Principles of Political Justice and its Influence in General Virtue and Happiness* (1793). The two were familiar with one another's work, and both were active in a group of writers led by John Johnson. However, as Wollstonecraft traveled to Paris to investigate the culture poised to execute King Louis XVI, Godwin continued to produce social commentary in London. Among his writings was a critique of societal inequity and injustice in his novel *The Adventures of Caleb Williams* (1794).

While in Paris, Wollstonecraft began an affair with the American adventurer and entrepreneur Gilbert Imlay. She became pregnant and eventually had to hide from the terrors occurring in Paris in a lonely cottage outside of the city while Imlay moved on. Despite her public declarations regarding the importance of individualism, dignity, and equality for women, for two years Wollstonecraft pursued Imlay with a desperation that belied her philosophy. After the 1794 birth of their daughter, Fanny, she twice attempted suicide in the face of Imlay's relationships with other women.

Wollstonecraft returned to London and became reacquainted with the 40-year-old William Godwin. He was attentive and supportive, and Wollstonecraft was pregnant with Mary by 1796. She and Godwin attempted living apart in the same neighborhood, which suited both well, the situation supporting their disbelief in the institution of marriage. Both held that the marriage requirement turned women into servants, and it also caused couples to remain together due to the law, rather than love. However, they departed from ideology to accept civic realities and married to protect the rights of their child. Wollstonecraft delivered Mary on August 30, 1797. She contracted blood poisoning due to a botched delivery and died on September 10, leaving Godwin to parent both Fanny and Mary.

In his grief, Godwin published Wollstonecraft's incomplete novel *Maria, or the Wrongs of Woman* in 1798 as part of *Memoirs of the Author of a Vindication of the Rights of Woman*. Godwin hoped to celebrate Wollstonecraft's contribution to society. Unfortunately, the autobiographical novel and other personal details of Wollstonecraft's various relationships scandalized much of the book's audience, and the publication had the opposite effect, eliciting harsh criticism of her. Godwin continued his own writing career and focused on educating both Fanny and Mary, although he remarked that he felt unfit for that position. He attempted to follow Wollstonecraft's ideas regarding education and patterned his attempts after the writings of Rous-

Illustration entitled "The Polygon, Somers Town, 1850," published in 1878. The Polygon was the London housing development where Mary Shelley was born and spent her early years.

seau and others. Wollstonecraft clearly remained in his thoughts, evident in his later edition of *Political Justice*. As Betty T. Bennett explains, he added "private affections" to reason as guides for social behavior.

Mary was clearly his favorite, and he delighted in taking her with him to visit writers such as Charles and Mary Lamb, to the theater, and to pantomimes. Godwin remained widely recognized as an outspoken political activist. With the help of a housekeeper and governess, Louisa Jones, he also attempted to build a solid home in a residential development known as the Polygon, in the Somers Town neighborhood of London. Jones helped Mary learn to read, and Mary followed her father's advice to read multiple books from his ample library at the same time. Even without her mother's physical presence, Mary matured in a household that encouraged her to regard herself as an agent of social change, with the philosophy that every individual should seek to promote such change.

When Mary was four years old, Jones ran off with one of Godwin's protégés. Certain that he could not provide alone the attention required by his daughters, Godwin decided to remarry. After two rejections, a neighbor, a woman he knew as the widowed Jane Clairmont, accepted his proposal. She brought two children into the family, six-year-old Charles and four-year-old Jane, later known as "Claire" Clairmont. In reality, Clairmont was a spinster named Mary Jane Vial, who had lived abroad with expatriates in France and Spain. That she had two children out of wedlock did not bother Godwin, and evidence indicates that she may have been pregnant when they married; she miscarried a short time later.

Others described Clairmont as staid and dependable, with no spark of intellect or imagination. She stood in great contrast to Mary's mother but would serve Godwin's purpose. The treasured days of enjoying the exclusive attentions of her father came to an end for Mary, particularly when Mr. and Mrs. Godwin had a son, William, in 1803.

The new Mrs. Godwin naturally favored her own children over Fanny and Mary, who became close as they shared their disregard for their stepmother. She believed in education but focused most of her efforts on Charles and Jane. Mary Jane Godwin reportedly read Mary's mail, limited her privacy, and restricted the time she was allowed to spend with her father. Situated in the middle of five children, Mary learned to cope. She became independent and willful, but she benefited from exposure to the visitors to her house, including the poet Samuel Taylor Coleridge. Mary would later quote Coleridge's *The Rime of the Ancient Mariner* in her most famous novel, *Frankenstein* (1818). According to some accounts, Mary hid with Jane behind a parlor sofa to listen to Coleridge recite his epic work. When they were discovered, her father told them to leave, but Coleridge requested that they stay. In addition to Coleridge, other visitors included the essayist and children's writer Charles Lamb and his sister Mary, William Wordsworth, Thomas Holcroft, John Johnson, Humphry Davy, and William Hazlitt. All of their works would be among those faithfully listed later in Mary Shelley's reading journal, where she accounted for all of her reading materials.

Mary adored her father, later writing that her attachment to him bordered on the "romantic" and was "excessive." Godwin, however, was often distracted by a need for money. He and Mary Jane Godwin opened a bookshop and publishing endeavor for children in 1805, naming it M. J. Godwin & Company. They relocated the successful business in 1807 to 41 Skinner Street, where the family lived in an apartment either above or next to the shop, depending on which source one consults. The business added to the overall support in the Godwin household of reading and writing by all family members. Not everyone enjoyed those activities as much as Mary. Her stepsister Claire complained later that those who could not produce an "epic novel" that would be included among the best books ever published were "not worth acknowledging" in the Godwin home.

Mary continued to enjoy her father's many books in a library where her mother's portrait hung. A famous image promoted by reports is that as Mary matured, she spent many hours reading at her mother's grave in St. Pancras Churchyard. She probably read not only Wollstonecraft's *Memoirs,* and the critical attacks that work had prompted, but also all of her mother's work. Thus, Mary Wollstonecraft's influence remained strong even in her absence, or perhaps especially because of that absence.

Even while distracted by work, Godwin attempted to educate his daughters based on Wollstonecraft's precept in her *Vindication of the Rights of Woman:* "The most perfect education, in my opinion, is such an exercise of the understanding as is best calculated to strengthen the body and form the heart. . . . to enable the individual to attain such habits of virtue as will render it independent." That would be accomplished primarily through exercise of reason, considered a male approach to learning during Wollstonecraft's era. Her ideas complemented those held by Godwin, who strongly believed in the use of imagination along with reason, the latter strengthened through study of fables and classic history. Such reading encouraged critical thinking.

Mary ignored public condemnation of her mother, claiming the name Wollstonecraft as part of her signature for years. She would eventually depart from her parents' focus on equality through peaceful revolution to support equality within a society that would soon narrow its focus to a rigid Victorian class structure and a worship of materialism. Her egalitarian approach was informed by her unusual family. They were often marginalized by a judgmental society, which also devalued women. From the beginning, her work reflected what was for Mary an everyday circumstance: the emphasis of politics, family, and self-expression through writing.

Mary's formal education consisted of attendance at Miss Caroline Perman's school at Ramsgate from May to December 1811. Known as a school for daughters of religious dissenters, it seemed a perfect fit for Mary while allowing her to distance herself from the conflict with her stepmother. Eventually, all of the children would attend school when finances permitted.

Mary settled in with her family in Somers Town, near London, reportedly publishing her first story, "Mounseer Nongtongpaw," in 1808 through her father's press. It was a reworking of Charles Dibdin's five-stanza song by the same title. Her work was so popular that it was later published in illustrated version with artwork contributed by the celebrated artist Robert Cruikshank. But it was her time away from the family and her trying relationship with her stepmother that would provide Mary with her best opportunity to relax, observe, and write.

In 1812, Mary spent a crucial few months with the family of one of Godwin's admirers, William Baxter, in Dundee, Scotland. She suffered from an unspecified condition in one arm, described merely as a "weakness," and Godwin hoped that her time spent near the ocean would act as a therapy. His concern for his beloved daughter is obvious in a note to Baxter, in which he wrote:

> I cannot help feeling a thousand anxieties in parting with her, for the first time, for so great a distance . . . It can . . . seldom happen that [a father] is the confidant of his child, or that the child does not feel some degree of awe or restraint in intercourse with him. I am not, therefore, a perfect judge of Mary's character. I believe she has nothing of what is commonly called vices, and that she has considerable talent.

He goes on to apologize for any trouble her visit might cause Baxter and requests that Mary bathe in the ocean regularly.

Mary loved the time apart from her conservative, controlling stepmother and became close friends with Christina and Isabel Baxter, with whom she would maintain contact. The family atmosphere of love and trust would inspire the sketching of family relationships in Mary's later fiction, and the Scottish dunes, beach, and hills that surrounded Dundee would provide the background for her novella *Mathilda* (1820; published 1959). Her surroundings greatly contrasted, to her benefit, with those of London. She wrote later that in that stable family environment she at last discovered her "still centre." The hills and woods both literally and figuratively grounded Mary in reality, something her home life failed to do. The critic and author Muriel Spark wrote that the experience caused Mary Shelley's imagination to differ from that of her future husband, the poet Percy Bysshe Shelley. Although Shelley later described her imagination as taking "airy flights," that phrase better described her husband's approach. Mary Shelley's imagination was grounded in reality, a far more reliable substance than the ethereal sphere in which her husband worked.

The same year that Mary visited the Baxters, she met Percy Shelley. He had sought out and pursued a friendship with Godwin, whose work he greatly admired. The two men shared a passion for social equality and the philosophical belief in revolution, although they approached the topics differently. Shelley was born to aristocracy, while Godwin's background was as the son of a common dissenter. Already an established writer, Shelley had published two popular gothic romances (see GOTHIC FICTION), *Zastrozzi* (1810) and *St. Irvyne* (1811), both of which owed much to the era's popular horror fiction. He would later encourage Mary to immerse herself in such writing, providing a tutelage that helped to nourish *Frankenstein*.

While Mary was used to a continuing stream of Godwin's followers and acquaintances in her home, Percy was different. He was much younger than most of Godwin's visitors, openly impassioned, and focused on the future and possibilities for change. As a man born into privilege, he was able to contribute large sums to Godwin's endeavors. He also socialized with Mary's family, bringing his wife, Harriet, to dinner. Percy had married Harriet a year earlier when she was 16 out of pity for what he perceived as mistreatment by her family. He later wrote of his regret for that impetuous act when he fell completely in love with Mary Godwin. Both the confession of regret and his desire for ever more heightened emotional relationships without the accompanying responsibility symbolized Percy Shelley's approach to life. His free-love philosophy extended his desire beyond Mary, as is clear in a

1814 letter written to his friend Thomas Jefferson Hogg: "The contemplation of female excellence is the favourite food of my imagination." He added that "Love makes men quick-sighted, and is only called blind . . . because he [man] perceives the existence of relations invisible to grosser spirits."

A married man of 22, Percy could not resist his attraction to Mary. He arranged meetings for the two at Wollstonecraft's grave, sometimes chaperoned by her stepsister Jane but other times clandestinely. They confessed their love to one another and then tried to end their relationship in deference to his marriage. However, Shelley declared that he could not be without Mary. After deciding to separate from Harriet, he left London for a time. During his absence, in the letter noted above, he told Hogg of Mary.

> I do not think that there is an excellence at which human nature can arrive, that she does not indisputably possess, or of which her character does not afford manifest intimations. I speak thus of Mary now . . . and so intimately are our natures now united, that I feel whilst I describe her excellencies as if I were an egoist expiating upon his own perfections.

He also explained his desperation to leave Harriet, writing that he realized "the full extent of the calamity which my rash & heartless union with Harriet . . . had produced. I felt as if a dead & living body had been linked together in loathsome and horrible communion."

Upon his return to London, Shelley demanded to see Mary, threatening suicide in front of the Godwins. Alarmed by Shelley's behavior, Godwin forbade Mary to see him and guarded her activities, restricting her ability to move about the city. Ironically, such vigilance contradicted the individual freedoms he supported in his writing, freedoms that had also been supported by Wollstonecraft.

No doubt Godwin's conflicted attitude helped prompt Mary, accompanied by Jane (now called Claire Clairmont), to run away to France and Switzerland with Shelley in 1814, spending three months abroad. When they returned to England in September, Mary and Percy expected rejection by their families, who were vocal in their dismay over the couple's actions. However, the pair was surprised by their friends' rebuff. A major loss for Mary was her relationship with the Bridge sisters.

Not yet a married couple—Percy was still married to Harriet—Mary and Percy were forced to adjust to isolation, and they began to rely on one another for all social and intellectual outlets. In addition to being lonely, Mary had to deal with Percy's debts, as he did his best to avoid the many individuals to whom he owed money. Part of Shelley's philosophy of equality was that he who had money best served by giving it away, a philosophy from which Godwin and others benefitted. Unfortunately, his generosity caused him to have to borrow to meet his own family's needs.

Mary delivered a daughter in February 1815, but the baby died on March 6. A journal entry she made shortly after the baby's death may have had an effect on her later writing of *Frankenstein*. In the entry, Mary describes a dream in which she and Percy rubbed the baby beside the fire; their action brought the child back to life. As Mary told Shelley in explaining the dream, the baby had just been cold and only needed warmth for revival. Mary would have continuing reasons to dream of birth and death over the next few years. Critics have noted strong parallels between her seeming fixation on the topics of maternity, life, and birth in real life and her use of those same themes in *Frankenstein*.

The family moved to Bishopsgate, Windsor, where their son, William, was born on January 24, 1816. A few months later, Mary moved with Percy and Claire to Lake Geneva. Claire had had an affair with GEORGE GORDON BYRON (Lord Byron), resulting in her pregnancy. She hoped to persuade Byron to establish a long-term relationship with her, so they could raise their child together. Mary, Percy, and Claire moved close to Villa Diodati, Byron's home, where Claire launched her campaign, but Byron rejected her as a serious love interest.

In 1817, Mary drew on her travel journal entries and letters written home to Fanny to write and publish *History of a Six Weeks' Tour through a part of France, Switzerland, Germany, and Holland, with Letters descriptive of a Sail Round the Lake of Geneva, and of the Glaciers of Chamouni*. The book also included parts written by Percy, including his great poem "Mount Blanc." Although Mary used her mother's *Letters Written During a Short Residence in Sweden, Norway, and Denmark* (1796) as a model, her approach was different. She wrote as an outsider critical of foreign cultures. Later, she would adopt a more sophisticated approach in her travel writing.

Mary described the eight years spent with Percy as happy but also "chequered," an understated description of the upheaval and distress the couple suffered. To begin with, Shelley left his wife, sparking unrelenting personal conflict for Mary. Her life and work would always be marked by what the critics Sandra Gilbert and Susan Gubar term "emotional extremes." Increasing her burden of guilt, Mary, like her mother, suffered strong social prejudice against her position as a mistress, an indiscretion made more grave by Percy's abandonment of his family. Furthermore, Percy did not seem to share Mary's conflict and guilt over their lifestyle. On the contrary, he remained excited by the idea of a free love that embraced open sexual relationships. Mary had suspicions that he provoked Claire's affections, and her emotional conflict further increased when he encouraged her to return the sexual advances of their friend Hogg. Her later fiction would reflect her deep belief in the importance of a strong family unit to mitigate against social ills and the challenges to that strong unit by the male drive for power, both social and sexual. While she supported free love in theory, she also believed that males and females should assume equal responsibilities in care for the family, and that its preservation should take precedence over all. That seemed less possible for men involved in what Eve Sedgwick and others have termed *homosocial* relationships—strong but conflicted relationships with other men.

At the same time, Mary was reading voraciously, and both she and Percy wrote down each title they read in their journals. Their isolation spurred reading, an activity they could share. Many of the early books were horror, including Veit Weber's *The Sorcerer* (1795) and Matthew Gregory Lewis's *The Monk* (1796), among others. In 1814, Percy visited a press that specialized in horror literature, and Claire and Mary together read Anne Radcliffe's *The Italian: or the Confessional of the Black Penitents* (1797). During December, while six months pregnant, Mary read three volumes of *Plays of Passions* (1798–1812) by Joanna Baillie, of whom she had been a consistent fan, in six days. Percy worked on a drama titled *The Assassins*, while Mary and Claire both began writing horror stories. While the group was in Paris, Hogg joined them and they continued their focus on tales of fear. Claire especially was vulnerable to such stories. Mary relates in a journal entry how Claire burst into their bedroom one night, her face "distorted most unnaturally by horrible dismay . . . The skin of her face and forehead was drawn into innumerable wrinkles," her eyes wide and ghastly. Scholars see these incidents as crucial to the production of Shelley's most famous story. They also detect a note of disgust toward Claire, who would be a lifelong thorn in her stepsister's side.

Mary began work on *Frankenstein* in 1816 and completed it in 1817, despite continuing complications in her already stressed relationship with Percy. The circumstances surrounding the birth of *Frankenstein* (1818) are by now quite familiar to fans of the work, although critics dispute some aspects of Mary's account. Mary described those circumstances in the introduction to the 1831 edition of the novel, partially in answer to what she describes as a question frequently asked: "'How I, then a young girl, came to think of, and to dilate upon, so very hideous an idea?'" She points in the introduction to the literary heritage passed down by her parents, both of "distinguished literary celebrity" and of her history as a "scribbling" child, when she indulged in "waking dreams." Her fantasies provided her refuge from an early age as she matured in the country "on the blank and dreary northern shores of the Tay, near Dundee." After marriage, reality replaced fiction until she visited Switzerland in 1816 with Shelley, where they lived close to Lord Byron. One stormy evening, Byron; his personal physician, JOHN WILLIAM POLIDORI; Shelley; and Mary discussed Byron's proposition that each one of them should write a ghost story. She describes the efforts of each, but the group of poets, at last "annoyed by the platitude of prose," gave up the task. Only she continued to think of a story.

10 Critical Companion to Mary Shelley

Photograph of the Villa Diodati in Geneva, Switzerland, taken in 2008. Mary Shelley conceived the idea for her novel *Frankenstein* while spending time at the Villa Diodati with Percy Shelley, Lord Byron, and John Polidori.

Preoccupied, she could not sleep and in bed that night began with eyes closed to conjure the tale that would make her forever famous. She wrote that "the idea so possessed my mind, that a thrill of fear ran through me . . . I could not easily get rid of my hideous phantom; still it haunted me." (It is interesting to note, as the critic Harley S. Spatt points out, that although Byron had proposed ghost stories, Mary's resultant novel contains no ghost.) By the time of the writing of the introduction, the novel had become extremely popular, and Mary should have felt vindicated regarding her abilities.

The novel has always been immensely popular, despite its several inherent contradictions. While it seems on the one hand to celebrate a rational approach to education, it simultaneously undercuts the value of such rationalism, noting the lack of humanity it breeds. Its subtitle suggests a celebration of PROMETHEUS and the idea of Prometheanism, suggesting the ability of humans to recreate themselves. Yet, in actuality, according to Harley Spatt, Mary writes of the irresponsibility and inhumanity of such ideology. The novel has been labeled *gothic*, yet it inverts most assumptions about that genre. Robert Hume calls it a "horror-Gothic" work. Rather than emphasizing the gothic's focus on external circumstance and the suspense such circumstance arouses in the reader, *Frankenstein* invites readers to consider the ambiguous nature of morality by delving into the psychological universe of the novel's two major characters. James P. Davis finds it interesting that Mary adopted the perspective of males, rather than a female, to write her first novel, particularly in light of the fact that her mother was a women's rights radical. Mary Shelley probably did not consider these contradictions when writing the story at age 19.

Compounding the effect of the loss of her first child, Mary suffered through the suicide of her half sister, Fanny Imlay, on October 9, 1816. Two months later, Harriet Shelley's body was discovered in the Serpentine River in Hyde Park, London. Despite the turmoil, Mary and Percy married within a month. Public censure against the two increased. They found some relief in the company of other writers who would eventually be declared the most influential of the romantic poets, including Byron. Byron bore his own scandalous reputation as a womanizer and one who was rumored to have engaged in incest with his half sister, an act that caused his informal expulsion from Britain. In 1817, Claire Clairmont gave birth to Byron's daughter Alba, later called Allegra. Claire's flighty presence through 1820 exacerbated the Shelleys' emotional burdens.

Not only were the Shelleys emotionally strapped, Percy Shelley still lacked income. His father, Sir Timothy Shelley, had cut off all financial support in light of Percy's outrageous behavior toward Harriet and the children. Percy further increased their financial demands by beginning a protracted battle to gain custody of his two children; he would never succeed. When he did have money, he lost it easily, his tenderness causing him to donate much of his funds to others. William Godwin also supposedly accepted more than £7,000 from his son-in-law, convincing Shelley of his responsibility to those members of society not born to privilege. Some scholars focus on Godwin's attitude as petty and opportunistic. However, such support was not only expected but honored by the 19th-century British arts culture.

After the Shelleys relocated to Italy in 1818, Mary lost another daughter, Clara Everina, to dysentery, and her son William died in Rome in 1819 of malaria. The Shelleys moved to Florence, where Mary gave birth to Percy Florence Shelley on November 12, 1819. She and Percy then began a protracted series of moves, relocating next to Livorno (Leghorn), where Mary began work on *Mathilda*, despite, or perhaps because of, suffering depression from William's death. That novel's theme of incest, a popular fictional theme of the day, framed what critics agree are autobiographical references. *Mathilda*'s subject matter so upset Godwin that he would not allow its publication, even though all proceeds from its sale were to go to him.

Mary's attempts to cope with William's death included the belated placement of a headstone at his grave. In a letter dated June 20, 1820, she wrote to Amelia Curran in Rome, "I am afraid that you find great difficulties in executing our unhappy commission Shelley & I are therefore induced to entreat you to have the kindness to order a plain stone to be erected to mark the spot with merely his name & dates—(William Shelley born January 24, 1816–June 7, 1819)—You would oblige us more than I can express if you would take care that this should be done." She made an unsuccessful attempt to draw hope from the future when she added, "Our little Percy is a thriving forward child but after what has happened I own it appears to me—a faded cloud—all these hopes that we so earnestly dwell upon." Throughout these events, the rarely absent Claire constantly pleaded for the Shelleys' assistance in taking custody of Allegra away from Byron.

Mary almost completed *Mathilda* in 1820, following another move to Pisa. A prolific period of writing produced *Castruccio, Prince of Lucca*, which Godwin later retitled *Valperga*, a novel that focused on 14th-century Italian political ambition and intrigue. Mary wrote the verse dramas *Proserpine* and *Midas* during April and May 1822, despite another personal tragedy: Claire and Byron's daughter died from typhus in April. Mary wrote of Claire in a letter that "she reconciled herself to her fate sooner than we expected . . . she was forever forming plans from getting her child from a place she judged but too truly would be fatal to her." Having known Allegra since her birth and understanding too well the grief of a parent who has lost a child, Mary again slipped into depression, exacerbated by weakness following a hasty departure from Pisa to Italy's lake country.

Soon after the move, Shelley bought the sailboat he had long desired, which Mary described as "a beautiful creature." However, Mary was too weak to join Shelley often when he sailed, and in June she miscarried during her fifth pregnancy. She probably would have died due to hemorrhaging had Shelley not had the presence of mind to immerse her in ice water to slow the blood loss. Mary later credited that episode with relieving her of any fear of death. She wrote that at the time she felt if her spirit left her body, it would "be received & sustained by a beneficent & gentle Power . . .—I had a passive satisfaction in death." Unsure whether her loss of blood had been the cause of that "tranquility," she still valued the "blessed effect" and that hour's "perfect resignation." Shelley took gentle care of his wife, even protecting her by hiding Godwin's nagging letters. A man who had never been physically or emotionally strong, Percy suffered from the tension of secrecy, reportedly experiencing daytime hallucinations and episodes of anxiety.

Shelley's rumored affairs with other women, including Emilia Viviana, daughter of the governor of Pisa, began to wear on Mary. He wrote *Epipsychidion* (1821) in Emilia's honor. He was also attracted to Jane Williams, wife of Edward Williams, the man who would later drown with him. Jane sometimes accompanied Shelley on his sailing outings, fulfilling Percy's desire for discussion not focused on his family. He may also have had a previous affair with Claire, based on evidence from Mary's letter dated June 1820. Scholars remain unsure whether Claire is the unnamed mother and Percy Shelley the father of "the Neopolitan child" referenced by Mary as Elena Adelaide Shelley. The Shelleys were secretly registered as her parents, but so were Sophia Stacey, Emilia Viviana, and Jane Williams. Not surprisingly, Percy's unfaithfulness added to Mary's feelings of distance from him in their final weeks together. Her emotions would add to the guilt that she felt when Shelley drowned on July 8, 1822, in the Bay of Spezia, one month before his 30th birthday.

Shelley had set out that Monday morning with Williams from Leghorn to sail for Letrici in order to meet the family of Shelley's friend, the writer and critic Leigh Hunt. When the men did not return, Mary and Jane Williams assumed they had traveled elsewhere, but when no word arrived by Wednesday, they began to worry. She later described the scene to a friend in a letter:

> At 12 noon our letters came—there was one from Hunt to Shelley, it said—"pray write to tell us how you got home, for they say that you had bad weather after you sailed monday [sic] & we are anxious"—the paper fell from me—I trembled all over—Jane read it—"Then it is all over!" she said. "No, my dear Jane," I cried, "it is not all over, but this suspense is dreadful—come with me, we will go to Leghorn, we will post to be swift & learn our fate."

The two women continued to hope their husbands had returned to Leghorn, but all anyone there knew was that the pair had sailed on Monday. Shelley's friend EDWARD JOHN TRELAWNEY set out to search for the men. He returned on July 15 with the news that both Shelley's and Edward's bodies had washed ashore.

In a lengthy letter dated August 15, 1822, written from Pisa to her friend Maria Gisborne, Mary recounted events from her final few weeks with Shelley. She confessed that in May and June, while Shelley was in fine spirits, "I was not well in body or mind. My nerves were wound up to the utmost irritation" while she experienced a great "sense of misfortune." She described nearly dying from the miscarriage but noted Shelley could not have lived without her—"the sense of eternal misfortune would have pressed to [sic] heavily upon him." She then offers a harrowing account of Shelley's dreams that drove him screaming into her room. On one occasion, he dreamed of Edward and Jane Williams that he found them "in the most horrible condition, their bodies lacerated—their bones starting through their skin, the faces pale yet stained with blood." Supposedly, Edward told Shelley that "the sea is flooding the house & it is all coming down." The dream continued with Shelley strangling Mary; he confessed the following day to having experienced many visions.

Grief-stricken, Mary was unhappy when Jane left in September to return to England. The two widows both lacked financial support, and both refused to give up their children to wealthy relatives; Sir Timothy would try to give Percy Florence to Byron to raise. Both women eventually received support from their dead husbands' families. However, while Mary would gain independence through a writing and publishing career and never marry, Jane would move in with Thomas Jefferson Hogg, the man who had once romanced Mary. Although both Jane and Hogg would later betray Mary, she would continue a voluminous correspondence with Jane and even support Hogg's attempts to publish a novel in 1830 and to find employment.

Claire had moved on to Vienna to stay with her brother, and a lonely Mary sought to ease her mourning by working with Leigh Hunt in publishing his newspaper, *The Liberal*. She was anxious to see some of Shelley's manuscripts published. However, Hunt's attitude toward Mary was cold and unfriendly, and he focused in conversation on only the final few weeks of the Shelleys' marriage, when Mary had felt physically and emotionally incapable of her former warmth toward her husband. Hunt's belief that she had done little to support her husband shocked her and added to her guilt. In an October 1822 journal entry, she expressed her feelings of isolation and separation, writing,

> For eight years I communicated, with unlimited freedom, with one whose genius, far transcending mine, awakened & guided my thoughts. I conversed with him; rectified my errors of judgment; obtained new lights from him; and my mind was satisfied. Now I am alone—oh, how alone! The stars may behold my tears, & the winds drink my sighs; but my thoughts are a sealed treasure, which I can confide to none.

Mary had clearly idealized her existence with Percy, blocking the memory of conflict.

Left to raise her son alone and struggle to support herself through her writing, Mary's next move was to Genoa in 1823. She wrote with some optimism in February that year, "I have talent, I will improve that talent . . . and if, while meditating on the wisdom of ages . . . any discovery occurs that may be useful to my fellows, then the balm of utility may be added to innocence." Her language was far less idealistic than in the entry of the previous October, and she indicated an ability and willingness to move ahead to discover her life. On March 19, she added to her journal, "Study has become to me more necessary than the air I breathe," adding that the "searching" nature of intellectual endeavors offered some relief for those of "reverie." She hoped to "become more worthy of my lost one," no doubt remembering Percy's support of her writing. However, because her sense of worth seemed always to depend upon others, she would not reach that fulfillment.

In Genoa, she published *Valperga*. She soon began publishing in various periodicals, and in July 1823 she saw a play by Richard Brinsley Peake, based on her novel, called *Presumption, or, The Fate of Frankenstein*. Mary took her son to London, where the second edition of *Frankenstein* was published in August. Through her travels, she continued to correspond with the Hunts, feigning happiness.

In London, she moved in with Godwin, and he accompanied her to call on Shelley's father. While Sir Timothy would not commit to permanent support, his solicitor gave Mary £100, which allowed her the freedom to live on her own. Best of all, she again became friends with Isabel Baxter, her childhood friend. She was pleased to see Jane Williams again and wrote often to Jane as a sympathetic friend, sending detailed letters about personal subjects, such as Mary's decaying relationship with Lord Byron. While visiting Italy in July 1823, Byron reneged on a promise to give her funds to support her return to London. Fortunately, Trelawney agreed to finance what she described as possibly a slow journey home, due to Percy Florence's delicate health. She told Claire of her "mischances . . . I do not feel them. My life is a shifting scene, & my business is to play the part allotted for each day well . . . as for money difficulties—why having nothing, I can lose nothing."

Despite various problems in her relationship with her husband, Mary felt she bore a lifelong debt for his support of her writing, and she freely expressed her gratitude. She noted in a letter in 1827 that she often felt the importance of the heritage her parents had left her, a heritage about which Shelley frequently reminded her. Her mother's "greatness of soul" combined with her father's "high talents" provided motivation for her own writing. Critics remain unclear as to Shelley's part in his wife's production; for some time, many felt that he actually wrote *Frankenstein: or the Modern Prometheus*, noting it unlikely that a young girl could have produced such a weighty work. Others argue that Shelley proved a hindrance, quoting Mary's own words in the introduction to the 1831 edition of her novel. She wrote of Shelley that "at this time he desired that I should write, not so much with the idea that I could produce any thing [sic] worthy of notice, but that he might himself judge how far I possessed the promise of better things hereafter." In her letters, she wrote that Shelly helped foster her ambition to write, but critics note that fostering could have become burdensome; following such an ambition would mean that she could not focus on her family. At first published anonymously, *Frankenstein*'s author was later identified as a woman, at which time one critic used the common phrase to denote a woman of intellect in describing the author: She possessed "masculine understanding." However, others were complimentary, for the most part.

The conflict Mary felt regarding her husband's relationship to her writing surfaced in a journal entry when she wrote that she felt so timid regarding her ability to participate in conversation between Shelley and Byron that she was reduced to "incapacity." In the introduction to the 1831 edition of *Frankenstein*, she opens with the statement, "I certainly did not owe the suggestion of one incident, nor scarcely of one train of feeling, to my husband," her tone clearly defensive. Yet in the same introduction, she adds that she would never have developed the tale had Percy Shelley not urged her on. One indisputable fact is the presence of Shelley when his wife conceived the idea for her novel.

Mary's personal writings reveal that she felt at a terrible loss of motivation following Percy's death. She noted a lack of confidence, writing that she only desired to keep his memory alive for his reading public. As late as 13 years following Shelley's death, she wrote in a letter that she had always been dependent, needing the support of others, and at that stage felt little worth.

Scholars have found Mary's letters of great value in helping understand her multifaceted character and interests. Her writing in all genres reflected the multiple effects of the time in which she wrote, influenced by political and social revolution, Enlightenment ideas, British Jacobinism, the romantics and their lyricism, the historical novels of Sir Walter Scott, women writers of both the period that preceded her and the one that would follow, and the ongoing struggle between nationalism and imperialism that would influence her contribution to the new genre of travel writing. While later audiences would know Mary Shelley almost exclusively through her first novel, she produced a body of writing extraordinary for a woman of her era. In an 1830 letter to John Murray III, she suggested a number of additional topics for publications, including "an History of the Earth," "The Lives of Celebrated women—or a history of Woman—her position in society & her influence upon it," and "A History of Chivalry."

While devoting herself to young Percy's welfare, Mary produced five novels, a novella, poetry, many articles and reviews, 20 short stories, a travel book, and two biographies. Scholars classify much of the article and short story output as drudgery, done only for income, in contrast to her far more creative novels. In addition, she published critical editions of Percy Bysshe Shelley's works. She had to deal with a doubting public readership while continuing to contend with her contentious father-in-law. Sir Timothy Shelley had strict ideas regarding proper behavior for women that did not fit Mary Shelley. In his opinion, she had committed a breach of propriety by carrying on a writing career. He gave her a small allowance for the sake of his grandson but constantly threatened to withdraw it, becoming particularly unhappy regarding her publication of his son's biography. In 1824, he protested against her making public what he considered private information regarding his family.

Encouraged by the acceptance of her work for publication, Mary continued work on fiction. While she enjoyed some semblance of a private social life, receiving a marriage proposal from John Howard Payne, an American actor and playwright,

Illustration of the American actor John Howard Payne as Hamlet in 1813. Payne proposed to Mary Shelley after her husband's death.

As concerns Mary Diana Dods, the Shelley letters revealed for the first time that Dods was actually the author known as David Lyndsay. Under that name, she published multiple articles in *Blackwood's Edinburgh Magazine*, as well as the well-known *Tales of the Wild and Wonderful* (London: Hurst and Robinson, 1825). Mary was particularly fond of her, perhaps due to her outcast status. Dods was described by the Scottish author Eliza Rennie as "grotesque-looking . . . with a cropped curly head of short, thick hair, more resembling that of a man than of a woman." She stated that upon first beholding Dods, one might imagine "that some one of the masculine gender had indulged in the masquerade freak of feminine habiliments." She did add that she discovered Dods to have an "extraordinary talent . . . was a great linguist . . . and . . . a person of very remarkable mental endowments." Mary refers to "Mr. David Lindsay" in several of her letters, as well as to "Doddy," her nickname for Mary Dods. Without the increase of Shelley scholarship in the 20th century, the true identity of Lyndsay would not have been discovered.

Following Percy's death, Mary developed an enduring friendship with Jane Williams as a fellow widow, which she hoped would provide strength and direction for her life. But Williams betrayed her in 1827, choosing to live with Hogg as his common-law wife and starting a rumor that Mary had rejected Percy in his final year of life. Mary would wait until 1828 to confront Jane and would eventually forgive her, choosing to preserve a relationship that had proved vital to her. Also in 1827, Mary wrote to Sir Timothy, again asking for support, explaining her acknowledgment of the fact that upon receiving "Bysshe's" inheritance, she would gladly refund any advances he had given to her. She tactfully reminded Sir Timothy that only he could supply the means for his grandson's support, writing that she felt confident he would not allow circumstances beyond her control "to interfere with the welfare of your Grandson and the respectability of his Mother." She stated that she regretted not being allowed to see Sir Timothy and asked that he try to place himself in her situation "and not to delay in relieving me from the humiliations & distresses to which I am subjected." In

in June 1825, her focus remained on her son and her work. In 1826, she published her novel *The Last Man*, which focused on the end of man in a futuristic fantasy set in the 21st century. Mary idealized Percy Shelley in the form of the novel's hero, Adrian, Earl of Windsor, in what has been labeled her darkest creative vision. It is the only work that later critics compared favorably with *Frankenstein*, and it seems to express Mary's feeling of isolation and despair over having survived so many of the people she loved.

In addition, Mary's travel articles appeared in *Westminster Review* and *London Magazine*. She also worked as collaborator with Thomas Moore on Byron's biography. Mary participated in subversive activities in her own right. She helped two women friends, Isabel Robinson and Mary Diana Dods, elope to Paris along with Isabel's illegitimate daughter, by securing their passports.

an enormous correspondence in English, Italian, and French, Mary referenced her writing, especially with publishers, but spent far more page space sharing intimacies and anecdotes with friends and acquaintances made over her lifetime of travel.

In 1828, Mary began work on *The Adventures of Perkin Warbeck*, which she would publish in 1830. Modeled after the historical fiction written by Sir Walter Scott, it was not successful, in part due to her lack of any personal knowledge about Ireland. However, she began a successful 10-year stream of contributions to THE KEEPSAKE, a collection published annually as a ladies' gift book. During that same year, she visited friends in Paris and caught smallpox, from which she recovered. She also became acquainted with the French novelist Prosper Mérimée, who proposed marriage, which Mary refused. She told another good friend who proposed to her in jest that the name Mary Shelley would appear on her tombstone. Although rumored to have had romances with various men, including an unreturned interest in the American writer Washington Irving and an affair with the politician Aubrey Beauclerk, she remained true to her word and never remarried.

Mary's often expressed belief in her journal entries and letters regarding her inability to make a successful career, despite evidence to the contrary, may have supported her forced adoption of society's view of the proper role for a woman. Her personal stance on women's roles remains a topic of lively discussion among critics who point to what they see as subversive messages in her fiction that support the feminism first expressed by her mother. She has been labeled a revolutionary by some and a conservative by others. She was never the professed feminist that her mother had been, and some of her personal writing does not support Wollstonecraft or Godwin's belief in social equality, particularly following her son's inheritance of the family estate. In one instance, she vowed that the best way to care for the lower classes was to make sure they had plenty of work to perform. On the other hand, she showed concern for the starvation of Irish laborers and noted that she and Percy Florence donated funds to help relieve the needs of workers near Percy's estate. Such indecision and seeming equivocation was part of the fabric of Mary Shelley's life and is reflected in her work, which in turn reflects the upheaval of her culture.

Throughout her life, Mary was aware of the costs of publicity. When Edward John Trelawny approached her regarding writing a life of Shelley, she asked him to delay such a project, which she herself hoped to accomplish at some point. She told Trelawny in an April 1829 letter, "Could you write my husband's life, without naming me it were something—but even then I should be terrified at rousing the slumbering voice of the public—each critique, each mention of your work, might drag me forward." She added that she had no wish to assert herself but rather had "the desire to wrap night and obscurity of insignificance around me." Although that was a wish that would never be granted, she tried to adopt a low profile and focus on her son.

Percy Florence entered Harrow, a famous private school in London, in 1832, the year after publication of the revised third edition of *Frankenstein*, and Mary decided to move to London to stay close to him. She adjusted to her long-term widowhood by keeping up friendships and spending evenings at the theater and the opera. Political interests were never far from her heart. On November 11, 1830, she wrote to congratulate General Lafayette on his victory in France: "May England imitate your France in its moderation and heroism." She described fear of the economic consequences of over-taxation in England and excused herself as a woman "for intruding these observations." She explained, "I was the wife of a man who—held dear the opinions you espouse, to which you were the martyr and are the ornament; and to sympathize with successes which would have been matter of such delight to him, appears to me a sacred duty."

Mary continued publishing with her first and second volumes of *Lives of the Most Eminent Literary and Scientific Men of Italy, Spain and Portugal*. While writing that work, she requested information from Gabriele Rossetti (1783–1854), the Italian patriot, poet, and professor at King's College London, and father of Dante, William Michael, and Christina Rossetti, founders of the Pre-Raphaelite movement. Next, Mary published the novel *Lodore* in April 1835. *Lodore* has been described as autobiographical, in that its focus is on the relationship between a mother and daughter. Shelley had used the same triangle of mother, daughter, and father in the tragic *Mathilda,* but unlike that novel, *Lodore* has a happy ending. Critics remark of *Lodore*'s independent intellectual character Fanny Derham that she represents the life of the mind not yet available to women in Shelley's time.

In 1836, after removing Percy from Harrow and relocating to Regent's Park in London, Mary suffered another emotional blow with the loss of her father on April 7. While he had complicated her life at times, Godwin had been a consistent creative force for her. Her constant seeking of his approval reflected her writings about the relationship of daughters to their fathers. Despite the fact that her early relationship with Mary Jane Godwin had not been positive, Mary, ever conscientious, made sure that her father's widow would be provided for.

In October 1837, Percy enrolled at Trinity College, Cambridge University, and Mary published the third volume of *Lives.* Sir Timothy at last agreed to allow publication of his son's poems, but he protested against a biographical memoir. Mary knew that her father-in-law would not live forever and began to write detailed and expansive notes in preparation for publishing the memoir. That same year, she also published her final novel, *Falkner,* yet another tale with a mother-daughter and father-daughter focus. Critics note that its sentimental and unrealistic conclusion results from Mary's personal pursuit of an impossible relationship with both of her parents. Eleanor Ty labels *Falkner* one of Mary's best works due to its description of psychological torture and guilt, a reflection of Mary's own continued emotions. In January 1837, she had again expressed feelings of isolation and deprivation. She wrote to Edward Trelawny of a life often filled with challenges, asking the rhetorical question, "What has my life been?" and following with the explanation, "Since I lost Shelley—I have been alone—& worse—I had my father's fate for many a year a burthen pressing me to the earth—& I had Percy's education & welfare to guard over—& in all this I had not one friendly hand stretched out to support me. . . . I toiled on my weary solitary way."

In August 1838, Mary published the first volume of *Lives of the Most Eminent Literary and Scientific Men of France.* She wrote to Leigh Hunt that the work was "pleasant writing enough—sparing one's imagination, yet occupying one." Shelley scholars often note that she had to undertake this type of "hack" work, a necessary evil to generate income. Her four-volume edition of Percy Bysshe Shelley's poetry was a far more lovingly rendered project, published in 1839 and dedicated to Percy Florence "By His Affectionate Mother." That same year, she published a second volume of *Lives of . . . Men of France.* By year's end, a single edition of *Poetical Works* was released, and she also published a two-volume edition of her husband's *Essays and Letters from Abroad, Translations and Fragments.* She remained true to her vow to keep her husband and his works constantly before the public.

In 1840, Mary stopped writing long enough to enjoy a Continental tour with Percy and some friends from Cambridge. The group traveled to Germany, Switzerland, and Milan. After her son and his companions returned to England in September, Mary lingered in Paris through the end of the year and wrote of witnessing Napoleon's funeral. (He died on St. Helena in 1821 but was returned to Paris for a state funeral in 1840.) She returned to London in time to celebrate Percy's gaining an allowance from his grandfather due to his February 1841 graduation from Cambridge. At long last she could relax, as she told an acquaintance, feeling "a little above water in my affairs."

Although death never seemed far away from Mary, who lost her stepmother, Mary Jane Godwin, in June 1841, she continued to enjoy her son's company and affection. They traveled again to the Continent in 1842, this time visiting Berlin, Dresden, Venice, Florence, Rome, and Paris. While in Paris, she struck up a friendship with Ferdinando Luigi Gatteschi, an Italian expatriate. It was one of several relationships she established based on her intense interest in revolution and politics, which did not diminish as she grew older.

Two years later, Percy inherited Sir Timothy's estate and title when his grandfather died on April 24, 1844. Mary could at last feel confident of her son's future security and her own. In 1844, she published her final work, *Rambles in Germany and Italy in 1840, 1842 and 1843*. In 1845, her life was again disrupted when Gatteschi attempted blackmail by threatening to make public Mary's private letters to him. His attempt failed, but his actions validated her lifelong aversion to publicity.

Mary enjoyed a fairly uncomplicated existence for the next few years. Although in March 1846 she reported severe back pain, and by some accounts chest pain as well, the discomfort did not debilitate her. She celebrated Percy's marriage in June 1848, to a widow, Jane St. John, with whom she apparently shared a positive relationship. Jane would recall that even late in life, Mary often spoke of Percy Bysshe: "It was always: 'Shelley would think this; Shelley would say that; how amused Shelley would have been by this thing . . . He always lives with me', she would say." In December 1848, she complained of chronic headaches that continued over the next two years; doctors discovered a brain tumor in December 1850.

Mary returned to Lake Como in Italy, and in one of her last letters, written to Isabella Baxter Booth, she wrote of a recent visit to Nice, where she was too weak to walk but was able to ride a donkey and spend more time than she should have traveling through the countryside. She told Isabel in closing that she felt fairly well, and "with the sun shining the blue lake at my feet & the Mountains in all their Majesty & beauty around & my beloved children happy & well, I must mark this as a peaceful & happy hour." She returned to London and died at home in February 1851 at the age of 53. Jane, Lady Shelley, requested that the bodies of William Godwin and Mary Wollstonecraft be exhumed from St. Pancras and moved to Bournemouth, where Mary was also buried.

In the final stages of Mary's life, Percy and Jane Shelley shielded her from much of the Victorian revisionism focused on the Shelleys' lives. These revisionists denied or underplayed the Shelleys' reformist interests and the unconventional lifestyle that had gained them equal parts admiration and infamy. Such revisionism lingers today, with many critics continuing to prefer the image of Mary Shelley as a lesser light when compared to her husband. They often portray her merely a victim of circumstance and psychological struggles, rather than seeing those factors as informing and strengthening her work. In the 1922 publication of *Proserpine and Midas*, André Henri Koszul wrote the following in his introduction:

> The force of style which even adverse critics acknowledged in *Frankenstein* was sometimes perilously akin to the most disputable kinds of romantic rant. But in the historical or society novels which followed, in the contributions which graced the 'Keepsakes' of the thirties, and even—alas—in the various prefaces and commentaries which accompanied the publication of so many poems of Shelley, his wife succumbed to an increasing habit of almost Victorian reticence and dignity. And those later novels and tales, though they sold well in their days and were kindly reviewed, can hardly boast of any reputation now. Most of them are pervaded by a brooding spirit of melancholy of the 'moping' rather than the 'musical' sort, and consequently rather ineffective as an artistic motive. Students of Shelley occasionally scan those pages with a view to pick some obscure 'hints and indirections', some veiled reminiscences, in the stories of the adventures and misfortunes of *The Last Man* or *Lodore*. And the books may be good biography at times—they are never life.

Recent scholarship based on Mary Shelley's personal writing and an expanded study that includes her entire body of work continues to challenge this still dominant traditional view. A newly informed readership with a 21st-century sensibility appreciates, rather than diminishes, Mary Shelley's "spirit of melancholy" and at the same time celebrates the presence of literary "music" in her work.

FURTHER READING

Aldiss, Brian W. *Billion Year Spree: The True History of Science Fiction*. New York: Schocken Books, 1974.

Bennett, Betty T. "Mary Shelley's Letters: The Public/Private Self." In *The Cambridge Companion to Mary Shelley*, edited by Esther Schor, 211–225. Cambridge: Cambridge University Press, 2004.

———. "Newly Uncovered Letters and Poems by Mary Wollstonecraft Shelley." *Keats-Shelley Journal* 46 (1997): 51–74.

———, ed. *Selected Letters of Mary Wollstonecraft Shelley.* Baltimore: Johns Hopkins University Press, 1995.

Bennett, Betty T., and Charles E. Robinson. Introduction to *The Mary Shelley Reader.* New York: Oxford University Press, 1990, 3–10.

Bennett, Betty T., and William R. Little. "Seven Letters from Prosper Mérimée to Mary Shelley." *Comparative Literature* 31 (1979): 134–153.

Bowerbank, Sylvia. "The Social Order vs. the Wretch: Mary Shelley's Contradictory-Mindedness in *Frankenstein.*" *ELH* 46 (Fall 1979): 418–431.

Carlson, Julie A. *England's First Family of Writers: Mary Wollstonecraft, William Godwin, Mary Shelley.* Baltimore: Johns Hopkins University Press, 2007.

Clemit, Pamela. "*Frankenstein, Matilda,* and the Legacies of Godwin and Wollstonecraft." In *The Cambridge Compassion to Mary Shelley,* edited by Esther Shor, 26–44. Cambridge: Cambridge University Press, 2004.

Clery, E. J. *Women's Gothic: From Clara Reeve to Mary Shelley.* Tavistock, Devon, U.K.: Northcote House, 2000.

Davis, James. P. "*Frankenstein* and the Subversion of the Masculine Voice." *Women's Studies* 21 (1992): 307–322.

Dunbar, Clement. *A Bibliography of Shelley Studies: 1823–1950.* Reprint, Abingdon, Oxford, U.K.: Taylor & Francis, 1976.

Dunn, Jane. *Moon in Eclipse—A Life of Mary Shelley.* London: Weidenfeld & Nicolson, 1978.

Feldman, Paula R., and Diana Scott-Kilvert, eds. *The Journals of Mary Shelley.* Baltimore: Johns Hopkins University Press, 1994.

Ferre, Rosario. "From Ire to Irony." *Callaloo* 17 (1994): 900.

Fisch, Audrey A., Anne K. Mellor, and Esther H. Schor, eds. *The Other Mary Shelley: Beyond Frankenstein.* New York: Oxford University Press, 1993.

Frank, Frederick S. "Mary Shelley's *Frankenstein*: A Register of Research." *Bulletin of Bibliography* 40 (September 1983): 163–188.

Gerson, Noel B. *Daughter of Earth and Water: A Biography of Mary Wollstonecraft Shelley.* New York: Morrow, 1973.

Gilbert, Sandra M., and Susan Gubar. *The Madwoman in the Attic.* New Haven, Conn.: Yale University Press, 1979.

———. "Mary Shelley." In *The Norton Anthology of Literature by Women: The Traditions in English,* 2nd ed., edited by Sandra M. Gilbert and Susan Gubar, 353–356. New York: W.W. Norton, 1996.

Golding, William. *Mary Wollstonecraft Shelley.* Edited by Harold Bloom. New York: Chelsea House, 1986.

Grylls, Rosalie Glynn. *Mary Shelley.* New York: Oxford University Press, 1938.

Haskell, Francis. "The Shelley Memorial." *Oxford Art Journal* 1 (1978): 3–6.

Hitchcock, Susan Tyler. *A Cultural History of Frankenstein.* New York: W.W. Norton, 2007.

Hodges, Devon. "*Frankenstein* and the Feminine Subversion of the Novel." *Tulsa Studies in Women's Literature* 2 (Autumn 1983): 155–164.

Hoeveler, Diane Long. "*Frankenstein,* Feminism, and Literary Theory." In *The Cambridge Companion to Mary Shelley,* edited by Esther Schor, 45–62. Cambridge: Cambridge University Press, 2004.

Homans, Margaret. *Bearing the Word: Language and Female Experience in Nineteenth-Century Women's Writing.* Chicago: University of Chicago Press, 1986.

Hunter, Paul J., ed. *Frankenstein.* New York: W.W. Norton, 1995.

Hustis, Harriett. "Responsible Creativity and the 'Modernity' of Mary Shelley's Prometheus." *Studies in English Literature, 1500–1900* 43, no. 4 (Autumn 2003): 845–858.

Jacobus, Mary. "Is There a Woman in This Text?" *New Literary History* 14 (Autumn 1982): 117–141. Republished in Jacobus's *Reading Woman: Essays in Feminist Criticism.* New York: Columbia University Press, 1986, 83–109.

Johnson, Barbara. "My Monster/My Self." *Diacritics* 12 (Summer 1982): 2–10.

Jones, Frederick. "The Letters of Mary Shelley in the Bodleian Library." *Bodleian Quarterly* 8 (Spring, Summer, Autumn 1937): 29–310, 360–371, 412–420.

———, ed. *Mary Shelley's Journal.* Norman, OK: U of Oklahoma Press, 1947.

Kiely, Robert. *The Romantic Novel in England.* Cambridge, Mass.: Harvard University Press, 1972.

Kucich, Greg. "Biographer." In *The Cambridge Companion to Mary Shelley*, edited by Esther Schor, 226–241. Cambridge: Cambridge University Press, 2004.

Lederer, Susan E. *Frankenstein: Penetrating the Secrets of Nature.* Newark, N.J.: Rutgers University Press, 2002.

Levine, George, and U. C. Knopeflmacher, eds. *The Endurance of Frankenstein.* Berkeley: University of California Press, 1979.

Litquotes. "Mary Shelley Quotes." Available online. URL: http://www.litquotes.com/quote_author_resp.php?AName=MaryShelley. Accessed June 20, 2009.

Literature Network. "Mary Wollstonecraft Shelley." Available online. URL: http://www.online-literature.com/shelley_mary/. Accessed June 20, 2009.

Lyles, W. H. *Mary Shelley: An Annotated Bibliography.* New York: Garland, 1975.

Lynch, Deidre. "Historical Novelist." In *The Cambridge Companion to Mary Shelley*, edited by Esther Schor, 135–150. Cambridge: Cambridge University Press, 2004.

Marshall, Florence A. *The Life and Letters of Mary Wollstonecraft Shelley.* 2 vols. London: Bentley, 1889.

McInerny, Peter. "*Frankenstein* and the Godlike Science of Letters." *Genre* 13 (Winter 1980): 455–475.

Morrison, Lucy, and Staci L. Stone. *A Mary Shelley Encyclopedia.* Available online. URL: http://www.scribd.com/doc/10048669/A-Mary-Shelley-Encyclopedia. Accessed July 27, 2009.

Mary Shelley: National Museum of Women in the Arts. (Sage Colleges; WAMC Public Radio, 1994), audiocassette.

"Mary Wollstonecraft Shelley Chronology & Resource Site." *Romantic Circles: Scholarly Resources.* Available online. URL: http://www.rc.umd.edu/reference/chronologies/mschronology/mws.html. Accessed June 20, 2009.

Mellor, Anne K. "Making a Monster." In *The Cambridge Companion to Mary Shelley*, edited by Esther Schor, 9–25. Cambridge: Cambridge University Press, 2004.

———. *Mary Shelley: Her Life, Her Fiction, Her Monsters.* New York: Routledge, 1989.

Moore, Helen. *Mary Wollstonecraft Shelley.* Philadelphia: Lippincott, 1886.

Morton, Timothy. "Mary Shelley as Cultural Critic." In *The Cambridge Companion to Mary Shelley*, edited by Esther Schor, 259–273. Cambridge: Cambridge University Press, 2004.

Neth, Michael, ed. *The Hellas Notebook.* Bodleian Shelley Manuscripts, Ser. 16. New York: Garland, 1994.

Nitchey, Elizabeth. *Mary Shelley—Author of Frankenstein.* New Brunswick, N.J.: Rutgers University Press, 1953.

Poovey, Mary. "My Hideous Progeny: Mary Shelley and the Feminization of Romanticism." *PMLA* 95, no. 3 (May 1980): 332–347.

———. "The Proper Lady and the Woman Writer: Ideology as Style in the Works of Mary Wollstonecraft, Mary Shelley, and Jane Austen." *Modern Philology* 83, no. 4 (May 1986): 434–437.

Rafferty, Terrence. "Shelley's Daughters." *New York Times Book Review* 26 October 2008, 12–13.

Randel, Fred V. "*Frankenstein*, Feminism and the Intertextuality of Mountains." *Studies in Romanticism* 23 (Winter 1984): 515–533.

———. "'The Political Geography of Horror in Mary Shelley's 'Frankenstein.'" *English Literary History* 70, no. 2 (Summer 2003): 465–491.

Robinson, Charles E., ed. *Mary Shelley: Collected Tales and Stories with Original Engravings.* Baltimore: Johns Hopkins University Press, 1990.

Rolleston, Maud. *Talks with Lady Shelley.* London: George G. Harrap & Co., 1925.

Schor, Esther, ed. *The Cambridge Companion to Mary Shelley.* Cambridge: Cambridge University Press, 2004.

Sedgwick, Eve Kosofsky. *Between Men: English Literature and Male Homosocial Desire.* New York: Columbia University Press, 1985.

Seymour, Miranda. *Mary Shelley.* London: John Murray, 2000.

Shelley, Lady Jane, ed. *Shelley and Mary.* London: privately published, 1882.

———. *Shelley Memorials.* London: Smith, Elder, 1859.

Shelley, Mary Wollstonecraft. *The Frankenstein Notebooks.* Edited by Charles E. Robinson. 2 vols. New York: Garland, 1996.

———. Introduction to *Frankenstein: or the Modern Prometheus*. 1831. Reprint, New York: Bedford/St. Martin's, 2000, 19–25.

———. *The Journals of Mary Shelley, 1814–1844*. 2 vols. Edited by Paula R. Feldman and Diana Scott-Kilvert. 1987. Reprint, Baltimore: Johns Hopkins University Press, 1995.

———. *The Mary Shelley Reader*. Edited by Betty T. Bennett and Charles E. Robinson. New York: Oxford University Press, 1990.

———. "Mythological Dramas: *Proserpine and Midas*." Edited by Charles E. Robinson. In *The Bodleian Shelley Manuscripts*, vol. 10, edited by Donald H. Reiman. New York: Garland, 1992.

———. *Notes to the Complete Poetical Works of Percy Bysshe Shelley*. Project Gutenberg. Available online. URL: http://www.gutenberg.org/etext/4695. Accessed June 20, 2009.

Small, Christopher. *Ariel Like a Harpy: Shelley, Mary and Frankenstein*. London: Victor Gollancz, 1972.

Spacks, Patricia Meyer. *The Female Imagination*. New York: Avon Books, 1975.

Spark, Muriel Spark. *Child of Light—A Reassessment of Mary Wollstonecraft Shelley*. Hadleigh, Essex, U.K.: Tower Bridge Publications, 1951.

———. *Mary Shelley: A Biography*. New York: Dutton, 1987.

Spatt, Hartley S. "Mary Shelley's Last Men: The Truth of Dreams." *Studies in the Novel* 7, no. 4 (Winter 1975): 526–537.

St. Clair, William. *The Godwins and the Shelleys: The Biography of a Family*. 1989. Reprint, Baltimore: Johns Hopkins University Press, 1991.

Sterrenburg, Lee. "*The Last Man*: Anatomy of Failed Revolutions." *Nineteenth-Century Fiction*. 33 (December 1978): 324–347.

Stoneman, Patsy. Review of *The Mary Shelley Reader, Containing Frankenstein, Mathilda, Tales and Stories, Essays and Reviews, and Letters. RES* 45 (1994): 118–119.

Sunstein, Emily W. *Mary Shelley: Romance and Reality*. Baltimore: Johns Hopkins University Press, 1991.

Ty, Eleanor. "Mary Shelley." In *British Romantic Novelists, 1789–1832*. Vol. 116 of *Dictionary of Literary Biography*, edited by Bradford K. Mudge, 311–325. New York: Gale Research, 1992. Available online. URL: http://people.brandeis.edu/~teuber/shelleybio.html#MainEssaySection. Accessed June 2, 2009.

Walling, William. *Mary Shelley*. New York: Twayne Publishers, 1979.

Williams, John. *Mary Shelley: A Literary Life*. New York: St. Martin's Press, 2000.

Wolfson, Susan J. "Mary Shelley, Editor." In *The Cambridge Companion to Mary Shelley*, edited by Esther Schor, 193–210. Cambridge: Cambridge University Press, 2004.

Wollstonecraft, Mary. *Posthumous Works of the Author of a Vindication of the Rights of Woman*. 4 vols. Edited by William Godwin. London: J. Johnson, 1798.

Part II

Works A to Z

"The Bride of Modern Italy" (1824)

Mary Shelley published her short story "The Bride of Modern Italy" in *London Magazine* in April 1824. The Shelleys had spent much time in Italy during the previous five years moving from Leghorn to Bagni di Lucca, Venice, Este, Naples, Rome, Florence, Pisa, and Bagni di Pisa before settling in San Terenzo in 1823. As they traveled, they developed strong friendships with Jane and Edward Williams, EDWARD TRELAWNY, and others, including Emilia Viviani, the 19-year-old daughter of the governor of Pisa. During that time period, Shelley scholar Betty Bennett notes, Mary's relationship with PERCY BYSSHE SHELLEY increased in "complexity." That was due in part to Percy's belief in "expansive rather than exclusive love." Mary shared Percy's beliefs to some extent. Thus, as he turned to other women for affection and inspiration, Mary viewed them not through the lens of jealousy but with curiosity and interest. According to her journals, she actually befriended Emilia Viviana, who became the inspiration for Percy's autobiographical love poem "Epipsychidion." Mary and Percy took pity on Emilia, who had spent years confined to the convent of Santa Anna. She began as a pupil, but when the Shelleys knew her, she remained in the convent as her parents arranged for her marriage. She probably served as inspiration to Mary for "The Bride of Modern Italy," whose main character, Clorinda, is also confined to a convent and trying desperately to escape her parents' plans for an arranged marriage.

According to Emily W. Sunstein, Mary wrote of her amusement over the convent of Santa Anna. Rather than resembling "the dim Gothic vaults of fiction," with all of their mysterious attraction, it was simply an old, dirty building in disrepair that always smelled like garlic. That image probably inspired the story's opening, in which the convent garden is described as "weather-stained" with only a few cabbages in the winter garden that "perfumed the air with their rank exhalations." Mary felt that Emilia, "pale and elegant," with her striking "black hair and languorous eyes, seemed romantic and pathetic." Mary enjoyed visiting Emilia, bringing her writing supplies so that she could produce poetry. In her correspondence, Mary noted that she had seen a marriage contract that contained an account of the "groom's attributes" but not his name. She "abhorred" the system that victimized Emilia. However, her fascination with Emilia faded, according to Bennett, when she perceived "the triviality of Viviani's character." In "The Bride of Italy," in order to depict Clorinda's shallow character, Mary quoted a remark made by Emilia, who noted of herself that "she changed saints everytime she changed lovers." In the story, Teresa teases Clorinda by saying, "for you change your saint as your lover changes name;—tell me, sweet Clorinda, how many saints have been benefitted by your piety?"

Shelley loved Italy, and in her 1826 book review titled "The English in Italy," she compared Italy's power of attraction and effect on the English to that of the addictive lotus flower. The English preference for Italy produced "a new race or sect" dubbed the "Anglo-Italian." According to Shelley, some characteristics of the Anglo-Italian included knowledge of the language and a loss of a desire to visit monuments and churches while consulting a guide book. Instead, in a desire to adopt native customs, the Anglo-Italian attached "himself to some of the most refined among" the natives in appreciation of their "talent and simple manner; he has lost the critical mania in a real taste for the beautiful." In the same review, Shelley warned against intermarriage between the English and the Italian, which always ends in disaster, as neither can fully accept the others' habits. Her remarks perfectly describe the young English artist Alleyn in "The Bride of Italy" and, probably, herself.

SYNOPSIS

The story opens in the winter garden of an Italian convent where two young women, Clorinda and Teresa, walk the paths. The scene depicts neglected walkways, "not overgrown, but strewed with broken earthen-ware, ashes, cabbage-stalks, orange-peel, bones," the refuse compared to that which may surround a "disorderly mansion." Still, its appearance is unlike a building in England, due to the presence of orange trees and geraniums, "unharmed by frost" growing among the cabbages. The girls await the arrival of Teresa's brother, Giacomo de' Tolomei. When he arrives, they move from the garden into a parlor where a near-deaf nun serves as chaperone. Giacomo hands Clorinda a paper to read, saying he has written a marriage proposal. It states the desire to ally "a noble family of Sienna . . . with the noble family of the Saviani of Rome." The proposal describes the groom as "well-made, good-looking, healthy, studiously inclined and of irreproachable morals." The document includes the amount of his fortune and a request for a specific dowry payment from Clorinda's family.

Clorinda cries, telling Giacomo that the proposal will not be accepted by her parents. It demands a dowry of 12,000 crowns, and she knows her parents will not offer more than 6,000. Giacomo states that in actuality his father will probably not accept less than 20,000 crowns. Should her parents agree, he will have to work hard to win his father's consent. When the dinner bell rings, Giacomo must depart.

The narrator describes the convent meal in great detail—"the tables covered with no white cloths; cellars with black salt, bottles of sour wine, and small loaves of bitter bread." The reader learns that the beautiful Clorinda Saviani is 18, has lived in the convent for five years, and has waited for her father to find a man who would accept a small dowry in exchange for marriage to her. Clorinda had attached herself to several young men, written letters, prayed, wept and loved. The narrator urges her "fastidious English" audience to resist any feelings of disgust, explaining that the Catholic religion "crushes the innate conscience by giving a false one in its room" and that the maxim in Italy is, "the dishonor attaches itself to the discovered not the concealed fault." After dinner, the girls go to Clorinda's room, which includes a print of St. Giacomo and various shabby appointments.

Clorinda despairs whether she and Giacomo will ever marry, and she talks of running away. Teresa warns that she must think of her honor and reminds her that she cannot get out of the convent. "Clorinda's tears mingle with her coffee," and she notes that the nun who complains of coffee without rum is "fishing for a present." She means that the nun is covertly requesting a bribe of liquor from Giacomo. The girls send him a note explaining the request, and the following day he returns with a large quantity of rum for the convent's superior. She accepts the gift and then leaves the young man alone with his sister and Clorinda.

Giacomo confesses that the marriage proposal was not accepted, and Clorinda despairs that she will be sacrificed to the man chosen by her parents for her to wed. She asks Giacomo to run away with her. He states he would sacrifice his life but explains that her ignorance of the world prevents her understanding that such an action would cause an irreversible loss of her honor. Giacomo declares he will travel to Sienna the following morning to try to convince his father to accept the small dowry offered by Clorinda's parents. In the meantime, he will send an English artist living in Rome with whom he has become friends to care for Clorinda. The Englishman sends a letter of five pages of introduction to Clorinda the following day and arrives with curiosity at the convent, as he has never seen one. He imagines the novices within, "fearful as brides, but not so hopeful," and those who have dreamed of the outside world. He also imagines a lovely garden and long inner halls, thinking that "if I do not lose my heart, I shall at least gain some excellent hints for my picture of the Profession of Eloisa."

The artist meets with the two young women, introducing himself as Marcott Alleyn. Alleyn charms Clorinda, and the narrator explains that in Clorinda's country, "either downright love is made, or the most distant coldness preserved between the sexes." She pours her heart out to the 17-year-old Alleyn, who is smitten and returns often over the next several days. He quickly wins the favor of the nuns through gifts and teasing and "establishe[s]" himself" with more freedom than Giacomo had ever enjoyed. He soothes Clorinda's longing for Giacomo by making her laugh, and when she complains about the nuns, he helps her plot "some droll revenge." Although he plays jokes on the nuns, he appeases them through his soft speech and gifts.

Clorinda feels happier than ever before and eagerly looks forward to Alleyn's visits. She all but forgets Giacomo and avoids Teresa, spending her time alone walking the garden paths. She no longer tends to her devotions as no saint named Marcott exists. Alleyn does not notice her growing passion until, one morning, he sees her blush, and the two kiss just as Teresa and a nun enter the room. The narrator explains of Alleyn that such young men "look on women as living Edens which they dare not imagine they can ever enjoy; they love, and dream not of being loved; they seek, and their wildest fancies do not picture themselves sought." Thus, Alleyn enjoys an innocent rapture when he departs and plans to return frequently. Teresa falls ill and remains in her room, leaving the two alone together often.

One day, Clorinda asks Alleyn whether he will "be under the walls to receive me" that evening if she carries out her escape plan. He asks whether she is seriously considering such an escape, and she replies that she cannot climb the wall, but she gives him wax with the impression of the convent key. He is to make a key and enter to free her; she has prepared a disguise and "all will go well." As he leaves, Alleyn thinks, "The devil it will!" He paces about, telling himself he can never enter the convent again: "I have sown a pretty crop, but I am not mad enough to reap it."

Giacomo returns and asks of news about Clorinda, and due to feelings of guilt, "Alleyn wished himself hanged." Giacomo explains that he could not convince his father to accept a lesser dowry, in addition to which he has learned that Clorinda's parents have brought the man for whom they intend Clorinda to Rome. In tears, Giacomo declares that if Clorinda still loves him, he will take desperate measures to be with her. Although Alleyn agrees to accompany his friend to the convent the next day, he sends an excuse, and Giacomo meets with Clorinda alone. Later in the day, Alleyn receives a note from Clorinda declaring her devotion to him, rather than her former lover, and she asks him to see her the following day.

Alleyn goes to Tivoli in order to avoid Giacomo until the appointed time, when he goes to the convent. Both Teresa and Clorinda look angry, and when Teresa leaves the parlor, Clorinda bursts into tears. She has suffered Teresa's scorn and cannot tolerate Giacomo's "looks of grief." She adds that "this heart has escaped from my control" and explains that she had to meet her intended the day before. Her "cruel mother" upbraided her for being deceitful, the convent superior having discovered a letter she had written to Giacomo. In order to avoid disgrace, she must marry immediately. She pleads with Alleyn to rescue her, as he remains her only hope.

That evening, Alleyn receives another note that expresses Clorinda's increasing horror. Plans have advanced for her marriage to the stranger, Romani. She understands that Alleyn will not marry her, and Giacomo has no hope of changing his father's mind. The note explains that Clorinda used to love a gentleman whose father also objected to their marriage, but that father has now died. She begs Alleyn to find that man and determine whether he still loves her and will marry her to provide "some alleviation to my cruel fate." She pleads with him to come to the convent the next day to at least "console your miserable friend."

Alleyn does not keep that appointment. He later learns that Clorinda had written him an additional lengthy letter that was intercepted by her parents. The following day, another note arrives, in which Clorinda bewails her fate and the fact that she is "the cause of a thousand griefs to others." She wishes herself dead, as now others hate her; even Alleyn seems to no longer care for her. She asks him to convince Giacomo to "desist from further pursuit" as her parents will never consent to the union. She now is focused on escaping her prison. More letters follow over the next month, begging Alleyn to come to the convent.

One morning, the superior visits Alleyn at his lodgings. She praises the tenderness of Clorinda's parents and notes that she had always been against men visiting the convent. However, Alleyn's "politeness and known integrity" had caused her to relax her rules in his case, and she invites him to visit whenever he pleases. After she departs, Alleyn decides not to go to the convent but instead to take a walk to distract himself. However, he finds himself standing before the convent door and enters the hall to see a sobbing Giacomo appear and fling himself into his friend's arms. He explains that Clorinda had married Romani the day before and moved to Spoleto.

Alleyn experiences a wave of relief over not having fallen into a matrimonial trap, feeling as if he had been "stayed by a friendly hand." He wonders why the superior had visited him and invited him to the convent, knowing that Clorinda had departed, and asks Giacomo whether they nuns might have lied about Clorinda's marriage and departure. Giacomo invites Alleyn to enter the convent, as the nuns will welcome him and fill his pockets with sweets, because they miss his "good cheer." He launches into a long statement about Englishmen and the fact that Alleyn is

> a heretic; words which, interpreted into pure Tuscan, mean an untired prodigal, and one, pardon me, whose conscience will no more stickle at violating yon sanctuary than at eating flesh on Fridays. Go by all means, and make the best of your good fortune.

Alleyn replies that perhaps Giacomo should ride after Clorinda. Then he adds that neither one of them should take the actions they have described. Instead, he will paint his Profession of Eloisa.

COMMENTARY

Shelley loved Italy, despite the tragedies that she experienced there. She expressed her fondness for the country in "Recollections of Italy," printed in *London Magazine* on January 9, 1824. In that essay, her narrator represents an individual who is ecstatic about a few moments of pleasant weather in London and argues that the English weather and countryside are every bit as uplifting as those of Italy, a statement that all readers would accept in its intended ironic delivery. The voice that defends Italy, dubbed Edmund Malville, represents Shelley herself. The trip though Italy that he describes closely follows that of the Shelleys' trip from Pisa to Vico Pisano on September 15, 1821, described in Mary's journal. The narrator notes, "We English often feel like a sick man escaping into the open air after a three months' confinement." As the inhabitants of Henley upon Thames meet each other, they exclaim, "What enchanting weather! It has not rained these two days . . . we shall perhaps enjoy a whole week of sunshine!" Such description stands in stark contrast to that of Tuscany. Malville describes the scene in rapture:

> The balmy air of night, Hesperus in his glowing palace of sunlight, the flower-starred earth, the glittering waters, the ripening grapes, the chestnut copses, the cuckoo . . . heaven disdains a plain; but when the beauteous earth raises her proud head to seek its high communion, then it descends to meet her, it adorns her in clouds, and invests her in radiant hues.

Shelley pokes gentle fun at her countrymen, who must naturally be products of their inhospitable weather and geography. Where England represents common sense and demands a cheerful acceptance of its environment, Italy exudes a seductive passion that seems a natural product of its climate and physicality. That contrast inherent to cultures provides the major focus of "The Modern Bride of Italy." Shelley presents the story as a cautionary tale, one that warns readers, not away from the Italy she so loved but, rather, that they remain onlookers and not marry into Italian culture. The physical beauty and warmth that thoughts of Italy evoke do not always suggest the positive. Rather, the manners of those living within that beauty must be carefully considered and lead to the rejection of any plans for intermarriage.

Shelley immediately makes her warning clear through the imagery of geraniums depicted in the opening scene of "The Modern Bride of Italy." They survive in the winter garden, traditionally symbolic of the female, and add a much-needed splash of color. But the rotten, smelly cabbages that surround them imply that the geraniums, representative of the convent's young women, do not foreshadow a happy conclusion to the story that will follow. Instead, they suggest the situation of the native Italians Clorinda and Teresa, young, fresh, and pretty like the geraniums, yet outnumbered by the ancient unsympathetic nuns who serve as their jailers. While a garden traditionally symbolizes temptation and the woman's sphere of power, the condition of the convent garden, littered and uninviting, counters that symbolism.

Shelley begins her critique of the Italian marriage contract in her story's title. The term *Modern* serves as an ironic description. As her story will demonstrate, the arranged marriage, considered a feudal concept in England by the 19th-century, remains a fact of Italian life for young women such as Clorinda. It is not only an outdated procedure but a cruel one, in light of its effect on the group Clorinda represents as well as on men like Giacomo, destined to never fulfill their love.

Through the contrast of Alleyn's more sensible English personality to that of the passionate Giacomo, the story emphasizes the dangers inherent to an individual from outside a culture who challenges its social rules. Shelley also featured this topic in her novel *Lodore* (1835) through the disastrous marriage of Englishman Horatio Saville to the Italian Clorinda. One may assume that the adoption of the name Clorinda for her novel's character was inspired by that of the young woman in "The Modern Bride of Italy." Through both works of fiction, Shelley warns young Englishmen that exotic Italian women are best given a wide berth. The clash between cultural expectations predicts disaster when the casual and enjoyable flirtation is advanced to matrimony. On the one hand, Shelley seems to recommend the classification of *Anglo-Italian* over that of tourist, as the first label suggests a deeper understanding and appreciation of Italy. At the same time, the fact that the Anglo-Italian rejects typical tourist destinations to instead admire the local more everyday attractions creates the challenges to relationships on which her story focuses through Alleyn's involvement with Giacomo and Clorinda.

Shelley does not blame the populace per se but instead places the blame for the barbaric marriage system squarely on the shoulders of the Catholic religion. Her description of the shabby Catholic convent and the nuns as aficionados of rum and chewing tobacco is anything but complimentary. In addition, the nuns pretend to supervise boarders like Clorinda in order to collect money from their parents, but they shirk their duties by assigning deaf and decrepit attendants to serve as chaperones. Simultaneously, they accept bribes from the young men they allow to enter the convent, masterminding a corrupt social system. The emphasis on the nuns' advanced ages also suggests they are relics of a time past who refuse to accept any change to an outdated centuries-old tradition. While the convent superior tells the Englishman Alleyn that she trusts him due to his "politeness and known integrity," he remains, as Giacomo makes clear at the story's conclusion, "a heretic" who breaks all of the rules that Giacomo must scrupulously maintain. The nuns' hypocritical favoring of Alleyn over that of one of their own religion is a strong indictment on Shelley's part.

Feminist critics would naturally find Clorinda's imprisonment of interest. While Clorinda is not the passive heroine who so often appears in traditional fiction, in the end, none of her plans come to fruition, and she complies with the social system that traps its most beautiful young women in loveless marriages. Her struggle is reminiscent of a bird beating its wings to no avail within its cage bars. She is reminded several times about the importance of her reputation in a society with a double gender standard. Even had she effected an escape with her lover, as Giacomo explains, she could no longer move in proper social circles. Shelley may reflect in that passage on her own elopement with the married Percy Bysshe Shelley, an act that forever placed her outside the acceptance of her own society.

Feminist and Marxist critics alike would also note Clorinda's position as a commodity. She is subject to financial barter as if she were a work of art or a piece of farm property. Ironically, she goes to the lowest bidder in this instance, the prospect who will accept her parents' stated dowry amount and not demand more. Interestingly, Giacomo is also a prisoner: Despite his membership in the nobility and his gender, he remains trapped by social, rather than civic, law.

While Clorinda's and Giacomo's reactions are hyperbolic, particularly to the sensibility of today's readers, those same readers must keep in mind the hopelessness of the characters' situation. They are both members of the upper class, generally representative of power, but they are not allowed to act on their love to marry. They are doomed to remain apart, despite what readers sense are strong feelings for one another. Although Clorinda's multiple romantic involvements mark her sincerity as suspect, she obviously prefers Giacomo to Romani.

Twice the story alludes to Eloisa, also known as Eloise and Heloise, when the artist Alleyn considers a painting in which he wants to depict that famous subject. The tale of her tragic love for the medieval French philosopher Abelard had been celebrated repeatedly in art, with Alexander Pope's 18th-century poem "Eloisa to Abelard" being one of the most famous of those representations. Eloisa, member of an upper-class medieval family, was tutored by Abelard, an intellect whose work questioned church teachings; some of his writings were considered heretical. The two fell in love and secretly married, after which Eloisa moved into a convent to help keep their secret. Eloisa's father mistakenly believed that Abelard had raped Eloisa, destroying her reputation and chance to marry. He punished Abelard by ordering him castrated. Abelard became a priest while Eloisa took her vows, and the two continued a lifelong relationship through correspondence.

Like Eloisa, Clorinda writes lengthy emotional letters to her various loves. While not dismissing her, Shelley makes light of Clorinda through the Eloisa reference, for Clorinda's love in no manner measures up to the classical devotion of Eloisa. In addition, through the story of Abelard, Shelley ironically suggests the fate that could befall Alleyn should he succumb to Clorinda's charms.

CHARACTERS

Clorinda Clorinda appears to be the protagonist, because the plot centers on her victimization as the subject of an arranged marriage. However, her character does not develop as do most protagonists. She remains flat throughout, lacking an epiphany, other than realizing that she will not be able to escape cultural conventions. To a 21st-century reader, she appears shallow and without substance, due to her focus on impressing men. However, readers must keep in mind her difficult situation. Her only "job" as a member of the upper class is to marry well, and she has been kept literally imprisoned in a convent, with little exposure to the world and to men. She is the traditional bird kept caged for the delight of males who view her as an object. Her parents assess a specific monetary value for Clorinda and make her part of a barter system in which she represents a simple commodity. Therefore, she should be viewed as a sympathetic character, one who appeals to reader pity, just as her real-life inspiration, Emilia Viviana, appealed to Mary Shelley.

Teresa and Giacomo The sibling pair upon whom Clorinda hangs her hope for a future involving love and a modicum of free will on her part, Teresa and Giacomo are minor characters who serve to advance the plot and to aid reader understanding of Clorinda. The reader quickly understands the hopelessness of Clorinda's situation with the siblings as her only allies. Teresa shares Clorinda's prison in the convent; thus, her brother is the only means of support she can offer Clorinda. She does act to distract the nun who supervises Clorinda's meetings with Giacomo, thus acting as a coconspirator. Naturally, she supports her brother's suit, and when it becomes clear that a match will not be made between Giacomo and Clorinda, Teresa loses interest in Clorinda's plight.

Giacomo appears to be a young man honestly in love with Clorinda. However, he has no power to sway his parents' determination to receive a specific amount of money from Clorinda's parents before their respective offspring can marry. Thus, Clorinda's love for Giacomo only serves to further frustrate her as she realizes that she may never be able to marry a man for whom she has any feelings. Giacomo proves important in introducing Alleyn, his British friend, to Clorinda, but that acquaintance also proves frustrating and borderline cruel in its empty promise.

Alleyn Readers may very well view Alleyn as the story's protagonist. Although he does not appear until well into the plot, he does enjoy an epiphany of sorts, which usually comes only to the protagonist. He realizes that he should not become entangled in the Italian system of marriage brokering that is so foreign to him. He is "sobered at once" after learning of Clorinda's marriage, as he considers how close he came to falling into an emotional abyss. While he is attracted to Clorinda, he eventually understands that physical attraction will not compensate for their vast cultural differences, a point that Mary Shelley makes in her later review, "The English in Italy." The reader does not learn much about Alleyn other than that he is British, which for Shelley's readers would have held great significance. Italy was one of the most popular European retreats for her countrymen, and much had been written for tourists. However, Alleyn represents the individual Shelley later labeled *Anglo-Italian,* adopting the term from usage by GEORGE GORDON BYRON (Lord Byron). It describes the individual who is no longer interested in seeing the "tourist traps" but would rather admire the local natural beauty. Alleyn does just that in his time spent with Clorinda.

FURTHER READING

Bennett, Betty T. *Mary Wollstonecraft Shelley: An Introduction.* Baltimore: Johns Hopkins University Press, 1998.

"A Medieval Love Story." Medieval History. Available online. URL: http://historymedren.about.com/od/peterabelard/a/love_story.htm. Accessed February 10, 2011.

Pope, Alexander. "Eloisa to Abelard." In *The Works of Alexander Pope.* Available online. URL: http://www.luminarium.org/eightlit/pope/popebib.php. Accessed February 11, 2011.

Shelley, Mary. "The Bride of Modern Italy." In *The Mary Shelley Reader,* edited by Betty Bennett and Charles E. Robinson, 263–273. New York: Oxford University Press, 1990.

———. "The Bride of Modern Italy." Available online. URL: http://www.horrormasters.com/Text/a1098.pdf. Accessed February 1, 2011.

———. "The English in Italy." *Westminster Review* 6 (October 1826): 325–341.

———. "Recollections of Italy." In *The Mary Shelley Reader,* edited by Betty T. Bennett and Charles E. Robinson, 255–262. New York: Oxford University Press, 1990.

Sunstein, Emily W. *Mary Shelley: Romance and Reality.* Boston: Little, Brown and Company, 1989.

"The Dream" (1832)

Mary Shelley published her short story "The Dream" in the ladies' annual titled THE KEEPSAKE in 1832. One of many stories published in such yearly publications, "The Dream" catered to its audience of mainly middle-class women by presenting a passionate love story placed in an exotic foreign setting, both in a time and a geographic sense. The story is historical fiction, its action taking place near Nantes in the Loire Valley of France at the beginning of the French king Henry IV's reign. The timing is crucial to Shelley's theme that love for the living does not devalue one's feelings for loved ones who have died. That theme is possibly an autobiographical reflection in light of her own husband's early death.

Henry's assumption of the French throne ended a long period of discord between Catholics and Protestants known as France's Wars of Religions, lasting from 1562 to 1598. Nantes had long been important to the area because of its proximity to the Loire River, making it a vital port town and seat of trade during the medieval era. Taking its name from the Namnates, who settled along the river during the first millennium, Nantes was invaded in 843 by the Normans, who remained there for about 100 years. They were eventually vanquished by Alain Barbe Torte, who took the title Duke of Brittany and made Nantes his capital city. As Duke Francois II later encouraged increased trade, Nantes became the first Atlantic port town. The French court remained mobile, moving about the area and building enormous chateaux along the river. One of those aristocratic chateaux provides the setting for "The Dream."

Henry, a character in the story, had been raised a Huguenot Protestant and would later convert to Catholicism, but not until 1593. In 1598, he began his reign by signing the Edict of Nantes, guaranteeing freedom of religion as well as civic rights to French Protestants. The edict reinstated agreements contained in previously broken treaties with Protestants, becoming the first European document celebrating religious toleration. One of its statements is particularly pertinent to Shelley's story of forgiveness, declaring: "First, that the recollection of everything done by one party or the other between March, 1585, and our accession to the crown, and during all the preceding period of troubles, remain obliterated and forgotten, as if no such things had ever happened."

By inserting Henry into her story, Shelley constructs historical fiction, a subgenre many critics credit Sir Walter Scott with creating. Shelley openly admired Scott. Their relationship grew after she first sent him correspondence that gently corrected his misguided assumption that *Frankenstein* had been written by her husband. He had offered that opinion in his printed critical review of the novel.

At least two strong possibilities exist for the real-life saint that Catherine represents. One is Catherine of Alexandria, who tried to convince Emperor Maximus of the superiority of Christianity to the worship of false gods. At first tolerated by the emperor, who was impressed by her great intelligence, Catherine later angered him by besting his court philosophers in argument and by her ability to convert others to her faith. When he tried to execute her on the wheel, angels destroyed it, causing the furious Maximus to behead Catherine. Angels carried her body to heaven, and a chapel was built in her honor on Mt. Sinai. She was considered among the most helpful of the saints and was celebrated with her own feast day through the Middle Ages. Poets including Adam of St. Victor and Jacques Benigne Bossuet immortalized her in verse. Multiple chapels were erected in her name, and her statue could be found in many churches, the wheel becoming her symbol. She became the patroness of young maidens and women students, watching over cloisters and their virgins. Her popularity waned when, in the 18th century, no chapel erected in her honor was found on Mt. Sinai.

Another possible candidate is St. Catherine of Sienna, born in 1347. Her parents wanted her to marry and live a traditional life, but she wanted to forego marriage for a life of celibacy, worship, and helping the sick and the poor, becoming famous for nursing sufferers through a plague. For three years, she experienced celestial visitations, and in 1370, through visions and trance, she acquired understanding of divine mysteries and later received the stigmata. Catherine gained a reputation for intelligence and the ability to bring conciliation to feuding parties throughout the region of Italy. During the Great Schism in the Catholic Church, she prayed at St. Peter's tomb and felt the weight of the church problems fall upon her shoulders, for which she prayed for martyrdom. She suffered agonies for three months and then died in her early 30s after writing hundreds of letters that were preserved for later generations for their wisdom. Her correspondence was said to lead readers, including women in cloisters, to mystical heights during meditation.

"The Dream" is regarded negatively by some as "hack writing," one of many of Shelley's works written specifically for money—in this case, to support herself and her son during the many lean years prior to Percy's inheritance of title and wealth. Other critics do not view writing for money as a negative. The story is categorized in various ways, including as literary Gothic (see GOTHIC FICTION), a label also often applied to *Frankenstein*.

Shelley may have drawn on a number of influences, one of the most obvious being Shakespeare's *Romeo and Juliet*, a tale of lovers whose families were enemies, which made theirs a forbidden romance. The story may also have drawn on PERCY BYSSHE SHELLEY's 1817 poem "Marianne's Dream," with its emphasis on the ability of dreams to reveal things unseen in the light of day. The first two stanzas read:

> 1.
> A pale Dream came to a Lady fair,
> And said, A boon, a boon, I pray!
> I know the secrets of the air,
> And things are lost in the glare of day,
> Which I can make the sleeping see,
> If they will put their trust in me.
>
> 2.
> And thou shalt know of things unknown,
> If thou wilt let me rest between
> The veiny lids, whose fringe is thrown
> Over thine eyes so dark and sheen:
> And half in hope, and half in fright,
> The Lady closed her eyes so bright.

One may hear echoes of the "Fair Lady" in Constance's statement that "I will rest tomorrow on St. Catherine's bed: and if, as I have heard, the saint deigns to direct her votaries in dreams, I will be guided by her."

While she set her story in France, Shelley adds a line from an Italian song beneath her title that reads: *Chi dice mal d'amore / Dice una falsita!* This translates: "Whoever speaks badly about love / Utters a falsehood!"

SYNOPSIS

Constance de Villeneuve is an aristocratic Catholic who lived through the "private feuds" that preceded the ascension of Henry IV to the French throne. She lost her brothers and her father in the wars and, like many others, finds it difficult to come to terms with a suddenly united country. Shelley describes the tension still existing in Constance's world: "Often did the hands that had clasped each other in seeming friendly greeting, involuntarily, as the grasp was released, clasp the dagger's hilt." Before the war, Constance had loved Gaspar De Vaudemont, a local Protestant, but now she feels they cannot be together as her union with Gaspar would defame the memory of her father and brothers, both sacrificed in battle for Gaspar's cause.

Constance is the last remaining member of her family. Thus, she is an "orphan countess" whose beauty and inherited wealth attract much attention. However, she never attends court and contemplates entering a convent. King Henry forbids such action until he has the opportunity to visit Constance to determine the motive of "one so beautiful, young, and gifted with fortune's honours, to desire to bury herself in a cloister."

Constance's grief knows no bounds, and she cries constantly, with the narrator comparing her to Lady Olivia in Shakespeare's *Twelfth Night*. She walks about her estate, finding comfort in the soothing breezes and sun, "the motion and change eternally working" in nature. She unconsciously seeks a particular nook in the park where she sits dejected, holding the king's letter that announces a visit to her estate. She questions fate as to why, "so young, unprotected, and forsaken," she now has also to struggle with the king's impending visit and his attempt to unite her with a husband. She longs to simply be allowed to remain in her home and grieve those she has lost, where she once dreamed "a mad dream of happiness."

As she sits in the nook, Constance is startled by a nearby rustling and for a moment hopes it is her former lover, Gaspar, who used to meet her in that spot. More realistically assuming it is one of her attendants, she then notes that the step is too strong for a woman, and Gaspar appears. She knows that she should rush from the spot, but she longs to see him one more time before she takes vows that will forever separate them. Shelley informs readers that the couple had once taken their own vows of "constancy" before Gaspar fought for the Protestant cause as a knight. He tells her he also wants to see her one more time before leaving for the Crusades in the Holy Land. Constance tells him that he will not be sent away, as he is too valuable now to the king, who will not want to lose his "favorite cavalier."

Gaspar reveals that one word from Constance will cause him to stay. She replies that never again will a smile or word from her be his and states that it was a sin for her to have opened her father's door in the past to their enemy. When Gaspar reminds her of happier times, Constance retorts that they were miserable days when she could imagine happiness as the result of her disobedience to her family, members of which she now mourns. He argues that they are both the last of their families and describes the positive aspects of their former relationship, asking whether their honest and loving vows should now be broken. Constance replies that they should never have been caught up in love and happiness when war and misery "were raging around." She tells him to leave and be happy serving the king, adding that other women will receive the vows he once gave her. She adds that she will do as all Christians should and pray for her enemies.

Constance returns home and speaks with her serving woman, Manon, sharing with her a plan to sleep on St. Catherine's couch. Manon reacts with fear, stating that no one has ever slept there without falling into the river and drowning. Constance declares that she will sleep there the following night, hoping for righteousness through a holy experience. Manon reminds her that the king will visit the next day, but Constance is firm in her resolve, noting that she hopes St. Catherine's votaries will guide her during her dreams.

Gaspar visits King Henry, who has stayed overnight close by Nantes, and explains Constance's resistance. He adds that he is most sad that she has resolved to sacrifice her own happiness by destroying his. The king had planned to present Gaspar to Constance as a possible husband, but Gaspar explains that he believes she will disobey even the king, so set is she on entering a convent. He declares that he will fight in Palestine, as a soldier of the Cross. The king tells Gaspar that he knows women better than does the knight, and that they should follow their original plan.

When the king's party arrives at Chateau Villeneuve the following day, he expects to be met by a pale and downcast Constance. Instead, she is animated and flushed, causing the king to believe that she either does not love Gaspar or has already decided to be with him forever. During dinner, when the king mentions Gaspar, Constance asks that they wait until the next day for that discussion. The king replies that this must mean she does not hate De Vaudemont. Constance states that "we are taught that we should forgive, that we should love our enemies." Gaspar emerges, having been disguised as the king's serving man, Dan Apollo. He wonders at Constance's radically changed demeanor, thinking of her now animated appearance and speech as "a riddle hard to solve." Constance faints upon recognizing him; then, when revived, she faints again and has a fit of weeping, bitterly disappointing Gaspar. She promises the next morning to disclose her purpose to the king. The king replies "Tomorrow—again tomorrows!—Does tomorrow bear some charm, maiden?" But he agrees and leaves.

Constance carries out her plan to sleep in St. Catherine's bed, "a narrow ledge overhanging the deep rapid Loire." The narrator describes her action as a madness that would shock even the king, who would not believe "any woman capable" of daring to invite the "disturbed visions" that such a sleep might deliver. To the onlookers, Constance,

a woman whose "beauty was so highly intellectual," and whom the king had heard praised for "her strength of mind and talents," was engaging in a foolish and rash act. But Constance's gentle spirit was crushed by guilt over undertaking "forbidden pleasures" with the enemy of her father, causing her to dare to "sacrifice all" and risk danger and death for redemption.

The night turns stormy as Manon accompanies Constance down a hill and into a boat that travels to a chapel. Constance's emotions are churning as she recognizes the love that she feels for Gaspar. Her thoughts predict "pleasant dreams," but then Manon calls her attention to a boat with four rowers in black cloaks that moves silently by their own boat. Manon calls on St. Catherine to protect the two women, and Constance recognizes Gaspar in the other boat. When she calls out to him, he does not reply. She slips into visions, imagining various shapes along the river, including her father waving and her brothers frowning from the shore. When they land, Manon tries to convince Constance to return home, but she rushes into a chapel and tells her waiting maid to remain behind.

Constance moves through a "narrow tortuous passage" to end up on a cliff above the rushing waters of the Loire, which seems to run faster than normal beneath thick black clouds. She has to remove her mantle, a requirement "of the spell," and then lie on the narrow precipice. Sleep does not come easily, but eventually she begins to dose, and she wonders whether the saint will send dreams "to drive her to despair, or to bid her be blest forever." As she falls asleep, Gaspar keeps watch beneath the hill.

When morning arrives, Gaspar clambers up the hill, finding a hold where none seemed to exist. The hill is not high; the danger that exists to the occupant of the "couch" is plunging into the waters below, rather than suffering a long fall. He finds Constance with her hands folded on her chest, her dark hair about her, in serene sleep. She smiles in her sleep, then tears fall, and she cries, "No!—he shall not die!—I will unloose his chains!—I will save him!" Gaspar catches her as she might fall, and she opens her eyes from her "dream of fate" to see him.

When Manon awakes in the chapel, it is decorated, and the altar is adorned with "golden chalices"; a priest is chanting to kneeling knights and the king. Constance and Gaspar enter together and are married. Constance waits a long time to speak of what happened to her during her sleep on the couch, hesitant to consider the days of "terror" when she felt that love was a crime. She had a full vision of being herself in "Paynim land" and an invisible St. Catherine guiding her through the city of infidels. She had visited a palace to see the infidels rejoicing and then entered a dungeon to find a ragged, skeletal prisoner. She later realized the prisoner represented Gaspar, and that she had been the enemy. She tells Gaspar, "I then knew for the first time what life and what death was. I was bid believe to make the living happy was not to injure the dead; and I felt how wicked and how vain was that false philosophy which placed virtue and good in hatred and unkindness." She knew that she had to release Gaspar from his metaphorical chains and bid him to "live for love." She first felt the true value of life when she sprang forward from St. Catherine's couch to fall to her own death, had not Gaspar been there to save her, his voice blessing her "for evermore."

COMMENTARY

"The Dream" provided Shelley a venue in which to express her own feelings that an individual should be able to pursue the future unburdened by the past. As evidenced in her letters, she felt constant pressure following her husband's death to hide from the public, which continued to intrude on her personal life due to her husband's and his circle's infamous activities. Mary Shelley took part in those activities, but only peripherally; many consider her more of a spectator than a participant. She remained all too aware of the problems involved with trying to convince the public not to look back to another age in light of her father's attempt to clear her mother's public reputation with his publication of *Memoirs of the Author of A Vindication of the Rights of Women*. The public focused only on MARY WOLLSTONECRAFT's more sensationalistic activities, not accepting WILLIAM GODWIN's book in the spirit in which he published it. As the critic Amy Sterling points out, a literary encyclopedia of that time contained a single entry under the term *prostitution*: "Mary Wollstonecraft."

In addition, Mary Shelley had to learn to forgive her own husband for his philandering and his practice of the romantic sublime, an ideology that promoted the importance of "saving the world" through practice of romantic ideals over that of caring for family. Furthermore, she had experienced a lack of forgiveness on the part of her own father following her elopement with Percy Shelley, a married man; her estrangement from her father lasted a full two years. The fact that Constance felt tremendous guilt in pursuing "forbidden love" with Gaspar surely had autobiographical significance for Shelley.

Never a religious person herself, Shelley may have tried to emphasize the foolishness and tragic waste in religious wars of any kind. Neither Catholicism nor Protestantism appear in a positive light in "The Dream," with the exception of an emphasis on the Catholic convent as a haven of sorts for women. Later feminist critics would emphasize the importance of the independence afforded by communities of women, freed of societal gender expectations. Feminist critics would find of interest additional aspects of the story, including Constance's intellect being equated to her beauty. She is also an active character when she plots her own solution to her quandary and courageously faces possible death in search of spiritual truth.

Shelley emphasizes the superiority of nature to religion as a key to the discovery of such truth, a key facet of romantic belief. Constance is first seen seeking solace outdoors. While she feels "pent up" beneath the roof of her undoubtedly lavish home, she is enticed to spend countless hours beneath "the clear sky, the spreading uplands, the antique wood," with nature's eternal workings the only thing able to call her "out of that dull sorrow" that proved unrelenting beneath her "castle roof." One certain location symbolizes her strongest and most enduring passion for Gaspar; it is "thickset with tall umbrageous trees" and filled with flowers. Although she vows not to go there, she continually returns to a space that Shelley suggests serves as a substitute chapel. As does Victor Frankenstein, Constance seeks a place in nature where the spirits of the dead wander, perhaps cursing the person "who permits their murderer [Gaspar] to disturb their sacred repose." Constance also turns to nature to test her resolve and to gain clarity of vision, choosing to sleep outside in the elements on St. Catherine's couch. Shelley emphasizes the rugged hillside, the churning waters, the mournful wind in the trees, and the "bed" itself—little more than a rock shelf covered with moss. While Constance prepares to suffer from the chill, instead she falls into a soothing slumber as nature affords her the dreams that she needs in order to determine her future.

Readers familiar with Shelley's works will recognize the importance of dreams and visions to the self knowledge gained by her protagonist. They have been used in that way since the first popular version of the HERO'S JOURNEY, or the quest: Homer's *Odyssey*. Where in "The Dream" it is a saint who enlightens Constance, in *The Odyssey* the Greek goddess, Athena, brings wisdom to Odysseus through visions and dreams. She also offers rest to Penelope, who has often worked through the night weaving a funeral shroud to fend off advances from neighboring men in the absence of her husband. The romantic poets believed in the use of drug-induced visions, as evidenced, for example, in Samuel Taylor Coleridge's poem "Kubla Kahn; or, a Vision in a Dream: a Fragment." William Godwin's contemporary, William Blake, engaged frequently in visionary writing, producing work largely unrecognized for its importance during his own time.

In addition, both Godwin and Blake rejected not only religion but also civic law as man's best path to self-enlightenment. Blake wrote in *The Marriage of Heaven and Hell* several "Proverbs of Hell," one beginning, "Prisons are built with stones of Law, Brothels with bricks of Religion." Shelley may have felt her father's and his contemporary's influence when she caused Constance to reject the king's direction. Henry represents the law of Constance's era and tries to impose his will, albeit gently, to counteract what she considers the best plan for her future. While Shelley did not strongly speak out against either civic law or religion, the subtext of her writing suggests her belief in the destructive nature of both. Just as she suffered for the dogma of religion with its attacks against her mother and her own lifestyle as a young woman, she struggled against the laws that controlled her son's inheritance and her culture's views of activities suitable for women.

"The Dream" begins with some promise to vary from the stock romantic tale through Constance's active stance. She does, in the end, assume responsibility for her future, choosing of her own volition to marry Gaspar. Had her choice not matched that of her king, one wonders if the tale would end so happily.

CHARACTERS

Constance Shelley's protagonist has a symbolic name, which is echoed in the story as the two lovers speak of their vows of constancy. Constance's actions also emphasize the meaning of her name as one who remains steady and devoted, seen in her focus on duty to her family, as well as in her unflagging love for Gaspar. One might say that her constant nature helps cause the conflict that she suffers. Described as a beautiful orphan countess, she is also deemed to have intellect and is "Mistress of herself," standing strong against outside visitors. Shelley reveals the influence of Shakespeare in her comparison of Constance to Lady Olivia in *Twelfth Night*. Also a countess, Lady Olivia will not marry, having chosen to suffer seven years of solitude following the death of her father and then her brother.

However, while Constance begins the story as an active agent, she soon turns passive and, despite her intelligence, ultimately behaves as a stock fairy-tale heroine. She dissolves into tears at the sight of Gaspar while in the king's presence, and assumes a helpless prone position on several occasions, fainting and lying down, like Sleeping Beauty, eventually to be awakened by the touch of her lover, who is required to rescue her. Thus, true love conquers all in "The Dream," besting religious warfare, the call of duty to the Holy Crusades, and traditional mourning for a familial loss. Shelley knew her readers and offered them exactly the type of tale they would have expected and desired, one of escape and fulfillment despite all odds. Still, they were left with their own vision of another era during which women seemed to have greater control over their fates.

Shelley does round her characters by presenting them with an unusual challenge not seen in fairy tales. They do not combat dragons or evil spells; instead, they must confront the evil of man in the form of war and the spell of guilt that man's rules cast over Constance. She does literally save Gaspar from the horrible death predicted in her dream had he joined the Crusades in reaction to her rejection of him. And Constance is a dynamic character, undergoing an epiphany that leads to a permanent change in her ideals and behavior.

Gaspar Like Constance, Gaspar plays the part of a traditional fairy-tale character, that of a prince. He woos his love and, despite her resistance, eventually supplies the requisite rescue from her predicament. He meets all of the requirements for the traditional hero. He is young, handsome, charming, and completely devoted to Constance, so much so that he vows to sacrifice himself in the Crusades should she not agree to marry him. Although not a true prince, he is an aristocrat, and as the king's favorite courtier, he remains as devoted to Henry as a flesh-and-blood relation. While Gaspar is obedient to the king's civic law, he does resist the call to additional war on behalf of religion, helping Shelley make one of her most commonly emphasized points: The private needs of family should always trump those of public demand.

FURTHER READING

Farmer, David Hugh. "Catherine (Katharine) of Alexandria." The Oxford Dictionary of Saints. 3rd ed. New York: Oxford University Press, 1992, 88–89.

Mousnier, Roland. *The Assassination of Henry IV.* New York: Charles Scribner's Sons, 1973.

Shelley, Mary. "The Dream." Available online. URL: http://worldlibrary.net/eBooks/WorldeBookLibrary.com/dreamshelley.htm. Accessed September 10, 2009.

"St. Catherine of Sienna, Virgin—1347–1380." EWTN Global Catholic Network. Available online. URL: http://www.ewtn.com/library/mary/csiena.htm. Accessed May 30, 2010.

Sterling, Amy. Introduction to *Falkner*, by Mary Shelley, 5–9. Doylestown, Pa.: Wildside Press, 2002.

Sussman, Charlotte. "Stories for the *Keepsake.*" In *The Cambridge Companion to Mary Shelley*, edited by Esther Schor, 163–179. Cambridge and New York: Cambridge University Press, 2003.

"The Evil Eye" (1830)

When Mary Shelley published her short story "The Evil Eye" in the ladies' annual THE KEEPSAKE, she offered her readers not only the happy-ending love story they expected from that journal but also the opportunity to vicariously experience an exotic locale. Stories from the Far East grew in popularity along with trade between England and Eastern countries, especially China and India. Set in Greece and Turkey, Shelley's story tells of a girl foundling who, through a traditional plot sequence turning on secret identity and coincidence, is reunited not only with her kidnapped son but also her long-lost father. Topics include revenge, family infighting over inherited wealth, the abuse of friendship, courage, and dedication to family. The story is best enjoyed in a version with footnotes that clarify terms which the common reader will find unfamiliar.

Shelley's decision to set her story in a foreign culture is not surprising, based on her own experiences and friendships. She had traveled widely on the Continent with her husband, journeys that she had featured in *History of a Six Weeks Tour* (1817), focusing on France, Switzerland, Germany, and Holland. She would feature foreign locales again in *Rambles in Germany and Italy in 1840, 1842, and 1843* (1844). She had also lived in several locations in Italy from 1818 to 1822. It was while in Italy that PERCY BYSSHE SHELLEY drowned in the Gulf of Spezia on July 8, 1822. In addition, the Shelleys had become friends with EDWARD JOHN TRELAWNEY, a devotee of Percy Shelley. A self-proclaimed adventurer, he shared many stories with his companions, and Mary Shelley would remain his friend for years, eventually helping him publish a book.

dered garments, fair to see; / The crimson-scarfed man of Macedon." The influence of that description may be seen in Shelley's detailed description of Dmitri as he prepares to undertake the journey to comply with Katusthius's request. Shelley also uses the term *Mainote* in her story, as Byron did in his poem "The Giaour: a Fragment of a Turkish Tale" (1813), to refer to "island pirates" from Maina. Maina provided a gathering place for Greek independence fighters under the guidance of Dmitri Ypsilanti in the War for Independence, which began in 1821. In the same poem, Byron refers to the Arnaoots, the band of Albanian mountaineers who play an important part in Shelley's story. Her reference to the village where Cyril and his band gather clues as to Dmitri's whereabouts as "monastic Zitza" also comes from "The Giaour."

Other Eastern narratives that influenced Shelley were *Anastasius* (1819) by Thomas Hope and *La Guzla* (1827) by Prosper Mérimée. The latter was a collection of folk ballads supposedly based on the original Illyrian, but Mérimée eventually revealed his "translation" to be a hoax. Shelley had reviewed Mérimée's work for the *Westminster Review* a few months before the publication of "The Evil Eye," suggesting it as a strong source for geographic details for her story.

While the setting and background for "The Evil Eye" differ greatly from that of Shelley's other stories, its emphasis on justice, the enduring power of love, and family do not. These are common themes in Shelley's fiction, as is the emphasis of the importance of nature. She brings the story to life for readers through the inclusion of detail such as her description in the story's opening of the village of Corvo, set in "a romantic folding" of Mount Trebucci and containing "minarets, crowned by a dome rising from out a group of pyramidal cypresses." The village is literally framed by nature, which also provides a basis for the dome, reflecting human dependence on nature's landscapes and its bounty.

SYNOPSIS

Katusthius Ziani, a Moreot, has traveled through robber-infested regions to a village in the wilds of Albania. The only Greek among Turkish inhabitants, he assures his safety by stating that he is

Lord Byron in Albanian dress from an 1835 portrait. Byron's poem about his travels in Greece, *Childe Harold's Pilgrimage,* influenced Mary Shelley's short story "The Evil Eye." *(Painting by Thomas Phillips)*

Perhaps most important to this particular story was the Shelleys' intimate friend, GEORGE GORDON BYRON. Lord Byron had traveled to Greece in 1823 with Trelawney to assist the Greeks fighting against the Turks; he died of illness at Missolonghi the following year. Shelley incorporated into "The Evil Eye" many ideas that she drew from Byron's time in Greece and, more specifically, from his four-canto poem, *Childe Harold's Pilgrimage* (1812–18), in which he described the travels of a pilgrim through Portugal, Spain, the Ionian Islands, and Albania. Shelley begins her story with an epigram that is a quotation from Byron's work: "The wild Albanian kirtled to his knee, / With shawl-girt head, and ornamented gun, / And gold-embroi-

a friend, a *pobratimo,* of Dmitri of the Evil Eye. Katusthius's relationship to the Albanian Dmitri demands respect from all. He eventually finds Dmitri in the mountain village of Corvo, where Dmitri has distinguished himself, developing a reputation for courage and loyalty.

Although now considered a fearsome warrior, Dmitri is rumored to have been gentler in the past, revealed in a section that highlights his history. An educated man, he had married a Sciote girl named Helena, and, contrary to the women-hating ways of his fellow Albanians, he loved Helena dearly and treated her with great respect. His passion for Helena was "a portion of his living, beating heart—the nobler part of himself—the diviner mould in which his rugged nature had been recast." However, tragedy strucks, and Dmitri returned from an expedition to find Helena murdered and his home destroyed by Mainotes who had also stolen his infant daughter. Despite his wealth and power, Dmitri's life became desolate as he spent three failed years in search of the baby. He was so bold as to attack a Mainote port, where he sustained a deep gash that ran from one eyebrow to a cheek. After his wounding, Katusthius saved him from death, whereupon Dmitri vowed eternal friendship. The two remained together for a time until Dmitri decided to return home, his friend's farming pursuits too mundane for his taste. Although once the most handsome member of his band of Arnaoots, following the loss of his family, Dmitri assumed a new brooding character that matched his savage appearance, accentuated by the scar. He now takes delight in drawing blood and has developed a "dark countenance" that causes both men and women to tremble. His steely gaze and fiendish laugh have supernatural powers over others, powers both feared and admired by his band.

When Katusthius arrives, Dmitri and his group have just returned with great spoils and riches, and the other men celebrate. However, Dmitri does not join their revels, remaining serious, apart, and brooding. Upon seeing Katusthius, he is overjoyed and enthusiastically welcomes his old friend with a lavish meal. Katusthius reminds Dmitri that he once rescued him from the Kakovougnis of Boularias and that Dmitri had pledged to repay his debt. He explains that he needs Dmitri to help him recover property that had belonged to his wealthy merchant father but had unjustly been given to his cousin, Cyril.

According to Katusthius, as a young man he had been captivated by "some superstition" and traveled abroad until he met a young Fanariote woman from Constantinople whom he wanted to marry. Because he had no money, he returned to Corinth to claim his fortunes. He discovered that his father's wealth indeed had grown during Katusthius's absence. However, he had died the year before not knowing the whereabouts of his son. Thus, his inheritance had gone to Cyril, who was married with a young son of his own. When Katusthius approached Cyril regarding the inheritance that he considered his own, Cyril immediately agreed to give Katusthius half of the inheritance. This did not satisfy Katusthius, who wanted the entire fortune as his birthright. He considered murdering Cyril, but his cousin was well regarded in Corinth, and Katusthius hesitated to kill a family member himself.

Having convinced Dmitri that Cyril is "a base interloper," Katusthius persuades him to assist in removing Cyril, so that Katusthius may regain all his wealth. After Dmitri agrees to help, Katusthius leaves, and Dmitri follows two days later, having purchased a fine horse and munitions to accomplish his purpose.

The next section of the story introduces readers to Cyril Ziani; his wife, Zella; and their young son, Constans. When Cyril returns home one day and finds Zella trembling, he learns that during his absence, a stranger had turned what seemed to be an "Evil Eye" upon Constans, a rosy-cheeked, golden-haired boy. The couple forgets the incident until Cyril returns a week later after traveling to conduct business to find Constans' nurse sobbing and Zella in the chapel, weeping. Cyril asks what happened, but Zella is too emotional to reply, and Constans also begins to cry. Cyril leaves the chapel wondering at the fate of fortune and what has happened.

When Zella comes out of the chapel, she explains that the Evil Eye had again been on the child. This time, the dark Arnaoot had emerged from a nearby grove mounted on a black steed and raced up to the house's threshold. When Constans ran out to greet him, the man said the boy was lovely and commanded him to look up. After looking into the man's face, the boy shrieked and fell on the ground, gasping, causing the women to run forward to grab him as the man galloped away. The women revived Constans with holy water and prayers.

Although disturbing, the event loses its power to frighten the group over time, and they return to their normal routine. As the weeks pass, Constans continues to mature "in intelligence and beauty." When Cyril jokes about the Evil Eye on occasion, Zella hushes him, not wanting to invite disaster.

Katusthius visits Cyril and Zella, who receive him with love and respect due to a trustworthy family member. He explains that he is traveling to Istanbul and wonders whether he might do any business on behalf of Cyril while there. They enjoy a pleasant evening with discussions about politics and trading, and the next day, Katusthius asks whether Cyril and Zella will go with him to Naples, where he plans to depart by ship. Zella overcomes her reluctance to leave home, and they go with Katusthius. Upon returning the following day, the couple speak of their fortunes and how lonely the life of the wanderer would be. As they grow close to home, they know something is wrong when they arrive at their farm and see a team of oxen deserted in the middle of a plowed furrow. No one is at work, and the waterwheel does not turn.

Cyril and Zella race home to discover that Constans has been taken by the man with the Evil Eye. The man came to the door of the house pretending to be exhausted, and when the nurse brought him a drink, he grabbed Constans from her arms and rode away. All the domestics had attempted to follow the man. Upon learning what happened, Cyril rides away, telling Zella not to worry, that he will return with the child. The workers return having been unable to discover the route taken by the Albanian kidnapper.

Cyril returns the following day, also with no report of luck. He departs again the next day and is gone for several days, while Zella remains despondent. In his absence, the domestics report having seen Arnaoots sneaking around the area. When Cyril returns, again unsuccessful, he does have some news, but not the news for which Zella has hoped. He discovered that Katusthius had not traveled to Naples but instead joined the Arnaoots and sailed for the shores of the Gulf of Lepanto; thus, the couple understands that their kin has betrayed them. Cyril plans to depart again but does not want to leave Zella alone, so they decide she should stay at her father's home during his journey.

The narrator supplies a history of the warfare between the Mainotes, Zella's ancestors, and the Kakovougnis, a more dark, squat race than the Mainotes. Then readers learn that Cyril was once on a ship that came upon a fortress besieged by a band of Kakovougnis that prevented a captain and his family from leaving in a commercial vessel. When able, the captain slipped away, arriving at Cyril's boat with his family. He requested refuge for his family and his treasure. Cyril agreed and transported them safely to Naples, where he later fell in love with the captain's beautiful daughter, Zella. They married and departed, and Zella's father, Camaraz, prospered, becoming the chief of a large tribe and the captain of Kardamyla.

When Zella and Cyril arrive at Kardamyla, Camaraz states that he will accompany Cyril in the search for Constans. While they are absent, Zella often visits the sea, not minding the gales or tempests because "the wild winds spoke to her." Described by the narrator as "this orphaned child of happiness," Zella spends hours on an outcropping rock, watching for a vessel that may signal the safe return of her son, husband, and father. She sees visions supplied by the Moirae, "the old fates of her native Grecian soil," howling about her son, whom she sees "pining" under the influence of the Evil Eye. Her cheeks turn pale, and she grows weak waiting and watching.

Cyril and Camaraz race about the country, chasing various clues regarding the whereabouts of Dmitri and Katusthius. They lead a band of Camaraz's tribe and decide to split into groups so as not to attract attention as they travel. At a monastery in Zitza, they rest and learn that the group they hunt had been there two weeks previously. The man with the Evil Eye is well known to the area.

During their stay, the child claimed to the monastery caloyers (monks) that Dmitri and Katusthius had carried him away from his home, but the two men in unison denied the child's claim. However, the caloyers could see that the two men were at odds regarding the child. While Dmitri was visibly fond of the boy, Katusthius appeared ready to kill him. The two began to quarrel more often and eventually became violent over the boy's fate, after which Katusthius took the boy and sneaked away in the middle of the night. A furious Dmitri chased after him on the following day.

Cyril and Camaraz pursue Dmitri back to Corvo, where Dmitri had gathered a band of his men to assist him. Cyril and Camaraz learn from a man who had been injured and was unable to join the group that Dmitri had succeeded in tracking Katusthius and forcing him to hide in the monastery of the Prophet Elias, on a mountain peak eight leagues from Ioannina. He temporarily left Constans with the monastery caloyers, who had refused to turn the child over to Dmitri, despite the fierce warrior's impassioned demands. Eventually, Dmitri and his followers succeeded in tearing down the iron door blocking their admittance to the monastery. When Constans saw Dmitri, the delighted child slipped away from the caloyer holding him and ran into Dmitri's arms, convincing the inhabitants of the monastery that he belonged with Dmitri. In the meantime, Katusthius had convinced the local Sagorians that his little nephew suffered under the evil influence of others, and a band joined him to climb the hill to the monastery to take and protect the boy.

Dmitri traveled away from the monastery, placing Constans in front of him on his horse until the band of warriors stopped for the night. One of Dmitri's Arnaoots warned the group that Katusthius approached with his supporters. As Dmitri and Katusthius planned to confront one another, the Moreots led by Camaraz and Cyril appeared, and Cyril called out to Constans. Camaraz threatened Dmitri with the ferocity of the Mainote pirates if he did not return the child, stating, "I am the grandsire of that child—give him to me!"

Dmitri became enraged to think the child was an offspring of the dreaded Mainotes who had murdered his wife and kidnapped his daughter. The narrator describes the effect of the news on Dmitri by telling readers that "a snake, which he felt awakening in his bosom, could not so suddenly have changed his cheer." For a moment, he is poised to dash Constans on the rocks. He cried to Katusthius that he had been driven by "resistless fates" to betray his friend's trust in him, but now he will kill the child, "a victim of . . . just revenge." However, Cyril and Camaraz worked their way up the low cliff, and the boy jumped into his father's arms when Dmitri hurled a dagger at Camaraz.

Although wounded, Camaraz told Dmitri the information on which Shelley's entire plot turns. He explained that Constans is innocent. His mother had been left behind as a child when Mainote pirates murdered her mother years ago. He added that Constans's father is a Corinthian, his mother a Sciote girl. The murder of Constans's grandmother happened 15 years previously, when Camaraz was among a group of pirates who believed an old lady living in a village on the coast of Scio hoarded treasure in her cottage. The group of men killed both women in their attack, only later understanding that the young woman was the real treasure of the home. Camaraz had not participated in the murders, and he rescued the girl child, who was about two years old, and raised her as his own. She was Constans's mother. Dmitri realized that the child Camaraz referred to was his own long-lost daughter and that Constans was his grandson. The child's confidence in Dmitri returned, and he embraced the old man.

In the final scene, Zella spent some nights on the "couch" of a cliff over the sea, watching for her husband and father. She could not eat and could not sleep, despite the opium given to her by her attendant. She thought she saw a vessel and began to move down the hill, but she stopped halfway down, fearful of disappointment. Exhausted and succumbing to the opiate, she fell asleep, her shawl pulled around her and her head on a rock pillow. When she awakened, she realized she was no longer on the ground and discovered she was on the deck of a vessel skimming over the waves. Possessed by wonder, she pulled aside the sail that blocked her view to see Dmitri sitting nearby, cradling Constans in his arms. When she cried out, Cyril turned and folded her in an embrace.

COMMENTARY

Shelley offers readers a tale populated with irresistible characters: a beautiful young woman, her devoted husband, and her spirited, intelligent son; an aging Albanian bandit who remains miserable due to the loss of his own beautiful wife and lovely daughter; a greedy, scheming ne'er-do-well; and a devoted and fierce grandfather willing to risk all for his grandson by an adopted daughter. Shelley's plot is a variation of a well-used story based on hidden identity and coincidence. It incorporates the popular foundling story line, in which a baby is adopted by a stranger, and its true identity is not learned until later, with stunning effect. In such stories, the child is often revealed to have an aristocratic background that entails inheritance. Such plots formed the basis for various mythological tales and the biblical tale of Moses, as well as novels such as Charles Dickens's *Oliver Twist*. It endures into later centuries and is seen as a pivotal element, for instance, of the *Star Wars* movie series, a 20th-century pop culture phenomenon. In Shelley's case, she employs that element to support themes including the importance of adult stability to a healthy family and the power of love to overcome the fiercest desire for revenge.

Shelley's readers also find her traditional use of natural elements to emphasize their ability to elevate human existence in "The Evil Eye." Her emphasis on an exotic locale allows the introduction of geographical specifics that Shelley had not employed previously. However, her romantic movement message regarding the power of nature to influence and better human character and ease their suffering is easily recognizable. For instance, when she describes the location of "monastic Zitza," she notes it "is situated on a green eminence, crowned by a grove of oak trees, immediately behind the village." Her selection of terms such as *eminence* and *crowned* both figuratively and literally elevate the importance of the natural setting in which the human-made structures exist. The narrator continues, "Perhaps there is not in the world a more beautiful or more romantic plot, sheltered itself by clustering trees, looking out on one widespread landscape of hill and dale, enriched by vineyards, dotted with frequent flocks," with the far away blue mountains forming a backdrop. Shelley also privileges the ocean, symbolic of the HERO'S JOURNEY and the ebb and flow of the life cycle, as she has in other stories. All of the males in the story are associated with the ocean as a source of employment and income. After Constans is kidnapped, Zella finds comfort only close to the ocean, where she wanders along beaches and climbs the hills. She is not frightened by "the shadows of the wide-winged clouds, when the roar of the surges" come to shore and the waves crest. The narrator compares the whitecaps to "newly shorn sheep scattered along wide-extended downs," as if to associate the uncontrolled energy of the sea with the more peaceful surroundings commanded by humans. Zella does not feel "gale nor inclement cold" due the fact that "the wild winds spoke to her," making her a figurative sister of the natural elements. That association immediately identifies her as a positive character, one whom readers understand they can trust and should support.

Critics who look for autobiographical aspects in Shelley's stories may find something here in the orphan state of Zella, a state shared by many of Shelley's characters. With the early death of her mother and her father's remarriage, the young Mary often felt marginalized by her suddenly inattentive father and a stepmother with whom she had little in common. In her childhood, she seemed to have most enjoyed the summer spent in Scotland, with its rugged geography and sea imagery reappearing in a number of her works. In addition, she may have identified with Zella's later state as an orphan of fortune, which seems to have deserted her with the kidnapping of her son and her husband's and father's absence. No doubt Shelley felt as if fortune had abandoned her, following the loss of several infants and Percy Shelley's death. Other personal connections reflected in "The Evil Eye" include those to her friends, Edward Trelawney and Lord Byron, mentioned in the introduction. Those connections would be seen most vividly in Shelley's final novel, *Falkner* (1837), a work also discussed in this volume.

CHARACTERS

Cyril Cyril is a flat character, remaining the same from the beginning of the story until the end. He represents the devotion to family that Shelley always supported in her fiction. The safety and well-being of his wife and child supersedes all, making him a noble figure. Interestingly, Shelley adds a touch of realism to Cyril, emphasizing that he held back when Dmitri had Constans, in contrast to the older and more courageous Camaraz.

Dmitri Dmitri is a man whose life is twice changed by fortune or fate, depending on one's point of view. The initial change is negative, with the loss of his wife and child, but the next is positive when he regains his daughter and a grandson. He is meant to symbolize both the best and worst aspects of human nature under the influence of passion. Love makes him an admirable character, whereas revenge perverts his natural tendency toward goodness and justice. Through Dmitri, Shelley suggests that one should never use love as an excuse for one's motivation to commit destructive acts. She provides a detailed description of her protagonist, a wealthy, well-dressed warrior with long, straight hair that falls from beneath a shawled cap to his waist, "a shaggy white capote" around one shoulder, a face that reflects the elements in its wrinkles and a brow "furrowed with care." He sports long, black mustaches and moves with "barbaric grace," supported by "bandit pride," but with a stamp of ferocity so strong that many believe "a supernatural spirit of evil" inhabits him. He represents the consummate BYRONIC HERO with a dark past and haunted aspect that make him fearful to those who do not understand his passionate drive. Although he does not undergo a true epiphany observable by the reader, the conclusion to the story guarantees a change in his life. Once a lonely, bitter old man, he has been returned to his family through the same chance that caused him to lose that family.

Katusthius Katusthius serves as the prototypical antagonist. Greedy, grasping, self-centered, and a man who has abandoned his own family, he suffers a blow of fate in losing his fortune. His loss may be compared to that of Dmitri, an approach that will allow the reader to also compare the manner by which the two men deal with their fates. Katusthius's lack of a moral code is revealed when he involves a man who is supposedly his friend in his own dastardly deeds with attempts to steal from Cyril, although Cyril has treated him with justice and respect. Thus, Katusthius defiles not only friendship and faith but also family bonds. He is a hypocrite, professing to believe that he should not desecrate family ties, but is not hesitant to ask Dmitri to do the dirty work for him. A man of purpose, his focus never wanders from his prize, even when Dmitri turns against him.

Katusthius's fate is not revealed to the reader. It could have been quite unpleasant had the pirates taken hold of him, especially because his own supporters would probably have not protected him once they discovered that he had deceived them in the ethics of his purpose. On the other hand, Cyril might well have forgiven him with Dmitri's support, due to Cyril's naturally good nature and Dmitri's dismissal of a desire for revenge. One hopes that at least the pirates would hold him for ransom after his family had left, demanding his portion of his fortune for their troubles.

Zella Zella is a stock female character in need of rescue, but she is also a devoted mother and wife, again emphasizing the importance of family leadership by a strong couple. Like another Shelley heroine, Constance, in "The Dream," Zella falls asleep on a stone couch to awaken in the arms of her lover, her positive future assured.

FURTHER READING

Byron, George Gordon Byron, Lord. *Childe Harold's Pilgrimage.* Project Gutenberg. Available online. URL: http://www.gutenberg.org/ebooks/5131. Accessed June 10, 2010.

———. "The Giaour: a Fragment of a Turkish Tale." Available online. URL: http://readytogoebooks.com/LB-Giaour.htm. Accessed June 10, 2010.

Sussman, Charlotte. "Stories for the *Keepsake.*" In *The Cambridge Companion to Mary Shelley,* edited by Esther Schor, 163–179. Cambridge and New York: Cambridge University Press, 2003.

Falkner (1837)

Falkner was Mary Shelley's final novel and one she was anxious to publish. She referred to *Falkner* when she wrote to her publisher, Charles Ollier, on January 7, 1837:

> You will have seen my New Novel advertized by Saunders & Otley. I offered it thro' you to Mr. Bentley, but you would not treat till it was finished. My necessities forced me to conclude with a publisher who did not object to advances—which were the more necessary—as ill health delayed my finishing till now.

This is one of several passages in Shelley's correspondence that reveals her constant need for money to support herself and her son. Some critics have used her financial straits to devalue her fiction. Their underlying logic is that fiction written under financial duress will lack the quality of true art. However, other critics, such as Amy Sterling Casil, believe *Falkner* represents a strong finish to Shelley's production of novels. She views it as supplying a fitting "book end" to Shelley's novel-writing career, which began with *Frankenstein* (1818) and spanned almost 20 years. Most writers' techniques are honed over time; their voices mature, and favored character types, topics, and themes clearly emerge. This is certainly true of Mary Shelley.

Falkner features the moral ambiguity that Shelley enjoyed offering in her later characters, emphasizing questions of morality through a subtext that questions a romantic ideal. That ideal held that morality based on human law remains inferior to the natural morality echoed by nature's elements. Shelley does not, on the other hand, enthusiastically support civil law, revealing its flaws through her plot. In that lack of support, she echoes her father's early attitude. In his idealistic writings, WILLIAM GODWIN had expressed a belief that all civil law should be abolished and civil institutions destroyed, as humankind's better nature would direct them toward their best behavior. Shelley scholar Betty Bennett supports William St. Clair's claim that Godwin believed that in "an unevolved state individuals had to compromise their ideals to safeguard themselves and their families." Such compromise generates the moral ambiguity that in the real world haunts all humans.

Shelley supported neither civic law nor that of nature as the singular best path to morality. Rather, her fiction suggests that morality lies in one individual's ability to remain committed to the good of others, regardless of the challenges of fortune or fate. Certainty does not exist, and disaster always awaits one, despite his or her best attempts to live a moral life. In Casil's opinion, *Falkner* echoes *Frankenstein* in its message that "passion condemns and kills, yet social propriety has no less deadly effect."

The shaping of the Falkner character is strongly influenced by the lives of Shelley's friends GEORGE GORDON BYRON (Lord Byron) and EDWARD JOHN TRELAWNY. Both Byron and Trelawny traveled to Greece, hoping to fight on the side of those seeking Greek independence. In addition, Lord Byron's *Childe Harold's Pilgrimage* (1812–18) focuses on an individual who, like Falkner, is a wanderer. The first two cantos of the poem are written in the voice of Childe Harold, but Byron switches to his own voice in the third canto. Thus, the statement in the fourth canto that underpins both the romantic ideal and provides a sort of motto for Rupert Falkner is Byron's own: "[M]an's greatest tragedy is that he can conceive of a perfection which he cannot attain." It is not an original idea, but rather one rejuvenated in art by each thoughtful generation.

The idea that perfection is desirable but ever out of reach could foster the moral ambiguity of which Falkner is repeatedly guilty. Falkner bases choices and actions on a false logic, as summarized by the narrator early in the novel when Falkner decides to change his life's direction: "We all are apt to think that when we discard a motive we cure a fault, and foster the same error from a new cause with a safe conscience." Falkner constantly "perceived of . . . perfection" and could not be satisfied with life after Alithea's death, caused by his hands. He first seeks escape through suicide and then through fostering a new life for Elizabeth, as if the new life could redeem the one lost.

Sadly, Byron fell ill and died in Greece without participating in the freedom fighting there as he had hoped. That same Greece in the midst of conflict frames Falkner's early action, as he hopes to die in war. However, as Casil claims, despite Falkner's BYRONIC HERO persona, it is the Shelleys' friend Trelawny who most strongly inspires the character. Trelawny, an adventurer extraordinaire, had proposed marriage to Mary Shelley. Whether that unrequited love was truly a love lost that continued to haunt him, as was Falkner's love for Alithea, or simple transient passion is not known. Trelawny continued a long relationship with Mary, despite his bizarre behavior at PERCY SHELLEY's cremation when he grabbed the poet's heart from the flames.

Most critics point to *Falkner*'s focus on a group of orphans as notable. Falkner, Elizabeth, and Gerard are all orphans, cut free from family when young and forced to make do with being fostered or surviving on their own for a time. Casil notes that the three characters find one another through links of "fate and tragedy" that include the loss of their parents as they seek "truths that bind" them together. The young Falkner ends up in an abusive boarding school and later military school, where he is bullied and becomes violent in self defense. His behavior makes him a loner. In Gerard's case, his "orphaning" results from desertion by his mother and "ill treatment" by his father, leading to his emotional isolation as a young boy. A bewildered Elizabeth, barely more than a toddler, cannot understand her parents' deaths and believes they will return, daily haunting their graves. A complete innocent, she must live with a woman who neither wants nor loves her. Elizabeth's needs become secondary to those of Mrs. Baker's natural family. But Falkner, as the center of the tale around whom all other characters orbit, remains decidedly the most tragic of the three.

Indeed, Shelley compares Falkner to PROMETHEUS, a mythical character who had long fascinated Mary, as he did her husband. Prometheus had supplied the secret of fire to humans. For that traitorous act, he was doomed to have his internal organs eaten away each day, only to have them regenerate during the night, with the cycle eternally repeated. Falkner's mental fate may be worse than that of Prometheus and his own physical disintegration. The narrator tells us that Falkner's "mind refus[ed] to acknowledge the bondage to which his body was the prey." He will find a search for any truth difficult while living in such denial, his state mainly a product of self-loathing, guilt, and isolation. Only when he adopts Elizabeth and comes to know Gerard, the son of the woman he loved and whose death he caused, can Falkner find any sense of grace or redemption. As in almost all of her fiction, Shelley structures characters who will allow her to emphasize the importance of the family nucleus to the discovery of universal truth. In essence, that importance may actually *be* the universal truth she wishes to share with her characters and readers alike.

Julia Saunders does not see the author of *Falkner* as the traditional follower of early Victorianism who idealized the family. Instead, Shelley's voice echoed her parents' criticism of gender inequities that affected the sharing of familial responsibilities by the parents. Shelley injected this theme into most of her novels, and she incorporates into *Falkner* one of her strongest plot lines, that of a criminal father who is, in essence, an emotional absentee. In allowing Elizabeth, as Falkner's adopted daughter, to be the unwitting instrument of the law, Shelley may have shaped her characters to model those in William Godwin's novel *Caleb Williams* (1794). In that book, Caleb is an innocent avenger for the victim of his father figure, named Falkland. Anne K. Mellor sees an additional literary parallel between Elizabeth Raby, repeatedly described by Falkner in angelic terms, and Lord Byron's character Aurora Raby in his poem *Don Juan* (1818–24). In canto 14, Byron's speaker describes Aurora as "a young star who shone . . . A lovely being, scarcely form'd or moulded, / A rose with all its sweetest leaves yet folded." He continues, "Early in years, and yet more infantine / In figure, she had something of sublime / In eyes which sadly shone, as seraphs' shine. / All youth—but with an aspect beyond time; / Radiant and grave—as pitying man's decline; / Mournful—but mournful of another's crime." Aurora ministers, as if an angel, to Byron's Don Juan by offering him a taste of heaven on earth. Shelley's narrator repeatedly refers to Elizabeth as an angel and offers this early description of the child, as seen through Falkner's eyes:

This sentiment became far more lively when so beautiful and perfect a creature as Elizabeth Raby was thrown upon his protection . . . her silver-toned laugh went to the heart; her alternately serious or gay looks, each emanating from the spirit of love; her caresses, her little words of endearment; the soft pressure of her tiny hand and warm, rosy lips,—were all charming as beauty, and the absence of guile, could make them.

In this novel, Shelley includes the same emphasis on the importance of the family as in her previous work and fashions yet another strong daughter-father relationship, as she had in *Mathilda* (written 1819–20; published 1959) and *Lodore* (1835). Most critics see these relationships as parallel to the one Shelley shared with her father, William Godwin. The fathers dote on their daughters to the point that they isolate the girls from society and raise them to serve themselves and men in general. An additional strong autobiographical element may be seen in Elizabeth's regular visits to her mother's grave, where, even though a very young child, she reads and wiles away hours of loneliness. The record of Shelley's own frequent visits to her mother's grave where she spent hours reading and writing and even met secretly as a teenager with Percy Shelley is one known to all Shelley aficionados.

As in all of her books, Shelley reveals important literary models in *Falkner*. Shakespeare's *Hamlet* plays a crucial part in helping Elizabeth better understand Gerard, and he teaches Elizabeth about many literary figures, both past and contemporary. Shelley quotes from poets throughout the novel, including her favorite, Samuel Taylor Coleridge, as well as William Wordsworth, William Shakespeare, and Alexander Pope, among others.

SYNOPSIS

Volume 1: Chapters 1–6

The novel's first volume opens with a history of the Raby family, who, two years previously, moved to the seacoast town of Treby with the hope of improving Mr. Raby's poor health. Treby is described by the narrator as having "neighboring fields . . . pranked with all the colors of Flora" and with a "festive and genial atmosphere." Unfortunately, not only did Mr. Edwin Raby not improve, but he died shortly after the family's arrival to Treby. His wife's fragile condition suffered when she had to care so diligently for her husband, and she died within a year. Their child, Elizabeth, was left an orphan with no family relations in the village.

Few people of wealth inhabit the village, and the narrator notes, "The poor are not sentimental," with few visiting the graves of their loved ones. One of those few is Elizabeth Raby, who regularly visits her parents' graves and talks with her mother. Despite her young age, she remains devoted to their memory. She is cared for by a Mrs. Baker, who had originally rented a cottage to the family. Mrs. Baker had hoped to find the means to care for Elizabeth following Mrs. Raby's death, but all she had discovered in the cottage was a bit of money and a letter Mrs. Raby had been writing. The would-be recipient of the letter is identified [only] by a first name, Alithea, so Mrs. Baker cannot contact her to fulfill Mrs. Raby's wish, revealed in the letter, that Alithea would care for Elizabeth. Her letter hints that although Edwin Raby had come from a wealthy family, he was estranged from them, for which the family partly blamed Mrs. Raby. When she had alerted them regarding Edwin's death, they had offered to take in Elizabeth, but not Mrs. Raby. She had declined the offer, knowing they would be cruel and haughty to the child.

Mrs. Baker does what she can for Elizabeth, although she considers the child a financial burden. In June, a stranger arrives, described by the narrator as self-possessed and energetic, at "the verge of thirty." However, he is often possessed by a passionate, restless, fierce mood. He has the appearance of one in charge of his fate, but when he is not under public view, he is transported into a rage. He becomes completely distraught over an unexplained action on his part and suffers guilt so sustained and destructive that he is compared to the mythical Actaeon being torn into pieces by his hounds. Remorsefully, he remembers thinking that he could bend fate to his own will, but he has failed miserably, tragically: "She was dead—the loveliest and best of created beings . . . he had heaped the earth upon her clay-cold form;—and he the cause! he the murderer!"

Unable to bear up under his grief and guilt, the stranger decides to go to the cemetery and shoot himself. He unknowingly sits on Mrs. Raby's grave, causing Elizabeth, unseen in the shadows, to object. He must hide his gun from the child and is unable to follow through on his plan. He thinks Elizabeth one of the loveliest creatures he has ever seen and accompanies her to Mrs. Baker's house. Learning her history, he requests to see the letter that Mrs. Raby had been writing, thinking he might assist in identifying its intended recipient. He sustains a shock when he reads the name Alithea, as he understands that Mrs. Raby's friend was also the woman he loved whose death he had caused.

The stranger walks all night, considering what he has learned and suffering terrible conflict. He recognizes that Elizabeth saved his life and considers it an important turn of fate that makes his living imperative. He must assume responsibility for her life, and that will in some way appease the life he took. He understands from having read Mrs. Raby's letter that Elizabeth would be miserable if allowed to join her father's family.

The next day, he identifies himself to Mrs. Baker as John Falkner, a captain in the Native Cavalry of the East India Company. Satisfied that he must be trustworthy, Mrs. Baker allows him to take Elizabeth. They begin by living in London but Falkner sets out to travel the world because, as the narrator explains, he believes the "glaring character" in his own consciousness is "visible to the whole world." He comes to adore the child, whom he thinks of as a beautiful angel, and Elizabeth adores him. He could never have traveled with only "memory and remorse" as his companions and understands that "he did not live in himself, but in the joyous being at his side." Elizabeth holds in her heart tenderness, fidelity, and unshaken truth, like seeds that will develop later. She tries to cheer Falkner during their travels, which move them from Paris to Odessa over the next six years. At Odessa, Falkner decides that Elizabeth needs a companion/governess and hires the dour Miss Jervis. Solemn and taciturn, Jervis cannot fill the role of a friend that Elizabeth needs. However, she does offer the child the education that Falkner did not have, teaching her "masculine studies" as well as needlework and "habits of neatness and order."

Volume 1: Chapters 7–12

Three more years pass, so Elizabeth is 13 when they settle in Baden. There they meet many visiting English travelers whom Falkner tries to avoid. Elizabeth settles her attention on a 16-year-old boy who attracts her due to his obvious sadness and self-isolation. Reckless and aloof, he takes a spill from a horse in the presence of Elizabeth and Falkner, who help him. He is identified as Master Neville by Jervis, causing a jolt to Falkner, who realizes he is the son of the woman whose death he caused. Jervis explains that his mother has left the family and his father, Sir Boyvill, hates the boy. Thus, the young man becomes an orphan, and Elizabeth can identify with him. Falkner feels renewed guilt, understanding the boy's life might have been quite different had his mother lived. Falkner leaves for the night and does not return home, worrying Elizabeth.

The next morning, Elizabeth prepares for her normal early morning ride, thinking of Master Neville, when she receives a note from Falkner. He explains that they must depart Baden, asks her to tell Jervis to oversee the packing, and says they must come in a carriage to meet him at Mayence. At first annoyed by the shattering of her plans to get to know Neville, Elizabeth notices a postscript that mentions Falkner is not well. She immediately hurries to direct their departure, first determining that Neville's horse, which is in their stables, can be led to Sir Boyvill's stables. When she reunites with Falkner, Elizabeth is surprised to learn they will return to England. While she wonders at Falkner's decision, she remembers that Neville is English and hopes to see him later.

During the journey, Falkner slips back into melancholy from the cheerfulness he had developed over several years. He considers the sullen resentful Neville and how sad it is that the gifts from his mother had been sullied by the ill nature of the boy's father. He chides himself for having slipped into acceptance of his life's sentence—"like the galley slave, the iron which had eaten into the flesh, galled less than when newly applied." Reminded all too clearly of his guilt in causing the death of Gerard Neville's mother, he again determines to seek death, this time by volunteering to fight in Greece for the independence movement. He tells Elizabeth that he will travel to the north of England to speak with her father's family and ask that she be allowed to live with them. Hurt and alarmed, Elizabeth begs him to allow her to accompany him, declaring that he is her true father despite his argument that she has seen the darkness in his heart and his "fits of distress and anguish." She argues that is all the more reason that he needs her near and she does not wish "to claim the kindness of those who treated my true parents ill." Falkner still resists, explaining that he has debts to repay, he is a coward, and he would be dead had she not saved his life. He believes that by fighting and dying for a good cause, he can in some way pay for his sins, and she should not be exposed to that suffering. She clings to him and cries, moving him to agree to her plan; she argues that in Greece, she will find "good Christians" to help protect her. Falkner later contemplates his situation, thinking that after his death, people may curse his name, but they will add that he died to "expiate [his] guilt." Elizabeth will profit from her good name of Raby, and then no more misery will derive from his acts. Elizabeth's only sorrow on leaving England is that Miss Jervis chooses to stay behind.

Elizabeth lives some miles from the fighting in Greece, and she passes the time by constructing a daily ritual and meeting her duties. The narrator notes that over the next three years, Elizabeth engages in impeccable behavior and total devotion to Falkner, who is aided by an Albanian Greek named Vasili. Elizabeth matures into a beautiful 16-year-old, a stage that the narrator describes as the time "when the human heart is nearest moral perfection, most alive and yet most innocent, aspiring to good, without a knowledge of evil." She is "no dreamer," filling her mind with duties and affections, wandering by the ocean when thoughtful, and checking daily news of combat. Vasili visits Elizabeth from time to time, telling her of Falkner's "harrowing" behavior, and Elizabeth realizes that he is seeking death, taking unnecessary risks. When Egyptian forces arrive, the warfare grows more perilous, and she eagerly anticipates an impending visit from Falkner. Before he can return, she receives a letter from Vasili, who writes that Falkner is in grave condition, having sustained a severe wound that came on the heels of illness. Elizabeth joins Falkner, the narrator stressing her independent nature in traveling on her own, and finds him on the verge of death. She overcomes many obstacles to remove him to the cooler surroundings of Zante. Falkner attempts to recover over several months, during which time he tells Elizabeth that she must understand the sin he committed. He explains that he left a brief explanation in England but has written a more thorough one that he carries with him in a small rosewood box. Elizabeth refuses to read it but promises that she will at the right time.

Falkner becomes ill again, and Elizabeth arranges their departure aboard a ship to travel northward after a surgeon warns of the danger of Falkner's remaining in Greece with the hottest of the seasons soon arriving. After a delay, they set sail at last, parting sadly with Vasili. Again stopped for a time while the ship is in quarantine, Elizabeth meets an English family headed by Lord and Lady Cecil, who have several children. While Lady Cecil is not pretty, she has a wonderful character, and Elizabeth is attracted to her. Then she notices Miss Jervis among the group, acting as a governess to the children. Jervis complains about having had to leave England again and the challenges of the many languages that she does not understand. Jervis introduces Elizabeth to Lady Cecil, who has been "struck by Elizabeth's beaming and noble countenance, which bore the impress of high thought, and elevated sentiments." Elizabeth also has a tall and graceful figure that has "sprung into womanhood." The two women become friends, with Lady Cecil expressing concerns about Elizabeth and Falkner, whose condition is again failing. The ship finally sails, and Elizabeth must leave her new friends behind.

The entire crew pities Elizabeth and observes her with admiration as she never leaves Falkner's side. One day, a young man appears and assists Elizabeth, volunteering to attend Falkner while she rests. The narrator tells readers, "It was a new and pleasant sensation to the lone girl to feel that there was one sharing her task, on whom she might rely." She notices the stranger gazing out to sea "with an air of softness and sadness," for which she immediately feels sympathy. Falkner improves slightly, and the stranger helps move him to another boat in Marseilles, as Elizabeth's sense of camaraderie with the stranger grows. He volunteers to accompany them on the next leg of their journey to Lyons, admiring Elizabeth more daily as he respectfully listens to her engage in concerned and informed conversations with Falkner.

As Elizabeth considers the fact that the stranger reminds her of someone, she suddenly thinks of Baden and Gerard Neville. The stranger must be he, although he has changed, having lost his fierce and sullen disposition, but he is still melancholy and seems unhappy. At one point, Falkner's health seems to have improved, but when Elizabeth introduces him to Neville, he faints, realizing the young man is Alithea's son. Falkner instructs Elizabeth not to allow Neville to accompany them. She is disappointed, having come to depend upon Neville's assistance, but she wants to do what Falkner wants and decides not to mention Neville's name ever again.

Gerard Neville comes aboard the ship to tell Elizabeth goodbye, and she notices when meeting him that "His large eyes seemed two wells of unfathomable sadness." He tells her how meaningful their relationship has been, that he has felt called to a sacred purpose, and she has caused him to strengthen his resolve. He must not forget his resolve but resume his focus, even if he must pay with his life. Elizabeth says he must not think in that way and asks whether he remembers her from Baden. With sudden recollection, Neville tells her that he thought of her as a sister at the time. He explains it is best that she is not involved in the evil that pursues him. The two part with regret, Elizabeth's feelings absorbed by "affection and solicitude" for Neville.

Volume 1: Chapters 13–17

Falkner slowly recovers, and he and Elizabeth enjoy the trip on the Rhine. Elizabeth continues to be concerned for Falkner and the cloud that seemed to darken his mood. She also thinks about Neville and wonders whether, for one so young, friendship and kindness, along with his youth, might not remedy whatever troubles him. When they arrive in London, Falkner's fever has gone, but his wound remains painful, the bullet having grazed a bone. They live a tranquil life in a new home that Elizabeth enjoys putting in order, never speaking of Neville. They read together, with Elizabeth leading discussions about stories of heroes of old, enjoying their imaginative aspects. Falkner, on the other hand, compares the tales to his own experiences and criticizes their lack of realism.

One day Lady Cecil visits, bringing her usual atmosphere of cheerfulness. Falkner, who had previously been unable to pay much attention to her, immediately likes her, especially when she praises Elizabeth's care of him. She invites Elizabeth to visit her near Hastings, as her husband is absent for some time in Ireland, and the two leave together with plans for Elizabeth to visit for two months; Falkner will join them in one month. Caring for Falkner has taken its toll on Elizabeth, who Lady Cecil feels will be back to her old self with a bit of care. Lady Cecil reminds her that Miss Jervis will be there as well as her brother Gerard. As she describes Gerard, Elizabeth cannot help but think of Neville.

Within a week, Elizabeth feels much better, and she enjoys everything except for the large number of visitors. Used to isolation, she finds the more frivolous visitors intrusive and talking with those with whom she shares nothing in common a challenge. She is delighted to see Mr. Neville and even more so to discover that he is the highly praised brother of Lady Cecil. Lady Cecil is pleased to see what she thinks at first is a "sudden intimacy naturally sprung" between the two, as she has believed they have much in common. She explains that Gerard is not related to her by blood: Sir Boyvill had been married to both of their mothers, but she had a different father. When Lady Cecil learns of their acquaintance, she asks why Elizabeth had not mentioned that she already knew her brother. Elizabeth had been unsure that the Neville she knew was Lady Cecil's brother and had hesitated to remark on the possibility. As for Neville, he had decided not to pursue a relationship with her, due to the personal resolve he had to fulfill. However, the narrator explains, he is unaware of "that shadow of the shape, which the Latin poet tells us flows from every object" that serves to fold round him, and those like Elizabeth, who "became mingled up for evermore with his identity."

When Gerard is gone one morning, Lady Cecil is concerned. However, he soon reappears to announce that Sir Boyvill has sent a message that he is coming to visit. Gerard assumes the purpose of the visit is to discourage him from acting on what may be new information regarding his mother. He explains to Elizabeth that he must redeem his mother's good name, comparing himself to Hamlet, who had the charge to avenge his father. Elizabeth discovers Boyvill to be a thoroughly disgusting man; he is the first human that she has hated. He verbally tortures everyone he comes near and is disagreeable and insulting. After he departs, Lady Cecil invites Elizabeth on a long carriage ride, promising to explain the history behind the disappearance of Alithea Neville.

Alithea was 19 when she married Boyvill Neville, who was not knighted at that time and was in his 40s. Her sea-captain father used her to barter a better position for himself. Good-natured and imaginative, Alithea determined to make a good marriage, despite Neville's naturally disagreeable and egoistic character. When things did not go well for the couple in town, mainly due to his jealousy and disagreeable temperament, she suggested that they move to the country, where she could be free from absurd accusations and be a satisfied and happy housewife and mother to their son, Gerard. Neville did enjoy Alithea and admired her domestic skills; he also liked Gerard well enough. The couple took a trip to the Continent, where Alithea gave birth to their second child, a daughter on whom Neville doted.

When they returned home, all seemed to go well until Neville returned one day from a trip to find Alithea had gone missing. According to the servants, she had left the day before with Gerard, and neither returned. A search was launched, and Gerard, a nine-year old, was found on a road, ill from exposure. When he recovered, he explained that his mother had taken him with her through a gate, spoken with a man who made her cry, and then the man put her into a carriage that suddenly appeared. The man had called for Gerard to jump into the carriage, but the child was too slow. As the carriage raced away, he heard his mother screaming for him. The servants then recalled that a man had visited the home and spoken with Alithea, but he had upset her, so he was not permitted entrance when he returned. Continued searches produced no trace of Alithea, but a note was eventually found that was signed only with the first name *Rupert*. It asked Alithea to meet the author of the letter one more time, and it gave her directions to unlock the gate and go outside to speak with him, after which he promised to depart.

Because Alithea had taken Gerard with her to meet the man, at first everyone believed Alithea had no ill motives in meeting the man. However, as time passed and no one received word from Alithea, Neville became more gloomy and sullen and then began to speak of Alithea with scorn, accusing her of running away with a stranger and abandoning her family. To make matters worse, within a year of Alithea's disappearance, a careless act by a nursemaid caused the death of the Nevilles' baby daughter. Neville blamed the death of the last remaining joy in his life on his wife; had she been present, such carelessness would never have been permitted. His anger against his wife built, as did his accusations. This enraged Gerard, who swore to find his mother and avenge the shame the stranger had brought to her. As a child of 10, he told his father, "I know what you think, but it is not true. Mamma would come back if she could. When I am a man I will find and bring her back, and you will be sorry then!" Gerard continued to seek his mother's abductor, although his father constantly berated him for seeking a woman who had besmirched her reputation and run away from her responsibilities.

Volume 2: Chapters 1–5

Volume 2 begins with the continuation of Lady Cecil's story. She relates that Gerard's heart had been broken over his mother's disappearance and the scandalous accusations against her. One day, he called his nurse and asked her to record what he remembered of the day that his mother had been taken. His details made plain that she had no intention of leaving with the stranger, whom Gerard described as tall, more handsome than his father, and stronger than two men. He had bodily lifted the protesting Alithea into the carriage after tricking her to move closer to the road, apparently having arranged for the carriage to arrive at that moment.

After he finished his tale, Gerard asked the nurse if it were not obvious that his mother had been taken and was blameless. The nurse agreed but added the question everyone had asked: Why had Alithea Neville not contacted her family over the many months she had been missing? Gerard pushed the nurse away, declaring she was evil like everyone else, and the answer to that question was that his mother was either dead or imprisoned.

Gerard changed from a happy child, "his boyish spirit dashed." He refused to spend time with others or see his father, who continued to attempt to find the fugitives but in vain. Many believed they had traveled to America, and word was sent to New York City and other major towns, but to no avail. The most mysterious aspect of the situation was the identity of the stranger. Neville decided that Alithea must have met him and formed a relationship during their marriage, and the thought "poured venom on the time gone by." His pride made him hate her for feeling affection for another while married to him. She had caused the first defect in his perfect life, detracting from his wealth, power and position, for which he hated her. After two years with no news and Sir Boyvill's hate festering, he divorced Alithea. The divorce required an act of Parliament, which led to wide publicity regarding Alithea's disappearance and subsequent silence. The worse aspect of the proceedings was that Gerard had to testify as to events of that day, contributing against his will to the indictment of his mother. After the testimony, he ran away in an attempt to find his mother, traveling to the ocean. He wandered for two months in an area called Dromore. He was eventually recognized and his father contacted, but his journey was publicized,

and Sir Boyvill was even suspected of abuse. Gerard was tied up at home to prevent his escaping again. Eventually released, he had become ferocious and filled with despair.

Lady Cecil, whose name was Sophia, and her mother arrived at Baden just after Elizabeth had departed several years earlier. While there, Sophia's mother met and married Sir Boyvill. It was Sophia who had nursed the broken leg that Gerard suffered when he fell from his horse, the accident that Elizabeth and her father had witnessed. The two became friends, and Gerard found the first person in whom he could confide. Sophia eventually married Lord Cecil, and when Gerard reached the age of 21, he announced his intention to continue the pursuit of his mother, infuriating Sir Boyvill.

Elizabeth is fascinated by the story and views Gerard as heroic. She asks what news Gerard has recently received, and Lady Cecil explains that a man named Gregory Hoskins, knowing Gerard has offered a reward of £200 for information about his mother, has sent a letter that he has that information.

Lady Cecil tells Gerard that Elizabeth now knows of his story. He writes to her that the Hoskins lead reached a dead end; he suspected the man, recently returned from America, knew nothing helpful. He expresses concern about how Elizabeth has received the story of his mother, writing, "In telling your lovely friend the strange story of my woes, you have taught her to mourn my mother's fate, not to suspect her goodness?" He is annoyed that he has not already explained the situation to Elizabeth. Lady Cecil knows that Gerard loves Elizabeth, and she can tell by Elizabeth's reaction to his letter that the feeling is mutual. Elizabeth adds some words of encouragement to Lady Cecil's response to Gerard. Lady Cecil wonders whether Mrs. Neville has been carried off to America and thinks about the nature of love.

When Gerard returns, he tells Elizabeth and Sophia that he at last discovered his mother's fate: She is dead. He explains that he found Hoskins, who related a story he had heard while living in America from a man named Osborne. Upon first arriving in Boston, Osborne had been suspicious and fearful, suffering night terrors. He at last told

Hoskins that he had assisted a friend to take a woman away from her home. Osborne had believed it was a love match, but "never did girl take on so for leaving her home with a lover." Tragedy struck when she managed to escape and drowned. He assisted his friend in burying her body, digging a grave in the sand close to the ocean. The details caused him nightmares, and he muttered about "no parson; and the dark breakers of the ocean—and horses scampering away, and the lady's wet hair." Whenever any correspondence arrived from Europe, Osborne would hide, afraid of his part in the crime being discovered. He believed his friend to have also died.

Gerard labels his mother's death a "murder," a label with which the two women disagree, believing the death sounded more like an accident. Gerard swears he will find the murderer and speaks with emotion about his mother's horrible, terrifying death, which has caused him to have nightmares in which he sees her drowning. Hoskins has informed him that Osborne is assisting the English ambassador in Mexico, and Gerard intends to travel there and interview him.

Lady Cecil asks Elizabeth to help her persuade Gerard not to undertake the dangerous journey, but Elizabeth feels sympathy for Gerard's emotions, again comparing him to Hamlet. This annoys Lady Cecil, who thought she had found an ally in Elizabeth. Gerard appreciates Elizabeth's support, and the two grow closer. Elizabeth is moved to write to Falkner about what has happened, knowing that he will not want to hear about Gerard based on his previous reaction to the young man, but feeling she must share these momentous events. Soon after she sends her letter, she receives a note from Falkner asking her to return home to "hear the fatal secret that will divide us forever." He is first going on a trip but will contact her when he returns.

Volume 2: Chapters 6–10

During Elizabeth's absence, Falkner had been alone for the first time in a long while, lost in his suffering and bitterness. He had been on the verge of joining Elizabeth when her note arrived. He had also received a letter from Lady Cecil hinting at her desire that the two young people marry, as they are such a good match for one another. Falkner decides he can best honor Alithea's memory by helping her son achieve happiness, and he concocts a plan to reunite Elizabeth with the Rabys, her real family. While she would suffer dishonor as Elizabeth Falkner, as Elizabeth Raby she would be an acceptable match for anyone. However, when he visits the Raby estate, he is dismayed and infuriated by Oswi Raby, the family patriarch. Raby has no desire to know Elizabeth, the child of a son who abandoned the Catholic faith and married a person of low social status, someone whom Raby believed to have been a servant for a Mrs. Neville. Falkner flinches at the reference to Alithea but remains focused on his purpose. When Raby disparages Elizabeth, Falkner grows angrier with every word. Raby believes that Falkner must want to "disembarrass" himself of Elizabeth and says he will discuss her with the daughter-in-law whose son will inherit the Raby fortune. Falkner leaves, telling Raby that he has made an enormous mistake in not comprehending Elizabeth's worth. He later feels guilty about having kept Elizabeth from her family, who could have provided wealth and a name for her.

Falkner wanders about for several weeks, delaying his return home. He finds a packet of letters from Elizabeth, who, encouraged by the kind words for Gerard that Falkner had included in a letter to her, writes more about her love. Falkner suddenly understands from Elizabeth's account that Alithea had suffered disgrace following her disappearance, something he had not previously considered. Filled with shame, he knows that he must immediately confess his actions in order to clear her name. He writes and asks Elizabeth to meet him at home in Wimbledon. When Falkner falls ill, he fears that he will die before he is able to confess. He realizes that a worse punishment than he could have realized has begun. His repentance will not be as he desired, through a glorious death; rather, it will be beneath "the slow grinding of the iron wheels of destiny, as they passed over him, crushing him in the dust."

When Elizabeth arrives home, she and Falkner spend a delightful evening together, and he saves his confession for the following day. She awakes happy because Gerard is to visit her before he sails for Washington, D.C., where he is to meet

Osborne. They talk happily after his arrival, both knowing they are in love. Falkner enters and is shocked when he sees Gerard, not knowing of his visit. He notices how much the young man resembles his mother. Elizabeth explains that Mr. Neville is visiting her before he departs for America, at which point Falkner explains there will be no reason for a journey. Neville need not travel to America to find his mother's killer, for "he stands before you. I am he . . . I am Rupert Falkner, your mother's destroyer." Then Falkner promptly leaves the room.

The two young people are stunned and assume that Falkner must be mad, until Gerard realizes that Falkner called himself Rupert, the name of the man who took his mother, although everyone knew him as John. Elizabeth is appalled that Gerard believes there is truth in her father's statement. She thinks the outlandish confession must result from illness and tells Neville to return on the following day.

Elizabeth finds Falkner and, grasping his hand, realizes he is not feverish and does not appear ill. He speaks calmly and clearly, telling her "all will soon be well" and asking her to read the account he has written. He reminds her that she has known for some time that he carried a terrible secret. Elizabeth declares that she shall never accuse him of guilt, and she will always think him the best of men. As they embrace, she at first turns away from the papers in disgust, but then reads the narrative, which constitutes all of chapters 9–12 in volume 2.

Falkner writes of his passion and the aspect of human nature that makes us all want to possess something that is not ours. He considers himself a criminal and is filled with self-loathing. He states that he covets death and that "this is my last labor—my legacy to my fellow beings." Falkner supplies his own sad history. His mother died when he was four, and his father was an abusive gambler and a drunk. After his father's death, he lived with his uncle's family, where he was neither cherished nor loved. His father's bad qualities influenced his own self-willed nature, and although he tried at first to be compliant, hostile treatment made him disobedient and reckless, and he was sent away to school. He got into trouble there and was confined to a room, but one day a carriage came to pick him up. It took him to cottage where a woman said to him, "I know you from your likeness to your mother—dear, dear Rupert." He remembered that his mother had called him by that name. He was raised in the cottage by the woman, Mrs. Rivers, who was remotely related to Falkner's mother and had been educated with her. This was how Falkner came to know Alithea Rivers, Mrs. Rivers's daughter. They spent much time together and he fell in love with Alithea, even as both were children.

Eventually forced to return to school, Falkner cared for a nest of mice in his room as his pets. Discovered by an usher, the mice were killed when a cat was released into Falkner's room. The boy struggled with the heartless usher, who hit him with a stick and pulled out a knife. The usher was cut on the head as the two fought, and Falkner escaped out the window and returned to the Rivers cottage, where he slept nearby. At that point, he was 16 and unsure of his future. He felt he had betrayed Mrs. Rivers, who had asked him to be "brave, generous, and true." He decided to join the military and travel the world, but first he sent a note to Alithea, asking her to meet him where he was hiding in the woods. Alithea finally came and asked him to return to the cottage, where Mrs. Rivers did not reproach him but instead was filled with joy to see him.

Falkner remained there, studying on his own during the day and wandering about the countryside with Alithea in the evenings. Mrs. Rivers corresponded with Falkner's uncle, who sent a cadet to pick up Falkner and take him to East Indian Military College. Falkner promised Mrs. Rivers and Alithea to become all they desired him to be. He had to spend a month with his uncle before going to college and was able to behave properly only due to the Rivers's influence. He spent two years at the military college, exchanging letters with Alithea. When Mrs. Rivers fell ill, Alithea wrote to ask for Falkner's help, and he was with them when Mrs. Rivers died. Before he returned to military school, he realized that he truly loved Alithea, and he dreamed of returning to marry her.

Alithea was placed in a boarding school, and Falkner saw her there only once. Later, her father returned home from the sea, and she was able to live with him. When Falkner visited them and expressed his desire to marry Alithea, Captain Rivers laughed at him, regarding Falkner as little more than a beggar. He struck Falkner, who did not return the blow and told Rivers he had taught him "one lesson—I will die rather than leave Alithea in the hands of a ruffian, such as you." When he contacted Alithea, she promised to meet Falkner in the woods again if he would not see her father. "She lavished careless words of endearment" on Falkner but was unable to contemplate disobeying her father, and she never declared the love for Falkner that he felt for her.

Falkner served 10 years in India, hoping only to raise his station to the point where Captain Rivers would allow him to marry Alithea; he also hoped that she would be moved to love him as he loved her. Suddenly, he learned that his uncle and his male cousin, heir to the family fortune, had died, and the entire fortune would pass to him. Free of the need to serve, he "lived in a dream" and returned to England obsessed by thoughts of Alithea.

Volume 2: Chapters 11–15

Falkner was bewildered and shocked to find her married and with a family. By coincidence, he met Alithea's husband, Neville, and found him "cold, proud, and sarcastic, withal a decayed dandy, turned cynic." Falkner arranged to meet Alithea and, thinking she must be miserable, begged her to run away with him. She had not at first even recognized Falkner and did not confess to the "disappointed joyless married state" that Falkner believed she suffered. Falkner writes that "had I not, with a serpent's subtlety, glided on imperceptibly; had I not brought forward her mother's name, and the memory of childhood's cloudless years, she had been mute with me." She tried to convince Falkner that her marriage is not all bad. Falkner told her bitterly, "Poor innocent bird . . . think you at once to be free, and in a cage? At once to feel the fowler's grasp, and fly away to heaven?" He told her she deceived herself, but she explained that she is "happy in my children" and that if he would stay and meet her son, he would also love him. Falkland became more focused than ever on possessing her.

When she would not see him again, he threatened to murder her husband.

Alithea agreed to meet Falkner one last time, and he concocted a plot to buy a carriage and horses, enlisting the help of Osborne as a driver. He felt that once he got her away from her husband, he could convince her to join him. In his account, Falkner confesses that he lacked self-command, although he seemed to be in control externally. In truth, "within I was the same slave of passion I had ever been." He describes the moment that he forced Alithea into the carriage as the moment that a devil whispered in his ear. The cries of her son as they drove away made her struggle, and she fell to his feet, convulsed in fear and anguish, her screams drowned by a tremendous storm. They stopped at a cottage near the sea, close to the Rivers home, where Falkner carried Alithea inside and tried to bring her back to consciousness. Osborne watched in fear, understanding that she had been forced to make the trip. Suddenly Falkner, realized the damage he had done to her and only wished her to live, so that he could return her to her son. Filled with self-revulsion, Falkner promised Osborne that he would take her home, and they again harnessed the horses. Falkner placed her in the carriage, and the two men walked beside the horses, leading them through the dangerously high water that had resulted from the storm.

As Falkner and Osborne moved forward through the high water, he saw the white caps in the water ahead but noticed something else, another bit of white. With horror, he realized it was a person, and that person was Alithea. She had awakened in the carriage and, not understanding that Falkner had decided to take her home, or that the water in the river had risen so high, she had attempted to escape. By the time Falkner reached her, she appeared lifeless. He struggled to reach the shore, terrified and frantic. When he reached the bank, the trembling Osborne helped him to lay Alithea on the ground, but she was beyond their help. Falkner writes that no matter where he has traveled or in what circumstances, even while fighting in Greece, he can hear the angry surf crashing and see Alithea "pale, drenched and lifeless." Osborne agreed to assist in burying her. Falkner had considered suicide to destroy himself beside her, but Osborne's "miserable terrors" would not permit it.

The remainder of the narrative deals with Falkner's devotion to and love for Elizabeth, the only salvation in his otherwise despicable existence, "the unmitigated influence of the demon forever" at his side. He realizes how he has cursed Elizabeth by burdening her, particularly in light of her new love for Gerard. He closes the document by telling Elizabeth that she is free of him, and he shall soon "have a soldier's grave."

Stunned, Elizabeth tries to imagine Alithea's feelings before her death. She had attempted escape for the sake of her son—that was obvious: "To the last she was all mother; her heart filled with that deep yearning, which a young mother feels to be the very essence of her life, for the presence of her child." She had given her life for that child, the man that Elizabeth now loved. Falkner has directed her to give the narrative to Gerard. As Elizabeth considers the fact that Gerard would now be triumphant, "Falkner humiliated and fallen," she feels closer to her father than ever. Alithea at least has "her reward" now in heaven without strife, and she will gain a new reputation as a heroine. It is Falkner who most needs forgiveness and consolation. Elizabeth quickly writes a note to Neville expressing her feelings, and she places it in a packet with Falkner's narrative. He has ordered that the narrative be delivered to Neville with his message that he will remain at his house, awaiting further word from Gerard. Falkner believes that Gerard might want to speak with him to ask questions or to move forward with any legal actions he deems necessary.

As Elizabeth watches Gerard receive the packet at the gate from a servant's hands and peruse the contents, then leave, she understands their relationship has changed forever. She contemplates their situation for a long time, deciding that for her future, "patience and resignation must henceforth take place of gladness and hope." Her duty must be to Falkner, who had rescued her from a miserable existence and sacrificed much for her well-being.

Falkner waits for Neville to appear, confident that he will demand justice, that the "law of honor would be resorted to, to avenge the death of Alithea." But many days pass, and Neville does not appear. As they wait, Falkner tells Elizabeth of his visit to the Rabys and that she should expect a visit from her aunt. He continues to await Neville and becomes again fearful that the vengeance he has hoped for from Gerard will not materialize. What will that mean for his future? "In what frightful shape would the ghost of the past haunt him?" The thoughts cause him to pity Elizabeth and to shrink "from himself as one doomed to dishonor, and unspeakable misery."

Volume 3: Chapters 1–7

The third volume begins with a summary of Gerard Neville's actions after leaving his sister's house. He visits Sir Boyvill, who has heard from Lady Cecil about Osborne and about Gerard's plans to sail to America. For the first time in a long while, Sir Boyvill is more open to hear of what Gerard has learned and does not berate his actions, encouraging them instead. He does strike a deal with his son that Gerard will take no action without first consulting him. Gerard is surprised and gratified, and the two men talk longer than he can remember. The following day, when Gerard visits Elizabeth, his hopes are high, not only in regard to settling the facts about this mother but in the security of his love for Elizabeth. However, Falkner's explanation claiming credit for Alithea's death has both confused and thrilled him. Falkner's association with Elizabeth and his familiarity with the Nevilles has caused confusion, while Gerard is also thrilled at the news, having so long hoped to learn some word of his mother's end.

When he returns to Falkner's house the following day and receives the narrative, he reads it quickly and takes it directly to Sir Boyvill. Leaving the older man to carefully study the narrative, Gerard remains in emotional turmoil. He thinks of Falkner's fragile physical condition and the fact that death seems imminent, but he also wants to avenge his mother's death. He knows that any action will forever damage his relationship with Elizabeth. He had thought just that morning that she "was all the universe of hope and joy" and that he would never have hurt her, but he writes that "now I meditate a deed that is to consign her to eternal grief."

After anxiously waiting the appointed length of time, Gerard returns to his father's house, where he is gratified to at last hear that his father, who seems unusually calm, will vindicate Alithea's name. Sir Boyvill adds that "her destroyer shall die to expiate her death." Gerard retires to better read the entire account, but first his father calls on him to remember to take no action until they have consulted. Sir Boyvill understands that Falkner is awaiting Neville's arrival for a duel at that very moment.

As Gerard rereads the complete account, he experiences feelings of compassion as he understands Falkner's complete misery. When he reads all of Falkner's negative statements about his father, he wonders that Sir Boyvill could have been so calm when he saw him a few minutes before. Gerard does not sleep until late into the night and awakens late in the morning to learn his father has departed to Dromore, leaving Gerard a note reminding him to take no action yet. Filled with anxiety, Gerard follows his father and continues to think about Falkner. His compassion is replaced with anger, not only over Falkner's crime but his willingness to make his own daughter, who is "beautiful, generous, and pure," miserable.

When Gerard arrives at Dromore, his father has already departed again, and Gerard is conscious of his surroundings as the very area in which his mother met her doom. He rides to the hut of which Falkner had written as the first stop following Alithea's kidnapping to find his father and a group of men there. In his position as magistrate, Boyvill has summoned another magistrate, Mr. Ashley, to witness the act of digging to find Alithea's remains. Her grave and bones are discovered, causing Gerard to want to join her in the grave, but he resists due to all of the witnesses. Sir Boyvill reminds them all of the disappearance of his wife and relates that the murderer is nearby, to which they all mumble angrily. He sends for a coroner, and when he and Gerard can speak alone, he tells Gerard that he will be sure that Falkner is hanged for his crime. His desire for "foul disgrace" to be brought on Falkner greatly differs from Gerard's plan for an honorable duel.

Gerard leaves and later returns to the grave along with his father, the coroner, and a large gathering of locals who mutter about Alithea's terrible end. She was from that part of the country, and many had enjoyed her kindnesses. Sir Boyvill is filled with hate and a desire for the most shame-provoking revenge on Falkner. Gerard must answer a large number of questions by the authorities regarding his acquaintance with Falkner. When Elizabeth's name is mentioned, the emotion is too much for Gerard to bear. The "coarse remarks" made by his father "harrow[s] up his soul." Frustration mounts as there is clearly no way he can "take from her the name and association of the child of a murderer." The narrator notes of Gerard that "there [is] poetry in his very essence, and enthusiasm for the ideal of the excellent," which makes him "exalted and refined." He stands conflicted; he has reached his goal and avenged his mother, regaining her pristine reputation, but in doing so he has brought misery to the person he most loves, Elizabeth. He determines to write Lady Cecil and ask for her help.

Elizabeth thinks of how much she loves Gerard. They have great sympathy for one another, and Gerard has taught her much of literature, for "with her he gave way freely to the impulses of a heart" and had poetry in his nature. However, "there was more of the genuine attachment of mind for mind in her sentiment with Falkner," whom she knows she will never abandon. Since his confession, Falkner's appearance has changed, "the passions of his soul, which had before deformed his handsome lineaments, now animated them with a beauty of mind."

When Elizabeth returns home from her normal early morning ride the fifth day after Falkner's confession, the servant tells her he has left with two men, and they were *not* gentlemen. She hears nothing from Falkner for days; then she finds out he has been taken to Carlyle and accused of murder. She mistakenly believes he has dueled with and killed Gerard, until a servant explains he has been accused of the murder of a lady some years ago. As she prepares to leave to see him, two women arrive at her door, one being Lady Cecil. Elizabeth grows excited, assuming they have news of Falkner's release.

The woman with Lady Cecil is Edwin Raby's sister-in-law, Elizabeth's aunt and the widow of

Edwin's eldest brother. She had always been fond of Edwin and regretted his rejection from the family. Upon discovering Elizabeth's existence, "her heart warmed . . . and . . . she felt all the repentance which duties neglected bring on a well-regulated mind." Lady Cecil had read Gerard's "incoherent" letter that morning, in which she could tell that were it not for Elizabeth's precarious position as Falkner's relation, Gerard would not be able to feel compassion toward Falkner. As it is, he wishes the older man saved for the sake of his "heroic" daughter. Mrs. Raby had arrived at Lady Cecil's home inquiring after Elizabeth, only to find that she had gone home to Falkner. The two women had learned the news of Falkner's arrest and imprisonment in London, but none of the printed accounts mentioned Elizabeth. He has obviously taken care to keep her from disgrace.

The two women tell Elizabeth they have come to take her away, and that all is well, but Elizabeth can speak only of Falkner, "my father." She argues that she cannot desert Falkner, who has done so much for her and suffered so greatly; he is a dying man. Mrs. Raby explains that she must come away with them in order to fulfill his wishes, as he has taken care not to contact her or try to involve her in his problems in any way. Elizabeth refuses to desert her father, causing Lady Cecil great annoyance. Mrs. Raby notes Elizabeth's sense of duty and uses that to argue persuasively that Elizabeth must join her real family. All of the Raby family members await her, and she reminds Elizabeth that they have themselves been persecuted, due to their religion. Elizabeth again resists, coldly replying that her real family had rejected her father and mother, causing her to feel "gratitude, obedience, duty, all due to the generous benefactor" who raised her to be "the child of his heart." A lengthy discussion follows, but Elizabeth does not relent, promising that she will give up all claims to family and "the name of Raby shall not be tainted." She shall retain the name Falkner to demonstrate her gratitude to "him who bestowed that appellation on her." The two women depart, Lady Cecil sullen but Mrs. Raby admiring Elizabeth's courage and remaining focused on bringing her into the Raby fold.

Volume 3: Chapters 8–13
Gerard visits Elizabeth in Stratford as she travels to Carlyle to see Falkner, and he warns her away from the scene, which will be improper for a young woman. He then expresses admiration for her selflessness and strong character, as she asks that he simply address her as Elizabeth, due to his distaste for the name Falkner. Gerard obviously loves her, and she is appreciative while remaining devoted to Falkner. Meanwhile, Falkner feels calm in prison. Unlike the normal person, he has so long anticipated imprisonment that it arrives as a relief. "Apprehension" had been the greater and more fearful prison. He feels "unnaturally glad" to be in the cell, except for his grave concerns for Elizabeth. He does begin to miss the freedom of nature, and now that he can barely see a few stars through the window, he becomes a "cannibal of his own heart." He has no release from his thoughts and feels "the curse of God upon him." When Elizabeth enters his cell, Falkner suddenly no longer feels imprisoned; her face causes him to dismiss the possibility of "the existence of evil."

Both Falkner and Elizabeth are convinced that he will ultimately be found innocent of murder. While what he did was disgraceful, it was not murder. Elizabeth hopes against hope that Falkner's case will be dismissed at the grand jury stage, because despite Sir Boyvill's passionate desire for public revenge against Falkner, she knows that Gerard "abhor[s] the course pursued" and will be able to influence proceedings. Yet despite Elizabeth's hopes, the grand jury does not dismiss the charges and still plans to try Falkner for murder. Falkner's solicitor informs him that the trial will be delayed until March to give Osborne time to arrive. Gerard Neville has spoken so passionately of the necessity of Osborne's appearance that he has broken the "prejudice" against calling the witness, to whom the court has agreed to grant immunity for his testimony. Falkner speaks of Osborne, describing him as "a poltroon, but kindly hearted—fearful of his own skin, to a contemptible extent, but looking up with awe to his superiors, and easily led by one richer and of higher station."

Elizabeth moves into an apartment nearby, continuing her ritual of early morning exercise, moving her tapestry frame into Falkner's cell to work as he reads to her, or reading to him as he sketches; they also share music. They can never forget the reality of the outer world, but they draw even closer during their many days together. While alone, Elizabeth feels miserable and often thinks longingly of Gerard Neville. As December arrives, there is no news of Osborne and whether or not he has been located, nor has Elizabeth heard from Gerard or Lady Cecil for some time. The narrator comments on the nature of the English people; they can be so generous to friends but not to strangers of whom they are often suspicious. That trait partially accounts for Elizabeth's lack of friends and her feeling of isolation. One day, she notices Gerard on the street, watching her, and although he does not signal to her, her spirits lift. Soon, after she and Falkner are told that Hillary, the man sent to Washington, D.C., to persuade Osborne to return with him, has failed in his mission. Osborne denied even knowing Falkner. When Hillary brought up the name Hoskins, Osborne visibly panicked and left the room, then immediately departed and ended up in New Orleans. Hillary pursued but never found him.

Falkner is livid that they should have to trust in such a dishonorable person to be responsible for his freedom. While noting that Osborne's cowardice is a "grievous blow," he remains convinced that the jury will hear him and never convict him of murder. As she returns home, Elizabeth concocts a plan to travel to America herself, feeling confident that Osborne cannot refuse her once she explains the situation. She is disappointed not to see Gerard outside again, but a few minutes later he arrives, and they both rejoice to see each other, despite his pessimistic attitude toward Falkner's chance of release. Sir Boyvill is celebrating the fact that Osborne will not appear, and Gerard feels confident that Falkner will be convicted. However, upon seeing Elizabeth's optimism, he comments that he wishes he could have her sense of hope. He explains that he wholeheartedly supports Elizabeth's opinion that Falkner does not deserve the trial and sentence that his father seeks, and that he has tried without success to soften Sir Boyvill's heart. He is appalled to learn of Elizabeth's plan to seek Osborne herself, and after seeing how determined she is, he volunteers to go in her place. When he tells Sir Boyvill of his plan, the older man "boil[s] over with angry denunciations" and calls his son a family disgrace and "the detractor of his mother's fame." Gerard leaves with a heavy heart, understanding that he and his father can never be on agreeable terms. He departs for Liverpool and travels to London shortly after, affirming that Osborne has left his government position in Washington. Lady Cecil is dismayed at Gerard's plan but agrees that Boyvill's vulgar pursuit of a gentleman and Elizabeth's part in it are terrible.

Neville's ship hits bad weather, and it only arrives in the harbor of Liverpool after three days on the ocean. He chafes beneath the delay and searches for another merchantman prepared to leave immediately. After identifying a ship, he is directed to a tavern to locate the captain, but instead he finds Hoskins, who shares the startling news that Osborne has just left the tavern. Although it seems odd that he would come to England when he had run away from Hillary specifically to avoid Falkner's trial, Hoskins explains it. He says, "They tell of a rattlesnake . . . that fixing its eye on its prey, a bird becomes fascinated, and wheels round nearer and nearer till he falls into the jaws of the enemy." Although Neville searches diligently, he cannot find Osborne, and as ships depart for America, he wonders whether Osborne might be on one of them. He hurries to pack and book passage on one of the ships but receives a letter at his lodgings that changes his mind.

Volume 3: Chapters 14–20

Falkner and Elizabeth have known nothing of Neville's efforts, supposing him at sea somewhere. One day, Elizabeth tells her father that she feels certain "the wind has changed" in their favor. Shortly thereafter, Osborne arrives at the cell, but he does not recognize the debilitated Falkner. Both Falkner and Elizabeth thank him for coming to offer assistance, but he tells them he does not intend to testify. He did not know the lady who died, and his testimony "must be worth nothing, for he had nothing to tell." Falkner grows contemptuous of Osborne's cowardice, while Elizabeth tries to convince him that he risks nothing by testifying; no charges will be brought against him. At last, Osborne, pale and squirming, agrees to surrender himself to the jailer, but Falkner rejects his so-called "sacrifice." However, Elizabeth tells him that they will accept his help, and after a few moments, Osborne apologizes to Falkner for his behavior. Elizabeth sends a note to Gerard Neville that goes to Liverpool to be delivered to him, not knowing that he is in that city. It is her note he received when he did not book passage, understanding that he need not do so.

As Falkner and Elizabeth await trial, more optimistic than ever, a letter arrives from Neville explaining that Sir Boyvill lies on his deathbed. He has asked Gerard to stay with him, and in his final hours he has finally expressed his love for Gerard. He also confesses to having mistreated Alithea and expresses his wish that Rupert Falkner not be punished in the way that Sir Boyvill had intended, as he knows that Falkner is innocent of murder. He also asks Gerard to forgive his cruelties and notes of himself that his "awakened conscience urges me to repair a portion of the evils I have caused." Gerard had fully intended to testify at Falkner's trial but must remain with his father until he dies, and he fears he might arrive too late. With Osborne's presence, things will surely go well, and he will arrive in Carlyle as soon as possible. Falkner goes to trial understanding that "man and all his works were but a plaything in the hands of Omnipotence," and he submits himself to his destiny.

Mrs. Raby visits Elizabeth at Gerard's suggestion. He has made the point that Elizabeth most needs Mrs. Raby's support before the trial, as he feels secure that Falkner will be acquitted, and Elizabeth will not later feel the need for her real family. Mrs. Raby strongly sympathizes with Elizabeth and wants to bring her to their Belleforest estate. Even the elder Oswi Raby, now mostly senile, bids her to do what is best for the family. Elizabeth is glad to see her aunt, who argues for the younger woman to separate herself from Falkner after the trial in order to be with Gerard, who clearly loves her. Again, Elizabeth states that she cannot—she will remain loyal to her father until his death. As they speak, they hear a knock at the door, and Osborne enters to announce that Falkner has been freed. Osborne's "evidence was clear and satisfactory." In addition, Gerard Neville had declared his father's change of heart and showed that Falkner had made a lengthy confession of the crime as soon as he realized it was necessary to free Alithea Neville from all accusation of improper behavior. Falkner's testimony added to the other statements to convince the jury of his innocence. The jury did not even leave to consult but rendered the verdict on the spot.

Mrs. Raby is able to persuade Falkner to live with Elizabeth at Belleforest, although all parties realize that Gerard Neville will probably never marry Elizabeth: The pain of association of Elizabeth and Falkner with the death of his mother would not permit it. However, Elizabeth receives a letter from Gerard declaring his love and asking for time to gain perspective on events; Elizabeth feels confident that the two will reunite at the appropriate time. They eventually marry and live at the seat of the estate in Bucks, while Falkner purchases a villa to live near them and their growing family. The novel concludes with the statement that all still live there, suffering little from the passage of time, "and Neville has never for a moment repented the irresistible impulse that led him to become the friend of him, whose act had rendered his childhood miserable, but who completed the happiness of his maturer years."

COMMENTARY

Formalist critics can find much to admire in *Falkner*, as Shelley makes clear her skill in the use of formal elements such as irony, foreshadowing, symbolism, and figurative language. An example of inescapable irony appears when Gerard explains the pain he suffers in considering what he knows to be false charges against his mother, asking Elizabeth, "What would you do . . . if your father were accused of a crime?" Elizabeth replies, "My father and a crime! Impossible!" The irony exists in the fact that, unknown to Elizabeth, her father, Falkner, has committed the worst crime, and it is against Gerard's mother. Gerard continues a short time later, declaring, "It is dreadful, very dreadful, to be told—to be persuaded that the idol of one's thoughts is corrupt and vile." His statement provides foreshadowing for Elizabeth's later discovery about her own "idol," Falkner.

Many symbols appear in the novel, some traditional and some literary, specific only to the novel. One traditional symbol is that of the snake, which can represent temptation in its connection to the temptation of Eve and Adam in the Garden of Eden. Shelley often uses snakes to represent the infection of a character with an evil passion that eats away at the character's heart in a metaphorical sense. The narrator notes of Falkner, soon after he meets the child Elizabeth, that "his fond aspirations had been snakes to destroy others, and to sting his own soul to torture. He writhed under the consciousness of the remorse and horror which were henceforth to track his path of life." In using the verb *writhed*, Shelley further aligns Falkner with a snake, suggesting that humans may take on the characteristics of creatures of torture. Falkner is also compared to the mythical Greek god Prometheus, doomed to eternal torture by Zeus, and Shelley extends that comparison by constant reference to Falkner's ongoing torture by the knowledge of his crime and its resultant guilt and remorse. Another traditional symbol is that of Eve, who, in addition to representing temptation, may also represent the state of innocence of the first woman prior to the Fall. Shelley compares Elizabeth to Eve as she creates a life in the foreign surroundings of Greece.

An example of a literary symbol in *Falkner* is the rosewood box in which Falkner keeps his letter of confession. It functions like a Pandora's box, waiting to set loose terrible consequences once opened. In addition, Shelley employs clouds the way other writers, and she herself at times, use birds—to symbolize freedom. She plays on that traditional metaphor, giving the clouds themselves wings in place of birds. As Falkner stares out of the window of his cell, he sees clouds flying "fast to other lands, and the spirit of liberty rode upon their outstretched wings."

Falkner stresses many of the topics common to Shelley's other fiction. Nature remains an important force, and the novel contains numerous references to nature in its abundant figurative language. For instance, early in the book, the narrator describes the faculties that are developing in the young Elizabeth, who does not yet even recognize her predispositions. She is unconscious of any "train of feeling" as described by the narrator, as it

> was the microcosm of a plant, folded up in its germ. Sometimes looking at a green, unformed bud, we wonder why a particular texture of leaves must inevitable spring from it, and why another sort of plant should not shoot out from the dark stem: but, as the tiny leaflet uncloses, it is there in all its peculiarity, and endowed with all the especial qualities of its kind.

The metaphor of a young plant also traditionally has been applied to virginal young women. Later, Shelley extends her metaphor as the narrator notes of Jervis in her care for Elizabeth that she "might be compared to the rough-handed gardener, whose labors are without elegance, and yet to whose watering and vigilance the fragrant carnation owes its peculiar tint, and the waxlike camellia its especial variety." The ocean plays an important part in the novel, as in other of Shelley's stories. When Falkner plotted to kidnap Alithea, he thought he could convince her to leave her husband once he took her away into nature—"in the wide, free scenes of nature, the ocean, parent of all liberty, spread at our feet; the way easy to escape, no eye, no ear, to watch and spy out the uncontrolled and genuine emotions of her heart." Nature also carries messages to the young lovers. Elizabeth dreams of Gerard as she awaits Falkner's trial, and "as she took her morning ride, or looked from her casement at night upon the high stars, and pale, still moon, Nature spoke to her audibly of him, and her soul overflowed with tenderness." In addition, Shelley uses nature to help explain the heart of man, writing of male passion: "With some analogy to the laws which govern the elements—they now sleep in calm, and now arise with the violence of furious winds."

The passage comparing man's passion to nature's destructive powers would prove interesting to feminist critics in its gender reference. Another appears in Gerard Neville's view of Elizabeth, when he thinks, "Not in human form had he ever seen embodied so much wisdom, and so much strong, yet tender emotion—none but woman could feel thus, but it was beyond woman to speak and to endure as she did." His reflection is stimulated by his observation of Elizabeth's care of her father, Falkner, a nurturing activity expected of a woman. Yet Gerard himself is compared to a woman when Elizabeth remarks that he has prepared a couch for her using a woman's touch. That description allows stronger contrast to the other main males in the story, Falkner and Sir Boyvill. Because both of those men are fathers to Elizabeth and Gerard, Shelley may suggest a change in generations as to their ability to behave in a more sensitive—that is, feminine—manner. Shelley adopts the traditional feminist symbol of a caged bird on multiple occasions. An early example is when Alithea is described by Lady Cecil as being "like a poor bird, that with untired wing would mount gaily to the skies, when on each side the wires of the aviary impeded its flight."

Psychoanalytic critics recognize allusions to the act of father/daughter incest in *Falkner,* as in Shelley's novel *Lodore,* and incest was a major theme in her gothic novel (see GOTHIC FICTION) *Mathilda.* Shelley's fictional families were generally missing a supportive mother figure. The families instead remain dependent on a father figure who establishes an unnatural or borderline unnatural relationship with his child. In *Frankenstein,* that monstrous parent-child relationship is between father (Victor Frankenstein) and his "son," the monster that he "birthed." In other novels, including *Falkner,* the predatory relationship is between father and daughter. Anne K. Mellor describes the heroines of *Lodore, Mathilda,* and *Falkner* as "indistinguishable" from one another. All are supposedly in an idyllic relationship with controlling fathers made to appear protective and adoring of their daughters, when in reality they are predatory and controlling. The narrator tells readers in *Falkner*'s first volume that Elizabeth learns early "the woman's first and hardest lesson, to bear in silence the advance of an evil, which might be avoided, but for the unconquerable will of another."

Psychoanalytic critics would also find interesting the fact that both Falkner and Gerard Neville dream of Elizabeth, confusing her in their dreams with Gerard's mother and Falkner's love interest, the tragically dead Alithea Neville. Falkner's dream could prove threatening symbolically because, although not with malice aforethought, he drove Alithea to her death, and now it appears he could do the same, if only metaphorically, to Elizabeth. Also, it suggests that he seeks to replace his lost "wife" with his foster daughter. To support this point, one might select the passage describing Falkner's feelings for Elizabeth after he has been arrested, is in jail, and plans to sustain his future relationship with her: "He loved her with a feeling, which, though not paternal, was as warm as ever filled a father's breast." That sentiment is sincere, as is the following thought: "He had looked on her, as the prophet might on the angel, who ministered to his wants in the desert; in the abandonment of all mankind . . . she had been his sweet household companion, his familiar friend, his patient nurse." That is one of several passages that makes clear the nurturing due a child by its parent had flowed in the opposite direction. It was Elizabeth who did the nurturing, a mother figure to the immature, frightened Falkner. Gerard's confusion of Elizabeth's sympathies with those of a mother figure suggests that she will bear responsibility for Gerard in a way that a wife should not, should the two ever marry.

However, seen from a different vantage point, the orphaned Elizabeth Raby's relationship with John, aka Rupert, Falkner, allows Shelley to again emphasize her own commitment to the family union that remains the focus of each of her novels. Falkner isolates Elizabeth from others through frequent travel and develops a dependency on her, but it may be seen as part of his parental love. Shelley celebrates Falkner's devotion by writing, "What is so often a slothful, unapparent sense of parental and filial duty was with them a living, active spirit." On the other hand, given free rein to exercise influence on the orphaned Elizabeth, Falkner attempts to shape her as a type of Eve, the perfect, untried and unsullied woman. In the first volume, chapter 9, Shelley writes of Elizabeth upon her arrival to Greece that "it was as if a new Eve, watched over by angels, had been placed in the desecrated land, and the very ground she trod grew into paradise."

In *Falkner,* as in *Mathilda* and *Lodore,* Shelley emphasizes punishment of the father for his sins against his daughter. Mary Poovey has noted that Elizabeth Raby makes her father figure assume responsibility for his past actions. This begins in a subconscious manner but later becomes fully conscious on Falkner's part as he realizes the possible harm association with him, and bearing his name, might do to Elizabeth. Unaware of the truth regarding Gerard's and Falkner's pasts, Elizabeth unwittingly acts as a persecutor and innocently wreaks revenge. Anne Mellor sees her as an avenging fury, albeit an unintentional one. Shelley portrays Elizabeth as completely justified while she acts on the courage of her convictions. However, she will remain just as convicted by the unshakable loyalty that she feels to Falkner. Through an eventual confrontation, he confesses his crime and suffers humiliation, forced on him by Alithea's husband, Sir Boyvill. According to Poovey, Shelley views Falkner's sins as among the worst. Not only did he deprive Gerard Neville of his mother; he created a scandal that caused public indictment of an innocent woman. Her absence provoked the false rumor that she had deserted her husband and children; she is slandered and libeled even in death. In his defense, Falkner does not realize this until Gerard tells Elizabeth about it many years after Alithea's accidental drowning.

Neville has agonized over that ghastly rumor, always believing that his mother was faithful to her children and loved them. Gerard's attentions to her served to alienate him from his father, who then missed the chance for a relationship with his son. That alienation is another factor that would interest psychoanalytic critics, as well as feminist critics, due to its focus on gender roles and relationships, this one between father and son. Their enmity is caused by the relationship of each with their wife/mother, suggesting oedipal elements.

Elizabeth may also be seen as avenging her own isolation, forced upon her by Falkner as he constantly travels from place to place, never allowing her to form lasting relationships with others, which fosters her total dependence on him. He also deprives her of the education she deserves and removes her from her native culture and her real family. Although he does hire a governess when Elizabeth is 12, the woman offers no companionship. Miss Jervis is, according to the English families living abroad who have enjoyed her services, "precise, and formal, and silent, and quiet, and cold," reminiscent of the caretaker hired for Mathilda in Shelley's novel of that title. Jervis teaches Elizabeth basic needlework skills and self-discipline, but Elizabeth needs friends and confidants. She turns to Falkner to fill that gap, sharing all of his activities and learning much through his intellectual pursuits. Her ironic rescue of him from suicide as a child and again from sure death in the war for Greek independence allow her to later negotiate the revelation of, and punishment for, his youthful crime. As she tends to Falkner during his recovery from wartime injuries, she also brings him into contact with Gerard, who constantly reminds Falkner of his shame. Only Elizabeth's passionate support of Gerard's attempts to vindicate his mother can force Falkner to admit his abduction of Alithea and his part in driving her to her heroic death.

Even in his confession, Falkner becomes the target of what some critics see as Elizabeth's repressed anger. He believes that when he confesses, Gerard will demand satisfaction through a duel, in which Falkner will use an empty gun, assuring his death. However, he is instead arrested and forced into a public confession. Thus, Elizabeth does not cause his physical death but, rather, the death of his pride. Pride remains a critical factor in the myth of the romantic sublime, an element of the romantic movement's ethos against which Shelley often wrote. The male ego caused damage to the domestic scene by removing the father from the personal circle of the home in order for him to attend to more personally gratifying public activities, for the benefit of strangers. As Mellor writes, most of the male characters in Shelley's fiction sacrifice without hesitation the welfare of their family members, friends, and loved ones to advance private ambition, or to protect misplaced pride and reputation.

After all she has done to force Falkner's atonement, Elizabeth remains devoted to him, so much so that she cannot marry Gerard until Falkner clears his name. Feminist critics would point to her lack of identity apart from her relationship with her father as responsible for Elizabeth's inability to imagine life without him. Even when she at last enters London's society scene, she feels alienated and isolated because, as the narrator explains, "Her mind was quite empty of conventional frivolities." Because Elizabeth's adopted father had shaped that mind, he had to bear responsibility. In this aspect, she greatly resembles Ethel in *Lodore,* raised in the wilds of America and unused to high society.

On the other hand, Elizabeth's dedication to her parent may be seen as a positive. Elizabeth's devotion allows Shelley to emphasize the importance of the parent-child bond, but it is seen in an even stronger light as a mother-child bond, as exemplified by the dedication of Gerard to Alithea Neville. The redemption of his mother's good name remains paramount to Gerard and serves as a high moral calling in the novel. Mellor believes it echoes Shelley's desire to clear her own mother's name as she honors her memory. While Shelley's father, William Godwin, had intended to celebrate MARY WOLLSTONECRAFT when he published *Memoirs of the Author of a Vindication of the Rights of Woman* (1798), he merely served to strengthen public condemnation of his wife's ideals. Shelley may reveal her desire to correct his failure through her characters.

Betty T. Bennett makes another suggestion regarding Elizabeth Raby, claiming that she represents a "reversioning" of an earlier Elizabeth, referencing Elizabeth Lavenza from *Frankenstein* (1818). Similarities between the two Elizabeths, in addition to their names, are that they are each semi-orphans, born of the Catholic faith and living in surrogate families. According to Bennett, Elizabeth Raby represents Shelley's "consistent reformist sociopolitical ethos." Shelley was that one author of many who lived to see her own work, *Frankenstein,* become an accepted part of her culture. Even members of the more materialistic culture of 1837 who read *Falkner* also read and enjoyed *Frankenstein.* However, that readership rejected the romantic radical politics on which Shelley based *Frankenstein,* embracing instead a romantic aesthetic. In *Frankenstein,* Elizabeth Lavenza remains passive, educated but seldom active, finding a strong voice only when she speaks in defense of Justine Moritz, condemned for supposedly killing William Frankenstein. Elizabeth denies Justine's guilt when other members of the family have accepted it, perhaps because she feels more closely related to Justine, as both girls have been taken into the Frankenstein family from marginalized groups. Elizabeth remains elevated above Justine, having descended from a nobleman, but still calls attention to injustice based on class difference. However, Justine is executed, neither woman having the required standing within their culture to allow their defenses to be heard and seriously considered. This is not true of Elizabeth Raby/Falkner, who constantly speaks on behalf of her foster father in the name of civil and social justice. She is strong enough to rescue Falkner from suicide at his own hand and by war, in the second instance keeping him alive through sheer willpower. She also convinces Gerard, son of the woman Falkner is accused of killing, to literally go to the ends of the earth on her behalf, despite her connection to Falkner. Gerard compliments Elizabeth for proving more selfless and loyal than he. Elizabeth also has the opportunity to reject Falkner's last name and resume her true family name, which would bring her high social status and disassociate her from any shame that Falkner brings on his own name. But she roundly rejects the repeated proposal and proves victorious in not only assuming her rightful name and social station but also in persuading her family, the Rabys, to accept Falkner into that family.

In examining autobiographical aspects of *Falkner,* readers often associate Gerard Neville with Percy Shelley, who affected Mary Shelley in ways similar to Gerard's influences on Elizabeth Raby. While Mary retained her father, like Elizabeth she had lost her mother, and she watched her relationship with her father weaken following his remarriage. In a letter to her friend Isabella Hoppner, written in August 1821, Mary offers a description of Percy that may be compared to Gerard: "Shelley is as incapable of cruelty as the softest woman—To those who know him his humanity is almost as a proverb." When Gerard helps Elizabeth care for Falkner on the ship between Greece and England, the narrator tells readers that when Gerard sent Elizabeth below deck to rest while he watched

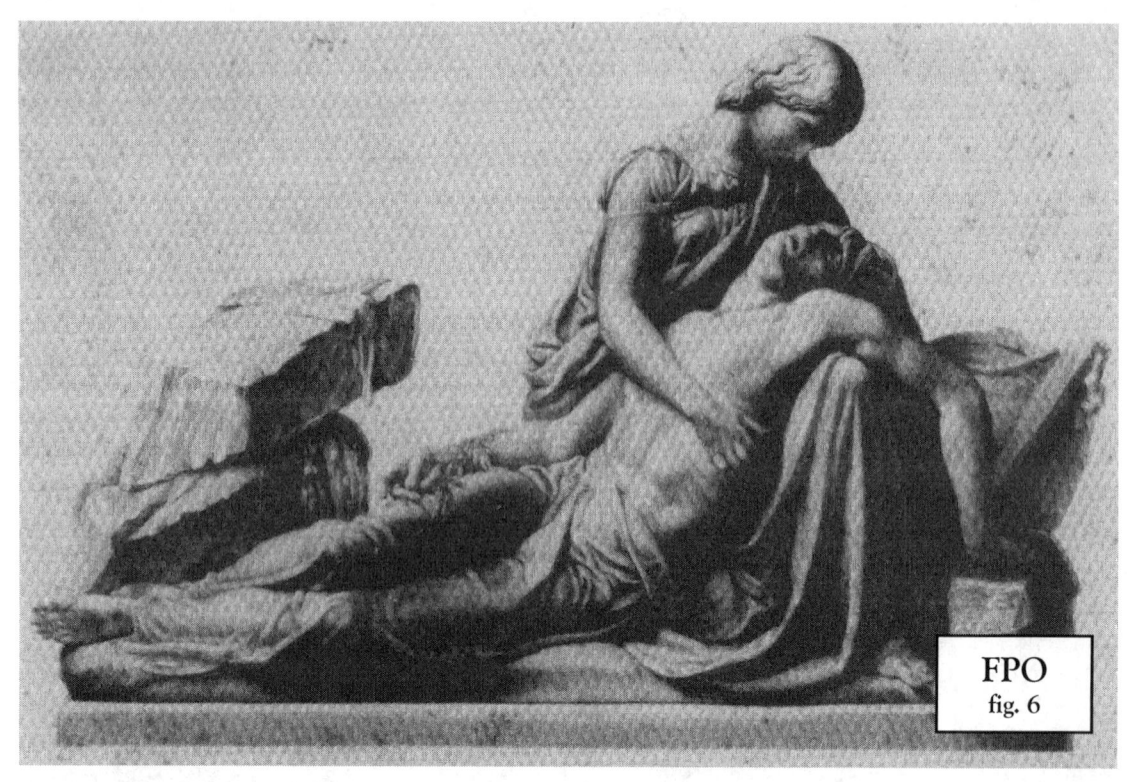

Monument of Percy Bysshe Shelley in Mary Shelley's arms. This engraving is from 1853. *(Monument by Henry Weekes; engraving by George J. Stodart)*

Falkner, "she found a couch had been prepared for her with almost a woman's care by the stranger." Just as Percy Shelley helped Mary expand her knowledge of literature, Gerard introduces Elizabeth to writings by Chaucer, Spenser, Pope, Gray, and Burns, as well as many modern poets. As Percy had done for Mary, Gerard helps Elizabeth build the self-confidence that compensates for her feelings of isolation and alienation from society, caused in large part by her parents' actions. Where Elizabeth feels forced to choose between Falkner and Gerard, Mary had to choose between her father and Percy. First, her father forbade her to associate with Shelley and then refused to see her upon her return to London after the two lovers "eloped" while Percy was still married. Still, Mary remained loyal to Godwin, even urging Percy to give her father money that the couple sorely needed. As Mary wrote to her good friend Maria Gisborne, "I look upon fidelity as the first of human virtues," explaining that she intended to write a novel about that virtue.

That intention surfaces in *Falkner*, in which the characteristic of fidelity is stressed continually. Elizabeth's devotion to Falkner remains unshakable, as does Gerard's determination to clear his mother's name. Elizabeth is described as "devoted to her duties, commanding herself day by day to fulfill her task" and "filled with matchless fidelity." Gerard tells her that he hates his own weakness "when I see your fortitude. You are more than woman, more than human being ever was." He recognizes that they both share that trait, "to see our duties in a strong light." Mary nursed her father to the point of exhaustion, as did Elizabeth, but that devotion was permitted due to the fact that Percy had died years earlier. Elizabeth shows marked integrity by remaining unswayed by many logical arguments against her devotion to a man who was not even a blood relation. The novel's overly sentimental conclusion, in which Gerard, despite Falkner's devastating effect on his life, accepts Elizabeth's adoptive father into his home, may reflect what some critics view as Mary Shelley's familial fantasy.

Many specific scenes and passages in *Falkner* may be somewhat confidently labeled autobiographical, based on Shelley's letters and journal entries. In any author's works, some novel passages may appear to be autobiographical on the surface, but upon closer study, they reflect general life experiences that many people share, such as the loss of a loved one. Parallels between such fictional passages and real-life private statements by an author, however, help support the claim for specificity to an author's experiences, some of which are demonstrated above. For instance, when Elizabeth is living by herself in Greece, awaiting word of Falkner, Shelley compares her feelings at 16 to those of a more mature person. The grief of the young is pure and almost sweet, as compared to the grief of those with more experience. Shelley writes of Elizabeth that she filled her days with "duties" and a set routine, always beginning with a ride along the beach. As a teen, "morning was not so fresh as her," and her thoughts of Falkner and the resulting sense of resignation

> mingled with a hope that warmed into an ardent desire to see him again. Surely there is no object so sweet as the young in solitude. In after years—when death has bereaved us of the dearest—when cares, and regrets, and fears, and passions, evil either in their nature of their results, have stained our lives with black, solitude is too sadly peopled to be pleasing.

By comparison, in 1823 Shelley wrote to her friend Leigh Hunt of her own feelings of sadness and isolation, a solitude interrupted by people who constantly reminded her of happier days:

> On Saturday Aug. 30th I went with Jane to the Gisbornes. I know not why, but seeing them seemed more than anything else to remind me of Italy. Evening came on drearily, the rain splashed on the pavement, nor star, nor moon deigned to appear—I looked upward to seek an image of Italy but the blotted sky told me only of my change. I tried to collect my thoughts, and then again dared not think—fir I am a ruin where owls & bats live only and I lost my last singing bird when I left Albaro.

CHARACTERS

Falkner While *Falkner* is seen by many as a woman's novel, and it contains a strong woman character in Elizabeth Raby, its protagonist is clearly John/Rupert Falkner. Falkner is repeatedly described as an individual of honorable bearing, one whose value may be seen in his expressions and mannerisms. He is also a man who behaved in a most dishonorable way, betraying the woman he loved and causing her accidental death. Falkner's suffering is constantly emphasized, as is his love for Elizabeth. That concern for the girl is seen by some critics as completely self-centered, despite his constant claims of remorse over the precarious social situation in which he places Elizabeth. He has been labeled a Byronic character due to his dark, brooding nature, relieved of a suicidal focus only by Elizabeth. He also possesses the mysterious background of the Byronic hero to be revealed in a lengthy letter, delayed until volume 2. He suffers moral conflict but does not serve as the moral center of the novel. That position some might claim for Elizabeth, but it would more properly be appointed to Gerard Neville, as discussed below. Falkner has exercised an error in judgment that he based on a false morality. He claims that he rescued Alithea Neville from a loveless marriage, but his true motive was to kidnap her for himself to realize a lifelong fantasy. The coincidental occurrences common to 19th-century novels forces him to face his error and suffer for it. While some time must pass before he makes a true confession to Elizabeth and others, he ostensibly does so in order to rescue Alithea's reputation. That motive is pure and represents a crucial alteration of Falkner's character.

Elizabeth Elizabeth Raby/Falkner has been discussed thoroughly above, with emphasis on the importance of her absolute fidelity to her foster father. She is a young person who owes her parent everything and realizes it. Not only does he rescue her from a loveless, near-poverty existence with Mrs. Baker, but he also prevents her being raised by her true family, the Rabys, who would have marginalized her due to what they envisioned as her father's disgrace. Shelley shows through Elizabeth that a loving environment proves more important than breeding; wealth does not equate to happiness. However, Elizabeth is raised with privilege, much of her education coming from travel that a working-class person could never enjoy. She remains a strong but static character, not changing much from the beginning of the story to its end. Although dominated by Falkner, she is an exception to the traditional female rule of inactivity, drawing compliments for her spirit and fortitude from Neville, who tells her she is not only more than the normal woman but more than the normal human. Her dogged devotion and courage are first revealed when she lives alone in Greece as a young teenager in order to be close to Falkner. It surfaces again when she declares that she will travel to America to locate Osborne, secure in the belief that she can talk him into returning to England with her. She declares in a masculine way that "so much is left undone, because we fancy it impossible to do; which, upon endeavor, is found plain and easy." There is little of sentimentality in Elizabeth, and she rarely engages in fantasy and daydreaming. The narrator tells the reader of a young Elizabeth engaged in conversation with Falkner about characters from "heroes of old" that "she dwelt on the moral to be deduced, the theories of life and death, religion and virtue."

Gerard Neville As noted above, with a listing of many similarities, Gerard Neville is based on Percy Shelley. Elizabeth holds to her early view of Gerard that "there was poetry in his very gloom that added charm to every thought spent upon him." A sensitive boy raised with the pain of seeing others betray his mother's memory when he holds true, he fights that battle alone. Unlike Elizabeth, who has Falkner as her champion, Gerard is truly alone in life. While Lady Cecil offers him friendship, and they share an antipathy for Lord Boyvill, she does not understand Gerard's dogged devotion. He exists in the novel as a love interest for Elizabeth and must bow to her wish to remain with her foster father, regardless of the love that she feels for Gerard. While most young men with any pride would not want to know they were second to a woman's father, Gerard embraces that situation, as do the Rabys and Lady Cecil, because Elizabeth "was too dear a treasure to be voluntarily renounced." Like Elizabeth, Gerard "cared not for the world, and when they did enter it, the merits of both commanded respect and liking; they were happy in each other, happy in a growing family, happy in Falkner." Gerard completes the triangle of the three "orphans" united by their devotion to one another.

Alithea Neville Although Alithea Neville has died before the plot of *Falkner* begins, she is the linchpin for its action. The love of Falkner's life, she is married to someone else, with whom she has two children and to whom she is determined to remain faithful, despite Falkner's appeals. A thorough description of Alithea appears in the novel's first volume, chapter 16. The narrator emphasizes her youth in comparison to her husband's age and her astute manner of dealing with his aggression, self-centeredness, and ego. Hers is a cautionary tale, for she is a woman who met all of society's standards and yet still fell prey to its harsh judgment based on rumor and innuendo. She allows Shelley to emphasize the crucial need of a woman to retain a spotless reputation, making clear that despite her best efforts, society may cruelly indict her due to no fault of her own. Haunted by gossip and public attacks all of her life, Shelley no doubt felt sympathy for Alithea, who is meant to be a positive character. Hers was a sacrificial heroic death for the sake of her children.

FURTHER READING

Allen, Graham. "Public and Private Fidelity: Mary Shelley's 'Life of William Godwin' and *Falkner*. In *Mary Shelley's Fictions from Frankenstein to Falkner*, edited by Michael Eberle-Sinatra, 224–242. New York: St. Martin's Press, 2000.

Bennett, Betty T. *Mary Wollstonecraft Shelley: An Introduction*. Baltimore: Johns Hopkins University Press, 1998.

———. "'Not this Time, Victor!' Mary Shelley's Reversioning of Elizabeth, from *Frankenstein* to *Falkner.*" In *Mary Shelley in Her Times*, edited by Betty T. Bennet and Stuart Curran, 1–17. Baltimore: Johns Hopkins University Press, 2000.

———, ed. *Selected Letters of Mary Wollstonecraft Shelley*. Baltimore: Johns Hopkins University Press, 1995.

Bennett, Betty T., and Charles E. Robinson. *The Mary Shelley Reader*. New York: Oxford University Press, 1990.

Ellis, Kate Ferguson. "*Falkner* and Other Fictions." In *The Cambridge Companion to Mary Shelley*, edited by Esther Schor, 151–162. Cambridge: Cambridge University Press, 2004.

Lahti, David. "George Gordon, Lord Byron: Childe Harold's Pilgrimage, 1812–1818." Available online. URL: http://www-personal.umich.edu/~lahtid/literature/vicenglish/byron/chldharold.htm. Accessed June 10, 2010.

Mellor, Anne K. *Mary Shelley: Her Life, Her Fiction, Her Monsters*. London: Routledge, 1989.

Poovey, Mary. "My Hideous Progeny: Mary Shelley and the Feminization of Romanticism." *PMLA* 95, no. 3 (May 1980): 332–347.

Saunders, Julia. "Rehabilitating the Family in Mary Shelley's *Falkner.*" In *Mary Shelley's Fictions from Frankenstein to Falkner*, edited by Michael Eberle-Sinatra, 211–223. New York: St. Martin's Press, 2000.

St. Clair, William. *The Godwins and the Shelleys: The Biography of a Family*. 1989. Reprint, Baltimore: Johns Hopkins University Press, 1991.

"The False Rhyme" (1828)

"The False Rhyme" appeared in the ladies' annual journal *The Keepsake for 1829* (1828). It is among the many stories that Mary Shelley wrote and sold as a means of support, a fact that some critics use to devalue such examples of her work. However, the story proves valuable in reflecting Shelley's interests and capabilities. "The False Rhyme" displays her knowledge of the value of poetry and its format, as well as her grasp of history, literary tradition, and the French language. The story ranks as historical fiction, adopting as its main characters the French queen Margaret of Navarre (1492–1549), also known as Marguerite de Navarre; Margaret of Angouleme, the duchesse d'Alençon; and Margaret of O. Margaret was the sister of Francis I (1494–1547); Shelley's audience would know her also as the grandmother of the French king Henry IV. The ruler of Navarre from 1544 to 1549, Margaret was known as a patron of learning and a writer, producing a seminal collection of tales titled *The Heptameron of Margaret, Queen of Navarre*. Today readily available in e-text, the five volumes of *The Heptameron* may be accessed through the Gutenberg project. That version of volume 1 also contains an essay written by George Saintsbury as well as many of the collection's original illustrations.

The Heptameron was not published in London as a trade book until 1853, a version translated by Walter K. Kelly, with the first widely printed version in French appearing in 1858. The dates of publication suggest that if Shelley had read the collection, it would have been in the original French in another form. She indulges in the inclusion of French phrases in the vernacular inserted into the story's opening scene. The phrases, which are rhyming couplets, form the framework for the plot and the source of a friendly wager on the part of Margaret with her brother Francis. The couplets and the ensuing wager hinge on a debate over the inconstancy of women. Thus, Shelley introduces one of her favored topics, the contrast between the genders and their perceptions of devotion and fidelity. The topic of fidelity was emphasized throughout the 72 tales included in *The Heptameron*. For instance, the first tale begins with this statement:

> The wife of a Proctor, having been pressingly solicited by the Bishop of Sées, took him for her profit, and, being as little satisfied with him as with her husband, found a means to have the son of the Lieutenant General of Alençon for her pleasure. Some time afterwards she caused the latter to be miserably murdered by

her husband, who, although he obtained pardon for the murder, was afterwards sent to the Galleys with a sorcerer named Gallery; and all this was brought about by the wickedness of his wife.

A footnote informs the reader that "the incidents of the story are historical." Thus, Shelley skillfully incorporates not only Margaret as a "true" historical figure but also her topic matter and her own tongue-in-cheek suggestion that the events of the story are truthful. Furthermore, she exhibits her poetic ability in fashioning couplets crucial to the story's premise. In his comments that accompany *The Heptameron*, Saintsbury notes that "prose tales" were long delayed in development due to a preference for verse fabliaux. He refers to 13th- and 14th-century French bawdy tales in verse form that later inspired the production of Giovanni Boccaccio's *Decameron* and Geoffrey Chaucer's *Canterbury Tales*. Shelley places herself in quite sophisticated company in her own fashioning of a simple story inspired not only by Margaret Navarre's writing but by the woman herself. Containing fewer than 1,200 words, no doubt to meet restrictions set by *The Keepsake*, the story remains fully self-contained, another tribute to Shelley's skill.

SYNOPSIS

"The False Rhyme" opens with a verse written by Thomas Moore that reads:

Come, tell me where the maid is found
Whose heart can love without deceit,
And I will range the world around
To sigh one moment at her feet.

Margaret Navarre is visiting her brother, King Francis, and she decides to host a party. However, her brother declines to attend, to Margaret's disappointment. Her disappointment intensifies when inclement weather spoils the party. Her own disposition dampened, she goes into the castle to find Francis doodling on his window. She has heard rumors that he is melancholy due to "a lover's quarrel with a favourite dame." As she walks into the room, he hurriedly hides what he has written on the window, obviously embarrassed, and jokes that he has committed treason by writing it. Her curiosity piqued, Margaret examines the verse he has written and counters with her own verse. The conversation runs as follows:

"What have we here?" cried Margaret: "nay, this is lèse majesté—

'Souvent femme varie,
Bien fou qui s'y fie!'

Very little change would greatly amend your couplet:— would it not run better thus—

'Souvent homme varie,
Bien folle qui s'y fie?'"

Loosely translated, the passage reads as follows:

"What have we here?" cried Margaret: "nay, this is a crime

'Often women change,
Crazy men who confide!'

Very little change would greatly amend your couplet:—would it not run better thus—

'Often men change
Crazy women who confide!'"

Francis replies that he will be content to hear even one tale of female fidelity. Margaret challenges him to find an example of infidelity on the part of "a noble and high-reputed dame." Francis immediately states an example in Emilie de Lagny.

The narrator supplies exposition, explaining that Emilie had been Margaret's favorite lady-in-waiting who married the Sire de Lagny. Tragedy visited the couple a year later when de Lagny was falsely accused of treason for yielding a fortress to the enemy. He was ordered into perpetual imprisonment. Deeply distressed, Emilie often visited her beloved in the miserable dungeon. The visits took an emotional and physical toll on Emilie, who remained inconsolable. Suddenly, she simply disappeared. Rumor held that she left France with all of her jewels, taking the handsome young page Robinet Leroux with her and sharing his bed. At that point, Margaret gave the order to stop the search for Emilie that she had instigated.

Now, under her brother's taunting, Margaret declares that she would prove Emilie's innocence in a month's time. She strikes a bargain with Francis. She will bear his "vile rhyme" as her "motto" to the grave if she cannot fulfill her vow to prove Emilie's innocence. Francis rejoins that if she wins, "I will break my window and grant thee whatever boon thou askest."

The story of their wager spreads through the songs of wandering minstrels. During the ensuing month, Margaret sends 100 emissaries "everywhere" seeking word of Emilie, ready to give many jewels to find her, but with no success. On the eve before the final day of the wager, de Lagny's jailer requests an audience with Margaret, saying that if she will ask de Lagny's pardon as her boon and obtain permission for him to appear before the king, she will win her bet. Margaret enthusiastically agrees, and that evening she jubilantly meets with Francis. The narrator adds that the timing is perfect, as Francis has received word of a great victory that day from a mysterious soldier. Everyone agrees this soldier is the bravest knight in the land for his courage in battle. Francis wants to reward him, but a vow he has taken prevent the soldier from revealing his identity beneath his lowered visor.

The gathering takes place in Francis's rooms, where "the sun shone on the lattice on which the ungallant rhyme was traced." The jailer ushers in his gaunt, thin prisoner, who walks with "tottering steps." When he kneels before the king and pushes back his hood, long, golden hair reveals the prisoner is a woman. Incensed, Francis demands to know the location of de Lagny and accuses the jailer of treason, but the voice of Emilie responds, "Wiser men than he have been deceived by woman." She quickly explains that in order to help her husband prove his innocence, she "assumed his chains" in prison, while he sneaked out with the page, Robinet, in disguise as a woman. De Lagny joined the king's army, and he is the courageous soldier hero that Francis had sought to reward earlier in the day.

Both women kneel before Francis as Margaret requests that Francis grant her boon. The king shatters the window, destroying the couplet that had touted female inconstancy, and then issues de Lagny his freedom. In the celebration that follows, Emilie is no longer the most beautiful woman present, as she has sacrificed her health and beauty for her husband. Despite her condition, more loveliness sits on her cheek than on any other woman's, due to her love for and fidelity to her husband.

COMMENTARY

While Shelley's stories have not yet received focused critical attention, they are apt subjects. "The False Rhyme" remains ripe for a formalist approach. To begin, the story's title suggests multiple possible meaning for the term *false*, which could mean an incorrectly formed rhyme, or one that does not offer the truth. In the case of the verse that captures Francis's and Margaret's interest, the latter is the most likely meaning. Francis has written a couplet suggesting the inconstancy of women, a suggestion that Margaret's revision of the couplet reverses. As the reader follows the simple plot, the term *false* is also applied to the love of a specific man and woman, suggesting inconstancy on their part and giving the two rhymers another focus, on which they stage a wager. The suggested metaphor of a game, which begins with the attempt on Francis's part to hide his rhyme from Margaret, continues in their sparring with the rhymes, their eventual wagers, and the production of a winner and a loser at the story's end. Love is often viewed as a game of the sexes, and this particular game involves disguises, which heightens the game's tension and aligns the plot with the traditional romance, in which disguises abound. The tie to the romance tradition also permits hyperbole, or exaggeration, which begins with the verse by Thomas Moore that opens the story. Emilie's substitution for de Lagny in prison and war itself may also be viewed as games, as may the tournament that concludes the story. Implicit in the concept of a game is a winner and a loser, and by proving Emilie's constancy, Margaret wins the game between the siblings. However, the concept of a loser proves ironic, as everyone wins in this particular competition. When Francis shatters the window in the story's conclusion, he symbolically shatters the false rhyme, destroying the lie about women that he had written on the window. The window's destruction also suggests the destruction of the lie in relation to the broader world, which is not open to receive the truths revealed within the castle.

Feminist critics would find the gender issues of interest. Margaret's active character—who makes plans, accuses her brother of treason, matches her brother's ability to rhyme, and concocts a competition—speaks to the female power prevalent in this tale. Readers need not know the historic Margaret to understand that she is the powerful figure. The metaphoric duel between the sexes as to which is the most constant is another show of feminine power, as Emilie receives Margaret's complete support in the competition. Emilie's constancy shows that females conquer the male propensity for inconstancy, making them the more sexually powerful as they withhold their sex as a prize for a special love. She delivers perhaps the most ironic line in the story when she states of the jailer, "wiser men than he have been deceived by woman." Her statement contradicts the story's main point, which is that women are not deceivers of men. It also strongly suggests a reference to Francis himself, who at the tale's opening was "melancholy" due to betrayal by a woman. Shelley would not add such a line without thought, and it begs critical reaction. Did she want to alert readers to the fact that women are intelligent enough to be selective in their use of deception, calling on that skill only when it produces a positive result? Can the immoral act of deception ever be viewed as a moral necessity? Are all men equally weak and vulnerable, regardless of social rank, when it comes to love? Certainly Shelley suggests those possibilities and more in that line. The black-and-white world of medieval tales, understood through dualities such as right/wrong, male/female, and purity/impurity, has been updated to apply to her contemporary audience.

Feminist critics will also notice Emilie's loss of physical appeal as she has martyred such traditional feminine traits in support of her husband. She wears the chains of prison, balancing the chain mail that de Lagny wears in order to fight and regain the king's favor. Despite Emilie's emaciation, she retains great value, based not on the traditional weight of external beauty but on her faith and stalwart love. Only her sacrifice permits de Lagny's military triumph, and the gains of the kingdom through battle would not have been possible if not for her moral strength. While both women kneel before Francis at the story's conclusion, they simply follow convention and show fortitude in their willingness to bend to his authority. His raising of the women from their "supplicatory posture" demonstrates a reversal of the traditional power roles.

From the New Historicist point of view, Margaret's real-life reputation as an intelligent queen, whose work *The Heptameron* inspired many later writers, brings an element of value to Shelley's story by lending it the support of Margaret's authority. Simultaneously, Shelley herself assumes that authority to join the storytelling tradition by placing Margaret within her tale. The story takes its place in a popular romance tradition as well as that of the fabliaux, explained above, offering it a rather rich literary pedigree. The mostly female readers of *The Keepsake* may have used the strong women in stories such as Shelley's to indulge in escapism from their own measured and restricted lives. In 1828, Shelley was herself experiencing the turmoil of inconstancy, although not of a sexual nature. Shelley learned that year that her supposed friend, Jane Williams, had betrayed her by engaging in vicious gossip about Mary's final months with PERCY BYSSHE SHELLEY. Some members of the couple's inner circle claimed that Percy had complained about Mary's lack of support during his final days, gossip that deeply hurt Mary. To learn that Jane had engaged in such gossip proved especially painful, as Jane's husband had died along with Percy, both drowned in a storm. The two had grown close as they coped with the sudden fear and loneliness in the shared traumatic aftermath of the loss of their husbands.

Many of the story's details, in addition to the cross-dressing and metaphoric gender-swapping would interest queer theorists. They might note Francis's remark that "Robinet was a pretty boy" as a display of homoeroticism, and Margaret's disappointment in her lady-in-waiting's misbehavior could represent jealousy based on erotic tendencies. The fact that Robinet could pass as a woman, particularly one as beautiful as Emilie, suggests his femininity. The close living arrangements of royals with their various attendants has long been viewed as a situation conducive to sexual interaction. Francis is described as reposing on a settee shared by his sister, adding further support to the theory that he practiced an alternative lifestyle. Many critics have noted the homoerotic relationships that rulers shared with their knights, although Shelley firmly emphasizes de Lagny's relationship to Emilie in this story. However, he abandons her to what had to be a terrible existence in prison in order to participate in male-centered activities peculiar to soldiers.

Any critic would observe the emphasis on the arts and imagination within Shelley's tale. The story includes two verses, and the plot turns on the truth or falseness of Francis's sentiment in his couplet. Margaret's sharp imagination permits her design of a competing couplet. The narrator states that "the result" of the royal wager "was long sung by troubadour and minstrel," emphasizing the importance of music as well as of storytelling to the medieval culture. Everyone in the area knew of the wager, to the point that the jailer learned of it and shared it with Emilie. Finally, celebrations both open and conclude the story, suggesting the additional importance of song and dance to the community.

CHARACTERS

Margaret Navarre That the real Margaret Navarre was a well-known historical figure brings much moral currency to Shelley's story. The fictional Margaret also echoes her real-life counterpart's imagination in her concoction of the wager that pits her wits against those of her royal brother. While she does not solve her conundrum alone and would have lost the bet, save for the assistance of the prison jailer, her grace in accepting the jailer's word and faith in this lowliest of subjects stands her in good stead. Margaret is not quite the traditional stock character, in that she did permit her faith in her lady-in-waiting to lapse after hearing the gossip against her concerning her interaction with Robinet. However, her own belief in feminine constancy, revealed in her dialogue with her brother, propels both into a renewal of faith, supported by swift action on her part.

Francis Like Margaret, Francis I is also a historical character. However, he had not captured Shelley's and the reader's imagination as had his sister, whose writing represented her great capacity for storytelling and invention. In the story, he serves as a foil to Margaret and, through his melancholy over lost love, represents everyman, despite his royal blood. Thus, readers can identify with him. Although Margaret becomes the more active of the two characters as pertains to their wager, Shelley ensures that readers keep in mind Francis's grave responsibilities as a king as the narrator references the waging of battles. The reader understands that while the king may lose a wager with his sister, he first wins a serious battle, or his knight does for him. His royal status elevates him above what could have been the role of a clown who loses a wager. His grace in accepting this sister's victory distinguishes him as a male willing to dispense with unflattering stereotypes of women and to revel in his knight's victory over challenges to love. To readers, he represents the ability of men of high intellect and sensitivity to understand when surrender to another's opinions results in moral victory.

Emilie A flat figure and a minor character, Emilie is nevertheless crucial to the plot and its resolution. She speaks one of the more important lines in the story: "Wiser men than he have been deceived by woman." While acting as the figure who convinces Francis that women can be constant, she simultaneously proves that they can also be deceitful for a good cause and suggests that Francis himself is one of the "wiser men" to whom she refers. Her willing surrender of her beauty, an important commodity for women, represents the ultimate sacrifice, near comparable to death on the part of the knight. Thus, her own fortitude balances that of her soldier husband.

FURTHER READING

Navarre, Margaret. *The Tales of the Heptameron.* Volume 1. Available online. URL: http://www.gutenberg.org/ebooks/17701. Accessed January 31, 2011.

O'Dea, Gregory. "'Perhaps a Tale You'll Make It'; Mary Shelley's Tales for *The Keepsake*." In *Iconoclastic*

Departures: Mary Shelley after Frankenstein: Essays in Honor of the Bicentenary of Mary Shelley's Birth, edited by Syndy M. Conger, Frederick S. Frank, and Gregory O'Dea, 62. Madison, N.J.: Fairleigh Dickinson University Press, 1997.

Shelley, Mary. "The False Rhyme." Available online. URL: http://underthesun.cc/Classics/Shelley/falserhyme/. Accessed January 31, 2011.

Sunstein, Emily. *Mary Shelley: Romance and Reality.* Boston: Little, Brown, 1989.

Sussman, Charlotte. "Stories for *The Keepsake.*" In *The Cambridge Companion to Mary Shelley,* edited by Esther Schor, 163–179. Cambridge: Cambridge University Press, 2003.

The Fortunes of Perkin Warbeck (1830)

The Fortunes of Perkin Warbeck deals with a popular topic that had interested audiences for centuries. A young man named Perkin Warbeck, born in Belgium in 1474, had claimed to be Richard Plantagenet, duke of York. His claim that he was the youngest son of Edward IV and heir to the English throne occupied at the time by Henry VII was plausible. Edward had been succeeded by Richard III, and Edward's two sons, Richard and the boy king Edward V, were imprisoned in the Tower of London at the time. No record exists of the two boys' fates, and Richard III, usurper of Edward IV, was thought to have ordered the children killed in 1483 to protect his claim to the throne. That version of history—believed by many modern scholars to be inaccurate—had been popularized by several writers, including William Shakespeare in his drama *King Richard III* (ca. 1591). Shelley quotes often from Shakespeare, along with other works, including poetry by her husband, at the beginning of each chapter. Richard was defeated by the duke of Richmond, who became King Henry VII. In addition, the story of Jane Shore, Edward's mistress, was made famous through ballads. Nineteenth-century readers would easily recognize her through Shelley's characterization as a romanticized character in her novel.

Warbeck gained the support of France's King Charles VIII; Margaret of Burgundy, his aunt; and James IV of Scotland. James also supervised the marriage of Warbeck to his cousin Katherine Gordon. Warbeck and his followers waged a failed war against Henry, invading England twice. He escaped following a 1495 failed attack but was captured by Henry at Beaulieau in 1497. Warbeck was first confined to court, but when he tried to escape in 1498, he was imprisoned in the Tower of London. For the next seven years, he continued claiming to be Richard, and once again he attempted a revolt, joining with the earl of Warwick, a fellow prisoner and a cousin who did hold a legitimate and recognized claim to the throne. He had been a playmate of Elizabeth, the daughter of King Edward IV whom Henry VII married to unite the Lancastrians and Yorkists, symbolized respectively by red and white roses. The King's Council found out about the plot, and Warbeck confessed to being an impostor, the son of Katherine de Faro and John Warbeck, a minor French official. Henry ordered both Warbeck and Warwick executed, and they were hanged on November 23, 1499. Many scholars, including Mary Shelley, believed that Warbeck had confessed under duress and that he was not an impostor but actually was Richard.

Warbeck was the subject of multiple artistic presentations during the 17th–19th centuries. In addition to Shakespeare's drama, John Ford wrote *Perkin Warbeck: A Strange Truth* (1634), Freidrich Schiller wrote *Warbeck* (1798), and L. M. Fontan wrote *Perkins Warbec* (1828); all were probably read and studied by Shelley. Novels based on the Warbeck tale include *Le Prétendant, ou le Faux Duc d'York* (1716), by La Paix de Lizancour; *Nouvelles historiques* (1774–1783), by Baculard D'Arnaud; *Warbeck: A Pathetic Tale* (1786), by Sophia Lee; and *Perkin Warbeck: Or the Court of James the Fourth of Scotland* (1830), by Alexander Campbell.

According to the critic Emily Sunstein, Shelley decided to write the story as a historical novel. When she mentioned the project to her publisher, Henry Colburn, he was initially not interested. Shelley worked on her novel over several years, during which time she faced her normal shortage of funds. In 1828, her friend Thomas Moore offered to

fig. 7

Portrait of Mary Shelley's friend Thomas Moore from the 1840s. This image is from Edmund Blunden's *Leigh Hunt and His Circle,* published by Harper & Brothers in 1930.

take her to his publisher, John Murray, ostensibly to discuss a writing project about GEORGE GORDON BYRON (Lord Byron). However, Shelley had sworn never to use Byron to make money and would not agree to write the project herself, though she would consult on such a project. Instead, she spoke with Murray about *Perkin Warbeck.* Murray hesitated to publish anything by Shelley due to her lingering reputation as a member of the infamous Shelley/Byron romantic circle as well as the daughter of the revolutionary writer MARY WOLLSTONECRAFT. He eventually gave Shelley £100, but he would not publish *Perkin Warbeck.*

Later that year, while Shelley visited Paris, she attended a drama based on Lord Byron's death and, probably, a drama by Louis Marie Fontan entitled *Perkins Warbec.* In 1829, she received a letter from her friend Prosper Mérimée, who dismissed the value of historical fiction, not knowing that Shelley was at work on *Perkin Warbeck.* His remarks did not dampen her enthusiasm.

Shelley wrote to Colburn in November 1829, reminding him of their earlier discussion about historical romance. At that time, she informed Colburn through her friend Leigh Hunt that she wanted to send him "a Romance on which I was occupied on the subject of Perkin Warbeck—You asked to see the first Volume—which I was not able to send . . . I may now say that it is ready for the press." In January 1830, she signed an agreement for publication of three volumes of *Perkin Warbeck* with Colburn and Bentley, for which she would be paid £150, relinquishing all rights to the publisher. Shelley had expected much more for an advance and was quite disappointed. And although the *Athenaeum* had previously ranked her the most distinguished contemporary English woman of letters, her novel did not sell. One event that undoubtedly contributed to the depressed sales was that on May 13, 1830, just prior to publication of Shelley's *Perkin Warbeck,* another novel based on the same character had gone on sale.

A thorough and detailed synopsis of the first volume of *Perkin Warbeck* is provided here to give readers a sense of how Shelley blends history with fiction. Summaries of the final two volumes will be brief, emphasizing the novel's romantic aspects.

SYNOPSIS

Introduction
In the novel's introduction, Shelley states that Perkin Warbeck had been suggested to her as a topic for a novel, and she decided that the romance aspect of the story merited exploration. She defends the plausibility of Warbeck's claims to being a Plantagenet by noting that the king of Scotland would never have offered his kinswoman as a bride to a person who had not thoroughly convinced him of his royal blood. According to Shelley, records exist in the Tower of London to substantiate the duke of York's, Richard's, survival. She adds that her purpose is not to argue that question but to focus on the fact that Perkin Warbeck was much loved by his contemporaries.

Volume 1: Chapters 1–6
The novel opens with three knights fleeing the defeat of King Richard III. One separates from his two companions, the three agreeing on a later location for rendezvous. The knight pushes his horse to

the point of exhaustion, fearing capture. He rests at a church where the service is led by a monk whom the knight soon recognizes as a member of his own order of the White Rose, supporters of the Plantagenets. The knight sees a sword hanging above the monk's fireplace, and when he remarks on it, the monk confirms that he had once been in the order but had left it due to a shameful act. As the two talk, they realize that the knight knows the monk's foster son, who had appeared at the field of battle. The young man had identified himself as King Richard's son, Edmund Plantagenet, and expressed a desire to join the knight in battle. The knight had believed him to have been killed and is on the verge of sharing that information with the monk when the boy bursts into the room. Edmund Plantagenet recognizes the knight as Lord Lovel, and he tells the two men that he saw his father's body hoisted over a mule to be presented to the townspeople in disgrace. The duke of Richmond had defeated Richard III and claimed the crown, although Richard had appointed the earl of Lincoln as his successor.

The next day, the boy and Lord Lovel—"the Noble Cavalier and gentle Squire"—ride together toward London. The knight learns of Edmund's background. When his mother died, the king did as she had asked on her deathbed, sending the boy away to live far from court and be raised by a trusted former knight who had fought with Richard in previous battles between the duke of York and King Henry VI. Always performing nobly, the knight had accidentally killed his twin brother on the battlefield and retired to the contemplative life of a monk in order to repent for the crime against his brother. When Richard's legitimate son died, he visited Edmund, giving the boy his first sense of connection to the outside world. Edmund has ventured into the world to fight for his father's cause, and the events he has observed have given him a new cause. For the first time in his life, "feeling was the parent of action."

When Edmund asks what became of King Edward's children after his defeat by Richard III, Lovel explains that his daughter, Lady Elizabeth, took refuge in Yorkshire while Edward, the older of Richard's two sons, died in the Tower. The younger boy, Richard, duke of York, "is said to have died." Lovel speaks in a grave voice that might have excited suspicion in someone more sophisticated than Edmund. He explains the question of succession by noting first that Edmund's father, the duke of Gloucester, caused suspicion of illegitimacy regarding Edward's children. As their uncle, the duke could legally rise to be king, and he named his son the Prince of Wales. Lovel and others at court did not rise against Richard, as Edward's son was too young to lead them, and many lives would be sacrificed.

The fissures caused by the Wars of the Roses had not healed, and if the Yorkists had fought among themselves, they would have lost all they had gained from the Lancasters. After Richard's son died, he declared the son of the duke of Clarence, the earl of Warwick, his successor, but the earl was now imprisoned. Presently, the son of Richard's sister, John de la Poole, Earl of Lincoln, laid claim to the throne. Whether he could stand up to the new Lancastrian king remained to be determined, but Lord Lovel would support him if he did. In the meantime, Richard III had decided to remove the stigma from his brother Edward's children and marry his niece, Elizabeth. Her mother, Elizabeth Woodville, at first refused the union, but after consideration she consented, in hopes of restoring her existing children's rights and her own status. Those at court still desired Elizabeth as their queen and pressed the earl of Richmond to take Richard's widow as his wife. Lovel hopes that Richmond will do so, which might lead him to "fall into a pit" of his own design.

Arriving outside London, Lovel and Richard wait until dark to approach the home of the earl of Lincoln. The narrator describes the earl as brave, wise, handsome, perceptive of what was right, and resolving to fulfill it. He did not approve of his uncle usurping the rights of Edward IV's children. And at this point Elizabeth had been so accepted as a royal that it was difficult to question the legitimacy of the boy proclaimed Edward V. Even the earl of Lincoln, now nominated to inherit the York throne, believed that Edward V should take the tile. However, Edward died in the Tower, leaving his brother, Richard, described as an ingenious and sprightly boy between the ages of 10 and 11, to support the York dreams on his immature shoulders. The boy went to live in the country, having been visited by the earl of Lincoln, who found him a fine young man. His mother, Elizabeth Woodville, the dowager queen, had given away her own son's future, and perhaps his life, by agreeing to allow his sister, Elizabeth, to marry Richard III.

As Lincoln considers the future, he hears noises without, and a woman is suddenly announced as "Lady Brampton." She sweeps into the room to tell Lincoln that "all is lost," King Richard is dead, and Lincoln must immediately declare his son, Richard IV, king of England. Stunned by the news of the death of his uncle, the king, Lincoln takes a moment to consider the fact that the king can no longer see the stars on which Lincoln gazes: "The past is his; with the present and future he has no participation." Lady Brampton demands to know why Lincoln lingers and does not come to the aid of his cousin.

Lord Lovel enters, and Lincoln asks him who survived the conflict and how things stand. When Lovel explains that the earl of Richmond has taken the crown as Henry VII, Lady Brampton retorts that the Yorks can undo that move. As the three confer, she continues to urge immediate action, while Lovel also wants to bring all Yorks together to support Richard. Lincoln hesitates to enter armed combat that will cause more deaths and favors keeping Edward's young son safe and a secret for the time being. They decide that Lovel should escort young Richard to Colchester and await the development of events. Lady Brampton will travel north to join her husband and unite the York loyalists, and Lincoln will remain in London to test the opinions of the nobility. They decide not to tell Dowager Queen Elizabeth that her son lives.

Lovel travels to the home of the moneylender named Jahn Warbeck, where the young Richard is staying. When the boy joins the two men, he learns that his uncle has been defeated and killed and announces that he is king of England; his brother, Edward, had taught him the succession to the throne. They travel to Colchester, where Richard stays in a farmhouse belonging to Sir Humphrey Stafford. Everyone waits impatiently to hear from Lincoln that the time has come to take up arms.

The narrator describes Henry VII as a prudent man of "strong sense and strong understanding," but totally without generosity and having a tendency toward cruelty. Although the young Richard's body had never been found, Henry had spread a rumor that both boys died in the Tower of London. In the meantime, it was important to emphasize the illegitimacy of the children of Edward IV and Elizabeth Woodville in order to argue his own right to the throne. For the moment, fortune was with Henry. The young, widowed Elizabeth was anxious to marry him, and the public seemed pleased at the thought of "the entwining of the two Roses" through that marriage.

The scene shifts to the young Elizabeth, who walks in a garden with her cousin, the Earl of Warwick. At 16, he is the same age as the 19-year-old Elizabeth's brother, Edward. Having recently claimed the throne only to be removed by Henry, Warwick sadly notes that he will go to the Tower while Elizabeth goes to court. She urges him not to lose hope; as soon as she is queen, she will bring him to court to be in her service. He is not as optimistic as she and asks only for a strand of her blond hair to keep when she departs. He moves as if to embrace her but then kneels and kisses her hand, the proper show of respect for one in her position. As Elizabeth travels to London, she is filled with hope to do well for her people, to rescue Warwick, and to support her mother. She well understands that for royals, emotions do not enter into marriage decisions. But when Elizabeth meets with her mother, she understands that revolution by the Yorkists is still a possibility. Prince Richard, her brother, has never been found, and while Henry's coronation is imminent, many commoners are not happy. Henry proceeds with his plans, and his coronation takes place on October 30.

Elizabeth comes to fear and dislike Henry and mourns the fate of Warwick, whom she is unable to assist. Her mother continues to stir controversy among the people, hoping to force Henry to immediately marry her daughter, although Elizabeth begins to hope ardently against the union. A marriage in which she could assert no influence on her husband would be no more than bondage. When she expresses that thought to her mother, the older Elizabeth works to convince her that she must go through with the marriage.

Henry pays little attention to Edward's daughter, seeing her only once prior to marriage, and despite the younger woman's concerns, her mother secures her "troth" with Henry. The dowager queen cries bitter tears at the prospect of the union, understanding it to be a necessity. She tells her daughter that she should have preferred to place her hand in that of her noble cousin, Warwick. Elizabeth responds that she has been a dutiful daughter, "plastic clay" in her mother's hands. Had her mother spoken those words two hours earlier, she would have married Warwick and been a happy woman, "but you have given me away; this ring is the symbol of my servitude."

On January 18, Henry marries Elizabeth, and those who would have moved against him appear silenced. The narrator notes, "The Red Rose flourished bright and free—one single white blossom, doomed to untimely blight, being entwined with the gaudier flowers." The king orders factions that would confront him, including Lincoln, into sanctuary.

Henry sends the queen, with her mother, sisters, and the countess of Richmond, away to hold court at Richmond. Richard's existence remains a secret that only Lincoln and Lovel share. They do not disclose his location even to the Staffords, who have worked to advance their own Yorkist interests. Hoping to build loyalty, Henry decides to "progress" across the country, not realizing that the Staffords are planning to advance to Worcester because Lovel is amassing a force of several thousand men to move against Henry. Lovel is joined by Sir Edward Brampton and his wife, Lady Brampton. She had established a friendship with Edward IV and became a court confidant, incensing the then Queen Elizabeth who now, as dowager queen, hates Lady Brampton despite her efforts to support the Yorks and Elizabeth's son. During Edward's reign, Lady Brampton refused any offer of gifts and advancement in order to remain above suspicion. That does not prevent the dowager queen from making clear her dislike of Lady Brampton, labeling her presumptuous to take up the support of the sons of the king's widow. The earl of Lincoln supports Lady Brampton, appreciating her loyalty and intelligence.

Lincoln would like to have Richard declared king immediately, but he has decided for safety's sake to wait until the York forces have taken back the power lost to Henry. If Lord Lovel's attempt fails, the prince will be secreted away to the Continent until he becomes of age and can himself organize a revolution. Lady Brampton suggests that if the forces fail, before leaving the country the prince should be recognized by his mother in Winchester as the heir to the throne and depart to the Continent from there.

The narrator mentions a Richard Simon, or Symond, present in the chronicles of the time, who had been a playmate of Elizabeth Gray's elder children and a lover of learning with a quick wit. When Elizabeth Woodville became queen, Simon remained in her good graces and served the court, barely escaping Henry's wrath when Edward was killed. Not loyal to either party, but rather to self interest, Simon has shifted his loyalty according to the side from which he has received the best treatment. He thrives on gossip and conspiracy and has planted rumors to seed revolution. His fidelity to the dowager queen seems firmly in place, and so Lady Brampton asks Simon if he can secure an audience for her with Elizabeth. The dowager queen agrees to meet with Lady Brampton, feeling certain she has important news to share, but she remains cool and aloof upon receiving the countess.

In an emotion-filled exchange, Lady Brampton asks Elizabeth whether she would prefer for her daughter to continue as queen or for her son to overthrow Henry and take the crown. Elizabeth is shocked at the mention of her son Richard, and at first she thinks Lady Brampton refers to an impostor. Lady Brampton is insulted by Elizabeth's lack of belief, understanding that old jealousies probably prevent the dowager queen from trusting her. She remarks that the earl of Lincoln himself has established a plan for overthrowing Henry. Upon hearing the earl's name, Elizabeth cannot contain her excitement, and all pretense drops away. Lady Brampton remarks that the dowager queen has insulted her when her only desire has been to "conduct the tempest-tost fortunes of this ill-starred boy into the safe harbor of maternal love." Simon steps forward, not wanting the meeting to end in a feud that would not support his own interests. He volunteers to ask Lincoln whether Lady Brampton speaks the truth and to discover why the existence of the prince had been hidden from him. Elizabeth weeps at the thought of her son's existence, causing Lady Brampton to abandon her cold manner and become more sympathetic toward an obviously grieving mother. Soon after the meeting, Queen Elizabeth appoints Lady Brampton to join her attendants at court with her.

Lovel's and Lincoln's attempts fail, and Lovel again finds himself fleeing cross-country with the prince. As they stop for rest at a hut, a group of men arrives, led by the moneylender, Jahn Warbeck. Two women accompany him, and the party comes into the hut to dry their clothing, dampened by the wintry mix of sleet and snow. Warbeck is surprised to learn the identity of the young prince, who continues to sleep on the hut's floor. After the women fall asleep, Lovel asks Warbeck's opinion on whether he can safely move the duke of York to Worcester to be recognized by his mother. Warbeck explains that his own son, whom his sister Madeline was to escort to the Low Countries, has died. He suggests that perhaps Duke Richard can assume the role of Warbeck's son and his last name and be spirited out of the country in that manner. Madeline agrees to assume the danger and responsibility of escorting the fair boy out of the country. The other young woman, who is Madeline's daughter, plays with Richard when he awakens the following morning. When Madeline explains to the prince that he will travel with her under the name of Perkin Warbeck, he is not surprised. That is the name he had used when previously living with Warbeck. Lovel discusses with Richard the necessity for complete secrecy and then sadly watches the group depart. Declaring the momentary melancholy that he experiences when forced to separate from Richard "womanly," he bids his men to mount and follow him.

At Winchester, Lady Brampton visits the cathedral daily, looking for a silver heart suspended near the altar. That is the signal on which she and Lovel have settled to mean the prince is in the area and ready to visit his mother. Elizabeth Woodville remains on edge waiting for her son, as the rest of the country wait to hear that her daughter, Queen Elizabeth, is pregnant with an heir to the throne. One day, Lady Brampton finds the heart, and Madeline emerges from the shadows to take her to the prince and explain Lovel's plan that she escort young Richard to Flanders. They agree that Lady Brampton will bring the widowed queen to one of the small chapels that are part of the cathedral of Winchester.

Mother and child share an emotion-filled reunion, each knowing it may be the final time they meet. The dowager queen explains that no pains will be spared "to elevate an offspring of the White Rose." She stresses that until Richard grows old enough to lead men to battle, others will fight and die for his sake. In the meantime, he should never forget his title, "yet suffer not unquiet ambition to haunt you." She charges Madeline to care for him, should he become orphaned, and does not rest easily until she later receives word the party is safely in France.

The birth of Arthur, Prince of Wales, soon confirms Henry Tudor on the throne, and staunch Yorkists hide in the court of the duchess of Burgundy. Lincoln remains at court in London, operating to keep the Yorkist schemes alive in great secrecy. Richard Simon has become a priest; because the sword has been removed from his hand by his robes, the energy and cunning that should have been employed on the battlefield have made him restless for intrigue. Although apart from Elizabeth Woodfield, he remains dedicated to her, in honor of their childhood friendship.

Simon develops a scheme to use a baker's son, Lambert Simnel, to come forward as an impostor in order to discover the type of reaction he would receive. After training Lambert, who proves an apt student, Simon sends anonymous letters to various nobles, stating that Prince Richard will soon be revealed; he plans to substitute Simnel for Richard. Believing that, based on the letter, Richard will soon appear, Sir Thomas Brouton begins to gather forces and then travels to Winchester to meet with Richard's mother and share the news.

He is stopped on the street by Simon, who confesses to having orchestrated the scheme. Simon asks Brouton to arrange a meeting with the dowager queen. Elizabeth agrees to meet Simon but remains in turmoil as she awaits his arrival, receiving news that the earl of Warwick has fallen from the Tower and drowned. Most believe his "accident" was actually enacted on King Henry's orders. At the appointed time, the dowager queen receives not just Simon but also Lincoln, Brouton, Lovel, and Edmund Plantagenet. They draft a new plan to allow Simnel to impersonate the earl of Warwick, rather than Richard, negating the story of his death. The story will be spread that Warwick has escaped and is gathering arms. If the news fails to incite the Yorkist sympathizers to action, no harm would be done, but if they did arise, the way would be paved for claims by the duke of York. He would first appear in Ireland.

Volume 1: Chapters 7–12
At the same time, Elizabeth Woodville suffers for the fate of her daughter. All hopes that her presentation of a son to Henry would cause the king to soften toward her have been dashed; he barely acknowledges the younger Elizabeth's presence. She is to obey without protest, and he often separates her from her son. Although she has practiced self-restraint in the hope of gaining her husband's favor, she at last gives up any idea that she and Henry might enjoy a positive relationship and complains to her mother. Henry suspects that his wife is involved with the rumors of a plot by her brother Richard to mount an attack against his kingdom. The shameful scenes of anger between the king and her mother humiliate and agonize the young queen.

When news arrives of the appearance of the Earl of Warwick in Dublin, the narrator compares it to "the bursting of a thunderstorm." Earl Kildare of Ireland has received the supposed earl of Warwick with honors, but Henry's English subjects appear unmoved. Henry dispatches spies to Ireland to gain intelligence, and they learn that the dowager queen has supported the plot against him. Henry hates Elizabeth Woodville and hates that he had been forced to marry a penniless queen instead of a royal from another country who could have brought funds into his coffers. He calls on council aristocrats loyal to him and also two priests whom he highly favors, both of them bishops, John Morton and Richard Fox. The group decides a pardon will be issued for the insurgents, and the true earl of Warwick will be revealed in London. Finally, the dowager queen is to be forced to forfeit all her lands and goods for having consented to the marriage of her daughter and Richard III. Should she pledge reliance on the king and reveal the location of her son, she could gain pardon.

When Sir William Stanley brings her the news, the dowager queen receives him with disdain and admonishes him for having shifted his loyalty from the Yorks to the Lancastrian monarch. She appeals to his emotions, asking how she, a loving mother, should sacrifice her own son. Embarrassed, Stanley withdraws. Henry exalts in taking his mother-in-law's wealth but realizes that knowledge of young Richard's location would be the much greater treasure. He appeals to another of her sons, the marquess of Dorset, son of Sir John Gray, who had opposed Richard III. Normally, Henry finds Dorset entertaining and witty and enjoys his presence. However, in this instance, Dorset defends his mother and annoys the king, who arrests him and sends him to the Tower, later to be released.

The king commits Elizabeth Woodville to a convent at Bermondsey, removing her from her five young daughters. Lady Brampton tries to buoy Elizabeth's hopes by noting that such shameful treatment of her might galvanize the Yorkist sympathizers against Henry. "The heartless tyrant" remains unmovable, as the dowager queen can only hope that her son will one day appear at her prison door to release her. Henry then acts on his plan to let the public know that the real Earl of Warwick had not fallen from the Tower and died after all. As Elizabeth Woodville travels to the convent, Warwick is made the center of a parade to St. Paul's Cathedral. Although emaciated, weakened by his year's imprisonment, and dejected, he is surrounded by many Yorkists, helping to prove Henry's claim that the person in Ireland is an impostor. Without hope and unwilling to chance reaching out to those around him, Warwick does not resist his return to the Tower.

When Lincoln learns of the dowager queen's arrest, he hastens to the home of his aunt, the duchess of Burgundy, in Flanders, procuring her support of the Prince of Wales, the deceased King Richard's son and also her nephew. She donates a large sum that allows the group escorting the Warwick impostor to continue their progress to Ireland. The real English Warwick in no way affects celebration of the Warwick who appeared in Ireland, where word goes out that it was King Henry who had produced an impostor. The Ireland earl of Warwick is proclaimed King of England, and a parliament is invoked in his name, in order to organize forces to invade England.

The Yorkists in England believe in the identity of the Warwick they have beheld, so the impostor in Ireland does not gain widespread support from those of the White Rose in England. Lovel and others gather to mount an attack against England, knowing they will most surely perish. Lincoln gathers his forces within England, and Henry decides to mount a crushing blow against those in revolt. After two years on the throne, he finds he must defend it as he had forced Richard III to defend against his own attack. The narrator states that Henry knows his crown is "a usurpation" and he is "conversant with overthrow and death." The following day, at the battle of Stoke, the Yorkist forces are defeated with the deaths of most of their leaders, including Lovel, and the devoted young Plantagenet is left for dead on the field. Simon and the impostor Warwick are imprisoned. Under torture, Simon reveals the existence of the duke of York, and Henry feels sure that in time he can discover his whereabouts. Meanwhile, his only enemy is the 13-year-old prince in exile, and the forces of the White Rose have been destroyed.

The narrator makes the point that in days of old, men earned reputations through valor, depended on and enjoyed the friendships of their brothers-at-arms, and were more dependent on nature than men of the present day. Plantagenet, who had been raised in the woods, swoons from injuries on the field and wishes to join his friends in death. Instead, he is rescued and nursed back to health by a friar. Upon his recovery, he decides to travel to Flanders to find the prince. As he travels and makes plans to dedicate himself to his cousin, he enjoys an "extactic mood that soared above the meaner cares of life." Edmund is well received by Madeline and her family, who are delighted that the 21-year-old young man could provide a "manly guardianship" for the prince. Each day, Madeline expects the return of her husband, a Spanish mariner, who will probably want her to return to Spain with him. Edmund begins to consider taking the prince to his aunt, the duchess of Burgundy, for safekeeping. Richard, now 14, hears of the imprisonment of his mother and death of all those who defended his cause, and he decides to travel alone to the duchess as Edmund goes to Brussels.

Henry's French secretary, Stephen Frion, has followed Edmund, having identified him after the battle and hoping that he will lead him to the prince. Described by the narrator as possessing a serpentine spirit, Frion had served both Spanish and French monarchs before joining Henry's court. Although Frion has lost Edmund's trail, by coincidence he has arrived at Madeline's home, where he shares shelter with the young prince. Frion suspects the young man of being something other than a Flemish local but does not know his identity for sure. When Richard accuses King Henry of being a mere Welsh earl who has mistreated the English, he arouses Frion's suspicion. At length, Frion feels confident that he has found the prince and plots that night to get the boy on a ship bound for England. The following morning, he requests that the boy guide him to Lisle. His urging alerts Richard to be careful, and the prince points out the route, telling Frion he is going back to the house. Frion tempts Richard by telling him that he is going to visit the sire of Beverem, and he wants to introduce the young man to him, due to Richard's lordly composure. When Richard's pride causes him to agree to accompany the wily Frenchman, Frion knows his task will be difficult. The distance to Lisle was long, and the boy is "wild as a bird" and likely to run away. Frion plans to deliver him to Lord Fitzwater, who has been detained at Lisle. Fitzwater will take the boy, whom Frion will identify as "a pretended son of the traitor Earl of Lincoln" to King Henry.

When they enter the hall of Lord Fitzwater, Richard thinks that he recognizes the badges the men wear as those of England. Frion quickly moves him away from the men. He knows that if Richard hears the English language spoken, rather than the French in which Frion has conversed with him, he will realize that Frion has not taken him to the sire of Beverem. When the two arrive at the chamber of Lord Fitzwater, Frion brazenly enters, quickly closing the door behind him. Richard thinks he hears an exclamation in English from behind the door, which he has. Lord Fitzwater berates Frion for taking the liberty to enter his chamber without a proper request for an audience. As Frion looks around, only a teenage boy is in the chamber. Fitzwater dismisses the boy, allowing Frion to hand a paper from the king to Fitzwater and to explain his plan.

As the boy goes outside the room, he recognizes the duke of York, just as Richard recognizes him as Robert Clifford, a boy called Robin with whom he had been imprisoned and had become friends. When Robin alerts him to the danger, Richard says he must flee, but Robin convinces him that is impossible. He urges Richard to play along with the men as if innocent of their plan, and he will later assist the prince. When Richard follows Frion to a room, he hears the bolt thrown over the door after it closes, confirming that he is now a prisoner. While admitting to himself that he had been foolish to trust Frion, the Prince pledges, "I will not fail myself," and he paces about, planning his later actions.

When a servant brings food to Richard, Robin pushes in behind him, stating that Fitzwater has asked him to keep their guest company, as two lads so close to the same age would have much in common. Robin then asks the servant to bring them wine and, after he leaves, laughs heartily over the trick he has played. Richard corrects him by reminding Robin of their time in the Tower, and Clifford sobers, telling the prince that he has a merry tale to share. He relates how, when he reentered Fitzwater's chamber and pretended to prepare some flies for fishing, his lord had paced about and then asked what Robin thought of the boy he had seen in the hall. Robin had replied that he looked English rather than Flemish, causing the lord to reveal to him the story Frion had told Fitzwater. But Fitzwater believed Richard was Lincoln's son and knew where a treasure was hidden. Fitzwater hesitated to turn over such a noble-looking lad, at which point Robin promised to speak with the boy to try to draw information from him. Fitzwater would have agreed, except that Frion had told him no one should see the captive boy. When Frion, "the subtle fiend," reentered the chamber, Robin told him that the Sire of Beverem had heard that a Flemish citizen might have been captured, and an attempt to kidnap him might be made. Therefore, if anyone boarding a boat the following day "appeared in durance," he should be rescued. Thus, Fitzwater ordered that Robin's services should be used to keep the young man in good humor until the following day. Frion agreed to the plan, and Robin was allowed admittance into Richard's room.

Learning of Fitzwater's sympathy, Richard suggests that he reveal his true identity, but Robin makes plain that Fitzwater "wears the blushing rose." While he would feel sympathy for a distant relative of Lincoln, he would not for the Yorkist prince. And while Robin has pledged his loyalty to King Henry, he will help Richard escape. Richard sulks at the thought that Robin will not recognize him as liege, but after a short resistance, he agrees to follow Robin's plan of escape.

As they plot, unseen to the boys, Frion enters the room. He notes their sincere and urgent tones and approaches them, listening. When Richard notices Frion, he is startled and starts to draw back, but the wilier Robin continues with the same tone and allows Richard to recover his wits. Robin leaves the room, singing as befits a page, while Frion feels embarrassed to have mistrusted the boys. Shortly thereafter, Frion is summoned to an audience with Fitzwater, after which Robin returns and directs Richard to run down the back staircase to where Robin's horse will be waiting, and not to go back to Madeline's house. Richard agrees that he will go to Brussels, but he adds that he must stop at his cousin's house to let her know that he fares well. As the two go outside where a groomsman holds the horse, Robin pretends Richard is a girl, asking for a kiss before "she" mounts the horse to be led to the gate. Both boys smile at the trick, and soon Richard is free of the city walls.

The Fortunes of Perkin Warbeck 81

As he gallops toward Madeline's home, Richard realizes he is taking a chance delaying his trip to Brussels, but he must repay her kindness. He hears someone call his name and is joined by a cloaked rider who identifies himself as Hernan de Faro, Dame Madeline's husband. When they arrive at their destination, de Faro promises to serve as Richard's protector. Suddenly, Robin bursts through the door, telling Richard he has only a few hours to escape. They agree that he will sail to Spain with Madeline and de Faro and Robin will let Edmund Plantagenet know that the prince has gone to Malaga, Spain.

Shortly thereafter, Robin shares the information with Edmund. Plantagenet had returned to take Richard with him to stay with Lady Margaret, the Duchess of Burgundy, but found the cottage empty. He could not ask questions about his friends' whereabouts for fear of raising suspicion. Upon returning to the cottage for a third time, he finds Robin, who explains what has happened. He does not linger to talk in depth with Edmund, and Plantagenet wonders whether he can trust Robin. After learning Robin's identity and that certain details of his story are true, Edmund decides to visit Jahn Warbeck in Paris before traveling to Spain.

In Paris, Warbeck assures Edmund that he has heard from his sister, verifying Robin's story. Lady Brampton is in Paris, where her husband took refuge following the Yorkist defeat. She agrees to go to Brussels to explain the situation to the duchess and then go to Spain. From Warbeck, Edmund learns of de Faro's valor and trustworthiness, and the Spaniard is well-received in Andalusia, which the narrator describes in detail. The reader also learns that de Faro, originally a Muslim but now a Christian, if horrified to find Christians and Moors locked in deadly battle.

When Edmund finds Richard, he discovers the young man's feelings of "warlike enthusiasm" within the religious conflict, feelings that Edmund soon shares. The region will prove a perfect "school" for Richard as he observes the effects of a country's invasion. When Edmund declares that he will serve one of the Catholic captains, Richard states, "I will be your squire, your page, your stirrup boy—but I follow!" They become known on the battlefield as the Englishmen, one with the golden spurs of a knight, the others as "el muchacho" due to his youth. The knight's protection of the boy becomes legendary. If ever the boy is threatened, the knight's "eyes flashed fire, and mortal vengeance fell upon his foe." In one battle, Plantagenet is injured, and the battle is won as he recovers. The men return to Madeline and her daughter, both of whom Richard loves as family, particularly his "angel sister," Monina de Faro. The girl is described as wild and impassioned but a good person who wishes only what is best for others.

More battles take place in which Edmund and Richard fight heroically. When two Moors kidnap Monina, Richard manages to rescue her. But when Richard and Edmund return to de Faro's home, they find Madeline dead of wounds suffered in trying to prevent the kidnap of her daughter. De Faro is still at a distance, on the battlefield. Both men mourn the death and destruction resulting from the Moorish wars, including that of their home. Many relics and documents testifying to Richard's royal lineage have also been destroyed.

Monina descends into despair until she hears Richard declare his intention to avenge the death of her mother, declaring he would prefer death to watching Monina suffer. His declaration forces her to regain her more cheerful character as she realizes that those around her depend on her fortitude. Preparations continue for the siege of Granada, and Edmund looks forward to continued adventures with Richard, even as he worries that Richard might be mortally wounded. He pledges to die protecting Richard, and the two return to the Spanish army, welcomed as fabled heroes. Richard shows such courage in battle before Queen Isabella that Count Tendilla knights him. In another battle, Richard kills one man whose friend continues to try to slay Richard. When he cannot succeed, he throws a spear with a note attached that challenges Richard to meet him in hand-to-hand combat the following morning. When Edmund seeks Richard the next day, he learns that the Moor had been seen toppling from his horse to die of his wounds, but Richard has not been found.

In the meantime, de Faro returns home to learn from Monina of Madeline's death, and he is filled with grief. He brings with him the Irish Lord Barry, baron of Buttevant, who fought at Stoke. He has brought news of Irish support for the duke of York, and also that France and England are on the verge of war. Barry is anxious for the prince to join Lady Brampton, who waits at Lisbon. Monina takes Barry to meet the cousins while de Faro goes to Malaga to bring his vessel to the Port of Almeria. As Monina and Lord Barry rest, flies bite his horse, and it runs away, with Barry in pursuit on foot. While Monina waits his return, she hears the approach of Moors and gallops away on her mule, but she becomes lost. At last finding water, she stops for refreshment, when suddenly a mare crashes through the underbrush. She recognizes the horse as Richard's mount and finds a man lying nearby on the bank. She tends to Richard, who has been wounded in his side, and he revives. They try to make it to a nearby village, but Richard nearly falls from his horse; Monina is just able to ease him to the ground. She cries out for help, and some passing Christians make a litter and carry the prince to the Alcade, where he begins to recover. The following day, he is transported to a town where he can find medical care, Monina walking beside him. She hires a man to find Edmund Plantagenet to share the news with him.

Monina nurses Richard for three days, and "it was dangerous for their young hearts thus to be united and alone in a fairy scene of beauty and seclusion." Edmund appears and is joyfully received as the three exchange stories of what has happened since they last were together. They soon depart, and the narrator says, "Farewell to Spain! to boyhood's feats and light coursing of shadows as he ran a race with the swift-footed hours. A kingdom calls for Richard! the trials of life attend him, the hope of victory, the fortitude of well endured defeat."

Volume 1: Chapters 13–16

The narrator begins the next chapter by explaining developments in France that affect Richard's future. Charles VIII, king of France, has attempted to subdue forces in Burgundy composed of supporters of its duchess, Anne, who want her to assume the throne and whom England supports. Henry does not want war and has delayed any action, to the dismay of many of his nobles. Charles finally prevails and marries Anne, uniting France and Burgundy. At this point, Henry is forced to listen to his nobles who want to fight Charles; this would work to the benefit of the Yorkists.

As the months pass, Richard educates himself regarding state situations. Henry continues to enjoy a peaceful reign, the existence of Richard still hanging over his head. He had dismissed Frion after Richard had escaped, angry that not only did he not produce the prince, but continued rumors of Richard's existence have stirred the people. Henry's spies continue to alert him when it seems Richard's forces will rise, and he learns that Lady Brampton is probably involved. Henry employs the efforts of one Meiler Trangmar, who has been driven to near madness by the deaths of his three sons, which he blames on the Yorkists. Presently serving as a priest, he has "dedicated himself to revenge" and offered his services to Henry.

Trangmar knows of Richard's existence; as a priest, he had heard a confession from George Nevil that confirmed the young prince lived, which Trangmar shares with Henry. In the guise of a sympathizer, he manages to obtain from the dowager queen the fact that Richard is in Spain. In April 1492, Trangmar follows Lady Brampton's path to Lisbon with a plan to capture the prince. With letters from the dowager queen, he easily contacts those entrusted to care for Richard, convincing them that the prince should return to England immediately. Details in the letter support Trangmar's claim that Lord Surrey and others were waiting to fight for Richard. Lady Brampton and Monina will go to the French court to gain the king's support, and de Faro will escort Lord Barry home to Cork. Plantagenet and Lady Brampton are uneasy about allowing Richard to leave with Trangmar, and Monina recognizes how strongly she feels about Richard when she has to face separating from him. She cannot force any joy; she only feels happy that she is able to accompany Richard's good friends.

While onboard the merchantman sailing for England, Richard is so happy to be among his countrymen that he does not realize he is a prisoner. Trangmar has made no plans beyond getting the prince onto a ship, but he has hired two men to help guard Richard, without revealing the boy's true identity to them. Richard yields to the priest's authority and impresses the crew members with his wit and spirit. As the narrator notes, "It was not in the power of his wily adversary to prevent him from ingratiating himself in the hearts of all around him." Richard becomes familiar with each crewman, and when the ship stalls due to a lack of wind, he helps amuse the group. Then a fearful storm hits, and the crew has to work furiously around the clock, bailing water from a leak and attempting to keep the merchantman afloat. Their tiny boat is "borne as a leaf on the stem of the wind." Fear overcomes the captain, who can no longer direct his crew, and Richard's natural leadership instincts take over as he encourages each man during three terrifying days of struggle. First, they are driven into the Atlantic, and then the winds reverse to blow them into the Bay of Biscay. When all the men face death, Trangmar's heart softens toward Richard, especially as he observes the young man's selflessness and courage. However, once the danger passes, Trangmar suggests they continue by land through France. His intention is to secure delivery of Richard to Henry, although he states it is for their safety. The boy sees through the ruse and asks why the priest's courage fails him now, when he had shown so much valor during the storm.

Trangmar is again filled with hate as he retorts that the boy has no right to accuse him of cowardice and mutters words that would have betrayed his intent had Richard heard them. Then he apologizes for not giving the prince the respect he deserves, and Richard accepts his apology, assuming part of the blame for not encouraging a more respectful relationship.

Trangmar plots to throw Richard overboard and orders the two hired men to help him. They refuse, reminding Trangmar that the order is to deliver this boy, whom they believe is named Fitzroy, to prison in England. Supporting their refusal is the positive attitude everyone on board has developed toward Richard. The narrator notes: "It is the fortune of those hurried into crime by violent passion, that they can seldom find accomplices as wicked as themselves." Richard berates himself for not having recognized the priest as an enemy. He wonders what he will do, isolated and alone on a ship, surrounded by an English crew who owe another man their allegiance.

One evening, when Richard feels that the natural elements one enjoys on the ocean have served to soften Trangmar's heart, he tells him of his loss of his brother and father and his sorrow about the treatment and fate of his mother. He notes a change in Trangmar's attitude toward him and pursues his baiting of the priest Trangmar. After first wrapping a rope around his arm to secure him to the boat, unnoted by Trangmar, he bluntly asks whether the priest is not a "treacherous spy . . . Henry Tudor's hireling murderer?" Trangmar replies, "I am no hireling; sacred vengeance pricks me on!" He lunges for Richard who swings aside on the rope, and Trangmar goes overboard, drowning. One of Trangmar's hired men yells out to the crew, identifying the prince as a prisoner of King Henry who should be seized. Richard identifies himself as Edward's son, to which one crewman yells, "Foulest treason!" Richard replies, "Or fairest loyalty . . . which of you will lay hands on your liege, on Richard the Fourth of England?" The captain and first mate argue over what to do; they finally decide that for the safety of their crew and the ship's goods, they will grant Richard's request to be dropped off in Ireland.

While still on the boat, Richard wonders whether or not Lord Barry has returned to Ireland and what type of reception he will receive. Before leaving the ship to set foot on land at Cork, a place he feels is his own, he dresses in the finery provided him in Spain. The ship departs, the captain having persuaded the mate not to sail to England and share what had happened with the king for fear of their own lives.

Cork is described as "an asylum for civilization in the centre of a savage district." Richard goes immediately to the service in progress at the cathedral, partly to atone for the sin of his part in the death of Trangmar. Cutting a startling figure in his finery, Richard attracts much attention; his golden spurs signal that he is of "honorable rank." The mayor welcomes the young cavalier and invites him to a celebration at his home. While feasting with many of the important persons of Cork, the mayor requests to know the visitor's identity. In a lengthy speech, Richard reveals himself to be the duke of York, son of King Edward IV.

The people gather in wonder around the prince, and then more festivities commence. The "mad exhultation" is compared by the narrator to the arrival of a heavenly being. Later, the prince is installed at court with all respect due him. The following day, he is urged to take the title of king but declines, explaining he should wait until he receives his crown at Westminster.

The earls in Ireland have recently engaged in conflict, which the prince's presence promises to rectify. He sends letters to the earls of Kilmond and Desmond asking them to come to court to meet with him. The prince shows a "fearless confidence" and reliance on the local wisdom that endears him to all. The former mayor, named O'Water, had loved Richard's father and pledges his loyalty, dispatching emissaries to travel in all directions with the news of the prince's arrival. Everyone waits impatiently for the arrival of de Faro and Lord Barry. Richard decides to visit Barry's seat, where he hopes to find the abbot of Kilmainham, an exile able to greatly influence the Irish.

As he travels, Richard encounters the strangest-looking group of humans that he has ever seen. Marked by their long, shaggy hair and saffron-colored garb, they contrast greatly with the Spanish and the English. He learns the lore of Ireland from his riding companion, Hubert Burgh, foster brother of Lord Barry; "the English-born prince, nursling of romantic Spain, felt as if he were transplanted into a new planet." Recently the site of war between the earl of Desmond and the chief of the Macarthys, the area bears the ill effects of conflict. Richard soon realizes that while arousing the Irish to support him would be a simple task, due to their disorganized, passionate nature, they would suffer at the hands of the disciplined English troops.

Upon his arrival in the area of the abbey, he receives a message from the priest he seeks, named Keating. However, Keating chooses to meet Richard in a secluded dell, causing the Prince to think him arrogant or cowardly. Richard is startled by Keating's ancient appearance; the narrator compares him to a withered white leaf. After looking the prince over, Keating questions the truth of his claim, startling Richard, who has not yet had that experience. When Keating notes Richard's irritation, he apologizes for his poor eyesight, noting he now sees there is no question that Richard hails from royalty. He asks Richard to command him as he will. He apologizes for the unusual meeting place, explaining that a bounty has been placed on his head. He then tells Richard that a meeting is taking place that includes the earl of Desmond and the Macarthy chief, and Richard eagerly expresses a desire to attend the meeting. He then sees the form of a young woman approaching them, and she exchanges comments with Keating. Keating tells Richard that the girl, an orphaned victim of the recent war, can act as his guide.

The narrator informs readers that the meeting has already concluded as Richard and his guide cross difficult terrain to reach the location. The earl is traveling to Marlow, surrounded by warriors and native chiefs. All of the attendants are described and their family histories supplied. Their costumes feature the native saffron color and is in the outmoded style of courtiers of Edward III. As they travel, they meet Lord Barry, who states that he must immediately find "an eaglet I have nursed" before it comes to harm. The earl replies that if the eaglet is a true bird, it will wing its way to Barry. More important now, his presence is needed by the king of Eagles, Lord Desmond, his cousin. When Barry tells him the young bird is the duke of York, the earl counters that they must conquer their Irish enemies before they can be of help to the duke. Recognizing all of his ancestral foes among the enemy names the earl has noted, Barry agrees to postpone his trip to Buttevant to meet the prince until the following day.

Richard agrees to the delay, charming Lord Desmond and others by stating that they should eventually place the crown on his head, rather than his doing so. Soon an embassy arrives from France to invite Richard to the court of Charles VIII. The messenger is none other than Frion; having been discharged by Henry, Frion has returned to his native country to serve the French monarch. While Frion's reappearance displeases Richard, Barry argues that Frion's service would work to the young royal's advantage. He knows many secrets of the Lancasters, and the fact that he has tried to kidnap Richard means he feels confident of the prince's true identity. He will know how to negotiate between the identities of Perkin Warbeck, Richard Fitzroy, and the duke of York. The duke accepts the invitation and prepares to go to France. Many of his new friends and supporters escort him onboard the ship and watch it depart on a smooth sea.

Volume 1: Chapters 17–18
Upon Richard's arrival in Paris, he is warmly received at the French court by its members and 100 exiled Yorkists. King Charles enjoys great prosperity, having recently married the duchess of Brittany and, by doing so, gained peace for the country. He is so well settled that he is looking for another war in which to engage and has turned his thoughts to invading Naples. The Parisians engage in grand celebrations—balls, tournaments and hunting parties—and greet the duke of York warmly. With the naïveté of youth, he believes that his future remains secure. His welcome by the English exiles and entertainment in grand style by the French make him forget the modest wilds of Ireland.

Jarring Richard's seemingly secure relationship with the French, Henry lands at Calais on October 6 with a force of 1,600 men at arms and an infantry of 25,000 men. Despite his lust for war and promises to Richard, Charles does not want to engage the English, who will surely defeat the French forces. Henry willingly agrees to depart if Charles will deliver the duke of York.

Lady Brampton understands the French motivation and at last convinces Richard that even while inwardly on the verge of betraying him, the French would grow outwardly more and more congenial. Shelley writes: "Richard, basking in the noon-day of regal favour, of a sudden felt a cloud spread athwart his sun-shine, and a chill take place of the growing warmth." He receives many visitors who suddenly all urge him to go to Brussels and confer with his aunt, Lady Margaret. He is forced to recognize that the French monarch plans to sign a treaty with Henry as soon as Richard leaves the country. Fortunately for Richard, Charles does not agree to deliver him to Henry.

Richard bears up under the insult by focusing on meeting with his aunt for the first time. The duchess receives him warmly, reassured by his presence and character that all she had heard from Lincoln, Lovel, Lady Brampton, and Plantagenet was true. Moved to tears by his resemblance to her dead brother and the memories that resemblance stirs, she happily presents Richard to all at her court. She establishes a court for Richard, dubbing him the White Rose of England and supplying 30 halberdiers to guard his safety. Loyal Yorkists join him at his court, and "the rumour of this new White Rose became a watch-word of hope for York, of fear for Lancaster." Head of the formerly distinguished house of Burgundy, Margaret treats the duke of York to pomp and richness that rivals that of the French, and her affection is "worth more than Charles' politic and courteous protection." However, Richard misses his friends, especially Monina. He does not know that while in Paris with Lady Brampton, Monina had volunteered to carry letters to the dowager queen, as she would not be recognized in the guise of a pilgrim visiting the convent that serves as Elizabeth Woodville's prison.

Richard's "apparition" in Ireland and in Paris has shocked Henry, who waits in vain to hear from Trangmar. He tightens the guard on Elizabeth Woodville, who has resided in the convent prison for six years. Thin and emaciated, she lingers near death, and "her eyes alone—last retreat of the spirit of life—gleamed brightly amid the human ruin." When Monina arrives disguised as a religious pilgrim and asks to see the dowager queen, she is admitted to Elizabeth's chamber and kneels beside her bed. Upon hearing Monina's whispered words, the queen revives briefly. Knowing she has too little time to say all she wants to say, she rejoices in the news of Richard's existence. She tells Monina to visit Sir William Stanley and ask him not to draw the blood of her son. She commands Monina, "Say to the Dean of St. Paul's, His sister must not doubt his truth; Henry must not shed the blood of his wife's brother." Monina requests a token to take to Queen Elizabeth. Elizabeth Woodville has only a daily prayer she has offered for Richard to give to Monina in the form of a beautifully illustrated missal. Within the next few moments, the dowager queen dies, receiving release from her troubled life.

The following day, Monina arrives at the king's palace at Shene and requests to speak with the king's chamberlain, Lord Stanley, whom she informs of Elizabeth Woodville's death. She explains that couriers will arrive by noon with the message for the king. She has hurried to arrive before them to request an audience with the queen, bearing the dowager queen's final words to her daughter. Stanley knows the king desired no contact between the queen and her mother, and he tells Monina he cannot grant her request. She asks whether she might not make the request of the king, to which Stanley agrees.

Stanley meets the king's hunting party as it returns to the castle. He relays the news of Elizabeth Woodville's death, and those in the party who remember her grow solemn. Among the group is her son, the marquess of Dorset, who comes forward to hear the news directly from Stanley. Filled with remorse for recently having forgotten his mother, he requests to bear the news to his sister, to which the king, taking pity on his grieved state, agrees. As the party returns in some disarray to the castle, Stanley looks for Monina at the gate where he had told her to wait for the king, but she is not there. The king enters the palace, and still she does not appear.

Dorset rides with grim thoughts to his sister's court, berating himself for not having tried to persuade the king to treat his mother more kindly. It is small consolation that Henry will probably agree to the holding of funeral masses at which prayers for her soul can be offered. As fate has it, he comes upon Monina and her servant waiting to speak to the king. He stops to ask her business and, when she explains, tells her he is Elizabeth's son and that he will take her to see his sister, Queen Elizabeth. Shelley makes the point that our lives hang on the thin thread of fate. The king would surely have denied Monina's request, which now has been granted by Dorset.

The queen expresses extreme remorse at the news of her mother's death and receives the missal from Monina, as she asks many questions about her mother's final moments. When she reads the missal, she asks Monina to tell her everything that she knows about her brother Richard. The astounded and terrified Elizabeth can hardly believe what she hears. Stanley interrupts to announce that the king has come to visit Elizabeth. Surprised by Monina's presence and put on guard by the sight of the missal in the queen's hand, he rushes Monina out of the room.

Stanley escorts Monina to the queen's garden, a sacred place in which no commoner, and few men, are allowed to enter. He is shocked to discover a youth within the garden who jauntily identifies himself as Robin Clifford, stating that he and the Lord Chamberlain are now "brothers in wildness." Annoyed by the young man's cocky and familiar attitude, Stanley demands that Clifford step aside and let the young woman pass. Recognizing Clifford's name from the discussions with Richard and his supporters, Monina says that she knows Clifford would not harm her. Stanley "writhe[s] with impatience" as Clifford makes his usual ironic comments before exchanging a few words with Monina.

As they walk on, leaving Clifford behind, Monina shares the contents of the missal with Stanley. He immediately feels uneasy about what might be seen as his part in her delivery of the message to the queen. Adding to his "consternation" is the fact that, based on Robin's interaction with Monina, he is also privy to the information regarding the duke of York. Concerned for his own compromise, Stanley strongly advises Monina to leave England immediately. He turns to leave her and then turns back as if to ask the many questions he longs to ask. However, he remains silent and in the end departs the garden, "as if to escape from his better self."

When Stanley walks back through the garden, he observes Clifford pacing about, no doubt considering the news he has just learned from Monina. Since rescuing Richard from Frion, Robin has "run a headlong, ruinous course." The narrator adds that "[t]hough overgrown and choked up by weedy vices," Robin's character is far from evil. He can be generous and bold but also undisciplined and at times cowardly. Longing for adventure and a secure future, he wonders now how he might benefit from his knowledge about Richard, and when Stanley passes him, he asks the Lord Chamberlain for the name of the girl messenger. They both are aware that they share the same secret about Richard's existence. Clifford abandons discretion to tell of his adventure in Lisle, while Stanley laments the self-destructive path taken by the duke of York. The first volume concludes with Clifford determined to visit the daughter of de Faro that same evening.

Volume 2: Chapters 1–7

The second volume opens with Monina changing her plans to join Lady Brampton and appeal to her protection. Robin Clifford's arrival inspires her to remain and continue to support Richard's cause. The narrator notes that while the chances are slight that "a young foreign girl" could accomplish much "in the heart of the usurper's power," Monina remains determined to pursue even "the most distant prospect." She resolves "to busy herself in replanting, in Tudor's own city of London, the uprooted rose bush, parent of the spotless flower." Rather than sailing the following morning, she sends a letter to Lady Brampton describing what she hopes to accomplish for "the idol of her thoughts."

When Clifford arrives, however, Monina is taken aback by his declarations that sound more focused on romance with her than service for Richard. She requests him to forget her personage and regard her only as a voice to guide him. He knows he cannot do that and holds her hands as she tells of Richard's travels and adventures. Robin becomes jealous of her tone of obvious admiration. He tells Monina:

> ". . . you have cast a spell on me, so that at this moment I would readily swear to perform your bidding, but that, when I do not see your witch's eyes, nor hear your magic voice, another wind may blow me right to the other side. Do not call this courtly gallantry, would by Saint Cupid that it were! for I am not pleased to behold my sage self fined down into a woman's tool: nor is it love;—Thor's hammer could not knock a splinter from my hard heart, nor the Spanish sun thaw its sevenfold coat of ice. I never have loved; I never shall: but there is some strange sorcery about you. When I next see you, I will draw a circle round, knock my head three times on the eastern floor, and call out 'aroint!' This twinkling light, too, and darkling hour—I must away:—sunshine shall, when we next meet, protect me from your incantations."

Robin's words sound incoherent to Monina, but she lets him finish. She crosses herself and sends him away with a saint's blessing.

Annoyed by his distraction with Monina, Robin decides to visit Lord Fitzwater to obtain advice. Fitzwater had gained the king's distrust with the escape of Richard and has been treated like a poor servant at court. When Robin tells Fitzwater of the rumors that "a phantom duke" has appeared in Ireland, referring to himself as Edward IV's son, Fitzwater declares that were it true, he would readily help "sever the entwined roses." Clifford assures Fitzwater that, having been a childhood friend of Henry, Fitzwater could validate this Perkin Warbeck's claim. He asks Fitzwater whether the two of them should not support Richard for the throne and then claim their rewards. Fitzwater's eagerness to support Richard's cause motivates Robin to spread the word to others.

Meanwhile, Monina does the same, visiting the dean of St. Paul's, as advised by the queen, and stirring up much interest. Many want to see the lovely young woman reported to support Richard, while others are too frightened to take up the cause. When Clifford sees her again, he believes that she speaks to him in a special way, significant in its softer tone. Although "he did not love her," if "she loved him, could saints in heaven reap higher glory?"

Intelligence gathered from the continent brings news of Richard's positive reception in France, his reception by the dowager duchess of Burgundy, and "the brilliant figure" he was while in Brussels. "Sedition" springs up "in England on every side." The discontented join common adventurers and soldiers of fortune to begin to plan revolt.

As Monina travels to the Cliffords' family home for a meeting, she shudders at the frozen white wilderness before her. She had for a time forgotten the beauty of "her Flemish home," but it floods back to her mind: "Bright Andalusia, its orange groves, myrtle and geranium hedges, the evergreen forest." But her heart is gladdened by the appearance of so many men—clergy, aristocrats, and servants, some angry over the death of the dowager queen, others disgruntled over a change in their fortunes for the worse since the arrival of Tudor rule. Shelley includes historically correct and important figures, explaining their connections to the House of Lancaster. After many debates and consultations, decisions are made as to how to proceed. The village where they are meeting will house arms, and they agree to tax themselves in order to financially support the revolt.

Monina returns to London with Clifford, her spirits high. They speak of Richard but also of news such as Columbus's voyage and discovery. Clifford has never before enjoyed such a conversation, considering such topics the stuff of fantasy and not worthy of wise consideration. Monina's voice seems like a melodious harp, enthralling him with tales of lands far away. His jealousy turns to anger, confusing Monina, who in her innocence does not understand his passion for her.

Soon Clifford travels with Lord Barley to Brussels to meet with the duchess and with Richard. He is able to appear congenial and decides to "insinuate himself into Richard's affections," hoping to guide the prince to do what he wishes after gaining his confidence. Richard's spirits are high, and when emissaries from Henry arrive, he leaves the palace and finds a safe haven. They meet with the archduke and demand Richard's ejection from the Low Countries, but the duchess reminds them that their decisions have no bearing on her own. Richard will receive her dowry, and the archduke has no jurisdiction over her lands. As the two emissaries, Mr. Poynings and Dr. Wemmings, enjoy cups of wine following the meetings, Clifford joins them, meeting their rebuff of him as a traitor with humor and light banter. Then he tells them all about Richard, his adopting the name of Perkin Warbeck, his travels, and all of the people who have assisted him. Dr. Wemmings carefully notes the names mentioned and invites Clifford to rejoin the Tudor cause. Clifford thinks of the hate he feels for Richard, but also of all the nobles he would betray if he turned once again to support the Tudors, "His brow became flushed; his lips worked with internal commotion." Before he can reply, an emissary from the duchess appears, and he slips away, not trusting his ability to continue as he knows his wit has been dulled by wine.

Shelley continues the character development of Robin Clifford as well as of Frion, sketching Clifford as the more complicated and conflicted of the two "villains." Both continue to execute a balancing act between the Houses of York and Lancaster. A love triangle develops between Robin, who loves Monina, and Monina and Richard, who love one another, although Monina does not recognize her emotions as love for some time. Monina also becomes devoted to Stanley, who takes up their cause.

Shelley continues to identify multiple historical persons involved with Yorkist schemes who are captured and martyred for the cause. She references riots among workers in Holland as a result of the embargo Henry places on imports from that country. De Faro resurfaces as a captain who has earned a reputation for helping to engineer peace in Holland. His actions are viewed as supporting Henry's cause and result in an invitation to visit King Henry and Queen Elizabeth's young son, the duke of York. The boy wants to know more about the explorer Columbus and his recent discoveries, and the Spaniard seems a likely source of information. Monina and de Faro are then used in an attempt by Henry to capture Richard, during which Richard discovers that Robin Clifford has betrayed him. Of his discovery, the narrator notes, "The whole wide world of misery contains no pang so great, as the discovery of treachery where we pictured truth; death is less in the comparison, for both destroy the future, and one, with Gorgon countenance, transforms the past."

In explanation of Robin Clifford's dishonorable actions despite his honorable heritage, Shelley dedicates much space explaining Clifford's feelings of rage and jealousy. Those emotions are sparked by a frustrated love for Monina and the realization that Richard represents honor, a state that Clifford can never attain. Maddened by the ever-increasing tension he experiences, Clifford attempts to kidnap Monina but fails. At that point, Clifford is viewed as a traitor by both King Henry, who sees him as conniving with the Yorkists, and Richard, who recognizes that anything Robin does will be only to advance his own self-interest. While Clifford avoids punishment, Stanley, perceived as a follower of Richard, is sentenced to execution by beheading and imprisoned in the Tower of London.

In chapter 6, Richard makes a harrowing secret entry into the Tower by climbing its walls. He hopes to meet with both Stanley, to whom he feels he owes a debt of gratitude, and his cousin, Lord Warwick, the latter still wasting away in prison 10 years after Richard's escape. Richard finds Stanley's cell, where he and Warwick meet briefly with the condemned man, who is kept company by Monina. She gains admittance by pretending to be Stanley's relative, determined to ease Stanley's isolation. Monina, disguised as a page, and Richard manage to escape the Tower, escorted by Lord Desmond. In danger in the nearby wood, they are rescued by Gypsies who secret Desmond from the area, while an old crone who claims to have known Richard's father escorts Richard and Monina to a safe haven.

Volume 2: Chapters 8–13
The old lady takes them to the home of Jane Shore, once mistress to King Edward, Richard's father. Shelley writes a long passage about Jane's loyalty to Edward and the bitter sorrow that fills her in his absence.

The following day, Richard and Monina hear bells signaling Stanley's death. The narrator notes in describing Monina's reaction: "Women nurse grief—dwell with it." Frion locates a safe place for Richard to stay; he later attends a wedding celebration in order to speak with his supporters and to test the public attitude toward the Yorkists. He is escorted by Lord Surrey, once loyal to the Yorkists but now loyal to Henry, to speak with Elizabeth, widow of the duke of Norfolk. As a child, Richard had been affianced to their daughter, Anne. As he speaks of occurrences in the past, he convinces the duchess of his identity as Edward's son, referencing a broach he had given her, which she pulls from the bosom of her dress. Touched by the scene and humbled in Richard's presence, Surrey defends his service to Henry, Richard's enemy. He argues that he does not want to serve Henry, but as a father and husband, he has to look to the best interests of his family. He prefers the peace that presently reigns in England to the war that Richard's claim to the throne must inevitably bring. Poverty and suffering will naturally accompany war, and Surrey hopes to avoid them.

When Richard moves to another safe spot, Robin goes to Frion with a ransom demand of 1,000 golden crowns from the duchess of Burgundy. If the ransom is delivered, he will not reveal Richard's whereabouts to Henry. He also surprises Frion by demanding Monina's hand in marriage.

Frion decides to consult with Monina at Canterbury, where she lives in disguise. Upon hearing of Robin's threat, she states that her father will double the money Clifford demands if she can remain free. Frion explains that Robin wants her, not more money. Alarmed by Robin Clifford's threats, Monina directs Richard to live for a time with a poor scrivener that Clifford has not considered important enough to suspect as one who might hide the prince. Clifford meets Frion again and is incensed over Monina's refusal to marry him, as well as over Richard's escape.

When a fleet of ships appears with Richard's supporters aboard, Clifford is exasperated by his inability to warn King Henry, who has moved to the north of England. Richard later organizes and leads a group of 600 men against Lancaster supporters at Kent and then makes his way to the ocean, where he, Monina, and some of the men board the ships and sail for the safety of Ireland. When onboard, Richard, Lord Barry, Edmund Plantagenet, and Sir George Neville mourn together for those lost in the skirmish.

Although received well enough in Ireland, due to a change in political circumstances, Richard accepts advice to move on to Scotland. Monina decides for Richard's sake to depart with her father on a dangerous voyage to India. Understanding that Richard's royal blood dictates certain plans for his future in which she cannot be included, she pretends to be lighthearted and joyous when she tells him of her plans. He, wanting to conform to Monina's actions, does not betray his devastation over thoughts of losing her. He tells her that he will see her again the next day, but when he goes among the people the following morning, he cannot find her. Richard remembers the "sweet Spaniard" as he had last seen her, "light, laughing" with "soft-beaming" eyes. As his ship sails away, Monina sheds bitter, anguished tears.

When Shelley shifts the scene to Scotland, she tells readers its history is "dark, tumultuous, stained with blood, and rendered foul by treason." James III had been weak and ill-tempered, but the present ruler, James IV, imbues his subjects with his own strength of character. His excellent government has brought peace and other benefits to Scotland. The age of chivalry survives there and Henry VII is its bitter enemy. Hatred for Henry will inspire the Scottish to battle England in support of the duke of York.

Shelley explains James's two love interests. First in love with his older mistress, Mary Boyd, producing several children with her, James then became infatuated with Jane Kennedy, daughter of the earl of Cassils. Members of his court have suffered from split loyalties between the two women, characterized by a fight between the women's two trained birds. Shelley symbolically demonstrates the seriousness of the conflict. However, in the descriptions of the reactions of the audience, she makes clear that the competition between two women will not distract from serious political pursuits.

Frion, Sir Edward Brampton, and Lord Barry go aboard Richard's ship when he lands at Weith. Barry makes clear the contrast in class structure between Scotland and England or France: In Scotland, poor people live intermingled with the rich in contrast to the segregation of the poor from the wealthy in England. Richard's men notice that "a new light" seems to have "broken in upon his soul," giving Richard a maturity and confidence he had not formerly possessed. In Edinburgh, Richard is impressed by both King James's appearance and his character. For his part, Richard impresses the Scottish lords by referring to James as the "strong north wind" that will fill his sails as he battles the English king for victory. James's and Richard's relationship continues to strengthen, as their personalities complement one another: "James drew toward himself the confidence of men; Richard bestowed his own upon them." All of Richard's men are content to practice patience except for Frion, ever the schemer, who becomes restless if not involved in intrigue.

James introduces Richard to Lady Katherine Gordon, describing her with lavish praise. Shelley devotes a long passage to her description, noting that others may be more beautiful, but Katherine is graceful, honorable, and represents truth itself. Richard agrees that she possesses an "unearthly spirit-stirring beauty," and he falls in love with her, although another in the royal family, Sir Patrick Hamilton, is known to love Katherine.

One man not happy about Richard's power is James's uncle, the earl of Moray, but even less pleased is Sir John Ramsay, laird of Balmayne. Despite the objections of these men and others who want Richard to promise much land and wealth in exchange for James's support, the Scottish king signs an agreement to fight with Richard against Henry's forces.

Shelley injects a discussion between James and Richard about the nature of love, as James moves closer to uniting Richard with his cousin Katherine. The narrator notes that "the threads were spun, warp and woof laid on, and Fate busily took up the shuttle, which was to entwine the histories" of Richard and Katherine. Her father, Lord Huntley, does not support the union, fearing Richard's early death and possible tragedy for his widow. That she should become England's queen is beyond his hopes; that she should marry a failed pretender would prove a nightmare. James finally convinces Lord Huntley to support the union. Huntley's only request is that Richard should live like a king, with all of the attendant wealth and festivity due him and his relations.

James takes Richard to Huntley's castle, and as he meets Katherine, Richard remembers Monina, his heart aching for a moment as he wonders about her fate. While Katherine is already a queen of her own castle, he is a homeless, wandering entity, some would say without identity. When James makes clear that he offers Richard Katherine's hand in marriage, Richard feels unworthy and then wonders whether he would have to remain in Scotland, her home. In spite of his concerns, the couple marry that evening. Katherine is obedient in accepting Richard as her husband. She remembers the tale often told to her that at her birth, a soothsayer had predicted she would marry a king: "All must be endured; for it was the will of Heaven." The narrator makes clear that for Richard, Katherine will become a "medicine for all his woes," the better part of himself.

Volume 2: Chapters 14–18

The couple enjoy a celebration of their nuptials upon returning to Edinburgh. Anti-Yorkist factions in Scotland continue to target Richard, and Frion grows unhappy now that he has to deal with both James and Katherine as Richard's intimates. Both recognize him for what he is and refuse to be tricked by his flattering ways, often barring him from seeing Richard. As spring returns, the Scots again consider battle, and Lord Audley travels to England to gather information.

By chance, Audley encounters de Faro, who describes an ill young woman onboard his ship, requesting that Audley take her to England. The reader understands that the young woman is probably Monina. Soon after, the royals depart Edinburgh in pomp and festivity, with dreams of noble battle. Katherine bids Richard to return to her, telling him that should he find England to be false, he could always return to be "sole monarch" of her.

Frion meets with Lord Bothwell, Henry's spy, and they conjure a plan to murder Richard, Frion knowing he will be well paid for his efforts. Frion guides Bothwell and a robed assassin named Wiatt into Richard's tent. Suddenly, footsteps outside warn the three that they have been discovered. A page has pretended to be the sleeping Richard, and he leaps from the bed. In the confusion, Wiatt's hood slips, and he is revealed to be Robin Clifford, who escapes. They decide not to disturb the sleeping Richard with news of the attempt on his life until the following day. With a "plausible tale," Frion later convinces Richard of his innocence.

Henry offers James a treaty, and Richard feels a change in James's attitude toward him, even though James seems to remain devoted to their friendship. James leads his forces into England, spurred by the hatred of his ancestors toward the English for their many grievances against the Scots. In various skirmishes, the Cornish insurgents are defeated; in one, Lord Audley is killed. Richard feels each loss, deeply regretting deaths on his behalf. When war broke out, "a thousand destructions waited on him; his track was marked by ruin." Shelley includes gruesome details of the deaths of innocent villagers. The Scottish forces must retreat, and Shelley concludes chapter 17 with a plaintive and emotional letter from Richard to Katherine, expressing regret that he has failed in his attempts to become king and may never see her again.

Irish support forces arrive too late, as James signs a treaty with Henry. He refuses to give up Richard, although many of his confidants urge him to do so. The earl of Surrey continues to ravage Scotland. Richard's followers appeal to the duchess of Burgundy, but she is unable to assist. The second volume concludes as James tells Richard that he must leave Scotland for safety's sake. James says, "I lose what I can ill afford; a kinsman and a friend," to which Richard replies with a noble speech regarding their loyalty to one another.

Volume 3: Chapters 1–5

Volume 3 opens with a comment that Frion believes himself a puppet master holding all the strings to his future fortunes. Katherine insists on leaving the country with Richard despite her father's pleas, as James prepares a fleet for their use. The earl fears that his daughter will end up simply wandering the seas, but she insists that she desires "to perform a wife's part unopposed." The earl of Huntley departs enraged, and Frion uses that emotion to gain his help in a trap to capture Richard. The earl thanks Frion for offering him an opportunity for revenge. However, after his anger passes, Huntley decides against assisting the entrapment of Richard's fleet, and Henry's final plan to encourage Scottish treason against James and Richard fails. Frion is captured, and the Scots prepare to hang him, but Katherine asks for mercy. Richard orders Frion to "tell my sister's husband that I bear a charmed life," and he is placed aboard a boat on which Robin, still under the name of Wiatt, hides.

Richard's English supporters look forward to accompanying him to Ireland in the hope of gathering force there to return to fight defenders of the Red Rose. The depressed duke of York considers how, since his birth, fortune has scorned him, and Katherine tries to cheer him. Because "solitary nature is the true temple of love," while at sea the couple's relationship strengthens and grows. Plantagenet, Barry, Keating, and Neville speak of war schemes, and Richard listens, although his heart is not in the discussion.

Richard and Katherine are well received in the Cove of Cork, and his heart is joyous as he returns to the only place that now resembles anything close to a home. However, Keating tries and fails to gain a promise of military support in a land that enjoys its peace with England. But after much urging and talk of freedom from England, an Irish force gathers and marches against the town of Waterford, which refuses to recognize Richard as the duke of York. They lay siege during a dreadfully hot summer, and in August, after fighting admirably in several skirmishes, Richard is reunited with de Faro, who sails into the harbor. Finally forced to retreat back to their boats, the Irish forces suffer more casualties from canon fire, and Richard falls to be rescued by de Faro. The Spaniard swims with Richard to his ship, the *Adalid*, where both men are pulled aboard.

Katherine has faithfully watched for the return of Richard and his men, receiving reports of destruction and retreat. At last, the *Adalid* appears on its way to Cork. Katherine asks Edmund Plantagenet to take her out to the ship, so that she may join Richard. When Plantagenet sees de Faro, he wonders where Monina is, and de Faro explains that she is in England, waiting to welcome them. They see two of the York vessels sail by the damaged *Adalid* and then note two Waterford vessels giving chase. When the Waterford vessels spot the slow-moving *Adalid*, they turn to attack. But de Faro takes advantage of shifting wind to evade the enemy. Propelled again upon the sea to new scenes and new hopes, all of Richard's schemes are thwarted, but he takes comfort in Katherine's love and devotion. Rather than urging him to continue his struggles, Katherine prefers to keep Richard to herself on the ship. By contrast, in England, Monina has "taught her soul to rejoice" at the news of Richard's marriage, because she remains devoted to his cause. Lady Katherine, on the other hand, "perceived that power failed most, when its end was good."

Edmund Plantagenet, more ambitious for Richard than he is for himself, disembarks in England at Cornwall to meet Monina, who has been urging the locals to support Richard. He tries to remain focused on his purpose but is smitten by Monina, now a beautiful, mature woman. Monina is shocked that an Irish force does not accompany Richard and stunned to learn from Edmund that they seek aid, rather than bring it. The leaders that Monina has organized are a poor group, a far cry from those who had given their lives for Richard in the past. Richard brings Katherine to shore and asks her to love England as he does, for the country is his mother.

Volume 3: Chapters 6–10

When Richard reaches a hill above the town where Plantagenet had told him his forces are gathered, he views 200 individuals that he labels "rabble," wondering aloud why they hide his troops. Edmund's cheeks burn with shame as the party passes into the town of Bodmin to be received by speeches delivered by the leaders of the disorganized bunch of Yorkists. Plantagenet calls them a "rout of shirtless beggars," but Katherine is struck by the humor of the situation, and she manages to elicit a laugh from Richard. Richard tells Edmund to be patient, believing that once his presence is known, support will appear. He issues a proclamation that declares him to be King Richard IV and announces plans to seize a town before Henry can become aware that he is in England. He stirs the troops, and Edmund regains his enthusiasm, leading the band to successfully assault a nearby fortress and steal arms. Richard hopes merely to redeem his honor, admitting he cannot win England.

Katherine acknowledges the "bare reality" of the weak support gained by Richard and tries to persuade him not to fight; she asks whether he sees death as victory, stating, "There is all to lose; naught to win." He explains that he cannot renounce his birth, nor he will suffer unbearable shame. In tears, she begs him to move to Burgundy with his aunt, but she cannot persuade Richard to change his mind. He remains determined to pursue what he sees as his birthright. Monina still believes that Richard will be victorious and that God supports his cause. Richard tells her that he will continue the fight, but he asks her to help Katherine reach the safety of the *Adalid* should he die. She agrees and then departs for London.

Henry's reign has long been established, and the peasantry, dependent on the nobles, remain tranquil. But others, such as the miners of Cornwall, wonder why they cannot escape Henry's demands. There are so many of them and so few nobles; could they not win their freedom? Sedition arises during a time when trade has expanded. The narrator states: "The spirit of chivalry, which isolates man, had given place to that of trade, which unites them in bodies." For the most part, however, Richard's claim to the throne is met with scorn. When Henry learns of Richard's arrival in England, he is overjoyed. He continues to circulate claims that Richard is a low-born imposter, not worthy of support, and tells his followers that "a flight of wild geese clad in eagles' feathers are ready to pounce upon us." He is gleeful in telling Elizabeth, who had been visited that morning by Monina, that he goes to capture Perkin Warbeck, and she is distressed by his tone. He tells her that he will not kill Warbeck, but if she shows any signs of sympathy toward the prisoner, or hints that he is truly her brother, Henry will execute him immediately.

Richard cannot scale the walls of Exeter, and Plantagenet is badly wounded. Richard then sends a challenge to Henry of Richmond. He offers to meet Richmond, which will allow Richmond the opportunity to defend his honor. The date is September 12, 1497.

The scene switches to Frion, now in prison in England, where he reigns among the prison rabble. He is visited by Robin Clifford, a mere shadow of his formerly bold self. The two conspire once again to plan Richard's fall. Richard marches on to Taunton; his original force of 7,000 has decreased to 3,000. As the country teems with soldiers bent on his destruction, Richard receives news of reinforcements and a request that he join the new arrivals. He rides into a trap orchestrated by Frion and by Clifford, who triumphantly leads Richard and his own men on a mad dash through the woods. As they stop to rest, Richard is left on his own, due to injuries that would seem to prevent any attempt at escape. Richard attempts to persuade Clifford to remember his noble ancestors and regain his honor, to "bid the fiend" that tortured him to depart. Clifford is so conflicted that he leaps to his horse and gallops away in "a fit," causing the men guarding Richard to decide to free him. Richard flies to his men, who have also traveled as prisoners with their captors, mainly composed of outlaws. Although fevered and weak, Richard bids his followers to continue their escape through the thick woods. They almost make it to the ocean but are blocked by English soldiers.

Volume 3: Chapters 11–16

Returning to the woods, Richard and his men thrash in thick undergrowth and are able to hunt for food. All sleep in turns except for Richard. His thoughts taunt him until he falls asleep at last. Finally, the group arrives on a hill above the crashing surf of the ocean. They plan to reach the shore but are blocked by English troops. Forced to fall back, they seek protection in the abbey of Beaulieu that had afforded protection to Queen Margaret. Richard believes that he hears a woman's voice speaking with a Spanish accent. He falls into a deep sleep close to the abbey gates.

Monina does as Richard had requested, offering to take Katherine to the *Adalid*, which will sail to Burgundy. However, when she explains that Richard is in Beaulieu, Katherine wants to join him. She and Monina stop on their journey at "St. Michael's Chair," a large rock on an outcropping above the sea where Katherine wants to pray. Monina accompanies her, and each woman, "sickened by disappointment, impatient of despair," broods "mutely over their several thoughts." Katherine continues to struggle with frustration over her inability to reach Richard, while Monina tries to practice patience. Suddenly, troops appear, led by the Lancaster supporter earl of Oxford, who is shocked to discover the beautiful and charming Katherine. She easily persuades him to take her to King Henry.

Meanwhile, Richard rises from his sickbed, pale and shaken, three days after his injury. Ever mindful of his goal of honor and responsibility for the lives of the men he left behind, he departs the abbey despite the abbot's protests, leaving all of his followers with the abbot except for Sir Hugh Luttrell and three of Luttrell's men. They ride back to Taunton, where Richard commands Sir Hugh to offer his surrender to the king. Richard is taken prisoner and chained in a cell, where he learns that Katherine is also Henry's prisoner. She has become known as "the Queen of Loveliness . . . the fairest White Rose that ever grew on thorny bush." Rumors spread that Katherine holds Henry in her power, and they seem confirmed when Richard is removed to London and better surroundings. In addition, the king orders two noblewomen, Lady Cheney and Lady Howard, to wait on Katherine, who is to be presented to Richard's sister, Queen Elizabeth.

Richard suffers the public humiliation of a procession from Westminster to St. Paul's, ordered by Henry in order for the curious crowds of rabble to gaze on him. He spends a few weeks heavily guarded at the palace of Westminster, with two large gloomy chambers for his use, wondering over his fate. Permitted to ride in unoccupied areas, he misses his followers and his beloved Katherine and begins to think of escape as the November days pass. Katherine is in an apartment in the same palace, keeping the company of the queen and her son Arthur, Prince of Wales. Elizabeth is jealous of Katherine, treated well by the same husband who abuses her and loved by her brother, whom Elizabeth does not know. Ten years after her mother's imprisonment, she has lost the ability to suppress emotion, and she weeps and shares her sadness with Katherine. Elizabeth finds the younger woman's naturally loving and warm spirit soothing.

Weeks turn into months, and the king continues his courteous treatment of Katherine, encouraging her friendship with Elizabeth. Meanwhile, Richard, "the chained eagle—was sick at heart," assuming everyone has forgotten him. Henry seems to have forgotten the joy of crushing a foe as he cultivates a relationship with Katherine, who fascinates him. Katherine hopes to persuade the king to free Richard, not realizing Henry is courting her until Monina makes that clear. Katherine asks to see Richard, but Henry refuses and plans to use Katherine to extract a "damning confession" from Richard that will "stamp him as a deceiver forever."

Months pass, and Katherine still does not see Richard. The following summer, Henry increases the number of guards that surround her, and she hears rumors that Richard has escaped. He had taken advantage of a terrible storm during vespers, which he was allowed to attend in Westminster Abbey in June, to slip away from his guards through the terrified crowd of worshippers. Richard is unsure where to find his followers. When he at last finds Monina, she celebrates his sudden appearance as a miracle. She tells Richard that she has recently met with his aunt, Duchess Margaret, who is filled with concern for her nephew. He also learns that Clifford has again been dealing in treachery and deceit.

Suddenly, Clifford comes into the meeting room, a seemingly changed man, warning Richard to escape to de Faro's ship, sitting at the mouth of the Thames, before he can be discovered. Clifford promises to return with a disguise for the duke's use, but the king's men arrive, and Richard leaves, attempting to get to the boat on his own. When Clifford reappears, he makes clear that he has been promised a reward by Duchess Margaret for aiding Richard's escape.

Shelley dedicates many pages to Richard's harrowing final escape attempt, including a last visit with Jane Shore and his thoughts of those he loves. He reaches a small craft that will transport him, de Faro, and Monina to the *Adalid*, but Clifford again betrays Richard and leaps aboard the small boat. He triumphantly declares that he has at last won the game, even winning Monina, whom he wildly grabs by the hair. De Faro cries out and unsheathes his knife. Richard tries to slash Clifford, but the boat moves, and he misses his mark. He flings himself at Robin, and they both fall overboard, while de Faro yells the order to his men to take their oars. The small boat, surrounded by other small craft, speedily moves toward the *Adalid*.

Volume 3: Chapters 17–21

In the next scene, Richard is again a prisoner. Eventually, Henry allows Katherine to see Richard, by that time pale and emaciated from his imprisonment. The narrator notes that love, which began "as an exotic" in Henry's heart, has "degenerated from being a fair, fragrant flower, into a wild, poisonous weed." His interval of fascination with Katherine passes.

Katherine hears various rumors regarding Richard. Henry places Richard in public view in what Shelley describes as "a kind of wooden machine," and Katherine visits him, falling to her knees before him as he sits in chains, obviously ill. When he confesses that he feels near to death, she admonishes him not to leave her. He tells her to seek "blessings apart from me." When she assists him to stand as the guard tells him he must leave, the guard knows the king will be upset that she has touched Richard. The crowd is staring at them, until their gaze is drawn to a thin, stooped old woman, recognized as Jane Shore, lover of Richard's father.

Katherine wonders what has happened to Monina, of whom she has heard no report, and Richard's other friends. She learns that Robin Clifford's body had washed up on the shore of the Thames. Rumor has it that he is one of the victims who drowned during a struggle in a "tiny bark" in which Richard was to have been taken to the *Adalid*. Clifford had not perished from drowning, however. He had a gash in his throat and still clutched long strands of golden hair in one fist. The narrator adds that he had been hunted through life by his own evil passions, and "they had tracked him to this death." In a flashback, readers learn that Richard had struggled underwater with one of Henry's men, then made it to the shore, awakening later to find himself alone; he saw no sign of the *Adalid*. He made his way to an abbey, where he hoped to take the sacraments; there, a prior identified him and gave him up to Henry. He had but to "pine out a miserable existence" in captivity.

As Katherine continues to keep Elizabeth company, the queen feels shame for the part her husband plays in Richard's misery and, by extension, that of Katherine. Edmund Plantagenet has recovered from his wounds at Exeter but has been "without compass or rudder" in the absence of Richard, his life's focus. He joins Katherine and tells her that, contrary to rumors, he heard that the *Adalid* had escaped and Monina and de Faro sailed away. Crushed to learn that no hope survives for Richard to ascend to the throne, he states he will go to the Western Indies, hoping to find Monina, and he departs in tears.

The days drag on with inactivity for Richard, who at last is able to visit his cousin, the earl of Warwick, thanks to his guard, Roger. He finds Warwick far healthier than when he had previously seen him and learns that he had inspired Warwick to recover. Richard explains all that has happened, and the two eventually plot to escape with the thought that they are "the last of the White Rose" and will "rise or fall together." However, they are caught in the prison courtyard, and Richard accepts that he will soon be executed. Katherine finds some comfort in Elizabeth's friendship. As they talk one evening, Elizabeth tells Katherine that she (Katherine) is the more fortunate of the two women, because she at least was able to marry the man she loved. When Katherine begs Henry for mercy, he tells her that she will benefit by the death of a "base impostor," for she is a royal princess. Elizabeth and Katherine manage to visit Richard one more time, and the final chapter ends with their emotional reunion and farewells.

CONCLUSION

Shelley adds a conclusion in which the reader learns that Katherine lives on, beloved by all, her friendship with Elizabeth strong. Years pass, and while visiting the seat of Sir Thomas Moyle, she wanders away from the frivolity and chances upon a gray-haired man, whom she recognizes as Edmund Plantagenet. When Katherine asks what happened to Monina and de Faro, Edmund tells her that in Spain he found Monina's tomb and learned that de Faro had sailed to the West Indies. Plantagenet had returned to England to take refuge in the beauty of the natural world. Katherine relates how, as a woman, she had sought love in Elizabeth and her children, who brought her much joy, noting that "if grief kills us not, we kill it." She confesses a need to love and be loved and asks Edmund not to judge her for that. The novel concludes with her statement: "Permit a heart, whose sufferings have been, and are, so many and so bitter, to reap what joy it can from the strong necessity it feels to be sympathized with—to love."

COMMENTARY

Mary Shelley has been criticized for writing a historical novel focusing on a topic about which she was not well informed. The historical aspects of *Perkin Warbeck* may seem forced to present-day readers, and Shelley's stepping into the story to point out ways in which her plot aligns with historical chronicles proves distracting. Other scholars note in her defense that she engaged in dedicated research to inform her version of the story of the real-life Perkin Warbeck, proven by the many historical parallels in the novel. She asked the assistance of acquaintances, such as Thomas Crofton Croker in Ireland, which is the setting for much of her romance. In a letter dated October 30, 1828, she confessed that without such help, "I must rest satisfied with a very imperfect sketch, as never having been in Ireland, & being very ignorant of its history, I shall fall into a thousand mistakes." Shelley also personally appealed for assistance to Sir Walter Scott, with whom she had established a relationship after his review of *Frankenstein*. On May 25, 1829, she wrote:

> I am far advanced in a romance whose subject is Perkin Warbeck ... Your [sic] are completely versed in the Antiquities of your country, and you would confer a high favor on me if you could point out any writer of its history—any document, anecdote or even ballad connected with him generally unknown, which may have come to your knowledge.

Sources to which she alludes in that letter include George Buchanan's *History of Scotland* (Edinburgh: Alexander Arbuthnet, 1582); a translation from Latin, Robert Lindsay's *The History of Scotland (1436–1656)* (Edinburgh: Baskett Co., 1728); and John Pinkerton's *The History of Scotland from the Accession of the House of Stuart to that of Mary*, 2 vols. (London: C. Dilly, 1797). Shelley wrote to her father in 1828 that she was writing each morning, presumably working on *The Fortunes of Perkin Warbeck*. She would complete the novel over the next two years, all the while soliciting supporting facts and information from GODWIN, John Murray, Prosper Mérimée, and Croker.

Lidia Garbin and David Vallins theorize the strong influence of Scott's *Ivanhoe* on Shelley, who sought to revive chivalric virtues in her culture. Several times her narrator comments on the virtues of a life of chivalry as compared to a life based on trade, the description applying to Richard's era. As Emily Sunstein explains, Shelley condemned the feudal social structure but valued the "fidelity, self-devotion and chivalric attachment" represented by Richard and Katherine. Other scholars believe that Shelley, like Scott, was exceedingly opposed to the violence that supported the ideals of chivalry and wrote in order to feature the negative elements of what was presumed to be a highly moral code. Recent scholarship asks readers to understand *Perkin Warbeck* as Shelley's condemnation of the chivalric code, which led individuals to commit horrors in the name of glory and personal gain to the exclusion of any universal benefit. Readers see this in the details of war that she supplies, particularly in her emphasis of the horrors inflicted upon innocent bystanders. She emphasizes the same theme in *Lodore* (1835) and also in *Falkner* (1837), extending her condemnation beyond the feudal code to the "romantic sublime," the belief that men feel they must accomplish a personal agenda and follow egocentric patterns in order to fulfill their destiny. It was an important aspect of the romantic idea put forth in the character of PROMETHEUS, adopted by both PERCY BYSSHE SHELLEY and Mary in their work. Mary Shelley recognized the romantic sublime as an attitude that greatly threatened the health and viability of the family. The character of Richard, duke of York, known as Perkin Warbeck, constantly laments the deaths of those who support his cause, yet he accepts them as necessary.

Other critics think Shelley was simply focused on the romantic story within the tale. More recent scholarship by Betty T. Bennett makes a different claim. Bennett links *Perkin Warbeck* to Shelley's other historical novel, *Lodore*, as illustrating that love proves ineffectual when competing with male ambition. Like Castruccio in *Lodore*, Richard, duke of York, or a pretender to that title, loves two women, Monina and Katherine, but sacrifices romantic passion to the passion of destruction. Shelley needed to revise history, as did Scott, in order to make her point. Shelley had noted that the story of Perkin Warbeck—an attempt by Richard, or a pretender, to take the crown from Henry VII—had been suggested to her as a topic, probably by William Godwin, in "historical detail." However, she decided that its romantic elements would make the story impossible "for any narration, [sic] that should be confined to the incorporation of facts related by our old Chroniclers, to do it justice." She probably was impressed by Scott's focus on the way the past shaped his present, as well as his skill in weaving fact into fiction, which caused her to adopt his work as a model for her own.

In his most famous work, *An Inquiry Concerning the Principles of Political Justice and its Influence in General Virtue and Happiness* (1793), Godwin had wondered whether a "rational man" could be the least bit concerned over whether "Henry the sixth or Edward the fourth should have the style of king of England." He made the point that regardless of the personal characteristics of specific historical individuals, the fact that they would involve innocent people in a war for the right to rule made them unreasonable human beings. Shelley shared this belief against the value of violence and aristocratic control. Like her father, she firmly supported the ideology of individual freedom within a republican government, or within little to no government. *Perkin Warbeck* emphasizes the forces that control individual destinies. Just as more recent scholarship has characterized Scott's focus on chivalry, it also suggests that Shelley was not as concerned with the feudal trappings of history as with the forces that helped shape the present, particularly the development of the social institutions that her father so opposed. She famously apologized for her lack of the activist nature of her parents (as described in the biography section); however, her novels took an important place in the 19th-century reform movement, which focused on the rights and dignity of the individual.

In *Perkin Warbeck,* as in her other novels, Shelley supports her father's notion that a rational individual is fully capable of self-government and does not require control by civic government. Like Godwin, Shelley opposed arbitrary power by any source, as Bennett explains. She modeled the character of Richard on Godwin's character Falkland in his novel *Caleb Williams* (1794). Falkland cannot escape the false principles of his education. While he may be a moral character, even admirable in his pursuits, in order to protect his name and reputation, he moves outside the law to commit murder, trading a human life for his own pride. In *Perkin Warbeck,* Richard has no plan that will benefit his subjects, other than a vague idea of ruling as a benevolent monarch. He still desires absolute control over others. Bennett sees Richard as culpable, as are Falkland and Castruccio; none of these individuals may be characterized as heroes.

As Bennett elaborates, because Richard accepts the promise of his supporters in the novel's opening to restore to him his rightful power, regardless of the results—success and honor, or defeat and death—he is unreasonable. His pledge to support the efforts of those who plan to stage a revolt will lead to the death of many. Those deaths will advance a goal that, in Bennett's opinion, is little more than self-aggrandizement. However, an alternate reading reveals Richard's conflict over efforts to take power. An important support for his assuming what he views as his rightful title comes from Monina. As a nonroyal and a Spaniard, Monina has no stake in gaining power or titles. She truly believes that Richard will be the better ruler. She has seen him perform in battle and so is assured of his physical prowess and leadership abilities. While Monina has romantic feelings for Richard, they do not tarnish her ability to see him as king because she realizes early on that they cannot be together in any substantial way.

As Richard recognizes Monina's devotion, he also sees the constant conniving on the parts of Frion and Robert/Robin Clifford. He understands that the power he seeks can turn at a single moment. In addition, at this point in time, life was acknowledged to be short and filled with pain and sacrifice by most. Dying in glory added extra dimension to an afterlife. One would be celebrated not only in heaven but also on earth in ballads and tales that had filled Richard's ears as he matured. Readers must keep in mind the setting for the novel at a time, Shelley reminds us, when knighthood still had to be earned rather than bought, and chivalry was a private moral code. Richard provided hope and motivation for many White Rose supporters that enriched otherwise vacant existences. Finally, the competition between the various military forces had been entrenched by centuries of quarrels, fighting, and hatred. To fight a particular foe was to honor one's ancestors. The caveat to all of these points, however, is that they apply mostly to the upper social classes, at least traditionally. Shelley does demonstrate the worker's ability to protest, however, when the tradesmen stage a revolt, having lost work due to Henry's political machinations.

Shelley may attempt to demonstrate not that Richard fails as an individual but, rather, that he fails because of the atrocities committed in his name. One critical view holds that Richard's renunciation of crimes against the people incriminates him even further. His pronouncement "let not the blood of my subjects plead against my right; rather would I pine in exile for ever [sic], than occasion the slaughter and misery of my countrymen, my children" proves that he well understands the cost of his drive for glory. In addition, he does not pine in exile but instead witnesses firsthand the blood of his followers and innocent bystanders spilled. Such political ambition proves destructive to many more people than it proves constructive. Richard believes he has the right to the crown, and that right supersedes all humanitarian concern. He clearly recognizes the implications of his actions, illustrated in his letter to Katherine that reads, in part,

> What am I, that I should be the parent of evil merely? Oh, my mother, my too kind friends, why did ye not conceal me from myself? Teaching me lessons of humbleness, rearing me as a peasant, consigning me to a cloister, my injuries would have died with me; and the good, the brave, the innocent, who have perished for me, or through me, had been spared.

The reader recognizes not only Richard's realization of the costs of his ambition but also the fact that, rather than take responsibility for his actions, he chooses to blame them on his family, who failed to save him from himself. Another view of this passage is the culpability inherent to his education in chivalry and its false ideals. However, the reader might point out that this passage appears at the novel's conclusion and may reflect a true wish for redemption on Richard's part. As Bennett sees it, the novel's tragedy is not in Richard's defeat and execution but, rather, in his inability to control his ambition, even after recognizing it for what it is. Had he been victorious, Richard would have differed little from Henry once placed in power. The need for policies to keep him and his supportive political forces in power would have resulted in tyranny. On the other hand, Richard clearly believed in fate, which he constantly cursed. He seemed defeated from the time of his birth; his spirit kept him moving forward in the hope that the wheel would eventually turn in his favor.

The comparison of support characters in *Perkin Warbeck* to those in Shelley's other novels may be further extended to aid understanding of her themes. Bennett points out that in both *Perkin Warbeck* and *Valperga*, two women of similar types support the male protagonist. As Richard's wife, Katherine corresponds in several ways to Euthanasia in *Valperga*. Both women plead with the men not to pursue individual glory. Although Katherine loves and supports Richard, she can see the folly of his actions and pleads with him to change his course: "Believe me, careful nights and thorny days are the portion of a monarch." She notes that a king attains the heights "only to view more clearly destruction beneath," adding that "fear, hate, disloyalty" all surround a king. Unlike Euthanasia, however, Katherine offers no alternative. She also must know that regardless of Richard's fate, she will survive as a royal princess and probably remarry. While Euthanasia supports the idea of a republic, Katherine simply wants Richard to withdraw from his efforts in order to preserve his life and their relationship. Likewise, the character of Richard's Spanish love, Monina, parallels that of Beatrice in *Valperga*. These women are complete partisans, supportive of their leaders regardless of personal or public costs. Bennett suggests that Monina's love for Richard causes her misinterpretation of conditions that help lead to his downfall.

As do Shelley's other novels, *Perkin Warbeck* suggests a personal connection to Shelley. Katherine may speak for Shelley as she would like to have spoken to her dead husband, Percy, asking that her personal love prove sufficient in the face of Percy's many interests that drew him away from their relationship. That idea adds to Bennett's theory that in her later novels, Shelley moved away from the romantic ideal of the power of universal love. Instead, Shelley supported individual relationships as having the power to exert change. In *Perkin Warbeck*, Katherine proposes that each individual possesses an "angelic portion" that permits our feeling the joy and pain of others. Ethel in *Lodore* takes that view a step further in stating, "Angels could not feel as she did, for they cannot sacrifice to those they love." Katherine also speaks of the individual capacity for benevolence, as Euthanasia in *Valperga* calls for "content of mind, love and benevolent feeling" on the part of each human being. In *Perkin Warbeck*, no alternative universal plan like Euthanasia's exists because both Katherine and Richard, as Bennett notes, cannot operate outside of an established political and social system in which they are assigned specific roles. Shelley desires that individuals operate on an individual basis to pursue ideals such as human dignity and the destruction of a social structure that devalues so many lives. However, they will all face the restrictions brought about by personal circumstance, whether social, political, or in some other way based on demographics. Also important to note are value systems that mutate across generations. Trust is one important value that has not changed from the time of Perkin Warbeck to the 19th century; betrayal remains just as bitter. When Richard learns of his betrayal by his childhood friend Robin Clifford, the narrator tells the audience, "The whole wide world of misery contains no pang so great, as the discovery of treachery where we pictured truth; death is less in the comparison, for both destroy the future, and one, with Gorgon countenance, transforms the past." Here Shelley examines the betrayal of trust at the human level, rather than merely on the level of a would-be monarch and a man who serves him. Betrayal as an aspect of human weakness remains a frequent topic in much of her writing.

Nature plays a featured role in the novel, with Shelley adding minute detail regarding the ever-changing physical surroundings. Readers become familiar with the landscapes of Spain, France, and Scotland, in addition to those of England. Scotland's untamed wilds become a dramatic stage for the tumultuous passions Richard experiences as he contemplates marriage to Katherine. Shelley's familiarity with Scotland due to her childhood trips there causes her descriptions to ring true. It is during Richard's journey from Edinburgh to Katherine's home that Shelley makes clear the contrast between Scotland and the other more refined locations. She personifies the crags on the steep hills, symbolic of a warning to Richard:

> York paused: The scene appeared to close in on him, and to fill him, even to overflowing, with its imagery . . . below, above, the dark pines, in many a tortuous shape, clung to the rifted rocks; the fern clustered round some solitary oak; while, beetling over, were dark frowning crags, or the folding of the mountains, softened into upland, painted by the many coloured heather.

Various passages point to moments or thoughts in Shelley's own life. She often felt fearful while living in Casa Magni in Italy, despite being literally surrounded by friends in the tiny converted boathouse where she and Shelley lived. Sunstein describes the ferocious storms over the water that the group endured, details of which Shelley includes in various novels and stories. More frightening to Shelley, perhaps, was the human habit of asking some invisible force, a deity, for comfort. Never a fan of religion, she writes later in *Perkin Warbeck*: "[A]nd we ask the voiceless thing—wherefore, when the beauty of the visible universe sickens the aching sense; when we beseech the winds to comfort us, and we implore the Invisible for relief . . . ?" She adds that when humans intuit the approach of evil, they want to "soar beyond the imprisoning atmosphere" of their own identities. Thus, those attempting to console us are simply mocking our destinies and may make a normally intelligent human grasp at any hope offered. Shelley compares that situation to one she may have known well: that of a mother who smiles "on the physician who talks of recovery while her child dies."

Sunstein notes a change in style in the second half of the novel, written during 1829 as Shelley negotiated the "emotional and philosophic ramifications" not only of her characters' actions but of her own and those who she loved. She casts Henry as a materialistic and avaricious individual who has the same flaw as Victor Frankenstein and Lord Raymond of *The Last Man* (1826). It is a flaw that she believed present in herself and Percy Shelley as well: Humans see themselves as the center of a universe either too complicated to notice them or too cold to care. Although each generation inherits and eventually identifies that flaw, it continues to reappear. If human intelligence were used correctly, evil might become good. However, no matter how strongly the wise may emphasize the folly of egotistical behavior, it continues. While retribution might take its time, it always followed what Sunstein labels "wrongdoing." It is important to notice that Henry does, if only momentarily, find the ability to look beyond himself when he becomes infatuated with Katherine. However, that infatuation does not last, and he undergoes no softening of his attitudes due to it.

Sunstein feels that when Shelley employed the "unromantic fact" that Katherine remained at court and, for those who know their history, enjoyed three more marriages after Richard, she is sending her longtime friend and romantic hopeful EDWARD JOHN TRELAWNY a clear message. She seeks to defend her desire to form emotional attachments with others, although in her case, she would never remarry. Although Katherine still feels duty-bound to her environment and remains in love with Richard, she does not have a heart of stone and celebrates "the freer impulses of our souls." Her "dependence on others" and habit of "clinging to the sense of joy" is what makes her who she is. Katherine states, "I am content to be an imperfect creature, so that I never lose the enobling attribute of my species, the constant endeavour to be more perfect." When Katherine states she is "doomed to a divided existence" to which she submits, Sunstein makes clear that Shelley does not describe herself. According to Sunstein, Shelley "submitted based on a sense of reality belatedly acquired, her drive for the preservation of herself and her son, and the mature branching of her rooted philosophy." At the time of her writing *Perkin Warbeck,* she no longer lived her life for her dead husband. She continued to deal with what she labeled the "'domestic enemy': discouragement, protest and brooding. English society, moreover, never forgot her past."

CHARACTERS

Warbeck/Richard Shelley's rendering of Perkin Warbeck/Richard, the duke of York, is positive, as would be expected for one portraying the male lead in a historical romance novel. Readers find him sympathetic, following his maturation from a child into a brave, chivalric, honor-bound man who stands in great contrast to the heartless, cold, misogynistic King Henry. The fact that informed readers understand from the beginning that Richard is doomed to die could cause them to lack interest in him and his various predicaments. However, Shelley's skillful use of detail successfully causes readers to be fond of Richard. Examples include his mourning of his brother Edward early on and the inclusion of several references to Edward's death in the Tower that reflect on Richard to sympathetic effect. In addition, Richard assumes a commanding presence early on, and his pride and courage are notable as he states, even as a teen, that he is the true heir to the throne. He shares many tender moments with both of his love interests, and in the end he writes a letter to Katherine brimming with desire and tenderness, something that Henry could never do. Katherine feels loved and cherished while poor Queen Elizabeth is abused, frightened, and lacking in courage, due to a lack of the support from Henry that Katherine has received from Richard. Thus, he is seen as an empowering figure for women. All in all, readers probably wish that Shelley's incarnation of Richard had made it to the throne. Reader affection for him supports a clearer understanding of Shelley's point regarding fate, and that none of us can predict our end. We must simply live with the courage of our convictions.

Katherine Cousin to the Scottish king James III, Katherine proves a boon to Richard. She is early described as "Truth," and readers learn later that Richard finds in her "a magic mirror, which gave him back himself, arrayed with a thousand alien virtues; his soul was in her hands; plastic to her fairy touch, and tenderness and worship and wonder took his heart . . . so that they could never depart." She acts as a foil to Monina, whose passion for Richard is fueled by her ardent belief that he should, and will, become king. Ironically, Katherine comes to be symbolized by the Yorkist White Rose, even bearing that name, although she beseeches Richard to stay with her and not to continue a fight that he cannot win. She does not understand the need for honor at the cost of all. Shelley shapes Katherine in her conclusion as a typical woman, guided by love and sacrifice. She cannot live without love and fully expects her needs to be fulfilled, while still carrying a lifelong love for her deceased husband.

Queen Elizabeth Elizabeth represents one of Shelley's sadder female characters. Possessing no agency of her own, she is duty-bound to doom herself to a loveless marriage. Not only does Henry not love her, but he abuses her by withholding royal privileges, such as interaction with her mother and brother that are her birthright. At no time does she attempt to use wit to help shape Henry into a husband better suited to her needs; her only tools are forbearance, patience, and a gentle demeanor, attributes to which Henry will never respond.

Monina Monina provides a foil to Katherine and the romantic focus for several men. Richard loves her but never considers marriage. Throughout life, he appreciates her strength and unflagging optimism that he will prevail. Also loved by Robin Clifford, she serves to demonstrate through his twisted fixation on her that love confused with power results only in destruction. Finally, Edmund Plantagenet represents courtly love in his admiration and measured passion for Monina.

He admires her spark and shares her devotion to Richard, but he waits too long to act on his feelings in deference to Richard. Monina represents the novel's center, as every important character is strongly attracted to her. She remains of spotless reputation, beautiful and desirable. However, she also represents the blind aspect of idealism in her inability to face the reality that Richard cannot win the day. Shelley also reflects Shakespeare's influence in Robin's speech comparing Monina to a witch. His dramatic dialogue is part renunciation, part surrender, in deference to the power that women hold over men.

King Henry Shelley's negative characterization of Henry proves necessary in order to encourage sympathy for Richard, Henry's nemesis. Her characterization mimics that of Shakespeare, and she uses quotations from his drama to help emphasize Henry's cold, calculating demeanor. She emphasizes questions of Henry's legitimacy to claim the throne that may be seen as equal to questions about Richard's legitimacy. Henry is at his most despicable in his dealings with his wife. From the beginning, he abuses Elizabeth, a woman who earnestly tries to please him. He terrifies her as often as possible, rendering her life an unending terror. He enjoys manipulating others to gain his ends, offering a contrast to Richard, who behaves honorably, regardless of the personal cost to him. The historical Henry VII may be best known for fathering Henry VIII, a great ruler who himself sired England's greatest ruler, Queen Elizabeth I. Shelley's Henry is a pronounced elitist, a characteristic true of the real Henry VII, who allowed his children to marry only other royals and no offspring of the baronage.

Robin Clifford Clifford at first plays the part of the fool, a character who often proved crucial to Shakespeare's dramas. Cunning and self-serving, he also cannot seem to avoid doing good for others in the first portion of the novel. He is always ready with a clever or sarcastic remark that misleads or confuses those with whom he interacts into dismissing him or his actions as less important than they are. His remarks disintegrate into cynicism later in the novel. He also plays the part of a rogue where women are concerned. For example, when he discusses Richard's situation with Monina, she asks him to consider her nothing other than a messenger. He thinks, "As soon forget sunshine or moonshine or the chance of play when the dicebox rattles." Insolent and self-absorbed, he detests Richard, duke of York, because they stand in such great contrast. The narrator explains: "While he was a cankered bloom, his heart a waste, his soul crusted over by deceit, his very person sullied by evil deeds and thoughts, Duke Richard stood in all the pride of innocence." Robin's characterization shifts as he gives in to his weaker instincts, betraying his aristocratic ancestry. Not only does he turn against Richard, mainly due to jealousy over Monina's devotion, but he attempts to kidnap Monina. For that act of violence, he pays with his life. Readers may find difficult the continued success with which Clifford convinces both Richard and Henry that he represents their best interests.

FURTHER READING

Bennett, Betty T. "The Political Philosophy of Mary Shelley's Historical Novels: *Valperga* and *Perkin Warbeck*." In *The Evidence of the Imagination*, edited by Donald H. Reiman, Michael C. Jaye, and Betty T. Bennett, 354–371. New York: New York University Press, 1978.

Garbin, Lidia. "Mary Shelley and Walter Scott: The Fortunes of Perkin Warbeck and the Historical Novel." In *Mary Shelley's Fictions from Frankenstein to Falkner*, edited by Michael Eberle-Sinatra, 150–163. New York: St. Martin's Press, 2000. Available online. URL: http://www.erudit.org/revue/ron/1997/v/n6/005752ar.html?lang=es. Accessed June 27, 2010.

Jones, Frederick L., ed. *The Letters of Mary W. Shelley*. Norman: University of Oklahoma Press, 1944.

———. *The Letters of Percy Bysshe Shelley*. Oxford, U.K.: Clarendon Press, 1964.

Powers, Katherine Richardson. *The Influence of William Godwin on the Novels of Mary Shelley*. New York: Arno Press, 1980.

Shelley, Mary. *The Fortunes of Perkin Warbeck*. Available online. URL: http://www.feedbooks.com/book/1353. Accessed June 27, 2010.

———, ed. *Selected Letters of Mary Wollstonecraft Shelley*. Edited by Betty T. Bennett. Baltimore: Johns Hopkins University Press, 1995.

Sunstein, Emily W. *Mary Shelley: Romance and Reality*. Boston: Little, Brown and Company, 1989.

Web of Mind. "Perkin Warbeck Project." Available online. URL: http://www.radford.edu/~webofmind/pwp.htm. Accessed June 27, 2010.

Frankenstein (1818)

"This is a novel, or more properly a romantic fiction, of a nature so peculiar, that we ought to describe the species before attempting any account of the individual production." Thus opened Sir Walter Scott's now well-known *Blackwood's Edinburgh Magazine* review of Mary Shelley's anonymously published *Frankenstein*. While viewed as peculiar in her own time, Shelley's novel—and, more correctly stated, its monster—would arguably become the most recognizable representative of her era in later centuries. The monster continues to appear in every conceivable media, from comic books and graphic novels to Halloween costumes and breakfast cereal boxes. The term *Frankenstein*, along with its variants, has become ubiquitous in our vocabulary. For example, in the 2004 movie *Supersize Me*, filmmaker Morgan Spurlock used "McFrankenstein" to describe the enormous quantity of food contained in "supersized" offerings from McDonald's. But while the monster may be immediately recognizable in all of his various incarnations to later generations, fewer people have actually read the novel that introduced his unnamed character. Thus, the monster is usually incorrectly referred to as "Frankenstein," though that is, in fact, the name of his creator.

In the preface to the 1831 revised edition of *Frankenstein* (the edition most often read today), Mary Shelley famously wrote that she had tried to conceive a story "which would speak to the mysterious fears of our nature, and awaken thrilling horror—one to make the reader dread to look round, to curdle the blood, and quicken the beatings of the heart." Based on the novel's continued popu-

Frontispiece to the 1831 edition of Mary Shelley's *Frankenstein* (Illustration by Theodor von Holst)

larity, one may assume that the story has affected readers as Shelley intended. It has been in print continuously since its original publication in 1818. Modern literary critics have examined it from almost every critical perspective—psychoanalytic, feminist, Marxist, deconstructionist, formalist, New Historicist. The novel also stands up well to even newer critical approaches, such as ecological criticism and postcolonialism, the latter of which aids in reader understanding of concepts of the alien other, as well as colonization of the physical body. Mary Shelley could not possibly have anticipated the longevity of her novel and its ability to capture the imagination of multiple generations over almost two centuries.

The reception of *Frankenstein* in its own era was enthusiastic, although its author was at first mistakenly identified as PERCY BYSSHE SHELLEY. Sir Walter Scott was among the reviewers who made that error, one that Mary herself set right in a courteous letter to Scott. Since that time, a few scholars have attributed much of the novel's creative genius to Percy Shelley, but little proof exists that Mary Shelley should not continue to be proclaimed its author and credited for an amazing and revolutionary work.

BACKGROUND

Mary Shelley's story of the novel's creation, as recounted in the introduction to the 1831 edition, has become legend. While historians have questioned the accuracy of some details of Shelley's account, for the most part its truth has been confirmed. She begins by sharing with her readers the request of her editors to explain "How I, then a young girl, came to think of, and to dilate upon, so very hideous an idea." She then describes the following: While enjoying the company of her husband and their friends GEORGE GORDON BYRON (Lord Byron) and his personal physician, JOHN WILLIAM POLIDORI, she received Byron's challenge for each member of the group to compose a ghost story. Polidori tried to do so but did not know how to properly conclude his tale, while "the poets," as Shelley refers to her husband and Byron, "annoyed by the platitude of prose, speedily relinquished their uncongenial task." Shelley, however, kept at it. Informed by her nightmares, Shelley's novel began to grow into the story that would not only allow her to meet Byron's challenge but also to astound readers for centuries. Shelley tells of whiling away long rainy days in Switzerland by reading German ghost stories translated into French. It was good preparation for Byron's challenge. Just as important were her interests—and her culture's interests—in artistic expression, the sciences, and philosophy.

Frankenstein is a kind of SCIENCE FICTION informed by gothic (see GOTHIC FICTION) plot and style. In some ways, it is based on literary theories expounded by Edmund Burke's treatise *A Philosophical Inquiry into the Origin of Our Ideas of the Sublime and Beautiful* (1756). Burke noted that beauty found in art derives from pleasure, while the sublime has pain as its foundation. The sublime is a "delightful horror," seductive in its power to elicit strong emotions. Horace Walpole's gothic novel *The Castle of Otranto* (1765), born in its author's nightmare about a gigantic hand in armor, clinging to a staircase banister, aligned with Burke's definition of the sublime. William Beckford followed with *Vathek* (1786), a book of terror written in French that Byron referred to as his Bible. One may compare its Faustian theme, captured in a didactic statement to its readers, to that of *Frankenstein*: "Such shall be the chastisement of that blind curiosity, which would transgress those bounds the wisdom of the Creator has prescribed to human knowledge." The modern science fiction writer Brian Aldiss sees *Frankenstein* also representing the modernized Faustian theme as it touches on science as well as humanity's dual nature.

Aldiss cites Shelley as "the author whose work marks her out as the first science fiction writer," titling the opening chapter in his well-known work *Billion Year Spree* (1973) "The Origin of the Species: Mary Shelley." He defines the science-fiction subgenre as "the search for a definition of man and his status in the universe which will stand in our advanced but confused state of knowledge (science), and is characteristically cast in the Gothic or post-Gothic mould." In order to consider what he calls "the brilliant context" from which Shelley found inspiration, he insists that one must consider the "literary, scientific, and social" theories and practices of her age.

Contemporary scientific discoveries and technological developments were clearly influential to the development of *Frankenstein*. Carl Linnaeus (1707–78) and Captain James Cook (1728–79) challenged the public's imagination through studies of newly discovered flora and fauna. Cook especially excited Europe with reports from his explorations, which included previously unknown landscapes as diverse as the Antarctic and the Easter Islands. When *Frankenstein* appeared in 1818, travel was soon to reach a new pinnacle, with the first steamship crossing the Atlantic in 1819. Other technological advances made life more challenging and interesting. For instance, steam locomotives would soon cut through England's landscape, passing foundries with hard-at-work furnaces; gas was already employed to produce light; and travel was becoming more convenient as new roads and bridges appeared. The world was changing at an alarming rate, challenging the limits of human understanding and acceptance. Her own culture formed a backdrop to Shelley's creation of what Aldiss describes as a combination of "social criticism with new scientific ideas."

Trained by her father, WILLIAM GODWIN, and her husband, Percy Bysshe Shelley, to read widely, Mary Shelley absorbed much information about the developing study of science that informed her novel. Godwin and his circle discussed the writings of the poet, physician, and botanist Erasmus Darwin (grandfather of Charles Darwin; 1731–1802), who focused on the natural world and was greatly influenced by Cook's writings and descriptions. In Erasmus Darwin's long poem *The Loves of the Plants*, he refers to the Antarctic, its icy setting soon to be integral to Shelley's novel. He adopted poetry rather than scientific prose to describe a wondrous new world in couplets such as "Slow o'er the printed snows with silent walk / Huge shaggy forms across the twilight stalk." Victor Frankenstein's pursuit of the monster across the ice floes clearly reflects Darwin's influence, by way of Cook. Of special importance was Darwin's 2,000-line long poem *The Temple of Nature; or, The Origin of Society*; the 1804 edition was illustrated by the artist Henry Fuseli, who coincidentally had been linked romantically to Shelley's mother, MARY WOLLSTONECRAFT. Darwin's accepting view of nature and its challenges can be seen in an excerpt from that poem's last canto: "Shout round the globe, how Reproduction strives / With vanquish'd Death—and Happiness survives; / How Life increasing peoples every clime, / And young renascent Nature conquers Time." He predicts various developments, such as the building of skyscrapers, eventual overpopulation, water made available to all through pipes from a distant source, and a dispute between religion and science. Darwin and Shelley's father never met, but in the publication *Anti-Jacobin*, they were both criticized as atheistic.

Darwin also famously described the investigation of theories regarding the spontaneous generation of life. He summarized an experiment in which a piece of a worm from the group scientifically labeled *vermicelli* moved with involuntary motion while contained in a glass jar. Mary Shelley also overheard Percy Bysshe Shelley and Lord Byron discussing this experiment. That discussion was one of many in which, according to Shelley's 1831 preface, "various philosophical doctrines were discussed, and among others, the nature of the principle of life." Victor Frankenstein would muse in the novel, "perhaps a corpse would be re-animated; galvanism had given a token of such things; perhaps the component parts of a creature might be manufactured, brought together, and embued with vital warmth." Mary Shelley also knew well Percy's poem *Queen Mab* (1813), itself influenced by Erasmus Darwin's ideas, which would continue to excite him.

Darwin initially believed, as had Aristotle, that only the male was responsible for producing a seed or embryon, while the female provided nourishment for the seed. He also believed the female was responsible for any "monstrous" reproductions, as in babies born with any deformities. In his *Zoomonia* (1794), he claimed that male imagination at the moment of conception determined the baby's sex and various physical characteristics:

[T]he act of generation cannot exist without being accompanied with ideas, and . . . a man must have at this time either a general idea of his own male form, or of the forms of his male organs; or of an idea of the female form, or of her organs, and that . . . marks the sex, and the peculiar resemblances of the child to either parent.

However, he revised that theory in his 1801 edition of *Zoomonia* after in-depth observation of animal and plant life convinced him that males and females both contribute innate characteristics to their offspring. As Anne K. Mellor comments, when Frankenstein as a male propagates alone, Shelley suggests that his ideas conflict with the more advanced ideas of Darwin.

In addition, Darwin wrote about "the economy of vegetation" in *Phytologia* (1800), emphasizing the importance of recycling organic matter over many years. Victor Frankenstein would challenge this idea by seeking to create a man instantaneously, through chemistry. He disrupts the life, death, decay, life cycle described by Darwin by removing bones and human matter from graveyards where they should decay and contribute to future life. In so doing, Mellor contends, Frankenstein not only "perverted evolutionary progress" but also parodied creationist theory by assuming the role of God and producing life in monstrous form. Mellor believes that Shelley invokes Darwin's theories to "suggest both the error and the evils of Victor Frankenstein's bad science." When Frankenstein makes no mother available to his offspring, he denies the monster sustenance that Darwin associated with the female gender. The poet Samuel Taylor Coleridge described Darwin as the "first literary character of Europe," but his poetry would soon be forgotten, though the ideas expressed in them would not. (Coleridge's own influence on Shelley is clear not only from her direct quotations of his work but also from the description of Victor Frankenstein's death on a ship swathed by mist in a becalmed sea, much like the ship on which Coleridge's Ancient Mariner sailed. Family legend says that the young Mary Godwin actually heard Coleridge read the tale aloud in her father's parlor.)

Another theory of her era that Shelley invoked in her novel was galvanism, a direct application of electricity for revival of the dead. Galvanism was a widely discussed and popular topic in the late 18th century. As Mellor notes, the process became commonly known following a series of studies by the University of Bologna anatomy professor Luigi Galvani. Galvani produced movement in a frog's leg using a bimetallic arc and wrote that his experiments confirmed the existence of a type of "animal electricity." His nephew toured Europe performing public demonstrations of the effect of electricity, astounding London audiences by making the eyes of a decapitated ox head open.

Mellor describes an experiment on a prisoner following an 1803 execution that further highlighted the use of galvanism. During application of electrical current, the dead man's face muscles quivered, and one eye opened. The public was mesmerized by the gruesome and startling event. However, not everyone believed in Galvani's science. Italian physicist Alessandro Volta disputed Galvani's findings, explaining that the arc, not the animal, was the origin of the electricity. Volta confirmed his theory through a series of experiments, but his identification of the true source of the movement did not diminish its immediate and astounding effects.

As Mellor explains, in the wake of the public's reaction to experiments on the dead, the practice was declared immoral. By 1804, Prussia had issued an edict against electrical experiments on the heads of decapitated criminals, but other performers continued astounding audiences and fascinating scientists and physicians. Andrew Ure animated a criminal's body in Glasgow in November 1818, the year of *Frankenstein*'s publication, and recorded the results: "Every muscle in his countenance was simultaneously thrown into fearful action: rage, horror, despair, anguish, and ghastly smiles, united their hideous expression in the murderer's face."

Earlier experiments with electricity also inform the novel. Benjamin Franklin's work frames Victor's early scientific interests, as he recreates the kite and key experiment to harness and control electricity, "that fluid from the clouds." The English had been fascinated by Franklin's work, along with that of Father Beccaria, who used the Leyden jar to define the existence of atmospheric mechanical electricity. Mellor explains that scientific exploration of the day was based on "Newton's concept of the ether as an elastic medium capable of transmitting the pulsations of light, heat, gravitation, magnetism, and electricity." Scientists continued work on the theory that a charged fluid in the atmosphere acted as an "animating principle" that could be recognized as light, heat, magnetism, or additional "guises." Darwin had written that human breathing predicted the existence of some such animating principle available in the air requiring constant replenishment. In his days at Dr. Greenlaw's Syon House Academy in 1802, Percy Shelley had engaged in experiments involving the Leyden jar and various chemical experiments resulting in holes in his own clothing and carpets; he even attempted to experiment on his sister, Elizabeth, and, according to Mellor, "electrified the family cat." He and Mary celebrated one of his birthdays by sending aloft "fire balloons." His fascination with electricity and its association with life forces including love is clear in his popular play *Prometheus Unbound* (1820). Like PROMETHEUS, Victor would steal fire, but his transgression was far worse than that of the mythic titan: He stole "a spark of being," as he describes it, which would animate his miscreant. Aldiss emphasizes that the public speculated regarding theories of evolution and also natural selection by the late 18th century, an aspect of the "debate" as to whether "species were fixed or mutable."

Furthermore, new medical discoveries and procedures also informed *Frankenstein*'s plot. For instance, attempts to revive those who were near death included the new effort of blood transfusion. Based on study of the circulatory system by English physician William Harvey in the 17th century, the earliest transfusions were from animal to human. Two centuries later, the English physician James Blundell introduced human to human transfusion in efforts to save women who hemorrhaged following childbirth within the decade in which Shelley published. Blundell also investigated surgical treatment of the pelvic organs, and his success was published and widely circulated in *The Lancet*. Shelley would have read or heard of his description of the simplicity of blood transfusion and the physician's charge in that article:

[H]is principal cares are—first, to see that the cup never empties itself entirely, otherwise air might be carried down along with the blood. Secondly, to make sure that blood which issues by dribbling, from the arm of the person who supplies it, may not be admitted into the receiver, as its fitness for use is doubtful. Thirdly, to watch the accumulation of blood in the receiver, and to prevent its rise above the prescribed level; and, lastly, to observe with attention the countenance of the patient, and to guard, as before stated, against an overcharge of the heart.

Just as important as Blundell's work was his argument against his critics that gains made during experimentation justified the mistreatment of dogs in his laboratory. Victor Frankenstein also believed that the end justified the means employed in his lab. His desire to save the world through his discoveries shaped him as a seeker after the "masculine divine." This notion of the romantic age empowered poets such as Percy Shelley to constantly seek higher levels of creativity and contribution to the public good, often to the detriment of their families and personal relationships. Victor Frankenstein well represents that notion, as would the majority of male figures in Mary Shelley's later novels.

Finally, older ideas are also powerfully reflected in *Frankenstein*. Victor Frankenstein studies theories by Renaissance philosophers such as Albertus Magnus, Cornelius Agrippa, and Paracelsus, the name adopted by the Swiss physician and alchemist Theophrastus Phillippus Aureolus Bombastus von Hohenheim. These theories serve as background supporting his quest to create new life. Other influential accounts and events that Shelley almost certainly learned of included the death of G. W. Richmann in 1753, electrocuted during a thunderstorm when conducting experiments with lightning. She also knew the story of Prometheus, who in Greek mythology created humans from mud and water, popularized by Aeschylus, and she had watched Percy Shelley creating *Prometheus Unbound* over several years. Jupiter curses Prometheus for providing fire to humans, to which Prometheus offers his own curse. He must withdraw the curse from Jupiter in order to free himself, but he cannot recall the words of his curse. In the first act of Percy Shelley's drama, Prometheus tells Jupiter,

> Heap on this soul by virtue of this Curse
> Ill deeds, then be thou damned, beholding good,
> Both infinite as is the Universe,
> And thou, and thy self-torturing solitude.
> An awful Image of calm power
> Though now thou sittest, let the hour
> Come, when thou must appear to be
> That which thou art internally.
> And after many a false and fruitless crime
> Scorn track thy lagging fall through boundless space and time.
> (1: 292–301)

One can hear echoes of the monster speaking to Victor Frankenstein in Prometheus's turning Jupiter's curse for a damned existence back on him. Both Frankenstein and his monster would suffer "self-torturing solitude."

Many readers of *Frankenstein* note that Shelley provides little detailed description of Victor Frankenstein's experimentations. Walter Scott not only accepted but praised Shelley's approach. He classified it as among writing of a certain type of "fictitious narratives" in which the author

> opens a sort of account-current with the reader; drawing upon him, in the first place, for credit to that degree of the marvellous which he proposes to employ; and becoming virtually bound, in consequence of this indulgence, that his personages shall conduct themselves, in the extraordinary circumstances in which they are placed, according to the rules of probability, and the nature of the human heart. In this view, the *probable* is far from being laid out of sight even amid the wildest freaks of imagination; on the contrary, we grant the extraordinary postulates which the author demands as the foundation of his narrative, only on condition of his deducing the consequences with logical precision.

For Scott, it was the reactions of the characters in the tale to the monstrous marvelous that most mattered and to which readers would want to relate. He added,

> It is no slight merit in our eyes, that the tale, though wild in incident, is written in plain and forcible English, without exhibiting that mixture of hyperbolical Germanisms with which tales of wonder are usually told, as if it were necessary that the language should be as extravagant as the fiction. The ideas of the author are always clearly as well as forcibly expressed; and his descriptions of landscape have in them the choice requisites of truth, freshness, precision, and beauty.

Brian Aldiss explains that the most successful science fiction portrays man in relation to a shifting environment, challenged by changes in abilities to comprehend and create. Scott apparently would have agreed with this much later opinion.

Shelley herself wrote in the preface to her first edition:

> The event on which the interest of the story depends is exempt from the disadvantages of a mere tale of spectres or enchantment. It was recommended by the novelty of the situations which it develops; and, however impossible as a physical fact, affords a point of view to the imagination for the delineating of human passions more comprehensive and commanding than any which the ordinary relations of existing events can yield.

Later critics would take her to task for glossing over details of the scientist's work, which resulted in a living human being. However, Aldiss makes the point that science fiction writers often take a page from the gothic novel to set their stories in an environment where readers cannot compare occurrences to their own experiences. Just as gothic novels were often set in a mysterious, darkened landscape, Shelley fashioned a laboratory surrounding that would appear completely foreign to her readers.

Various detailed versions of the creation scene were later imagined for film, many of which also gave Victor a lab assistant, often a miscreant in his own right. However, Scott concluded,

Upon the whole, the work impresses us with a high idea of the author's original genius and happy power of expression. We . . . congratulate our readers upon a novel which excites new reflections and untried sources of emotion. If Gray's definition of Paradise, to lie on a couch, namely, and read new novels, come any thing near truth, no small praise is due to him, who, like the author of Frankenstein, has enlarged the sphere of that fascinating enjoyment.

Five years later, a reviewer of Mary Shelley's novel *Valperga* (1823) opened with this comment:

Frankenstein, at the time of its appearance, we certainly did not suspect to be the work of a female hand; the name of Shelley was whispered, and we did not hesitate to attribute the book to *Mr* Shelley. Soon, however, we were set right. We learned that Frankenstein was written by *Mrs* Shelley; and then we most undoubtedly said to ourselves, "For a man it was excellent, but for a woman it is wonderful." What we chiefly admired, in that wild production, was vigour of imagination and strength of language; these were unquestionable attributes, and they redeemed the defects of an absurd groundwork and an incoherent fable; and, moreover, they tempted us, and every body [sic] else, to forgive the many long passages of feeble conception and feeble execution, with which the vigorous scenes were interwoven.

Whatever its faults, *Frankenstein* would forever be considered the best of Shelley's works. Despite later critical praise of her additional novels, they continue to languish in the broad shadow cast by her first novel as it renews itself in the imagination of one generation of readers after another.

SYNOPSIS

In the 1831 edition, the novel begins with its full title, *Frankenstein or the Modern Prometheus*, beneath which appears a quotation from Milton's PARADISE LOST (10: 743–745): "Did I request thee, Maker, from my clay / To mould Me man? Did I solicit thee / From darkness to promote me?—." A dedication follows: "To William Godwin Author of Political Justice, Caleb Williams, etc., these volumes Are respectfully inscribed by the Author." Mary Shelley explains to readers that she added the introduction to the 1831 edition because the publishers "expressed a wish that I should furnish them with some account of the origin of the story." She notes that she complied with their request in part to answer the question often put to her by readers: How did the novel originate? Emphasizing that she does not like to draw attention to herself, she says that she is supplying the explanation because it is a small addition to matter already in print and will not be considered intrusive to the novel itself. Noting her parentage's effect on her early "scribbling," Shelley describes story writing as a favorite pastime but adds that as a child she enjoyed even more "the formation of castles in the air—the indulging in waking dreams." She describes what she wrote down as intended for an audience but her dreams as being hers alone, where she has found refuge and pleasure. She describes her life while in Scotland as a child and the effect of her surroundings on her: "They were the eyry of freedom" where she could "commune with the creatures of" her "fancy." Sitting beneath trees, she wrote in a common way, not recreating herself as a heroine and never suspecting that "romantic woes or wonderful events" might be in her future. Later, "reality stood in the place of fiction" and life's obligations stopped her writing, despite her husband's interest that she might fulfill the destiny put in motion by her parents. According to Shelley, her husband had hoped to judge her talents, but she did not write for some time.

Next, Shelley relates the story of the summer of 1816 in Switzerland when she and her husband passed time during rainy weather reading French translations of German ghost stories. The characters proved miserable, doomed beings bringing death to visit their loved ones. On one particular evening, Lord Byron and his physician Polidori joined the couple. Byron issued a challenge to all to write their own ghost stories. He managed to produce a tale and later published "a fragment," while Percy Shelley created a fiction based on incidents in his own life. Polidori wrote "something very shocking," but both poets eventually gave up the challenge to create a full ghost story.

Mary Shelley remained focused, hoping to produce a tale that would "awaken thrilling horror" in its appeal to the baser elements of human nature. Despite her hopes, she produced nothing. Then, she writes, "Every thing must have a beginning, to speak in Sachean phrase, and that beginning must be linked to something that went before." Eventually, Shelley succeeded, and she claims that her invention issued from chaos. Her imagination gave form to dark substance after "seizing on the capabilities of a subject." That subject grew in part from conversations she heard between Percy Shelley and Byron of Dr. Darwin's experiments, which gave "voluntary motion" to a dead worm in a jar. Galvanism had been of great interest to their culture, and its effect combined with these additional influences to lead to a sleepless night for Shelley. Her imagination sparked vivid images of "the pale student of unhallowed arts" beside the "thing" he had assembled, causing her mind to be so possessed by the terrible tale that she could still see the images the following day. Shelley wanted to frighten the reader as she had been frightened, and her tale was born. She began, "It was on a dreary night of November." However, her husband suggested that she add more to her slight tale, and the novel took shape. Shelley notes that all these years later, she again bids the novel that is like a hideous child to "go forth and prosper," adding that she now much better understands grief and sorrow than when she wrote the tale. She concludes by explaining changes to the novel in the new edition are "principally those of style"; she has introduced no new ideas.

Preface

The preface to the 1831 edition (which is separate from the introduction) also appeared in the original 1818 edition, written by Percy Shelley in Mary Shelley's voice. Its opening lines emphasize that the fiction that follows could possess an element of truth, referencing studies by Dr. Darwin and "the physiological writers of Germany." The narrator states that she did not merely weave "a series of supernatural terrors," and she has attempted "to preserve the truth of the elementary principles of human nature." She invokes great models, such as the *Iliad* and works by Shakespeare and Milton, all of which follow the rule that allows a fine writer to "apply to prose fiction a licence [sic]" that has led to the production of works mimicking human emotions, resulting in fine poetry. The narrator includes a brief relation of the story's circumstances, noting its production for amusement but also that it is the result of exercising "untried resources of mind" and mingling additional motives, such as a challenge from friends during the summer of 1816 while in Geneva. The narrator concludes that the tale that follows was the only one completed in response to that challenge. The preface is given the byline "Marlow, September, 1817." Four numbered letters follow.

Letter 1

Letter 1 is addressed to a Mrs. Saville in England, sent from "St. Petersburgh, Dec. 11th, 17—." The speaker notes he is far north of London in the cold breeze of Petersburgh, filled with a delight that results from his anticipation of traveling further north to "icy climes." He labels the breeze a "wind of promise" and notes that his daydreams grow more vivid. To him, the North Pole to which he hopes to travel is not a seat of desolation, but rather one of "beauty and delight" filled with light from a seldom-setting sun. He addresses Margaret, soon identified as his sister, and attempts to explain his anticipation of "a country of eternal light." His eagerness to "tread a land never before imprinted by the foot of man" conquers any fears, causing him to feel like a child partaking in a new adventure. He hopes to discover "the secret of the magnet" and feels exuberant about his purpose: "a point on which the soul may fix its intellectual eye."

The narrator reminds Margaret of his reading, when a child, volumes written about voyages of discovery in their Uncle Thomas's library. Before dying, their father had told his uncle to prevent the narrator from spending a life at sea, but that is precisely the life he later pursued. First, he spent one year "in Paradise" when he became a poet after immersing himself in Shakespeare and Homer. He failed as a poet and took up his present avocation, first gaining experience on a whaling ship in the North Sea, enduring much physical discomfort.

He performed so well that a captain offered him the second mate position. He tells Margaret that he could have enjoyed his inherited wealth and position but instead prefers glory, although he is sometimes depressed by his decision. He must sustain not only his own spirits, but also those of his companions. He describes the season as the best time for traveling in Russia, as the sledges are well equipped to travel over snow, and Russians wrap in furs to avoid suffering from the cold. He plans to depart for a town called Archangel in two to three weeks, hire a ship and sailors, and set off on his adventure, not knowing when he might return. He blesses his sister and asks that Heaven help save him, signing his letter, "your affectionate brother, R. Walton."

Letter 2

Again addressed to Mrs. Saville, England, the second letter is dated "Archangel, 28th March 17—." Walton notes the slow passage of time. He has hired a ship and sailors but longs for a friend with whom to share the joy of his future success or to support him should he fail. He will commit his feelings to paper but notes that it is a "poor medium for the communication of feeling." He regrets his early self-education and his focus mainly on books about voyages. Although he also read poetry, he should have studied languages, finding at the age of 28 that he is less educated than many schoolboys. His complaints are useless; he will find no friend in Archangel or on the ocean. He describes his lieutenant, an Englishman whom he praises as noble. The ship's master is bright, gentle, and courageous and possesses integrity. Walton credits his own abhorrence of the brutality often found on ships to his sister's nurture as he matured.

Walton next describes a sad story of lost romance attached to one mariner in his crew that recommends him as noble, though he is uneducated and "silent as a Turk." Walton assures Margaret that while he may complain in his letter, he has not lost his enthusiasm. He tries his best to describe his overwhelming emotions as he prepares to go "to unexplored regions," to "the land of mist and snows," quoting a line from Samuel Taylor Coleridge's *The Rime of the Ancient Mariner*. He concludes by wondering when he and his sister will be together.

Letter 3

In a brief third letter to Margaret dated July 7, 17—, Walton informs her he is in good spirits, along with his men, although they realize they will not be home again for years. They are moving through an icy sea, his having sent the letter to England via a ship sailing from Archangel. He notes some warmth is present due to southern winds and that he has nothing exciting to report, promising Margaret he will exercise prudence and not seek danger. However, he will have success, which he compares to a crown, asking, "What can stop the determined heart and resolved will of man?"

Letter 4

Dated August 5, the fourth letter begins with reference to a strange accident. Walton writes that he will describe it, even though he will probably see Margaret before a letter can reach her. He reports a dangerous situation the previous week when the ship was enclosed by ice and surrounded by a thick fog that halted progress. Once the mist cleared, the crew groaned to see enormous spans of ice, and then they noted something unusual. The group watched "a low carriage, fixed on a sledge and drawn by dogs" a half mile away, apparently guided by a giant. After its disappearance, they wondered if they had not seen an apparition. They could not follow, although they noted his track. Two hours later, the ice broke, freeing the ship, and Walton decided that they would depart in the morning. However, when morning arrived, a new sledge was discovered with only one living dog and a driver with a different appearance than the "savage" seen the day before. The stranger asked the destination of the ship, which surprised Walton, who assumed a person on the brink of death would desire rescue by anyone, regardless of their direction of travel. The stranger came aboard upon finding the ship's destination was the North Pole. Walton describes the stranger as almost frozen, emaciated, and exhausted; he fainted when carried inside.

After two days, the "guest" could finally speak. Walton describes how the man beamed "with benevolence and sweetness" unequaled, but his manner was "melancholy" and "despairing." He explains that he is chasing someone, and when Walton tells the stranger of having seen the giant on the previous day, the stranger is quite interested. Walton is curious but says he does not demand an explanation from a man in such a weak state, to which the guest replies that "you have benevolently restored me to life." A new spirit that Walton finds attractive seems to fill the stranger, prompting Walton to begin "to love him as a brother." Walton concludes the letter by telling Margaret he has at last discovered "the brother of my heart."

Walton stops writing and begins again on August 13, explaining how his affection for the stranger grows, describing him as gentle, wise, and cultivated, yet seeming to have been destroyed by grief. He shares with the stranger his desire for acquiring knowledge that would allow him "dominion" "over the elemental foes of our race." The stranger grows gloomy and proclaims, "Do you share my madness? . . . Hear me,—let me reveal my tale, and you will dash the cup from your lips!" Walton is amazed and shares with the stranger how much he has desired a friend; he thirsts for "a more intimate sympathy with a fellow mind." He has felt he could never declare himself happy without that blessing. The stranger agrees and speaks of having enjoyed such friendship, but he says that he has lost everything, pointing out that Walton still has hope and a bright future. Walton then explains to Margaret that despite the stranger's broken spirit, no one can enjoy nature's beauty to the extent that he can, describing him as having "a double existence," miserable yet able to retire into himself, assuming a celestial spirit. Walton notes that due to Margaret's refinement, she would appreciate the stranger whose voice he compares to "soul-subduing music."

The fourth letter contains a final section dated August 19, in which the stranger prepares to share his complete story with Walton, who is anxious to hear it but expresses concern that the exertion might be too much for his guest. The stranger appreciates the concern but notes that nothing can change his destiny. He says he will begin his tale on the following day, when Walton is free to listen. Walton tells Margaret he will construct a full manuscript of the story and describes remembering well the stranger's voice and appearance, one of "melancholy sweetness." He closes using a maritime metaphor to compare the stranger to a gallant and wrecked vessel.

Chapter 1

With the shift to numbered chapters, the stranger's voice takes over the first-person narration. He opens with an explanation of his Genevese heritage and the fact that his family is one of the most prominent in Geneva. Due to political interests, his father did not marry and begin a family until a mature age; the strange tells the story of his father's eventual marriage. When a dear friend lost his wealth and retreated from society, the narrator's father spent 10 months searching for him. He found his friend ill and in the care of his daughter, Caroline Beaufort. The daughter had a strong mind and much courage, and she took a job plaiting straw to help support her family. Her father eventually died in her arms, leaving her in poverty. The speaker's father placed her in the care of a relative and married her two years later, the vast difference in age seeming to bring them closer.

The narrator's father had a marked sense of justice and doted on his wife, whose virtues he revered, protecting her "as a fair exotic is sheltered by the gardener," spoiling and pampering her. They traveled to Italy, Germany, and France, and Walton's visitor was born in Naples, remaining the only child of two appreciative parents for some time. From his parents, he received lessons in patience, charity, and self-control; he was guided as if by a "silken cord."

The speaker's mother wanted a daughter. When the speaker was five years old, his mother discovered a poor family to care for, as she had cared for those living in poverty on Lake Como. She took her son with her to the family's home and noticed among their five children one little girl who contrasted with the others by her light coloring, thin build, and gold hair, which the speaker compares to "a crown of distinction." They discovered the child had been fathered by a Milanese nobleman; her German mother had died in childbirth. The father had disappeared in a political struggle, and the child stayed with the foster family. The speaker and his mother took the girl, described as a cherub, home to become, as the narrator states, "my more than sister." His father also loved the child, who became an adored and beautiful companion for the speaker. His mother had had the thought that she would bring the girl, Elizabeth, home as a gift for her son, now identified as Victor. While everyone loved her, Victor notes that she was his own possession. They referred to one another as cousin, and he knew she would be his until death.

Chapter 2

Elizabeth and Victor are raised together, with "harmony" as "the soul" of their relationship; about a year separates them in age. Elizabeth is calm and focused, and she pursues poetry, while Victor is passionate, intense, and more interested in knowledge than she. He enjoys investigating causes for occurrences in nature that Elizabeth admires from afar. For Victor, the world is "a secret" he "desire[s] to divine." Learning the hidden laws of nature brings him joy. A new baby, William, joins Victor, Elizabeth, and another son, Ernest, in Geneva, where they lead a blessed childhood existence in the country. Victor does not enjoy crowds but does appreciate a few close relationships, especially with a schoolmate named Henry Clerval, son of a merchant. Clerval enjoys hardship and danger; reads romances and chivalric tales; and writes songs, stories, and dramas. Clerval wants his friends to act in his plays, their characters drawn from tales of knighthood. Although sometimes demonstrating a violent temper and always passionate, Victor remains a scholar, focused specifically on "the secrets of heaven and earth" and the metaphysical mysteries of nature and man. He contrasts himself to Clerval, who is attracted to moral relationships, studying man's heroism and virtue and hoping to become a famous philosopher and writer. Meanwhile, Elizabeth's "saintly soul . . . shone like a shrine-dedicated lamp" in the idyllic home. Her gentle nature helps subdue Victor's rougher and more sullen personality. Clerval matures into a gentle, kind, and tender men, but he is still passionate for adventure. Elizabeth influences him to turn his soaring ambition to thoughts of doing good.

Victor remembers his childhood as positive. However, as a young adult, a passion arises that will rule his destiny: He begins to study natural philosophy, beginning at age 13 by reading work by Cornelius Agrippa. While Victor finds Agrippa's ideas exciting, his father dismisses them as "trash." In his narration, Victor wonders whether, had his father taken time to explain to him that new, more viable theories had replaced those of Agrippa, he might not have pursued their offer of "chimerical" powers, rather than the "real and practical" powers of more modern science. Victor reads as much writing by Agrippa, and also Paracelsus and Albertus Magnus, as he can find, studying their "wild fancies" with delight but always feeling dissatisfied. He equates his feelings with those expressed by Sir Isaac Newton when he compared himself to a child picking through seashells "beside the great and unexplored ocean of truth." Victor discovers that the most learned philosopher knew little more than he does; no one can speak of a "final cause" for life.

Victor continues reading 18th-century theory while following a routine education route, still in search of the philosopher's stone. He does not desire wealth but instead wants to learn the secret to banishing all human diseases and allowing man to avoid death, except of a violent nature, altogether. He even practiced incantations in the hope of raising ghosts until an accident alters his course. When he is 15, he and his family experience a violent thunderstorm during which he witnesses a "string of fire" descend from heaven, strike an oak tree, and demolish it in an explosion of light. While familiar with electricity, Victor seeks to learn more about it and also galvanism, a practice that astonishes him. Suddenly, he abandons his previous fixation, adopting a disdain for natural science and all "its progeny as a deformed and abortive creation." He studies mathematics and has the feeling that he has averted a storm "ready to envelope me." He enjoys feelings of peace and tranquility, but he concludes the chapter by stating, "Destiny was too potent"; his utter destruction is already assured.

Chapter 3

Victor leaves home to study at the University of Ingolstadt when he is 17. Before he departs, the first misfortune of his life occurs. Elizabeth has scarlet fever, and their mother cares for her, although others ask her not to. Elizabeth survives, but their mother does not. On her deathbed, she places Victor's and Elizabeth's hands together and tells them that all her hopes for happiness have been grounded in their future marriage. That expectation will continue to be their father's sole consolation. Victor experiences a natural grief that verges on bitterness, but eventually he decides that he has to overcome his feelings. He needs to accept that his mother is dead, and he must continue with his plans and duties. He delays his departure to the university for a few weeks, unwilling to leave his family and especially Elizabeth, who tries to comfort everyone. Victor has never found her so enchanting. Clerval spends the evening with the family prior to Victor's departure, and Victor can tell he wishes he could also have a university education. Parting is difficult, and Victor promises to write. He knows he must form new friendships at university but feels he is unfit to be with strangers.

On the day after completing the long and tiresome journey to Ingolstadt, Victor takes letters of introduction to his professors. Chance is "the evil influence, the Angel of Destruction" that takes control. Victor will work with Professor Krempe, a natural philosophy instructor, uncouth in appearance but steeped in the secrets of his profession. He terms Victor's study of the 18th-century sources a complete waste of time, noting someone should have told him of the folly of such focus; he should instead focus on modern science. Krempe sketches a plan of study for Victor and explains that another professor, M. Waldman, will instruct him in chemistry. Victor mourns the loss of his vision of boundless grandeur in exchange for what he characterizes as "realities of little worth."

Victor finds the self-aggrandizing Krempe contemptible, but Waldman is intriguing. When Waldman refers to the ancient teachers and philosophers, he explains they could perform miracles that modern science cannot as "they penetrate into the recesses of nature, and show how she works in her hiding places." Victor again focuses on pioneering and exploring unknown powers to reveal "mysteries of creation" to the world. (In this passage in the book, he first notes that his last name is Frankenstein.) So excited that he cannot sleep, he dozes in the morning and then begins to pursue the ancient studies. He discusses his past studies with Waldman, who does not dispute that men of genius, even if misdirected, generally make positive discoveries. After Victor explains in cautious terms what he hopes to accomplish, Waldman states that he views Victor as his disciple and explains that chemistry is a branch of natural science in which the greatest improvements have been made. He gives Victor a list of books to study.

Chapter 4

Over the next two years, Victor becomes close friends with Waldman and even learns to appreciate Professor Krempe's input. He spends many entire nights at work in his laboratory and improves some chemical instruments, gaining fame at the university. He no longer needs instruction and considers going home, but he discovers "the cause of generation and life" and understands he has the ability to bestow "animation" on lifeless matter. Victor has studied the human body intensely and has searched for the source of life, spending time in vaults and charnel houses (repositories for human bones). Nothing frightens him due to the intensity of his focus on preventing the beauty of humankind from becoming worm food. He is astonished to have discovered the secret, which, while overwhelming, also delights him. In his narration, he explains that he did not immediately understand how to reach his goal directly but instead could fashion his endeavors to point them toward the goal. He compares his situation to that of the Arab in a tale in which, buried with the dead, he finds a passage to life.

In the present, aboard the ship, Victor addresses Walton's eagerness and the wonder and hope in Walton's eyes. Victor asks him to be patient and listen to the entire story, promising not to lead him on. He asks that Walton try to learn from the story.

Back at the university, Victor hesitates in making plans to animate matter, realizing it will be a challenging feat. He debates whether to attempt to create a human or a simpler form. His imagination presses him to create the complex and wonderful human, understanding that his work may be somewhat imperfect. He spends months collecting and preparing materials. In his narration, he describes the great emotional upheaval he felt. By creating life, he will "pour a torrent of light into our dark world," and he thinks of the many blessings a new species will bestow on him as its father. He thinks if he can begin by bestowing life on something inanimate, he might eventually be able to recall people from death. He engages in a "secret toil" to collect body parts that he describes as horrible, all of his actions taking place at night with the moon watching him. He describes having lost all sensation and soul in favor of his one pursuit. He collects bones from charnel houses and "disturbs" secrets of the human frame. Although he loathes the activity of assembling body parts, he cannot stop his pursuit, which encompasses an entire summer.

Victor forgets his friends and family and ignores the beautiful and bountiful summer season. He thinks of his father's expectations to hear from him. Years later, looking back, Victor now understands that his father was correct: Any human should preserve a calm mind, regardless of the activity in which he engages. If study weakens affections, then it is not worth pursuing. He includes a list of tragedies that would not have occurred had humans enjoyed domestic affections: "Greece had not been enslaved; Caesar would have spared his country; America would have been discovered more gradually; and the empires of Mexico and Peru had not been destroyed."

Victor's father does not scold him in his letters; he simply inquires about Victor's activities. But Victor continues to ignore his family and spends another year in the laboratory, comparing himself to one who toils in the mines. He begins to suffer the consequences of his intense emotional journey, lack of exercise, and poor eating and sleep habits, but he ignores his deteriorating state, assuming that once he has completed his quest and the intense focus it requires, his health will return.

Chapter 5

The chapter opens: "It was on a dreary night of November," setting the tone for its events. Victor Frankenstein collects instruments in order to "infuse a spark of being" into the body he has assembled. As soon as his creation opens a yellow eye, Victor judges his work a catastrophe, the being a wretch. Although limbs are proportionate, the body muscled, hair a luminous black, and teeth white as pearls, those aspects make more horrible the "watery eyes," shriveled complexion, and straight black lips. He judges his two-year work a dream vanished, replaced by a feeling of "breathless horror and disgust." Victor runs from the room and throws himself onto his bed, where he suffers a nightmare in which he looks for and finds the beautiful Elizabeth, who then transforms into a dead corpse that further transforms into his mother's worm-riddled corpse. He awakens to find the "miserable monster" gazing at him, then grinning and attempting to speak. Victor escapes its outreached hand to race into the courtyard, where he spends the night.

Victor compares his creation to a hideous mummy brought to life, a wretch, something "even Dante could not have conceived." Victor feels as if he is in hell, opening his eyes after a restless night to see the steeple of a church. He runs through the city streets, explaining his feelings with a quotation from Coleridge's *The Rime of the Ancient Mariner* that concludes, "Because he knows a frightful fiend / Doth close behind him tread."

Victor stops in front of an inn and sees Henry Clerval; his delight at seeing his friend causes him to temporarily forget his misfortune. Clerval walks with Victor toward the university, explaining that he finally convinced his father of the value of taking "a voyage of discovery to the land of knowledge." Victor asks about his family, and Clerval tells him they are well, but he comments on Victor's ill appearance. Victor explains that he has been busy. When they reach his apartment, he fears Clerval seeing the monster, but a quick search of his room and laboratory reveal the monster has left. A servant brings breakfast, and Victor is so delighted by circumstances that he clasps his hand and runs and jumps like a child, alarming Clerval, who declares him ill. Victor imagines that he sees the creature enter the room, faints, and falls into a "nervous fever" that confines him for several months.

Clerval nurses Victor back to health and does not alert the family to the severity of his condition for fear of their reaction. Victor constantly sees the monster and raves in his fever, making Clerval decide his distress stems from a disturbing event. Victor slowly recovers and discovers the season is spring, its "divine" nature supporting his recovery. He begins to feel joy and affection, which replace the gloom, and expresses remorse to Clerval, who has missed classes in order to care for him. Clerval notes his recovery will be payment enough, but that he wants to speak with Victor about something. His statement frightens Victor, who for a moment supposes that Clerval must have discovered the truth about the monster. However, he simply asks Victor to write home, a chore Victor happily agrees to undertake.

Chapter 6

Chapter 6 opens with a letter from Elizabeth to Victor that begins "My dearest Cousin" and tells him that a single word from him will calm the family's fears. She has restrained his father from making the journey to Ingolstadt in his frail condition and wishes she had made the trip and been able to care for Victor. She tells him of the family's happy state, offering details of his brother Ernest's maturation and referring to the fact that their contented hearts "are regulated by the same immutable laws" that govern nature. Elizabeth reminds him of their servant Justine Moritz, who joined the family when her loving father died and her mother could not tolerate her. She had moved to the Frankenstein household at the age of 12, at Mrs. Frankenstein's suggestion. Elizabeth expounds on the freedoms allowed by "the republican institutions of our country" as compared to the monarchies around it, remarking that a servant in Geneva does not "mean the same thing" as one in France or England. Justine was a favorite of the family, particularly of Victor, and was afforded dignity and some education. Justine has repaid the family through her complete dedication and loyalty. Her siblings died, and her mother repented her hard feelings toward Justine and asked her to return home. Justine did not want to leave the Frankensteins but did as asked. However, her mother soon began harassing Justine, blaming her for her siblings' deaths. When her mother died, Justine returned to the Frankensteins.

Elizabeth next describes the youngest child, William, identifying a little girl whom he likes, and she shares some gossip. She concludes by again asking Victor to write. The letter is dated March 18, 17—.

Victor responds to Elizabeth and then takes Clerval to the university to introduce him to professors. Clerval rearranges Victor's apartment and his laboratory, having understood that they had bothered Victor. But when Victor and Clerval see M. Waldman, he "inflict[s] torture" with his praise for Victor's achievements in the sciences, making Victor "writhe" as if undergoing a cruel death. Victor tries to hide his discomfort from Clerval but can see that his friend recognizes his distress. Clerval does not ask about its source, for which Victor remains grateful. M. Krempe also praises Victor generously.

Clerval has no interest in science but instead desires to learn "oriental languages" as part of his literary pursuits. Finding a study of Persian, Arabic, and Sanscrit intriguing, Victor joins Clerval in his studies for temporary amusement. He finds the languages soothing, quite different from "the manly and heroical poetry of Greece and Rome." He passes another year in such pursuits and then plans his departure to travel home, enjoying long walks in nature with Clerval, who touches the "better" aspects of Victor's heart, making clear his love for his friend. Clerval "rejoices" in Victor's "gaiety" and begins to also invent tales based on eastern culture.

Chapter 7

When the friends return home one day, Victor finds waiting for him a letter from his father in which the elder Frankenstein warns him of "horrible tidings" that he must share. William is dead. He had disappeared when the family took a walk in Plainpalais. Having at first been with Ernest, William had run away to hide and never reappeared. The family searched until nightfall with no luck, but Mr. Frankenstein discovered his son's body at 5 A.M., the murderer's print still on William's neck. When Elizabeth saw the mark on William's neck, she exclaimed that she had "murdered my darling child!" She fainted and, upon revival, explained that she had permitted William to wear a miniature of his mother in an expensive locket and assumes its theft was the motive for the murder. Mr. Frankenstein writes that only Victor can console Elizabeth, and he must come home at once. The letter is dated May 12, 17—.

Clerval reads the letter and bursts into tears, then agrees to accompany Victor to order horses to take him to Geneva. As they walk, Clerval attempts to comfort Victor. He says that William now "sleeps with his angel mother" but also states how miserable it would have been for the child to have died in the way he did. He wants to take comfort in the fact that William now knows no pain. Victor immediately takes a carriage homeward, engrossed with melancholic thoughts. He is filled with dread, although unable to name its specific source. He weeps when he sees Mont Blanc, one of the mountains that represent his youthful innocence, an innocence now lost. As night closes around him, he foresees that he will become the most wretched of persons.

When he reaches Geneva, Victor cannot rest and decides to go to the scene of William's murder, which involves a short boat trip to Plainpalais. He watches lightning flash around the mountain peaks signaling a storm as he goes ashore. Terrific thunder crashes occur, and the fierce lightning makes the lake appear to be on fire. He describes the "temptest" as "beautiful yet terrific," the "noble war in the sky" elevating his spirits, proclaiming that it serves as William's funeral dirge.

Suddenly he sees a figure. When illuminated in the lightning, the figure is clearly Victor's "daemon." He shudders to think the monster may have murdered William, then becomes convinced that he did so. He chases the monster up to the summit of a nearby mountain and stands in the thick darkness, understanding that he has sired a criminal. As he comprehends the result of his actions, he is gripped by deep anguish. At dawn, he turns toward town and considers informing the authorities about the monster and the fact that he is the murderer. Second thoughts cause him to change his mind, as he worries that he would not be believed and might be thought mad. In addition, seeing the agility with which the monster raced over the ground and ascended a mountain, he doubts that a group of men could catch him.

He walks home and enters his house for the first time in six years, fixing his gaze on his mother's portrait, below which is a miniature of William. Ernest welcomes him sorrowfully, stating he wished his brother could have arrived three months previously, when the family was happy. He weeps as he explains Elizabeth cannot be consoled and remarks that the murderer has been caught. This news shocks Victor, who comments that he saw the murderer the night before and is puzzled as to how anyone could have caught him. His remark confuses Ernest, who explains that Justine Moritz has been accused, and he wonders how a person treated as a member of the family could suddenly become capable of this horrible crime. Victor expresses dismay and cannot believe Justine would murder anyone. Ernest says they all felt the same, but the irrefutable proof was the locket William had been wearing discovered in the pocket of one of Justine's garments. Their father joins them and states he had rather remained ignorant of Justine's actions than to learn of such depravity in a person he so valued.

Victor says Justine is innocent, and his father explains she will be tried that day. Victor remains convinced that she will be proven innocent and that he will not have to tell his tale of horror, madness, and vulgarity, which would alert his family and friends to the terror he has released on the world. Elizabeth tells Victor, calling him her "dear cousin," that his arrival fills her with hope. Victor thinks of how much he loves and values Elizabeth, and he tells her that Justine is innocent. Elizabeth cries, telling Victor how kind and generous he is. Their father adds that should Justine be innocent, "the justice of our laws" will free her.

Chapter 8

As the family awaits the beginning of the trial in the courtroom, Victor thinks that the decision will be made whether his "curiosity and lawless devices" would be the cause of death for two innocent people, Justine and William. He continues to focus on the fact that Justine's future will be obliterated by shame and the grave, which will be his fault. He thinks he would confess to the crime, but people would believe him insane, and that act would not save Justine. Justine, calm and dressed in black, appears confident in her innocence and is tranquil but seems confused. The facts do not support her claim of innocence: She was known to have been out late on the night in question and the next morning was seen close to the place where William's body was discovered. She became hysterical when shown the body, and then the locket was found in her clothing. At the mention of that discovery, everyone in the room murmurs in horror and indignation.

Justine attempts to defend herself with "a plain and simple explanation of the facts." She tells the court that Elizabeth gave her permission to visit her aunt in a nearby village on the night of the murder. Upon her return, she learned of the missing child and helped to search for him. She spent much of the night in a barn belonging to acquaintances and explains that she awoke at dawn after being disturbed by the sound of steps. As for the locket, she did not understand its presence in her pocket; she suggests perhaps the murderer placed it there. She did not realize that she had walked close to the place where William's body was discovered, and she states her innocence, pleading for the mercy of the court.

Several character witnesses speak well of Justine, and Elizabeth makes an emotional plea on her behalf, despite being the "cousin" of the murdered child. She explains that Mrs. Frankenstein had placed complete faith in Justine, who was responsible for William's care. She adds that despite the value of the locket, she would have willingly given it to Justine, so much is Justine valued in their family.

Victor becomes increasingly agitated at the thought that not only had the daemon committed murder, he had planned the execution of an innocent: "The tortures of the accused did not equal mine; she was sustained by innocence, but the fangs of remorse tore my bosom." He spends a wretched night and is crushed the next morning when a verdict of guilty is handed down. Victor is surprised to find that Justine has confessed to the crime. Elizabeth visits Justine at her request, although Mr. Frankenstein does not want her to. Victor accompanies Elizabeth, and when they enter Justine's cell, she falls to the floor before Elizabeth. She explains that she confessed in order to gain absolution, adding that her confessor had frightened her into doing so, threatening her with excommunication. Elizabeth declares that she will persuade the judges to withdraw their verdict.

Victor retires to a corner of the cell to consider his situation, believing that even Justine did not share his "deep and bitter agony." He knows he is the true murderer and understands that "the never-dying worm" in his heart that fills him with anguish and despair blocks all hope. He again feels he suffers more than Justine. Although she may be miserable, her innocence makes her troubles like a cloud that passes over the moon; his sorrow is permanent.

Elizabeth's plea for mercy fails, Victor again decides he cannot defend Justine by explaining about the monster or he will be declared mad, and Justine is executed on the scaffold. Victor feels guiltier than ever, especially when facing Elizabeth's "voiceless grief." His soul is "torn by remorse, horror, and despair" over the first victims of his "unhallowed arts."

Chapter 9

Victor cannot rest or sleep and wanders "like an evil spirit." He mentally reviews his actions in creating the monster, wondering how such benevolent intentions could have turned so wrong. His health suffers, and he seeks solitude. Hoping to help his son cope with what he supposes is grief over Justine's guilt, Mr. Frankenstein tries to convince Victor that they must help others by hiding their "immoderate grief." He also expresses concern that such sorrow will affect Victor's health and his ability to enjoy life.

The family stays at their house at Belrive, hoping the change will help them adjust to their sorrow. Away from home, Victor feels liberated and passes many hours on the water in the boat, even in stormy weather, at times considering suicide by jumping into the waters. The thought of his family's dependency on him for stability restrains him. He weeps often over the bitter loss of hope and abhorrence of "the fiend," his "hatred and revenge" bursting "all bounds of moderation."

His father is in failing health, and Elizabeth appears despondent, no longer the happy "creature" that Victor had cherished. As they talk, she speaks of how changed the world now appears following Justine's conviction and her realization of how "falsehood can look so like the truth." She is especially upset that the murderer escaped and may even hold a respected place in society. She also notes Victor's distress and asks him to release his passion for revenge, wondering whether his loved ones no longer help to relieve his problems. She states that if the family members remain true to one another, they will enjoy peace and happiness. But Victor knows that nothing, "not the tenderness of friendship, nor the beauty of earth, nor of heaven," will be able to redeem his soul. He seeks release through exercise and notices that over the six years during which he has destroyed his life, nature has not changed the "savage and enduring scenes" that he recalls.

In mid-August, almost two months after Justine's execution, Victor hikes through villages and into the Alps, admiring Mont Blanc as he climbs. His spirits are lifted, and he relives the "light-hearted gaiety of boyhood." The winds sooth him like a lullaby, and he sleeps well.

Chapter 10

Victor continues his climbing, admiring nature and its "immutable laws," evident in "sublime and magnificent scenes" that help console him, elevating him above his bitterness. He extols the restorative effects of nature at some length and climbs Montanvert to consider all that has happened. Recalling the moving glacier scenery, he wants to recover the "sublime ecstasy, that gave wings to the soul" from the past. Victor again extols nature, speaking of its "awful and majestic" effects. Lines from Percy Shelley's poem "Mutability" (1816) help illustrate Victor's thoughts regarding man's imprisonment by his emotions, something that differentiates humans from beasts. As he ascends to the peak, he speaks aloud: "Wandering sprits, if indeed ye wander, and do not rest in your narrow beds, allow me this faint happiness, or take me, as your companion, away from the joys of life."

He starts to see a sudden movement as a man moves toward him with superhuman speed, and he recognizes the "wretch" he created. The monster confronts him, and Victor screams at him, calling him a devil. The "daemon" responds that he expected such a reception and knows Victor wants to kill him; then he reminds the man that Victor is his creator. He adds, "Do your duty towards me, and I will do mine towards you and the rest of mankind." If Victor will not meet his demands, the monster will "glut the maw of death" with the blood of Victor's friends and family. Victor jumps toward the monster, who easily moves out of reach and requests that Victor be calm, asking whether he has not already suffered enough due to Victor's actions. He again reminds Victor that he is his creature, and he will comply with his "lord and king" if only Victor will give him what he deserves: "Remember, that I am thy creature; I ought to be thy Adam; but I am rather the fallen angel. . . . Every where I see bliss, from which I alone am irrevocably excluded. . . . Make me happy, and I shall again be virtuous."

The creature tells Victor that he owes him the opportunity to tell the story of what happened to him since leaving Victor's laboratory. He presents a logical argument, reminding Victor that the guilty are allowed to speak in their defense before being condemned. He reminds Victor again that he is Victor's creature: "Listen to me; and then, if you can, and if you will, destroy the work of your hands." He places his own hands before Victor's eyes to block the sight that Victor "abhors" and asks for compassion in honor of the virtues that he did once possess. Victor follows him across the ice for the first time, feeling "what the duties of a creator towards his creature were." As the monster begins his tale, rain falls.

Chapter 11

The monster describes a scene resembling that of the birth of a baby, noting that he vaguely remembers in the beginning seeing a light, experiencing strange sensations, being engulfed in darkness again, and at last noticing objects around him in the light. He took a walk, the light and heat bothering him. He found relief in the forest near

Ingolstadt, where he relieved his great hunger with berries and his thirst at a stream. He enjoyed the gentle light that later appeared and beheld a "radiant form" above him that lit his path so he could find more berries. He found a cloak to ease his discomfort and had no distinct ideas, only sensations. The moon was the only object that he could clearly distinguish.

As a few days passed, he began to distinguish between his sensations and focused clearly on the stream and the trees, delighting in pleasant sounds of nature. When he tried to imitate the sounds, he made only inarticulate grunts and noises. His eyes at last adjusted to the light, and he learned to distinguish one plant from another as well as differentiate between the various types of birds. He discovered a fire left by "wandering beggars" and learned that it inflicts both pleasure and pain. He also learned to add more wood to feed the fire. He observed that a breeze fanned the flame and then, at night, saw that it provided light as well as heat. After discovering some bits of cooked food, he tried placing his berries near the fire but found they were spoiled by the exposure, while roots and nuts were improved.

Due to a lack of food, the creature left the spot and traveled for three days through a new snowfall. He discovered a small hut and peered in, seeing an old man near the fire. When the man saw the monster, he screamed and ran away. The monster was "enchanted" by the hut and its ability to shield him from the elements: "[I]t presented to me then as exquisite and divine a retreat as Pandaemonium appeared to the daemons of hell after their sufferings in the lake of fire." He ate the food and slept until noon, then traveled over fields to arrive at a village, where he was amazed by the sight of people at work and play, the gardens, the animals, and the various styles of houses. However, when he attempted to enter the village, people immediately shrieked in fear, and he quickly departed. He discovered another cottage but did not enter, instead crawling into a "hovel" attached to it that provided shelter from the elements. He rested, contemplating "the barbarity of man." He stole some food and decided to remain there for a time.

Later, the monster discovered he could observe the inhabitants of the cottage by looking through a chink in the wall of the hovel that allowed him to see their movements outside. He observed a sad young girl who went outside to get a pail with milk and was soon joined by a young man with an even sadder expression who took the bucket to carry it into the cottage. The monster discovered another chink that permitted him to gaze into the cottage. He describes all that he saw but did not fully understand at the time: the family members interacting, an older man with a "benevolent countenance" playing an instrument, and the three people treating one another with kindness and affection. He observed them bringing wood for the fire and small amounts of food that they enjoyed. Each time the young people entered the cottage, the older man was happy. The monster enjoyed the contrast between the silver-haired, bent old man and the slight and graceful young man. He was amazed by the use of tapers for light at night and watched the people engage in "various occupations which I did not understand." He later understood that they sometimes read aloud, but at the time he "knew nothing of the science of words or letters."

Chapter 12

The monster continued to be touched by the family's gentle treatment of one another. He soon realized the old man was blind and admired the young people's respectful treatment of their elder. He wondered why they often cried and what was the source of their unhappiness. His lack of knowledge led him to believe they had every luxury, with the cottage for shelter, fire, excellent warm clothes, and their enjoyment of one another's company. He eventually figured out that part of their problem was lack of food: They had only one cow for milk and a few roots from the garden for sustenance. The monster was moved by the young people often sacrificing their food for the sake of the old man. He had been stealing from their food for himself and stopped when he realized the pain he was causing. He discovered that he could collect wood for the family to help them. He enjoyed their astonishment when they discovered the wood and the fact that his taking over that task allowed them time to work more in the garden.

The monster comments on the "godlike science" of the cottagers' communication of emotions and knowledge through "articulate sounds." He studied their use of words and began to learn language, using the entire winter to observe them and continue his education. He learned the young people's names—Felix and Agatha—and enjoyed watching the old man encouraging them through a change in the tone of his voice. Felix was apparently the saddest of the three, but he tried to be cheerful with his family. The monster noted several examples, including Felix bringing a flower in early spring to cheer Agatha. With further observation of the old man, the monster realized that when he read, he uttered many of the same sounds as when he spoke, suggesting the symbolic importance of something on the book's pages. The monster had a negative experience when he saw himself in a pool of water; compared to the beautiful forms of the family, his own ugly form filled him with feelings of mortification and despondence.

As the light lingered longer during the day, the snow vanished, and Felix could work more and produce more food. He conducted the old man on a daily walk. The monster observed rain and wind and took notice of all the changes around him. When the moon provided light, he collected wood for the cottagers that he left outside their door and enjoyed their reaction to these deeds by "an invisible hand." He learned words like *good, spirit,* and *wonderful* but did not yet understand their meaning. He loved the cottagers and viewed them as the "arbiters" of his future destiny. The monster worked hard to learn "the art of language." His spirits rose with the passing days of the new season that brought "bright rays of hope, and anticipation of joy."

Chapter 13

Felix seemed sad but appeared "ravished by delight" upon the arrival of a lady on horseback. The monster describes her as beautiful, dressed in a dark suit with a veil, having a musical voice and black braided hair. Felix kissed her hand and called her "his sweet Arabian." Agatha also kissed her hand and was just as happy. The monster understood that the lady, like him, was attempting to learn their language, repeating some of their words. Felix called her Safie when he told her good night. The monster wanted to understand the family's discussion but still lacked the necessary grasp of the language.

The next day, Felix went out to work, and Safie sat with the old man, playing the guitar and singing to him, her sounds like those of a nightingale. She persuaded Agatha to also play the instrument. Happy days passed as the creature continued his observation and noticed the blooming of plants, the warming weather, and the increased pleasure brought by his nighttime rambles. His speech improved as he learned "the science of letters," which opened a field of delight and wonder. He began to learn history as Felix read aloud Volney's *Ruins of Empires*. He wept at the fate of humans conquered by other humans and wondered at mankind's vicious nature. He wondered how people could be simultaneously powerful, virtuous, magnificent, and base, at times evil, but at other times noble. The creature listened in wonder to details of the book, often turning away in "disgust and loathing." The reading and discussions continued to open new doors to knowledge.

The creature's learning also provoked him to consider his own situation. He learned the importance of possessions, realizing he lacked possessions. He also had no knowledge of his creator and no friends. Such reflections caused him agony as he wondered whether he was merely a monster disowned by all humans. He began to think he would have been better had he remained in his "naïve wood." The nature of knowledge was complicated, he realized, offering both joy and sorrow. He also learned that the state of death would end all, and he came to understand that the gentle ways of the family were something he would never enjoy; he labels himself an "unhappy wretch."

The creature grew increasingly unhappy as he learned of the normal way of life, from the baby's birth to its development in childhood. No father had blessed his upbringing; his past was just "a blot, a blind vacancy," and he had seen no other creature resembling him. He repeatedly asked himself,

"What was I?" He continued to love the cottagers and thought of them as his protectors, but he would later learn how he had deceived himself with such thoughts.

Chapter 14
The creature learns the name of the cottagers: They are the De Laceys, descended from good French stock. He relates their history, beginning with the fact that they once lived prosperously in Paris. De Lacey's son, Felix, met Saphie when attempting to free her father, a Turkish merchant who had been imprisoned in France, presumably because of his prosperity and religious beliefs. Saphie's father caused the family's downfall. All of Paris was scandalized by the Turk's situation, understanding his innocence. The Turk at first offered Felix riches as a reward if he would help him to escape prison, but Felix refused. Then the Turk observed the fact that Felix was in love with Saphie, so he promised Felix his daughter's hand in marriage in exchange for Felix's assistance in his escape. Felix corresponded with Saphie with the help of an interpreter. At this point in the story, the creature tells Victor that he has the letters to prove the truth of his tale and will later give them to Victor.

Safie explained that her mother was a Christian imprisoned by the Turks, and she spoke highly of her mother's beauty and intelligence. She had instructed Saphie in her religion and stressed the importance of the "higher powers of intellect, and an independence of spirit, forbidden to the female followers of Mahomet." After her death, Saphie had clung to the lessons she learned. The Turk's execution was ordered and date fixed; Felix agreed to aid in his escape.

After rescuing the Turk, Felix, Saphie, and her father fled to Italy, where the Turk encouraged Felix's attentions toward Saphie, although he loathed Christians and had no intention of allowing Felix to marry his daughter. Meanwhile, the French government, outraged by Felix's actions, imprisoned Agatha and De Lacey. Felix returned to France in an attempt to secure the release of his sister and father, leaving the Turk and Saphie behind, where Saphie was to wait for him. Months passed before the trial, in which they were exiled and relieved of their fortune. Ultimately, the De Laceys moved to the cottage in Germany where the creature was vicariously absorbing his education in life and learning. The Turk betrayed Felix and withheld his daughter's hand. However, Saphie found some letters that provided the family's location. She took action despite her father's telling her that Felix had lost his money. When he told her he had to flee because the French authorities pursued him, she developed the plan to take some jewels and go to Germany. The girl who accompanied her fell ill and died, but Saphie found friends in the house where she temporarily lived. A woman there found a guide to take Saphie to join the De Laceys.

Chapter 15
The creature next tells Victor that at that stage, crime still was "a distant evil." He explains that he found a satchel in the woods containing three books: *The Sorrows of Werter, Paradise Lost,* and *Plutarch's Lives,* with which he begins to educate himself, referring to his findings as a "treasure." The monster read each book as factual, questioning his identity and purpose. They produced "an infinity of new images and feelings" that both excited and dejected him, provoking never-ending "speculation and astonishment." *The Sorrows of Werter* caused him to feel "something out of self" and filled him with wonder over its ideas about death and suicide. He began to see himself in the readings. He would feel hopeful, but he lost his sense of hope when he saw his reflection or his shadow in the moonlight.

From Plutarch, he learned to admire past heroes, although the information about kingdoms and countries confused him. The information about humans killing other humans upset him, and he admired the peacemakers. While reading *Paradise Lost,* the monster conceived the notion of a "creator" and identified with Adam due to his solitude and no link to any human. However, he felt slighted when he realized that Adam was crafted in the perfect image of his creator, while he was a monster and was left alone. He compared his existence with both Adam and Satan and felt he was in a worse condition than either, since he had no companionship, no Eve to soothe him at day's end.

The creature pieced together the mystery of his origin after reading Frankenstein's journal, which had been left in a pocket of his clothing. He descended into a state of self-loathing and began to crave companionship. In telling his story, he again returns to a comparison with Satan, stating, "Satan had his companions, fellow-devils, to admire and encourage him; but I am solitary and abhorred."

Despite the disappointment that his awakening sense of self-identity brought, the creature continued to enjoy nature and feel kindly toward the cottagers. He planned to approach the old man while the others were out, realizing it was his appearance that frightened others, and the blind man could not see him. He put his plan in motion, speaking to De Lacey, who was kind to him, stating that "this was the hour and moment of trial."

After he knocked on the cabin door, and De Lacey invited him to enter, the creature explained that he was a stranger who hoped some friends who live in the area would help him. The old man explained that he should not be afraid because humans were basically filled with "brotherly love and charity," and he urged the creature not to lose hope. De Lacey asked the stranger to tell him his story. The creature thanked him and called him his benefactor. De Lacey asked if he might know the identity of the stranger's friends. The monster cried out that the old man and his family were his benefactors, which confuses De Lacey. At that moment, Felix, Safie, and Agatha entered the cottage and were horrified at the sight of the visitor. Agatha fainted, Safie ran from the cottage, and Felix pulled the monster away from his father, where he clung to De Lacey's knees. He struck the monster with a stick. Although the creature could have easily killed Felix "as the lion rends the antelope," he resisted that urge. Heartsick, he left the cottage and sneaked back into the hovel.

Chapter 16

The creature cries to Frankenstein, "Cursed, cursed creator! Why did I live?" and asks why Victor did not destroy him before he became consumed by despair. He explains that he passed a miserable night in the hovel and departed the next day knowing the rest of the world was in peace and repose.

He no longer enjoyed the bird songs or nature; again he compares himself to "the arch-fiend," noting he "bore a hell within." Eventually, as he hid in the woods, the fine spring day restored some tranquility to him. He reconsidered the cottage experience, thinking perhaps he acted too hastily, had shocked the De Laceys, and should have introduced himself slowly. Calmed, he slept and enjoyed peaceful dreams, then found food and returned to the cottage. He waited, but the De Laceys did not return, although he observed two other men passing by, saying things he did not understand. Then Felix appeared with another man, and the creature heard them discussing a sale of the cabin, due to the fact that Felix felt the family was in danger and could no longer live there. The creature never again saw his family.

He remained in the hovel in despair, his emotions out of control as he experienced waves of feelings of revenge and hatred. Thoughts of the gentle Agatha and the old man would calm him, then anger him again as he considered their reactions to him. After the moon came out, a fierce wind "produced a kind of insanity" in the creature, who burned down the cottage as he danced around it. He ran into the woods and thought of what he had learned of geography in listening to Felix teaching Saphie as he decided where to travel. He again cursed Frankenstein for creating him able to experience emotions, while making him completely isolated from men who hated him due to his appearance.

As the creature traveled, "Nature decayed" around him, "and the sun became heatless." He was cold in the rain and snow and could find no shelter as he traveled toward Switzerland. When spring again arrived, it merely made him more bitter. He rested during the day and traveled at night. One morning, however, he again felt moved by the beauty of nature and walked through the woods in the restorative warmth of the sun. He heard voices close to a nearby river and walked in that direction. A young girl fell into the water and was in danger of drowning when the creature rescued her. Her father tore her from his arms and ran away, the creature running after them. When the man saw him following, he fired his gun at the creature, who escaped into the woods, wounded and in terrible agony. The creature vowed "eternal hatred and vengeance to all mankind" before fainting from the pain.

He survived for weeks in the woods as he healed, each day desiring revenge. At last, the creature arrived at Geneva. Exhausted, he fell asleep, and upon awakening, he saw a beautiful little boy approaching. Believing the child would not yet be prejudiced toward his appearance, he decided to seize him "and educate him as my companion and friend" in order to ease his loneliness. He grabbed the child, who struggled, and he told the boy he meant him no harm. The child demanded that the "ogre" release him or he will alert his father, to which the creature responded that he would not see his father again. The boy responded by identifying his father as the powerful M. Frankenstein, who would punish the creature.

Suddenly, the creature realized that he had in his grasp a member of Victor's family; he describes the "hellish triumph" he felt at the thoughts of destroying the boy in revenge. He noticed and took the locket with the picture of Victor's mother, which made him even angrier as he thought that such a beautiful creature would have rejected him. He murdered the child and then sought a hiding place in a barn that he believed to be empty. There he found a woman asleep and whispered for her to awake, "thy lover is near." The woman stirred, but did not awake. The creature thought that had she awakened, she would have reacted to him with horror, which angered him and made him decide that she should pay for his crime. He placed the locket in her pocket, having learned from Felix about the law and how to "create mischief." He remained close to the scene for days and then escaped to the mountains, waiting to confront Victor. The chapter closes with the creature's demand that Victor create a companion that shares his defects.

Chapter 17

When Victor looks confused, the creature repeats his demand, and Victor refuses, stating that "no torture shall ever extort a consent from me." The "fiend" tells Victor he is wrong, and he will convince Victor through the application of reason. He then presents the argument that because of Victor, he is shunned by all humans, although he would weep with gratitude if someone would offer him acceptance. However, he understands now that "the human senses are insurmountable barriers to our union." Because he remains unable to inspire love, he will inspire fear, and if Victor does not comply, he will destroy him. He contorts with anger temporarily but then again calmly speaks, repeating that he intends to use reason rather than passion. The creature labels his request reasonable, as he and his companion will disappear once united. He knows they may not be truly happy, but they will at least not be lonely.

Victor feels a stirring of compassion, understanding that he must bear responsibility as the creator of his own problems, feeling that he owes the creature "all the portion of happiness that it was in my power to bestow." The creature can see that Victor's mind has been changed and continues to speak, promising that he and his companion will travel to South America and live in the wilds. Victor asks whether they would not eventually return to the company of humans, but the monster responds that he "will quit the neighbourhood of man, and dwell as it may chance, in the most savage of places." He adds that his evil passions will abate, and he will die not cursing his creator. Victor's feelings soften under "the strange effect" of the creature's words. He wants to console his creation but sickens as soon as he looks at him and sees "the filthy mass" that speaks. The monster demands a response, as Victor reflects on the power of the creature and the potential for destruction. He decides that he must comply for the sake of his fellow humans. The monster swears that he will watch the progress of Victor's labor, and once it is completed, he will disappear forever. He ascends the mountain in his superhuman state more swiftly than an eagle.

As the sun sinks, Victor descends, his heart heavy and his steps slow. He weeps bitterly and yells at the stars and clouds, "if ye really pity me, crush sensation and memory; let me become as nought; but if not, depart, depart, and leave me in darkness." His return takes all night, and he immediately leaves for Geneva. The family is concerned by his haggard appearance, but they ask for no explanation, and he offers none, believing he has no right to play on their sympathies. Everything except for the reality of the task before him seems like a dream.

Chapter 18

Victor must devote several months of study in preparation for assembling the creature's female companion. The focus helps restore his health and spirits, a change that his father notices with pleasure. On occasion, however, a "devouring blackness" still overcomes him, but he takes walks to help pull himself back from the brink. His father tells him that he anticipates Victor's marriage to Elizabeth, but he asks whether Victor considers her more as a sister than a future wife, allowing that his son may have met someone else whom he loves. His father speculates that this may be the reason for Victor's occasional depressions. Relieved that his father has not guessed the truth about his distraction, Victor still recognizes that he cannot marry while completing his obligation to the creature. He knows also that he must travel to England to gather more necessary knowledge for his task. Victor does not want to assemble the female in or close to his father's house, where he might be discovered. Once he fulfills his promise, he knows the monster will be gone forever. In addition, the chance exists that the creature might suffer an accident and die even before Victor has made him a mate. Victor tells his father he wants to visit England for a few months. His father is pleased that Victor feels good enough to travel but wants Clerval to join him at Strasburg. Although Victor knows his friend will disrupt the solitude required to complete his task, he still rejoices in the thought of his company, because he will be rescued from countless lonely hours. He might even discourage the creature from intruding on Victor's work.

Victor prepares for his journey, thinking of the day that he might be free from his slavery and able to claim Elizabeth. He does fear leaving his family vulnerable to an attack by the monster, but then he remembers the creature vowed to follow and stay with him, so he will probably go to England. Victor regrets being "the slave of my creature," because he must be governed by impulses. Toward the end of September, he departs, with Elizabeth asking that he return soon. He packs his chemical supplies and leaves, unable to enjoy the majestic scenery through which he travels.

In Strasburg, Clerval joins Victor, who is struck by the contrast between himself and his friend, who is "alive to every new scene," extolling nature and enjoying existence, expressing his concern for Victor's seeming depression. They travel about and end up at the Rhine River, where Victor's spirits lift as he lies in the bottom of a floating boat on a lake. He feels transported to a fairy land, and he is filled with tranquility. Clerval extols the virtues of the location, labeling the river "divine." He states that the spirit of the place seems more in harmony with humans than that of the glaciers close to their home. Victor envies Clerval and admires the fact that he is a being formed in the nature of poetry, with an overflowing imagination, and he quotes from William Wordsworth's "Lines composed a few miles above Tintern Abbey" (1798) to capture the mood, saying he is part of "The mountain, and the deep and gloomy wood, / Their colours and their forms, were then to him / An appetite; a feeling, and a love." Victor asks, "Where does he now exist?" Walton (the narrator) then understands that Clerval will not survive, as Victor continues to wonder what happens to people after death. He asks Walton's forgiveness for his expression of sorrow, a light tribute to Henry Clerval's great value. He says that he and Clerval traveled on to Rotterdam and then to Britain, visiting London and its many historical landmarks.

Chapter 19

For several months, the two friends in London, where Victor finds the philosophical documents he needs to study in preparation for his work. Henry's voice helps soothe him when he is sorrowful, but Victor decides that following the murders of William and Justine, he will no longer be able to participate in normal activities with his fellow humans. He sees his former self in Clerval, who is interested in so many things and always busy working toward his eventual goal of traveling to India. Each time that Clerval leaves, Victor collects materials for his experiment.

They remain in London for several months and then receive an invitation from an acquaintance to visit Scotland. They depart for Perth in February, planning to spend one month exploring. Victor brings his instruments and supplies, deciding that "an obscure nook in the northern highlands" will offer an excellent place for his work.

They pass through Oxford, and Victor speaks of its history and the inhabitation of the city by "the spirit of elder days." But, however enjoyable the sights, Victor continues to suffer, comparing himself to "a blasted tree," where "a bolt" has entered his soul. He attempts to shake off his chains, "but the iron had eaten" into his flesh, and he remains miserable. As they move on, Clerval states he could live in their new Scottish surroundings forever, so strongly does the scenery affect him. Victor fears disappointing the creature and knows he must complete his mission. He anxiously awaits each letter from home with dread, afraid the monster has wreaked havoc on his family, the result of the horrible curse upon Victor's head. Clerval accompanies their friend on a tour of the country around Perth, giving in to Victor's plan to stay behind. After they leave, Victor walks out of town through an area of poverty and squalor and locates a miserable hut on an island that is perfect for his work. He repairs the hut, brings in furniture, and moves in, stating such an event would have surprised most people, but the villagers suffered from such poverty that they barely noticed. He works every day and almost finishes his labor, but his heart is sick at the work of his hands. His labor is advanced, and he anticipates its conclusion but feels a foreboding of evil.

Chapter 20
One evening in his laboratory as the moon is just rising, Victor reflects on what he is doing, wondering whether his new creation might not be "ten thousand times more malignant than her mate." She might refuse to comply with the monster's plan to leave the region, or she might leave him in disgust, seeking instead the beauty of humans. They might have children, "a race of devils," and if in they live in the wilds, their offspring cold prosper and again attack humans. The entire human race might be at risk. Then Victor sees the wretch watching him through the window with a malice and treachery on his face that makes Victor decide his occupation is mad, and he tears the female form to bits. The creature howls with "devilish despair and revenge" as he witnesses the act, and then he leaves.

Victor locks the room and returns to his apartment, where he stares at the sea beneath a quiet moon. He hears the door creak open, and then the wretch appears, demanding how Victor dared to break his promise. He declares that he has sneaked along, following Victor on all of his travels, suffering privation and fatigue, only to see his hopes destroyed. When Victor tells him to leave, the creature replies,"You are my creator, but I am your master—obey!" Victor states he will never resume the task, and the monster questions why every other man and beast should have a mate, but he cannot. Why should Victor be happy while he must remain wretched? He vows to watch Victor like a snake "that I may sting with its venom. Man you shall repent of the injuries you inflict." He departs, vowing to be with Victor on his wedding night. Victor tries to seize the creature, but he gets away to his boat and shoots across the waters. Victor later regrets not having pursued him to try to kill him, as he does not fear the monster, but he is worried about Elizabeth.

Then next day, Victor experiences a greater calmness, only because he has sunk to the depths of despair. He wanders like a spectre, thinking of the fiend's last words, which seem like a dream and yet are distinctly realistic. The sun sets, and Victor receives letters from home, as well as one from Clerval in which his friend requests that Victor join him. He determines to depart the island within two days, but first he must clean out his laboratory. He is sickened by the remnants of the body he destroyed, momentarily feeling that he killed a real woman. After collecting his instruments, he gathers the remnants of the female creature, feeling stronger than he had the day before. Although he understands that he must still accept the consequence of his actions, he also feels as if "a film" has been removed from his eyes. In the early morning beneath the moon, he goes out onto the solitary water, feeling as if about to commit a crime to dispose of the remnants of his experiment. After he drops the bag overboard, clouds cover the sky, and he sleeps soundly in the boat. When he awakens, the sun is up, the wind high, and the waves rising, threatening to flood his boat. He attempts to change course but makes matters worse; without a compass, he cannot tell which way to turn. He fears being driven into the Atlantic to starve or drown as the water roars around him. Tormented by thirst, he assumes the water will be his grave and curses the fiend, thinking of his family. After several fearful hours, the storm subsides, and Victor spots land. Although he is exhausted from his efforts during the storm, he constructs a new sail from his clothing and heads toward the land, musing over the strength of his desire to live.

Victor heads for the town and pulls his boat onto the shore, when a crowd begins to gather. They seem surprised at his appearance and whisper to one another, no one offering assistance. When he asks the name of the town, Victor is told that he will discover the name soon enough, and he is surprised by the rude response. He states that the English generally receive strangers in a more polite manner. A man replies that may be true, but in Ireland villains are not well received. The crowd grows, and the expressions the people assume alarm Victor. They follow and surround him, and one man tells him he must follow him to Mr. Kirwin, a magistrate where Victor is to give an account of the death of a man found murdered the previous night. While startled, Victor knows that his innocence will be proven. Although he feels weak and hungry, he struggles to maintain his composure and receive the charges. Little does he anticipate, he tells Walton, the frightful events that will occur.

Chapter 21

The magistrate speaks severely to Victor and then bids nearby men to tell their story. They relate how they discovered a man's body after setting out to fish the evening before. They believed him to have drowned at first, but then they discovered his clothing was dry and his body not cold. The victim appeared to be about 25 years old and had been strangled. Hearing the details of the strangulation, Victor becomes agitated. Additional witnesses relate having seen a man, believed to be Victor, in a boat. Others testified that in the strong wind of the previous night, Victor's boat might have come from far away to land at their village. Mr. Kirwin asks Victor to see the body, and he remains calm, knowing several people witnessed him on the island at the time the victim was believed to have been murdered.

When Victor views the body and sees that it is Clerval, he is overcome with grief and horror. He exclaims, "Have my murderous machinations deprived you also, my dearest Henry of life? Two I have already destroyed. . . ," and then he faints. He develops a fever lasting two months, during which visions of the murders of his loved ones torment him. He feels as if the monster has hold of his neck at times and screams for those caring for him to help him kill the fiend. Only Mr. Kirwin understands French, but Victor's voice and gestures frighten the others. He wishes to die, wondering why, when so many children and young lovers are lost, he would be allowed to exist, but he "is doomed to live."

Victor at last awakens one morning, and a sleeping old woman serving as nurse addresses him in English and asks if he feels better. She tells him he would be better off dead, as things will go hard on him due to the man he murdered. Memory floods back, and Victor feels isolated, with no one to sooth him or support him. He learns that Kirwin treated him well, placing him in the best cell and providing physician visits. As Victor sits dozing in a chair one day and wondering whether he should declare himself guilty and accept the punishment, Mr. Kirwin enters and addresses him in French. He explains that he believes Victor to be innocent. He had found letters on Frankenstein attesting to his home, and he wrote to Geneva two months previously, but he has received no answer. However, Victor's father has arrived, and he enters the cell, assuring Victor that Ernest and Elizabeth are fine. When his father mentions Clerval, Victor declares that a horrific destiny hangs over him, and he must survive to fulfill it. His father's presence is like that of an angel, and Victor begins to recover, although "absorbed by a gloomy and black melancholy." He tells Walton that his destiny will at last claim him sometime soon, but at that time, death was far away.

The grand jury acquits Victor, who continues to feel trapped in a dungeon, "the cup of life poisoned forever" and visions of the monster's watery eyes in his mind. He wants to return to Geneva, knowing he needs to protect the family and kill the fiend. Although his father believes him too weak to make the journey, he allows Victor to persuade him to return home. As they travel, Victor views the past as "a frightful dream," recalling his "mad enthusiasm" while creating the monster. He increases the laudanum he has been taking in order to sleep, and his father notes his restlessness. He awakens Victor, who hears the waves dashing against the boat and enjoys a brief sense of security, a "calm forgetfulness."

Chapter 22

When Victor arrives home, his father begins a program to reenergize his son, assuming he needs social contact, which is the one thing his son abhors. Victor feels he no longer has the right to seek amusement with other humans, having unleashed death upon them. They would all hate him were the truth revealed. After giving in to Victor's reluctance to partake in social events, Mr. Frankenstein tries to convince him of the "futility of pride" in the face of his son's self-accusation in the murders of William, Justine, and Clerval. The elder Frankenstein has never asked for a full explanation, nor has Victor offered one, despite the fact that he longed for a sympathetic ear. He cannot burden his family with the "unnatural horror" that he feels. Victor's father asks him to stop claiming responsibility for the deaths, to which Victor proclaims that he is not mad, and that all the elements of nature can bear witness to the truth of his claims. His father assumes Victor borders on derangement and never alludes to any of the deaths of family and friends in hopes of helping to "obliterate" their memory and speed Victor's recovery.

Victor becomes less emotional with the passage of time, feeling calmer than at any time since "my journey to the sea of ice." He receives a letter from Elizabeth that expresses happiness upon her learning that he is in Paris, safe and recovering. She has suffered all winter from an "anxious suspense" but hopes now for peace for the family. She takes that opportunity to express to Victor thoughts that she has previously kept secret. Reviewing facts of their childhood attachment, she reminds him that "as brother and sister" they "entertained a lively affection towards each other, without desiring a more intimate union." She wonders whether Victor might have fallen in love with someone else, and perhaps that has contributed to his melancholy. Had he done so, she can understand, as he has engaged in wide travel and they have lived apart for several years. She explains that should he feel duty-bound to fulfill their promise to marry, that would be false reasoning. While Elizabeth still loves Victor and wants the two to remain close, she desires his happiness as well. Marriage would be miserable for her if he did not enter into it freely. She requests that he treat the situation honestly, for if he could find happiness in another relationship, he must take that opportunity. He need not answer immediately; she bids him think about it for a time. She wants to see only one smile on his face due to her communication.

Victor recalls the monster's admonition that "I will be with you on your wedding night" and understands the demon will do whatever possible to kill him and destroy his chance for happiness. He thinks of death positively in that the monster's power over him will end. Death would grant him such freedom. Victor compares that independence to the freedom the peasant "enjoys" when his family has been massacred, his house destroyed, and he is left homeless. He is alone but free, and Victor's liberty would be similar. However, Elizabeth proves such a treasure that she is balanced by the "horrors of remorse and guilt" that pursue him until death. He rereads her letter multiple times, his heart daring "to whisper paradisiacal dreams of love and joy," but then he understands that "the apple was already eaten," meaning he sacrificed his future by yielding to temptation to gain the ultimate knowledge. He states he will die for Elizabeth's happiness, and if his marriage hastens his fate, so be it. Recalling that the monster had murdered Clerval as he awaited Victor's marriage, he reasons that his marriage would provoke an encounter with the creature and therefore would protect his father and Ernest from any retribution.

Victor calmly responds to Elizabeth that while little happiness may remain for them on earth, if any is to be gained, it will be through their union. He confides that he has a tale of misery and woe to share with her, which he will do the day following their marriage, as he desires complete confidence between them. A week later, he and his father travel to Geneva, where Elizabeth receives them warmly, but Victor notices that she has lost weight and "much of that heavenly vivacity" that had previously charmed him. However, that change is more suitable in a companion for one as wretched as he. He understands that the tranquility he has enjoyed will not endure. At times, he becomes filled with rage, despondent, and possessed by "a real insanity," countered by Elizabeth's gentleness and sweetness. She weeps with him, and when his reason returns, she tries to inspire him to endure, although he knows that "for the guilty there is no peace." His father admonishes Victor to transfer the love for those lost to those who still exist and look forward to the birth of a new, dear generation. Rather than taking hope from his father's comments, Victor can only think of the murders the monster has committed. He notes that his death is not an evil when balanced with Elizabeth's love.

At that point in his story, Victor cries, "Great God!" and tells Walton that had he known the future, he would have banished himself from Geneva and wandered about the earth. However, the monster seemed to have "magic powers" that blinded Victor to his true intentions. When Victor prepared for his own death, he instead "hastened that of a far dearer victim."

As the wedding day approaches, Victor maintains a cheerful appearance and brings joy to his father, but Elizabeth cannot be deceived. She seems to fear that hope may "dissipate into an airy dream." Victor arms himself with pistols and a dagger.

Victor learns that through his father's efforts, the Austrian government will restore much of Elizabeth's family fortune. They marry surrounded by friends and family and agree to have their honeymoon at Villa Lavenza near Lake Como, part of Elizabeth's restored estate. Elizabeth is tranquil and seems happy, and Victor's father is overjoyed. The couple depart via water to spend a night at Evian, and Victor experiences happiness for the last time. They enjoy the beautiful scenes of nature, and he comments again on the majesty of Mont Blanc. He looks upon the mountains as an insurmountable barrier to the monster. Although Elizabeth appears sorrowful, when Victor attempts to comfort her, she tells him her heart is content, particularly surrounded by the natural beauty; they can see the fish and pebbles through the clear water. As the sun sinks, they pass the river Drance, and Victor describes its relationship to the mountains. The wind remains soft, and the flowers give off a pleasant scent. However, when their boat comes to shore, Victor again experiences fear; he notes that such fear and concerns would soon "cling to me for ever."

Chapter 23

After enjoying a short walk as darkness falls and commenting on the lovely scene, the couple retire. The wind rapidly escalates "with great violence" as the moon begins to descend, with clouds sweeping across it "swifter than the flight of the vulture." Victor's previous calm turns to anxiety, and he remains watchful, determined to "sell my life dearly" and not shrink from conflict. Elizabeth becomes fearful as she watches Victor, detecting his terror, and asks the source of his agitation. He bids her to be at peace, telling her they must pass through this "dreadful" night and then all will be safe. Elizabeth goes up to bed as Victor explores the house, inspecting any place that might hide the monster. Suddenly he hears a "shrill and dreadful scream," and the "whole truth" rushes through his mind, causing him to be unable to move for a moment. Then he rushes to the room.

Victor exclaims to Walton, "Great God! Why did I not then expire! Why am I here to relate the destruction of the best hope, and the purest creature of earth?" He describes Elizabeth's lifeless body thrown across the bed, her head hanging and her hair covering her distorted features. Even now Victor continues to see her bloodless limbs and "form flung by the murderer on its bridal bier." He faints and falls to the ground, awakening to find himself surrounded by people all looking terrified. He describes their feelings as only a shadow of his own. He rushes back to the bed to see Elizabeth's body now rearranged so that her head is on the pillow, a handkerchief covering her face and neck. He embraces her, but her lifeless nature is soon clear. Victor then notices the "murderous mark" on her neck. He looks up to see the fiend peering at him through the window, illuminated by the pale moonlight. The creature grins and points to the corpse, causing Victor to rush the window, drawing his pistol and firing. The monster runs "with the swiftness of lightning" and plunges into the lake.

A crowd gathers, alerted by the pistol shot, and helps cast nets into the water in hopes of catching the creature, but without result. While many in the group think that Victor may have just imagined the "form," they divide into search parties. When Victor attempts to join them, he falls down utterly exhausted, a "film" over his eyes and his skin "parched with the heat of fever." He is carried to bed and remains barely conscious, arising after some rest. He crawls into the room with the corpse, around which women are weeping, and adds his tears to theirs as his thoughts wander. He remains "bewildered in a cloud of wonder and horror" as he considers the many deaths he has caused, thinking that his father and Ernest might even be dead. The thought fills him with resolve to return to Geneva. Because no horses are available, he must return by lake, although a storm rages. He attempts to row the boat along with others but is "incapable of any exertion." When the rain stops, Victor can see the fish and is reminded of the trip recently made in the opposite direction with Elizabeth. He remarks that nothing proves more painful to humans than change, a pain that he is experiencing; nothing will ever appear the same. The fiend has stolen all possibility of future hope for happiness.

Victor pauses to remark to Walton that he should not dwell on the events following Elizabeth's murder. His tale has been one of horrors; what is left to relate will be tedious. Although his strength is exhausted, he will add a few details.

Victor arrives at Geneva, and his father is greatly affected by the news of the death of Elizabeth, "his more than daughter." Within a few days, he dies in Victor's arms. Victor experiences darkness and chains pressing in on him, although he occasionally dreams of pleasant scenes. He suffers what others call madness for months, existing in a "solitary cell." He awakes to a desire for revenge and is possessed by rage when thinking of the monster. He prays that he might be able to kill him.

Eventually, Victor is able to tell the magistrate of the monster's acts, labeling him "the destroyer of my family" and seeking the assistance of the law to apprehend and punish him. He warns the magistrate that his tale is strange but "too connected to be mistaken for a dream," noting that he has no motivation to lie. He maintains a calm manner and briefly relates his history with precision, including accurate dates. The magistrate is incredulous but listens intently. When Victor tells him it is his duty to pursue the creature, he responds that the accused's superpowers would render any of his efforts useless. Victor suggests that the creature is probably in the Alps and can be hunted like any other animal. The magistrate agrees to pursue the suspect but advises Victor to prepare for disappointment, as he will probably elude pursuers. He also suggests that Victor control his desire for revenge. Victor states that his rage is unspeakable in light of the magistrate's reaction to his "just demand." He will devote himself to apprehending the creature. He trembles and seems to possess "that haughty fierceness which the martyrs of old" supposedly had. When the magistrate attempts to sooth him, Victor responds, "How ignorant art thou in thy pride of wisdom!" He departs to contemplate his next act.

Chapter 24

Victor has almost lost the capability of rational thought; fury and rage consume him, but thoughts of revenge give him strength and help bring calm and calculation. He decides to leave Geneva, taking some money and family jewels to support himself as he begins a wandering lifestyle that will cease only with his death. He will travel widely, enduring much adversity and at times longing for death, but revenge will keep him alive.

Upon first deciding to leave Geneva, he does not have a good plan and wastes time wandering about the town, unable to decide upon a path. He goes to the graveyard where his family members are buried and speaks aloud near their tomb. He notes that their spirits seem to gather around him and cast a shadow. Victor's grief gives way to rage and despair as he considers the fact that all of those dear people are dead while he and their murderer live. Kneeling, he kisses the earth and vows "by the shades that wander near me . . . and by thee, O Night, and the spirits that preside over thee," he will pursue the demon to death and remain alive until he can fulfill that act. He requests that the "wandering ministers of vengeance" help him and cause the monster to "drink deep of agony." A fiendish laugh rings out in reply, and the mountains echo it, tormenting Victor. Then he hears a voice whisper, "I am satisfied: miserable wretch! You have determined to live, and I am satisfied." Victor runs toward the voice and sees the creature flee in the moon's bright light.

For months, Victor pursues the monster through Germany to the Mediterranean, where he sees "the fiend" hide himself on a vessel bound for the Black Sea. Although Victor boards the same boat, the monster inexplicably escapes. Victor continues tracking the creature through Tartary and Russia where peasants frightened by the sight of the monster sometimes help guide Victor after him. He endures cold, hunger, and fatigue, feeling cursed by a devil and as if he carries with him a personal hell. He occasionally gains some relief by what seem to be good spirits that uplift him and provide food, with a fortuitous cloud dropping rain for drink, then vanishing. He follows rivers, but the demon avoids them as congregating places for humans. Victor gives villagers meat from animals that he kills and money to help him. Only when he sleeps can he feel any peace. The good spirits send hours of happiness in pleasant dreams to help him retain strength to complete his pilgrimage; the hope of the night sustains him during the day. His father, Elizabeth, and Clerval visit him in visions, and he sometimes pretends while he marches that he is in the middle of a dream. They haunt him so clearly that at times he convinces himself they still live. He continues his pursuit of the monster as if he were under some power over which he has no control.

Victor speculates on the feelings of the creature as he pursues him, occasionally finding writing, which the monster has cut into trees or stone to guide him. The creature invites Victor to follow him north to "the everlasting ices," where he will be miserable in the cold. Victor renews his vow of vengeance and thinks of death as an opportunity to join Elizabeth. Soon he sees only a few hovels, and rivers are ice-covered. He finds another message from the creature, advising him to find furs to wear and to procure a store of food as they begin a journey on which Victor's suffering will satisfy the monster's hatred. The words inspire Victor to continue, and he finally spots the monster on the horizon. He compares the iced water there to the blue seas of the south, but he thanks the guiding spirit for bringing him to the water's edge. He procures dogs and a sledge, hoping to catch the monster before he arrives at the shore. Victor enters a village and learns the monster had invaded it, taken over a cottage, and stolen supplies, a sledge, and dogs, then departed across the ice, to the villagers' relief. They believe he will perish by breaking through the ice, as he has traveled away from land.

Victor despairs, believing the monster has permanently eluded him. He will have to begin a surely fatal endless journey across mountains of ice. As a native of a "genial and sunny" climate, Victor will be unable to survive long. The thought that the monster may live while he might die enrages Victor. He rests and feels the spirits of the dead gather around him, renewing him. He trades his sledge for one designed to use on ice, replenishes his supplies, and departs the village, thereafter enduring days of misery.

Victor has no idea how many days passed before Walton brought him aboard. At times he had heard "thunder" that he thought was the ice cracking and feared falling through into the water, but frost would return and solidify the ice again. Judging by the amount of food he had eaten, he guesses that he traveled for three weeks. At one point, as he thought he might give up and one of his dogs died, he spotted the creature far away, "a dark speck," which made him weep. After resting and feeding his surviving dogs, he continued his pursuit, never losing sight of his prey for a time. But after a while, he could no longer see his foe, and he heard a ground swell beneath him. The wind arose, and the ice cracked, opening a gap of water between Victor and the creature.

Some of Victor's dogs died as he passed many hours on the ice floe. On the verge of losing all hope, he spotted Walton's ship and was astounded to see a vessel so far north. Losing strength, he guided his ice raft toward the ship and was taken on board, his task uncompleted. He wonders if his guiding spirit will allow him rest and also whether he will die, while the monster survives. Victor asks Walton to swear to kill the monster if he ever encounters him, should Victor die before he can complete the deed. He does not go so far as to request that Walton pursue the creature. He does warn him not to be fooled by the creature, who is "eloquent and persuasive," and not to trust him. Walton should call out the names of the monster's victims to give him strength to plunge a sword into the monster's heart, and Victor promises that his own spirit "will hover near, and direct the steel aright."

At this point, the journal entry stops, and the notation "Walton, *in continuation*" appears, followed by the date, August 26, 17—. Walton again addresses Margaret, asking whether the tale's horror has not congealed her blood. He describes Victor's "fine and lovely eyes," at times brightly lit and at others "quenched in infinite wretchedness," and how his voice occasionally breaks when speaking. Sometimes Victor retains control of his emotions, but at other times, he resembles "a volcano bursting forth," shrieking in rage. Walton judges the tale "connected" and told as if truthful, and it is supported by the letters of Felix and Saphie that Victor has supplied, as well as by the fact that Walton had spotted the creature on the ice. When Walton asks Victor for the details of the monster's creation, he refuses to share them, terming Walton's desire to know "senseless curiosity." He bids Walton to learn from his memories and not create the same miseries for himself. Victor amends Walton's notes to guarantee that all details are correct. A week has passed during the time that Victor has related the story.

Walton tells Margaret that he has become thoroughly involved with Frankenstein and his tale. He is consumed by interest in his visitor and hopes to help him gain peace before his death. Walton explains that Frankenstein truly believes his dead family and friends appear before him from "regions of a remote world." Victor's faith in their presence makes them almost as interesting to Walton as if he shared Victor's vision. They sometimes discuss subjects other than Frankenstein's tale, including general literature, in which Walton judges him to have enormous knowledge. Victor is eloquent and speaks so effectively that he brings Walton to tears. Walton writes that Victor "seems to feel his own worth, and the greatness of his fall." He tells Walton that as a young man, he believed himself destined for greatness, and upon his creation of a "sensitive and rational animal," he would rank himself above others. However, such thoughts now oppress him, and he is "chained in an eternal hell." He addresses Walton as a friend and wishes they could have known one another prior to his "state of degradation."

Walton expresses frustration to Margaret that he must lose the friend he has just discovered. He had found someone to "sympathise with and love me," but as soon as he has realized that friend's value, he will lose him. He has tried to urge Frankenstein to live but is repulsed. Frankenstein thanks him for suggesting that new friendships could be formed but states nothing can replace the loved ones he has lost, adding the companions of one's childhood always exert a certain hold that no later friend may replace. Those early friends may better judge one's actions and motives, with a sibling never capable of suspicion of one's actions like an acquaintance might be. Wherever he goes, the spirits of Clerval and Elizabeth accompany him, and he hears their voices. He must complete his task of killing the monster in order to fulfill his "lot on earth" and then die.

The next section is dated September 2. Walton wonders to Margaret whether he will ever see England and his friends again. The mountains of ice surrounding his boat threaten to crush the vessel. While he retains his hope, the thought of his responsibility for the other lives onboard is "terrible" as he realizes that his "mad schemes" could cause their loss. Then he wonders how Margaret will feel should he perish. He pictures her awaiting his return, perhaps for years, in despair and "tortured by hope." That prospect proves "more terrible" to Walton than his own death. However, he adds that she has a husband and children and bids her to be happy. He notes that Frankenstein regards him with compassion and tries to bolster his hope; he "talks as if life were a possession which he valued." Victor reminds Walton that other navigators who ventured to the north have had such accidents, which does cheer him. The sailors also benefit from his eloquence, and his voice and attitude uplift and fill them with energy. While strong, the effect is transitory, and Walton fears a mutiny fueled by the crew's despair.

In the following section, dated September 5, Walton begins by stating that a scene of "uncommon interest" has occurred that he will record, although he is aware that Margaret may never read the record. He describes the continuation of excessive cold and the threat from the surrounding mountains of ice; several of his comrades have already died, and Frankenstein's health continues to decline. While he is sitting in his cabin with his friend, Walton's crew enter. They ask him to promise that if an opening in the ice appears, he will take the opportunity to depart and not continue the journey. Before Walton can reply, Frankenstein answers the demand. He wonders how they are "so easily turned" from their plan. He reminds them they had labeled the undertaking glorious, not because it was easy but precisely because they anticipated and met danger and death. Overcoming those challenges requires courage and honor. They had longed to be "hailed as the benefactors of [their] species," but at the first imagination of danger, the first trial of that courage, they shrink, becoming content to be known as "poor souls" who could not endure the elements. Running away requires no preparation, he states, and then exhorts them to "be men, or be more than men. Be steady to your purposes, and firm as a rock. This ice is not made of such stuff as your hearts be." He urges them to return "as heroes who have fought and conquered." Walton praises Frankenstein's tone and inflection, then asks the men to depart and consider their guest's words. He agrees not to press them to go further north if they do not want to, but he hopes their courage to complete the deed will return. Walton concludes by telling Margaret that he would prefer death to the shame of returning without completing his purpose.

In a few lines written on September 7, Walton tells Margaret "the die is cast," and he has agreed to return if able to do so. His hopes are "blasted by cowardice and indecision," and he will return "ignorant and disappointed." He requires more "philosophy" in order to "bear this injustice with patience."

On September 12, Walton writes that he will return to England and that he has lost "hopes of utility and glory" as well as his friend. He describes the events of September 9, when horrendous cracking sounds from the ice in every direction greatly endangered the ship and its crew. However, Walton was busy tending to Frankenstein, on the verge of death. On September 11, a passage to the south opened, and the sailors shouted with joy, awakening Victor, who asked about the cries. Walton explained, and Victor replied that Walton might give up his purpose, but Victor would not. His desire for vengeance would strengthen him as needed. When he tried to jump from his bed, he fainted, and the ship's surgeon confirmed he had only a few hours to live.

Victor regained consciousness later and told Walton that although his emotions do not run as high as in the past, he still desires the creature dead. He reveals that he has been reviewing his past and does not regret his actions. The creation of a rational being resulted from "a fit of enthusiastic madness," and Victor feels that he fulfilled his duties to his creation. While he owed the creature some attention, he owed his fellow humans more. Their needs were greater in proportion to happiness or misery, leading him to refuse to create a female companion for the creature. In response, the monster displayed "unparalleled malignity and selfishness, in evil" through the subsequent murders. Because the creature showed such irrational thirst for vengeance, Victor feared it might not end. Victor should have destroyed the creature, and he renews his request that Walton do so. He understands that the ship is now leaving the North, and he asks Walton to use his own best judgment in deciding what to do with the monster.

Victor then tells Walton that he hastens to the arms of forms that flit before his eyes, anticipating his release at last from torment. He advises Walton to "seek happiness in tranquility, and avoid ambition," although he knows he has no right to pass along advice that he has not followed himself. He tries to speak again a short time later but cannot, and then he dies. Walton labels Victor's death "the untimely extinction of this glorious spirit" and regrets that he has no words to describe the depth of his sorrow. He weeps and experiences a cloud of disappointment overwhelming him; he hopes to find consolation with his return to England.

Suddenly, Walton hears loud noises and wonders what the sounds mean, occurring at midnight. He tells his sister he must investigate their causes and bids her good night. When the account begins again, Walton opens with the exclamation, "Great God! what a scene has just taken place!" He will try to describe "this final and wonderful catastrophe."

When Walton enters the cabin containing Frankenstein's body, he sees the monster. He describes him as gigantic and uncouth, with distorted features. He hangs over Victor's coffin, his long hair over his eyes, and extends a huge hand resembling that of a mummy. To Walton, the creature appears loathsome and hideous, and, trying to remember "his duties" toward the monster, Walton asks him to remain. The monster speaks to the corpse, labeling Frankenstein a "generous and self-devoted being" and noting it is too late for him to ask Victor for pardon. He takes responsibility for destroying Victor by destroying all that he loved. Walton slowly approaches, not wanting to look the monster full in the face. He tells him any repentance is now "superfluous. If you had listened to the voice of conscience, and heeded the stings of remorse" prior to wreaking vengeance, Frankenstein would remain alive.

The creature asks whether Walton dreams that he did not suffer agony and remorse. He claims that Victor suffered only a portion of his own agony, taking responsibility for "a frightful selfishness" with its roots in a heart poisoned by remorse. His heart had been fashioned for love and sympathy and endured

Photograph of Boris Karloff as Frankenstein's monster from the 1931 production of *The Bride of Frankenstein* (Universal Studios)

unimaginable tortures "when wrenched by misery to vice and hatred," repeating that no one can imagine the torture such change has wrought on him. He had pitied Frankenstein and hated himself. However, when allowed to hope for a companion and happiness and seeing that hope destroyed by one who sought his own happiness and joy, he was filled with a desire for vengeance and became a slave to such passion. Evil became his good.

Walton admits to being touched by the monster's words until he recalls Victor's warning that might happen, due to the creature's ability to speak and reason well. He calls the monster a wretch and a "hypocritical fiend," reminding him that had Victor lived, the creature would have killed him. Walton suspects the creature feels regret now simply because the victim of his "malignity" has been removed by death from his power. The creature responds that the accusation is untrue, but he knows he can gain no sympathy now. He repeats a litany of the destruction of his former hopes in several sentences that begin, "Once I . . ." He acknowledges that crime has degraded him to the point where he may no longer be recognized as that being with thoughts "once filled with sublime and transcendent visions." Although he destroyed Frankenstein's hopes, that did not satisfy his own desires, which were always for love and friendship and justice. Why should Walton think him the only criminal, when men like Felix drove him from his door, and the father of the child he rescued from death tried to kill him? He acknowledges he is a wretch and explains to Walton that he abhors himself far more than others can hate him and longs for the day his imagination will no longer haunt his thoughts.

The creature assures Walton he will commit no further mischief, but that he plans to kill himself. He will build a funeral pile and "consume to ashes this miserable frame," in part so no one else might make another creature like him. He will release himself from sufferings, knowing that once he is gone, any memory of either Victor or of him will vanish. He will seek happiness from the passing away of senses that once brought him joy from nature. Bidding Walton, the last man to ever see him, farewell, the creature also says "Farewell, Frankenstein!" He again declares that however "blasted" Victor was, he had experienced a superior agony. Soon he shall die and make extinct his "burning miseries" as he ascends to the funeral pile "triumphantly," exulting in the torture of the flames. If the monster's spirit will not "sleep in peace," it at least will no longer suffer painful thoughts. He leaps out of the cabin window onto a waiting ice raft and is "soon borne away by the waves, and lost in darkness and distance."

COMMENTARY

Frankenstein can be profitably examined by almost every critical approach. It offers through its formal elements of plot, character, setting, style, and point of view abundant material for traditional formalist critics and supporters of New Criticism. New Historicist critics look at connections between Shelley's life and times and her writings, an approach applied in the discussion of the introduction below.

Critics employing political approaches such as Marxism and feminism find much to appreciate in the novel, as do those peering through the lens of PSYCHOANALYTIC CRITICISM, postmodernism, deconstruction, and structuralism. In addition, *Frankenstein* offers ample material for still later critical approaches, such as queer theory. Intertextualist critics can view *Frankenstein* within its literary and linguistic context, studying the texts to which Shelley refers to better understand it. Finally, a critic may compare and contrast any work of literature to its author's additional works in order to focus on autobiographical elements and themes important to that author. Of course, various critical schools may examine the same passages and elements in a work of literature and discover they evoke more than one "meaning" to the reader. Thus, a critical discussion of *Frankenstein* presents many overlapping analyses of identical fictional elements and passages. Such overlap proves that varied critical applications offer different lenses through which to view the same work, depending on the ideology or methodology applied. While the following critical discussion does not claim to be exhaustive, it offers examples of many approaches. As *Frankenstein* is certainly Mary Shelley's most significant work, it is here discussed more thoroughly than other entries in this volume.

Frankenstein's Introduction

Mary Shelley's introduction to her 1831 edition of *Frankenstein* has surely become one of the most referenced introductions to any novel. Only here do critics find answers to questions regarding the novel's origin, and Shelley claims that her publishers requested that she discuss the topic. One understands the curiosity that contemporary readers must have had regarding the monster's genesis from the mind of "a young girl," as Shelley labels herself. Some may see Shelley's apology for her "personal intrusion" as the echo of a trope used by female authors from previous centuries who did not want readers challenged by their female gender. Others view Shelley's sentiment as a precursor to later years, when she claimed to desire no attention at all, in contrast to her husband's circle of friends, with their disreputable lifestyles. Still others look to the introduction as an attempt to replace the original preface to the novel, written for the 1818 first edition of *Frankenstein* by Percy Shelley. One effect of that preface and of comments by Mary Shelley in her later introduction has been to cause some skeptical readers to believe that Percy, not Mary, wrote the novel. They point to Mary's additional remarks about Percy in the introduction to further their cause. Some might interpret Mary's statement that "At this time he desired that I should write, not so much with the idea that I could produce anything worthy of notice, but that he might himself judge how far I possessed the promise of better things hereafter" and her additional claims of domestic duties and intellectual pursuits as excuses not to write to support a claim for Percy's authorship. However, another group reads Mary's complete remarks about Percy as indicting his attempts to interfere with her work, an intrusion that she managed to overcome. Mary, however, shares credit for the inspiration of the novel's birth with Percy, explaining that at first she wrote only a few pages, but her husband "urged me to develop the idea at greater length." She adds that while her husband was not responsible for any single incident in the novel, if not "for his incitement, it would never have taken the form in which it was presented to the world," except for the preface, which she credits to him.

Shelley also had to deal with expectations based on her parents' accomplishments: "My husband, however, was from the first, very anxious that I should prove myself worthy of my parentage, and enroll myself on the page of fame." While she has no qualms about admitting the great effect on her, "a devout but nearly silent listener," of exposure to Percy's conversations with Byron regarding "the nature of the principle of life," she makes clear that it was "my imagination, unbidden" that "possessed and guided" her. Those who know of the romantic ideal of the "masculine divine" would recognize a split between that ideology and Mary Shelley's statement that "supremely frightful would be the effect of any human endeavour to mock the stupendous mechanism of the Creator of the world. His success would terrify the artist; he would rush away from his odious handywork, horror-stricken."

Those who embraced the idea that imagination could move them beyond mere human capabilities would not necessarily see an attempt to imitate the Creator as undesirable.

Shelley's reference to the novel as "my hideous progeny" may reflect on her 1822 miscarriage, although she follows by bidding that literary progeny to go into the world and prosper, claiming that it represents for her that happier time prior to the loss of her husband, before she had personally experienced the "death and grief" that characterized her novel. She concludes the introduction by explaining that alterations to the new edition are in "style," rather than substance, perhaps developing from her maturity, not only as a person who had come to know intense grief and loss, but also as a storyteller.

The Letters

Shelley narrates the beginning of the novel through letters between Walton and Margaret, and she concludes the novel in the same format. In addition, letters scattered throughout the novel between Victor and his family members frame much of the novel's action. By adopting the letter format, Shelley draws on a tradition that dates back to Samuel Richardson's epistolary narrative *Pamela* (1741), which was, prior to feminist claims in favor of Aphra Behn's *Oronooko* (1688), long celebrated as the first English novel. While today's readers may find Shelley's approach odd or even annoying, her original readers would not. During their era, written messages were the norm, with documents of all sorts passed from hand to hand. Correspondence framed their lives, as it does Shelley's plot.

It was Percy Shelley who urged Mary to expand her novel. According to original plans, the story would have opened with Victor Frankenstein's narration in what eventually became the fifth chapter with the line "It was on a dreary night of November." Shelley decided, perhaps in reaction to her husband's advice, to provide an opening narrative scheme to lead readers into Victor's tale. She selected one that her readers would find familiar and plausible, that of letters from Walton to his sister.

The personal nature of the letter supported sentimental fiction, such as *Pamela*, in its attempt to stress emotion or personal feelings over rationality, and instinctive acts based on compassion over more measured actions dictated by duty. *Pamela* is also viewed as a work that prefigured psychological realism, emphasizing character motives as key to the translation of internal feelings to external actions. Authors of psychological realism were far more interested in why their characters behaved in a certain way than in the particular behavior itself. Shelley's story is simultaneously personal, sensational, hyperbolic, and realistic, with its emphasis on the senseless nature of man's attempts to control his own fate. It also focuses on motivations for Victor's and the monster's actions, the "why" of their behavior.

Shelley begins with four letters from Walton to his sister. Afterward, the story is told through journal entries, labeled as chapters, that feature Victor's story as well as the monster's tale embedded within Victor's. The narrative thus runs several layers deep and allows Walton's voice and desire for adventure and glory to parallel that of Victor Frankenstein. Shelley's format accommodates Victor's mentoring of Walton as he becomes the teacher, his instruction forcing him to examine his motives. The desires of the two men mirror each other, but Shelley makes clear that if Walton will view Frankenstein's life as a cautionary tale, he may be able to avoid the disaster he is courting through his desire for fame and glory. Readers are prepared early for Frankenstein's effect on Walton when Walton writes of his feelings of isolation and his longing to have a friend. As he explains to Margaret, he feels that in Frankenstein he has discovered a soul mate. He tells Frankenstein that he wants to hear his story, in part to possibly "ameliorate" the grim fate to which Frankenstein has alluded. He does not at first realize that the story's purpose will be to empower him to avoid that fate.

As the two men meet on a great expanse of white ice that symbolizes ultimate isolation, Shelley emphasizes the destructive power of the lack of friendship and family on an individual. Walton remains in a better situation than Frankenstein; his isolation is, for the most part, a physical one. He retains his sister as family and with her readily shares his fears, doubts, and aspirations. Frankenstein reminds Walton of the potentially destructive nature of passion that is allowed to escape the bounds of intellect. For instance, in the lengthy fourth letter, Walton remarks that his visitor must conquer "the violence of his feelings" and appears to "despise himself for being the slave of passion."

The endless expanse of ice also symbolizes Rousseau's tabula rasa, an untried element that offers immense potential. Frankenstein and the monster sully that innocence and potential by introducing the evil represented by their shared experiences. As did the Ancient Mariner in Coleridge's *Rime of the Ancient Mariner,* Walton may better recognize life's temptations and the potential for evil set against such an enormous, clean backdrop, where every speck is magnified in contrast. While his own ship, a male symbol of aggression and desire, has penetrated the virgin ice, it is held captive long enough for Walton to learn the lesson that Frankenstein's life provides. Realizing the importance of their setting, Frankenstein even tells Walton that were they "among the tamer scenes of nature," he might fear Walton's ability to believe the story he plans to tell. However, in such "mysterious regions" that suggest the "ever-varied powers of nature," Walton will find "evidence of truth" in the tale.

The critic Brian Aldiss is not alone in suggesting that Shelley may have been thinking of Lord Byron and Percy Shelley as models for Walton and Frankenstein. The two men greatly admired each other, holding long, in-depth conversations that deeply impressed Mary Shelley. She may have perceived herself at times as audience, student, and perhaps even voyeur, and she offers her reading audience the same role that she had played to her husband and Byron.

The importance of such personal information to understanding the novel is precisely the claim made by those who advocate critical approaches such as cultural poetics or the New Historicism. In taking one of these approaches, one could also propose that Mary is closely related to Margaret, a silenced female who is meant only to absorb her brother's information, not to contribute to the narrative. However, she emphasizes the importance to any writer of an audience and suggests that even when writing "private" journal entries, authors keep in mind the possibility of an eventual audience. Perhaps that audience will only consist of their future selves returning to their work with a new perspective that allows old words to assume different meaning. On the other hand, journal keeping was such a common practice that many nonprofessional writers engaged in that activity. They would see Walton and later journal keepers, such as the protagonist of Shelley's *The Last Man*, as engaging in the expected when recording for posterity their thoughts and occurrences. Such records proved crucial in contributing to the collective memory of family members and gave women who participated in journal writing a voice with the promise of it one day becoming public.

Victor Frankenstein tells Walton that he "had determined, at one time, that the memory of these evils should die with me." The opportunity to offer Walton a better future through the relation of his own trials drives Frankenstein to tell his story. Interestingly, he does not protest Walton's recording of the story, despite his earlier statement that he assumes he will not be remembered. He even offers to edit Walton's record to guarantee its accuracy. He hopes that Walton's attempts to gratify his desires will not "be a serpent to sting" Walton as Frankenstein's desires did to him. He also hopes the story will impart a useful moral to Walton. Indeed, Walton finds the story's startling originality and moral grounding irresistible as a tale to pass on to his sister.

The letters introduce Frankenstein as a sympathetic character, describing him as sweet and melancholy. Once readers come to know Frankenstein through the novel, they are likely to disagree with this generous assessment. Frankenstein is not naturally "sweet," a peculiarly feminine description. His ambition causes him to seldom think of the welfare of others. To clarify, he may often think of others and feel anguish over causing them distress, yet he is unwilling to alter his behavior or to confess his guilt to anyone other than the monster.

Walton's sympathy probably grows from his recognition of a kindred spirit: He states that Frankenstein has become a brother to him, and the two reflect one another in personality and desire. Walton may be seen as an alter ego of Frankenstein. He may represent the scientist's innocent stage, while the monster is the mature version, representative of Frankenstein's freakish desire. After all, it is not Frankenstein's desire for knowledge that perverts him, it is his desire for power. Walton seems to be closely related to Frankenstein, especially when he selects Archangel as his point of departure. An archangel is appointed by God for some specific duty and has been associated with both the Fall of man (Lucifer was an archangel) and his protector (Michael is an archangel). The city symbolizes Walton's final chance for rescue, but he follows temptation and does not turn back from seeking after glory. Thus, he leaves faith behind, instead choosing adventure.

New Criticism

One of the most common critical applications to any text is that of New Criticism, an approach based on formalism, or the analysis of the formal elements of literature in any work. New Criticism views every literary work as possessing an inherent meaning wholly independent from forces outside the text. It offers readers a systematic method of uncovering that meaning based on a "close reading" of the text, with careful attention paid to its formal elements.

An important aspect of the element of style is an author's use of symbolism. Some of the most obvious symbolism is often contained in character names, and this is true of Frankenstein. Victor's name remains ironic, as he obviously does not complete the hero's journey in a victorious manner. Elizabeth serves as a symbol of spiritualism, her name meaning "child of God," while the name *Clerval* suggests clarity of vision. Justine, her name symbolic of law and justice, is manipulated by the creature and by her culture, resulting in a most unjust death. *Felix* is Latin for lucky or successful. Felix is fortunate until taken advantage of by Safie's father. The name *Agatha* derives from the Greek for one who is good or honorable, characteristics that Agatha embodies. Safie, or Sophie, is a French name rooted in the Greek *sofia*, meaning wisdom. She enables the creature to learn language and to gain wisdom by sharing her own knowledge.

An important nature symbol throughout the text is the moon, which plays the role of revealing and concealing characters. The moon traditionally symbolizes the female. It produces no light of its own but must instead reflect the light of the sun, typically a male symbol. In addition, the moon is connected to cycles and controls such natural forces as the tides, strongly relating to woman's menstrual cycles and to the force of conception and birth. Thus, the moon is the first object of interest to the monster, who prefers its soft (feminine) light to the brutal (masculine) light and heat of the sun. Shelley comments on the displacement of the woman by a man in birth and nurture, clearly indicating the price to be paid for Victor's "unnatural" conception of the monster. The moon continues to provide light to the monster when he must travel at night in order to evade other humans, acting as a nurturing presence and literally affording the monster vision and a sense of life. In addition, light represents knowledge in many instances, so the moon's light helps illuminate the knowledge required by the monster for survival. It witnesses Victor's destruction of the female form that he had agreed to fashion as a mate for the monster, and it accompanies him onto the water, where he dumps her "body." Although prior to his going onto the lake, which joins the sea, "all nature reposed under the eye of the quiet moon," a short time later the moon is hidden by clouds, suggesting the feminine source of life as obscured by Victor's actions. The moon's "pale yellow light" in chapter 23 illumines Elizabeth's chamber of death and also reveals the monster's face in the window, while in the final chapter in the graveyard, "the broad disk of the moon" brightly reveals the monster's presence.

Traditionally a symbol for cleansing or new life, water also plays a crucial role in *Frankenstein*. The first water readers are introduced to is that in the oceans that Walton travels. He travels north into the grip of freezing weather, transforming the life-giving waters into ice that threatens his survival and that of the crew. Victor pursues his creation, his progeny, over ice, ironically representative of birth waters that will end rather than produce or sustain life. The sea and ocean are mentioned dozens of times. For example, in the final chapter in the four-paragraph section that begins "Some weeks before this period" and concludes "made the paths of the sea secure," Shelley uses sea references eight times. Victor often ventures onto lakes, generally seeking escape. One instance may be seen in chapter 9, following Justine's execution, when Victor goes alone onto a lake where he contemplates suicide. In chapter 20, Victor takes his boat onto the lake to dispose of the remains of the female creature he had intended to make but then destroyed. When he throws the basket of remains into the lake and it sinks, the water assumes reverse significance, suggesting death rather than life. After dozing in the boat for a time, Victor awakes to a storm and fears he may drown, be "swallowed up in the immeasurable waters that roared and buffeted" around him. Rather than representing the gentle birth waters associated with the female womb, the lake again represents death, due to the presence of a male who has murdered, not produced life. However, Clerval, who remains a child of nature, is delivered after death from the lake's birth waters, his ironic rebirth serving to publicly accuse Victor of murder.

Shelley uses other traditional symbols, such as colors, to make her point. Mont Blanc and the snow represent purity, due to their whiteness. Elizabeth's golden hair as a child symbolizes value, further emphasized by its description as a crown. Another traditional symbol in Western literature liberally employed by Shelley is the snake and the serpent. One example appears early in the story when Frankenstein tells Walton that he hopes desire will not serve as a serpent that stings Walton as it did him. In chapter 20, the monster tells Victor he will watch him like a wily snake and sting with a snake's venom. When the creature burns down the De Lacey cabin, the flames are described as forked tongues, calling to mind snakes. Darkness is traditionally evil and light good, and Shelley employs much light/dark imagery in that representative manner. However, she also inverts that dichotomy, which will be discussed at greater length below, to make dark more positive than light. An example is the night providing protection for the monster, who must remain hidden as he travels. Fire, like water, may symbolize new life or cleansing. Shelley uses it thus in chapter 16 when the monster burns down the De Laceys' cottage, effectively erasing his recent past, so that he may begin anew. Fire also represents hell, and in that same scene, the flames support Shelley's frequent use of the terms *devil*, *demon*, and *Satan* to emphasize the hell that life has become for Victor.

Additional symbolism may be seen in the depiction of various enclosed spaces, all representative of the female womb. Examples are the laboratory, hovel, hut, and house. The laboratory and hovel can be viewed as the creature's place of creation and gestation. He gains knowledge in the hovel through reading, the words birthing his intellect. He also learns of life by observing the cottagers, giving birth to emotions and self-awareness. The time spent in the forest and then the hovel both represent stages of childhood development, during which time nature nurtures the monster in the absence of his parents. The two-room hut in Scotland where Victor devotes "the morning to labour" as he creates the female creature also represents a womb, although its labors will produce a miscarriage of Victor's efforts. Victor focuses on "the consummation of my labour" and speaks of the fact that his "labour was already considerably advanced." Such language gives clues to the reader of the symbolic importance of the hut as a womb and Victor's actions as a substitute for the birth labors experienced by women.

Irony, another aspect of style, means basically that things are not as they seem, and it is abundant throughout the novel, with several instances already noted. Victor's open admiration of nature and its support of an inherent order is ironic in view of the fact that he attempts to pervert that order by usurping God's and woman's positions as creators. Irony exists in Victor's name due to his failure. It is also reflected by the knowledge that he can save Justine by identifying himself as the creator's monster. Generally, knowledge is liberating, but in this instance, it renders Victor helpless in his inability to communicate with others. That lack of ability is also ironic in its contrast with the monster, who communicates well. In addition, Victor's initial motivation for his creation of the creature is to bring special knowledge to the world.

Instead, he brings tragedy and reveals his own terminal ignorance regarding the ways of God and man. Additional irony may be seen in the monster's acute sense of self as contrasted with Victor's lack of self-awareness and recognition of his own monster within. Elizabeth's remarks about the superiority of Geneva's justice system and its more enlightened view of servants turns ironic when the innocent servant Justine is later executed. Also, her comments to Victor that as long as the family members are together they will experience peace and joy proves ironic, as Victor, the family's center, brings every family member destruction and death. Mrs. Frankenstein's dying wish for Elizabeth and Victor to be married in order to support hope for the future also becomes ironic as their marriage terminates Elizabeth's life. These examples represent a few of the many instances of irony in the novel.

Shelley also uses imagery to help set tone, an aspect of style, throughout the novel, her abundant detail another stylistic aspect that more modern readers may find distracting. Aldiss reminds us that we must keep in mind the narrative techniques of Shelley's day, because writers and readers did not yet consider "the novel as architecture" with the focus mainly on plot—the events or action of the novel. They viewed the novel as storytelling, which allows side ventures into environment and emotions. For instance, in the 10th chapter, Victor describes rain and mist that support his "dark melancholy." It greatly contrasts with his first feelings upon seeing the glacier that filled him "with a sublime ecstasy, gave wings to the soul, and allowed it to soar from the obscure world to light and joy. The sight of the awful and majestic in nature had indeed always the effect of solemnizing [his] mind." The many scenes in boats on water also incorporate imagery that may serve as a metaphor for a life challenged by outside forces, as sailors are by the natural elements. Storms arise when Victor confronts special conflict or feelings of desperation, his inner turmoil mirrored in Shelley's nature imagery.

Shelley masterfully emphasizes contrast thematically as well, particularly the contrast between man and God, and man and woman, as creators. In the 16th chapter, the monster tells Victor, "From you only could I hope for succor, although towards you I felt no sentiment but that of hatred. Unfeeling, heartless creator!"—making clear Victor's failure as creator. The monster's early experiences contrast greatly with those of Victor, who enjoyed traditional nurture by two parents. Victor tells Walton in chapter 2, "No human being could have passed a happier childhood than myself" due to his parents' "spirit of kindness and indulgence." He viewed them as the "creators of all the many delights which we enjoyed." He later labels his mother in chapter 3 "this best of women," and he notes her "fortitude and benignity." Shelley clearly depicts Victor as a weak and useless father figure, accomplishing much of her characterization through contrast with his own parents.

Shelley also incorporates abundant figurative language, or comparisons, in metaphors and similes. Victor speaks of "the cup of life," poisoned forever for him following Clerval's murder. In chapter 18, he compares his melancholy to a monster, terming it a "devouring darkness" that threatens to "overcast the approaching sunshine." Shelley includes another comparison in chapter 16 as the monster destroys the De Lacy cabin and remarks that the flames cling to the cottage "and licked it with their forked and destroying tongues." Flames are compared to serpents, a metaphor that supports Shelley's emphasis on temptation. In another type of comparison, personification, Victor says in chapter 8, "Thus spoke my prophetic soul."

The ability to read and write is labeled "the science of letters" by the creature, and Shelley calls attention to the scientific method by emphasizing all that the creature observes as he learns. Most of the women are, at some point, compared to angels to stress their good, caring, and innocent natures. They may then be seen as the opposite of the monster, who is often compared to Satan, a fallen angel. Victor's experimentation that produced the monster is compared in chapter 8 to "unhallowed arts," indicating the creative but evil nature of the experiments that produced the monster. In addition to using figurative language as an aspect of style, Shelley also inserts paradox on occasion. For instance, as Walton writes to his sister of Victor in the final hours of life, he describes his surroundings as "these desert seas." Juxtaposition of the terms *desert* and *seas* allows emphasis on the identical isolating effects of greatly contrasting geographic areas.

Theme acts as another element of fiction, important to the formalist critical approach. Brian Aldiss labels *Frankenstein* "a triumph of imagination; more than a new story, a new myth." He bases his judgment in part on its focus on morality as a major theme. While clearly a science fiction tale, *Frankenstein* emphasizes issues of morality and ethics more strongly than the topic of scientific pursuit. Victor Frankenstein's own sense of morbidity overtakes his passion for scientific inquiry as he explains to Walton in chapter 4. He describes having to spend all of his time in preparation for his creation in "vaults and charnel houses," causing him to sink "into a shadowy state beyond reach of other human beings." He shudders as he notes his obsession with "every object most insupportable of the delicacy of human feelings . . . I beheld the corruption of death succeed to the blooming cheek of life: I saw how the worm inherited the wonders of the eye and brain." When Victor discovers the secret of life, he compares himself to scientific geniuses and notes, "Remember, I am not recording the vision of a madman," adding that he experiences "delight and rapture" when he realizes the extent of the knowledge he possesses. And yet, as Victor attends court in Geneva after William's murder, he thinks that if he spoke of his creation of the creature, his declaration "would have been considered as the ravings of a madman." After suffering through Justine's execution due to his actions, Victor possesses a "voiceless grief" and his soul is "torn by remorse, horror and despair." The creature reminds him that he ought to be Victor's Adam but instead is "the fallen angel," or Satan.

Victor reacts to the monster's request to create a mate for him by imagining the two together as representing a "joint wickedness" that "might desolate the world." Later, he becomes slave to his creation and is consumed by melancholy resembling madness; he burns with rage to destroy the monster. Victor's thoughts of the monster extracting revenge upon Elizabeth cause his imagination to create "a thousand images to torment and sting me." His giving into his passions rather than acting in a rational, moral manner leads to the repeated sin of murder, for which he must take responsibility. He becomes possessed with hatred and the desire for revenge, which renders him "like a restless spectre," as if he already exists among the walking dead due to his immoral acts. Victor's loss of a moral center leads first to a metaphorical and then to a literal death, strongly communicating Shelley's message of the importance of morality.

The New Historicism

A reader may turn from formalism or New Criticism to New Historicism for an expanded view of *Frankenstein*. New Historicists believe one should not separate history and culture from literature, as each informs the other. Such critics cite Shakespeare as a major force behind such a view, crediting him with blurring the distinctions among history, literature, and politics.

Although no single creed unites New Historicist critics, they all maintain that the historical analysis that prevailed in the mid-1800s to the mid-20th century was inadequate, which would bring into question many of the sources with which Shelley worked and also explain her struggles and those of her mother. They, along with other active women, were often judged based on what appeared to be indisputable facts, such as the lack of women's influence on history and social matters. Only males were considered responsible for any cultural and historical achievements through all of time. With revision of such viewpoints, New Historicists would later reject the idea that one can objectively determine the events of an historical period and instead argue that history is interpretive. The founder of the movement, Stephen Greenblatt, argued that art and society are interconnected, and therefore New Historicism should be thought of as a way of reading, rather than as a critical practice. Such an approach has opened many classics like *Frankenstein*, as well as Shelley's other works, to new interpretations. Greenblatt renamed New Historicism *cultural poetics*, a term allowing for the concerns of the theory of how art and society affect one another and often contradict each other. That theory accommodates the conflict seen between the highly moralistic themes of Shelley's writing and lifestyle, and that of the romantics with whom she shared her time and their culture.

The cultural and political atmosphere of the 1960s through the 1980s largely impacted the formation of cultural poetics. This time period also saw the development of the feminist movement and FEMINIST CRITICISM; both critical approaches encouraged a rediscovery of traditional texts through the new openness to consider the effect of culture on art. Cultural poetics struggled with the concept of undecidability as practiced by New Critics and challenged the idea that one could approach history objectively. Critics admitted to their biases and began to view a text as culture in action. It is important to note that there is no single definition or creed of cultural poetics, so it may be easier to break it down into two generic schools: cultural materialism and New Historicism. Both share concepts crucial to critical work on *Frankenstein*. They each call for a reawakening of our historical consciousness, declare that history and literature must be analyzed together, and desire to place texts in an appropriate context. In providing the historical context for various texts, we are simultaneously learning about ourselves, our own habits, and our own beliefs. New Historicists would claim that Shelley used *Frankenstein* to accomplish that purpose, interrogating her culture's mores and social codes.

Like Shelley's other novels, *Frankenstein* focuses in part on challenges to the survival of the family unit by the independent male ego that seeks to satisfy itself at the cost of others. She thus challenges the 19th-century ideal of the family unit in which the male offers major support and the woman acts as a helpmate. The Frankenstein family is male-centered, rather than family or community-centered, interested in individual accomplishment on the part of its eldest son and service on the part of its women. Victor Frankenstein leaves the family and ignores Elizabeth in order to pursue the romantic notion dubbed the "masculine divine," a state in which the male commonly and, often without admitting he does so, rejects familial love in order to save the world. Shelley constantly critiqued the man who ignored his family responsibility, privileging his own desire for fame and accomplishment.

Many critics see Shelley's critique as focused on Percy Shelley. Although Mary adored him, her journal reveals that at times she did feel abandoned by Percy and often not deserving of sharing his company and that of his friends. In her novel, to strengthen her critique, she created the De Lacey family as a counter to the Frankenstein family. It celebrates its female members: Agatha and the independent and intellectual adventurer Saphie. In addition, the younger male of that household, Felix, unlike Victor, assumes responsibility for placing his family in danger and causing their exile by his activities in support of the treacherous Turkish merchant. For Shelley, prioritization and care of family represented a moral imperative, and *Frankenstein* strongly reflects her belief.

Feminist Criticism

A feminist critic would find much of interest in the novel. FEMINIST CRITICISM grew from the political movement in America, England, and France during the 1960s and reflects varying ideologies. While *Frankenstein* may easily be interpreted in terms of feminist issues, one must take care not to project the practice of feminism in the 20th century on Shelley, who in the second decade of the 19th century would not know the term or think to apply it to herself. Nonetheless, her mother's work was claimed by later critics as the first true feminist writing, and Shelley's works have been fruitfully examined by feminists two centuries after their publication.

In the late 1970s, the feminist scholar Elaine Showalter defined three phases of female writing. The *feminine* phase, during which women accepted social mores that defined their roles in patriarchal terms, lasted from about 1840 to 1880, following Shelley's career. The *feminist* phase, 1880 to 1920, produced women writers who developed oppressed female characters in their stories in order to display their own oppression in an overt way. In *Frankenstein*, Shelley was more interested in stressing the importance of family over female independence. However, in characters such as Saphie in *Frankenstein* and Fanny Derham in *Lodore,* she shaped individuals who, perhaps unconsciously, may have represented her own sense of frustration over the inability to fulfill her potential, due to her culture's gender attitudes. Finally, the *female* phase, which started around 1970, depicts women as more empowered, independent thinkers who reject the notion of being ruled by men's laws. Although some might argue that feminism slowed or disappeared altogether as a pure concept by the end of the 20th century, others argue that it still exists but has taken more flexible forms. Showalter also introduced the concept of gynocriticism, which basically offers the framework for evaluating women's literature through women's eyes. This final phase has allowed a new understanding and interpretation of Shelley, her famous novel, and her other works.

Some assumptions of feminist criticism have proven crucial to an analysis of *Frankenstein*. The most important is that all people—women and men—should be politically, socially, and economically equal; women are not inferior to men. In addition, women must define and articulate their roles in society. However, in *Frankenstein* and in many pre-20th century works, women in general are seen as the *other;* they are objects defined by the male, according to Western culture, which has historically claimed the superiority of the male, beginning with the biblical story of the Garden of Eden, in which the woman transgresses by accepting and offering temptation.

Feminist critics may search for a gendered subtext, a message beneath the surface message, in 19th-century works like *Frankenstein*. They may claim that the fact that none of the women in the novel are allowed individual identity apart from males and never attempt to define and articulate their separate roles serves as an important message that readers of Shelley's time did not recognize with a surface reading. Thus, Shelley includes in the novel, consciously or unconsciously, a subtext for readers. She may suggest that had Justine and Elizabeth more clearly and forcefully expressed their opinions and been allowed to develop a sense of self, Victor would have been forced to take responsibility for his actions, and they would not have been victimized. In addition, the fact that both young women represent fertility and motherhood, concepts perverted by Victor as he seeks to take over those gender roles, causes them to suffer a special victimization. The co-opting of their reproductive capabilities represents a symbolic sterilization and an elimination of the need for women that proves even more important than their physical deaths.

For feminist critics, a closely related topic of interest in *Frankenstein* is the silencing of women by men. For the most part, the women characters are forced to listen to the men and given little or no chance to respond. For example, Walton's sister remains a silent audience, and all of the other women characters are ultimately silenced by death. Victor's mother is silenced early on when she dies of a disease caught while she is working in her caretaker role. She remains a silent presence in the story as a frozen image shut up inside a locket, a symbol of containment. Justine, especially, becomes a pawn in a masculine game of revenge between the monster and Victor and, along with the portrait in the locket, stands accused by the monster as a motivation for his actions. She is silenced in her attempts to argue her innocence, both by the court and by her male confessor, who persuades her to present a false confession, leading to her death. The female creature that the monster has Victor assemble never matures to gain a voice, as Victor violently tears her into small pieces before she is complete. Elizabeth dies a terrible death due to Victor's ignorance in presuming the monster seeks his destruction, never thinking that he will silence Elizabeth. Strangulation, the monster's method of murder, acts both metaphorically and literally to choke off Elizabeth's voice. Anne Mellor writes that the feminine in *Frankenstein* is both silenced and sacrificed by the masculine, as these several examples show.

Objectification of women supplies an additional focus for feminist critics. *Frankenstein* consistently treats women as passive objects to be treasured, admired, and cared for by males. This supports a stereotypical idealization of women as spiritually superior to men. Thus, men require their guidance to live a wholesome life, and if men fail, women may be blamed for that failure. In an opposing, equally unrealistic, and stereotypical view, all women possess the capacity to act as temptresses, enchanting men with black arts and forcing them to commit evil acts while under their power. Both approaches clash with the reality of the marginalization of women: They are supposedly imbued with great powers, and yet they must be under the control of men. Reducing them to objects offers a simple way to control them.

Examples of objectification, stereotyping, and control begin when Victor supplies his family background for Walton in chapter 1. He describes his mother as an angelic caregiver for her father, sacrificing her own needs for his, and later as needing care by his father "as a fair exotic is sheltered by the gardener." He objectifies his mother using the traditional comparison of a woman to a flower and makes clear that she will perish without male protection. Victor's father is much older than his mother and thus serves as a controlling father figure as well as a husband. His mother tends to the sick and the poor and discovers and cares for Elizabeth, the female child who is immediately compared to a cherub with a crown of blond hair that resembles a halo. Elizabeth causes the mother's death by sharing her disease, and she must take the mother's place as caregiver to the family's four males. Victor also notes early on that Elizabeth, in her idealized role as the angel in the house, helps Clerval control his more base instincts. When the monster sees Mrs. Frankenstein's portrait—an objectification of her as artwork—around William's neck, "it softened and attracted" him, her beauty soothing the raging beast. But then he remembers "that I was for ever deprived of the delights that such beautiful creatures bestow." At that moment, Mrs. Frankenstein converts from a positive to a negative force, transformed by the monster's inability to control himself, into a temptress whose very image tortures him. She literally transforms from a goddess into something evil as the monster assumes that had she ever viewed him, the vision would have "changed that air of divine benignity to one expressive of disgust." His rage returns, and he commits murder, an act that can in part be blamed on Mrs. Frankenstein's beauty. In addition, Clerval later remarks that William "now sleeps with his angel mother," again idealizing a woman. When Victor returns to Geneva, he notices his mother's portrait hanging on the wall in the family home, where she has been reduced to a silent object of art. As these examples demonstrate, objectification of women and feminine stereotypes are well represented in Shelley's novel.

To continue that theme, Elizabeth literally follows in her adoptive mother's footsteps as an object for possession by a controlling male. In the first chapter, she is presented to Victor by his mother as "a pretty present," and Victor labels her as his "promised gift" and regards Elizabeth "as mine—mine to protect, love, and cherish. All praises bestowed on her, I received as made to a possession of my own . . . till death she was to be mine only." Elizabeth becomes responsible for the family's future upon the mother's death. Her union with Victor is labeled the family's only "hope" by both Mr. and Mrs. Frankenstein. Victor looks to her for moral guidance, as in chapter 2 he states that she possesses a "saintly soul" that shines "like a shrine-dedicated lamp in our peaceful home." When considering their marriage in chapter 22, Victor says that in Elizabeth "I possessed a treasure." He also wishes for love and joy but adds that "the apple was already eaten." He references the temptation of Eve by the serpent in the Garden of Eden, although in this instance it is Victor who has given in to temptation. He addresses Elizabeth as "my darling girl" and "sweet girl" and also in the third person, patronizing phrases that reduce her to the status of a child who requires control. It is Victor's influence that later further reduces Elizabeth's status as she now appears thinner and has lost most of her "heavenly vivacity," foreshadowing her loss of life. She continues to be useful in calming Victor but begins to act as a mirror, reflecting his melancholy. Just prior to their marriage, Elizabeth receives a portion of her family's lost Austrian fortune, further objectifying her to a commodity with a specific financial value.

Feminist critics may view the creature as "the other," a foreign and marginalized being, as women are often regarded. He expresses quite tender feelings with maternal characteristics as he first comes to know the world, and he is judged on his appearance rather than his intellectual capacity, as are many women. He considers his reflection, using water as a mirror, a traditional means for objectification of women as they pay close attention to their beauty. Such a reflection generally symbolizes an internal self-reflection for women, as well as the obvious literal reflection of the external. As discussed above, the creature is frequently connected to imagery of the moon, a strong female symbol. Like women, traditionally seen as descendants of Eve and temptresses set on the destruction of mankind, the creature serves as a temptation to Victor, who compares his error in creating the monster to "eating the apple." This allows Victor to escape assumption of responsibility for his actions, much as men in general use women as scapegoats for their actions.

Victor embodies some stereotypically feminine characteristics that interest feminist critics, such as his emotional reactions, which would be regarded as hysteria in most female characters. He spends much of his life in a prone position, ill or fainting, as do female characters in much traditional fiction, including fairy tales. Victor becomes often lost in his imagination, another traditional feminine characteristic, as women were believed to act on instinct rather than reason. While Victor begins the story as a rational being, a scientist who should operate in the arena of logic, he loses his grasp on logic and reality later in the novel. In chapter 22, it is Elizabeth who, in a letter, tries to convince him of possible "false reasoning" on his part. Such gender role reversal remains an excellent source for feminist critical analysis.

Feminism has many ways of "debunking" male dominance. Some critics choose to expose stereotypes applied to women throughout the ages. Others rediscover works written by women authors that were never given due credit. Monique Wittig goes as far as to create the lesbianization of language, eliminating gender specific pronouns to analyze the language itself within a text. Shelley's use of language echoes such theories, although she would probably not have thought in terms of gendered language. Anne K. Mellor explains that feminists view 18th-century scientific commentary as Mary Shelley did, with attention to the importance of metaphors in scientific rhetoric. For example, Francis Bacon wrote of science's ability to take "Nature and all her children" and enslave them to the male pursuit of science. His statement was imbued with gendered politics, in which science became aggressive male practice intent on directing a fertile, passive feminine natural world to comply with its wishes. In writing *Frankenstein*, Shelley proved her awareness of the dangers to women of such an attitude. She created science fiction in order to contrast two pursuits. The first pursuit is based on a male hubris determined to manipulate natural forces for male edification, while the second would be pursuit of the true and far more pure elemental science of nature.

Mellor sees Shelley's depiction as a challenge to "cultural biases" obvious in the popular gendered definition of science that operated on the hierarchy of male over female. Her critique of the political nature of science through depictions of the unimaginably horrible results of its forced application to create a human was all the more brilliantly imagined for its basis in her era's scientific thought. Victor Frankenstein's pursuit of "nature to her hiding places" results in quick and sure repercussions. As Mellor points out, nature turns the metaphoric table on Frankenstein, emerging as anything but a passive or nurturing force for the scientist. While the monster finds respite in nature, Victor feels the fury of nature's revenge. As a result of Victor's attempt to usurp nature and the female role, he suffers fevers, fainting, anxiety, and madness. Those same activities and sufferings were traditionally attributed to, and expected of, women in their passive roles, allowing Shelley to ironically project traditional female ills on the man who would stand in as mother in the reproductive process. When Frankenstein pursues the monster through the mountains, rain pours on him from a black sky, and he is exposed to vicious lightning storms. He is threatened by death from a storm at sea after disposing of the aborted female experiment and suffers from a terrible thirst. He dies in the bitter cold of the North Pole, arguably nature's most inhospitable setting. It is science that remains complacent in the shadow of nature. Mellor also believes that Ernest is the only survivor of the family because he remains close to nature. Elizabeth suggests that he become a farmer and enjoy a "healthy happy life; and the least hurtful, or rather the most beneficial profession of any."

Many critics, including Mellor, note Frankenstein's attempt to usurp the reproductive nature of woman, which, had he succeeded, would have resulted in theft of her value to culture. He is intent on creating a society devoid of women. Victor even seems set on destroying the mother figures in his life. His own mother sacrifices herself in caring for the ill, a role expected of her by all the males in her family. Justine, mother figure to William, is victimized by Victor, who allows her to go to her death in order to save his own reputation. She stands accused of killing her surrogate child, and Victor allows her to die, half believing that she is responsible for William's death, a monstrous subconscious act of vengeance against mothers on his part. The man he has created will not have a mate, due to Frankenstein's confidence that such a couple will produce a race of monsters.

Marxist Criticism

The core principles of Marxist literary criticism are that society shapes our awareness and that social and economic values influence the development of personal values. Marxist thought in general often promotes the elimination of bigotry, hatred, and conflict from society through the elimination of class structure, thus supporting class struggle to achieve equality. Marxist critics claim that in order to understand a work such as *Frankenstein*, one must understand the social forces at work at the time it was written. Certainly Mary Shelley suffered almost her entire life with a fear of lack of income. She well represents class struggle in the controlled conflict with her father-in-law over his lack of contribution to her son's family following Percy Shelley's death. Eventually her son inherited his grandfather's title and estate, allowing Mary to relax during her final years. But before that time came, she often expressed concern over her income to publishers in a tactful manner and to friends in a more open way. Although she wrote *Frankenstein* when she was a teenager, without having experienced much privation or struggle, she was made acutely aware of her culture's inequities through the writings of both of her parents. Her background and natural propensity to observe political struggle in her environment may have supported her inclusion of several telling passages regarding class structure and the material value accorded to women to help measure their worth in her novel.

For instance, as concerns material value, the Frankensteins are landed and moneyed people. Mrs. Frankenstein is "raised" above her father's errors, which led to a loss of his material wealth through marriage. Even in death, she retains her material and objective value, reflected in her portraits. The locket that contains her miniature is a valuable piece of jewelry, thus giving her value as a commodity. That one piece of evidence found in Justine's pocket, suggesting theft from the upper class, helps convict a member of the lower class.

The novel also shows class structure being enforced through civil law. Shelley calls the reader's attention to the struggle of the working classes and the arbitrary nature of human laws and social rules in contrast to the unchangeable and thoroughly rational laws that seem to guide the order one observes in nature. Thus, nature as God's creation remains superior to society, humans' creation. When Elizabeth writes to Victor in chapter 6, she first stresses nature's immutable laws that dictate a certain structure; the term *immutable* is used in multiple references to nature throughout the novel.

Later in the letter, Elizabeth references human law, mankind's weak attempt to construct order through civic and social laws, as she writes of their family servant, Justine. Justine greatly contrasts with the Frankensteins as a servant in the employ of a firmly established family. She shares Elizabeth's adopted status in the family, but because she hails from the working class, she could never be seen as a daughter, even though she acts as a surrogate mother to the Frankenstein's youngest child, William. Despite their informal adoption of Justine, the family cannot raise her to their socioeconomic level, thereby showing the inferiority of man's systems to nature's more equitable system. Ironically, in a letter, Elizabeth attempts to describe the law's positive attitude toward servants in Geneva:

> The republican institutions of our country have produced simpler and happier manners than those which prevail in the great monarchies that surround it. Hence, there is less distinction between the several classes of its inhabitants; and the lower orders, being neither so poor nor so despised, their manners are more refined and moral. A servant in Geneva does not mean the same thing as a servant in France and England. Justine, thus received in our family, learned the duties of a servant; a condition which, in our fortunate country, does not include the idea of ignorance, and a sacrifice of the dignity of a human being.

These words later prove painfully ironic when the civil courts convict Justine of William's murder, the conviction based mainly on her possession of a valuable material good that one of her class would not normally possess. Shelley may have attempted to alert England to its harsh class structure after having lived in Switzerland and observed their better treatment of servants.

While Elizabeth is also an adopted member of the family, she boasts an aristocratic Austrian heritage through her father, made clear by Victor when he discusses her joining their family. Her very appearance has set her apart from the working-class family that cared for her. Shelley makes that distinction clear through her physical appearance, with hair the color of gold, a valuable metal, and resembling a crown, symbolic of her distinctive background. One may discern her class membership with one look at her. Just prior to their marriage, Victor discovers that a portion of Elizabeth's family fortune has been restored to her, further emphasizing her upper-class stature as equal to his own and also reinforcing Elizabeth's economic value. Through her inheritance, she possesses a dowry, the traditional material value assigned to a woman and used in trade for marriage to a suitable male.

In addition, Shelley further calls attention to class structure when Victor retires to an island off Scotland's coast to perform the task with which the creature charges him, the production of a female companion. Victor remarks on the island's poverty, so acute that no one asks questions regarding his remodeling of one of the island huts; the local population remains so focused on meeting their basic requirements that such observation would prove a luxury. Victor tells Walton that "all the senses of the cottagers" were "benumbed by want and squalid poverty." Perhaps most damning of Victor's class consciousness to 21st-century readers is the passage in chapter 22 when he longs for the freedom of a peasant "when his family have been massacred before his eyes, his cottage burnt, his lands laid waste, and he is turned adrift, homeless, penniless, and alone, but free." His breathtaking blindness to the suffering of the poor reminds readers of the typical attitude toward the poor in Shelley's time. That attitude as seen in this passage might be summed up as: "Those who have nothing can lose nothing."

While the poor and the oppressed do not revolt in this novel, the supreme revolution is staged by the monster, who moves from servant to master in his relationship with Victor. In chapter 18, Victor declares himself "the slave of my creature," and in the next chapter he tells of his desire to "shake off my chains." The creature addresses Victor in chapter 20 as "slave" and reminds him of the power he holds over him, stating, "You are my creator, but I am your master—obey!" Victor manages to shake his servitude by destroying the partial woman he has produced, leading the creature to gain even more ferocity in declaring himself a snake who will eventually poison Victor. In the end, the monster's revolt is complete in his destruction of an entire aristocratic family.

Psychoanalytic Criticism

Psychoanalytic critical approaches have varied over time. They were at first based in the theories of Sigmund Freud, later expanded to include the dream world and mythic images of Carl Jung, and now also include what is known as *feminist semanalysis*, a methodology intended to "rescue" Freud from a male-dominated culture. For *Frankenstein*, the most often applied psychoanalytic approaches are based in the ideas of Freud, Jung, and mythology study.

Freudian critics are interested in Victor Frankenstein's fear of sexual involvement. Freud's psyche model proposes that the human unconscious houses two basic instincts, the sexual instinct (known as *eros*) and the destructive and aggressive instinct. Victor's many acts of destruction and aggression are easily catalogued. Some of his aggressive behavior may also be analyzed as a product of eros, his actions and attitudes toward women offering supporting examples. For instance, Victor reaches the heights of passion and aggression when engaged in dismembering the partial female body that he had constructed as a companion for the monster. It is not the idea of two such creatures communing together that he abhors; rather, it is the thought of sexual propagation, which he deems a monstrous act. In addition, the construction of Elizabeth's murder proves intriguing in light of psychoanalytic theory. The scene that Shelley constructs of Elizabeth Lavenza Frankenstein's death on her wedding night is believed to be based on a painting of a highly seductive scene by Henry Fuseli entitled *The Nightmare*. This famous work depicts a woman in a position of sexual submission while under attack by an incubus, a night spirit. The spirit arrives by riding a stallion, a strong symbol of male animalistic sexuality, which stands by the bed with a twisted expression as he stares at the woman.

Freudian critics also focus on certain types of symbols, including the phallic, or male penis symbol; and the yonic, a concave space such as a vase, flower, or cup, representing the vagina. Elizabeth died because the fearful Victor dreaded consummation of the marriage, leaving her alone in their wedding bed. Rather than employing his own phallus to consummate his marriage, Victor stalks the grounds carrying the phallic gun, ostensibly to protect himself from attack, ignoring the possibility that the monster would seek to kill Elizabeth. Once she is dead, Victor embraces her passionately, whereas when she lived, he reserved his passion, regarding her as a sister. Freudian critics also focus on the dream state in which Victor often exists. He frequently mentions feeling as if he is in a dream or, as in chapter 23, "a cloud of wonder and horror," and he constantly reports on the troubled state of his real dreams.

Victor's relationship with Elizabeth suggests incest, another common topic in Shelley's novels and of interest to psychoanalytic critics. In the original 1818 edition of the novel, Shelley portrayed Elizabeth as Victor's cousin, daughter of his father's sister. In the revised 1831 edition, Shelley instead described Elizabeth as an orphan. At first glance, one might understand the change as being for the sake of propriety—to avoid the taint of incest. However, during Shelley's era, unions between cousins were both legal and acceptable, particularly as families sought to retain property rights and ownership (Charles Darwin, for example, married a first cousin). As Miranda Seymour and other critics suggest, many of the changes that Shelley made to the 1831 edition of the novel shifted its focus away from individual choice, emphasizing fate as the supreme force controlling one's life. One might speculate that making Elizabeth an orphan rather than a cousin would better accommodate such an emphasis.

More important to psychoanalytic critics is that in the 1831 edition, Elizabeth fulfills more completely the contemporary ideal of the angelic female presence in the home, anticipating Victorian ideals. That role was to be clearly characterized in Coventry Patmore's later poem "The Angel in the House" (1854). Based on Patmore's wife, the poem emphasizes the most desirable characteristics in a Victorian Age wife and mother: passivity, meekness, grace, self-sacrifice, and lack of power. In *Frankenstein*, while Victor's mother fulfills that role at the novel's beginning, Elizabeth assumes the role upon his mother's death, therefore becoming a mother substitute.

Thus, even as an orphan and not a cousin, Elizabeth has a relationship with Victor that suggests incest. Freud's well-known stages of development suggest that infants begin in an oral phase, move onto an anal stage, and finally experience the phallic stage. In the phallic stage, the male child forms an erotic attachment to the mother and fears castration by the father, his competition for his mother's attention. Because Elizabeth replaces the mother in the Frankenstein family, she may be seen as fulfilling Victor's erotic needs provoked by his oedipal complex—that is, his desire to sleep with his mother. His mother may even be viewed as provoking that relationship, declaring on her deathbed that Elizabeth and Victor must marry, as their union has always been the hope for her future.

When writing more explicitly in her later novels about incest, Shelley generally focused on an opportunistic father who takes advantage of his daughter, training her to serve him as a wife substitute in every way except sexual. The novella *Mathilda*, not published until 1959 due to its depiction of the taboo father/daughter relationship, contains the most overt suggestion of sexual fixation by a father of any of Shelley's writings. Shelley's own father, William Godwin, who read the work, was so dismayed by its content that he withheld it from publication, even though Shelley had designated all income from the work to go to his support. Psychoanalytic critics have made much of the persistent incest themes in Shelley's work, even though incest novels were popular during her era (see the entry in this volume on *Mathilda* for a full explanation). When writing *Frankenstein*, she obviously found the incest theme interesting and helpful in depicting Victor and making clear his avoidance of all women except his mother. Shelley may use incest to suggest that all of Victor's relationships are irregular and disproportionate, even—or especially—those within his family. The fact that he regards Elizabeth as a sister rather than a lover from the beginning of the story foreshadows the complicated and nontraditional nature of later relationships.

Other Freudian aspects of *Frankenstein* include its focus on various elements of the psyche, which seem to correspond to what Freud later termed the *id*, the *ego*, and the *superego*. While the categories were not original to Freud, who drew upon the work of the German Georg Groddick to develop his theories, he popularized the terms. The id contains impulses and instincts and is strongest in infants who seek sensory satisfaction to the exclusion of everything else. The monster represents the id as described by Freud: the dark, hidden, passionate aspects of our personality generally seen as negative and contrasting with the more positive ego that exists only partly in consciousness and works to satisfy the id and the superego in a constructive manner that will promote a positive future.

Victor may represent the ego, his behavior modified by demands of the world and functioning with reason and logic, although he often feels out of control and unable to meet his responsibilities. For instance, in chapter 18, he notes, "I was aware also that I should often lose all self-command, all capacity of hiding the harrowing sensations that would posses me during the progress of my unearthly occupation." The ego is strongly present in children, and Victor often regresses, unable to control his basic instincts and passions. When he loses control in chapter 23, the magistrate seeks to soothe Victor "as a nurse does a child." At times, Victor's actions suggest that the id has overpowered him as, earlier in chapter 23, he notes that he does not know what happened: "I lost sensation, and chains and darkness were the only objects that pressed on me." He further explains that he often exists in a dream state, where previously in the novel he engaged in brief fantasies. By the end of the novel, one might speculate that Victor's id, his subconscious desires, have overcome his ego, the more rational aspect of his character.

At other times, the superego seems to take power. In chapter 24, Victor begins to imagine that his father, Elizabeth, and Clerval still live, and that he shares their company. He again feels overwhelmed by an outside force, but this time it is a powerful one. As he tells Walton, he pursued the demon more as a task ordered by heaven, "as the mechanical impulse of some power of which I was unconscious."

Freud's third element, the superego, aims for perfection, representing ideas and spiritual goals. It attempts to distinguish between right and wrong, and it generates enormous feelings of guilt for failure. The superego is our conscience, helping humans to maintain a sense of morality, and may be represented by Elizabeth or Clerval. In chapter 1, Victor describes Elizabeth as "the beautiful and adored companion of all my occupations and pleasures," and in chapter 2, he notes that he might have "become sullen in my study, rough through the ardour of my nature, but that she was there to subdue me to a semblance of her own gentleness." In chapter 2, he says of Clerval that he "occupied himself, so to speak, with the moral relations of things." Like the ego, Victor seeks, although unsuccessfully, to find a balance between passion and desires and the reality required in order to participate within a community. He must serve the id, the superego, and the world around him, a demanding task. Again in chapter 18, Victor notes of Clerval that he "might stand between me and the instruction of my foe," illustrating the mediating posture of the ego. Again, following the loss of Elizabeth, Victor slips from all control, allowing the monster both within and without to take over. While in the graveyard, he begins with a controlled expression of grief but concludes by describing himself as possessed by furies and choking with rage.

Jungian critics are interested in the novel's archetypal characters, such as that of the hero engaged in a quest. Analysis of quest aspects in a work of literature has been practiced most remarkably by American philosopher and scholar Joseph Campbell, who wrote the seminal text *The Hero with a Thousand Faces* (1949). Campbell found study of the myths crucial because he believed modern readers may better understand themselves and others by understanding ancient stories and themes. Victor could be viewed as an archetypical hero, as his life has taken new direction to change the outcome of a problem. However, Victor is plagued by his creation and spends the rest of his life seeking to correct his mistake and, therefore, forgive himself. Thus, Victor could more easily be classified as an ironic hero because he does not display signs of courage or excellence and, instead, plays the victim to his own creation. He embarks on a quest to discover the secret of life and suffers loss, like the traditional hero, but the loss is due to his incorrect behavior. He loses his guide in Clerval and may be seen to descend into Hades during his fever following Clerval's death, when he has visions. He faces the same monster multiple times, rather than the multiple monsters seen in a traditional quest, and he does not defeat the monster as do heroes.

While the traditional quest often features a son seeking to follow in his father's footsteps or to redeem his father's evil deeds, in *Frankenstein* Victor is the father of the monster and no redemption occurs. Victor does not achieve any of his goals, and while he returns home to Geneva, it is not a victorious return to celebrate his success. Instead, Geneva offers tragedy and sorrow, and Victor regresses mentally and emotionally while there. One might suggest that he establishes a new home to satisfy the required cycle of the quest, that new home being in the frozen north. He speaks in chapter 22 of feeling the most composed since his "journey to the sea of ice," referring to his confrontation with the monster. His encounter with his "son" and the accusations of having been an evil creator may have begun a new life that would conclude again in a sea of ice when telling Walton his story. That icy landscape also offers the backdrop to the son's reconciliation with the father, when the creature claims Victor's body and carries it away, and the traditional quest travel medium of the sea has become one of ice. Such a reclassification of home and the father/son relationship would fit the label of an ironic quest, or, at the least, a nontraditional quest. Additional quest imagery appears in chapter 24 when Victor refers to his departed friends and family as "shadows" and states that "the shades of my murdered friends" have heard of his devotion. The term shade is one applied in Homer's *Odyssey* to those who have died and exist in Hades, where heroes might visit them to receive advice and instruction. In Victor's case, however, he exists in the updated version of Hades, with Shelley inserting imagery evocative of hell as he hears "a loud and fiendish laugh" shatter the peaceful graveyard, and he feels "as if all hell surrounded me." This imagery and twist on the traditional further support the claim that Victor's proves an ironic quest. He gains new guides in the form of good sprits that help provide for his physical needs and show him the way to the frozen north. Victor tells Walton that he is engaged in a "horrible pilgrimage," in contrast to the triumphant pilgrimage of the traditional hero.

Walton represents a more traditional quest hero, complete with the pride he reveals in his early writings to his sister. He expresses a strong sense of destiny to become a conqueror and has as his goal or treasure the secrets of the North Pole, to be revealed to civilization. Margaret acts as his guide and his muse, and Walton reveals that she shaped much of his disposition. He travels over the ocean, which becomes a shape-shifter of sorts when the sea turns into ice that locks his boat in place. Victor serves as his most obvious guide in offering him a cautionary tale. Near the end of his storytelling in chapter 24, Victor tells Walton that as a young man he believed himself "destined for some great enterprise," but in the end, all of his "speculations and hopes are as nothing; and, like the archangel who aspired to omnipotence," he now exists in hell. Walton thus has made the traditional descent into Hades to gain wisdom from heroes, or in this case, an antihero, who has gone before. Walton tells Margaret that Victor tries to give him hope. He fears never seeing her again but tells his crew they have engaged in "an honourable undertaking" and will be "hailed as the benefactors of your species," just like the "brave men who encountered death for honour, and the benefit of mankind." In other words, they will become part of a storytelling tradition that has proved crucial to the romantic genre of hero tales: It grants heroes immortality. He also exhorts them to conquer the ice, which is not as strong as their hearts, and to "return as heroes who have fought and conquered." Walton then practices heroism by deciding to return home and save his fellow travelers, although he considers it an act of cowardice and lacking in ambition. However, that is exactly what Victor, as his guide, bids him do just before dying, when he says, "Farewell, Walton! Seek happiness in tranquility, and avoid ambition." Perhaps his greatest victory is in his practice of "curiosity and compassion," which prevents his killing the monster and granting Victor's dying wish. Thus, Walton does claim a treasure for his quest in Victor's extraordinary tale and his bequeathing of that tale to mankind. The reader presumes that he does return home, completing his quest.

The monster contains elements of various archetypes. The most obvious is that of a tempter, as he plays the role of Satan in the Garden of Eden, tempting Victor to eat the apple, a phrase he uses in chapter 22, referencing the forbidden fruit from the tree of knowledge consumed by Eve and offered to Adam. An additional comparison to Satan in temptation's form occurs in chapter 20 when the monster compares himself to a snake that will sting with venom. His words echo God's curse on mankind as he evicts Adam and Eve from the Garden in Genesis 3:15. He explains to the serpent that its relationship with woman and her seed (children) will forever be one of enmity: "He shall bruise you on the head, / And you shall bruise him on the heel." The monster may also be seen as fulfilling the role of a traditional child character, particularly at the novel's conclusion. He weeps over the death of his "father," exhibiting clear signs of remorse and yearning and embodying the actions of a child who has lost a parent.

While the monster has consistently acted as an archetypal child throughout the entire book, his actions after Victor's death are now focused on his own death, as he claims that "soon these burning miseries will be extinct. I shall ascend my funeral pile triumphantly, and exult in the agony of the torturing flames." This reference calls to mind the figure of the phoenix, a bird that sacrifices itself on a pyre every 500 years to be reborn into a new bird. The monster's archetypal references are ironic, as fire will neither purify him nor cause his rebirth. He literally represents the monsters encountered by all heroes, as well as a shape-shifter. As he matures, he changes from an open, trusting, and intelligent being into a twisted being that haunts Victor.

Victor may represent the archetypal wanderer in the end stages of his life. In chapter 20, following the destruction of the female creature, Victor "walked about the isle like a restless spectre." Later, he has no home following the multiple murders of his family and friends, noting in chapter 24 that he will quit Geneva, which has become hateful to him. He uses the family treasure to finance his wanderings and tells Walton he has endured hardships that befall travelers "in deserts and barbarous countries," having slept on sandy plains and "wandered many hours" around town, uncertain of his path. His sole guide by the novel's conclusion is the monster, who leads him along the Rhone River, to the Mediterranean, through Tartary and Russia, and then north, cursed by a devil and transporting hell with him. He becomes a shade, a member of the walking dead.

A final psychoanalytic critical interest to be discussed here is seen in Victor's relationship to the monster as a representation of two different aspects of his own personality. A common theory is that the monster represents Victor's alter ego, another aspect of his self. The term *alter ego* originated in the 19th century, applied in psychology in discussion of schizophrenia. It derives from the Latin term for "the other" and is most commonly defined as a second self, or the alternate side of one's personality. Victor may be viewed as a type of Dr. Jekyll to the monster's Mr. Hyde, caught up in an experiment gone terribly wrong. The fact that the monster is never named supports the theory that he is a part of Victor. Victor's multiple references to the creature as a demon and devil may be interpreted as references to his own darkly haunted personality. If an individual leading a double life may be thought of as insane, existing outside of reality, than Victor is such an individual. He even notes on several occasions that if he told the truth about the monster, others would believe him mad, a person who has lost a grip on reality. The creature's words reside literally in Victor's ears, as he states in chapter 20, "like a dream, yet distinct and oppressive as a reality." The fact that Victor and the creature are referred to as father and son suggest a close relationship and open the door for the two to be seen as one. Walton is the only individual in addition to Victor to clearly see and converse with both him and the creature. When he enters the cabin following Victor's death, Walton sees a form hanging over Victor that seems more a vision than reality. Both the monster and Victor at first experience transcendence and joy, but they dissolve into a desire for hatred and revenge, and both are compared to spirits and specters on multiple occasions.

Queer Theory

Proponents of queer theory also find much of interest in *Frankenstein*. Victor's strongest relationships are with men, not women. The most striking example is his relationship with Clerval, whom he describes as "the image of my former self." He also bonds quickly with Walton, who compares him to "a celestial spirit." As Victor lies dying, Walton tells his sister, "I have sought one who would sympathise with and love me. Behold, on these desert seas I have found such a one." Even the monster is described by Victor as "the great object of my affection," and Victor ignores Elizabeth, his future wife, in order to spend all of his time working on his creation. His destruction of the woman creature when only partially complete could also represent a preference for men, and even an intention to usurp women in the creative process.

Structuralist Criticism/Deconstruction

Structuralism and deconstruction offer additional related approaches to an analysis of *Frankenstein*. Structuralists often study binaries—opposites such as day/night, light/dark, good/evil, god/devil—to understand a text. Through such oppositions, they believe that the reader organizes, values, and interprets the text. Traditionally, the item that appears first in the "fraction," what could be seen as the "numerator" rather than the "denominator," possesses higher value; readers have learned to privilege day over night, light over dark, good over evil, and god over devil. The traditional approach privileges Victor over the monster, associating Victor with day, light, and goodness and the monster with night, darkness, and evil. Readers understand that good dwells in light, while evil exists in the dark. Much of such understanding comes from religious study in the Western tradition. For instance, the biblical gospel of John, chapter 3, verses 19–21 tell readers:

> And this is the judgment, that the light is come into the world, and men loved the darkness rather than the light; for their deeds were evil. For everyone who does evil hates the light, and does not come to the light, lest his deeds should be exposed. But he who practices the truth comes to the light, that his deeds may be manifested as having been wrought in God.

Structuralism emphasizes form over content in a work of literature. Language remains arbitrary and derives from a system created by humans in order to achieve meaning. Like all social and cultural practices, language depends on a certain code to be useful. Meaning resides in codes found in the text, something decided before a reader ever picks up a book such as *Frankenstein*. In chapter 2, Victor tells Walton that as a child, Elizabeth "shone like a shrine-dedicated lamp." In chapter 3, he experiences his first major scientific occurrence when lightning strikes the oak and creates a "dazzling light." In chapter 4, Victor has an epiphany regarding his theories and tells Walton, that "from the midst of this darkness a sudden light broke in upon me—a light so brilliant and wondrous, yet so simple" that it made him dizzy. A short time later, Victor says that his scientific breakthrough will "pour a torrent of light into our dark world." Here, light corresponds to knowledge and truth. Again, one may turn to the Bible for multiple similar expressions. The Gospel of John, chapter 1, labels God *light* and notes of Christ, "He was not the light, but came that he might bear witness of the light / There was the true light, which coming into the world, enlightens every man" (1:8–9). However, when the moment of triumph arrives in *Frankenstein*, it comes on a "dreary night of November" in the rain with a nearly burned-out candle that allows Victor to view the creature "by the glimmer of the half-extinguished light." That imagery cues the reader to the fact that the creature will not be "good," as it is a product of the dark. Victor returns to his room to pass a sleepless dark night, his dreams, occurring in the dark, becoming "a hell."

As order descends into chaos, dark imagery predominates. Victor spends more time immersed in dark moods and passions. The monster travels at night and dwells in shadow in the hut. Following his failed attempt to interact with the De Laceys, he wanders in the dark woods, but when the sun rises, it helps restore his tranquility. When night arrives again, the monster experiences a type of insanity and burns down the cottage in the dark. After Victor argues with the monster over his demands in chapter 17, he wanders home through the night when "the stars shone at intervals, as the clouds passed from over them; the dark pines rose before me," and the scene is solemn. He cries out to the stars to have pity and crush him or leave him in darkness. In the next chapter, Victor experiences fits of "devouring blackness" He destroys the female creature at night and returns to dispose of her remains at night when "clouds hid the moon." These constitute a few examples of the negative use of darkness. The monster has brought Victor into both literal darkness, forcing him to seek cover of night, as well as the metaphorical emotional darkness of fury and revenge, and it serves as the cause of his problems. The creator, associated with light, represents goodness, while the created, associated with dark, clearly represents evil.

Deconstruction follows structuralism to suggest that what a text purports to say and what it actually says may differ. A reader needs to take apart, or deconstruct, its words for a hidden meaning. One of deconstruction's strongest proponents, Jacques Derrida, stated that humans are rigidly "logocentric," centered on a variety of words, including *God, reason, origin, being,* and *truth,* to name a few. Each such term could serve as what Derrida labeled a "transcendental signified," a self-sufficient concept. Western thought is centered on binaries like those noted in the structuralism discussion above, and humans can not understand a concept without structuring an opposite concept.

Derrida suggested unprivileging the binaries. Thus, one could take those same binaries examined by structuralist critics for meaning and invert them to discover a new meaning. That would allow one to know something because it differs from something else, not because it can be compared to a transcendental signifier; Derrida termed this operation *différance.* Reversing binaries, making the higher status numerator a lower status denominator, allows readers to challenge the established value system and ideas. What if, for instance, one were to privilege the created over the creator, dark over light, monster over Victor? Readers might do so, viewing Victor as flawed or even bad. After all, he is a creator who abandoned his creation, a father who abandoned his child. Therefore, the creature may be viewed as a victim, rather than as inherently evil. He begins life as a rational being longing for human companionship. Forced to hide at night, the creature finds welcome refuge beneath the light of the moon, a feminine symbol, and broader nature to nurture him in the absence of a parent. Victor has challenged the power of nature in an attempt to take that power for his own ends. Like an innocent infant, the creature remains ignorant to the ways of the world and open to love and compassion, valuing education, language, and communication as he develops the ability to comprehend and share with others. Victor has forgotten the value of education, instead turning to his own obsessions and gaining only perversion through his knowledge. The creature sacrifices for the De Laceys and serves them by gathering wood and attempting to care for their needs, whereas Victor consistently shows himself to be a self-centered egoist, thinking of no one but himself. Where the creature lives in forced isolation due to his hideous appearance, Victor chooses isolation from family and Clerval. Where the creature always tells the truth, Victor withholds the truth, even though he realizes he could have saved Justine had he revealed the facts about the monster.

The creature lashes out only after he has been deprived, through no fault of his own, of human love and repeatedly denied the compassion that he so freely gives. He may be a demon haunting Victor's dreams, but that is the only way to gain Victor's attention. Deserted by his creator, he must follow him about and take something dear to him in order to force a discussion. He promises honorable behavior in exchange for the granting of a reasonable request and only turns again to murder when Victor withdraws his sole chance for a companion. The creature tells Walton of his actions, "I knew I was preparing for myself a deadly torture; was the slave, not the master, of an impulse, which I detested, yet could not disobey. . . . Evil thenceforth became my good." He asks, "Am I to be thought the only criminal, when all humankind sinned against me?" These examples illustrate the value of deconstruction and how easily it can be accomplished, allowing readers to view the same material in a completely different manner.

Postmodernism

Postmodern critics rejected the way of thinking that guided the development of critical approaches such as New Criticism and structuralism. Unlike earlier critical approaches, postmodernism (which is often said to encompass deconstruction) holds that objective reality does not exist. All definitions and depictions of truth are creations of the human mind. Truth itself is relative, dependent on the cultural and social influences on one's life. This thought could be applied in analyzing the monster's development of a social consciousness. Because postmodernists believe that many truths exist, but not *the* truth, as truth and reality are constructs of the mind, the monster in *Frankenstein* would be expected to develop his own perception of reality, particularly when left on his own to observe others and judge himself in relation to them.

According to the leading thinkers of postmodernism, modernity failed because it depended on an external point of reference—such as God, reason, and science—on which to build a philosophy. Postmodernists feel there is no such point of reference because there is no ultimate truth or unifying element in the universe, and thus no ultimate reality. Shelley's novel supports that idea in her counter of God, or faith, reason and science as offering ultimate pathways to understanding. All are corrupted by man's desire for power. The postmodern approach holds that the only reality that exists is the reality we create for ourselves, shaped by each individual's dominant social group. That explains why the monster is so easily influenced by the cottagers. He believes they offer the ultimate key to knowledge, commenting on the communication by "articulate sounds" as "a godlike science" that would allow him to "unravel the mystery" of speech. The postmodern critic, believing that each person's reality is different and no one has a claim for the absolute truth, would find the lack of tolerance among *Frankenstein*'s characters of one another's points of view of utmost importance.

When analyzing the monster's search for external reality, postmodernists might state that to be loved and accepted, to have a relationship with a fellow human being, represents his ultimate desire. Due to the monster's rejection by the cottagers and other humans, Victor serves not only as his creator but also as the only social construct on which he can build his reality. Rejection by his creator, the one who was supposed to love and accept him, turns the monster's desire for love and acceptance into a desire for vengeance. He speaks to Walton of how his heart "was fashioned to be susceptible of love and sympathy," explaining he was not created originally to be an instrument of evil. He then describes his despair upon discovering that Victor,

> the author at once of my existence and of its unspeakable torments, dared to hope for happiness; that while he accumulated wretchedness and despair upon me, he sought his own enjoyment in feelings and passions from the indulgence of which I was for ever barred, then impotent envy and bitter indignation filled me with an insatiable thirst for vengeance.

The monster makes a unique claim for absolute truth, playing on the duality of good/evil for self-definition. Victor is his God, and he sees himself as the devil to his God, as he references himself as "the fallen angel." However, he also quickly declares that "even that enemy of God had friends and associates in his desolation; I am alone." While the monster sees his reality as one of evil, the fact that humanity abandoned him equates to his ultimate reality; his isolation led directly to wickedness. With the death of Victor, his God, death becomes his reality.

Intertexuality

A final critical approach to assessing Shelley's novel is intertextual criticism. This approach encourages study and analysis of a text based on other works of literature alluded to or quoted from in that text. The idea behind the approach is that no text can be properly interpreted in isolation. Structuralists focused on intertextual criticism are interested not in the meaning of a text but rather in *how* an author conveys that meaning. Many readers may find it interesting to know what books influenced Shelley the most. It is notable that the major texts Shelley alludes to in the novel are real.

For example, Samuel Taylor Coleridge's *The Rime of the Ancient Mariner* surfaces often in the novel in theme and imagery. Shelley's setting of ice and snow, which traps Walton's ship, and the overall topic of the effect of isolation owe much to Coleridge's work. The poem's story of an individual who must for a time wear a dead albatross and later tell his story in order to pay for causing the death of his fellow sailors, relates to Frankenstein's sins against nature, which also lead to multiple deaths, and his telling of his own story as a cautionary tale.

The novel also alludes to and shares symbols and imagery with John Milton's *Paradise Lost*. The novel opens with a quotation from Milton's work, a clear message to readers regarding the story's topic. Victor specifically mentions and also alludes to

Satan and his fellow fallen angels are cast out of heaven in John Milton's *Paradise Lost*. Shelley would revisit Milton's themes of creation and damnation in her novel *Frankenstein*. (Illustration by Gustave Doré)

the conflict between heavenly and earthly forces, applying the term *fallen angel* to himself, and the monster also compares himself to a fallen angel. The monster is termed a *demon*, *devil*, and *Satan* and is compared to a serpent on multiple occasions, suggesting parallels to the biblical creation and temptation myth found in the biblical book of Genesis. *Paradise Lost* is one of the three books that the monster utilizes for self-education, with all three books helping the reader better understand the creature. In chapter 15, the creature compares himself to Adam, stating, "Like Adam, I was apparently united by no link to any other being in existence." He then contrasts Adam's happier state and his protective father to the creature's unhappy state and lack of a caring father. He also compares himself to Milton's Satan when he states, "Satan had his companions, fellow-devils, to admire and encourage him; but I am solitary and abhorred." Later in that chapter, when the monster considers confronting the De Laceys, he dreams of paradise but understands "it was all a dream; no Eve soothed my sorrows, nor shared my thoughts; I was alone" and abandoned by his own creator. The reader also compares the monster to Adam as the first created man as the creature goes through a symbolic birth and learns from his natural surroundings in chapter 11.

Another of the monster's books is *The Sorrows of Werter* (1774), by Johann Goethe. Goethe specifically separates his protagonist from the rational characteristics that marked the Enlightenment. Werter declares that art does not originate in reason, instead having its origin in the heart; he claims that that his knowledge may be shared by many, but his heart's emotions are his alone. A simple tale, *The Sorrows of Werter* leads the creature to consider his self-identity and the meaning of life. The book supports the creature's questioning of his place in the world and also his despondent attitude toward his treatment by others. When Werter commits suicide, the act puzzles and saddens the creature and contributes to his wondering whether life is worth living. It perhaps informs his decision to kill himself at the novel's conclusion.

The third book that greatly impresses the creature, *Plutarch's Lives*, allows Shelley to suggest the importance of learning through history so as not to repeat humankind's mistakes. Her use of the text is skillfully ironic, because Frankenstein specifically repeats such errors when he allows hubris to overcome logic and control his actions. The book also allows Shelley's emphasis on the pointless nature of wars and the seemingly limitless capacity of humans' inhumane treatment of others. The creature notes his admiration for the peaceable lawgivers and states, "I felt the greatest ardour for virtue rise within me, and abhorrence for vice." This statement shows that one may select models from the past to guide actions for the good. However, the thought becomes ironic when the monster later abandons all hope for a virtuous life and engages in multiple murders.

In other instances, Shelley references Dante, suggesting his circles of hell as Victor and the monster both claim to abide in a hell on earth.

Victor mentions in chapter 2 that Clerval reads about Arthur and the Knights of the Round Table, enthralled with knightly adventure. That interest supports Clerval's characterization as one who possesses a high moral sensibility, as well as his courageous service and dedication to Victor. Victor also mentions authors that he reads, particularly in natural science, some of whom Shelley also studied. For instance, Humphry Davy's 1802 lecture "A Discourse Introductory to a Course of Lectures on Chemistry" suggests that through study, one might mistakenly desire power over nature, which could lead to the type of mistake that Victor made in attempting to create a human. Luigi Galvani's experiments mentioned in the introduction to this section were well known to Shelley's generation and were immortalized in cartoons that she probably read.

Writings by her family also greatly influenced Shelley and her work. Her mother's novel *Maria, or the Wrongs of Woman* (published 1798) shows in part the damage incurred by a young woman whose stepmother regards her as "a creature of another species." Shelley must have drawn on her mother's novel and also from her father's 1794 novel *Things as They Are, or The Adventures of Caleb Williams*, which depicts social injustice and the consequences of a betrayal of friendship. She often alludes to the subject of her husband's popular work *Prometheus Unbound* in Victor's multiple references to metaphoric chains that hold and oppress him. For instance, in chapter 19, Victor says he "dared to shake off" his chains "and look around me with a free and lofty spirit; but the iron had eaten into my flesh, and I sank again, trembling and hopeless into my miserable self." Shelley contrasts Victor to her husband's mythological character, doomed by a god for his gift to man and chained to a cliff where vultures daily eat his liver, which grows back at night so that he suffers again. Where Prometheus eventually escapes his chains and eternal torture, Victor cannot. The novel's subtitle, *The Modern Prometheus*, most prominently calls attention to that myth and announces that *Frankenstein* will update the plot. In this modern characterization, Prometheus seeks to give humanity the gift of life but instead brings the gift of death.

The Monster as Pop Culture Icon

Another important topic in the critical study of *Frankenstein* is what popular culture has made of the monster. Many people first meet Shelley's monster not through the novel itself but via another medium, whether advertising, cartoons, games, comics, or film. The monster may be friendly and amiable or even more horrifying than characterized by Shelley. The fiction writer and critic Brian Aldiss labels *Frankenstein* the "first great myth of the Industrial age," noting that it has permeated every aspect of media and entertainment—but Aldiss also estimates that if one spoke to a thousand individuals who know of Frankenstein's monster, not one would have actually read the novel. In commenting on the creative license taken with Shelley's tale, he writes that "the monster has spawned Sons, Daughter, Ghosts, and Houses; has taken on Brides and created Woman; has perforce shacked up with Dracula and Wolf Man; has enjoyed Evil, Horror and Revenge." The conflict inherent to the human lust for power and the desire to exercise creative instinct for a higher good continues to resonate in ensuing ages.

The monster in many guises has entertained audiences for decades. His portrayal on screen began in the 1931 16-minute adaptation starring Charles Ogle as the monster. Various actors have endured layers of makeup and quite varied direction in English-language film versions since then, including, most famously, Boris Karloff, but also Lon Chaney, Jr.; Bela Lugosi; Christopher Lee; Kiwi Kingston; Susan Denberg; Peter Cushing; Freddie Jones; David Prowse; Michael Sarrazin; Leon Vitali; Randy Quaid; and Robert DeNiro. Non-English versions also abound, including films in Japanese, Mexican, and German. Many films utilize the character of the monster or Victor Frankenstein but vary the format. One version depicts a mad scientist assembling a monster from body parts of teenagers killed in car wrecks; another replaces electricity with nuclear power for a new kind of cautionary tale; another introduces the monster to nudists; another unites the outlaw Jesse James with Frankenstein's granddaughter; yet more expand the monster to even more monstrous proportions to do battle with gargantuan creatures; and one even establishes the monster as a military leader in World War II.

In addition, many movie and television parodies and satires of Mary Shelley's creation exist and continue to be produced. One of the best-known early television series was the American 1960s comedy series *The Munsters*, in which the character actor Fred Gwynne portrayed a Frankenstein-like family patriarch. A later use of Frankenstein themes and characters occurred as part of the post-modern 1990s dramatic series *The X-Files*. For those interested in the many refashionings of Shelley's characters and ideas, a multitude of informative popular culture books and websites exist.

CHARACTERS

Victor Frankenstein Victor Frankenstein's character serves as a cautionary tale. Through him, Shelley depicts the dangers inherent in the human pursuit of scientific answers and suggests that boundaries should exist to limit technological advances. Such advances, as in the creation of a monstrous human, may prove to be detrimental. Victor begins as a positive character, praised by Walton, who first meets him and introduces him to the reader as gentle, sensitive, remarkably intelligent, and the soul mate Walton has long sought. The background to his story encompassing his family suggests the possibility for domestic bliss or at least stability, where each member assumes responsibility for his or her traditional role. Such details have led critics to suggest that at that stage, Victor might represent Percy Shelley.

However, Victor wanders from that path through the temptation of science. His natural intelligence pushes him to question immutable laws of nature—that is, that people are born and die as a natural part of an intended cycle. Even after creating something that appeared monstrous, Victor could have redeemed himself by assuming responsibility for his actions as a parent and a leader in both his domestic and professional circles. Shelley makes abundantly clear through the monster himself that he was not born with the murderous instincts that overtake his remarkable ability to reason following consistent and unfounded rejection by every human he encounters. Although physically not desirable, the creature offers much promise, ignored by Victor, who operates on an instinctive repulsion.

In addition, despite modeling of compassionate behavior and the valuing of nature's inherent unbreakable laws by Clerval and Elizabeth, Victor rejects their approach and persists in wreaking havoc on those he loves. He seems to enjoy a moment of epiphany in chapter 11, saying, "For the first time . . . I felt what the duties of a creator towards his creature were, and that I ought to render him happy before I complained of his wickedness." However, he later decides he cannot complete those duties and thus denies his responsibility. His mistakes transform him, just as they do the monster, into a mass of wretched hate, regret, and rage. He seeks revenge as doggedly as he first sought the knowledge that he believed would bring light into a dark world by conquering human disease, suffering, and death. Unprepared for the role as birth parent, which he usurps from women, or even as a traditional father, Victor fails miserably in what had seemed a noble venture.

Victor blames his youthful desires, his destiny, for his later desperation, again assuming little personal responsibility. He finds blaming intangible "fate" and mysterious forces much simpler than blaming his own arrogance, concluding chapter 3 with the comment, "Destiny was too potent, and her immutable laws had decreed my utter and terrible destruction." He tells Walton, "When younger, I believed myself destined for some great enterprise," and he continues, "Oh! my friend, if you had known me as I once was, you would not recognise me in this state of degradation. Despondency rarely visited my heart; a high destiny seemed to bear me on, until I fell, never, never again to rise." This reference to falling demonstrates Victor's ignorance supporting his belief that he is destined to play the part of God. He speaks to Walton directly of how an early faith in his "talents" caused destruction, saying, "When I reflected on the work I had completed, no less a one than the creation of a sensitive and rational animal, I could not rank myself with the herd of common projectors. But this thought, which supported me in the commencement of my career, now serves only to plunge me lower in the dust." Victor clearly recognizes his folly at that late date; had he not held himself in such higher esteem while a young man, he would not have viewed creation of the monster as necessary. Thus, this creature from his past would not have haunted his future and led to his and many additional deaths. With the murders of his family and friends, Victor also loses innocence (William), a sense of justice (Justine), clarity and creativity (Clerval), and love and hope (Elizabeth).

Ultimately a failure, Victor will be successful in convincing Walton to follow another path. Near death, he admonishes Walton: "Seek happiness in tranquility, and avoid ambition, even if it be only the apparently innocent one of distinguishing yourself in science and discoveries." Because Walton represents Shelley's broader audience and learns from Victor's mistakes, Victor's sacrifice is not in vain. He gains some redemption by the story's end for not bestowing on Walton what might be an enduring legacy: the secret knowledge of producing life. Instead, he seeks to leave as his legacy a story that will serve to convince others not to make the same mistake. That story falls within the tradition of tales that celebrate great heroes, offering immortality through art rather than science. Shelley clearly transmits the message that imagination remains superior to misguided intellect, art superior to science.

The Monster Among the best-known literary figures of the 19th century, Frankenstein's monster represents science and man's desire for fame and self-aggrandizement gone wrong. Although born with the best instincts and intellect and imagination that science and metaphysics can bestow, the creature's isolation and lack of human nurturing and love prove tragic. Through him, Shelley suggests that the natural order must be preserved if humans are to avoid drastic consequences.

Born unnaturally, the creature also experiences an unnatural maturation, left alone in nature to find his way like an animal. Even though his prolonged exposure to the De Laceys supports the creature's development of language and intelligence, the literal wall that stands between him and that idyllic, loving community limits his ability to experience love. Without exposure to human affection and companionship, the creature is doomed to a life of misery, supporting Shelley's point that nothing proves more important than the support of a loving family unit. He explains his misery and heartbreak following the murder of Clerval and the fact that he pitied Frankenstein and "abhorred" himself. However, the creature reacts violently to the knowledge that "the author" of his "existence and of its unspeakable torments, dared to hope for happiness" while directing even more "wretchedness and despair" upon the creature. Meanwhile, Victor enjoys the life from which he has barred his creation, causing the monster to fill with "impotent envy and bitter indignation" and "an insatiable thirst for vengeance." Responsibility for the creature's tragic actions falls squarely on the shoulders of his self-indulgent and irresponsible scientist creator.

The monster does assume some responsibility in the novel's closing paragraphs, but he always measures his own capacity for vengeance against that of Victor. Ironically, the monster may be seen as the only of the three adventurers—Victor, Walton and himself—to find triumph and closure in his quest. While Victor and Walton do not fulfill their destinies or grasp their goals, the monster does. He tells Walton that he will "ascend my funeral pile triumphantly," choosing to die on a burning pyre that traditionally symbolizes a noble death. In part, he destroys himself so that no curious mind might find his body and try to duplicate his creation. He sees Victor dead and plans to eliminate the isolation he has so long suffered. It is proper that he follow in death the man "who called me into being." Although he tells Walton no one will remember him or Victor, the reader understands that Walton has immortalized them through the story that will be retold countless times. Such telling is the manner by which traditional heroes gain fame.

The monster has been viewed as a human alter ego, a physical manifestation of the evil man invites into his existence when he tampers with nature's immutable laws. In seeking to destroy the creature, Victor may be seen as desiring to kill his own evil nature. Neither the creature's superhuman physical capabilities nor his immense intellect can validate his existence when he lacks human affection and the satisfaction that acceptance of one's eventual death brings to humans. As he tells Walton, he cannot believe that he is "the same creature whose thoughts were once filled with sublime and transcendent visions of the beauty and the majesty of goodness." Critics believe the creature represented for Shelley the romantic sublime—the idea that a poet hero may change the world with transcendent thought and expression—gone wrong. The weakness of such ideology lay in its requirement that its pursuit should take precedence over commitment to family, leading to much suffering on the part of those forced to provide its support system with little return for that investment.

Elizabeth Lavenza Frankenstein Elizabeth Lavenza fulfills the role of the traditional supportive female, acting as an extension of Victor's mother after her death. In the original 1818 edition of the novel, Elizabeth was Victor's cousin, but in the revised 1831 edition, she became an orphan. More important, Shelley adjusted Elizabeth's characterization in the 1831 edition, according to critic Miranda Seymour, to shape her into a woman who anticipated Victorian Age sentiment, as can be seen in lines such as "Her soft voice, the sweet glance of her celestial eyes were ever there to bless and animate us." Seymour believes that changes to Elizabeth's character allowed Shelley to rehabilitate her own public characterization, helping her gain a "foothold in a circle of social, good-natured wives willing to ignore her disgraceful past."

Elizabeth's noble heritage is visible in the beauty first noticed by Victor's mother, her aristocratic station captured in the metaphor that compares her golden hair to a crown. As a small child who is "fairer than pictured cherub—a creature who seemed to shed radiance from her looks," she later possesses a "saintly soul" that shines as if part of a shrine in the Frankenstein home. Brought home by Victor's mother as Victor's playmate, her fate is to become his possession. When on her deathbed, Victor's mother joins the hands of Elizabeth and Victor and pronounces that all future happiness rests in their union, charging Elizabeth to become instant mother to her younger children. Following the mother's death, Elizabeth provides the family its soul and becomes the source of its virtue, her good characteristics struggling unsuccessfully to overcome Victor's evil characteristics.

Shelley demonstrates through Elizabeth that all of the cajoling, appealing, and love a woman may prove capable of giving pales before the male passion for self-aggrandizement. Elizabeth sacrifices herself first for her father, who does not want to claim her and foists her off on a lower-class foster family, for whom she must also sacrifice and work. Finally, she serves the Frankenstein family and later literally sacrifices herself on the altar of Victor's passion for success and then for revenge. Ignored by Victor, her needs deemed of little to no value, the objectified Elizabeth becomes in death, with her head lolling off the bedside, the toy doll that she proved to be throughout her life. She will have life after death, continuing as a helpmate to the hapless Victor, hers one of the spirits and shades that comfort and strengthen him in his pursuit of the creature.

Henry Clerval Clerval assumes the role of nature and imagination to contrast with Victor's penchant for science and rationality. Superior to Victor in creativity and goodness, he will exist mainly to serve Victor's needs. Of an artistic character, he also possesses intelligence that eventually qualifies him to attend university. However, once at Ingolstadt, where Victor has previously attended school, he is denied attendance, forced instead into the feminine role of caregiver and nursemaid for Victor. He has a propensity for language, suggesting a better developed penchant for communication than Victor, and lives to praise nature and its immutable laws—laws tragically ignored by Victor.

First described in chapter 2 as the son of a merchant and "a boy of singular talent and fancy" who "loved enterprise, hardship, and even danger," Clerval reads romantic chivalric tales, instructs his friends in plays as a child, and later writes drama himself. Like Elizabeth, he serves as a moral touchstone for his friend, focusing on "the moral relations of things" and "the virtues of heroes." Like Victor, he dreams of his name recorded among those "in story, as the gallant and adventurous benefactors of our species." Unlike Victor, he never loses sight of the ethical center of humanity in his ventures, although Victor attributes that in part to Elizabeth's positive influence; however, Victor still succumbs to temptation despite her influence. Clerval may be viewed in literary terms as Victor's foil; their contrast helps the reader better understand Victor.

Clerval remains for the most part a selfless individual, sacrificing months he might have spent in the classroom as he nurses Victor back to health following his creation of the monster. He makes himself available to travel with Victor, all the while extolling the wonders of nature and its immutable laws, his words falling on ears no longer able to hear them. In chapter 18, Clerval embodies both nature and the imagination as he speaks of the "divine river" and "the spirit that inhabits and guards" the area along the Rhone as having "a soul more in harmony with man, than those who pile the glacier." Victor tells Walton that Clerval "was a being formed in the very poetry of nature . . . his friendship was of that devoted and wondrous nature that the worldly-minded teach us to look for only in the imagination." He adds in the next chapter that in Clerval he saw the "image of my former self," indicating a time when he had first set out on the adventure that for him would end disastrously.

When Clerval leaves Victor behind to travel around Scotland, Victor begins shaping a woman for the creature, then destroys her and dumps her remains into the water. While describing his boat buffeted about by a storm, he confesses to having been terrified and states, "I had no compass with me." One might argue that Clerval had served as that compass. The next time Clerval makes an appearance, it is as a corpse, the creature's third victim. Upon viewing his body, Victor cries, "Clerval, my friend, my benefactor—." Clerval is among the spirits who later appear to Victor and accompany him as he chases the monster, ever present even in death to support and tend to his needs.

Victor Frankenstein's family Members of Victor Frankenstein's extended family—which includes the servant Justine, the adopted daughter Elizabeth, his parents, and two younger brothers, Ernest and William—exist to emphasize Victor's conflict. His mother, a paragon of virtuous, sacrificial womanhood must die in order to motivate Victor toward his goals of not only animating a body but also bringing the dead back from the grave. Justine represents service and justice, or its lack, as after serving the family loyally for years, she dies on Victor's account, saving him the mortification of accusations of madness, were he to confess.

William is a sacrificial lamb, innocent in his youth and wearing the mark of female beauty with his mother's picture around his neck, which motivates the monster to strangle him. In addition to unwittingly taunting the monster with his mother's forbidden beauty, William probably inspires jealousy in him over his relationship with Victor. The creature makes clear that it is William's familiar last name that leads to his murder.

Ernest provides interest as the family's sole survivor. As critics suggest, it might be his identification with nature that helps preserve him. In Elizabeth's letter to Victor in chapter 4, she writes of Ernest that he spends time "in the open air, climbing the hills or rowing on the lake." He also lacks Victor's "powers of application," which proves to be a blessing when one considers what such powers provided for Victor.

The family's father, Mr. Frankenstein, serves as a model for the traditional patriarch. Dependable, rational, in control, and strong for the sake of his family, he always manages to calm Victor. His visit following Victor's arrest for Clerval's murder helps return Victor, who declares him as a "good angel," to eventual health. Because he does not understand the cause of Victor's melancholy and unrest, he tries to correct what he believes might be "the futility of pride" in his eldest and works to help him become more socially involved. It is Mr. Frankenstein's efforts that procure a portion of Elizabeth's family fortune prior to her marriage to Victor. Upon news of her death, Victor describes him in chapter 23 as "excellent and venerable," his eyes becoming vacant, losing "their charm and delight." Too weak to bear the news of Elizabeth's murder in addition to the losses of William, Justine, and Clerval, he soon cannot arise from his bed and dies, ostensibly yet another victim of Victor and his monster.

FURTHER READING

Agrippa, Cornelius. *Three Books of Occult Philosophy.* 1531. Reprint, London: Chthonios, 1987.

Aldiss, Brian. *Billion Year Spree: A History of Science Fiction.* New York: Doubleday, 1973.

Aldrich, Marcia, and Richard Isomaki. "The Woman Writer as Frankenstein." In *Approaches to Teaching Shelley's* Frankenstein, edited by Stephen C. Behrendt, 121–126. New York: Modern Language Association, 1990.

Bann, Stephen, ed. *Frankenstein: Creation and Monstrosity.* London: Reaktion Books, 1994.

Batchelor, Rhonda. "The Rise and Fall of the Eighteenth Century's Authentic Feminine Voice." *Eighteenth-Century Fiction* 6, no. 4 (July 1994): 347–368.

Behrendt, Stephen. "Mary Shelly, *Frankenstein*, and the Woman Writer's Fate." In *Romantic Women Writer's Voices and Countervoice* edited by Paula R. Feldman and Theresa M. Kelley, 69–87. Hanover, N. H.: University Press of New England, 1995.

Belcher, R. "Psychoanalytic Criticism." Available online. URL: http://web.olivet.edu/english/rbelcher/lit310/310psy.htm. Accessed July 21, 2009.

Benjamin, Marina. "Elbow Room: Women Writers on Science, 1790–1840." In *Science and Sensibility: Gender and Scientific Enquiry 1780–1945*, edited by Marina Benjamin, 27–59. Oxford, U.K.: Basil Blackwell, 1991.

Bewell, Alan. "An Issue of Monstrous Desire: *Frankenstein* and Obstetrics." *Yale Journal of Criticism* 2, no. 1 (Fall 1988): 105–128.

Bok, Christian. "The Monstrosity of Representation: *Frankenstein* and Rousseau." *English Studies in Canada* 18, no. 4 (December 1992): 415–432.

Botting, Fred. "*Frankenstein* and the Language of Monstrosity." In *Reviewing Romanticism*, edited by Philip W. Martin and Robin Jarvis, 51–59. New York: St. Martin's Press, 1992.

Bronfen, Elizabeth. "Rewriting the Family: Mary Shelley's *Frankenstein* in Its Biographical/Textual Context." In *Frankenstein: Creation and Monstrosity*, edited by Stephen Bann, 16–38. London: Reaktion Books, 1994.

Brooks, Peter. "What Is a Monster? (According to *Frankenstein*)." In *Body Work: Objects of Desire in Modern Narrative.* Cambridge: Harvard University Press, 1993, 199–220.

Brown, Richard, dir. *The True Story of Frankenstein.* Produced by Zora Brown. Videocassette. A & E Home Video, 1994.

Butler, Marilyn. Introduction to Mary Shelley. *Frankenstein or the Modern Prometheus. The 1818 Text.* Oxford: Oxford University Press, 1993, ix–lvii.

Campbell, Joseph. *The Hero with a Thousand Faces.* 1949. Reprint, Princeton: Princeton University Press, 1990.

Chamberlain, Robert. "The Cultural Context of *Frankenstein* in Films: Oppression or Carnival?" *Proceedings of the Conference on Film and American Culture.* Williamsburg, Va.: Roy R. Charles Center, College of William and Mary, 1994, 7–14.

Clayton, Jay. "Concealed Circuits: Frankenstein's Monster, the Medusa, and the Cyborg." *Raritan* 15, no. 4 (Spring 1996): 53–69.

———. "Frankenstein's Futurity: Replicants and Robots." In *The Cambridge Companion to Mary Shelley*, edited by Esther Schor, 84–102. Cambridge: Cambridge University Press, 2004.

Clery, E. J. *Women's Gothic: From Clara Reeve to Mary Shelley.* Tavistock, U.K.: Northcote House, 2000.

"Contemporary Reviews." In *Romantic Circles: Mary Wollstonecraft Shelley Chronology and Resource Site*, edited by Neil Fraistat and Steven E. Jones. Available online. URL: http://www.rc.umd.edu/reference/chronologies/mschronology/reviews.html#Pres. Accessed January 2, 2010.

Corbett, Mary Jean. *Family Likeness: Sex, Marriage and Incest from Jane Austen to Virginia Woolf.* Ithaca, N.Y.: Cornell University Press, 2010.

Craig, Siobhan. "Monstrous Dialogues: Erotic Discourse and the Dialogic Constitution of the Subject in *Frankenstein*." In *A Dialogue of Voices: Feminist Literary Theory and Bakhtin*, edited by Karen Hohne and Helen Wussow, 83–96. Minneapolis: University of Minnesota Press, 1994.

Davidson, Jane P. "Golem—Frankenstein—Golem of Your Own." *Journal of the Fantastic in the Arts* 7, nos. 2–3 (1996): 228–243.

Davis, James P. "*Frankenstein* and the Subversion of the Masculine Voice." *Women's Studies* 21, no. 3 (1992): 307–322.

Dickerson, Vanessa D. "The Ghost of a Self: Female Identity in Mary Shelley's *Frankenstein.*" *Journal of Popular Culture* 27, no. 3 (Winter 1993): 79–91.

Dutoit, Thomas. "Re-specting the Face as the Moral (of) Fiction in Mary Shelley's *Frankenstein.*" *Modern Language Notes* 109, no. 5 (December 1994): 847–871.

Essaka, Joshua. "'Marking the Dates with Accuracy': The Time Problem in Mary Shelley's *Frankenstein.*" *Gothic Studies* 3, no. 3 (December 2001): 279–308.

Favret, Mary A. "The Letters of *Frankenstein.*" In *Romantic Correspondence: Women, Politics, and the Fiction of Letters.* Cambridge: Cambridge University Press, 1993, 176–196.

———. "A Woman Writer's the Fiction of Science: The Body in *Frankenstein.*" *Genders* 14 (Fall 1992): 50–65.

Fleck, P. D. "Mary Shelley's Notes to Shelley's Poems and *Frankenstein.*" *Studies in Romanticism* 6 (1967): 226–254.

Forry, Steven Earl. *Hideous Progenies: Dramatizations of "Frankenstein" from Mary Shelley to the Present.* Philadelphia: University of Pennsylvania Press, 1990.

Frank, Frederick S. "Mary Shelley's *Frankenstein*: A Register of Research." *Bulletin of Bibliography* 40 (September 1983): 163–188.

Fredricks, Nancy. "On the Sublime and the Beautiful in Shelley's *Frankenstein.*" *Essays in Literature* 23. no. 2 (Fall 1996): 178–189.

Galvani, Luigi. *Commentary on the Effect of Electricity on Muscular Motion.* Translated by Robert Montraville Green. Cambridge, Mass.: Elizabeth Licht, 1953.

Gilbert, Sandra, and Susan Gubar. "Horror's Twin: Mary Shelley's Monstrous Eve." In *The Madwoman in the Attic: The Woman Writer and the Nineteenth-Century Literary Imagination.* New Haven, Conn.: Yale University Press, 1979, 213–247.

Glance, Jonathan C. "'Beyond the Unusual Bounds of Reverie?': Another Look at the Dreams in *Frankenstein.*" *Journal of the Fantastic in the Arts* 7, no. 4 (1996): 30–47.

Glut, Donald F. *The Frankenstein Legend: A Tribute to Mary Shelley and Boris Karloff.* Metuchen, N.J.: Scarecrow, 1973.

Goldner, Ellen J. "Monstrous Body, Tortured Soul: *Frankenstein* at the Juncture between Discourses." In *Genealogy and Literature,* edited by Lee Quimby, 28–47. Minneapolis: University of Minnesota Press, 1995.

Goodson, A. C. "Frankenstein in the Age of Prozac." *Literature and Medicine* 15, no. 1 (Spring 1996): 16–32.

Hall, Jean. "*Frankenstein*: The Horrifying Otherness of Family." *Essays in Literature* 17 (1990): 179–189.

Heffernan, James A. W. "Looking for the Monster: *Frankenstein* and Film." *Critical Inquiry* 24, no. 1 (Autumn 1997): 133–158.

Helman, Cecil. *Body Myths.* London: Chatto & Windus, 1991.

———. *The Body of Frankenstein's Monster.* New York: W. W. Norton, 1992.

———. *The Body of Frankenstein's Monster: Essays in Myth and Medicine.* Cecil Helman, 2004.

Henry, John. "Magic and Science in the Sixteenth and Seventeenth Centuries." In *Companion to the History of Modern Science,* edited by R.C. Olby et al., 583–596. London: Routledge, 1996.

Higdon, David Leon. "Frankenstein as Founding Myth in Gary Larson's *The Far Side.*" *Journal of Popular Culture* 28, no. 1 (Summer 1994): 49–60.

Hindle, Maurice. "Vital Matters: Mary Shelley's *Frankenstein* and Romantic Science." *Critical Survey* 2, no. 1 (1990): 29–35.

Hitchcock, Susan Tyler. *Frankenstein: A Cultural History.* New York: W. W. Norton, 2007.

Hobbs, Colleen. "Reading the Symptoms: An Exploration of Repression and Hysteria in Mary Shelley's *Frankenstein.*" *Studies in the Novel* 25 (1993): 252–269.

Hodges, Devon. "*Frankenstein* and the Feminine Subversion of the Novel." *Tulsa Studies in Women's Literature* 2 (Autumn 1983): 155–164.

Hoeveler, Diane Long. "*Frankenstein,* Feminism, and Literary Theory." In *The Cambridge Companion to Mary Shelley,* edited by Esther Schor, 45–62. Cambridge: Cambridge University Press, 2004.

Hogle, Jerrold E. "Otherness in *Frankenstein*: The Confinement/Autonomy of Fabrication." In *New Casebooks: Frankenstein. Mary Shelley,* edited by Fred Botting, 206–234. New York: St. Martin's, 1994.

Hollinger, Veronica. "Putting on the Feminine: Gender and Negativity in *Frankenstein* and *The*

Handmaid's Tale." In *Negation, Critical Theory, and Postmodern Textuality,* edited by Daniel Fischlin, 203–224. Boston: Kluwer, 1994.

Howard, Jennifer. "The Birth of 'Frankenstein.'" *Chronicle of Higher Education* (November 7, 2008): B12–B15.

Huet, Marie-Hélène. "Unwanted Paternity: The Genesis of *Frankenstein.*" In *Monstrous Imagination.* Cambridge: Harvard University Press, 1993, 129–162.

Johnson, Barbara. "My Monster/My Self." *Diacritics* 12 (1982): 2–10.

Jordanova, Ludmilla. "Melancholy Reflection: Constructing an Identity for Unveilers of Nature." In *Frankenstein: Creation and Monstrosity,* edited by Stephen Bann, 60–76. London: Reaktion Books, 1994.

Ketterer, David. "Frankenstein's 'Conversion' from Natural Magic to Modern Science—and a Shifted (and Converted) Last Draft Insert." *Science-Fiction Studies* 24, no. 1 (March 1997): 57–78.

Kiceluk, Stephanie. "Made in His Image: Frankenstein's Daughters." *Michigan Quarterly Review* 30, no. 1 (Winter 1991): 110–126.

Kieckhefer, Richard. *Magic in the Middle Ages.* Cambridge: Cambridge University Press, 1989.

Knellwolf, Krista, and Jane Goodall. *Frankenstein's Science.* Aldington, U.K.: Ashgate, 2008.

Lamb, John B. "Mary Shelley's *Frankenstein* and Milton's Monstrous Myth." *Nineteenth-Century Fiction* 47, no. 3 (December 1992): 303–319.

Landsdown, Richard. "Beginning Life: Mary Shelley's Introduction to *Frankenstein.*" *The Critical Review* 35 (1995): 81–94.

Lauritsen, John. *The Man Who Wrote Frankenstein.* Boston: Pagan Press, 2007.

Lawrence, Christopher. "The Power and the Glory: Humphry Davy and Romanticism." In *Romanticism and the Sciences,* edited by Andrew Cunningham and Nicholas Jardine, 213–227. Cambridge: Cambridge University Press, 1990.

Lederer, Susan E. *Frankenstein: Penetrating the Secrets of Nature.* New Brunswick, N.J.: Rutgers University Press, 2002.

Levine, George, ed. *The Endurance of Frankenstein: Essays on Mary Shelley's Novel.* Berkeley: University of California Press, 1982.

Lew, Joseph W. "The Deceptive Other: Mary Shelley's Critique of Orientalism in *Frankenstein.*" *Studies in Romanticism* 30, no. 2 (Summer 1991): 255–283.

London, Bette. "Mary Shelley, *Frankenstein,* and the Spectacle of Masculinity." *PMLA* 108, no. 2 (March 1993): 253–267.

Malchow, H. L. "Was Frankenstein's Monster 'a Man and a Brother'?" In *Gothic Images of Race in Nineteenth-Century Britain.* Stanford, Calif.: Stanford University Press, 1996, 9–40.

Marshall, Tim. *Murdering to Dissect: Grave-robbing, Frankenstein and the Anatomy Literature.* Manchester, U.K.: Manchester University Press, 1995.

Martin, Philip W., and Robin Jarvis, eds. *Reviewing Romanticism.* New York: St. Martin's, 1992.

McLane, Maureen Noelle. "Literature Species: Populations, 'Humanities,' and *Frankenstein.*" *ELH* 63, no. 4 (Winter 1996): 959–988.

McInerney, Peter. "*Frankenstein* and the Godlike Science of Letters." *Genre* 13 (Winter 1980): 455–475.

McWhir, Anne. "Teaching the Monster to Read: Mary Shelley, Education, and *Frankenstein.*" In *The Educational Legacy of Romanticism,* edited by John Willinsky, 73–92. Waterloo, Ontario, Canada: Wilfrid Laurier University Press, 1990.

Mellor, Anne K. "Possessing Nature: The Female in *Frankenstein.*" In *Romanticism and Feminism,* edited by Anne Mellor, 220–232. Bloomington: Indiana University Press, 1988.

Michel, Frann. "Lesbian Panic and Mary Shelley's *Frankenstein.*" In *Frankenstein: Complete, Authoritative Text with Biographical, Historical, and Cultural Contexts, Critical History, and Essays from Contemporary Critical Perspectives,* edited by Johanna M. Smith, 384–395. Boston: Bedford/St. Martin's, 2000.

Michie, Elsie B. "Production Replaces Creation: Market Forces and *Frankenstein* as a Critique of Romanticism." *Nineteenth-Century Contexts* 12, no. 1 (1988): 27–33.

Milano, Ray. *Monsters: A Celebration of the Classics from Universal Studios.* New York: Del Rey, 2006.

Moers, Ellen. "Female Gothic." In *The Endurance of* Frankenstein: *Essays on Mary Shelley's Novel,* edited by George Levine and U. C. Knoepflmacher, 77–87. Berkeley: University of California Press, 1979.

Montag, Warren. "The 'Workshop of Filthy Creation': A Marxist Reading of *Frankenstein*." In *Frankenstein: Complete, Authoritative Text with Biographical, Historical, and Cultural Contexts, Critical History, and Essays from Contemporary Critical Perspectives*, edited by Johanna M. Smith, 384–395. Boston: Bedford/St. Martin's, 2000.

Morton, Timothy. *Mary Shelley's Frankenstein: A Sourcebook*. New York: Taylor & Francis, 2002.

Murfin, Ross C. "Cultural Criticism and *Frankenstein*." In *Frankenstein: Complete, Authoritative Text with Biographical, Historical, and Cultural Contexts, Critical History, and Essays from Contemporary Critical Perspectives*, edited by Johanna M. Smith, 396–409. Boston: Bedford/St. Martin's, 2000.

———. "Feminist Criticism and *Frankenstein*." In *Frankenstein: Complete, Authoritative Text with Biographical, Historical, and Cultural Contexts, Critical History, and Essays from Contemporary Critical Perspectives*, edited by Johanna M. Smith, 297–305. Boston: Bedford/St. Martin's, 2000.

———. "Gender Criticism and *Frankenstein*." In *Frankenstein: Complete, Authoritative Text with Biographical, Historical, and Cultural Contexts, Critical History, and Essays from Contemporary Critical Perspectives*, edited by Johanna M. Smith, 334–345. Boston: Bedford/St. Martin's, 2000.

———. "Marxist Criticism and *Frankenstein*." In *Frankenstein: Complete, Authoritative Text with Biographical, Historical, and Cultural Contexts, Critical History, and Essays from Contemporary Critical Perspectives*, edited by Johanna M. Smith, 368–380. Boston: Bedford/St. Martin's, 2000.

———. "Psychoanalytic Criticism and *Frankenstein*." In *Frankenstein: Complete, Authoritative Text with Biographical, Historical, and Cultural Contexts, Critical History, and Essays from Contemporary Critical Perspectives*, edited by Johanna M. Smith, 263–274. Boston: Bedford/St. Martin's, 2000.

Murray, E. B. "Shelley's Contribution to Mary's *Frankenstein*." *Keats-Shelley Memorial Bulletin* 29 (1978): 50–68.

Negra, Diana. "Coveting the Feminine: Victor Frankenstein, Norman Bates, and Buffalo Bill." *Literature Film Quarterly* 24, no. 2 (1996): 193–200.

O'Rourke, James. "'Nothing More Unnatural': Mary Shelley's Revision or Rousseau." *ELH* 56, no. 3 (Fall 1989): 543–569.

PBS. "James Blundell." *Red Gold: The Story of Blood*. Available online. URL: http://www.pbs.org/wnet/redgold/innovators/bio_blundell.html. Accessed October 3, 2009.

Perkins, Margo V. "The Nature of Otherness: Class and Difference in Mary Shelley's *Frankenstein*." *Studies in the Humanities* 19, no. 1 (June 1992): 27–42.

Perosa, Sergio. "Franklin to Frankenstein: A Note on Lighting and Novels." In *Science and Imagination in XVIIIth-Century British Culture*, edited by Sergio Rossi, 321–328. Milan: Unicopli, 1987.

Purinton, Marjean. "Mary Shelley's Science Fiction Short Stories and the Legacy of Wollstonecraft's Feminism." *Women's Studies* 30, no. 2 (April 2001): 147–174.

Randal, Fred V. "*Frankenstein*, Feminism and the Intertextuality of Mountains." *Studies in Romanticism* 23 (Winter 1984): 515–533.

———. "The Political Geography of Horror in Mary Shelley's *Frankenstein*." *ELH* 70, no. 2 (Summer 2003): 465–491.

Rauch, Alan. "The Monstrous Body of Knowledge in Mary Shelley's *Frankenstein*." *Studies in Romanticism* 34, no. 2 (Summer 1995): 227–253.

Reed, John R. "Will and Fate in *Frankenstein*." *Bulletin of Research in the Humanities* 8, no. 3 (1980): 319–338.

Richardson, Alan. "From *Emilie* to *Frankenstein*: The Education of Monsters." *European Romantic Review* 1, no. 2 (Winter 1991): 147–162.

Rieder, John. "Embracing the Alien: Science Fiction in Mass Culture." *Science-Fiction Studies* 9, no. 1 (March 1982): 26–37.

Rieger, James. "Dr. Polidori and the Genesis of *Frankenstein*." *Studies in English Literature* 3 (1963): 461–472.

———. "Mary Shelley's Life and the Composition of *Frankenstein*." In *Frankenstein: or, The Modern Prometheus*, edited by James Reiger. Indianapolis: Bobbs-Merrill, 1974. xi–xxxvii.

Robinson, Charles E., ed. *Mary Shelley: Collected Tales and Stories with Original Engravings*. Baltimore: Johns Hopkins University Press, 1976.

———. *Mary Wollstonecraft Shelley.* Volume IX. The *"Frankenstein" Notebooks.* New York: Garland, 1996.

Rogers, Michael. "Classic Returns." Review of *The Essential Frankenstein: The Definitive Edition of Mary Shelley's Classic Novel,* edited by Leonard Wolf. *Library Journal* (January 1994): 172.

———. "Classic Returns." Review of *Frankenstein,* by Mary Shelley; *Frankenstein,* by Mary Shelley, illustrations by Barry Moser; and *The Last Man,* by Mary Shelley. *Library Journal* (November 15, 1994): 93.

Rowen, Norma. "The Making of Frankenstein's Monster: Post-Golem, Pre-robot." In *State of the Fantastic: Selected Essays from Eleventh International Conference on the Fantastic in the Arts, 1990,* edited by Nicholas Ruddick, 169–177. Westport, Conn.: Greenwood, 1992.

Rubenstein, Marc A. "My Accursed Origin: The Search for the Mother in *Frankenstein.*" *Studies in Romanticism* 15 (Spring 1976): 165–194.

Sayres, William G. "Compounding the Crime: Ingratitude and the Murder Conviction of Justine Moritz in *Frankenstein.*" *ELN* 31 (1994): 48–54.

Schefer, Jean-Louis. "The Bread and the Blood." In *Frankenstein, Creation and Monstrosity,* edited by Stephen Bann, 177–192. London: Reaktion Books, 1994.

Schopf, Sue Weaver. "'Of what a strange nature is knowledge!': Hartleian Psychology and the Creature's Arrested Moral Sense in Mary Shelley's *Frankenstein.*" *Romanticism Past and Present* 5 (1981): 33–52.

Schor, Esther. "*Frankenstein* and Film." In *The Cambridge Companion to Mary Shelley.* edited by Esther Schor, 63–83. Cambridge: Cambridge University Press, 2004.

———, ed. *The Cambridge Companion to Mary Shelley.* Cambridge: Cambridge University Press. 2004.

Scott, Walter. "Remarks on *Frankenstein, or the Modern Prometheus;* a novel." *Blackwood's Edinburgh Magazine* 2 (March 1818): 613–620. Available online. URL: http://www.rc.und.edu/reference/chronologies/nschronology/reviews/benrev.html. Accessed June 24, 2010.

Seymour, Miranda. *Mary Shelley.* New York: Grove Press, 2002.

Shelley, Mary. *Frankenstein: Complete, Authoritative Text with Biographical, Historical, and Cultural Contexts, Critical History, and Essays from Contemporary Critical Perspectives.* Edited by Johanna M. Smith. Boston: Bedford/St. Martin's, 2000.

Silver, Alain. *More Things Than Are Dreamt of: Masterpieces of Supernatural Horror, from Mary Shelley to Stephen King.* New York: Limelight Editions, 1994.

Simmons, Eileen A. "'Frankenstein' for the Twenty-First Century: An Exploration of Contemporary Issues." *English Journal* 83 (1994): 30–32.

Slusser, George. "The Frankenstein Barrier." In *Fiction 2000: Cyberpunk and the Future of Narrative,* edited by George Slusser and Tom Shippey. 46–71. Athens: University of Georgia Press, 1992.

Smith, Crosbie. "*Frankenstein* and Natural Magic." In *Frankenstein: Creation and Monstrosity,* edited by Stephen Bann, 39–59. London: Reaktion Books, 1994.

Smith, Johanna M., 'Hideous Progenies': Texts of *Frankenstein.*" In *Texts and Textuality: Textual Instability, Theory, Interpretation, and Pedagogy,* edited by Philip Cohen, 121–140. New York: Garland, 1997.

———. Introduction to *Frankenstein: Complete, Authoritative Text with Biographical, Historical, and Cultural Contexts, Critical History, and Essays from Contemporary Critical Perspectives,* edited by Johanna M. Smith, 19–25. Boston: Bedford/St. Martin's 2000.

St. Clair, William. "The Impact of *Frankenstein.*" In *Mary Shelley in Her Times,* edited by Betty T. Bennet and Stuart Curran, 38–65. Baltimore: Johns Hopkins University Press, 2000.

Stryker, Susan. "My Words to Victor Frankenstein above the Village of Chamounix: Performing Transgender Rage." *GLO: A Journal of Lesbian and Gay Studies* 1 (1994): 237–254.

Swingle, L. J. "Frankenstein's Monster and its Romantic Relatives: Problems of Knowledge in English Romanticism." *Texas Studies in Literature and Language* 15 (1973): 51–65.

Thorne, Barrie, with Marilyn Yalom. *Rethinking the Family.* New York: Longman, 1982.

Three Faces of Evil: Frankenstein, Dracula, and Dr. Jekyll & Mr. Hyde. Laserdisc. Fairfield, Conn.: Queue, Inc., 1994.

Todd, Janet. "Frankenstein's Daughter: Mary Shelley and Mary Wollstonecraft." *Women and Literature* 4, no. 2 (Fall 1976): 18–27.

Travers, Peter. Review of *Mary Shelley's Frankenstein*, directed by Kenneth Branagh. *Rolling Stone*, 1 December 1994, 131–132.

Tropp, Martin. *Mary Shelley's Monster*. Boston: Houghton Mifflin, 1976.

Tuite, Clara. "Frankenstein's Monster and Malthus's 'Jaundiced Eye': Population, Body Politics, and the Monstrous Sublime." *Eighteenth-Century Life* 22, no. 1 (February 1998): 141–155.

Turney, John. *Frankenstein's Footsteps: Science, Genetics and Popular Culture*. New Haven, Conn.: Yale University Press, 1998.

Ty, Eleanor. "Mary Shelley." In *British Romantic Novelists, 1789–1832*. Vol. 116 of *Dictionary of Literary Biography*, edited by Bradford K. Mudge, 311–325. New York: Gale Research, 1992.

Ure, Andrew. *On Galvinism*. London: Privately printed, 1890.

"*Valperga; or the Life and Adventures of Castruccio, Prince of Lucca*. By the Author of 'Frankenstein.'" Review. *Blackwood's Edinburgh Magazine* 13 (March 1823): 283–293. Available online. URL: http://www.rc.umd.edu/reference/chronologies/mschronology/reviews/valpbw.html. Accessed July 26, 2009.

Veeder, William. *Mary Shelley & Frankenstein: The Fate of Androgyny*. Chicago: University of Chicago Press, 1986.

Vernon, Peter. "*Frankenstein*: Science and Electricity." *Études Anglaises* 50, no. 3 (July–September 1997): 270–283.

Vine, Steven. "Filthy Types: *Frankenstein*, Figuration, Femininity." *Critical Survey* 8, no. 3 (1996): 246–258.

Weissman, Judith. "A Reading of *Frankenstein* as the Complaint of a Political Wife." *Colby Library Quarterly* 12 (December 1976): 171–180.

Wilkinson, Charles Henry. *Elements of Galvanism in Theory and Practice*. 2 vols. London, C. H. Wilkinson, Murray-McMillan, 1804.

Willis, Martin. "*Frankenstein* and the Soul." *Essays in Criticism* 45, no. 1 (January 1995): 24–35.

Youngquist, Paul. "*Frankenstein*: The Mother, the Daughter, and the Monster." *Philological Quarterly* 70 (1991): 339–359.

Ziolkowski, Theodore. "Science, *Frankenstein*, and Myth." *Sewanee Review* 89, no. 1 (Winter 1981): 34–56.

Zonana, Joyce. "'They Will Prove the Truth of My Tale': Safie's Letters as the Feminist Core of Mary Shelley's *Frankenstein*." *Journal of Narrative Technique* 21, no. 2 (Spring 1991): 170–184.

History of a Six Weeks' Tour (1817)

Early in their marriage, PERCY BYSSHE SHELLEY urged Mary to "obtain literary reputation," as she reports in the 1831 introduction to *Frankenstein*. First published in 1818, *Frankenstein* would achieve that goal for Mary Shelley, its presence secure in the literary canon far before inclusion of works by women was the norm. At the same time that Shelley was at work on her novel, she wrote *History of a Six Week's Tour*, which included contributions from Percy. Shelley scholar Betty Bennett claims that *Frankenstein* and *History*, both published anonymously, "subverted current genres, using accepted forms for other than their presumed purpose, in the interest of her [Shelley's] reformist agenda." According to Bennett, Shelley's *History* "established a philosophic perspective and technique" that was missing from other travel writings and that would inform Shelley's future writing.

Publication of travel journals, generally composed of letters, was neither an unusual nor a new phenomenon. Shelley's mother, MARY WOLLSTONECRAFT, among others, had also written an epistolary travelogue, hers entitled *Letters from Norway* (1796), an account that the Shelley group read as they toured. Such travelogues appealed to readers for two reasons. First, they enjoyed learning about foreign populations and geography, particularly those they might never visit. Second, they were intrigued by the autobiographical content, as authors often included personal reflections on the meaning and effect of travel.

Shelley's *History* traces the couple's tour following their elopement and draws heavily on both

Title page of Mary Shelley's *History of a Six Weeks' Tour* from 1817.

her and Percy's journals. After a preface written by Percy, she begins her book with the first travel entry in her journal, dated July 18, 1814, as the Shelleys began winding their way through France, Switzerland, Germany, and Holland. The entries conclude on September 13, when the Shelleys ran short of funds and were forced to return to England. The 1814 portion reads like a memoir and serves as the bulk of *History*. However, the book also contains four letters written from Switzerland in 1816, two by Mary and two by Percy, as well as Percy's poem "Mont Blanc." As Bennett describes the work's content, she emphasizes that while the book has "the trappings of conventional travel diaries and correspondence," Shelley includes more than observation and travel advice. She also offers readers "advice about humanistic values."

In his preface, Percy Shelley explains that the writings recount the travels of the author, her husband, and stepsister (Claire Clairmont), who chase "like the swallow, the inconstant summer of delight and beauty which invests this visible world." The women travel on foot, unusual for females, and search for "delight and beauty" rather than the traditional visit to art and antique vendors and sites. That description foreshadows GEORGE GORDON BYRON's later label *Anglo-Italian*, a phrase employed by Mary Shelley in writing about the English visitor to Italy who becomes more than a tourist, learning the language and ignoring tourist attractions in favor of the pleasure of more natural delights.

Despite her philosophical and political focus, Shelley also included reflections on fashions and cultural habits, knowing that her readers would share her own interest in the mode of foreign countries. Although sickened and fatigued by the frightening trip across the English Channel from England to France, she was not so exhausted as to miss the women's costumes upon landing, so unlike what one would find in England. She describes with interest "the women with high caps and short jackets; the men with earrings; ladies walking about with high bonnets or *coiffures* lodged on the top of the head, the short hairs dragged up underneath, without any stray curls to decorate the temples or cheeks." In Paris, she describes the boulevards, which she prefers to the formal gardens. One boulevard is "eight miles in extent, and planted on either side with trees. At one end is a superb cascade, which refreshes the senses by its continual splashing."

Upon crossing from France into Switzerland, Shelley writes of the contrast between the two countries: "The Swiss cottages are much cleaner and neater, and the inhabitants exhibit the same contrast. The Swiss women wear a great deal of white linen, and their whole dress is always perfectly clean." She finds few kind words to describe the lower-class Germans with whom they later traveled, writing "nothing could be more horribly disgusting than the lower order of smoking, drinking Germans . . . they swaggered and talked, and what was hideous to English eyes, kissed one another." She does add that the few members of the merchant class with whom they traveled "appeared well-informed and polite." She also describes the only pretty woman they met, "a truly German beauty" encountered at an inn, who had "grey eyes, slightly tinged with brown and expressive of uncommon sweetness and frankness." In Holland, she noted Rotterdam's cleanliness, adding that "the Dutch even wash the outside brickwork of their houses."

The trio traveled through a Europe recovering from war, inviting Shelley's comments on war's politics and devastation. As Jeanne Moskal explains, the trio experienced a post-Napoleon Europe in spring 1814, and Shelley worried that Paris, one of their destinations, might suffer further destruction. She includes a warning by a Frenchwoman of the dangers of possible rape by the remnants of Napoleon's forces still prowling the countryside. Shelley notes that the group was quickly reminded of the "great and extraordinary events" that had recently occurred, describing the town of Nogent as in complete ruin, "entirely desolated by the Cossacks." She adds, "the distress of the inhabitants, whose houses had been burned, their cattle killed, and all their wealth destroyed, has given a sting to my detestation of war." In writing about the Swiss, she noted that they appeared to be "a people slow of comprehension and of action; but habit has made them unfit for slavery, and they would, I have little doubt, make a brave defence [sic] against any invader of their freedom."

Napoleon returned for his 100 days' rule prior to the group's second trip in 1815, and both Shelleys focused in their writing on his political defeat. They viewed it both philosophically and aesthetically, musing on forces that outlast those of politics, such as education and the beauty of nature. Rousseau's theories had been important to Mary Shelley's parents' educational ideals and key to their support of the French Revolution. Moskal notes that Rousseau's ideas had fueled the revolution and underscored the importance of equality; Wollstonecraft had labeled him "the true Prometheus of Sentiment." Mary Shelley includes in her *History* a description of viewing the obelisk dedicated to Rousseau, who would be exiled by the very men later executed at the site of the monument during the Revolution.

Shelley adopted the typical reference to her fellow travelers, meant to hide their identities, as she refers to C*** and P***, instead of Claire and Percy. However, Mary and Percy's elopement had become well known. Familiarity with their story allowed readers to vicariously participate in their perspective. Although readers may not have known that Shelley was incorporating her mother's views into her own writing, they would benefit from Wollstonecraft's techniques of reflecting on politics and social mores.

In Mary Shelley's letter in the travelogue, dated summer 1816, she describes the effect of their return to Geneva, where Mont Blanc often captured her attention. With the perspective of a now-seasoned traveler, both in a geographic and a life experience sense, she expresses optimism and hope for the future with Percy. They would be able to marry by December that year, following the suicide of his wife Harriet, and for a time, she could dream of years untouched by further grief. Although that vision would be repeatedly disrupted, her appreciation of her surroundings always survived. She closes her letter with a description of the area at the foot of Mont Blanc: "A more experienced bird may be more difficult in its choice of a bower; but in my present temper of mind, the budding flowers, the fresh grass of spring, and the happy creatures about me . . . are quite enough to afford me exquisite delight." As if afforded an unconscious presentiment of turbulent times to come, she adds that she will continue to draw life from nature, "even if clouds should shut out Mont Blanc from my sight."

FURTHER READING

Bennett, Betty T. *Mary Wollstonecraft Shelley: An Introduction.* Baltimore: Johns Hopkins University Press, 1996.

Moskal, Jeanne. "Travel Writing." In *The Cambridge Companion to Mary Shelley,* edited by Esther Schor, 242–258. New York: Cambridge University Press, 2003.

Shelley, Mary. *History of a six weeks' tour through a part of France, Switzerland, Germany and Holland: with letters descriptive of a sail round the Lake of Geneva, and of the glaciers of Chamouni.* Available online. URL: http://www.archixve.org/details/sixweekhistoryof00shelrich. Accessed February 27, 2011.

journals and letters

Like other authors, Mary Shelley reveals in her personal writings much about circumstances surrounding the production of her work. Collections of her letters and journal entries were finally published in the 1980s, revealing someone far different from the dependent and compromising author previously imagined. While discovery of details about her relationship with PERCY BYSSHE SHELLEY was crucial, her correspondence and journals also prove that she held her own ideas and lived a life of the mind previously not attributed to her. Mary Shelley's letters, journal, notes on manuscripts, and notebooks are housed in various places, and many have been gathered into collections, as noted in the further reading section below.

Shelley began recording her daily activities and her reactions to events in her life at an early age. Such journal entries gave later scholars a clear picture of her upbringing and early philosophy. As cited by the scholar Emily Sunstein, as a young teen Shelley wrote, "[t]he human heart is nearest moral perfection, most alive, and yet most innocent, aspiring to good, without a knowledge of evil." Years later, she would write in her journal about her childhood, describing such activities as her wandering about the St. Pancras Old Church (London) graveyard, dreaming of what she might be. In a December 2, 1834, journal entry, Shelley wrote of her daydreams: "They peopled the Churchyard I was doomed so young to wander in—hope drank at her [Fantasia's] fountain—and she fed on the Ambrosia of hope." That early image of Mary framed the imaginative years that would follow, years brought to life by her personal descriptions and commentary.

Shelley also revealed her earliest thoughts about Percy Shelley, writing as a teen that he had given her a notebook to use in translating the *Aeneid*. She noted in the book, "Shall I write a poem on receiving a cordial shake of the hand at parting from an esteemed and excellent person . . . ah I cannot write poetry." That notebook still exists, labeled the Percy Bysshe and Mary W. Shelley Notebook, Manuscript Division, held in the Library of Congress. As Mary's relationship with Percy developed, they frequently exchanged letters, many of which have been preserved. One of the earliest, written in October 1814, notes, "[D]earest Shelley you are solitary and uncomfortable why cannot I be with you to cheer you and to press you to my heart oh my love . . ."

A prolific letter writer, Shelley wrote for both professional and personal reasons. One of the professionally motivated notes went to Sir Walter Scott following his glowing review of *Frankenstein* (1818), which had been published anonymously. In the review, Scott hazarded a guess that Percy Shelley had written the work, a mistake that Mary politely corrected. She wrote, "I am anxious to prevent your continuing in the mistake of supposing Mr. Shelley guilty of a juvenile attempt of mine; to which—from it being written at an early age, I abstained from putting my name" (June 14, 1818). She also wrote to publishers as she confirmed agreements to sell her writing and corresponded with others for details to augment her work. For instance, through material gathered through correspondence, she informed her historical novels and the various biographies that she published, such as *Lives of the Most Eminent Literary and Scientific Men of Italy, Spain, and Portugal* (1835–37). She lacked what the scholar Betty Bennett refers to as "ready Spanish resources," a fact revealed in a letter, which Shelley concludes with the statement, "The best is that the very thing which occasions the difficulty makes it interesting—namely—the treading in unknown paths & dragging out unknown things—I wish I could go to Spain."

However, most of Shelley's correspondence is of a personal nature, interesting to those who wish to better understand her complicated relationship with Percy. Clearly gossip and speculation about his affairs bothered her, yet at times she expressed as much interest in the women who fascinated Percy

Photograph of St. Pancras Old Church in London. As a child, Mary Shelley often read by Mary Wollstonecraft's grave in St. Pancras's churchyard. *(Used under a Creative Commons license)*

as did he. She confided to friends through correspondence that upon first making the acquaintance of the beautiful young Emilia Viviana, daughter of the governor of Pisa in whose honor Percy would write "Epipsychidion," she was enthralled with her. Emilia would act as a model for the main female character in Mary Shelley's later short story "The Bride of Modern Italy." At other times, she employed her letter-writing skills to defend Percy, and later herself, from the gossip that so often surrounded them. When the Shelleys' Swiss nursemaid became pregnant by one of their servants, and both were dismissed from employment, the nursemaid told others that Mary's stepsister, Claire, was Percy's lover. In a letter to acquaintances dated August 10, 1821, Shelley wrote, "Mr. Shelley is at present on a visit to Lord Byron at Ravenna and I received a letter from him today containing accounts that make my hand tremble so much that I can hardly hold the pen . . . [The maid] says Claire was Shelley's mistress." She explains that she will include a portion of his letter, rather than writing out his message, because "I had rather die that [sic] copy any thing so vilely so wickedly false, so beyond all imagination fiendish."

Other personal correspondence captures the horror of her loss of multiple children, such as a lengthy letter written to her friend Maria Gisborne from Pisa, dated August 15, 1822. Shelley explains that her "nerves were wound up to the utmost irritation, and the sense of misfortune hung over my spirits," describing how much she detested their house. Then, on June 8, she "was threatened with a miscarriage," and after feeling ill for a week, she suffered the loss of her baby on June 16 at home. "I was so ill that for seven hours I lay nearly lifeless—kept from fainting by brandy, vinegar eau de Cologne etc—at length ice was brought to our solitude." This happened prior to the arrival of the doctor. Claire and Mary's friend Jane did not want to use the ice, but "Shelley overruled them & by an unsparing application of it I was restored." It is this entry that suggested to later scholars that Percy Shelley had saved Mary's life shortly before his own death. And it is in that lengthy letter that she shares details about his going missing and his body's later discovery.

Mary Shelley's journals intrigue readers also for the daily recordings of activities in which she and her husband engaged, particularly their reading and study. They famously read books together, and Shelly recorded each title in her journal. As Bennett writes, the journals and letters "indicate the collaborative nature of their intellectual relationship, which eventually included editing each other's works, translations, reacting and encouraging each other's writing and contributing to the same projects." Percy also engaged in massive correspondence, as did other members of the Shelley circle, including GEORGE GORDON BYRON (Lord Byron). Years after Byron died, a man who claimed to be his son threatened to blackmail Mary Shelley with letters purportedly written by Byron containing damaging information about Mary and Percy. Their letters were so widely circulated that many, no doubt, still await discovery.

One drawback to having access to the personal writings of an author is that they encourage readers to find autobiographical content in the author's artistic production. Writers naturally incorporate themes and facts from their own lives into their art. However, when readers care only to mine bits of fact about an artist's life from their art, rather than appreciate their art for its own sake, the work's value is cheapened. Whatever one's attitude toward Mary Shelley's personal writings, everyone must agree that they provide invaluable records of two lives that continue to fascinate readers.

FURTHER READING

Bennett, Betty T. "Mary Shelley's Letters: the Public/Private Self." In *The Cambridge Companion to Mary Shelley*, edited by Esther Schor, 211–225. Cambridge: Cambridge University Press, 2004.

———. "Newly Uncovered Letters and Poems by Mary Wollstonecraft Shelley." *Keats-Shelley Journal* 46 (1997): 51–74.

Bennett, Betty T., and William R. Little. "Seven Letters from Prosper Mérimée to Mary Shelley." *Comparative Literature* 31 (1979): 134–153.

Feldman, Paula R., and Diana Scott-Kilvert, ed. *The Journals of Mary Shelley*. Baltimore: Johns Hopkins University Press, 1994.

Jones, Frederick. "The Letters of Mary Shelley in the Bodleian Library." *Bodleian Quarterly* 8 (Spring, Summer, Autumn 1937): 29–310, 360–371, 412–420.

———, ed. *Mary Shelley's Journal*. Norman: University of Oklahoma Press, 1947.

Marshall, Florence A. *The Life and Letters of Mary Wollstonecraft Shelley*. 2 vols. London: Bentley, 1889.

Neth, Michael, ed. *The Hellas Notebook*. Bodleian Shelley Manuscripts, Ser. 16. New York: Garland, 1994.

Shelley, Mary Wollstonecraft. *The Mary Shelley Reader*. Edited by Betty T. Bennett and Charles E. Robinson. New York: Oxford University Press, 1990.

———. *The Journals of Mary Shelley, 1814–1844*. 2 vols. Edited by Paula R. Feldman and Diana Scott-Kilvert. 1987. Reprint, Baltimore: Johns Hopkins University Press, 1995.

———. *Selected Letters of Mary Wollstonecraft Shelley*. Edited by Betty T. Bennett. Baltimore: Johns Hopkins University Press, 1995.

Stoneman, Patsy. Review of *The Mary Shelley Reader, Containing Frankenstein, Mathilda, Tales and Stories, Essays and Reviews, and Letters*. *Review of English Studies* 45 (1994): 118–119.

Sunstein, Emily W. *Mary Shelley: Romance and Reality*. Baltimore: Johns Hopkins University Press, 1991.

Walling, William. *Mary Shelley*. New York: Twayne Publishers, 1979.

Williams, John. *Mary Shelley: A Literary Life*. New York: St. Martin's Press, 2000.

The Last Man (1826)

The Last Man elicited the most negative reviews of any of Mary Shelley's publications. One reviewer described it as "the product of a diseased imagination and a polluted taste." Not a single reviewer of the era appreciated the futuristic novel, although later critics would proclaim it her second best after *Frankenstein* (1818). One complaint against the book was its use of the term *last*, as, logically, one wondered for whom *The Last Man* was writing his account. Readers of the next century developed the sensibility to appreciate the novel's gender role reversals, reformist sociopolitical commentary, and dismantling of traditional cultural values. Where 19th-century critics focused on its "lady metaphysics," today's readers view *The Last Man* as much more than a reflection of the popular subgenre of apocalyptic fiction. With the perspective allowed by almost two centuries, today's audiences note Shelley's approach to what Betty T. Bennett labels "public and domestic politics" as well as "its essential Romanticism—and radicalism" (see ROMANTICISM). While it did not prove a commercial success when first published, substantial later critical reaction to the novel has revived interest in it by 21st century readers.

Commentators have characterized *The Last Man* variously as grief writing/therapy, a roman à clef, a feminist symbol for obstacles faced by 19th-century women writers, supportive of the traditional family, critical of the myth of the traditional family, and an indeterminate vision of the end of civilization. Others analyze it in terms of its theme of fragmentation, a theme shared by *Frankenstein*. Both novels reflect a profound sense of the inevitability of isolation and "last of their race" characterizations of the monster and of Lionel Verney. *The Last Man* may also reflect Shelley's anxiety about her future as a writer or the future of writing in general. Still others write of the novel in terms of its characterization of a vulnerable and perhaps insecure England. That view offers a disconnect from the general 19th-century perception of the country as an imperial giant—in Shakespeare's words, "This blessed plot, this earth, this realm, this England" (Richard II 2:1:40). Readers in both Shelley's day and today may read the novel for what many claim to be portraits of Mary Shelley's family and friends: Adrian as PERCY BYSSHE SHELLEY, Raymond as GEORGE GORDON BYRON (Lord Byron), and Perdita as Claire Claremont. However, with the arrival of the 21st century and the fragility of the earth becoming clearer day by day, *The Last Man* rings with a new authority. Plague and natural disasters destroy man in a setting at the end of the 21st century, the timing of which modern readers take note.

The labeling of the novel as grief writing has a strong basis. Its introduction tells of the narrator's and a companion's exploration of a cave in Naples. Because Mary and Percy Shelley often enjoyed such outings, they are seen as the two adventurers who discover the Sibyl's cave and in it the leaves that bear her prophesies. The narrator takes great pains to translate the story scrolled across the leaves, which tells of the last human to survive a plague and describes humanity's demise in detail. As is often noted by commentators of Shelley's work, much of the novel contains biographical reflections of her life and beliefs and those of her family and friends. Because she worked on *The Last Man* during a time of grieving for her drowned husband, scholars are not surprised to hear echoes of her personal situation in the book. A lengthy passage from its introduction is worth quoting in full in support of the theory that Shelley wrote to help her cope with great personal loss:

> My labours have cheered long hours of solitude, and taken me out of a world, which has averted its once benignant face from me, to one glowing with imagination and power. Will my readers ask how I could find solace from the narration of misery and woeful change? This is one of the mysteries of our nature, which holds full sway over me, and from whose influence I cannot escape. I confess, that I have not been unmoved by the development of the tale; and that I have been depressed, nay, agonized, at some parts of the recital, which I have faithfully transcribed from my materials. Yet such is human nature, that the excitement of mind was dear to me, and that the imagination, painter of

tempest and earthquake, or, worse, the stormy and ruin-fraught passions of man, softened my real sorrows and endless regrets, by clothing these fictitious ones in that ideality, which takes the mortal sting from pain.

Shelley mentioned the novel on several occasions in her letters. She wrote to her publisher, Charles Ollier, November 15, 1825, "The title of my book is to be simply 'The Last Man, a Romance, by the Author of Frankenstein.'—As soon as Mr. Colburn has made the communication of which he speaks it will be ready—that is two volumes are quite ready [sic] the third will be prepared long before those are printed—Mr. Colburn can therefore send it to the press immediately—." Originally published in three volumes, in its modern printed version, it runs almost 500 pages in length.

Shelley understood well the gender differences that so often inhabit her works, *The Last Man* included. On September 12, 1827, she wrote to Frances Wright, a social reformer born in Scotland who had been raised in England. At that time active, Wright was involved in American reform movements that emphasized the dangers inherent to women writers and reformists and the need to combat such threats. In 1824, Wright and her sister established the Nahoba settlement in Tennessee, where slaves could earn money to purchase their own freedom, an effort that eventually failed. Shelley told Wright that she honored women, a thought that "makes me tremble for you—women are so per[pet]ually the victims of their generosity—& their purer, & more sensitive feelings render them so much less than men capable of battling the selfishness, hardness & ingratitude which is so often the return made, for the noblest efforts to benefit others." Michael Eberle-Sinatra suggests that *The Last Man* functions as Shelley's extension of John Milton's PARADISE LOST, which reads in book II, lines 770–772, "Let no man seek Henceforth [sic] to be foretold what shall befall Him or his children." She includes those lines as an epigraph on her novel's title page and thus predicts humankind's eventual annihilation. In his history of SCIENCE FICTION, *Billion Year Spree* (1973), Brian W. Aldiss writes that *The Last Man* further emphasizes *Frankenstein*'s pessimism: "[I]t is the race, rather than the individual, which is hunted down to exile."

SYNOPSIS

Volume 1: Chapters 1–3

Volume 1 introduces the various romantic relationships among the characters that allow the reader to care for them and understand the motivations of each. Shelley does not introduce the threat of a plague into her plot line until the first volume's final chapter. The first volume is the longest of the three.

The novel's introduction opens with a detailed description of two adventurers touring caves in Naples with their guides. They discover a cavern believed to be that of a Grecian sibyl. Although warned against danger by their guides, who will not accompany them, the two venture into the twisting caverns. Their torch extinguishes, leaving them in total darkness, but they retain their wits and continue to walk through the underground cave until reaching an opening where they stop to rest. The narrator describes it as

> a wide cavern with an arched dome-like roof. An aperture in the midst let in the light of heaven; but this was overgrown with brambles and underwood, which acted as a veil, obscuring the day, and giving a solemn religious hue to the apartment. It was spacious, and nearly circular, with a raised seat of stone, about the size of a Grecian couch, at one end. The only sign that life had been here, was the perfect snow-white skeleton of a goat, which had probably not perceived the opening as it grazed on the hill above, and had fallen headlong.

They discover leaves that have been written upon by the sibyl in various languages, some familiar and some not, and the narrator takes on the job of translating the messages. The introduction concludes with the narrator excusing any errors and noting that the reader "must decide how far I have well bestowed my time and imperfect powers, in giving form and substance to the frail and attenuated Leaves of the Sibyl."

Following the introduction, readers are eased into the plot by the novel's narrator, who states,

"So true it is, that man's mind alone was the creator of all that was good or great to man, and that Nature herself was only his first minister." He describes how much he had loved England as a boy, and he writes of his father that nature had granted him "the envied gifts of wit and imagination, and then left his bark of life to be impelled by these winds, without adding reason as the rudder, or judgment as the pilot for the voyage." Everyone loved his father, who was invited to every social event to enliven it with his revered wit, his profligate lifestyle ignored or excused by the very individuals it harmed. Even the king supported him until he married, "and the haughty princess of Austria, who became, as queen of England, the head of fashion, looked with harsh eyes on his defects, and with contempt on the affection her royal husband entertained for him." When the king promised continued financial support only if his father would change his ways, his father agrees. Filled with momentary resolve to alter his behavior, he quickly lost that resolve and wasted the king's gift at the gambling table. He left London for self-exile in Cumberland, to be quoted and missed by his friends, including the king. While in Cumberland, he met a poor cottage girl who cared for him when he was ill; they married and had a family, which he could not support. On the verge of death, he wrote a letter, asking the king to care for his family. His wife never received any assistance and died in poverty, leaving two orphans.

At this point, the narrator identifies himself as the older child, age five when orphaned. He describes a vague feeling of superiority to others based on the stories he had been told about his father's court connections. He became a shepherd but rebelled against the lonely life by forming a band of shepherd boys and leading them in their misdeeds, receiving blame but also reward, even for those infractions that he does not commit: "But while I endured punishment and pain in their defence with the spirit of an hero, I claimed as my reward their praise and obedience." Such was his schooling, and he wandered about civilized England, declaring, "I owned but one law, it was that of the strongest, and my greatest deed of virtue was never to submit."

The narrator had to raise his sister Perdita, younger by three years, whom he describes: "[H]er eyes were not dark, but impenetrably deep; you seemed to discover space after space in their intellectual glance, and to feel that the soul which was their soul, comprehended an[sic] universe of thought in its ken." Although she had the appearance of an angel, Perdita was cold to others, a result of an upbringing that left her "unloved and neglected"; thus, "she repaid want of kindness with distrust and silence." She enjoyed solitude and spent much time in nature, which the narrator describes in great detail. Perdita had no memory of her parents but greatly resembled her father in that "a generous tide flowed in her veins; artifice, envy, or meanness, were at the antipodes of her nature; her countenance, when enlightened by amiable feeling, might have belonged to a queen of nations; her eyes were bright; her look fearless." She was self-sufficient, in contrast to her brother, who needed constant companionship.

At the age of 16, the narrator was strong and lithe; he neither feared nor loved any man. He describes himself as having a savage personality, being "in danger of degenerating into that which informs brute nature." On the verge of setting sail across "a sea of evil," the narrator notes that his fortunes changed and became "like the gentle meanderings of a meadow-encircling streamlet."

The time is 2073, and the king who had once befriended the narrator's father has abdicated his throne to allow the establishing of a republic. He dies, leaving a son, a daughter, and his wife, still mourning the loss of power to which she had been accustomed as a queen. Her son, Adrian, second earl of Windsor, is 15 years old and the focus of all of her energies, as she urges him to regain the crown. He resists, leaning toward the ideals of the republic.

After being sequestered for a time, Adrian visits Cumberland. The narrator wants to challenge Adrian, whom he sees as part of the family responsible for his own family's misery. He watches preparations for Adrian's arrival and wonders bitterly why he should be any different from the wealthy, simply because he wears poorer clothing. Angered by Perdita's excitement over the impending arrival, he tells her of the earl, "Why, all his virtues are derived from his station only; because he is rich, he is called generous; because he is powerful, brave; because he is well served, he is affable. Let them call him so, let all England believe him to be thus—we know him—he is our enemy—our penurious, dastardly, arrogant enemy." In this scene, the reader learns that narrator's name is Lionel.

Lionel is "driven half mad" by the reaction of the locals as they dress in their best clothing and cry "Long live the Earl!" His "blood boil[s]" to see the earl riding his fine horse, and he vows revenge. Lionel is imprisoned for poaching on royal lands, but the earl orders him freed. He returns to his poaching and is eventually caught again and attacks the gamekeepers with his knife. The earl finds the men struggling and startles Lionel with his greeting: "Lionel Verney, do we meet thus for the first time? We were born to be friends to each other; and though ill fortune has divided us, will you not acknowledge the hereditary bond of friendship which I trust will hereafter unite us?" Adrian's sensitivity, intelligence, and benevolence win even Lionel's affection. Adrian tells Lionel details about his father that the king had recorded in a letter urging Adrian to find the son of his great friend. Lionel tells readers that it is through his friendship with Adrian that he becomes more human. Exposed to poetry, philosophy, and history, he feels as if a curtain has been opened, allowing the light awakening "the sleeping ideas" in his mind and affording new ones. Perdita shares with her brother that she has also developed a great fondness for Adrian.

They next meet Adrian's younger sister as well as the woman Adrian loves, Princess Evadne, daughter of Prince Zamai, ambassador from the free states of Greece. Evadne does not return Adrian's affections, a fact clear to Lionel but not to Adrian. Witnessing his friend's unrequited love, Lionel asks, "What is there in our nature that is for ever urging us on towards pain and misery? We are not formed for enjoyment; and, however we may be attuned to the reception of pleasurable emotion, disappointment is the never-failing pilot of our life's bark, and ruthlessly carries us on to the shoals."

Adrian visits London and then returns with plans for his friends. Lionel is to serve as a secretary to an ambassador in Vienna and Perdita to go to London, with plans for Perdita to become Evadne's "younger sister." Anxious to embrace his destiny, Lionel writes, "Life is before me, and I rush into possession. Hope, glory, love, and blameless ambition are my guides, and my soul knows no dread." He is intoxicated by the material beauties at court and exclaims, "The mere flow of animal spirits was Paradise, and at night's close I only desired a renewal of the intoxicating delusion." He eventually recognizes the harmful effects of that delusion and becomes disillusioned with his surroundings, wishing "to be something to others."

Adrian has come to envy a man named Lord Raymond, of whom he has heard much praise from the Greeks. Suffering an insult to his pride as a young man, Raymond left England to gain fame for his war exploits in Greece: "Power therefore was the aim of all his endeavours; aggrandizement the mark at which he for ever shot. In open ambition or close intrigue, his end was the same—to attain the first station in his own country." Upon Raymond's return to England, Lionel shares with his audience, "The rumour went that Adrian had become—how write the fatal word—mad: that Lord Raymond was the favourite of the ex-queen, her daughter's destined husband."

After two years in Vienna, Lionel travels to England to morally support Adrian, first visiting Perdita in her cottage at the edge of Windsor Forest. He is surprised by her maturity, explaining: "Her person was formed in the most feminine proportions; she was not tall, but her mountain life had given freedom to her motions, so that her light step scarce made her foot-fall heard as she tript across the hall to meet me." He asks Perdita to explain what has happened to Adrian and why she has left Evadne's company. She explains that Adrian had devoted himself to Evadne and traveled the world: "In solitude, and through many wanderings afar from the haunts of men, he matured his views for the reform of the English government, and the improvement of the people." He made public his plans to diminish the power of the aristocracy. His mother came to hate him, and others distrusted him. As for Evadne, she "entered but coldly into his systems. She thought he did well to assert his own will, but she wished that will to have been more intelligible to the multitude. She had none of the spirit of a martyr, and did not incline to share the shame and defeat of a fallen patriot."

Raymond, the opposite of Adrian with his violent passions and desire for self-aggrandizement, held Adrian in contempt. Evadne fell prey to Raymond's tyranny and rejected Adrian. Perdita was distressed as she witnessed Adrian's emotional torture. Adrian went into seclusion, and Perdita departed London for the cottage.

Volume 1: Chapters 4–7

Lionel visits London and meets Lord Raymond. He nearly falls under Raymond's spell, but each time he speaks disparagingly of Adrian, Lionel recognizes Raymond's true character. Still, Lionel admires Raymond's "powerful and versatile talents, that together with his eloquence, which was graceful and witty, and his wealth now immense, caused him to be feared, loved, and hated beyond any other man in England."

Lionel describes Parliament as divided by three factions: aristocrats, democrats, and royalists, the last of which has faded away in light of Adrian's devotion to the idea of a republic. Much political conflict occurs, and England appears on the brink of civil war. Then Lionel notices that Perdita has fallen in love with Raymond. One day, while visiting his sister, Lionel meets Adrian's sister, Idris: "Her tall slim figure bent gracefully as a poplar to the breezy west, and her gait, goddess-like, was as that of a winged angel new alit from heaven's high floor; the pearly fairness of her complexion was stained by a pure suffusion; her voice resembled the low, subdued tenor of a flute." Idris requests support from Lionel and Perdita for Adrian and his interests, hoping they can persuade Adrian to come out of seclusion for the good of England.

Raymond appears to escort Idris back to the castle, then returns to Perdita's cottage and asks for her. Adrian follows her instructions and tells Raymond she is not available. Raymond discusses a political challenge from a man named Ryland who is going to introduce a bill "making it treason to endeavour to change the present state of the English government and the standing laws of the republic," an attack against Raymond. He asks Lionel to accompany him to Parliament and shares Adrian's location. He also announces that he will marry Idris for political advancement, regardless of the fact that she does not love him. He tells Lionel that "my first act when I become King of England, will be to unite with the Greeks, take Constantinople, and subdue all Asia. I intend to be a warrior, a conqueror; Napoleon's name shall bow to mine; and enthusiasts, instead of visiting his rocky grave, and exalting the merits of the fallen, shall adore my majesty, and magnify my illustrious achievements."

Lionel describes Ryland's speech to Parliament: "He compared the royal and republican spirit; [showed] how the one tended to enslave the minds of men; while all the institutions of the other served to raise even the meanest among us to something great and good." Ryland seems to convince many, but Raymond also speaks persuasively, assuring his audience that he means only to benefit England. Raymond enchants the group, so that "The motion was lost; Ryland withdrew in rage and despair; and Raymond, gay and exulting, retired to dream of his future kingdom." Later, flushed with victory, Raymond asks Lionel to describe him as "king-expectant, angel or devil, which?" Lionel is filled with passion, due to his jealousy over Idris's impending marriage to Raymond:

> This ironical tone was discord to my bursting, over-boiling-heart; I was nettled by his insolence, and replied with bitterness; "There is a spirit, neither angel or devil, damned to limbo merely." I saw his cheeks become pale, and his lips whiten and quiver; his anger served but to enkindle mine, and I answered with a determined look his eyes which glared on me; suddenly they were withdrawn, cast down, a tear, I thought, wetted the dark lashes; I was softened, and with involuntary emotion added, "Not that you are such, my dear lord."

The two continue their tenuous relationship, often discussing philosophy, with Lionel making clear that he supports Lord Ryland's view rather than that of Raymond. One day, they approach Perdita's cottage, and Lionel thinks, "I would assist Perdita to overcome herself, and teach her to disdain the wavering love of him, who balanced between the possession of a crown, and of her, whose excellence and affection transcended the worth of a kingdom." He hopes to convince Perdita to give up her feelings for Raymond. As far as Lionel is concerned, Raymond is foolish to value political power over the invaluable love of his sister. They find Perdita reading an account of what has happened in Parliament in the newspaper; Raymond surprises her by calling her "dear" and asking her to be his lover. Lionel then feels free to hope that Idris will now be free to become his wife.

The following day, Lionel travels in a balloon to see Adrian, his location having been revealed by Raymond. Adrian has been weakened by his trials and is ill, but he recognizes Lionel. That evening, the former queen, now a countess, arrives along with Idris. Adrian describes the countess, writing, "Never did any woman appear so entirely made of mind, as the Countess of Windsor. Her passions had subdued her appetites, even her natural wants." They all depart, with Lionel and Adrian going to Windsor to Perdita's cottage. Shelley allows Adrian several pages of praise for nature and man's relationship with nature and his creator.

When they arrive, they learn that Perdita and Raymond have married, leaving England for the Continent. Happy for his sister's security, Lionel considers his own situation. Although he is now related by marriage to the wealthy Lord Raymond and best friends with the earl of Windsor, Lionel is quite poor. He does not want to take advantage of their friendship to ask Adrian for an appointment to a post. In order to occupy himself, Lionel turns to reading and study, living in the cottage.

Still in the city, Idris asks Adrian, who has returned to London and is recovering, what Lionel is doing and how he fares. When she learns that he is in the cottage, she begins visiting Lionel regularly, requesting Adrian to accompany her. One evening, Idris and Lionel kiss, and their love for one another is clear. Adrian attempts to explain to the countess that Idris loves Lionel, hoping to make a successful appeal on the part of his sister for their marriage. However, the countess is furious. She exclaims that although Adrian may have overthrown her plans for him, she will not allow him to do the same to her plans for her daughter. She later reminds Idris that she is a princess of Austria and asks her to not see Lionel for one month, pretending to bargain with her. Idris refuses, but she does promise her mother that she will delay marriage to Lionel. Adrian is called to London, leaving his sister alone with her mother.

One snowy night, Idris arrives at Lionel's cottage, beating on the door and begging him to save her. Although Lionel does not yet understand what has frightened her, he agrees to escort her away from the cottage and her nearby mother. As they hurry on foot through the darkness, Idris grows weak from emotion and exertion, so Lionel hires a chaise carriage to take her to London, where she can join Adrian and feel safe. Idris manages to explain to Lionel that the countess blames him for the loss of Sir Raymond, as well as for Adrian's madness. Earlier that night, when Idris had gone to bed, she overheard her mother plotting with a servant to send Idris to Austria in order to separate her from Adrian.

Adrian contacts the countess the following day and informs her that he has become Idris's guardian. The countess replies coldly that she will return to her own country and simply forget that she has two children, because both have disobeyed her. With her departure, Adrian and Idris at last feel free to marry.

For a short, happy time Raymond and Perdita live near her previous cottage, and Adrian, Idris, and Lionel all live together at Windsor Castle. Both couples have children, and the entire group contributes to raising them. Lionel describes how well the various members of the group got along, even "the ambitious, restless" Raymond. He has decided that his dreams of glory are a small price to pay for his new existence with Perdita. When the time comes to select a Lord Protector for England, Lionel muses that the position would have been Raymond's had he married Idris, but Raymond had "exchanged a sceptre for a lute, a kingdom for Perdita."

As everyone—except for Idris, who stays behind to care for the children—travels to London, Perdita has a presentiment of disaster, which she tries to ignore. Raymond asks Lionel to support his nomination of Adrian for the Lord Protector position, but Adrian counters with a plan to nominate

Raymond. Raymond rises to the cause, becoming excited about the prospect of again joining the political game. His candidacy greatly concerns Perdita, who anticipates a calamity. Raymond is elected, and Perdita accepts their new roles, while their daughter, Clara, lives much of the time with Lionel, Idris, and Adrian. Adrian grows ill again but visits Raymond and Perdita when he can, bringing Clara with him to see her parents. Raymond directs the building of an art museum; he is a popular protector, and Perdita does well in her role as his wife.

Raymond brings a "mysterious Greek" to London to help him buy art and, visiting him one night, encounters poverty and squalor in his house, a new condition for Raymond. He also discovers Evadne Zaimi, at one time the recipient of Adrian's undying love. Embarrassed and saddened, she explains that before her father died, he arranged a marriage for her to a wealthy Greek merchant, but the war between Greece and Turkey caused them to flee with none of their riches. Five months after they arrived in England, her husband died. She has lived in poverty, serving wealthy Greeks; she had drawn the plan for the museum that the Greek had submitted to Raymond. She has had a checkered past, due to her ambition. She is also in love with Raymond. He promises to help her, but she explains that she deserves her poverty, as she had helped ruin her husband with her schemes.

Volume 1: Chapters 8–10
Raymond eventually feels passionate toward Evadne and continues visiting her secretly. Perdita discovers a letter between them and confronts Raymond, who explains about Evadne but declares he has committed no sin. He and Perdita discuss separation after their six happy years together, and he is conflicted, loving his wife but also reluctant to leave Evadne to her terrible fate. He determines not to see Evadne but is nonetheless drawn to her. Perdita expects him to change, but he continues his absences without explanation. She demands that he choose between her and the Protectorate.

Raymond finds Evadne near death due to his absence and sends a message to Perdita with a woman who takes his ring to assure her entrance into the palace. Perdita receives the ring and message in misery but valiantly entertains the guests at the celebration of the Protectorate. Raymond's infidelity effectively ends life for Perdita. They continue the sham of their marriage, but when Adrian visits, he suspects a problem.

Perdita and Clara visit Lionel and Idris, where Clara enjoys playing with their son, Alfred. Raymond visits, noticeably sobered, and Lionel tries to comfort Perdita in her distress; they remove to another house. She and Raymond later exchange letters, both bitter and both acknowledging a change is necessary after the many months of pretending. Raymond eventually tells Adrian and Idris what has happened, explaining that Evadne finally departed, unable to be the cause of Raymond's remorse. Raymond understands that he can never regain his former relationship with Perdita. To emphasize the seriousness of his actions, Lionel notes,

> Debasement of character is the certain follower of such pursuits. Yet this consequence would not have been immediately remarkable, if Raymond had continued to apply himself to the execution of his plans for the public benefit, and the fulfilling his duties as Protector. But, extreme in all things, given up to immediate impressions, he entered with ardour into this new pursuit of pleasure . . . without reflection or foresight. The council-chamber was deserted; the crowds which attended on him as agents to his various projects were neglected. Festivity, and even libertinism, became the order of the day.

Lionel and Adrian go to London to try to speak with Raymond and find him with various despicable men. When Adrian tries to reason with him, he resists, retorting that "my passions are my masters; my smallest impulse my tyrant." He announces he is going to Greece, and Adrian agrees to go with him. Everyone is caught up in a moral tempest following Raymond's abdication of the Protectorate and departure to Greece. Perdita turns away from him and ignores Clara. Lionel attempts to distract Perdita with lessons about literature, the artistic passion of his life. Perdita demands that no one pronounce Raymond's name, but she studies newspapers for word of him from Greece.

After a year of battle in Greece, where Raymond has become a hero, Adrian returns home, having suffered a wound. A short time later, Raymond is missing and feared kidnapped or put to death by the Turks. Perdita decides to go to Greece, and Lionel and Clara, no longer a baby, accompany her. They find all of Athens mourning for Raymond's loss. Adrian discovers that Raymond is a prisoner being treated cruelly, and he works for two months to secure Raymond's release. Adrian and Perdita travel in a small boat to greet the vessel that returns Raymond, injured and so weak he can barely rise from a chair on the vessel's deck. He receives a hero's welcome and is overcome with emotion at seeing his family. Raymond is determined to retake his command, and Perdita does not object. As Lionel explains, she is more frightened by another threat: plague. It had begun close to the Nile and was quickly spreading.

Volume 2: Chapters 1–3

Volume 2 begins as the group travels with a partially recovered Raymond to Kishan, arriving in July. Hearing of Raymond's arrival, the Turkish army retreats, and the Greeks prepare for battle. After an encounter that wounds and kills many, Lionel is thinking of how ashamed he is of humankind when he hears a scream and discovers Evadne, disguised as a man and dying of wounds sustained in battle. She dies placing a curse on Raymond: "I have sold myself to death, with the sole condition that thou shouldst follow me—Fire, and war, and plague, unite for thy destruction—O my Raymond, there is no safety for thee!" Raymond becomes melancholy but is determined to continue the fight, sending Perdita and Clara back to England, to Perdita's dismay. He explains that Evadne's final words have sealed his fate.

The Turks are crippled by blockades that cause famine, and the plague continues to advance. As the Greeks move toward their enemies, they meet less and less resistance. They arrive at Stamboul and find it deserted. Some Turks had attempted escape. One told his captors, "Take it, Christian dogs! Take the palaces, the gardens, the mosques, the abode of our fathers—take plague with them; pestilence is the enemy we fly; if she be your friend, hug her to your bosoms. The curse of Allah is on Stamboul, share ye her fate." The Greeks wonder whether "Death had become lord of Constantinople."

Raymond calls his troops coward but allows them to retreat. He is determined to plant a cross on the mosque, although Perdita pleads with him not to enter the city. Convinced that he will die during that year, 2092, Raymond vows to meet his destiny as a great ruler and enter the city. He sends Lionel to General Karazza to gain promises of more troops, as his own grow restless with rumors and exaggeration of the danger. The general states that this will take time. As Lionel returns, he uses his spyglass to see Raymond and others at the gates of the city. His men fall back, and Raymond enters alone, bearing the Greek flag. A few moments later, an enormous explosion occurs, and the city is on fire; soon, a heavy rain helps extinguish the flames. Lionel walks through the ruins of the city seeing charred bodies and "various articles of luxury and wealth," but there is no sign of Raymond. Exhausted, he finally sleeps in despair. When he returns home, he must explain to Perdita that the city is a heap of ruins, forming Raymond's tomb. He praises Raymond's courage and dedication, which died with him, and Perdita notes that her husband will live on in Clara. When Lionel returns to the destroyed city, Raymond's dog is discovered. Having stood over his master until the body was discovered, the dog died. The men carry Raymond's body to his Athens home, where Perdita waits. Lionel compares his sister's cold, white appearance to marble, the material of tombs. She asks that Raymond be buried in Athens.

A "melancholy train" of men wind through the mountains bearing their hero's body. Lionel describes the place outside of Athens where Raymond's body was buried and stones placed that identified him and his deeds:

> The chasm, deep, black, and hoary, swept from the summit to the base; in the fissures of the rock myrtle underwood grew and wild thyme, the food of many nations of bees; enormous crags protruded into the cleft, some beetling over, others rising perpendicularly from it. At

the foot of this sublime chasm, a fertile laughing valley reached from sea to sea, and beyond was spread the blue Aegean, sprinkled with islands, the light waves glancing beneath the sun.

As Lionel prepares to return to England in October, he returns to Raymond's tomb and finds a partly finished cottage. He again admires the majesty of the place, and Perdita says, "In such a spot death loses half its terrors, and even the inanimate dust appears to partake of the spirit of beauty which hallows this region." She has decided to remain behind with Raymond. Lionel tries to persuade her to return to be with Raymond's friends to help ease her grief, but she insists on remaining, a course that Lionel labels madness. He drugs her with laudanum, and when she awakes, she is aboard a vessel with Lionel and Clara on the way home to England. She leaps into the ocean in order to drown, tying her body to the vessel. When her body is recovered, she is clutching a note that reads "to Athens." Lionel returns her remains to land, placing them in the care of a trusted friend who will be sure that she is buried with Raymond, and he again departs Greece, filled with grief. He does not tell Clara that her mother's death was suicide.

He and Clara reach France, where they hear a strange tale. A ship had come to shore and a man who appeared to be "vanquished by malady and approaching death, had fallen on the inhospitable beach. He was found stiff, his hands clenched, and pressed against his breast. His skin, nearly black, his matted hair and bristly beard, were signs of a long protracted misery. It was whispered that he had died of the plague." It was determined the ship had sailed from Philadelphia in America.

Volume 2: Chapters 4–7

When Lionel returns home, he tells Idris and Adrian that they should all abandon the daily misery of the world and live a peaceful existence. Adrian's health continues to fail, but they celebrate the peace that reigns. They learn from Greece that all who entered the ruins of Constantinople died from the plague, and they wonder whether it will reach England. The country is agitated over the approaching election of a new Lord Protector; Ryland is outspoken, among others, regarding what the focus of the country should be. Many still feel there is no need for an aristocracy, saying, "Among a race of independent, and generous, and well educated men, in a country where the imagination is empress of men's minds there needs be no fear that we should want a perpetual succession of the highborn and lordly." Others disagree.

The plague reaches Athens, and many who had moved to Greece return home to England. Lionel muses, "Raymond's beloved Athenians, the free, the noble people of the divinest town in Greece, fell like ripe corn before the merciless sickle of the adversary." The question of rank seems unimportant to Lionel in the face of death and ruin. America is dying, and strange tales arrive from the East of a "black sun" that crossed the heavens, darkening the real sun and causing animals to twist in agony and birds to fall dead from the sky; no explanation could be given. Mosques and churches fill as everyone laments man's imminent destruction. Lionel takes refuge at Windsor with his family, which now include two children, one son having died while he was in Greece. At age 9, Alfred is a "manly fellow" and the baby a happy boy as well. Clara is living with Lionel, and Alfred attends Eton. One day, as Lionel watches Alfred with his playmates, he realizes the children are the future of England. As he considers his own mortality, for his son he thinks, "May your progress be uninterrupted and secure; born during the spring-tide of the hopes of man, may you lead up the summer to which no winter may succeed!"

The elements seem to turn against man, ravaging the land as nature becomes "dark, cold, and ungenial," prompting Lionel to construct a prose poem to the wind. He notes his fear of fire, even a small one in a stove, as an effect of the Constantinople blaze. Although England remains secure, thousands are dying of plague, and no one can determine how it spreads. It does not appear to be contagious in the traditional sense of one's exposure to an infected individual causing one to develop symptoms. Lionel remarks that France, Italy, Germany, and Spain stand between England and the scourge. Suddenly, nature is viewed as a menace as earthquakes, pestilence, and famine strike, first in Mexico, bringing many immigrants to England. Ryland serves as Lord Protector and finds it difficult to deal with the immigrants' poverty, the cancellation of trade, and other mounting problems that interrupt his plans. Many simply cannot believe that huge portions of the earth are being laid waste, and all are reminded of ancient plagues and destruction. Prompted by the changes, Lionel writes, "In this mortal life extremes are always matched; the thorn grows with the rose, the poison tree and the cinnamon mingle their boughs." Bankruptcies and financial crises challenge Ryland's attempt to institute equality, and he returns to plans based on the ruling manor in order to share resources. By August 2093, the plague reaches France and Italy. England fills to bursting, and Windsor Castle houses the homeless. The rich have to alter their lifestyles, and everyone understands the changes are permanent.

Alfred's birthday is celebrated with a small fair filled with music and dancing that lifts Lionel's spirits until he is stricken with the thought, "Ye are all going to die . . . already your tomb is built up around you." He thinks about halting the gaiety, but Idris stops him, and his friends are concerned. Ryland arrives and distracts them all. Lionel describes him as a man who wants to know everyone's desires; he continues, "Few people had discovered some cowardice and much infirmity of purpose under this imposing exterior. No man could crush a 'butterfly on the wheel' with better effect; no man better cover a speedy retreat from a powerful adversary. This had been the secret of his secession at the time of Lord Raymond's election." Ryland brings the bad news that the plague is everywhere, to which Adrian replies they must all now help the sick. Ryland speaks of abdicating his office, and Adrian accuses him of cowardice. Adrian determines to oppose the world. Although everyone will surely die, he is determined to care for them as much as possible and says if he can better one life, even keep the plague from one cottage, then he will not have lived in vain.

The plague arrives in London, and "universal misery" reigns, although Adrian attempts to help mask its effects to promote morale. When Lionel travels to London, he notices his is the only carriage on the street, and people stare at him as he moves through the city. He finds Adrian in improved health, apparently a result of increased meetings with his people to receive their requests. His effect on others is like that of a magician: Order and morale return. He asks Lionel to nominate him for the Deputy Protector position, as the present deputy has died. Ryland is much altered by fear but is pleased to learn he may soon leave London and retreat to his estate. Lionel agrees, but when he understands the danger in which Adrian will be placed, he nominates himself. They debate before Parliament, with Adrian for the first time claiming his rights based on his heritage. He tells Lionel he was born to take this job, to rule England in anarchy. He asks Lionel to return to Windsor to care for Idris, which Lionel agrees to do, but he decides he will eventually come back to London to help Adrian. He stops by Perdita's cottage and notes its disrepair with bitterness. He visits a man struck with the plague, seeing its effects for the first time. The man dies, after which no one will come near his body. Adrian searches a map for a place to take his family, but he decides that Windsor will remain their home. Men begin to rave and incite others to terror. Idris's nurse has died, and she is glad that Lionel has arrived to take control. Everyone except for Lionel is able to sleep that night.

Volume 2: Chapters 8–9

One calamity after another occurs. Lionel returns to London to assist Adrian and compares what has happened to a pack of wolves descending on defenseless prey. Wicked deeds mingle with those of heroism. With the approach of winter, hope increases that the plague might be slowed. Lionel notices that the largest strides in progress are made in small villages where everyone feels sympathetic toward their equals. Natural leadership has surfaced in various individuals, which Lionel encourages by suggesting that each village hold elections to select their official leaders. Spring arrives, with a beauty inspires everyone, and rich crops are planted. However, the plague returns. Idris and Lionel tend to the sick as the crops rot in the fields; too many have died to tend to the harvest.

In late summer, Lionel travels to London to visit Adrian, and he witnesses the over-packed horrible hospital scene, along with the laughing crowd in a local ale house and a theater where *Macbeth* is being performed. He pauses to enjoy the performance, which captivates everyone, and remarks on how much more meaningful many of the scenes are than they used to be. He relates a story of the daughter of a wealthy nobleman who falls in love with a common worker. The lord forbids the marriage and then dies along with every member of his family except for the "Juliet." As she sits alone in late September, her love returns, and she faints with joy into his arms.

In his narrative, Lionel recounts many anecdotes, including one in which Clara has to deliver the news to him that his son, Evelyn, has fallen ill. He searches for Idris and finds her with an astronomer who has completed his essay "The Pericyclical Motions of the Earth's Axis." Despite her grave concerns, Idris smiles at the irony in his pursuits. Her mood quickly darkens when she learns of Evelyn's illness. She, along with Lionel and Clara, sit with the boy all night until his fever breaks, and it becomes clear that he will survive.

At the end of the summer, the countess of Windsor returns to England, saying she has forgiven her daughter and will acknowledge her grandchildren, an act that Lionel labels "whimsical." She retains her false pride even in the face of so much death. More and more immigrants arrive, and Lionel moves his family to London, as Windsor lies in the line of their march from the west. London arms itself for protection from an invasion by those who had entered Ireland, with Adrian leading the forces. In the face of Adrian's leadership and compassion, they surrender their arms. Idris grows more fearful and depends on Adrian to help calm her. He confides that by the next summer, man's fate will be decided. The second volume closes with Lionel's musings regarding humanity and how it will deal with the death of hope.

Volume 3: Chapters 1–3
Volume 3 opens with Lionel's exclaiming that one would not know from the beauties of nature in the spring that extermination was eminent. People have returned to everyday duties after a time of chaos, when the poor entered abandoned castles and everyone became equal in material terms. But the material no longer matters; its value is greatly reduced, and people are focusing more on relationships. The children continue to thrive, although Idris has grown ill. Lionel ponders how much easier it would usually be for parents to die, knowing their children will carry on, but if he and Idris die, they will go understanding that the children will soon follow.

Only about 1,000 people remain in London, and Lionel expresses in a lyrical manner the mighty country's fall from power. He bids farewell to all accomplishments, technological and artistic. By autumn 2096, Adrian is planning the family's emigration. Lionel bemoans their leaving England, where eventually no one will exist to sing her praises. They plan to take beloved animals along but regret leaving what friends remain. They join Adrian in London, and Idris sees her mother for the first time in many years. Adrian has assembled a council of about 50 persons, undistinguished by social station; all are equal. He has selected 500 people to accompany him to Paris, where he will meet Lionel and his family. His compassion is obvious when he finds an orphan girl and decides to take her along.

While Lionel is gone, Alfred falls ill, and Idris goes to search for Lionel in a storm. A woman helps her, and Lionel later finds them and takes Idris home. He feels so ill, he believes he has the plague, and he can see that Idris is dying. Alfred dies, and Lionel and Idris try to find joy in the fact that they are together in their final moments. Lionel tells her, "Let us not, through security in the hereafter, neglect the present. This present moment, short as it is, is a part of eternity, and the dearest part, since it is our own inalienably. Thou, the hope of my futurity, art my present joy. Let me then look on thy dear eyes, and, reading love in them, drink intoxicating pleasure."

They both awake the next day, and Lionel becomes quite ill; Idris cares for him during three days of delirium. Lionel recovers as Idris grows weaker. Their departure for Paris has been delayed from November 25 to January 20. Most people have made the trip to Paris; Clara, Evelyn, a female attendant, and a servant traveled together, while

Adrian traveled with his mother. Lionel observes that "Plague had become Queen of the World." His family group lingers in Rochester as Idris wants to visit a friend, Lucy, and her mother. Lionel sends word to Adrian of this further delay, as the rest of the party waits for them at Windsor Castle. A snowstorm catches Lionel and Idris, and she dies in the storm, although Lionel carries her into a deserted cottage and tries for two hours to revive her. Determined to bury her with her family, he wraps her up and continues pushing through the storm. He carries Idris into the vault inside the castle to lay her with Alfred when the countess enters the vault. The countess at first remains haughty and angry, insisting on viewing Idris's body on her own, saying, "There at least, I may have her undisturbed." However, after seeing her daughter, she at last relents and says, "Lionel Verney, my son." She continues, "If our beloved angel sees us now, it will delight her to find that I do you even tardy justice. You were worthy of her; and from my heart I am glad that you won her away from me." They place Idris in the vault and cover it with the stone designed to do so, and the countess is no longer a "hard, inflexible woman."

Volume 3: Chapters 4–7

Lionel travels to Lucy, whose mother has died, and asks her to accompany him to care for the children now that Idris is gone. When they return to the castle, the countess relates a long story about her return to her family via Dover. Her tale includes her sighting three small suns that whirl around the main sun, sending animals into panic and creating an enormous wave that travels with startling speed toward the coast. It abates prior to reaching the shore, but the wind does not die down for three days. They learn that the two groups in Paris have sought to take over the city but have met resistance from the few natives still there. The Parisians note they have accepted death as inevitable, and they order the English who still desire to live to return to their island. Great political dissension arises, with evil committed in the name of religion in some cases. Adrian pleads for peace between the two factions; the men should not want blood on their hands for murder in their last days. They agree to keep the peace until February, when Adrian arrives.

At last Adrian, and 12 others set sail from Dover and round Calais, and then travel to Paris. Along the way to Paris, the men need new horses but can find only six, so the reduced group moves on. Adrian dashes on his white horse into the middle of feuding groups in the streets of Paris. An impostor-prophet appears to challenge Adrian, who continues to plead with the crowds for reason. Adrian tells his followers to meet him in Versailles; he spends the night in Paris. Lionel meets Juliet, the young woman he had known so many years previously, who now has a child and follows the impostor-prophet. Lionel is taken captive, blindfolded, and thrown into a dungeon because he has tried to convince Juliet of the prophet's foolishness. He fears execution, but then he is released by Juliet. She refuses to leave with him, as the prophet holds her child hostage, so Lionel travels alone to Versailles.

Fourteen hundred souls prepare to travel through the Alps. Lionel is to lead a group of 100 to scout for supplies and housing; the others break into small groups. Adrian's mother, now convinced that love is the purpose of life, travels with Adrian, Clare, and Evelyn. At one point, Adrian's resolve fails; then he recovers and promises not to complain again to Lionel. Lionel travels to Geneva, remarking that events during their "progress through France were so full of strange horror and gloomy misery" that he does not dare supply much detail. The plague arises again among their groups. He returns to Versailles with his group to reunite with Adrian, for whom Lionel has developed a near-worshipful attitude while watching him help calm the unruly men.

The impostor dies of plague, as does Juliet and her child, and the travel begins again. They see many strange occurrences, including a white-robed "specter" that turns out to be an opera dancer. Lionel writes, "It had been well, if such vain terrors could have distracted our thoughts from more tangible evils. But these were too dreadful and too many not to force themselves into every thought, every moment, of our lives." Many of their friends die, such as the young girl Adrian had rescued,

Lucy, and the countess, as they move through an empty France and into Switzerland. Lionel thinks of the countess as "the last tie binding us to the ancient state of things." He constantly contemplates the end of his race. Clara had cared for the countess, as she had for all the other ill members of the family, and grieves her death.

The group is still able to enjoy nature's beauties as they travel toward Geneva, and at one point they hear the organ sounds of Haydn's "New-Created World" reverberating across the hills. They pause to celebrate the sounds of music, which they had not heard in some time.

Volume 3: Chapters 8–10

The group continues to celebrate the natural wonder of Geneva, but Lionel mourns the lack of humanity; there is no one left there to save. He remarks on the irony of seeking relief, not in the lush areas of the world but in the middle of ice and snow. He draws comfort in the fact that "This solemn harmony of event and situation regulated our feelings, and gave as it were fitting costume to our last act. Majestic gloom and tragic pomp attended the decease of wretched humanity. The funeral procession of monarchs of old, was transcended by our splendid shews." Adrian and Lionel focus on what little time they have left with the children and are especially delighted by Clara. They wander through beautiful deserted castles and enjoy a lovely autumn as they travel to Milan. As they linger at Como, housed in a luxuriously designed palace, they take daily trips onto the lake in a small skiff. Clara becomes more beautiful by the day, gaining her former happy demeanor while sailing, and Evelyn is a delight to all. However, Evelyn contracts typhus and is dead within a few days. The three survivors leave Como in August.

Chapter 9 of volume 3 opens with Lionel expressing his deep melancholy and exhaustion as he pushes himself to record his final thoughts. He recounts his, Clara's, and Adrian's continued travel toward Greece, marking the many ruins they encounter along the way. While Adrian is enthusiastic about traveling to Greece, Lionel is fearful of the rough ocean. He gives in to Adrian's plan, and the tiny group selects a vessel from the many available and sets sail in the morning. Lionel grows uneasy as he sights what appears to be a storm. As their surroundings grow dark, the boat is tossed about in tall waves, and all three are filled with terror. They attempt to change course, but the darkness disorients them. Lionel describes the scene as the "darkness, palpable and rayless, hemmed us round, dissipated only by the lightning; sometimes we beheld thunderbolts, fiery red, fall into the sea, and at intervals vast spouts stooped from the clouds, churning the wild ocean, which rose to meet them; while the fierce gale bore the rack onwards, and they were lost in the chaotic mingling of sky and sea." They all wash overboard, and only Lionel swims to land.

He curses his survival and staggers inland, discovering shelter with food and provisions. After resting, he returns to the shore and calls out for Adrian and Clara in vain, then compares himself to Robinson Crusoe. He travels to Ravenna, where he spends three days and later wanders the countryside, isolated and on the verge of madness. When he enters a palace, for a moment he believes a wild man stands before him, but he realizes it is his own reflection in a mirror. He continues to wander, hoping for other survivors and leaving messages about himself in three languages as he travels. He reaches Spoleto and counts notches he has made on a wand that he carries, noting 25 days have passed since the accident at sea. He ends up at the Coliseum in Rome and remains in the ancient city, musing about its past and that of mankind. Lionel becomes resolved to his situation, writing, "A year has passed; and I no longer guess at my state or my prospects—loneliness is my familiar, sorrow my inseparable companion." His only company is a dog that he found still tending sheep, despite the fact that its owner had died. Lionel journeys with the dog to the Tiber, where he plans to launch out onto the ocean. The novel's concluding paragraph reads:

> I have chosen my boat, and laid in my scant stores. I have selected a few books; the principal are Homer and Shakespeare—But the libraries of the world are thrown open to me—and in any port I can renew my stock. I form

no expectation of alteration for the better; but the monotonous present is intolerable to me. Neither hope nor joy are my pilots—restless despair and fierce desire of change lead me on. I long to grapple with danger, to be excited by fear, to have some task, however slight or voluntary, for each day's fulfillment. I shall witness all the variety of appearance, that the elements can assume—I shall read fair augury in the rainbow—menace in the cloud—some lesson or record dear to my heart in everything. Thus around the shores of deserted earth, while the sun is high, and the moon waxes or wanes, angels, the spirits of the dead, and the ever-open eye of the Supreme, will behold the tiny bark, freighted with Verney—the LAST MAN.

COMMENTARY

While Shelley's first novel focused on the disaster wreaked by a single man that caused his family's obliteration, *The Last Man* extends destruction to the entire human race. In *Frankenstein*, a scientist reached beyond himself for extraordinary creative powers, seeking to control nature. In *The Last Man*, nature exerts the ultimate control by ridding the earth of humans and returning its control to the natural elements. Shelley shows the reader a microcosm of the world and its dismantling through the characterization of Adrian, heir to the English throne, and his entourage.

Adrian may best symbolize nature's power to destroy humankind's weak attempts to force its own order on the universe. As heir presumptive to the English crown, Adrian represents the most traditional means of order developed by humans, that of the monarchy. The monarch stands at the top of a hierarchical order placing humans in various social categories, dependent on arbitrary material possession or birth heritage. When Adrian's father declares an end of monarchy in the face of calls for a republic, perceived as a superior type of order, Adrian is left a prince without a future. Ironically, he will assume his destined leadership role only in the face of certain destruction of all forms of human-designed order. Nature's steady, methodical destruction of humankind reminds all involved that any power humankind claims pales in comparison to the true order of the natural world. Shelley's purpose in demonstrating human weakness and ultimate inability to escape fate may surprise readers familiar with her early support of romantic ideals, including the transcendent power of the imagination.

Shelley focuses on the power of writing early in *The Last Man* by constructing a layered narration, beginning with a prediction in the novel's opening of humankind's destruction. The prediction appears in the form of writings by an ancient sibyl, a divine female prophet. The divinity of the prognosticator gains authority from the best-known predictions of the destruction of civilization found in the Bible's Book of Revelation. The novel's author, who is its first narrator, claims to have found fragments of the sibyl's prediction and, in an attempt to amuse herself during a period of grief, assembles the pieces like those of a puzzle. Shelley makes clear the power of the act of writing as her narrator notes that use of the imagination "softened my real sorrows and endless regrets, by clothing these fictitious ones in that ideality, which takes the mortal sting from pain." Thus, Shelley, herself a writer, narrates how another writer supports her own efforts to transcend reality.

However, the third narrator in the scheme and the novel's protagonist, Lionel Verney, makes clear the shortcomings of the imagination when the plague intervenes. The cruel reality of disease supersedes the powers of imagination to destroy even, one must suppose, Lionel's imagined reading audience. That plot structure causes the novel's major weakness, according to critics of Shelley's own times: How can that writer claim to be the "last" human when he continues to record his actions and ideas, seeking the immortality through writing that others like him have sought since the earliest oral tradition? Whatever one may think of Shelley's plot structure, by demonstrating the limits of imagination, Shelley countermands a major tenet of romanticism.

Shelley's skepticism of the romantic ideal and her critique of the male ego willing to sacrifice all in fulfillment of ambition combine to provide a strong framework for her novel. Anne K. Mellor writes that Shelley not only attacks her own previously expressed ideology, but she attacks both conservative and liberal political ideologies, finally "denying the authority of all ideologies, all systems of belief." In *The Last Man*, conservative politics support control through a hierarchy based on materialism, while liberal politics support individual freedom and the destruction of all social class distinctions. In her novel, Shelley, who in real life favored the liberal ideal, supports the cynical position that such equality can be accomplished, but only through the great leveler of death. She emphasizes the futility of political systems through Ryland's abandonment of his position as Lord Protector in order to guarantee his own safety and prolong his life. He begins his term attempting to share all food equally. When that does not work, he reverts to the landed system, in which a ruling force establishes an order and disburses food. That conservative system also fails in the face of anarchy. The novel thus reflects poorly on the ideology of equality and socialism as well as the more conservative approach to order by rule. Mellor sees Ryland's failure as Shelley's message that socialism and an equal sharing of resources proves effective only in a time of plenty.

As part of her focus on romantic ideology, Shelley offers much praise for nature as a creative and sustaining force, but she also obviously undercuts it, ultimately characterizing nature as a force of destruction. Early in the novel, Adrian celebrates nature with an outpouring that resembles the Psalms in structure and rhythm. He also directly mentions God, strongly tying the passage to a statement of religious belief:

> "O happy earth, and happy inhabitants of earth! A stately palace has God built for you, O man! and worthy are you of your dwelling! Behold the verdant carpet spread at our feet, and the azure canopy above; the fields of earth which generate and nurture all things, and the track of heaven, which contains and clasps all things. Now, at this evening hour, at the period of repose and refection, methinks all hearts breathe one hymn of love and thanksgiving, and we, like priests of old on the mountaintops, give a voice to their sentiment."

Shelley will turn Adrian's praise of the permanence of God's creation to irony, later proving through the visitation of the plague that humans are not permanent. She also demonstrates through the sibyl's prediction of the end of the world that the earth itself lacks permanency. It will no longer generate or nurture, nor will voices rise in unity in thanksgiving and praise. Thus, Shelley devalues both faith in God and the romantic belief in nature as providing a transcendent medium. It is nature that obliterates man, after all, reminding him of his limitations and his complete lack of value to the earth. Nature has transformed from a revered life force, seen especially in *Frankenstein*, to a destructive force, or at least a passive one.

Lionel opens volume 3 with a catalogue of varied natural tragedies and asks the reader whether cataclysmic natural occurrences forewarn man's destruction. He answers his own question with a resounding "no" as nature goes about its business, even offering in some locations abundant food for man and beast, all the while advancing death: "Where was pain and evil? Not in the calm air or weltering ocean; not in the woods or fertile fields, nor among the birds that made the woods resonant with song, the animals that in the midst of plenty basked in the sunshine. Our enemy, like the Calamity of Homer, trod our hearts, and no sound was echoed from her steps." Man has lost his position as God's favorite, created in the image of the Father, with dominion over the earth. Now he has sacrificed that position, his beautiful form is ravaged by plague, and he has even grown accustomed to the threat of disease and death after several years of suffering. Lionel now identifies death with the same nature he previously celebrated as a sustaining force: "Plague is the companion of spring, of sunshine, and plenty. We no longer struggle with her. We have forgotten what we did when she was not."

Most scholars and readers assume the narrator, author of the book, and last man of its title, Lionel Verney, represents Mary Shelley. In short order, Shelley had coped with the deaths of several members of her own family, including her children and husband, as well as their friends Edward Williams and George Gordon Byron, Lord Byron. Others feel Lionel's poetic sensibility is modeled on that

188 The Last Man

Self-portrait of Edward Williams, friend of the Shelleys. Williams drowned with Percy Shelley after their boat, the *Don Juan*, sank.

of Percy Bysshe Shelley. Later critics, such as E. J. Clery, caution against such a reductive reading, reminding readers that Shelley's creative gaze was fixed firmly on traditional elements of the apocalyptic tale, which directed much of her plot and character shaping. "End of times" stories were well known, and Shelley's novel easily fell into that category. In addition, her era seriously considered Thomas Robert Malthus's theory that predicted the population increase would outpace the availability of resources to support that population. His theory represented a factual, scientific "end of times" prediction that humans would disappear due to starvation. Other writers followed by stressing difficult choices humans might be called to make in which simple moral axioms would no longer apply. Shelley's father, WILLIAM GODWIN, posed scenarios fraught with moral anxiety in his best-known writing. In one instance in his *Enquiry Concerning Political Justice* (1793), Godwin stated that if faced with the choice of rescuing the French theologian and political writer François Fénelon or his own father from a burning building, he would select Fénelon for the greater good of the human race. *The Last Man* presents an equally difficult moral conundrum in which the final human decides to record the horror of his final moments. If someone should ever discover his writing, he intends it to act as a cautionary tale rather than a simple tale of horror. In addition, both Shelley and her father viewed reason as the human attribute that, if allowed to be fully exercised, would free humankind from the need for any type of social institution, including government.

Shelley may also have been warning against the anticipated results for England if and when its power structure shifted. She seems to ask readers to consider the dangers of England's losing the glory and world leadership position it had always known in the face of social changes. For example, in the novel, when England becomes a final bastion for its own people who return from distant lands, as well as for enormous numbers of immigrants, it fails in its national duty to support them. Its leaders, Lord Raymond and later Ryland, cannot rise to the task. Even Adrian, pure of spirit and motivation, can do little more than comfort his peers and, in the end, fails in his leadership when he causes Clara's death. When Adrian's English survivors arrive in Paris, the Parisians seek to turn them away, basing their decision on the fact that the English unrealistically continue to insist upon survival, instead of accepting their fate. Rather than uplifting the Parisians, that attitude will increase the misery of their final days. Lionel states, in part, "England, late birthplace of excellence and school of the wise, thy children are gone, thy glory faded! Thou, England, wert the triumph of man!" As Lionel mourns London in the opening of the third volume, he subverts Shakespeare's famous lines from *Richard II* mentioned in this entry's introduction.

Shelley also calls to mind the gothic (see GOTHIC FICTION) tradition, which device she excelled in using in *Frankenstein*, yet she proceeds to subvert it by turning to her new "end of world" approach. The gothic may terrorize its characters and readers, but it ultimately offers some redemption by a tale's conclusion. The words spoken by Verney in the novel's opening relate strongly to the gothic sensibility, one most forcefully practiced by Shelley in her novel *Mathilda*, (written 1819–1820; published in 1959). However, by the time *The Last Man* was published (1826), the gothic had passed its prime and fallen from popularity. The novel's gothic excess hearkens back to that which appeared in the works Percy Bysshe Shelley had used to introduce himself to William Godwin in 1812, *Zastrozzi* and *St. Irvyne*, both of which would also have impressed Mary Shelley. Where *St. Irvyne* employed the motif of the "elixir of eternal life," *The Last Man* would deny its existence. Although Shelley attempted to turn away from the gothic approach as it faded in popularity, she obviously realized that it best supported her talents. She stubbornly evoked its spirit for another decade, employing gothic elements in her best-known short stories, such as "Ferdinando Eboli" (1829); "Transformation" (1830); "The Dream" (1831); and "The Mortal Immortal" (1833).

Like other Shelley novels, particularly *Valperga* (1823) and *Lodore* (1835), *The Last Man* warns against the application of the imagination without support of reason. The first volume's opening description of Lionel Verney's father includes imagery that compares the application of imagination without judgment and reason to a boat without a rudder or captain: "My father was one of those men on whom nature had bestowed to prodigality the envied gifts of wit and imagination, and then left his bark of life to be impelled by these winds, without adding reason as the rudder, or judgment as the pilot for the voyage." This theme may represent Shelley's reaction against application of the romantic ideal of the imagination in the way she had seen it practiced by her husband and others. It formed the basis of the "masculine divine," an ideology that encouraged men to preempt all traditional personal responsibilities with those needed to save the world. She warns repeatedly in her fiction against the harm that males do, particularly to their families, when they act on their fancy and do not take responsibility for those who depend on them.

Shelley might have been describing Percy Shelley when she wrote of Verney's father, "the accumulating pile of debts of honour and of trade, which would have bent to earth any other, was supported by him with a light spirit and tameless hilarity; while his company was so necessary at the tables and assemblies of the rich, that his derelictions were considered venial, and he himself received with intoxicating flattery." Both Verney's father and Percy Shelley, while blessed with a personality that drew others to them, often ignored their own families in order to serve and/or entertain others. Romanticism supports the pursuit of transcendence, which could too conveniently slip into a pursuit of pleasure without the moral obligations that true transcendence should bring. During that pursuit—a part of which was, for some romantics, experimentation with mind-altering substances—one could too easily ignore the consequences of stepping out of the reality of everyday life, mistaking self-indulgence for transcendence. Shelley demonstrates this as she again employs the extended voyage metaphor when the narrator writes: "My father felt that his fall was near; but so far from profiting by this last calm before the storm to save himself, he sought to forget anticipated evil by making still greater sacrifices to the deity of pleasure, deceitful and cruel arbiter of his destiny." Her strong language makes clear the warning against a worship of pleasure, a crime of which Percy Shelley and his circle might stand accused. Although she somewhat tempers her view by attributing some acts simply to personal destiny, her point is made. Mary Shelley's philosophy also surfaces in Lionel's thoughts as he reads what Adrian has written following the loss of Evadne's affections:

> "Life"—it began thus—"is not the thing romance writers describe it; going through the measures of a dance, and after various evolutions arriving at a conclusion, when the dancers may sit down and repose. While there is life there is action and change. We go on, each thought linked to the one which was its parent, each act to a previous act. No joy or sorrow dies barren of progeny, which for ever generated and generating, weaves the chain that make our life."

Those dancing to the rhythms of romantic ideology could find themselves holding a badly bruised partner as well as a hefty bill from the piper as the music ebbed.

One method to better understand any work of literature is through intertextual analysis. Almost all schools of criticism, with the exception of formalism, recognize this approach. For instance, *The Last Man* immediately alludes to Shelley's previous novel by identifying its writer as "the author of *Frankenstein*." Readers who know *Frankenstein* will assume similarities between that novel and *The Last Man* in plot, style, and theme. That assumption proves true in several ways, as already discussed. In addition, *Frankenstein*'s subtitle, *The Modern Prometheus*, alludes to the myth explaining the origin of fire, which brought order and survival to man, but at a terrible and eternal cost to the giver of that gift. In addition, it immediately connects the reader to other writers who have considered PROMETHEUS, most specifically Percy Bysshe Shelley in his epic poem *Prometheus Unbound*. It also suggests what later critics, including Anne K. Mellor, label "Promethean Politics," which she defines as revolutionary "politics urged by the young Wordsworth and Coleridge, by Blake, Godwin, and Percy Shelley, a program that advocated radical social change and utopian transformation of the social and political order." However, women writing during the same era, such as Mary Shelley, "offered an alternative program grounded on the trope of the family-politic, on the idea of a nation-state that evolves gradually and rationally under the mutual care and guidance of both mother and father."

The Last Man alludes to multiple classical and traditional texts and historical accounts, including the stories of Adam and Eve, Sampson, Solomon, Icarus, Apollo and Artemis; *The Arabian Nights*; accounts of Alexander the Great, Caesar, Napoleon, and Oliver Cromwell; and works by Boccaccio, Dante, Milton, Shakespeare, Marvell, John Cleveland, Wordsworth, Coleridge, Keats, Defoe, and Calderon de la Baca, to name only a few. By understanding those authors' stories, characters, and historical figures and their importance to understanding the cultural, political, and social structures and concerns during the times in which they wrote and lived, readers gain multiple contexts for better understanding those elements in Shelley's tale.

Feminist critics note the traditional characterization of the various women characters as important to understanding Shelley's attempts to support the female reaction against the masculine divine. Those women who serve as wives and mothers are more positively drawn than those who do not, such as Evadne. Not only does Evadne contribute to her husband's social destruction by adopting masculine ambition, but she later assumes the male dress and role of a soldier, for which she is punished by death. She claims Lord Raymond even from beyond the grave by placing a curse on him, equating her with witches and other evil female incarnations. By contrast, the countess, who also exhibits an active aggressive "manly" agenda, eventually repents and manages to reverse her evil status. At first, similar to Lady Macbeth, she places personal ideology above the care of her children, and then she temporarily abandons her family before reclaiming her traditional nurturing role. When Lucy, who had assumed Idris's motherly role, dies, Lionel writes that she had exhibited "those peculiarly feminine virtues conspicuous in her; uneducated and unpretending as she was, she was distinguished for patience, forbearance, and sweetness." While Shelley complies with the contemporary demands for the ideal domesticated female, she also uses that characterization to undercut an ideology supporting masculine independence at the risk of family unity.

Formalist critics find much to comment on in the various elements of Shelley's style—tone, vocabulary, the production of imagery, symbolism, and irony. In the story's introduction, the narrator's description of the sibyl's cavern contains strong imagery of a church, including words and phrases such as *dome-like roof, light of heaven, a veil,* and *a solemn religious hue.* Its "raised seat of stone" suggests an altar, and "the perfect snow-white skeleton of a goat" suggests a sacrifice. Shelley introduces the imagery of faith as a precursor to questions regarding faith that will occur later. She foreshadows those questions in this passage by noting that the apartment "was overgrown with brambles and underwood"—negative imagery. In addition, she employs irony when the only visible sign of life in the church-like area is death in the form of a goat skeleton. The bright whiteness of the skeleton may symbolize the purity in the simple concept of life versus death and the reader's naïveté, like that of Verney, in taking life for granted. The goat may also be seen as important in its connection to Old Testament sacrifices, demanded by a "jealous God" from his just people.

Shelley selects various character names for their symbolic meaning. Lionel echoes the word *lion*, the king of beasts, and when he notes of Adrian that "the might of his smile would have tamed a hungry lion," readers recognize it is Verney himself who is tamed. Adrian may derive from the Greek for "dark" but in Latin means "rich." The seeming contradiction between those two versions helps to illuminate the conflict faced by Adrian. The two names considered together also suggest that being born to wealth is not enough. Perdita, labeled with a word that means "lost," shares the name of Shakespeare's character from *A Winter's Tale*. Shakespeare's Perdita is abandoned by her father, who mistakenly believes she is not his child. She is raised by a shepherd who names her Perdita because she is lost, abandoned by her family. She later meets a prince, they fall in love, and they want to marry but cannot due to her low social class. However, when her true identity is discovered, they are allowed to wed. Readers of Shelley's novel would relate her Perdita to that of Shakespeare and see many parallels.

Shelley also traditionally uses the seasons as symbols, and this novel is no exception. Winter generally foreshadows death, either literal or metaphoric, and when Idris comes in a panic to Lionel's door, the snow is falling in a dark night, made darker by Lionel's disturbing dreams:

> At past midnight I was awaked by a violent knocking. It was now deep winter; it had snowed, and was still snowing; the wind whistled in the leafless trees, despoiling them of the white flakes as they fell; its drear moaning, and the continued knocking, mingled wildly with my dreams . . . I hurried . . . to open my door to the unexpected visitor. Pale as the snow that showered about her, with clasped hands, Idris stood before me.

Here, winter frames Shelley's negative tone, in preparation for the death of Lionel's hope to marry Idris. However, she later effects a skillful inversion, and winter comes to denote hope. The people believe that the frost and, later, snow will deter the effects of the plague, although that hope proves false. Another aspect of style employed in the above passage is that of personification, as Shelley projects human characteristics onto the wind.

Finally, *The Last Man* deserves consideration as a work of science fiction. It is also classified as fantasy, a broader classification than science fiction, which is itself an aspect of fantasy. In fantasy, readers are asked to suspend their belief in natural forces, such as gravity, which then allows characters to behave in a way they normally would not, such as when men fly or animals can talk. Fantasy elements in this novel include the appearance of multiple dark suns and strange behavior among animals. In science fiction, natural laws are also overcome, but by use of a believable technology. Travel is a popular subject of science fiction, which often features travel machines or other modes of movement not yet available. As Mary Shelley imagined the world centuries in the future, she saw its inhabitants moving by way of balloon as a common conveyance, something not yet true in her world. While this may seem less than adventurous to the modern reader, when Lionel travels by balloon in the first volume, it not only moves him from place to place but also affects his mood and stirs his imagination:

> The balloon rose about half a mile from the earth, and with a favourable wind it hurried through the air, its feathered vans cleaving the unopposing atmosphere. Notwithstanding the melancholy object of my journey, my spirits were exhilarated by reviving hope, by the swift motion of the airy pinnace, and the balmy visitation of the sunny air. The pilot hardly moved the plumed steerage, and the slender mechanism of the wings, wide unfurled, gave forth a murmuring noise, soothing to the sense. Plain and hill, stream and corn-field, were discernible below, while we unimpeded sped on swift and secure, as a wild swan in his spring-tide flight. The machine obeyed the slightest motion of the helm; and, the wind blowing steadily, there was no let or obstacle to our course. Such was the power of man over the elements; a power long sought, and lately won; yet foretold in by-gone time by the prince of poets, . . .

Shelley's use of such futuristic imaginings is slight. For instance, people still mainly travel by horse back and carriage, and cross the ocean in traditional vessels. Brian Aldiss argues against the novel's classification as science fiction due to the lack of any innovations, other than balloon travel, representing the future. He points out that, to the contrary, Shelley seems to move backward in time with the appointment of a Lord Protector, recalling Oliver Cromwell's era, and her descriptions of London reflect on Daniel Defoe. He also notes that vaccination against disease was common in Shelley's time, yet she supposes that in the 21st century, humans lack defense against a plague.

Shelley's defenders counter that she is not concerned with creating an entire new world for her readers. Rather, she wants readers to better understand their own world. Her main point may be found in the irony of her final sentence. By the novel's end, everyone understands that man's power is no power at all, as he is obliterated by a microscopic creature. More important, he is obliterated by his lust for power to the exclusion of all other concerns.

CHARACTERS

Lionel Verney Lionel Verney narrates the story, is the last survivor of its title, and is supposedly based on aspects of both Percy and Mary Shelley but most strongly suggests Mary. Mary and Lionel both suffered isolation as children, rejected by their social group. They both embraced the imagination as an escape mechanism. Both existed basically to support others and both were writers. Through Lionel, Shelley continues her critique of the romantic ideal of the imagination that had its birth in *Frankenstein* and runs through all of her novels. She demonstrates not only that the imagination proves ineffective when help is most needed, but that it can prove destructive. When Lionel is searching for Raymond in the ruins of Constantinople, he recognizes that his faith and hope are also ruins, mere shells of their former state. He tells readers that he experiences a momentary fantasy allowing him to imagine that Raymond lives, but that momentary relief is quickly followed by a reality almost too painful to bear. When all of his loved ones are gone, the only relief he experiences is through his writing, as he plans to "pour his soul" onto paper, exercising his imagination to provide what he realizes will be only a momentary and ineffectual release. He offers his soul to a nonexistent reader rather than to a deity. Lionel's actions are futile if he is, indeed, the last man on earth. Although most people in Shelley's age, as Mellor points out, at least cling to faith and God for a future even after death, for an atheist like Shelley, the disappearance of the reading audience equates to a permanent extinguishing of the imagination. No transcendence awaits her, no power that promises thoughts and dreams will endure. For her, time will terminate at some point; in the novel, the sibyl predicts that will happen in 2100 at the world's end. Shelley thus strongly critiques the romantic ideology that postulated one could transcend through the power of the imagination.

Perdita Perdita is Verney's sister and the wife of Lord Raymond. Her early poverty and orphan state breed a lifelong desire for independence. Shelley identifies her with nature, writing of Perdita as a child: "She was like a fruitful soil that imbibed the airs and dews of heaven, and gave them forth again to light in loveliest forms of fruits and flowers; but then she was often dark and rugged as that soil, raked up, and new sown with unseen seed." This statement makes clear Perdita's potential but does not assure that she will fulfill that potential. Shelley continues to identify Perdita with nature by placing her home near Windsor Forest, an area that various characters use as a retreat to seek mental and emotional renewal from the demands of city life. When Lionel sees his sister following a two-year absence, he describes her, in part, as moving "so that her light step scarce made her foot-fall heard," which identifies her with stealthy animals. She will not be able to survive the demands of civilization, much as a wild creature forced into domestication might not survive.

Perdita's talent is music, a sophisticated form of self-expression, which she uses to communicate her mood. When Lionel seeks later in life to educate Perdita in literature, he notes that music, like that found in birds' calls, is her artistic mode. When Perdita kills herself, she chooses to drown in the ocean, selecting nature as the instrument of death that will unite her spiritually with Lord Raymond.

Mellor and others see Perdita as modeled on Mary Shelley. Shelley uses her to define woman's identity as a reflection of the domestic sphere where she is ever ready to sacrifice herself, both physically and emotionally, for the dominant male. Perdita's loneliness as a child makes her reticent as an adult, a characteristic that others translate as aloofness. She also allows imagination free reign, constantly predicting disaster and making herself ill over her concern for her husband. She attempts to communicate through letters rather than speaking directly to Raymond, and when they do speak, he often misunderstands her because she will not say quite enough. Mary Shelley had at one time or another exhibited all of these characteristics.

Mellor explains that when Raymond first selects Perdita over Princess Idris, Perdita gains self-confidence, her music improves, and Adrian compares her to a blossoming flower. In describing that change in Perdita, Shelley describes her own artistic maturation following her marriage to Percy. As Perdita could only imagine herself in relationship to her husband, committing suicide to join him in death, so Mary had trouble conceiving of herself as an independent being. She also thought of death as an alternative to surviving her husband, expressed in her poetry. But while Perdita literally cannot survive without her husband, even for the sake of her child, Mary Shelley could and did. She may be expressing what would later be labeled "survivor's guilt." Shelley's projection far into the future of a lack of independence and continued strict gender roles for women expresses her lack of hope for any substantial change in women's roles, even 200 years beyond her own life time.

Adrian, earl of Windsor Adrian is the son of England's last king and the novel's hero. When his father abdicates the British throne in 2073 in order to establish a republic, Adrian shares his father's democratic principles and remains unmoved by his mother's demand that he reclaim the throne. He devotes himself to a life of the mind, immersing himself in studies, with the result that he is "imbued beyond his years with learning and talent." His physical description fits that of Percy Bysshe Shelley, on whom most critics feel he is modeled. His body expresses "the excess of sensibility and refinement" with which he is blessed, and his blond hair and association with light through specific imagery, such as "morning sunbeams" that touch his hair, suggest the countenance of an angel. He is kind and sincere, has a beautiful voice, and as a young man dedicates himself to poetry and is driven to the edge of madness over Evadne's rejection.

However, he is still capable of rallying his countrymen, urges equality for all, and fights in Greece with the natives against Turkish oppressors, reminiscent of Lord Byron's actions. Adrian actually regains strength when placed in a leadership role, suggesting that is his destiny. Courageous and energetic, he refuses personal political power, despite his title as earl of Windsor, supporting Lord Raymond's candidacy as England's Lord Protector. Eventually, he literally sacrifices himself for his country, thus becoming a Christ figure as he comforts and protects the sick. At the point that the plague threatens to destroy Britain, Adrian agrees to assume the title of Lord Protector of England. When he leads survivors toward the Alps, he stops a conflict between factions by placing himself between the two. He is compared to "an angel of peace" as a result of his efforts to again unify his countrymen.

In Adrian's choice not to marry but rather to serve as a universal father, critics including Mellor believe that Shelley comments on her husband's selfishness; Percy Shelley believed only he himself could satisfy his need for a soul mate; no one else could reach the perfection that he demanded. Adrian may also represent Mary Shelley's conflict regarding feelings for a husband that she at once idealized and resented, due to a perceived insensitivity to his family's needs. When Adrian insists, despite Verney's warning, in making the dangerous sea journey that leads to his death, Shelley may be expressing her extended anger over her husband taking a chance on the water, leading to his drowning. Again, she may be projecting what she saw as Percy Shelley's irresponsibility onto the character of Adrian. The fact that Verney's niece, Clara, who shares the name of the Shelleys' first daughter, also drowns, symbolizes her feeling that Percy did not take seriously the demands of family life.

Adrian is also important as part of Shelley's focus on gender inequality. Women are viewed as not only the creators of life but also as its preservers. Men do not appreciate life as do women—thus, masculine values threaten society. They must also assume the duty of respecting and preserving life. On the other hand, Adrian never marries due to unrequited love, suggesting him as an ideal that survives outside of culture's pressure on all men and women to marry. He is ill almost from the beginning of the novel, a traditionally feminine characteristic. Shelley also emphasizes Adrian's feminine side through his willingness to sacrifice himself for his larger family of English citizens.

Lord Raymond Lord Raymond is a nobleman who eventually becomes head of state. An adventurer and heroic type, he attracts the interest of Perdita and marries her. Mellor describes him as the character used by Shelley to critique male egoism and the "masculine divine," also allowing her to settle her conflict over her hostility toward Byron. Some parallel may be seen in Byron's early offer to help Mary Shelley following Percy's death but then reneging on his promise, due to his enthusiasm in supporting the Greek cause. That cause led to both the real and fictional characters' deaths.

Raymond serves as a foil for Adrian, infinitely stronger in both a physical and mental sense, capable of much passion. However, his passion is focused on fulfilling a destiny and gaining eternal fame rather than on humanitarian activity. He becomes so focused on fighting for Greek independence and distracted by an illicit love for Evadne that he abdicates his elected office as Lord Protector of England and ignores his obligation to his family, abandoning them.

Raymond is not a monolithic character. Shelley adds interest to his personality in some of his unexpected choices. Early in the novel, when he returns to England, he plans to marry Princess Idris, a scheme supported by the countess of Windsor, which would allow him to restore the monarchy and gain immense personal power. However, he rejects those plans for the love of Perdita Verney, allowing his romantic and sexual passions to supersede his political ambition. Mellor believes that Shelley might have been projecting her own fantasy that Byron would abandon his plans in order to marry her. But Raymond can only stand family bliss for five years. He is then elected Lord Protector and becomes sexually involved with Evadne, a Greek princess with whom Adrian had originally been in love.

Although Raymond eventually accepts Evadne's decision to leave him, he is emotionally unable to apologize to Perdita, who also separates from him. With neither woman willing to continue the tripartite love affair, Raymond selects a more easily fought battle, that with the Greek military, where he again becomes a hero. It is not enough that he is a hero for his daughter, Clara. His brash tendencies eventually destroy him as he ignores logic, leaving all of his men and charging alone on horseback into Constantinople. Planting the Greek Christian flag on Constantinople's mosque is his ultimate ambition, and it literally kills him. As she did in *Valperga*, Shelley frames a strong argument against such blind ambition, which ignores individual relationships and is willing to risk all for self-aggrandizement.

Princess Idris Princess Idris is Adrian's sister, the daughter of England's last king. Strong-willed and independent, she marries Lionel Verney against her mother's wishes, acting against the female stereotype to resist Raymond and the possibility of restoring the aristocracy, through which she would have gained much power. However, once married, she fits the stereotype of the 19th-century feminine ideal, foreshadowed early on when Lionel compares her grace in movement to that of an angel. She becomes the perfect supportive wife to her loving and attentive husband, wavering only slightly in her optimism for their future together at the death of one of their sons. As with other characters in this novel, Mary Shelley can also be seen as a model for Idris.

Evadne A Greek princess, Evadne attracts but rejects Adrian, instead romancing Raymond in spite of his being married to Perdita. She acts as a cautionary tale to women who do not choose wisely in marriage and also do not honor the institution as it applies to themselves or to others. In addition, she assumes the male role in several instances, allowing her unfeminine ambitions to destroy her husband, drawing architectural plans for the cultural museum that Raymond envisions, abandoning Raymond, and eventually assuming physical disguise as a man to fight in the Greek war against Turkey. Shelley depicts her evolution into a male substitute who, with her death, curses Raymond also to die. Evadne must be included in the male egocentrics that Shelley charges with failing to assume proper responsibility for their families and thus failing society. Evadne fails as a woman mainly because she abandons her prescribed societal role.

As a young beautiful woman, Evadne tempts and teases Adrian, who would be a fine candidate for marriage. She leaves him to later follow her mother's instruction to marry a wealthy merchant. One assumes that she married only to have the means to support her agenda. Although she realizes that Raymond is happily married with a child, she takes advantage of his protective feelings toward her as a "helpless" woman living in poverty to agree to an affair in which both parties are equally culpable. An intelligent woman, Evadne eventually realizes that if Raymond did leave Perdita, he would be so burdened by guilt that he would not make a satisfactory lover or husband. She abandons him but later follows him as a soldier rather than bowing to her fate as a woman. She curses Raymond to die when she dies, just as Raymond will later do metaphorically to Perdita by his own death. Evadne is more a failure as a woman than even the countess of Windsor, who at least supported her husband's political position and attempts, although erroneously, to construct a future for her two children. The countess is aligned with Evadne in her eventual dismissal of her children and her abandonment of her family, but in a hierarchy of sins, hers are diminished by Evadne's egocentric acts. The countess further redeems herself by returning years later to serve as a mother, ultimately symbolizing birth, while Evadne symbolizes death.

FURTHER READING

Aldiss, Brian W. *Billion Year Spree*. New York: Doubleday, 1973.

Clery, E. J. *Women's Gothic: from Clara Reeve to Mary Shelley*. Tavistock, Devon, U.K.: Northcote House, 2000.

"Contemporary Reviews: *The Last Man*." *Romantic Circles*. Available online. URL: http://www.rc.umd.edu/reference/chronologies/mschronology/reviews.html#Pres. Accessed on June 26, 2009.

Eberle-Sinatra, Michael. "Gender, Authorship and Male Domination: Mary Shelley's Limited Freedom in *Frankenstein* and *The Last Man*." In *Mary Shelley's Fictions: From Frankenstein to Falkner*, edited by Michael Eberle-Sinatra, 95–108. New York: St. Martin's Press, 2000.

———, ed. *Mary Shelley's Fictions: From Frankenstein to Falkner*. New York: St. Martin's Press, 2000.

Goldsmith, S. "Of Gender, Plague, and Apocalypse: Mary Shelley's Last Man." *Yale Journal of Criticism* 4, no. 1 (Fall 1990): 129–73.

Lederer, Susan E. *Frankenstein: Penetrating the Secrets of Nature*. New Brunswick, N.J.: Rutgers University Press, 2002.

Lokke, Kari E. "*The Last Man*." In *The Cambridge Companion to Mary Shelley*, edited by Esther Schor, 116–134. Cambridge: Cambridge University Press, 2004.

Mellor, Anne K. *Romanticism and Gender*. New York: Routledge, 1993.

Melville, Peter. "The Problem of Immunity in *The Last Man*." *SEL: Studies in English Literature* 47, no. 4 (Autumn 2007): 825–846.

Schuetz, Julie K. "Mary Shelley's *The Last Man*: Monstrous Worlds, Domestic Communities, and Masculine Romantic Ideology." Available online. URL: http://prometheus.cc.emory.edu/panels/4A/J.Schuetz.html. Accessed on August 23, 2009.

Shelley, Mary W. *The Last Man*. 3 vols. London: Henry Colburn, 1826.

———. *The Last Man*. In *The Novels and Selected Works of Mary Shelley*. Vol. 4. Edited by Jane Blumberg with Nora Crook. London: Pickering & Chatto, 1996.

———. *The Last Man*. Edited by Hugh Luke, Jr. 1965. Reprint, Bison ed., with introduction by Anne K. Mellor, Lincoln: University of Nebraska Press, 1993.

———. *The Last Man*. Edited by Anne McWhir. Ontario: Broadview Press, 1996.

———. *The Last Man*. Edited by Morton Paley. Oxford and New York: Oxford University Press, 1994.

———. *The Last Man*. Available online. URL: http://www.gutenberg.org/etext/18247. Accessed June 20, 2009.

———. *The Last Man*. A Hypertext Edition by Stephen E. Jones. Available online. URL: http://www.rc.umd.edu/editions/mws/lastman/index.html. Accessed on June 25, 2009.

———. *Selected Letters of Mary Wollstonecraft Shelley*. Edited by Betty T. Bennett. Baltimore: Johns Hopkins University Press, 1995.

Snyder, Robert Lane. "Apocalypse and Indeterminacy in Mary Shelley's *The Last Man*." *Studies in Romanticism* 17 (1978): 435–452.

Spatt, Hartley S. "Mary Shelley's Last Men: the Truth of Dreams." *Studies in the Novel* 7, no. 4 (Winter 1975): 526–537.

Sterrenburg, Lee. "*The Last Man*: Anatomy of Failed Revolutions." *Nineteenth-Century Fiction*, 33 (December 1978): 324–47.

Thomas, Sophie. "The Ends of the Fragment, the Problem of the Preface: Proliferation and Finality in *The Last Man*." In *Mary Shelley's Fictions: From* Frankenstein *to* Falkner, edited by Michael Eberle-Sinatra, 22–38. New York: St. Martin's Press, 2000.

Webb, Samantha. "Reading the End of the World: The Last Man, History, and the Agency of Romantic Authorship." In *Mary Shelley in Her Times*, edited by Betty T. Bennet and Stuart Curran, 119–133. Baltimore: Johns Hopkins University Press, 2000.

Wright, Julia M. "'Little England': Anxieties of Space in Mary Shelley's *The Last Man*. In *Mary Shelley's Fictions: From* Frankenstein *to* Falkner, edited by Michael Eberle-Sinatra, 129–149. New York: St. Martin's Press, 2000.

Lodore (1835)

Mary Shelley varied from her previous approach to fiction in writing her three-volume, 900-plus-page novel *Lodore*. Rather than serving as a gothic (see GOTHIC FICTION) burst of emotionality, or as a moral exposition, *Lodore* offers several characters that operate outside of what the critic Richard Cronin refers to as "a single hierarchy of moral judgment." In the vein of novels by Edward Bulwer-Lytton, an extremely popular writer of Shelley's era and one she greatly admired, Shelley produces a type of hybrid fiction that many reviewers of her day despised. Bulwer-Lytton was the first to excel in fiction that combined elements of sentimental fiction, the type in which Shelley also excelled, and silver-fork fiction, which focused on the fashionable, aristocratic elements of society. One story credits the label to a comment in the November 18, 1827, edition of the *Examiner* by William Hazlitt accusing the novelist Theodore Hook of a preoccupation with "silver forks" in his novels. Another explanation holds that *Fraser's Magazine* accused Bulwer-Lytton of being a "silver polisher." Due in great part to attacks by *Fraser's* reviewers, silver-fork fiction all but disappeared by 1840. It would be replaced by realistic fiction prompted by a rise in concerns regarding working class conditions. But for a brief time in the 1830s, fiction that featured aristocratic foibles captured the public's interest, including that of Mary Shelley.

A combination of the type of character shaping seen in silver-fork fiction, along with that of the sentimental fiction of her heritage, held tremendous appeal for Shelley. Like Bulwer-Lytton, she sought to shape a story that did not offer a simple moralistic view but, rather, complicated her fiction's themes and characters by adding satire and irony to sentimentality. The critic Betty Bennett writes of *Lodore* that more than Shelley's other novels, it should be read because of "its honest recognition of the contradictions" one notes "within her ideology of the bourgeois family." Those contradictions may plainly be seen in the more rounded characterizations. For instance, Shelley offers in Lord Lodore, according to Richard Cronin, a "moral anomaly." For the most part, readers expected lead characters to either represent pure goodness or pure evil.

One explanation supporting Shelley's more realistic characterizations is that they were clearly based on real-life characters. Although most authors do this to some point, with Shelley's fiction, parallels to her own life appear marked. That may partially be explained by the fact that scholars know so much about her life; few authors have been studied in such detail. However, readers of her own day immediately recognized the similarities, in part due to public fascination with the romantic circle in which the Shelleys participated. Shelley's stepsister, Claire Claremont, was so incensed by *Lodore*'s familiar characterization that she took Shelley to task, excoriating "a person of your genius, whose moral tact ought to be proportionately exalted," for gilding, embellishing and passing "off as beautiful what was the merest compound of Vanity, folly, and every miserable weakness."

Clairmont's vituperative response was prompted by *Lodore*'s similarities to her onetime lover, GEORGE GORDON BYRON (Lord Byron), from whom she had tried unsuccessfully to regain custody of their daughter, Allegra, before the child's early death. To Claire, rather than being the BYRONIC HERO that would grow increasingly more popular in fiction, *Lodore*'s characterization instead mimicked real details from Byron and Claire's life, most markedly Lodore's removal of the care of his infant daughter from her mother. Whether Shelley intended the similarity is doubtful, but Claire's assessment of Lodore's character as a mixture of "vanity, folly, and every miserable weakness" is correct. However, it is also incomplete, as Shelley adds touches of affection and remorse to Lodore's cynical attitude that more fully develops his character.

Early critics also approached the novel as an autobiographical artifact, attributing its value to its reflection of the lifestyles of the Shelley circle. Edward Dowden wrote in 1886 that one could find in Lodore "an almost literal transcript from [Mary Shelley's] life and that of [Percy] Shelley during the weeks of distress and separation in London," referring to their return home after running away to the Continent together in 1814. He also saw evidence of references to Emilia Viviani, the young woman with whom PERCY BYSSHE SHELLEY may have had an affair and for whom he wrote *Epipsychidion* (1821), as well as to Percy's first wife, Harriet Westbrook. In 1935, Frederick L. Jones, an accomplished Percy Bysshe Shelley scholar, agreed in a letter written to the *Times Literary Supplement* in which he labeled *Lodore* artistically "mediocre" and of value only due to its reflection of details

Miniature portrait of Mary Shelley from 1857 *(Painting by Reginald Easton)*

from the Shelleys' lives. Scholar Jane Blumberg described Shelley's later work as easy writing, symptomatic of Shelley's having abandoned her earlier political ideology in favor of "an artistically unchallenging, but emotionally tranquil life." Her point of view would later be challenged but is one that lingered until focused feminist scholarship came on the literary scene in the middle of the 20th century.

That scholarship would embrace the value and interest brought to the novel by its autobiographical aspects, but it would find much additional value. In Lisa Vargo's opinion, *Lodore*'s greatest importance is its insight into Shelley's "desire to remain true to Jacobin ideals" adhered to during the final decade of the 18th century, and also for its illustration of "ideological perspectives on women" related to progress toward equality gained by women during the 1830s, most importantly women's education. As an example of that illustration, Vargo quotes from a letter to Shelley's publisher describing the novel in which Shelley demonstrates a clear compliance with "her culture's representation of bourgeois domesticity":

> I do not know how briefly to give you an idea of the whole tale—[The] A Mother & Daughter are the heroines—The Mother who after safrifising [sacrificing] all to the world at first—afterwards makes sacrifices not less entire, for her child—finding *all* to be Vanity, except the genuine affections of the heart. In the daughter I have tried to pourtray in its simplicity,& all the beauty I could muster, the devotion of a young wife for the husband of her choice—The disasters she goes through being described—& their result in awakening her Mother's affection, bringing about the conclusion of the tale—Perhaps a fitting motto would be Sir Walter Scott's well known lines beginning "O woman in our hours of ease &C.

Such characterization of women as angels—self-sacrificing, innocent, and devoted to their families—would appear in Shelley's other works as well, beginning with *Frankenstein* (1818).

While Shelley's mother, MARY WOLLSTONECRAFT, chafed beneath such ideology and publicly argued for women's education as the key to independence, she would not adopt a private agenda supporting such independence. She fell in love with an American womanizer who left her with his child, and after chasing him around a foreign country and doing his bidding when asked, she became depressed and attempted suicide. After again becoming pregnant with the much older WILLIAM GODWIN, Wollstonecraft attempted to live apart from him as a protest against the public institution of marriage, but in the end they married in order for their child to reap the civic benefits due the offspring of a traditional couple. She enjoyed a few evidently happy months with her husband before dying of puerile fever following her delivery of Mary. Wollstonecraft's life, often sensationalized, clearly demonstrated how difficult ideology was to put into practice.

As Mary matured, Wollstonecraft's portrait hung prominently over a fireplace in the room that Sunstein refers to as "the heart of the house." Mary Godwin studied beneath the portrait, which remained even after Godwin's second marriage. Despite her devotion to her dead mother, which included hours spent reading near her gravesite, the mature Mary Shelley had little use for mothers in her novels. The mother was eliminated altogether in most and in others was, at the least, not present in her daughter's life. *Lodore* includes two absent mothers from Ethel's and Fanny's lives, one dead and one alienated from her husband. The one present mother, Ethel's grandmother, proves a bad influence on her own daughter, Cornelia, supporting Cornelia's choice of high society over caring for the family unit. Shelley was fascinated by daughter/father relationships, and her daughter characters adore their fathers and often live with them late in their lives. Shelley emphasizes the positives a girl raised by her father enjoys in chapter 3 of *Lodore*'s first volume, writing that a daughter's education by a father "tends to develop early a thousand of those portions of mind, which are folded up, and often destroyed, under mere feminine tuition." Many of the daughters in Shelley novels reflect her own experience as a child who idolized her father, retaining a strong relationship into her own adulthood.

Additional recognizable elements in *Lodore* from Shelley's life include the practice of dueling as a way for men to settle disagreements and/or seek compensation for a wrong. Byron was involved in dueling, and Shelley's father, William Godwin, mentioned it in his *Enquiry Concerning Political Justice*. In book 2, appendix 2 of the book's third edition, he wrote, in part,

> this despicable practice was originally invented by barbarians for the gratification of revenge. It was probably at that time thought a very happy project, for reconciling the odiousness of malignity with the gallantry of courage. But in this light it is now generally given up. Men of the best understanding who lend it their sanction, are unwillingly induced to do so, and engage in single combat merely that their reputation may sustain no slander.

Lodore engages in the duel that takes his life precisely for that reason. His evasion an earlier challenge moves him to self-exile because he fears slander against his good name.

Outlawed in 1819, dueling continued into the 1830s; 14 duels were reported in the *Times* during the end of 1835, the year Shelley published *Lodore*. In addition, she knew a man who died in a duel in 1827 following an argument over cards.

Shelley's background reading for the novel influenced her choice of setting, which proves quite a strong element in the novel. Lodore's escape to the wilds of Illinois in the United States prove key to Ethel's upbringing as one close to nature. According to Vargo, specific information on the upper Midwest came from sources including *A Year's Residence in the United States of America* (1828), by William Cobbett, and Morris Birkbeck's *Notes on a Journey in America, from the Coast of Virginia to the Territory of Illinois, With Proposals for the Establishment of a Colony of English* (1817), as well as Birkbeck's *Letters from Illinois* (1818). Claire Claremont also read those two authors, and conversation probably took place between Shelley and her about the books' contents. Scholars working out a chronology for *Lodore* estimate that Ethel would have been in Illinois in 1818, at the same time as Birkbeck. In *Letters from Illinois*, a letter dated March 23, 1818, reads in part:

> The toil and the difficulty, and even the dangers, attending the removal of a family from the hills of Surrey to the prairies of Illinois are considerable and the responsibility is felt at every step, a load upon the sprits of a father, for which his honest intentions are not at all less, and even triumphantly, to have secured a retreat for ourselves, and then, turning our backs upon care and anxiety, to be employed in smoothing the way, and preparing a happy resting place for other weary pilgrims, is an enjoyment which I did not calculate upon when we quitted our old home.

While Shelley does not describe in much detail the years that Lodore and Ethel spend in Illinois, she had a thoroughly painted backdrop in mind as she wrote. Lodore enjoys the changing seasons: "the moss grew thicker and greener upon the logs that supported his roof, . . . the plants he cultivated increased in strength and beauty, and . . . the fruit-trees yielded their sweet produce in greater abundance . . . the landscape became more familiar," and "so did a thousand associations twine themselves with its varied appearances, till the forests and glades became as friends and companions." Shelley had long shared the romantic view of nature's transcendent power that she projects into the novel. The wilderness has a marked effect on Lodore, bringing him peace. The narrator tells us that he "became enamoured of the independence of solitude, and the sublime operations of surrounding nature," and "he learnt to be contented with his lot." The years in the wilds of America positively affect Ethel, who, in the middle of her suffering on her husband's behalf in England, thinks longingly of the open spaces of Illinois.

Shelley also corresponded with Frances Wright, who founded a Tennessee colony for slaves that permitted them to work in order to gain their freedom. Wright also planned a colony for whites drawn in part on ideas of William Godwin and the Welsh social reformer Robert Owen (1771–1858), and Shelley met Owen's son. Birkbeck had visited an Indiana colony established by Owen, a colony that Shelley's friend the novelist Frances Trollope would also visit. Thus, Shelley remained quite aware of the United States and specifically of Illinois, having discussed the establishment of utopias with her circle.

Vargo also writes that Shelley may have featured Wales in the novel, based on what Percy had told her about his and his wife Harriet's visits there in 1812 and 1813. Mary Shelley could draw on her own experience living in Italy to develop scenes of Ethel and Edward Villiers visiting Saville in Naples and moving on to Rome. Not only had she lived there with Percy, but she also learned the language, continued correspondence with Italian friends, and wrote and published articles about the country. In addition, popular poetry of the day by Letitia Landon and Felicia Hemans depicted Italy's artistic and political interests, so the public would know of its attraction. Shelley had also visited Essex with Percy and may have located the Fitzhenry estate there because of its proximity to London, which allowed easy travel between the two cities, trips taken in the novel by Ethel and Lodore. And the name *Longfield* echoes the name of Shelley's home, Field Place in Sussex. A final prominent geographic influence was that of Lodore Falls in the Lake District in Cumbria, England, still a popular tourist retreat. The falls will be discussed in more detail in the critical section below.

Lodore did not prove particularly successful commercially, despite its shared characteristics with Bulwer's popular novels and a positive critical reception. That may have been because readers had come to expect a certain fiction from "the author of Frankenstein," the manner by which Shelley was often identified in her publications. Vargo writes that while *Lodore* may not "possess the mythic appeal of *Frankenstein* or topical interest of *The Last Man*" that does not mean it lacks significance. She supports Betty Bennett's statement that while some have evaluated Shelley's works as lacking a philosophical basis, we may simply not have recognized it. Therefore, the reader must take responsibility for knowing more about the time period during which Shelley produced *Lodore*. Vargo believes the novel can be used to learn much about women living in 1830s England through study of its female characters. On the surface, it celebrates the female ideal of virtue and service, but a subtext may be discovered supporting the value of the intellectual, active woman.

Shelley's educational references reflect her own experience in an early program based on the ideas of Jean-Jacques Rousseau, a plan that featured some aspects supported by her mother. Godwin taught Mary to read and write at an early age, assigning her to trace the inscription on her mother's gravestone. He supplied textbooks as well as Wollstonecraft's novels for her reading, establishing his role as teacher to his daughter's role as pupil. Mary loved learning, and it was so highly valued in the household as to cause her stepsister to complain that the only way to receive any attention was to excel in writing. Mary gained the education that her mother had to do without as a child, reading history, studying classical languages, pouring through Shakespeare and Milton, and reading poetry in various languages. Her father and his second wife founded a bookstore and publishing company, further emphasizing the vital importance of books and reading. As a child, Mary Godwin learned a study routine that she continued to practice as an adult. According to Emily Sunstein, she studied and wrote from the morning into the early afternoon; took exercise and enjoyed some recreation; and always read as a student, taking notes, developing chronologies, and learning to cross-reference sources.

While Wollstonecraft had strongly supported an education for females, she still worried about the consequences. She said of Mary's half sister, Fanny, due to the oppressed nature of women in her era, "I dread to unfold her mind, lest it should render her unfit for the world she is to inhabit." Godwin did not fear that Mary's education and training might cause her conflict while trying to fit into a society that demanded certain behavior of young women. However, Mary may have felt her own inner tension over what she had to view as her unconventional home life and upbringing. Such conflict over self-identity may be revealed in the fact that each of the five women characters in *Lodore* reflect a bit of their author-creator. While, at first glance, readers and critics rightly protest Ethel's too-good characterization as unrealistic, a steadier gaze reveals that Shelley used Ethel's angelic image to challenge the already emerging Victorian feminine ideal. Villiers is shaped for a similar purpose. He does not take responsibility for his initial actions, and thus Ethel must share the consequences. Shelley's culture defined marriage as a necessary convention; Shelley reveals that it proves successful only when each member of the couple fulfills their dictated roles in placing the family first in all considerations.

The topic of proper behavior for women during Shelley's time produced an industry based on the publication of conduct books. These books advised young women as to proper behavior to meet the Victorian mores of English culture. Ironically, they added to support for a woman's education, holding that women would learn to share the same desires and focus of their husbands and thus prove to be better mates. Their education would lend knowledge regarding economic conservation in the household; in other words, a woman would learn to follow budgets and construct her private domestic domain on a tightly shaped regime that complemented her husband's public activities. He would produce and earn in the workplace, and she would spend and consume in what the scholar and critic Nancy Armstrong terms a tasteful manner, bringing pride and honor to her household and the greater culture. Once placed in the consumer arena, women were automatically granted a power, in writing, that they had not previously enjoyed, and the conduct books entered the debate over the place of women in the society.

Mary Wollstonecraft commented on one of the most familiar of the conduct books, Dr. John Gregory's *A Father's Legacy to his Daughters* (1774), which had been read for more than 50 years. She criticized Gregory's ideas as well as some of Rousseau's. Of Gregory, she wrote that his advice was laced with a "paternal solicitude," adding that while some of his advice was sound, other advice "so speciously" supported ideas that she thought "have had the most baneful effect on the morals and manners of the female world." While he wrote with an "easy familiar style," and respect for his deceased wife permeated his work, he did not help his daughters by wishing mainly to make them "amiable." His various statements distressed Wollstonecraft, who passionately responded, "Hapless woman! What can be expected from thee when the beings on whom thou art said naturally to depend for reason and support, have all an interest in deceiving thee."

Wollstonecraft's lengthy comment is worth repeating here. In *A Vindication of the Rights of Woman*, she writes that she "entirely disapproves" of such "remarks relative to behavior" because

> A cultivated understanding, and an affectionate heart, will never want starched rules of decorum—something more substantial than seemliness will be the result; and, without understanding the behavior here recommended, would be rank affectation. Decorum, indeed, is the one thing needful!—decorum is to supplant nature and banish all simplicity and variety of character out of the female world. Yet what good end can all this superficial counsel produce? It is, however, much easier to point out this or that mode of behaviour, than to set the reason to work; but, when the mind has been stored with useful knowledge, and strengthened by being employed, the regulation of the behavior may safely be left to its guidance.

Wollstonecraft uses much stronger language to answer Rousseau, who "declares that a woman should never, for a moment, feel herself independent, that she should be governed by fear to exercise her natural cunning, and made a coquettish slave in order to render her a more alluring object of desire, a *sweeter* companion to man, whenever he chooses to relax himself." She accuses Rousseau of falsely basing his arguments in some sense of a natural order, insinuating "that truth and fortitude, the corner stones of all human virtue" should be restricted in women in favor of obedience. "What nonsense!" Wollstonecraft declares, and she asks "when will a great man arise with sufficient strength of mind to puff away the fumes which pride and sensuality have thus spread over the subject!"

Her writings elicited responses, many critical of Wollstonecraft, that added to the debate, such as *Letters and Essays, Moral and Miscellaneous* (1793), by Mary Hays, and *Strictures on the Modern System of Female Education* (1799), by Hannah More. Some agreed with part of Wollstonecraft's ideas but took issue with others.

Sarah Stickney Ellis in her 1839 "Characteristics of the Women of England" wrote about the "gentle, inoffensive, delicate, and passively amiable" young women, labeling "ungracious" her task of rousing "them from their summer dreams." However, a wake-up call proved necessary. She proclaimed that such listlessness would not do, telling her readers,

> You have deep responsibilities, you have urgent claims; a nation's moral wealth is in your keeping. Let us inquire then in what way it may be best preserved. Let us consider what you are, and have been, and by what peculiarities of feeling and habit you have been able to throw so much additional weight into the scale of your country's worth.

Here Stickney conflates morals and material worth, using the metaphor of weights on a scale, which evokes imagery of trade and balance. She next evokes architectural imagery, imagining the domestic sphere, with woman at its center, as the column helping to enforce the order that emanated from a strict class structure. She references England's "nation of shopkeepers" as a crucial part of its three social tiers:

> [T]he middle class must include so vast a portion of the intelligence and moral power of the country at large, that it may not improperly be designated the pillar of our nation's strength, its base being the important class of the laborious poor, and its rich and highly ornamental capital, the ancient nobility of the land. In no other country is society thus beautifully proportioned, and England should beware of any deviation from the order and symmetry of her national column.

All of these voices joined the growing debate regarding the woman question. Armstrong labels the female encroaching of "aristocratic culture" and resultant seizure of authority "The Rise of the Domestic Woman." Such claiming of authority was the unpredictable offspring of the concept that women in the domestic sphere also served as the "moral centers of networks" in support of capitalism.

With the disappearance of conduct books, other instructional rhetoric had to take their place. One type of publication known as the etiquette book appeared in the 1830s and entered the debate over the proper role of women. After Queen Victoria ascended to the throne in 1837, the definition of the ideal woman centered for a time on her. An era that bemused 20th-century sophisticates would view as straight-laced and well-controlled in actuality seethed beneath a calm surface and continued to reconsider Wollstonecraft's argument against female subordination.

Shelley undoubtedly absorbed much of her mother's attitude, if not her outspoken nature. She wrote to an acquaintance, "The memory of my Mother has always been the pride & delight of my life: & the admiration of others for her, has been the cause of most of the happiness I have enjoyed." Although not a political activist like her mother, Shelley channeled Wollstonecraft's attitude via her subtext and through the shaping of characters like Fanny Derham. Fanny's independent intellectual presence clearly countered that of the subservient Ethel. Critic Mary Poovey has labeled *Lodore* an "uneven development," stymied by such contradictions in gender representations. She notes a struggle for authority between the characters, indicating tension in the simplistic binary logic of Victorianism.

Reviews of *Lodore* were positive. Some sources note 16 journals and magazines that either reviewed or included excerpts of the novel. Of interest to later readers and feminist critics is the complete lack of reference to Fanny Derham, the character representing an intelligent, creative woman who chooses to live without marrying. A reviewer in *The Athenaeum*, number 387, from March 28, 1835, praised Shelley's novels as always possessing "a character of their own" that made them agreeable, although the essence of that character was difficult to explain: "Delicacy in conception of character, earnestness of purpose, such as draws the reader along . . . and a gentle harmony of language . . . they are essentially feminine too in their strength as well as their sweetness." The reviewer applies to Shelley the saying, "How divine a thing / A woman may be made."

On May 24, 1835, *The Examiner*, number 1425, opens with the thought that it is commonly remarked "that women are incapable of creating a strongly-marked masculine character." Women writers' male characters are titled, handsome, wealthy men who are proud of having "done their duty." However, "Mary Shelley is a remarkable exception to this rule." Her works are stamped by "a force, and individuality, and a subtle investigation of motives."

In May 1835, *Fraser's Magazine for Town and Country* II noted, "The publication of *Lodore* has gone a considerable way towards convincing us that Mrs. Shelley might have indeed been the author of *Frankenstein*—a work which we once believed could not possibly owe its existence to a female novelist." The review later notes, "The execution of the work is, upon the whole, extremely good . . . an original and thoughtful mind is visible throughout, and there are many passages of exceeding gracefulness, of touching eloquence, and of intense feeling." The novel's "faults" are seen in its "wild and quaint" imagery and in its analyzing and detailing too closely the tiniest sensation, which combine to "constitute a feeling or a passion," an approach that tires the reader.

On May 6, 1835, *Leigh Hunt's London Journal*, number 58, congratulated Mrs. Shelley on her "agreeable work" and her "ear for the musical in writing," while on March 28, 1835, the *Literary Gazette*, number 949, declared Shelley "one of the most original of our modern writers."

Despite such positive critical reception, sales of *Lodore* remained lackluster or, at least, did not meet Shelley's expectations. Shelley was obviously distressed over its lack of commercial success, revealed in an 1837 letter written to its publisher, Charles Ollier. Shelley informed him that she had published a new novel, referring to *Falkner*, reminding Ollier that he had hoped a new novel might spur sales of *Lodore*. In the letter, although she concludes with phrases of forced civility, she first admonishes him for taking advantage of her, writing:

> I hope you will still reap that benefit from it—Are you sure 700 are not sold & that 50 pounds is not due to me? It would be very welcome & considering the very insignificant sum which you gave & the fair success it had—I own I think it is a little hard that the sale should stick just a few copies this side of 700—or 600 or whatever the number was—But I trust to your kindness—& sympathy with a poor Author to get me the 50 pounds when it is possible.

The novel's tepid sales could also have resulted from the repeated critical attacks against Bulwer-Lytton's novels. William Makepeace Thackeray based a satire on Bulwer-Lytton's popularity, noting in ironic praise that one of Bulwer-Lytton's popular novels, *Eugene Aram*, had provided a model for mixing "vice and virtue up together in such an inextricable confusion as to render it impossible" for the reader to prefer one to another. In addition, Shelley altered her character and plot shaping to include witty statements, resulting in an unfamiliar edginess of style. Although her reviewers praised character development not dependent on passion, readers drawn to the emotional writhing of Victor Frankenstein and company may have been disappointed not to find the same in *Lodore*. Instead of banking so heavily on tortured and anguished descriptions to further illuminate her characters' suffering, Shelley allowed herself some narrative distance, resulting in more reflective statements. While her characters' self-assessment was still fraught with irony, they did not see themselves as helpless victims, diminished by outside forces. For instance, as Lodore reviews the weaknesses of his wife and mother-in-law, "against his will, his own many excellencies rose before him," one of which is "self-sacrifice for the good of others." Lady Lodore is not spared Shelley's critical eye, as the narrator writes, "To act in contradiction to her wishes was a crime beyond compare, and her soul was in arms to resent the insolence which thus assailed her majesty of will."

Despite some critical suggestions of Shelley's departure from the norm, her inclusion of Count Lodore's daughter Ethel as a strong representative of the contemporary ideal of submissive, angelic womanhood causes others to view the novel as firmly within Shelley's focus on such women. Newer scholarship, however, discusses the theory that Shelley calls attention to the false nature of any idealization through her shaping of Ethel, probably the least interesting character in the novel, transparent from the book's early pages, with no contradiction to suggest any dimension. Even Shelley's reviewers did not focus on Ethel; it was Elizabeth Fitzhenry, the mature spinster, whom they most often mentioned, again reflecting on the evolution of the woman question. By mid-century, the focus would turn to the "redundant" female or, as George Gissing phrases it in the title of his novel, *The Odd Women* (1893). Lisa Vargo suggests that when Frances Power Cobbe tried to respond to the challenge in her *Fraser's Magazine* article "What Should We Do With Our Old Maids" (1862), Shelley offered a "comforting answer" through Elizabeth Fitzhenry. In the first chapter, Shelley immediately counters the "innumberable precedents in the traditions regarding unmarried ladies," which held that the melancholy characteristic of such women must be attributed to a lost romance. In Elizabeth's case, she is concerned for her family, particularly the fate of her younger brother, as well as their estate, personal and material concerns that have nothing to do with romantic love.

Shelley's focus on the concerns of her society allows her to develop interesting characters who seem either to shatter or totally support stereotypes, thus offering readers what her critics have called "uneven development" of plot and characterization. Shelley's narrator may best celebrate that realistic "unevenness" when stating in the first volume that only through our acknowledgement of their "singular nature" will human "contradictions" reach "accord."

SYNOPSIS

The novel was published in three volumes, each inscribed with the following quotation from John Ford's *The Lover's Melancholy* (1629), 5.1.4–9:

> In the turmoil of our lives,
> Men are like politic states, or troubled seas,
> Tossed up and down with several storms and tempests,
> Change and variety of wrecks and fortunes;
> Till, laboring to the havens of our homes,
> We struggle for the calm that crowns our ends.

Volume 1: Chapters 1–4

Volume 1 opens with the history of the Fitzhenry family and a description of its present state. After an accounting of the family's gain of fortune, service in Parliament, and attainment of a title, the narrator notes their fortunes turned. No one outside of their estate of Longfield understands details of the downturn, and they are not even sure whether the male Lord Lodore survives. The remaining inhabitant, his older sister, Elizabeth, appears "a somewhat ancient but most amiable maiden, whose gentle melancholy was not . . . attributed to an ill-fated attachment, but to the disasters that had visited her house." Twelve years older than her brother, she awaits his return. Henry Fitzhenry, Lord Lodore, is described by those who remember him in his youth as "a fine, bold, handsome boy—generous, proud and daring," a skilled hunter with an "elegant figure and dark eyes" that women found quite appealing. However, he left the locals "like a dream" and returned years later with a wife.

During their visit of only three days, the wife left an indelible impression that over time has become mythology. The local inhabitants remember her as "an angel bright with celestial hues" for whom her husband simply serves as "background" for her "resplendent image." He has not been seen since, and the mention of his wife's name brings visible pain to Elizabeth's face. But she continues to adore her brother—"Lodore, in exile and obscurity, was in her eyes, the first of human beings"—and she holds faith that he will again "blaze upon the world." She seems able to ignore the passage of 12 years and the realization that her brother should now be 50 years old.

Chapter 2 serves as a flashback, removing the reader 12 years prior to the opening chapter. Lord Lodore is in Illinois, where "like magic" he builds a "commodious home" on the river. His neighbors know little about him other than that he is a decent hunter, but they admire the changes he makes to his property, which help support the town nearby. At first, the town struggles to develop, but later it enjoys rapid growth. However, another bigger community develops not far away, and the Englishman's neighbors wonder if he might move there, as it could better suit his more sophisticated tastes. But Lodore does not move, apparently appreciating the isolation his productive farm affords. The smaller town diminishes to the size of a village, left to those who desire tranquility and lack grand ambition.

Lodore is occasionally observed passionately gesturing or talking to himself when he believes he is alone. He wanders into the woods for days, seeking the isolation that will help him deal "with the fierce enemy that dwelt within his breast." Although he avoids others, he is not a misanthrope. He takes interest in the "rude and unlettered" and gains a reputation for benevolence. A man of powerful passions, he nonetheless conceals his sufferings, which does not suit his natural personality: "He groaned beneath the chains that fettered him to the spot, where he was withering in inaction." The narrator notes Lodore is in danger of becoming a "cannibal" of his heart, which is filled with regret and remorse. However, time eventually brings him peace, which his natural surroundings support. He draws relief from the steady unchanging rhythm of the seasons and begins to better appreciate his neighbors. He recognizes their love and devotion to one another and admires the men's courage and honesty and the women's kindness.

Fitzhenry has always loved the arts and misses them while living in Illinois. Upon his arrival, he had ordered books from New York, and he continues the habit, building a library. Books have become a boon and help him look to the future as he struggles with questions such as "Why do I live?" While he has no eager anticipation, he enjoys a calm reliance "upon the power of good."

The next chapter introduces the reader to Fitzhenry's daughter, Ethel. While as a toddler she elicited "the passion of his soul," he did not think of her often. The narrator shares that he adores her, but her presence often brings pain. However, as she matures, she occupies most of his energies. She benefits from the education that only fathers can supply daughters and becomes fearless, her personality matching that of the wilderness. She can effortlessly ride and ramble and rarely leaves her father's side. She is gentle and docile enough to not intrude on her father, amusing him with her spirit, and has been so good of heart that Fitzhenry would "tremble for her future happiness." She can remain silent for hours if necessary and read his expressions. With large hazel eyes filled with tenderness and sweetness, but backed by fire, she is "at once beseeching and tender" but also vivacious, frank, truthful, thoughtful, earnest, and without guile. Tall, slender, charming, and lovely, she has a "matchless sweetness of temper." She helps calm Fitzhenry's early anxiety resulting from exile, and before long their home becomes everything. He begins to lay aside ambition and vanity, opting instead for peace and security.

Ethel does not remember any other life. She began her time in Illinois in the company of a black woman and her daughter, hired by Fitzhenry in New York. Ethel is isolated from the settlers but does not seem to mind, not knowing any other way of life. She understands it as "the immutable order of things" and never questions her situation. Her father focuses on making her "generous, soft and devoted" without "vanity and petty passion," filled with honor but also sweet and gentle, with cultivated tastes and an education, but "to control her acquirements, as to render her ever pliant to his will" . . . a creature "half poetry and half love." He bases his treatment of her on "ideas from Milton's Eve, and adding to this the romance of chivalry, he satisfied himself that his daughter would be the embodied ideal of all that is adorable and estimable in her sex." The narrator compares Fitzhenry to an instructor and Ethel to a parasite that puts out tendrils, not knowing whether it clings "to a supporter or a destroyer." Ethel is raised to be totally dependent on her father: "She seldom thought, and never acted, for herself." Ethel "inspired her father with more than a father's fondness. He lived but for her and in her." Because she has nothing to compare to, Ethel is unaware of her good fortune. Their little village suffices as her world, and she turns 15 years of age unaware of her connection to England.

Chapter 4 opens by noting of Fitzhenry that as he ages, his early "violent passions" seem to have died away, but he retains a melancholy expression. An internal voice questions how long he might remain at peace. That peace is shattered in the next chapter by a visiting young Englishman named Whitelock. He sees an opportunity to worm his way into the wealthy family. In Fitzhenry's absence, he tries to take advantage of Ethel's innocence to gain her patronage with plans to persuade her to marry him, so that he may gain her wealth. When she explains upon her father's return that Whitelock had engaged in what Fitzhenry recognizes as improprieties, he decides it is time to leave America.

Volume 1: Chapters 5–9
Fitzhenry forgets the devotion to Illinois that he has so long practiced and moves "to reach the stormier seas of life." In chapter 6, upon their departure from the only home Ethel has known, she is at first saddened but also excited about the trip. Fitzhenry

asks whether she remembers anything before their coming to Illinois, and she answers that she remembers being caressed by a beautiful woman. Fitzhenry sighs when Ethel questions whether that woman is dead, and the narrator states that it is now necessary to relate Lord Lodore's history.

As a young man, he strove to follow the good example of his father and sister and was adored by the locals, "courageous as a lion," generally softhearted, but "roused to anger by opposition." He attended Eton at age 13, but he felt out of place among equals; he was used to leading those of lesser standing than his own. At school, he led a group of wild boys but did not resemble them and picked as a best friend a small, effeminate boy named Derham whom the other students disliked. Fitzhenry stopped them from humiliating their weaker peer, but he could not do the same with the schoolmasters who picked on Derham. Instead, he planned to escape and told Derham that he must also leave the school. Derham told Fitzhenry that he promised his mother he would tolerate his circumstances and could not break his promise. Fitzhenry continued to urge him to come away to the Lodore estate, telling Derham, "I am a boy here, there I am a man—and can do as men do."

Fitzhenry did return home, where he acquired his education through a private tutor, but he remained in contact with Derham. When Fitzhenry later attended Oxford, Derham went abroad to a German university with the goal of becoming a diplomat and taking advantage of his skills in modern languages. Derham retained his shy, quiet attitude into adulthood, a strong contrast to Fitzhenry, whose eyes often sparked with emotion. Fitzhenry visited Derham two years later and moved on to visit Italy, Poland, and Russia, until called home to attend his father at his deathbed.

Following his father's death and upon taking the family title, Lord Lodore declared his intention to return to Vienna. He greatly upset his older sister, Elizabeth, also called Bessie, who looked upon him as a god and hoped he would remain at Longfield. The narrator notes of Elizabeth that "Her affection, her future prospects, her ambition, were all centered in him; and it was a bitter pang to feel that the glory of these was to be eclipsed by the obscurity and distant residence which he preferred." In reaction to his sister's weeping, Lodore agreed to postpone his journey for one month. Elizabeth was happy just to see his head bent over his reading or letter writing and enjoyed hearing his pacing about, but "Too soon her sun set." Lodore hurt her feelings when he remarked that looking on the ocean waves reminded him that he would soon "leave this dull land." Despite the grief caused to his sister, he departed at exactly one month. As the years slipped by, Elizabeth often wondered how he occupied himself as she "had little except such meditations to vary the hours."

Despite Elizabeth's vision of her brother as a deity, he became one of those men whose youth promised greatness, but who in their maturity only gilded "the edges of the clouds in which they hide themselves, and arrive at the term of life, the promise of its dawn unfulfilled." While his soul once filled with ambition, now "weeds and parasites" twisted about it, threatening destruction. He disappeared for months at a time and ignored the attentions of his "fair countrywomen," apparently in love with him. He seemed able to flirt and converse and then move on unfazed, sometimes after weeks of socializing, leaving only a card as a farewell.

In the seventh chapter, Fitzhenry returns to England at age 32, apparently having untangled himself from a "voluntary servitude" in which he attempted to "tranquilize" a jealous and possessive woman. Attracted to the idea of marriage, he begins to look for a proper candidate for a wife and for a way to enter public life in England. He succeeds in amusing those around him but continues to feel isolated. As he considers his wasted youth, he envies the carefree ploughboy and sees "poverty and care as blessings; and the dearest gifts of fortune—youth, health, rank, and riches—were disguised curses." He travels to Wales and takes refuge in nature, enjoying climbing, lingering by waterfalls, taking long horseback rides, and escaping from people to calm his heart in the outdoors. After a year, he begins to tire of the isolation and decides to visit his sister in Essex. A storm delays him and causes him to notice "a vision of white muslin" stranded in the violent wind and rain. She is 15-year-old Cornelia Santerre, described as resembling an angel with a radiant and soft appearance that begs for protection. Confused, she does not at first want to leave the protection of a rock but eventually allows herself to be escorted toward her home. They are met by her servant, but Lodore continues to her house and meets her mother. He learns that Lady Santerre's husband died early in their marriage, and his family's fortune went to a brother who gives his sister-in-law and niece £200 yearly for living expenses.

Lodore is attracted by the mother and daughter and begins to think of marriage to the girl, who knows nothing "beyond obedience to her parent, and untaught in the guile of mankind." He imagines bringing them his fortune in exchange for "gratitude, tenderness" and "unquestioning submission." He feels fortunate to have turned away from "fair daughters of fashion" in order to embrace this simple country girl. He speaks only a few words to Cornelia before her mother agrees to his plans for marriage. Aware of her lack of education, Cornelia makes light of herself, and Lodore falls in love; "his wayward feelings were to change no more—his destiny was fixed." Because he has always thought of women as "white paper to be written on at will," to be shaped by a husband into acceptable material, Cornelia seems a perfect match.

While Lodore loves Cornelia, he focuses on her future potential, and due to the age discrepancy, he would never have considered marriage had not her mother helped to arrange matters. Lady Santerre convinces Lodore that he would "play a god-like part," lifting Cornelia from adversity to prosperity and happiness. It is a role that Lodore fancies, and he yields "with docility to her silken fetters." On Cornelia's 16th birthday, they marry. When they visit King's Theater in London, all eyes turn to behold the most beautiful "sylph-like girl, that ever trod dark earth." London society finds Cornelia entrancing, and her social career begins.

The new couple moves to Berkeley Square, where Lady Santerre comes to live with them. Mother and daughter are "familiar friends," but Lodore is excluded. Mrs. Santerre's presence blocks any development of the intimate "outpouring of the heart" that true love should produce. Seeing her second chance in life, Mrs. Santerre decides to "secure her empire" with her daughter. The narrator describes her interference as "a shadow—undefined—formless—nothing—yet every thing." Where Lodore had viewed Cornelia as nature's child, kin to the mountains and waterfalls with which she was raised, she has in reality been raised by her mother to "view society as the glass by which she was to set her feelings," ignoring her natural mental abilities, instead focusing on frivolity and charming ingenuity. Suddenly, Lodore is again homeless in his own house, not in control, unable to share any confidences with Cornelia, due to her mother's looming presence. Before meeting Cornelia, Lodore "had no lofty opinion" of women, although he "cherished an ideal." Where he expected to find "truth, clearness of spirit, and complying gentleness," framed by a charming lack of sophistication, he instead discovers that his wife complies only with her mother's wishes. A few feeble attempts to separate the two fail, and Lodore's existence suffers from his "wounded affections."

Lodore makes a grim error in withdrawing from the competition while Cornelia is still so young and malleable. The narrator compares the situation to those who would acquire power in politics—"they must in some degree follow, if they would lead," and by adapting themselves to their would-be constituents' "humors," they will eventually win the day. Because he cannot feel warmly toward Cornelia, offering her a role model, she turns to the only role model she has ever known. At times, his "overflowing heart" still seeks his wife, but Lady Santerre's domination makes impossible any meaningful interchange between the two. Lodore's pride causes him to become indifferent, and that indifference evolves into resentment and dislike. Cornelia enjoys high society, and Lodore turns to public affairs for intellectual and emotional excitement.

By chapter 9, the split between husband and wife is severe, despite the birth of a daughter within a year of the marriage. Lodore chafes and turns arrogant, finding his short political career unsatisfying, "to mingle with the senseless and the vulgar; and at home, to find a—wife, who prefers the admiration of fools, to the love of an honest heart." He remains excluded from his wife's daily activities, and when she falls ill, a nurse is called to care for the infant who is secluded in a corner of the enormous house. Lodore idolizes the child, but Cornelia serves to separate the two. Although she is suffering in ill health, Lodore ignores her needs, and Lady Santerre continues to interfere with the family's relationships. However, as their daughter grows older and becomes responsive to him, Lodore understands that she is worth every effort on his part. He begins to view Cornelia as a mere puppet to her mother, "endowed with the usual feminine infirmities." Cornelia is not heartless but naturally returns her husband's hostility and views his relationship with their daughter with jealousy and hatred. After three years of marriage, the couple exists in a state of "warlike neutrality."

The third summer following their marriage, Lodore returns home to find that his wife has gone to a ball, and he thinks with longing and anger of what a true home should be. He is shocked to find a note that sends him reeling back through time, feeling the "thrill and shudder as of an occurrence beyond the bounds of nature." The note is from a past acquaintance announcing that she is in the area with her husband and would like to meet Lodore and his wife. Lodore's obvious distress mixes with some tantalizing memories that focus on the mysterious writer of the note. He stays up all night thinking of her.

The next day, Lodore takes Cornelia to visit the mysterious lady, and the two beautiful and charming women take a great interest in one another, despite the fact that the Polish lady of rank is of Lodore's generation. Her name is Countess Lyzinski, and her son, Count Casimir, also finds Cornelia appealing. Lady Lodore eagerly accompanies the countess and her son in their interactions with high society, Cornelia taking charge of Casimir. Lodore observes the interaction without reaction of his own. He maintains an even temperament toward the countess, which she returns, although her demeanor is cold and silent. Lodore helps oversee Casimir's activities and acts as a guide, yet seems also to hate him. Generally polite and restrained, Lodore constantly corrects Casimir and silences him, the younger man tolerating Lodore's behavior for the sake of continuing to spend time with Cornelia. When Cornelia complains to Lodore regarding his behavior, he corrects her impudence. As for the countess, she seems to regard the escalating tension and discomfort on Lodore's part with hidden pleasure.

An incident at the Russian ambassador's house escalates the ill feelings. Cornelia neglects to join the women as custom warrants and finds herself in a room that the men have entered. When they notice her, they are embarrassed. Lodore asks her to leave, and she consents, but as they make their way from the room, she sees a glance pass between her husband and the countess that alarms her and raises her curiosity. Her mother has been unable to attend the dinner party, and Cornelia decides to seek her advice when they arrive home.

Volume 1: Chapters 10–13

When Lodore approaches Cornelia at home, she fears he is going to use his authority to tell her to stop flirting so much with Casimir, which she has already decided to do on her own. Instead, he shocks her by asking if she will go away with him. Thinking the reason for his question is that he might have had ill luck in gambling or business, she asks if all is lost. He replies, "My honour is . . . and the rest is of little worth." When she insists that he explain, Lodore reveals that he has insulted a gentleman by striking him, and that "he has requested satisfaction." Cornelia guesses the argument was with Casimir, and she suddenly realizes that Lodore refuses to offer him satisfaction through the traditional means of a duel.

Lodore tells Cornelia that he cannot explain the past, but that under no circumstances can he fight with the boy. She again wants to discuss the situation, but Lodore reiterates that he simply wants to know whether she will go away with him. He attempts to control his emotions and paces about the room as she asks if there is no other action they might take. Lodore explains there is not and frightens Cornelia as he speaks of crimes he has committed and their consequences. He tells her that if he participated in the duel, just standing by so as not to harm Casimir, he would be arming "kindred blood against kindred blood" and forcing the young man to commit patricide. Cornelia realizes what Lodore next confesses, that Casimir is his son, and she reacts with violent emotion. She resents his plan to withdraw her from everything she desires and loves and beseeches her mother to "Save me!" Lady Santerre takes Cornelia to a villa in Twickenham. When she later sends for her servants, she learns that Lodore has departed, and she and Cornelia are unprepared for the news that he has taken the child and her attendant with him.

Lodore had spent two hours after Cornelia and Lady Santerre's departure considering all that had happened and understanding that his early carefree attitude had sealed his fate. He had thought introducing his wife to his former lover and coming to know his son had been the correct thing to do. He had not anticipated the flood of emotion in reaction to Casimir's attitude toward his wife. He had spoken harshly to the boy one too many times and insulted him in public with a blow; Casimir had every right to seek satisfaction, having no knowledge that Lodore was his father.

Lodore had listened as Casimir's second had visited his house and spoken with a servant regarding plans for the enemies to duel. When he visited his child to say goodbye, she had thrown her arms around his neck and pleaded to accompany him. He took her into the country, thinking at first to return her after he made plans to leave England in shame. However, after considering the fact that Cornelia felt a stronger devotion to her mother and to high society than to him and the child, he reconsidered. Everyone would judge him a coward, running away from a challenge. He resolved to view the situation logically and to think through possible actions. Lady Santerre's "worldliness, her vulgar ambition, her low-born contempt for all that is noble and elevating in human nature" would combine with Cornelia's docility and careless "disregard for the nobler duties of life" to become a negative influence on the child. In contrast, he viewed his own "many excellencies" and his focus on the raising of his daughter to emulate his aspirations; she would obviously be better off with him. Cornelia had her mother as well as her reputation, home, youth, and friends, none of which he had.

Lodore hurries to Southampton and catches a vessel to Havre. He first writes a letter to the countess, bidding her to enjoy their son and telling her that he departs forever. He will not reveal his destination, as he does not want Casimir to follow him; she may decide whether to tell him the truth regarding his father.

Five days later, Cornelia receives a lengthy letter from Lodore, in which he again asks her to join him and the child, telling her she will have to forego rank and luxury and will instead have the "wide forest, the uninhabited plain" for shelter with her husband and child as "the sum and aim" of her life. He appeals to her to live with them in what will be a simple dwelling in a new world, from which she might learn a new lesson. He understands that he speaks an unknown language but asks her to pause and consider what will be lost if she does not join them. Their daughter's security and future is his chief concern. He depends on her "sense of delicacy" to remain silent and not reveal his location to others. The ship will sail from London in five days. As Cornelia considers her options, Lady Santerre takes the letter, reads it, and remarks that "you will not abandon a parent, who has devoted herself to you from your cradle—who lives but for you." Lady Santerre cries "My dear child!" while Cornelia cries out for her own daughter. Her mother calms her by promising that Lodore will soon regain his senses and not stay long abroad. She persuades Cornelia to remain with her.

Lodore supposes that Cornelia will at least come to see him to try to get the child at Havre. He begins to berate himself for not having volunteered to meet her in Hampton and watches for her arrival every day. When he at last receives and reads her letter, he is stunned by her reply. She makes clear that she will not accompany him. At first she begs, then demands, that he give her the child, adding that she will be quite content to never see him again.

Later, in the middle of the long voyage across the Atlantic, Lodore nurses the bitterness he feels toward Cornelia, at times believing he might go mad. Only the child's presence calms him and prevents him taking refuge in his passions. Like the storm outside that at last dissolves with sunshine breaking through the clouds, Lodore's anger is replaced by more gentle emotions toward his child. He softens as he imagines Cornelia and envisions her occasionally in tears as she recalls his promise to protect and care for her. He writes many letters during the voyage but immediately destroys them.

Resolved to write to Cornelia from New York, Lodore finds letters awaiting him. One from Lady Santerre announces to him that Cornelia has decided to end all communication; she does not want to hear from him. She refers him to a solicitor for future contact, at which Lodore shreds the heartfelt appeal he had been writing. But Lady Santerre has lied in the letter, because soon after Cornelia had written the letter delivered to Lodore before he left England, she regretted it. At age 19, she has not yet learned to sacrifice for others; however, her mother is able to soothe and flatter her wounded vanity. A short time later, Cornelia does give over all correspondence with Lodore to her mother. After a brief isolation, she enters society again, viewed as the injured virtuous wife. Her public views her as a bright star, and she enjoys her privileged position, isolated from temptations and rarely experiencing any passion as the years pass. She often longs for her child and hates Lodore all the more, then turns "to pleasure" to counteract her pain. The countess and Casimir have returned to the Continent, and Cornelia does not hear from them again.

Volume 1: Chapters 14–18
Chapter 14 of Volume 1 returns readers to the present, the background on Lodore having concluded. The narrator notes that while living in Illinois, Lodore used the name Fitzhenry, so as not to alert neighbors to his aristocratic status, as well as to hide his identity. His head is filled with ideas about how best to approach Cornelia upon his arrival in England with their daughter, Ethel. He wonders if they might reconcile in order to raise her together, not wanting to give her up at this stage in her life. While Cornelia will undoubtedly be able to integrate Ethel into society, he is the only parent she has ever known. Cornelia will now be more than 30 years old, and he might hope that for the sake of their daughter, she will soften her heart toward him. While she remains young, beautiful, and desirable, his best years are behind him, and his age shows on his face. He determines to "assert the brightness of his honour" for Ethel's sake and "sweep away the stigma attached to him." As soon as they reach New York, he writes to his sister, Elizabeth, to request news about Cornelia.

As Lodore and Ethel wait in New York, he helps acclimate his daughter to society and proper manners. Without any warning, he receives a singular request one day by way of a formal note from England that asks if he would consider escorting a young woman to that country. Lodore is amazed to discover the young woman is Fanny Derham, daughter of his Eton schoolmate and later friend. She had traveled to America in the company of another family, an experience that her father thought would be to her benefit. But Fanny has so missed her father that she cannot enjoy any of the adventures that her host, Mrs. Greville, has planned for her. Mrs. Greville explains to Lodore that Fanny has never been a child. She has cared for her father, who has tended to be sickly from a young age, and he has taught her "dead languages" and other subjects unusual to a girl's education. Mrs. Greville explains that Fanny has suffered due to her separation from her father, "what, in feminine dialect, is called fretting."

The narrator describes Fanny as pale, with penetrating blue eyes: "Intelligence, or rather understanding, reigned in every feature." Lodore is delighted to assume responsibility for his friend's daughter and buoyed by a supportive note that he receives from Derham. The knowledge that Derham would not reject Lodore, nor "participate in the world's blind scorn," makes him more hopeful about returning to England. The fact that Derham writes of his wish to resume their close relationship buoys Lodore's spirits. He visits Niagara Falls, which "mirror[s] the dauntless but rash energy of his own soul," and sees Fanny approach him to share a letter from her father. His hopes are confirmed when he reads Derham's words that his chilled heart warms to think of renewing his friendship with Lodore.

The days that follow are the happiest of Ethel's life as she develops a friendship with Fanny and loves her father even more. Lodore at last receives the packet of letters that will decide his fate. He reads Elizabeth's letter to learn that Lady Santerre has died, news that supports his hope that Cornelia might desire a reconciliation, although Lodore has little to offer her. However, when he reads Cornelia's reply to Elizabeth's letter informing her of Lodore's planned return, his hopes die. Cornelia desires no relationship with her husband, telling Elizabeth: "Persuade him that it will be unmanly cruelty to force himself, even by a letter, on me." Elizabeth adds that Cornelia has given herself up to flatterers and pleasure, that she has become an imitation of her mother, only lacking the motherly feelings that somewhat relieved Lady Santerre of guilt. Elizabeth offers to come to America to live with Lodore and Ethel. Lodore determines to set sail for England, thinking he might still change Cornelia's feelings toward him. He writes to Elizabeth to tell her to expect him, his enthusiasm and hope infecting Ethel, whose spirits rise high.

Lodore entertains the girls by telling stories of his childhood and expressing his enthusiasm to see Derham again. Ethel begins to view England as a paradise, and memories of Illinois fade. Her father maintains a frivolous and excited air. The narrator states that "A strange distortion of vision blinded this unfortunate man to the truth, which experience so perpetually teaches us, the consequences of our actions never die." While time and regret may change their appearance and effect, they remain, and shutting one's eyes will not affect "the inexorable destinies" that "spin the fatal thread . . . sharpening the implement which is to cut it asunder." He enjoys the brilliance of spring, visiting the vessel on which they will soon sail in order to make preparations. The narrator writes, "It was the first of May, realizing by its brilliancy and sweets, the favourite month of the poets."

Lodore goes for a ride with Ethel, and they discuss the wonders that await them in Europe. That evening, they join a dinner party at the home of Mrs. Greville that includes an American named Hatfield. He does not recognize Lodore, but as it turns out, Hatfield had witnessed Casimir's challenge of Lodore 12 years before.

Eventually the discussion turns to England, and the American insults Lodore's country before a group of about 20 people. The American labels Admiral Fitzhenry "scum of the earth," while his father had been a pillar of state whose title would be blackened. Lodore becomes furious. Hatfield then describes for the group the evening at the Russian Embassy. Incensed when Hatfield labels him a coward, Lodore strikes him, identifies himself, and challenges Hatfield to a duel. While some from the group support Hatfield, Lodore is left alone. A stranger who has witnessed the events identifies himself as an Englishman and volunteers his services to act as Lodore's second. Lodore reads the name Edward Villiers on the man's card and is favorably struck by his "silver-toned voice." Villiers tries in vain to persuade Lodore to find another way to settle the feud, but Lodore refuses, suddenly feeling cheerful, as if he were soon to recover his reputation.

Lodore accepts Villiers's offer to lend him a pistol to participate in the duel, described by the narrator as "that sad relic of feudal barbarism." The two go to his apartment, where Lodore writes a note for Ethel, which Villiers promises he will deliver. Lodore remarks, "I commit my daughter to a higher power than mine, secure that so much innocence and goodness must receive blessings." Villiers mentions that he has a slight acquaintance with Lady Lodore, and Lodore asks him to tell her that he has "invoked a blessing on her" and forgiven her, while requesting her forgiveness of him. Lodore faces Hatfield on the beautiful moonlit night, the narrator stating that "neither had ever been more alive, more full of conscious power, or moral and physical energy." A few moments later, Lodore is dead.

Devastated, Ethel travels to England, thinking constantly of her father and wanting nothing more than to visit "scenes once hallowed by her father's presence." Her Aunt Elizabeth retrieves an old will written years before by Lodore that reduces Cornelia's income from "several thousands" to "barely sixteen hundred per year." A requirement of the allowance is that she never see their daughter. In the will, which Lodore had meant to replace upon his arrival in England, Ethel will receive £5,000 per year until maturity but is only allowed to live on its interest until she becomes old enough to inherit his entire estate. Cornelia does not reply to Elizabeth's letter that informs her of that change and that her daughter is in England.

Elizabeth cares for Ethel, who constantly talks about her father, her aunt a willing audience. Ethel makes Illinois seem a paradise to her aunt, just as England had seemed a paradise to Ethel just a few weeks earlier. Elizabeth pours out all of the emotion she has so long held in—"her long-stored anecdotes, her sacred relics, the spots made dear by his [Lodore's] presence, all were a treasure poured out bounteously before Ethel." Elizabeth had been so long separated from her adored brother that she talks now of meeting with him in heaven. She and Ethel visit his remains in the family vault as if visiting a shrine. While his memory soothes Elizabeth, Ethel feels constantly exhausted, haunted by her father's vision, and she becomes depressed, wandering outside. While the outdoors give color to her cheeks, she grows thin and will not eat, causing her aunt to call the village doctor.

Ethel wants to die—"she was in love with death"—and nothing helps revive her natural youthful spirits. Alarmed, Elizabeth takes Ethel to London, hoping a change in scene will help her. In chapter 18, which concludes the first volume, Elizabeth takes Ethel to plays, exhibitions, and panoramas, all of which excite Ethel, but she still feels lonely and isolated while staring out of her carriage at all of the people she does not know. She can realize little of the wit and elegance her father had told her she would encounter. Elizabeth's plain appearance belies her aristocratic background, and the two draw little attention.

One day, they attend an opera, and when her aunt asks her to turn and meet her friend, Captain Markham, Ethel turns to see Villiers. All of the terrible memories of her father's last day rush into her mind, and she hurries from the room, her aunt bringing Villiers along to follow her. He explains to Elizabeth that he is not Captain Markham but Edward Villiers, and that he hopes one day to visit Miss Fitzhenry and not to upset her. Elizabeth is embarrassed to have mistaken him for someone who would be much older than he, as she recalled Captain Markham from Ethel's christening. Still, the resemblance between the two men was great. Ethel hopes to be able to apologize to Villiers for her overreaction and is delighted when he calls the next day. He and Ethel get on well, and when he leaves, he is lost in thought at the strange chance that brought him to Lodore's aid. He visits Lady Lodore's house but finds it locked up, and a servant tells him she is in Baden. That answer leaves him deep in thought.

Volume 2: Chapters 1–4

Soon Villiers becomes a constant fixture at Elizabeth's home, his presence always lifting Ethel's spirits. The narrator notes a great contrast between Villiers's "airy brightness" and Lodore's "wounded yet lofty spirit." Even so, Ethel happily anticipates each visit and comes to think of Villiers as an older brother, in her youth not recognizing the early stages of love. As an Eton graduate himself, he takes Ethel and Elizabeth to visit all of the places that Lodore had told Ethel about. When he asks Elizabeth whether Lady Lodore is in touch with her daughter, he is surprised by the vehement response that works to "tarnish to his mind the name of Lady Lodore" and also "make him rejoice" over the termination of "their more intimate connexion."

When they visit the opera, Lady Lodore is present, and her beauty and grace catch Ethel's attention. Ethel notices "something bewitching" in her smile, as "sensibility beamed from her long and dark grey eyes." Villiers has called a carriage, and Elizabeth hurries Ethel outside, telling her once they are in the conveyance that the woman was Lady Lodore. Ethel can hardly believe the woman she saw was her mother, due to the woman's youth and elegance and the fact that she did not seem a good match for her father. Villiers assumes that the chance "meeting" must have shocked Lady Lodore, and he decides to visit her, despite Elizabeth's recent verbal attacks on her sister-in-law. As soon as he sees her, he knows the attacks cannot be true.

The narrator then informs readers that it was partly because of Lady Lodore that Villiers had traveled to America, and his history is supplied. Born to a wealthy man whose wife soon died, Edward Villiers matured in the household of his uncle, Viscount Maristow, and developed a close bond with his cousin, Horatio Saville. Saville had an excellent mind but a frail body; he enjoyed Edward's sparkling personality, so different from his own. Only Edward understood Horatio's sensibility, although the older boy was admired by all for his intellect and high character. While his spirits could also rise, Horatio's weak body could not stand much exertion. He met Lady Lodore when he was 29 years old, and she was near his age. He knew her reputation was spotless, although no one completely understood her circumstances, and he admired her serene, fair, happy demeanor. The fact that she had remained cloistered from society's gossip and scandal and remained well thought of by all aroused Horatio's curiosity. He introduced himself, the two struck up a friendship, and he began escorting her to social events. She determined not to engage in any fancy or to dream of love, as she knew her perfect conduct had to continue.

Saville fell deeply in love with Cornelia and wondered how she might gain her freedom from Lodore. She explained that she could not. Even had she wanted to be free to marry again, or to regain her daughter, she knew that Lodore would fight her efforts, and England's laws would favor him. Saville contemplated how Lodore might be convinced of the cruelty of his actions, and he requested that Villiers travel with him to America to attempt to bring Lady Lodore's child back to her.

Villiers doubted whether Saville could stand up to the rigors of the journey, but the two set sail for America. As chance would have it, they crossed paths with Lodore and Ethel, finding when they arrived in Illinois that the two had departed for New York. As they returned to the East Coast, the two split up to pursue different activities, Saville seeking society and Villiers preferring to hunt and visit Niagara Falls. When, by chance, he met Lodore, he was astonished to find him an honorable and admirable man; Villiers could not understand why Lady Lodore would not want to be with him. When Villiers reunited with Saville for the return trip to London and shared with him the news of Lodore's death, Saville was too sophisticated to express his excitement. However, Villiers assumed that upon his arrival in England, Saville and Lady Lodore would marry.

While Saville was absent, Cornelia realized how much she loved him. She nursed her mother through her final illness with "exemplary patience and kindness" and then began to think of Lodore. She feared that he might believe her mother's death removed the final obstacle to their reunion, and she grew to hate him, seeing him now as the force that prevented her following her heart in her feelings for Saville. While feeling this way, she had sent the letter to Elizabeth that had been forwarded to Lodore. When the reply that Cornelia received from Elizabeth carried the news of her husband's death, Cornelia felt a stab of remorse over her behavior. She went into seclusion following her double personal losses and dreamed of being with Horatio. At the same time, he dreamed of nothing other than reuniting with Cornelia. However, the narrator comments that while each felt so close to the other, in reality, they had never been so far away. Cornelia's pride would continue to stall her developing a close relationship, while Saville felt undeserving of her love.

Friends and relations, particularly Saville's sisters, began to interfere with the romance. They told their brother that Lady Lodore was to marry another, the Marquess of C——, and Horatio's low self-confidence convinced him to step aside and "be no obstacle in the way of her ambition." Saville's immediate yielding annoyed Cornelia, who had expected to see some signs of jealousy and resentment, not the forbearance that Saville's natural dignity produced. Cornelia loved Saville but felt she should not have had to state her love. Thus, Saville left England. Still, Cornelia did not despair, expecting that he would return and that "the sincerity of their mutual preference would overcome the petty obstacles of time and distance." Unfortunately, Saville assumed her joyous attitude to be the result of his having left the field. Cornelia unknowingly "was at work in defacing the whole web of life, and substituting dark, blank, and sad disappointment, for the images of light and joy with which her fancy painted it." After five months, when Horatio did not return, Cornelia decided to "unbend" and visit his sisters to learn of any news. She was shocked when they told her that Saville had married a foreigner: "Her heart died within her. What had she done? Was she the cause? . . . It was over; the scene was closed. It were little worth to analyze the poison she had imbibed."

Cornelia determined to forget Saville, but she could not. She learned from the newspaper that Horatio had married Clorinda, daughter of the Principe Villmarian, a Neapolitan nobleman. She wondered whether Saville loved his bride and how he could so easily have forgotten her. She felt desolate and alone, humbled and without hope. After Cornelia's many years of suffering, she had hoped for a change with Horatio. Eventually she stopped thinking of Saville but still "wept over the vanished forms of delight." She could not hate Saville and eventually regained peace, based on her characteristic "firmness of purpose." Cornelia began to think of her daughter, and a sense of duty dawned. She decided to force the return of her daughter, understanding that she had to appear independent and a part of the society she had come to view with contempt and disgust. While attending the opera, she heard the name of Fitzhenry and spotted Elizabeth. She also noticed Edward Villiers, Horatio's favorite cousin, with great curiosity. The following morning, Villiers called upon Cornelia.

Volume 2: Chapters 5–9
The narrator uses the fifth chapter to describe Cornelia's fortitude. She masks her emotions before the world, and when Villiers finds her as serene, gracious, and lovely as ever, he despises her. He cannot accept her attitude in the face of the recent death of her husband; loss of her lover, Saville; and encounter of her daughter at the opera with no reaction. He does not understand her willpower and determination to not crack under the extreme pressure. As she chats blithely about having seen Miss Fitzhenry at the opera, Villiers is shocked by what seems to be a rather carefree attitude toward her own child. However, he soon realizes that she is talking about Elizabeth and had not recognized Ethel.

When Villiers explains that the beautiful, mature 16-year-old Cornelia saw with her sister-in-law is her daughter, Cornelia cannot hold back her tears. She had been silly to think of her daughter as still a small girl. She suddenly understands that striking up a relationship with a young woman who undoubtedly had been turned against her by her father would prove impossible and bring her shame and embarrassment. Cornelia tells Villiers that she must move to Paris to avoid any further chance meetings with her daughter, because such a meeting will lead to disaster for all. When another visitor arrives, she reassumes her mask of calm, and Villiers departs.

Villiers visits Ethel and Elizabeth and learns that Elizabeth has told Ethel they must leave London, even though it has improved her health, and return to Longfield. Ethel remains distraught over having seen her mother and the conflict that she feels due to loyalty to her father. He had never spoken of her mother until just before his death. Still, her aunt holds such a negative attitude toward Cornelia—who had, after all, deserted her child—that Ethel feels she must dislike her mother as well. She does not want to leave London, however, due to Villiers's presence; his attentions are largely responsible for her return to good health. He suggests that Elizabeth take a villa at Richmond, which will remove the ladies from London and allow them to enjoy a country setting, yet not take them so far from his home in the city. Elizabeth accepts and follows his advice.

Ethel quickly adjusts to Richmond, where she thrives, spending much time outdoors in nature. The nearby river is lovely, and although "the wide, dark lake, the endless forests, and the distant mountains, of the Illinois" are not present, Ethel still appreciates the "appearance of solitude, which habit [has] rendered dear" to her. Her imagination, when applied to the groomed gardens and wooded parks, can transform them into secluded areas, untouched by man. Love flows through Ethel's soul like an "even and unruffled stream." Thoughts of Villiers remain with her constantly, although she gives no outward appearance of her dependence, and "she so implicitly trusted to his truth, that she was unaware that she trusted at all."

The next chapter opens with a reminder to the reader of Villiers's privileged upbringing in his uncle's family. He had lived as a wealthy man and carried the expectations of the wealthy. Due to the laws of the time, Edward could expect an allowance. Although Colonel Villiers lived an extravagant lifestyle, accruing enormous gambling debts, Edward paid little attention. Everyone lived in debt, and Edward did not spend more "than beseemed a man in his rank of life." Following the "universal example," he "suffered no wants." When he came of age, his father was out of the country, but his uncle, Lord Maristow, wrote to Edward's father to remind him. Colonel Villiers wrote that upon his return to England, arrangements would be formalized for his son's future. However, he did not return, and Villiers's debts mounted. When his father asked him to cosign a mortgage, he agreed to everything without any understanding of his assumption of responsibility, and his father promised him an allowance "of six hundred a year."

Several years passed, and Edward's father never made good on his promise; then Edward saw him in a gambling hall. He had that same day received a note from his father, promising to pay Edward the first money that came into his hands. In disgust, Edward left the gambling room, "his young heart . . . pierced to the core." His father's betrayal deeply hurt him and helped him realize that "his parent had stepped beyond the line of mere extravagance; he had lost honorable feeling." Villiers never again appealed to his father for money.

Shamed when his son caught him gambling, the colonel did pay Edward a portion of what he owed to him. Edward had to hand the money over to his creditors, and his financial situation deteriorated. Raised never to correctly value and appreciate money, and having squandered all that he had, Villiers had no support. Lord Maristow rallied to his support, railing against his brother for his mistreatment of Edward. Lord Maristow appealed to his son, Horatio, to help his cousin, but Horatio's own "means were extremely limited." Embarrassed, Villiers turned to moneylenders. While he did not gamble, Edward lived extravagantly with no hope of inheritance until Colonel Villiers's death; his father was only 50.

Until he met Ethel, Edward had not considered altering his lifestyle. Now she has become his "star," "a bird of beauty, brooding in its own fair nest, unendangered by the fowler." But "bitter worldly considerations" damage Villier's fantasy, and he can no longer deny the threat of poverty that has already overcome his father. He decides to continue seeing Ethel but to withdraw, should she ever declare "exclusive regard" for him, in deference to her future security, which he cannot provide.

One morning at Richmond, Elizabeth reads aloud from the newspaper that Villiers is "about to lead into the hymeneal altar a young and lovely bride, the only child of a gentleman, said to be the richest commoner in England." As Elizabeth muses on the identity of Edward's supposed fiancée, Ethel hurries "into the shrubbery" to conceal the fact that the news has upset her. When Villiers visits later that day, he answers Elizabeth's question about the comment with humor, but he hurries to find Ethel. Although he had mentally rehearsed what he would tell her, in her presence, "the gossamer of the mind was swept away by an immediate appeal to his heart." The narrator notes that neither Ethel nor Villiers realize the love they feel for one another.

The two arrange to ride together, so that Edward may explain his situation to Ethel, accompanied by a groom. As they ride, he speaks of his father's financial difficulties, which have led to his own poverty. His situation makes it impossible for him to marry and care for Ethel; he has no desire to lead her into his own "discomforts." He does not want to stop seeing her, but at the same time, he understands that she should discard him as a beggar. His words are tender, and as Ethel listens "with complacency," he beams "adoration and sincerest love." She finally replies, "You cannot think that I care for fortune—I was happy in Illinois." Thus, Villiers believes he may continue with their present relationship, and their conversation seems to have drawn them closer.

Two months later, while at the opera, Cornelia hears the comment by another woman in the box that Edward Villiers is to marry a Miss Fitzhenry. Cornelia is overcome with pride and self-will and imagines Ethel suffering penury and want, all because of the plots of her father. She takes some solace in that self-indulgence, which the narrator pronounces an "emotion of revenge; the most deceitful and reprehensible of human feelings—revenge against a child." When Villiers enters the opera box, she offers what others view as a humorous remark, explaining that Villiers intends to marry a beautiful "and portionless" young woman, and that "his tastes of a hermit" will spur him to emigrate to America, where he can live simply and inexpensively in the wilderness. Villiers feels the hate in her remark but encourages her to proceed, viewing her anger with some interest. She then unleashes "the page of futurity," depicting his own recent thoughts regarding his inability to marry and support a wife. While he wants to leave, at the same time he remains fascinated by the "bitterness of spirit" he observes in Lady Lodore. When Edward does decide to leave the box, he comments that "it is all a dream," and he intends to marry no one, that he will not victimize anyone with his "selfishness and poverty." Cornelia thinks that she may have performed a good deed by preventing the marriage, even though Villiers is at least a gentleman. Villiers resents Lady Lodore, hating her for discovering and revealing his own thoughts. He passionately loves Ethel, and his generosity pushes him to finally sever their relationship. He vows to ride to Richmond and sacrifice his own wishes "at the shrine" of Ethel's welfare.

Meanwhile, Elizabeth Fitzhenry considers the impropriety of Ethel's relationship with Edward and decides they will return to Longfield. Ethel shocks her aunt by stating simply, "I would rather not." Villiers awaits her to join him on a walk to the river and a boat ride. While Elizabeth feels she should chaperone the couple, she never goes onto the river in a boat, always insisting that Ethel remain close to the shore. In the end, she accompanies them but waits on the bank.

The narrator describes the river in laudatory and poetic terms, describing it as "calm and free." In contrast to a lake, "there is always life in a stream." The river pursues the goal that God has designed for it. On this summer evening, the air is warm, "all nature reposed, and yet not as a lifeless thing," and it gladdens the hearts of the lovers. When Ethel tells Villiers she will soon return to Longfield, he is at first startled but then declares that will be the best thing for her. At that point, he explains that he has taken advantage of her innocence and loneliness, although he loves her. He reveres her excellence, but he is penniless and a beggar. He will soon need to either flee the country or go to prison. Ethel replies that she wishes she could comfort him, that she will never hate him, and that because she knows little of the world, she cannot understand his situation or offer any guidance.

They are interrupted by Bessie's voice, recalling them "from the fairy region to which their spirits had wandered." Villiers departs, but he promises to return the next day. While Ethel is confused, "her step [is] buoyant, her eyes sparkling and joyous" because she is in love and feels like "the queen of the world." However, Villiers does not return, and after two weeks, Ethel pines for him. A month passes, and "the silence of death" hangs between her and Edward. When she and Elizabeth visit London, she sees Villiers as she is riding in the park, but he looks grave and betrays no pleasure. He bows to Ethel and rides away, and she does not see him again.

Until Villier's disappearance in London, Ethel had enjoyed pleasure mingled with pain, but now she steels her heart against softer thoughts and tries to spend her time in studies and music. She loses weight, becomes pale, and struggles with the ferocious passion of her heart. She wonders where she and her Aunt Bessie will settle, no longer concealing "from herself that she and the worthy spinster [are] solitary wanderers on earth," with little contact with other humans. Desolate, she tries to think of death, but at this point in her life, "Nature and love [are] wedded in her mind," and she cannot bear the thought of "parting with life." She decides to focus her thoughts on her mother but can see no way that they can reunite, as a wall seems to have been constructed between them. Ethel thinks of leaving London, recalling her father's positive comments about Italy. Her aunt does not approve, wondering how women might travel as Ethel suggests, but she wants to humor her niece. Ethel's sweetness is "a loadstone to draw all hearts." Then Ethel receives a letter from Edward, apologizing for having ignored her and asking to visit her aunt. Her heart soars again at the thought of seeing Villiers.

During his absence from Richmond, Villiers has learned that his cousin Saville, older brother to Horatio, will marry the daughter of a wealthy earl. He joins the family and learns of all the wedding plans from the girl's cousins. At first, Edward's resolution not to draw Ethel into his assured poverty stands, and he enjoys listening to the sisters speak of the family, especially of Horace, as they refer to Horatio, whom they adore. He receives a letter from Horace and yearns to visit him but recalls that he cannot leave England and expect to be supported. Suddenly, he hears from his father, Colonel Villiers, of his own intended marriage. He requests Edward to sign an agreement not to seek further support from him, in exchange for which Edward's debts will be paid. Edward rejoices, assuming that he can now move forward with his own plans for the future.

Villiers visits Richmond, requests Ethel's hand in marriage, and the two are overjoyed. Elizabeth has some doubts regarding whether Ethel should marry at such a young age. Edward brings his family—Lord Maristow and the girl cousins Sophia, Harriet, and Lucy Saville—to visit at Richmond, and this has an immediate positive effect on "the recluses," Ethel and Elizabeth. The young women immediately embrace Ethel, although she feels "as a wild antelope among tame ones," observing their language and actions and considering how different they are from her own. The narrator observes that "a man is more thrown upon the reality of life, while girls live altogether in a factitious state." The family remains in London until the elder Saville son marries. Edward is anxious to sign the papers his father has mentioned to free himself for marriage. However, he learns his father's marriage is delayed, postponed for a time, news that staggers him. At this point, he moves forward with his plans, and he and Ethel marry. Word is sent ahead of time to Lady Lodore, who makes no reply. Following the wedding, Elizabeth returns to Longfield, and the new couple travel to the Continent.

Volume 2: Chapters 10–12

Ethel and Edward travel toward Naples, adjusting to their new relationship. Ethel's happiness is reflected on her face, but Edward is more sedate, because "the heart of a man is seldom as single and devoted as that of a woman." They visit Horatio and his new wife after first traveling through Switzerland, Florence, and Rome. Lucy Saville had told Ethel prior to their departure that when Edward left, all of the family's "props" will have been pulled away, explaining that Horatio's marriage had been "a sad blow to us all," as they had no opportunity to meet his bride. More important, she keeps him in Italy, refusing to leave her home to visit England. Lucy also shares that Horace had been "a discarded lover." She feels he married partly to gain revenge on the woman who had broken his heart.

Lucy continues her story, explaining that Clorinda Saville, Horace's bride, is a highly emotional woman from an abusive background, shut up in a convent for years by her jealous mother. Horatio had always said, "I am in love with an idea, and therefore women have no power over me," but upon meeting Clorinda, he felt protective toward her. His words of kindness to the young girl "elicited a whole torrent of gratitude and passion." While Horace wanted to move slowly to develop their relationship, Clorinda wanted immediate rescue. Lucy adds that since their union, Horace and Clorinda are constantly surrounded by her family, insulated by the Italian culture. To Lucy, it seems as if Clorinda wants to isolate Horace, rather than "link herself" to his friends. She hopes Ethel will find that she is wrong.

Immediately upon their arrival in Naples, Edward decides to search for Horatio. While he is out, Horatio calls on Ethel, and she notes he is quite shy. They exchange pleasantries until Edward appears. As they talk, Ethel examines Horatio closely and notices how attractive he is, particularly his expressive eyes and his manners, "marked by high breeding." She cannot know that he was feeling somewhat shy due to the knowledge that she is daughter of his onetime love, Lady Lodore. Because Ethel is so different from her mother, Horatio eventually becomes more comfortable in her presence. He explains that Clorinda will visit that afternoon. He adds of her that "not one atom of body, one particle of mind" bears "the least affinity to England." Ethel finds Clorinda beautiful, silent much of the time, and like a picture. She explains to Ethel that she does not hate England but rather fears it. She thinks no one will like her and that her pride will cause her to embarrass her husband. When Ethel later urges Clorinda to reconsider traveling to England, she becomes angry and declares that Horatio once loved an Englishwoman, knowledge that she finds tortuous. She would rather be "torn in quarters by wild horses" than to visit. If she knew Edward was considering a return, she could "strike him dead."

Several months pass as the new couple, "beelike, sipped the honey of life." Saville's presence adds "the living spirit of poetry" to their lives and "associated the treasures of human genius with the sublime beauty of nature." The only thing Ethel dislikes about him is his inability to arrive on time, which makes them all late for various excursions. Clorinda never joins them for rides or going out to dinner, as she has "an empire of her own," to which she gladly admits her friends. She especially enjoys musical performances and sings beautifully herself. Ethel enjoys her company but notes a "wall" between them. She tells Ethel that because she is Italian and Ethel English, "there is a natural war between my fire and your snow."

The two couples decide to visit Rome, but when they arrive in Terracina on the way to Rome, Clorinda has an emotional breakdown. Ethel watches Clorinda physically transform, turning ugly and casting "tiger-like glances" at Horatio. When she attacks him at dinner with a knife, Edward manages to grab her arm, and she sinks into convulsions. Ethel and Edward must travel on without them. Before they depart, Horatio explains that Clorinda's repentance is as violent as her attack. Her "vehemence neutralizes" all that is good in her, and he is "chained to the oar," powerless to change her or escape. He hopes with time and steady attention from him, Clorinda will change. Although he would like to flee, he will not desert her when she is so dependent. While Edward tells him repeatedly that they will delay their trip to wait for him and Clorinda, he bids them to continue and promises to reserve a house at Sorrento for the summer for them upon their return.

As Ethel and Edward travel toward Rome, they consider Horatio's situation, which demonstrates that not everyone is "fortunate in the lottery of life," as they consider themselves to have been. Ethel does not mind the separation from Horatio. Although she likes him well enough, she is delighted to have Edward to herself. Edward's thoughts turn in another direction, as he fears that Ethel may not be able to stand up to the trials that await them, and he tries again to discuss their financial situation with her. She again makes clear her lack of understanding or desire to understand his finances, stating "that is your affair" and telling him that all will be well. Villiers understands that her extreme youth and ignorance blind her to the truth. The narrator notes that Ethel is "ignorant of the mechanism of giving and receiving, on which the course of our life depends." They blend with the others during Holy Week at Rome, with Villiers seeing many people he knew.

Eventually the visitors from England and other northern locations return home, and Ethel and Edward consider the return to Naples. Happy at Rome, Ethel does not want to return. Edward again broaches the topic of their economic future, and Ethel again rebuffs him, preferring to enjoy the romantic evening as the couple sit outside the remains of the Coliseum. She has no fear as Edward discusses the possibility of borrowing from Horatio but then changes his mind, noting that his friend is "ill enough off himself." Ethel exults in the climate, the "calm majesty, a silent and awful repose in the ruins of Rome," the luxuriant plant growth in sunny soil, and feels in unison with nature. Because their souls feel "in perfect harmony," they delay returning to Saville, where Horatio suffers a conflict they want to avoid. Instead, they spend a month traveling to England, renting a home in London and hoping to avoid the social season, which is waning.

Though they had hoped to save funds by spending much quiet time at home, they find themselves pulled into the gaiety and round of social visits, "while still every settlement [is] delayed" by Colonel Villiers. However, they spend time away and together as Ethel, without Edward's vast social experience, is happy to improve her mind through independent study. She enjoys matching names that her father had discussed in Illinois with the persons she could now observe and read about in the newspapers on her own. Another reason she avoids society is because she has heard that her mother, Lady Lodore, is in London. While her mother has caught sight of Ethel a few times and smiled and nodded, Edward does not want them to come together for fear that Ethel might be hurt.

Ethel observes her mother in a box below her one evening at the opera and notices all of her visitors and how graciously and easily Lady Lodore interacts with them. However, to Ethel, her mother's smile often appears forced, like a shadow. Perhaps it is the shadows of the gas lights that causes it, but her mother appears less brilliant, altered in a way that suggests she is unhappy. One day, Ethel visits Parliament and hears a voice behind her that she identifies as belonging to Cornelia. All of her rehearsed greetings to her mother dissolve in the rise of emotion she feels. When her mother tells her, "Your ear-ring is unfastened, Ethel," Ethel's finger shakes as she reaches to fix it. Cornelia says, "Permit me," and when her hand touches Ethel's cheek, it seems that time stops. Ethel feels as if she were suffocating, and she cannot even manage to say "thank you." She sits quietly gathering her thoughts and at last turns to speak to Cornelia, but her mother is gone.

Ethel assumes that her mother does not want them to be friendly to one another. That saddens her, because the vision of a monster that Elizabeth had inspired when their discussion turned to her mother has dissolved. Ethel longs to wait on her mother and be allowed to love her. The chapter concludes with the narrator stating that the next time mother and daughter meet will not be at a palace.

Volume 2: Chapters 13–18

An event occurs that changes the Villiers' plans as they plan to visit Maristow Castle. They learn of the sudden death of Mr. Saville, Horatio's older brother, making Horatio the heir to his father's title. Lord Maristow tries to accept the fact that Horatio has remained abroad and would probably not take his place in Parliament. He has urged his son to return home in the past and, before Villiers had departed on his honeymoon, asked Edward to also try to persuade his son to come home. He thought that whatever Mrs. Saville's antipathy toward England might be, she would have to overcome it. Lord Maristow views Horatio as playing "a boy-lover's part," ridiculous at his age. Maristow bemoans to Villiers that friends who have seen Horatio and Clorinda have commented on their silliness. Maristow also regrets his part in urging Edward to depend on his eventual independence from his father, leaving him poor and now with a wife to support. He tells Edward that when the political tide turns, he will try to help him, or he can live abroad until the storm that is forming due to his debts has passed.

Villiers struggles regarding his future action. If he goes abroad, he will be a beggar. If he stays, he will expose himself and Ethel to insults and "dangers from which there was no escape." His sunny disposition does not allow him to wallow long in fear, as he thinks that surely his luck will change, and better days are ahead. He hopes for something unseen to save them, but he does not speak of his concerns to Ethel. She is anxious to leave town and prove through deprivation that she is willing to meet "the adversity which he [has] so much dreaded."

Ethel and Edward visit Longfield, where the time spent walking and horseback riding temporarily reinvigorates the pair. The lovely view of the sea, the country storms, and the silvery moon all raise their spirits. Villiers carries a gun, but Ethel, "though American bred," is distressed by death, so Edward never shoots birds or other game when she accompanies him. Edward considers the peaceful interlude a gift, and in their youth, the couple enjoys one another completely. Then the narrator reminds readers that such beauty does not last.

As the two are riding one day, shadows of clouds cover the path, but the sun reaches them and they could observe spring everywhere. Still, a "vague, uneasy restlessness . . . pregnant with melancholy" surrounds them. Villiers has received a letter from his banker that his credit is overdrawn. While Ethel understands that he is upset, she does not understand debt and so cannot comfort him. Edward remarks that the poets believe the wonder of nature makes earth a type of heaven, but reality contradicts that idea. Humans are, at the core, barbarians who abuse nature and its abundance and cut themselves off from nature's "generous but simple munificence."

Ethel tells Edward that where she matured in Illinois, "the simplest abode, food and attire, were all I knew of human refinements, and I was satisfied." Edward seems not to hear her. He tells her that man does not first desire wealth but rather "sympathy and applause." Humans rate one another simply by their possessions. If a human is merely learned and good but poor, that person will not be welcomed by society. The only individual that he despises for being poor is himself.

While Ethel thinks of Illinois as a paradise where such judgment might be avoided, Edward recalls their stay in Italy as positive. He thinks they might want to return there, but that they may first have to walk through "a fiery pass" like the "souls of Dante." He declares that he will go into London on the following day to face his creditors, and Ethel says she will accompany him. He tells her that she must remain behind, that he will stay a few days, and then he will return. He promises not to be absent for longer than a week.

When Edward leaves the following morning, the narrator notes that parting from a loved one is a "landmark" in life—"we begin our career out of illusion and the land of dreams, into reality and endurance." He promises to write every day. As Ethel looks down the road after he departs, she worries that something bad will happen to Edward, when instead he deserves to be rewarded for his goodness. She credits him for saving her from isolation following her father's death and her mother's rejection. Her passions are both "bitter and sweet." When Ethel goes back into the house in obvious distress, her Aunt Bessie thinks how glad she is to have remained single and avoided such "conjugal distresses."

Ethel passes the time at home worrying about Edward and writing many letters to him. She continues to remind him that she does "not even feel the want of those luxuries so necessary to most women." She explains that Lord Lodore rendered her "independent of the services of others." She also does not view solitude as evil and is no "object of pity" when fortune deprives her of wealth. Edward replies, explaining that his father's affairs are in greater disarray than ever, as he married in secret, leaving his new wife's father livid over their elopement. The colonel has attempted to raise funds, as his father-in-law declares he will withhold all of his daughter's inheritance unless she dissolves the marriage. Edward's hopes for any help from his father have at last completely died.

Feeling "in absolute beggary," Edward declares that he now must do whatever he can to raise funds. He asks Ethel to be patient, knowing that she wants to join him in London. Ethel gently scolds him for writing as if he believes her better off at Longfield than with her husband, regardless of his situation. Three weeks pass with no word from Edward. Ethel at last receives a letter telling her that Edward has visited his solicitor and must go again on the next day. Ethel struggles over whether to join him, regardless of his having asked her not to. When Ethel decides to go to London, she tells her aunt, who does not question her decision. Edward had made clear to Ethel that Aunt Bessie should know nothing of his financial problems. However, when Ethel decides to travel alone to forego the expense of a servant, knowing that Edward has dismissed his own faithful servant, Elizabeth is shocked.

Frightened but excited, Ethel departs on November 28, feeling pride in the fact that for the first time she will be paying the postillion and giving directions. However, as the day turns chilly, she becomes alarmed at how long the journey has taken and at the enormous size of London. She wonders whether Edward might be at his club and is unsure of his address in Duke Street, St. James's. As she and the driver face thick fog and the noise of the busy London streets, Ethel thinks it a wretched place for Edward to have to live. She feels as if their journey through Fleet Street and the Strand will never end. When they pull up to the door of the Union Club, a waiter tells Ethel that Mr. Villiers left town a week earlier, leaving her aghast. He mentions that the porter, Saunders, might know where Villiers lodges, so the carriage awaits while Saunders is found. Ethel anxiously watches the many pedestrians from inside her carriage, hoping to catch sight of Edward.

After a long wait, the waiter returns to tell her that the porter could not wait to speak with her, that he had to leave and has forgotten the number of the house in Duke Street. He recalls that the woman who owns the house is a widow named

Mrs. Derham. The carriage returns to Duke Street, and at last the driver finds Mrs. Derham's residence. Ethel rushes inside to find that Edward is not at home, so she waits for him. When Mrs. Derham questions her identity, and she states that she is Mrs. Villiers, Mrs. Derham doubts her, saying that Mrs. Villiers lives in the country, prompting Ethel to show her Edward's letters. Ethel then gratefully accepts Mrs. Derham's invitation to share her tea.

When Edward at last arrives home, their reunion is joyful. The narrator informs readers that "she was here, in her youth, her loveliness, her sweetness; these were charms; but others more transcendent now attended on, and invested her;—the sacred tenderness of a wife had led her to his side." They enjoy a wonderful supper together, the "fulfillment of perfect human happiness," and are "imparadised" by their union. In their private little room, their hearts can "build up bowers of delight, and store them with all of ecstasy which the soul of man can know." They speak of their long future together and their union "for better or for worse."

Villiers does not leave the room for a few days and enjoys his wife's presence during inclement weather. His father has left town, and Edward has attempted to raise funds on annuities, but he cannot pay the interest. Edward and Ethel spend the time talking, and Ethel learns for the first time of Horatio Saville's love for her mother; she can hardly believe that her mother would not desire to wed a man with a heart as pure as that of Horatio. As Villiers awaits his solicitor's actions on his behalf, another month passes.

On January 4, Villiers receives a request from Lord Maristow, who entrusts a commission to him that causes Edward to travel to Egham. In his absence, Ethel tries to write letters to Italy and to her aunt, but she is distracted by thoughts of Edward's safety. Suddenly, Saunders, the porter from the Union Club, is admitted to speak to Ethel and explains that Edward is in danger. He describes Edward as a good man who has treated him well; thus, he hopes to be able to help Villiers. Two men had appeared at the club looking for Edward, and before Saunders could stop one of the waiters, he had told them where Villiers lived. Saunders had recognized the men as bailiffs and realizes they are seeking to arrest Villiers, news that frightens Ethel. Saunders asks her whether he should go to Egham to warn Villiers. Confused, Ethel does not know what to do and asks Saunders for his opinion. They both agree that he should try to find Villiers. When Ethel tries to pay him, Saunders advises her to keep her money, as she may need it, knowing that Villiers will pay him later. She writes a note for Saunders to take to Edward, and they agree that he will return to Mrs. Derham's house by 9:00 the following morning.

Wanting to speak with someone, Ethel hurries downstairs and knocks on Mrs. Derham's door. She is shocked to see Fanny Derham sitting in the parlor. They hesitate to speak, Ethel due to confusion and Fanny because she has felt neglected by Ethel, who has not written to her in some time. Soon they recover from their shyness and study each other more closely. While Ethel has changed and matured since marriage, Fanny is "still a mere girl . . . her young ingenuous countenance . . . unaltered." Her intelligent eyes beam, and "her beauty [is] all intellectual: open, sincere, passionless, yet benignant, you approached her without fear of encountering any of the baser qualities of human beings." She is consulting a dictionary, and Ethel remarks that she seems to be continuing her past pursuits. Fanny replies she is more wed to them than ever, and she asks whether Ethel needs to speak with her mother, who is out, and whether she might assist Ethel in her mother's absence. Ethel explains the situation, for which Fanny has sympathy, telling Ethel that she has had some experience in the area, because "Adversity and I are become very close friends." She advises that if the porter is successful, no harm will come to Villiers and that Ethel should try to get some rest.

Fanny helps calm Ethel and then, in Ethel's room, explains her own history. Her father had died, and his family had treated her mother badly. A relative had assisted them to be able to procure a livelihood through the boarding house. Fanny does not feel diminished by such activities; she only disdains them because they have interfered with her philosophical pursuits and her enjoyment of nature. She desires only to help her mother and does not worry about any physical hardships. Ethel is able to take courage from Fanny, knowing that she also can face privation if called upon. God will comfort her and allow her to comfort Edward. As the second volume concludes, Ethel resigns her "destiny to a Power superior to any earthly authority."

Volume 3: Chapters 1–5

The novel's third volume opens with Ethel receiving a note from Edward, advising her that he cannot return until that evening, when he plans to meet her at midnight. She dresses and hurries downstairs to meet Fanny, who awaits her. Ethel thinks, "It was an unspeakable comfort to have one as intelligent and kind as Fanny, to communicate with, during Edward's absence." She learns that Fanny has already sent away the bailiffs who came to search the house for Edward.

Concerned not only for her own reputation but also that of Fanny, Ethel worries about what Fanny's mother will think of her. The two discuss Fanny's parents, with Fanny making the point that her mother did not make a good match for her father. She describes her father as one who was susceptible "to the world's scorn," adding that her mother is happy with Sarah, Fanny's older sister, who has given Mrs. Derham a granddaughter. She and her mother would "torture" each other if they spent much time together; Fanny lost her guide and preserver when her father died.

When Ethel asks whether Fanny does not merely "waste" her life in regret, Fanny has a quick reply. She references the independence that her father had "cultivated" in her, explaining that "an ardent thirst for knowledge, is as the air I breathe; and the acquisition of it, is pure and unalloyed happiness." Books are her passion. She has also worked with the poor and miserable to help improve their lives, and she praises the power of words, noting that she speaks up on their behalf whenever possible. She wishes that others would find their voices and speak against oppression, as only then will conditions change. Ethel later thinks of the passion that she feels for Edward: "Every other idea and thought, to use a chemical expression, was held in solution by that powerful feeling, which mingled and united with every particle of her soul."

When they are able to meet, they try to plan for the future.

Although Ethel would like to talk more with Fanny, the two women have contrasting attitudes: "Ethel had received . . . a sexual education. Lord Lodore had formed his ideal of what a woman ought to be, of what he had wished to find in his wife, and sought to mould his daughter accordingly. Mr. Derham contemplated the duties and objects befitting an immortal soul, and had educated his child for the performance of them." Where Lord Lodore had instructed Ethel to yield to her husband's will and focus on making him happy, Derham had instructed Fanny to be self-sufficient and independent. Ethel is guided by "the tenderness of her heart," while Fanny "consulted her understanding." The two do share a propensity to act from a sense of justice, never deviating from "the strict line of honour and integrity." Later, the narrator notes that Fanny sees "slavery" in Ethel's situation but still appreciates her friend's warmth and generosity.

Ethel can hardly wait for midnight to arrive, when she will reunite with her husband. She becomes more and more impatient until at last Villiers appears. His love for her is clear in his thoughts that the earth's "power and splendours" would mean nothing without Ethel. She worries about their financial situation, although she does not understand the details: "Money had always been placed like counters in her hand; she had never known whence it came . . . this was the faulty part of her father's system of education." They consider moving to Brussels or Paris until his affairs can be settled. He tells her he will return in a week.

Ethel wants to be with him, thinking "there could be no degradation in a wife waiting on the fallen fortunes of her husband." She wants to write down such thoughts in hopes of convincing Edward to let her join him, but no words can express the emotion that is "stronger than any reason in her heart." Only when she spends time with Fanny can she distract herself from her situation. She wonders over "a mechanism of mind so different from her own . . . each had been the favourite daughter of men of superior qualities of mind," but they had received opposite educations. What unites them is the "absence of every factitious sentiment. They acted from their own hearts—from their own sense of right, without the intervention of worldly considerations."

Ethel begins to visit her husband, who is in hiding, braving the January ice and freezing temperatures. Villiers wants to send an enclosed carriage to pick her up, but, wary of expense, Ethel takes a hackney coach instead, exposing her to the elements. When the cold makes her feel dizzy, she reminds herself that she vowed to bear the struggle cheerfully, as long as she could be with Edward. Once or twice, she faints when she returns home. Edward visits Mrs. Derham's house, and the widow explains that Ethel will become ill from all of the physical exertion she has been making during the winter cold. He wants to scold Ethel but is stopped by her obvious total devotion to him. He explains that his solicitor has made a plan for him to get some money after which they can stay at a country inn. Fanny wonders at her friend's naïveté regarding money but admires her elevation "above the common place of life."

While Ethel awaits Edward's arrival, she receives a letter from him, and Fanny tells her that the two bailiffs have been at the house again. Ethel decides to brave Edward's disapproval and join him, with Fanny accompanying her. Edward is predictably annoyed at first by Ethel's exposing herself to risk. However, when he sees Fanny, he understands there is danger associated with the visit, prompted by the bailiff visits. Fanny departs, and Edward and Ethel later decide to remove to a location close to an inn near Brixton, south of London. Ethel tells him that they will receive money the following day. She has asked Aunt Bessie for a loan, even though Edward has said he does not want her to do so. She feels his reluctance is "strange morality" and asks, "Are generosity, benevolence, and gratitude, to be exploded among us?" He gently rebukes her, reminding her they are not in the wilds of America, where the "simplicity of barter and exchange" exists. He chides her for acting against his will, but the conversation then turns to their devotion to one another, and Ethel thinks this is "speaking in a language" that she can comprehend, unlike their discussions of financial matters.

They can both better accept privation when together, as their hearts make a "fairyland" of any surrounding. In moments when Ethel feels the pressure of her situation, it can be relieved by her memory of the Illinois River and the beauty of the prairie, and she considers asking Edward whether he would want to move to America. Villiers loves her more than ever as "the difficulties of their situation exalted her." The narrator cautions readers not to indulge in pity for the couple, because "their pure natures could turn the groveling substance presented to them, to ambrosial food for the sustenance of love." They cannot pay the bill for their meal, and the following day, the waiter will not serve them until the bill has been paid. They wait patiently for Fanny, who is to bring them money from Aunt Bessie.

Volume 3: Chapters 6–10

Fanny eventually arrives with a letter that covers their bills, and they decide to move to Salt Hill, near Windsor. They drop off Fanny at Piccadilly and settle into their new establishment. Villiers must leave in the morning, and Fanny misses him when she awakens, but she takes comfort in the spring breeze—a comfort that does not last long. When Edward does not return, she at last goes to bed and is awakened the next morning by Fanny, who informs her that Edward has been arrested. Ethel joins him in the room that will be their debtors' prison. He tries to protest, but he can "read in her eyes" that she must complete her "hallowed" duty: "Angels could not feel as she did, for they cannot sacrifice to those they love." Although surrounded by "the world's worst adversity," Ethel's mind remains clear and serene. As Fanny later explains to Lady Lodore, Ethel "lives within the rules," renting lodging across the river from the prison.

In March, Lady Lodore returns home and experiences the loneliness of having no one there awaiting her. She misses her mother's company, and Saville's marriage is "a canker at her heart," although she has not thought of marriage for herself as a possibility for some time. She has "sacrificed all" to "the world she live[s] in." The narrator notes that pride masks her great sense of understanding and her "great kindliness of disposition," shutting up her positive qualities like "the wall of China." At this point, she is humiliated and sad, and her life seems worthless. She has had little interest in Ethel, whom she believes to be weak "in both character and understanding." Cornelia worries that she might go mad, thinking, "what greater madness, than to know that love, affection, the charities of life, the hopes of existence, are empty words for me?" Although her mother seemed a wretched character at times, she had at least valued Cornelia, as no one now does. Her misery increases one evening when an acquaintance describes Mrs. Saville, Horatio's wife, as a 20-year-old beauty with a little girl on whom her husband dotes. At the age of 34, Cornelia mourns the loss of her prime.

Fanny visits Lady Lodore and, after their conversation, decides that she had been wrong to think of Ethel's mother as "cold, worldly and selfish." She asks Lady Lodore to consider giving Ethel money, as Villier's father cannot, and they have no prospects. When Lady Lodore declares that Ethel must move in with her, Fanny explains that Ethel will never consent to do so. Cornelia considers that fact and decides to visit Ethel. The narrator emphasizes that "never before had the elegant and fastidious" Lady Lodore entered such a place, referring to her daughter's poor lodgings. Cornelia has tried to dress plainly, but her silks and furs contrast greatly with her surroundings, the housing Ethel occupies in order to be close to Edward.

Cornelia is so moved by her daughter's youthful grace and dignity in her self-sacrifice for Edward that she decides she can do the same for her daughter. She sees in Ethel "one of those rare examples sent upon earth to purify human nature." When she arrives home to her wealth and possessions, she declares that "never more . . . will I so waste my being, but learn from Ethel to be happy and love."

Volume 3: Chapters 11–16
Villiers is suspicious as to Lady Lodore's intentions when Ethel first tells him that her mother has visited, and he thinks of how naive Ethel is, having been raised in a backwoods, in contrast to his own sophistication. However, he then again wishes to be in the wilds of America, "or any part of the world where the majesty of nature" might surround him, believing he should be "less alive" to the "sinister influence" of his misfortunes. He vows that he will never be the poor father to his own children that his father was to him.

Lady Lodore completely rejects her wealth and social position, sacrificing all of her material possessions to rescue her daughter and son-in-law from imprisonment. She first works with Villier's solicitor to secretly pay his debts, delighting in carrying out her plan and feeling for the first time as if her life has purpose. Villiers is puzzled when his solicitor advises him that his financial circumstances have changed, as he cannot guess who might have rescued him.

Cornelia's new vision of life expands when she realizes how much she sacrificed in giving Ethel to Lord Lodore to raise and vows to "atone for the evils that were a consequence of this neglect." She plans to return to "the uncouth and lonely mountains of Wales," where Lord Lodore had first discovered her, to live "in poverty and seclusion." Cornelia fantasizes the excitement of Ethel and Edward when they are free. She especially exults in the fact that she, who had been too selfish and haughty to yield to Horatio and become Mrs. Saville, will make such sacrifice. She will not see Ethel again for a time, in order not to reveal her secret. The narrator notes that her newfound sensibility "cause[s] her to make more progress in the knowledge of life . . . than love or ambition had ever done before." Shelley devotes many pages to analyzing the change in Cornelia and to philosophizing as to its motivation and results. At one point during a carriage ride through Hyde Park, Cornelia thinks of Lodore and has a sudden desire to visit America to see where he lived and to visit his grave at Longfield. She begins to cry, not from guilt but more from a sense of sharing his fate as she plans her own "self banishment." Cornelia wonders whether he might hear her, if at his grave she said, "Be at peace! your child is happy through my means."

Her plans complete, Cornelia waits for Fanny to visit her on a June day and thinks of how much she had loved Saville. She writes a letter to Ethel, explaining her actions and promising to write again to let Ethel know where she has gone. Just before leaving the house, she glances at a newspaper and learns with great surprise that Horatio's young wife has died. Fanny arrives, and they converse, with Cornelia explaining that she feels confident they will see each other again. After Fanny departs, Cornelia considers contacting Saville, then convinces herself that without her youthful beauty and wealth, he will not be interested in her. She departs, falls ill at a country inn, and is there for several weeks.

Ethel gives birth to a daughter one month after Edward is freed. The narrator then summarizes how the relationship between Saville and his wife Clorinda had developed, eventually coming to a tragic conclusion. Much of the summary is a review for readers who previously learned that Clorinda had been an ignorant girl whom Saville educated and trained in the arts, all the while pining for Cornelia, whom he continued to desire. He never felt such passion for Clorinda but married her to help her. Although he confessed prior to the wedding that he loved Cornelia, Clorinda still desired marriage.

When Ethel visited Horatio in Italy, seeking news of her mother, Clorinda flew into a jealous rage so fierce that Horatio could not reason with her. She constantly tormented him with accusations and unfounded judgments as they expected their first child. The emotional tirade stopped for a time at the birth of their baby, but eventually Clorinda became jealous of her own daughter and the time that Horatio spent with her. Horatio's sisters visited their new niece in Naples and urged Clorinda to come to England, but she became so incensed at the mention of Saville's previous home that she declared to him she would die if she went there, particularly if she had to meet Lady Lodore. Saville's father, Lord Maristow, told Clorinda she must choose between her husband, who had to return to England, or her own country. In her fury, she burst a blood vessel and lay ill for a time under the close attention of her husband. In a moment of heroism, she said she would go to England but then regretted that declaration. The narrator notes: "Like all Italians, Clorinda feared death excessively; besides that, to die was to yield the entire victory to her rival."

Clorinda eventually calmed herself, but she lost weight and begrudged what she perceived as a lack of attention to her sacrifice for the sake of her husband. She eventually fell senseless after seeing a miniature and hearing her husband's relatives remark how much it resembled Lady Lodore. Again overcome by passion, Clorinda died. Saville deeply mourned her and took comfort in his daughter, also named Clorinda, who had never been as attached to her mother as she was to him.

Volume 3: Chapters 17–20

Saville returns to England and eventually sees Ethel again, but neither will speak of Lady Lodore, out of respect for the other. In September, Lord Maristow hosts a party, which everyone attends, including Elizabeth Fitzhenry. Lord Maristow appeals to Lord Derham to bestow an income on his granddaughter, Fanny. He agrees after seeing that Fanny is out in the world, enjoying the company of people of whom he approves. Thus, Fanny will be financially secure for life. Eventually the group speaks of Lady Lodore, with Fanny commenting on the strangeness of no one having received a letter from her. She recounts the last time she had seen her, speaking of what seemed to be a change in her character.

As several months pass, Villiers's solicitor makes inquiries about Lady Lodore. Ethel asks Villiers to help, but Edward notes that as an adult, Lady Lodore can do as she pleases. Ethel reminds him of her mother's sacrifice for them, which they have learned about, although not in detail.

Saville visits Villiers's solicitor and learns all of the details of Cornelia's self-sacrifice. He determines to find her, thinking, "It became a duty . . . to respect, revere, adore one so generous and noble." While he and Villiers search for Lady Lodore, the reader learns that she has ended up in her sister-in-law's village of Longfield, where she lives with a Dame Nixon. Elizabeth's servant reveals the visitor's identity. Not knowing of Cornelia's change of heart, Elizabeth has no desire to visit her. She is disturbed to receive a letter from Ethel explaining their search for Cornelia and that they will soon arrive to investigate the possibility that she is in the area. Elizabeth still will not consider forgiving Cornelia, something she sees as "desecration to the memory of her brother."

When Elizabeth at last visits Cornelia, it is to urge her to go away and never see Ethel, something her brother had desired. But almost immediately, Elizabeth observes a marked change in Lady Lodore. Cornelia explains that she does not want Ethel to see her in poverty, as she will feel that she needs to assist her mother, and the living conditions are what Cornelia desires. She cares for a widow who kindly gave her a home, and the role suits her. Elizabeth agrees not to reveal Cornelia's location to Ethel, and in turn Elizabeth will occasionally bring Cornelia news of her daughter.

Soon Ethel arrives at Longview and explains to Elizabeth all Cornelia's sacrifice to her benefit. An entire chapter is devoted to explaining all that has happened to Cornelia that caused her to end up in Essex, caring for the ill Dame Margaret Nixon. During Cornelia's delirium, she had visions of Ethel dancing around Lord Lodore's tomb and beckoning Cornelia to come to her. When she recovered, she did visit her husband's tomb and ended up staying in Essex. She will stay until Margaret dies and then execute her plan to move on to her native Wales and live in isolation.

Elizabeth informs Ethel of her mother's location, and they enjoy a reunion in the lovely garden where Cornelia has spent much time. In the final chapter, the narrator relates that Cornelia has married Saville, now the viscount of Maristow, and enjoys her new family, especially the second chance she has been given through Clorinda to raise a daughter. Villiers's hard-hearted father dwells in poverty and misery, his wife having deserted him to care for her father, who plans to bestow all he has on his daughter. The book ends with a statement about Fanny Derham's life. While "no details can be recounted," the narrator praises Fanny's intellect and her demeanor.

Volume 3: Conclusion

Shelley uses the conclusion to provide the reader with a synopsis of the characters' lives following the end of the novel's story. Critics find a major point of interest in the final section that focuses on Fanny Derham. The fact that the narrator will not venture to "relate the varied fate" of Fanny has led to speculation that Shelley had no role model for Fanny's active and independent woman, unafraid to exist without a husband or family. Critical reaction to the conclusion is examined in the commentary section.

COMMENTARY

The introduction to this entry emphasized, in part, the autobiographical nature of the novel and its fascination for those who want to see more revealed of the Shelleys' relationship. The plot works to support such revelations but, more importantly, showcases Mary Shelley's own attitudes about her past. Even with decades of perspective on her financial struggles while still Percy Shelley's wife, her emotions remain strong, evident in her passionate tone when addressing the topic of finances. For instance, in the seventh chapter of volume 1, while relating the history of Lady Santerre, Cornelia's mother, Shelley reflects on the stinginess of Percy Shelley's father, Sir Timothy Shelley, when she explains that Lady Santerre's own father-in-law "allowed them two hundred a year, and called himself generous." In Shelley's case, as in that of Lady Santerre, a grandchild needed and deserved more support from a wealthy but stingy grandfather. She continues to write of the widow's struggle to keep up appearances in society, adding that "poverty is a tyrant, whose laws are more terrible that those of Draco"—probably reflecting on her struggles as a single mother, but also on the betrayal of Percy's social network after he and Mary had run away together. In that same volume, she emphasizes Cornelia, symbolically widowed when Lodore departs for America, and her success in remaining free from even a whiff of scandal, an admirable accomplishment. Shelley had faced scandal herself a number of times, enduring false accusations and blackmail attempts in her widowhood, due to the scandalous activities of her circle.

Shelley's bitterness over the betrayal that critics assert she probably felt toward Percy Shelley when he left the family alone to pursue his ideals is reflected in Lord Lodore's engagement in a duel that he knows will kill him. His honor ranks more important than his daughter's future, which he is willing to sacrifice in order to redeem his good name and reputation. Ethel later sees her father's act as one of desertion, particularly when he had not trained her to be independent and wise to the ways of the world. Her ignorance over financial matters plays an important role in the book, helping at once to define her purity and naïveté, especially when she does not understand why Edward's friends will not help him. She views the lack of support as a betrayal, echoing Shelley's attitude toward Byron shortly after Percy Shelley's death, when he reneged on promised financial support. Due to her era's demands for restraint, Shelley does not report the incident with inflammatory language but makes clear Byron's actions in a letter to friends. She probably would have seen such an action more as a betrayal of her husband's memory than of herself, and that by an individual who had claimed to be a close friend.

Some scholars believe that Shelley's characterization of the youthful Ethel developing a relationship with the older socialite, Villiers, recounts her own experience with Percy Shelley. They stress the parallels between Villiers's financial problems and those of Percy. Despite the fact that both were from wealthy families and had the potential to be wealthy, both literally had to hide from creditors. Villiers is another irresponsible male fashioned by Shelley, in her ongoing focus in her fiction on the gender inequality present in families in terms of responsibility. Although in her youth Shelley had supported romantic ideals and retained an optimistic outlook, in her later novels she did not, instead demonstrating that the focus of the romantic poets on saving the world came at a great cost to their families. The poets at times prioritized social causes above familial needs.

Shelley appears to be torn over her support of the romantic ideal that proved so critical to her husband and his circle. On the one hand, she often criticizes men who desert their families in pursuit of the "masculine sublime," seeking to rescue the world but simultaneously leaving those closest to them in need of rescue. On the other hand, she continues to see nature as the romantics did, celebrating its uplifting and emotionally healing aspects in much of her writing and bemoaning the lack of recognition of nature's importance to many. For instance, in the second volume, Villiers notes that "poets tell us" of the beauty of the world, and they form "an argument for their creed from the wisdom and loveliness displayed in the universe." Such delights "make earth a type of heaven," but as he continues to contemplate, he adds, "How false and senseless all this truly is!" He notes that people who can make the earth's spaces their home, eat its fruits, and kill its animals but do not attend to property and culture are labeled "barbarians and savages—untaught, uncivilized, miserable beings." At the same time, those more civilized feel themselves "the greater, the wiser, the nobler," despite the fact that they place barriers between themselves and nature. The majority of humans take no account of nature, unless it is measured as a possession.

Shelley depicts America, more specifically Illinois, as a type of Eden, despite the more realistic depictions that she studied. Lord Lodore raises Ethel in the wilds of Illinois, suggesting the positive effects of nature, a mother substitute of sorts. Later, as Ethel suffers privation with Edward, for relief she can return to nature in her imagination: "The thought of . . . the Illinois and the measureless forest rose before her, and in her ear was the dashing of the stream . . . her light feet again crossed the prairie." She wonders whether she and Edward should not move there to escape his creditors and enjoy "the pleasant labours of cultivation, the rides, the hunting, the boating, all common-place occurrences, which, attended on by love, were exalted into a perpetual gorgeous procession of beautified hours." These passages and many more demonstrate Shelley's enduring belief in nature's grandeur and its power to heal and nurture.

One way for readers to understand *Lodore* is through its comparison and contrast to Shelley's other novels. As noted in the introduction above, it contrasted in its use of "moral anomaly" in the shaping of all its characters except for Ethel. But many similarities to Shelley's previous works exist. It so closely shares themes with *Mathilda* (1819; published in 1959) and *Falkner* (1837) that they are often discussed as a group by Shelley scholars, an approach that falls within the purview of intertextual analysis. This approach holds that nothing is written in a vacuum; texts reflect the influence of other texts. For instance, as Lisa Vargo reminds us, early in *Lodore,* Shelley compares Ethel to Miranda, Shakespeare's character in *The Tempest,* and Mary Wollstonecraft had featured five excerpts from that play in her *The Female Reader* (1789). Vargo notes that in Wollstonecraft's hands, Miranda is fashioned as a model for middle-class culture, and that modeling is reflected in the characterizations of both Fanny and Ethel. While intertextuality most commonly examines texts by other authors that influence the writer, the approach may expand to also include texts written by Shelley.

Shared themes in Shelley's novels include incest, of interest to psychoanalytic critics; and the idealization of the Victorian family, of interest to feminist and psychoanalytic critics. The latter is thoroughly developed by both *Falkner* and *Lodore* in their lengthier format, whereas the former is further developed and is an overt theme in *Mathilda.* All three novels feature father/daughter relationships of an unnaturally heightened emotional nature. All three offer daughters who represent the angelic and self-sacrificing personality that the public wished in its women, and those daughters in all three instances are surrogate wives for their fathers. In Lodore's case, he marries a child bride in Cornelia, a situation also suggestive of unnatural affections. Her childlike purity is made clear when he first sees her dressed in white muslin, material used for infant clothes and suggestive of purity. Lodore metaphorically steals a child from her crib, fathering her first child when she is only 17. His teen wife later takes an interest in Lodore's illegitimate son, and the novel's incestuous overtones—or at least its suggestion of aberrant sexual relationships—strengthen.

Lord Lodore takes his daughter Ethel away from her mother at puberty, literally moving her into isolation, where she matures under his instructions to obey "his will." Freudian critics would view this as the perfect scenario for development of the Electra complex, which corresponds to the Oedipus complex for boys. In a two-parent household, a girl will be discouraged by her mother from pursuing her father romantically, and vice versa. However, in Lodore's American residence, no such controls exist, and Ethel is framed by a wild and, by suggestion, lawless landscape that would turn a blind eye to unnatural relationships. The narrator states that "Her earliest feeling was love of her father" and that she "grew into the image on which his eye doted, and for whose presence his heart perpetually yearned." The reader also learns that Lodore loves Ethel "with more than a father's fondness," a clearly suggestive statement to Freudian critics. He "fashioned his offspring to be the wife of a frail human being, and instructed her to be yielding, and to make it her duty to devote herself to his happiness." Readers may be forewarned of Lodore's patriarchal attitude early in the novel in his interaction with Cornelia: Women are to be used, and no affection for them is required. One could counter that Shelley simply reflects in that final passage influence by Milton and his shaping of Eve through specific dialogue as Adam's servant.

Like most women of her time, Ethel is fashioned to lack any sense of self, including a desire for personal happiness or fulfillment outside of a relationship with a male. In the end, such women remain without identity, apart from the male to whom they are attached. As Anne K. Mellor has written, Ethel and Shelley's additional heroines lack mothers and sisters who might offer a constructive model that would allow them to develop any sense of self. Mellor notes that Ethel's education is based on the teachings of Jean-Jacques Rousseau, studied by both Shelley and her mother, Mary Wollstonecraft. Rousseau wrote in *Emile* that a woman must possess "good-nature or sweetness of temper; formed to obey a being so imperfect as man . . . she ought to learn betimes even to suffer injustice and to bear the insults of a husband without complaint." Ethel fills this description; she is depicted as "gentle and docile" and one for whom pleasing "her father was the unsleeping law of all her actions, while his approbation imparted a sense of such pure but entire happiness, that every other feeling faded into insignificance in the comparison." Later readers view such a description as a negative, rather than as the positive the Victorian times intended it to be.

Feminist critics take note of Lord Lodore's definition of woman as a pre-Fall Eve or as a proper lady permitted by males to exist within a male domain. He basically dooms all women to sacrifice themselves for the sake of their families, a crucial aspect of his feminine ideal. Although he references an innocent Eve, the suggestion of temptation in that reference looms large, as does that of sexual exploitation. Women may define themselves only through their relationships with others, and that definition begins in relationship to males. Ethel adores her father and will naturally search for a husband who can step into a patriarchal role. She meets and develops a relationship with Edward Villiers due to his relationship with her father; he is literally Lord Lodore's "second," the closest she can get to her dead father, and he will continue her father's domination. When the two begin to see one another in England, readers are told that Ethel does "not think of love," and as Villiers becomes an important part of her existence through daily habit, "she entertain[s] his idea chiefly as having been the friend of Lodore." She thinks of him as "a fond elder brother." Villiers characterizes Ethel as an angel and scolds her on occasion as he might a child, two views of women encouraged by the pre-Victorian era. When they are separated she suffers from a complete lack of survival skills, noting that fact as a weakness in her father's education. In the scene where they wait for Fanny to bring money to pay for their meal, Ethel "employed herself in netting a purse, (the inutility of which Villiers smilingly remarked)" as he reads Shakespeare aloud to her. His intellectual activity should be taken seriously, while her artistic activity is seen as frivolous. When she attempts to discuss the injustice of the rich not sharing with the poor, a point that would interest Marxist critics, Edward dismisses her ideas by labeling her "eloquent" but a "little wild American" who states a "philosophy" applicable only to the backwoods—that is, to people who lack civilized sensibilities.

Feminist critics also note that Shelley has placed Fanny Derham in the novel to demonstrate that not all women needed to be dependent on men. The narrator makes clear the contrast between Lodore and Derham in describing the education of their daughters:

> The one fashioned his offspring to be the wife of a frail human being, and instructed her to be yielding, and to make it her duty to devote herself to his happiness, and to obey his will. The other sought to guard his from all weakness, to make her complete in herself, and to render her independent and self-sufficing.

However, that lack of dependence results in cultural disapproval. Fanny pays a price for her independence and her scholarly pursuits, which make her an outcast in her patriarchal society. She has no place in a society that values marriage above all, again made clear by the narrator: "Such a woman as Fanny was more made to be loved by her own sex than by the opposite one. Superiority of intellect, joined to acquisitions beyond those usual even to men; ... forms a kind of anomaly little in accord with masculine taste." Women feel no threat from Fanny, so they can trust her and even appreciate her unusual attributes.

Shelley desired a life of the mind, out of reach to a woman of her era, and she may have projected her desires onto Fanny. She also created Fanny in opposition to her celebration of the bourgeois pre-Victorian family, again perhaps undercutting that fantasy and supplying a subtext that works against the story's surface message. The reader also realizes that without Fanny's assistance, Ethel and Villiers might never have been relieved of their burden. She acts as a buffer against the bailiffs who visit her mother's home searching for Edward, she brings the letter of credit from Aunt Elizabeth that literally allows the couple to eat again, and she visits Cornelia with news of Ethel's plight. Fanny's father had required Lord Lodore's protection, but Lodore's daughter clearly requires hers.

While the reader discovers the fates of all other women in the novel, Fanny's remains a mystery. Fanny is an "odd woman," as George Gissing, in his novel *Odd Women* (1893), would later label women who were unmarried and unable to make a career. Fanny admits that her older sister, properly married and with a child, is the better confidante for their mother, having fulfilled the traditional role. Still, Shelley saves information about Fanny until the novel closes when she devotes a long paragraph in which the narrator paradoxically explains why one cannot explain Fanny's "varied fate":

> She continued for some time among her beloved friends, innocent and calm as she was

beautiful and wise; ... One who feels so deeply for others, and yet is so stern a censor over herself ... so single-minded and upright, and yet open as day to charity and affection, cannot hope to pass from youth to age unharmed. Deceit, and selfishness, and the whole web of human passion must envelope her, and occasion her many sorrows; ... still she cannot be contaminated. She will ... pursue her way unflinching; and in her ... love of truth and in her integrity, she will find support and reward in her various fortunes. What the events are ... cannot now be recounted; and it would require the gift of prophecy to foretell the conclusion.

The adjective *varied* surely indicates a fate that varies from that of the norm. Mellor believes that Shelley could not allow her narrator to predict Fanny's "conclusion" because no model yet existed for Fanny. Mellor writes that Fanny represents Shelley's "recognition of the limits and failures of her own ideology." But possibly inherent to the fact that Fanny could live an existence unimagined is Shelley's belief that such limits are meant to be shattered.

Feminist and psychoanalytic critics would also be interested in the role of the mother—or, in the case of Shelley's fiction, her absence. In all of Shelley's writing about families, the mother dies early on or is absent, causing her offspring to feel acute abandonment and males to take center stage. Victor Frankenstein's mother dies; Mathilda's mother dies immediately following her birth, and the aunt who raises her dies when she is a teenager; Elizabeth Raby's mother in *Falkner* dies; and Lady Cornelia Lodore prioritizes social activity over the care of her daughter. Psychoanalytic critics would note that in the case of incest, such abandonment by death or selected absence may be viewed by the young woman left behind as betrayal.

In *Lodore*, the fact that Cornelia resurrects and acts upon her love for Ethel 20 years following her abandonment of her daughter redeems the relationship, but only after Cornelia pays an enormous personal price in an act that places her safely in the realm of the sacrificial female: She literally gives up her identity when she gives away her material possessions, including her home, and leaves her friends. Prior to her final acts, she stood in stark contrast to her daughter, as she sacrificed for her social position while Ethel sacrificed for her husband.

Most critics view Lord Lodore as a reproduction of the controlling aspects of Shelley's own father. Lodore insists on absolute obedience, and Ethel responds perfectly, bending to his will while adoring him. She sacrifices all independence and semblance of spirit in response to a simple look from him and is compared to a puppet through an allusion to "a silken string." Ethel does not fear her father but, rather, idealizes him. She is completely honest and exists to serve others, meeting Coventry Patmore's later Victorian requirements for the "Angel in the House," described in his 1854 poem. She is sweet, joyous, buoyant, and educated to "enlarge her mind," yet she still obeys her father's every command. As for Lord Lodore, Shelley writes, "He lived but for her and in her," a troubling suggestion of unhealthy obsession. His death devastates the 18-year-old Ethel, who feels that she may as well have died with him. She falls "in love with death, which alone could reunite her" with her father. This passage echoes one in Shelley's *Mathilda*, written in 1820 but not published until 1959, when, at the story's conclusion, the title character notes, "In truth I am in love with death; ... Alone it will unite me to my father when in an eternal mental union we shall never part." On at least one occasion, Shelley herself seemed to contemplate taking her life, but she moved past the moment in consideration of her son's best interest.

Those who seek to see Shelley's life reflected in her fiction speculate that she was looking for the family life that she herself lacked. If that is true, her seeking a satisfying fictional family life to replace her own discordant one fails repeatedly. Mellor suggests that Shelley's fictional families might have failed because she was incapable of imagining a fulfilling daughter-parent relationship, based on her personal experience. Some may see such a judgment as too harsh in light of Shelley's often positive relationship with her father. Although he was a controlling force in his daughter's life, such was the ethos of his era. He did serve as her adviser and editor, but Shelley also wrote material, like that in *Mathilda,* with the power to make him so self-conscious that he would not publish it, even though he lost the income it might have generated. And she seemed to enjoy an affectionate relationship not only with her surviving child, Percy, but also with her daughter-in-law, suggesting that, if not in fiction, perhaps in reality she did at least learn to live with disappointments from her own youth in order to enjoy her maturity.

As a father figure and as a husband, Villiers follows Lodore in betraying his responsibility to Ethel, eventually moving her near debtors' prison where he was confined. Ethel's self-sacrifice for the sake of her husband is the central action of the last portion of the novel, moving her mother to resurrect their relationship. Cornelia sacrifices her identity, severing social connections and leveraging her small fortune to pay her son-in-law's debt. Once Cornelia becomes a "good woman" like her daughter, Shelley rewards her sacrifice with a new husband in the form of Horatio Saville, viscount of Maristow and Shelley's ideal man. He is learned, "mild . . . and forebearing," adjectives that also described Ethel under her father's tutelage. By the novel's conclusion, then, Ethel and Cornelia are safe in relationships with adoring husbands, on the surface validating Lord Lodore's edict. But feminists may read this conclusion in reverse, instead recognizing that it is the women who rescued the men.

As Lisa Vargo notes, of the various daughter/parent relationships, Shelley spends the most effort developing that between Cornelia Lodore and her mother, Mrs. Santerre, but it is doomed from the beginning. In Mrs. Santerre, readers see a stereotype of the meddling mother who alienates her son-in-law from his wife by insisting that Cornelia enjoy the society to which Lodore has introduced her. The narrator notes of Lodore that "he, with strong pride and crushed affections, gave himself up for a disappointed man. He disdained to struggle with the sinister influence of his mother-in-law." Feminists would note that he turns a hypocritical blind eye to the fact that he is actually the tempter of his teenage wife; her mother simply supports his actions. He quickly yields to Mrs. Santerre's force and blames the victim, for "while he cherished a deep and passionate hatred for the cause, he grew to despise the victim of her arts. He thought that he perceived duplicity, low-thoughted pride, and coldness of heart, the native growth of the daughter of such a mother." Lady Santerre teaches Cornelia to value social success above that of her family relationships. A child herself, Cornelia cannot behave toward their daughter in the manner required by Lodore; rather, she turns back to the social role at which she has become so adept. She views Lodore as selfish, "incapable of the softness of love or the kindness of friendship."

For the sake of her daughter, Cornelia "had signed away all that she possessed—she had done it with a smile—and her voice was unfaltering." Unlike males who dream of accolades for their sacrifices, Cornelia assumes that following her disappearance, "her name and memory would equally vanish from the earth, and she be thought of no more. If Ethel ever entertained a wish to see her, Villiers would be at hand to check and divert it." She reverses the actions of her own mother, who blocked her husband from developing a normal relationship with his wife. Feminists would also point out that Cornelia's action is far more heroic than any previous actions of Lord Lodore or even Villiers, whose situation demands sacrifice of his child bride, rather than of himself.

If Villiers was modeled on a realistic view of Percy Bysshe Shelley's irresponsibility, Saville represents the idealized Percy. The narrator describes him as one of that group who is "tolerant of the follies of their fellows—who sympathize with, and assist their wishes, and who apparently forget their own desires, as they devote themselves to the accomplishment of those of their friends, . . . they can divest themselves of selfishness, and incorporate in their own being the pleasures and pains of those around them." This reads like a description of the female ideal to which Lodore subscribed. Again, Shelley strongly suggests that in order for the family to function, men as well as women must assume the burden of placing the family before self. The narrator also makes the point that Saville's forbearance may have made him appear cold and withdrawn to others. After all, Cornelia disastrously misinterpreted that forbearance and, without perceiving how he would interpret her actions, almost ended all hope of either for future happiness. Some critics suggest that Shelley describes herself in that aspect of Saville, answering the charges against her of "coldness" from Percy at times during their relationship, and from Leigh Hunt and Jane Williams following Percy's death.

In another approach, Fiona Stafford theorizes that Shelley made a business decision in regard to subject matter and style and responded to a marketplace that demanded silver-fork fiction. But Stafford does see the subject matter as timely in relation to social unrest, which could affect attitudes toward the upper social classes. Through *Lodore,* Shelley analyzes what Stafford labels "aristocratic degeneration." Lodore makes questionable decisions specifically based on his social class. He loses his wife through a social gaffe; dies defending his aristocratic honor; and leaves as an inheritance for his daughter isolation, loneliness, and a lack of logistical survival skills. Villiers, as Lodore's metaphoric double, almost does the same, saved only by Ethel's one-dimensional goodness, Fanny's intellect, and her mother's wealth.

The influence of the romantics' writings on Shelley remains clear in all of her stories, with *Lodore* being no exception. Critics point out that although her choice of name for Lord Lodore is never explained, it must relate to Lodore Falls, mentioned by almost all romantics in their poetry. Coleridge especially describes the falls' effects, which are echoed by Lodore when he first sees Niagara Falls. Lodore emphasizes not just the wild nature of the falls but the resemblance of that nature to his own impetuous, uncontrollable character. Water falls where natural forces direct it, with disregard for human needs, and the irresponsible Lodore goes his way, reacting to forces around him, rather than being proactive for the sake of his family.

Cornelia Lodore, whose largest role in the story is as a socialite and a disreputable mother, ends her time on the page experiencing maternal passions while observing Mother Nature. She thinks, "[N]ature is the refuge and home for women; they have no public career—no aim nor end beyond their domestic circle; but they can extend that, and make all the creations of nature their own, to foster and do good to." She comes to believe that through nature, women can learn to turn their "steps to the habitation which God has given as befitting his creatures, contemplate the lovely ornaments with which he has blessed the earth," activities far preferable to becoming "the mere puppet of one's own vanity." The reader recalls the scene in which Cornelia was introduced, trapped in the hills in a terrific thunderstorm, under attack by nature and disoriented by the deluge. By the novel's end, she has made peace with her own role as a mother, and apparently Mother Nature has also made peace with her. While the passage echoes the romantic belief in the majesty of nature, it also supports Shelley's message regarding the importance of the family unit.

CHARACTERS

Lord Lodore Henry Fitzhenry, later Lord Lodore, has been perceived in various ways by readers, depending on the era. Readers of Shelley's time found him both admirable and a scoundrel, while later readers have viewed him more sympathetically as a man doomed by a code of honor inherited along with his title. Critics postulate that Shelley uses Lodore, along with his later surrogate, Villiers, as a cautionary tale that focuses on the perils of membership among traditional 19th-century aristocracy. Whether she precisely asks for sympathy from readers is doubtful, but just as audiences have for centuries enjoyed catharsis when watching members of the aristocracy reach a tragic ending resulting from "overweening pride," they may find such a release in watching Lodore's self-fashioned doom.

Lodore is only one representative of pride in the novel, as it appears in various forms in Villiers, Cornelia, and even Ethel, often misconstrued and misdirected. Contemporary critics took issue with the novel's title, as its namesake disappears so early in the novel. However, others point out that even in death, Lodore's presence looms large and acts to control much of the plot beyond his demise. Shelley would have seen that presence as realistic based on her husband's influence on her whole life following his accidental death only a few years into their marriage.

One could argue that Shelley does not shape Lodore to be a one-dimensional womanizer, as he undergoes visible conflict and seems to change as a result while living in Illinois. Yet the overall impression that he makes on readers may lack depth. That lack could be due to the accepted one-dimensional, colorless character of Ethel, his seemingly single positive accomplishment. One can envision his absence long before it occurs, knowing that Ethel will struggle without him, and that struggle will curiously help define those around her more than it does her. Lodore is born to live in mental anguish, his particular blend of intellect and passion causing him to reject humanity at the same time that he longs to embrace it. However, the humanity for which he longs is a fantasy, one that he passes along to Ethel in his gender stereotypes. When struggling over his decision to leave London for America, Lodore is described as "the reverse of a philosopher; and the more he gazed and considered, the more imperfect and distorted became his perception."

Lodore resembles the waterfall for which he is named, and the passage in which he visits Niagara Falls is a seminal scene for any reader who wants to better understand him. The narrator tells the reader that Lodore watched the falls, "whose everlasting and impetuous flow mirrored the dauntless but rash energy of his soul," and the next statement that he momentarily considered plunging into the water is not surprising. This is particularly true if we recall the statement about the younger Fitzhenry that Shelley quotes from Byron's *Childe Harold's Pilgrimage* (1816), originally written about Napoleon: "Quiet to quick bosoms is a hell." Lodore momentarily envisions himself "a blot in the creation; his hopes, and fears, and resolves a worthless web of ill-assorted ideas, best swept away at once from the creation." Such passages support the suggestion by some that Lodore represents a Byronic hero, but he lacks the mysterious background generally attributed to that characterization. On the contrary, it is clearly his aristocratic background that causes him so much trouble, again perhaps a strong message from Shelley.

Lady Cornelia Lodore At first, Lady Lodore attracts readers, appearing as a young innocent with a questionable future. That appeal later lessens when she retains her loyalty to her mother, rather than forming a new loyalty to her husband. She chooses to construct an active social life that restricts her contact with her family. Because one's husband and child are prioritized by Shelley and readers, Cornelia Lodore appears to be abnormal, rejecting the traditional wife and mother roles. Instead, she chooses to remain primarily a daughter and becomes locked in a youthful fantasy of high society. Even when Lord Lodore removes Ethel from Cornelia's care and takes her to America, Lady Lodore continues her lifestyle and suffers little. Her occasional bitter thoughts of her husband's betrayal cannot be labeled remorse; rather, they result from pride. Because she listens to her mother rather than obey her own instincts, she misses opportunities to enjoy a traditional existence with her husband and daughter.

Although Cornelia lives apart from Ethel, her natural effect on her daughter is strong, made clear in a passage early in the second volume as Villiers observes Ethel before she has met her mother:

> There was something in her gesture and manner as she left them, that reminded Villiers of Lady Lodore. It was one of those mysterious family resemblances, which are so striking and powerful, and yet which it is impossible to point out to a stranger. A bligh (as this indescribable resemblance is called in some parts of England) of her mother struck Villiers forcibly.

Cornelia's profile softens somewhat years later, following her mother's death, but that results from her feelings for Saville. She has remained admirable in her years of restraint, living an exemplary existence during which time not a whiff of scandal has touched her. Finally she has found a man to whom she is attracted, and with the news of the death of her husband, she has a chance to find happiness. However, her pride interferes, and she pays dearly for her mother's strict training in role playing and appears to lose forever any chance for true love. Cornelia remains a character with a lesson to be learned. It is a lesson that will be taught to her by her daughter in a role reversal of parent and child.

When Cornelia learns that Villiers is living in the debtors' prison and Ethel in poverty and observes Ethel's complete devotion to Villiers, she practices self-sacrifice as well for the first time. Cornelia barters away her own sense of self as she rids herself of her wealth in order to redeem Villiers's debt. With her loss of social standing comes a loss of self-identity, and she removes to nature, allowing Shelley to emphasize the importance of nature to the romantics. It is specifically associated with women and nurture, as Lady Lodore muses: "[N]ature is the refuge and home for women; they have no public career—no aim nor end beyond their domestic circle." However, they can avoid "feelings which are pregnant with disquiet or misery" by turning to God as found in nature. The term *pregnant* further aligns nature with women and Lady Lodore with Eve, her first husband's model of perfection. In addition, she ends up living in an older woman's house and caring for that woman, thus in the second half of her life fulfilling the caretaker role expected of women, a role perfectly modeled by her daughter. The fact that Cornelia gains a decidedly excellent second husband in Saville, complete with wealth and connections, as a result of her self-sacrifice alerts the reader to the rewards inherent to such behavior. Cornelia serves as a didactic figure for Shelley's readers, along with Lodore, Villiers, and Ethel.

Ethel Ethel has been thoroughly discussed above. Suffice to say that her goodness renders her a flat character, one of little interest other than as a conduit for the passions of several key characters and as their foil. Shelley excuses her lack of intrigue by rendering her a child of nature, naive to the ways of humans due to a lack of socialization during her youth. Shelley does not offer the reader balance between the innocent, nonsocial Ethel and the wise, complete social creature of Cornelia. However, she does seem to privilege isolation and nature, granting those rewards to both daughter and mother and thus forming a strong parallel between them. Cornelia ends up finding her best self while at work in a garden, just as Ethel has her strongest thoughts while outdoors. Ethel does her best thinking in nature and often with a book in her hand, although she cannot be labeled a true student of either. Ethel desires to love and serve and, of all the characters in the book, becomes the most fulfilled in doing just that.

Edward Villiers Readers of later generations would not find Villiers a sympathetic character, seeing him as a man who will not take a job in order to pay his debts. However, he served Shelley's purpose to emphasize silver-fork society and to remove the gilt from the view of upper society adopted by her contemporaries. Lisa Vargo sees Villiers, along with Cornelia and Saville's sisters, as a means for Shelley to offer a social critique.

Fanny Derham Fanny's appeal to feminist critics is discussed above, as well as the fact that she has the last word, so to speak, in the novel, ironically through her silence. While Anne K. Mellor comments that Shelley concludes the novel with Derham's story that "cannot be told" to emphasize the limitations of her beliefs regarding women and their power, or lack of it, Lisa Vargo disagrees. She counters Mellor's claim by suggesting that Shelley's conclusion focuses on Derham in order to "challenge . . . her society to recognize the possibilities of social transformation." Fanny's independence and desire for intellectual pursuits sets her apart from her early years, but she has the strength of character to value that isolation, in contrast to Ethel and Cornelia. She is also used by Shelley to emphasize the difference between her father and Lord Lodore in their attitudes about raising not just children but specifically girls. Where Lodore raises Ethel to serve others, Derham raises Fanny to serve herself, not in a self-absorbed way but more to tend to her own needs and not lead a life of complete self-sacrifice. That is why she can assist Ethel as she does. Had Fanny been a carbon copy of Ethel, she could not have been so active on Ethel's behalf. She seems to take Ethel on as a project of sorts, recognizing in Ethel's weakness her own strength. The two are too different to become true friends, as were their fathers. Although Lodore sees Derham as his only friend and supporter, that thought exists only after

Lodore's years of self-exile, during which time he never saw Derham. The two go separate ways early on, emphasizing their character differences, which will be further emphasized in their daughters.

As are other of Shelley's characters, Fanny is aligned with nature, particularly in the scene by Niagara Falls when she delivers her father's letter to Lodore. When Lodore first notices her standing nearby, "the thunder of the waters prevented speech." Fanny is silenced by the force recently compared directly to Lodore, representing the silencing of bright women by powerful men. She hands the letter to Lodore and blushes, a sure sign of discomfort in the one-on-one interaction with a male, foreshadowing her later choice to reject romance and love. When she departs, her description aligns her with a deer or antelope: "[S]he sprung away up the rocky pathway," emphasizing her free spirit.

FURTHER READING

Armstrong, Nancy. *The Ideology of Conduct: Essays in Literature and the History of Sexuality*. London: Methuen, 1987.

Blumberg, Jane. *Mary Shelley's Early Novels: This Child of Imagination and Misery*. London: Palgrave Macmillan, 1993.

Cronin, Richard. "Mary Shelley and Edward Bulwer: *Lodore* and Hybrid Fiction." In *Mary Shelley's Fictions: From Frankenstein to Falkner*, edited by Michael Eberle-Sinatra, 39–56. New York: St. Martin's Press, 2000.

Eberle-Sinatra, Michael, ed. *Mary Shelley's Fictions: From* Frankenstein *to* Falkner. New York: St. Martin's Press, 2000.

Ellis, Sarah Stickney. "Characteristics of the Women of England." In *The Women of England*. London: Fisher, Son & Co., 1839, 9–38.

Jump, Harriet Divine, ed. *Silver Fork Novels: 1826–1841*. Vol. 6. London: Pickering & Chatto, 2005.

McCracken, David. *Wordsworth and the Lake District*. Oxford: Oxford University Press, 1984.

Mellor, Anne K. *Mary Shelley: Her Life, Her Fiction, Her Monsters*. London: Routledge, 1989.

Mitchell, L. G. *Bulwer Lytton: The Rise and Fall of a Victorian Man of Letters*. New York: Hambledon and London, 2003.

Rosa, Matthew Whiting. *The Silver-Fork School: Novels of Fashion Preceding* Vanity Fair. New York: Columbia University Press, 1936.

Shelley, Mary. *Lodore*. Edited by Lisa Vargo. Peterborough, Ontario, Canada: Broadview Press, 1997.

———. *Selected Letters of Mary Wollstonecraft Shelley*. Edited by Betty T. Bennett. Baltimore: Johns Hopkins University Press, 1995.

Stocking, Marion Kingston, ed. *The Clairmont Correspondence*. 2 vols. Baltimore: Johns Hopkins Press, 1995.

Sunstein, Emily W. *Mary Shelley: Romance and Reality*. Boston: Little Brown, 1989.

Vallins, David. "Mary Shelley and the Lake Poets: Negation and Transcendence in *Lodore*." In *Mary Shelley's Fictions: From Frankenstein to Falkner*, edited by Michael Eberle-Sinatra, 164–179. New York: St. Martin's Press, 2000.

Williams, Nicholas M. "Angelic Realism: Domestic Idealization in Mary Shelley's *Lodore*." *Studies in the Novel* (December 22, 2007): 397–415.

Wollstonecraft, Mary. *A Vindication of the Rights of Woman: With Strictures on Political and Moral Subjects*. London: J. Johnson, 1792.

Mathilda (1959)

Mary Shelley's second work of fiction, the 80-page novella *Mathilda*, is described by the critic E. J. Clery as "a tale of incestuous desire and suicidal remorse." Shelley wrote *Mathilda*, sometimes spelled *Matilda*, in 1819 and 1820, and had designated all income from the project to support her father, WILLIAM GODWIN, who read and commented on her manuscripts. However, Godwin was distressed by its subject matter and withheld it from publication; it would not be published until 1959. Shelley wrote the novel following the death of her infant daughter Clara in September 1818 and her toddler son William in June 1819. Well along in pregnancy with her son Percy Florence, Shelley was revising the manuscript just before his birth. Scholars have been fortunate to have Shelley's rough draft, titled *Fields of Fancy*, as well as the complete manuscript with which to compare the published novel. Both the draft and finished work, along with introductory material, are available in electronic form online through Project Gutenberg.

The manuscript's three notebooks were lodged in several locations following Mary's death. The Bodleian Library held one portion as part of the Shelley papers, with instructions from Mary Shelley that they be available only to serious scholars and then with restrictions. Family members had other portions of the manuscript and did not make them available to the public for study for many decades. Sir John Shelley-Rolls, PERCY BYSSHE SHELLEY's grandnephew, did offer his third notebook for public review. Eventually all parts came together as the only complete Mary Shelley manuscript in existence. All three notebooks contain portions of other crucial works by both Shelleys including, Percy's *Prometheus Unbound* and *A Defence of Poetry*.

Elizabeth Nitchie, the editor of an electronic version of *Mathilda*, adds this note:

> The finished draft, *Mathilda*, still shows Mary Shelley's faults as a writer: verbosity, loose plotting, somewhat stereotyped and extravagant characterization. The reader must be tolerant of its heroine's overwhelming lamentations. But she is, after all, in the great tradition of romantic heroines: she compares her own weeping to that of Boccaccio's Ghismonda over the heart of Guiscardo. If the reader can accept Mathilda on her own terms, he will find not only biographical interest in her story but also intrinsic merits: a feeling for character and situation and phrasing that is often vigorous and precise.

SYNOPSIS

As the novel's narrator, Mathilda explains to her reader, "I am alone—quite alone—in the world—the blight of misfortune has passed over me and withered me; I know that I am about to die." She explains that for a time, she thought she should not share her horrible tale, but now that she will soon die, its "mystic terrors" are diluted. The narrator addresses someone; readers will later discover it is Woodville, a man Mathilda meets in the woods. She explains the motives for the actions she is going to relate, noting they were not evil; rather, she lacked judgment. She adds that her fate has been governed by "a hideous necessity," and then she begins her tale.

Chapter 1

The novel's first chapter details the story of Mathilda's father, a wealthy youth to whom Shelley gives no name. After his father's death, he is indulged by his mother and allowed to read and enjoy his freedom with plenty of money to spend. By nature, he is vain and extravagant, but he is well educated, attending Eton and university. Although self-centered, he enjoys pleasing others. However, "By a strange narrowness of ideas he viewed all the world in connexion only as it was or was not related to his little society."

He falls in love with a wealthy neighbor's eldest daughter, Diana, and her good nature helps guide his passions for the good as well: "He looked up to her as his guide, and such was his adoration that he delighted to augment to his own mind the sense of inferiority with which she sometimes impressed him." Of her mother, Mathilda states, "There were few who could boast of so pure a heart, and so much real humbleness of soul joined to a firm reliance on her own integrity and a belief in that of others." She was a child when she lost her mother, and her father devoted himself to her education, sparking her joy of reading. Diana particularly favored the classics and spoke to Mathilda's father of her high morals and ethics, as well as her political ideology. Mathilda's father also reads widely, but little of works written during the most recent 50 years. His mother died when he was 19, and he married Diana just before his 20th birthday, casting off his frivolous friends in favor of her superior wisdom. She has torn the veil that obscured his vision, and he can now hardly believe he had "joined in the cant words and ideas of his fellow collegiates." Mathilda is born 15 months later, but Diana dies, and Mathilda's father deserts her, seeking to escape his grief over the loss of his wife.

Mathilda matures in Scotland in the care of an aunt, his father's sister, who says of her father that following Diana's death, "she never heard him utter a single word: buried in the deepest melancholy he took no notice of any one; often for hours his eyes streamed tears or a more fearful gloom overpowered him." He wrote once to his sister to assure her of his safety in Hamburg, and Mathilda carries the letter with her. Later, her father writes to his sister, explaining that he plans to travel to the East. Mathilda reveals the contents of the letter, which reads, in part, "When I leave this place do not expect to hear from me: I must break all ties that at present exist. I shall become a wanderer, a miserable outcast—alone! alone!" He also bids his sister to care well for Mathilda, whom he may one day see. He leaves Hamburg and travels to Turkey, changing his name to prevent his family from locating him.

Chapter 2

In the second chapter, Mathilda's story begins. For almost 16 years, she lives with her aunt, whom she describes as coldhearted. During her first seven years, she is attended by a servant who had previously been with Diana. Mathilda wanders the countryside of Loch Lomond, developing a passion for nature; she declares that she loves every object, every animal. When the servant departs, Mathilda is heartbroken, and her isolation begins. Her only pleasure arises from nature, as her aunt shares little in the way of physical love. This causes Mathilda to truly revel in the outdoors; she writes, "When rocked by the waves of the lake my spirits rose in triumph as a horseman feels with pride the motions of his high fed steed." Her aunt does encourage her to learn to play the harp, at which Mathilda excels, and she practices escapism by pretending herself to be a Miltonic and Shakespearean heroine. Her "aerial creations" often involve her parents and incorporate ideas of the sublime. A voracious reader like her parents, she balances her reading of fancy with the Enlightenment logic of Alexander Pope and also learns history, engaging in rational thought as well as emotional expression. By the conclusion of the second chapter, Mathilda is fantasizing the scene of reunion with her father in detail.

Chapter 3

Chapter 3 opens with the receipt of a letter from Mathilda's father; she is now 16 years old. He asks whether Mathilda's aunt will bring her to London, or whether he should travel to Scotland. The decision is made for him to come to Scotland, and Mathilda anxiously waits during his three-day journey. She is on the lake when he arrives, and Shelley's hyperbolic description fits GOTHIC FICTION's demand for excess: "As I came, dressed in white, covered only by my tartan *rachan*, my hair streaming on my shoulders, and shooting across with greater speed than it could be supposed I could give to my boat, my father has often told me that I looked more like a spirit than a human maid." With that description, Mathilda's father joins her fantasy world, attributing metaphysical power to her and predicting his daughter's early demise into spirit form.

Mathilda is delighted with her father's stories of exotic lands and is touched by the change that has taken place in him as compared to the descriptions she had heard. He has a "feeling of unreality" and speaks of what seems a dream world. Mathilda remarks, "He talked of my Mother as if she had lived but a few weeks before; not that he expressed poignant grief, but his description of her person, and his relation of all anecdotes connected with her was thus fervent and vivid." Mathilda feels herself reborn and compares her life to a river, flowing with new ideas. She foreshadows the future by telling Woodview, "I lament now, I must ever lament, those few short months of Paradisaical bliss; I disobeyed no command, I ate no apple, and yet I was ruthlessly driven from it." As for her father, "He was, as it were, now awakened from his long, visionary sleep."

With Diana dead and his friends at a distance, all her father has is Mathilda. She enjoys showing him the Loch Lomond area, and all is wonderful, but Mathilda says, "I drank of an enchanted cup but gall was at the bottom of its long drawn sweetness," warning the reader of changes to come. Those changes begin with her aunt's death. Mathilda's father compares her grief over the loss of her aunt to his grief over the loss of her mother. The two return to London five months after their reunion, and her father constantly fixes his gaze of love and affection upon Mathilda. Again she reminds the reader, via Woodbine, that supreme happiness would soon become despair.

Chapter 4

The fourth chapter begins in the London setting where, as to be expected, a young man becomes attentive to Mathilda. Although she does not return his affection and is relieved when it ends, the brief relationship disturbs her father, evoking a change in his attitude and behavior. E. J. Clery notes that the suitor's rejection begins "a Fall from Paradise," reflecting on Mathilda's previous use of the term *paradisiacal bliss*. Mathilda compares the sudden nature of the change in her father's demeanor to a bolt of lightning. One day her father adores her, and the next he shuns her. She compares her condition to that of Proserpine, who, while gathering flowers, was kidnapped by the "King of Hell." Mathilda tries to pretend it is all a bad dream. The predatory nature of the evolving relationship is foreshadowed when Mathilda says, "I was dashed down from heaven to earth as a silly sparrow when pounced on by a hawk." She terms her father's mind "diseased," perhaps as an excuse for the actions that will follow. He announces that they will travel to Yorkshire, where he spent his childhood. He goes first and sends for Mathilda four days later, instructing her to meet him at the home he shared with her mother. She determines to persuade him to explain his change in attitude toward her and to learn what secret he hides. The chapter closes with her comment, "Half I accomplished; I gained his secret and we were both lost for ever."

Chapter 5

In chapter 5, Mathilda puts into action her resolution to rescue her father from his negative state, with the time frame being a year following their reunion. She turns to nature and its divinity to urge his communication, hoping that if he will talk about the cause of his change in attitude toward her, she can alter that attitude. However, he chides her for her presumption, saying, "In the heart of one like me there are secret thoughts working, and secret tortures which you ought not to seek to discover." She argues that she must know whether she is in any way responsible for his torments and goads him to speak. In a reflection on the importance of the "word," the focus of the poet and storyteller, he replies, "One word I might speak and then you would be implicated in my destruction; yet that word is hovering on my lips. Oh! There is a fearful chasm; but I adjure you to beware!" Reflecting on Mathilda's comparison of herself to the Furies, mythical female creatures who stalk those who break nature's rules and drive them insane, he adds later, "I tell you I am on the very verge of insanity; why, cruel girl, do you drive me on: you will repent and I shall die."

Her father requests that Mathilda read Dante's writing to him, as that is what Diana used to read, then he changes his mind and requests to hear instead the descent of Sir Guyon to the Halls of Avarice. His attempted substitution of Mathilda for his dead wife, and the change in reading material to a tale of temptation and fall, again clearly signals readers as to the tragic nature of the rising action. Mathilda describes their retreat as more peaceful than their time in London, as her father often watches over her artistic pursuits. Still, he seems more melancholy and cannot sleep, problems Mathilda attributes to his having been reminded of Diana. She also wonders if, perhaps, he had fallen into unrequited love while in London. She determines to help relieve his misery, hoping to force him to speak with her about its cause. "Breathless" with emotion, she pleads with her father, "Listen to me, dearest friend, and permit me to gain your confidence. Are the happy days of mutual love which have passed to be to me as a dream never to return? Alas! You have a secret grief that destroys us both: but you must permit me to win this secret from you. Tell me, can I do nothing?" He finally confesses that she is the cause of his grief and warns her against pushing him to say more. She counters that his speaking his secret will bring peace, telling him, "do you think that I can live thus fearfully from day to day—the sword in my bosom yet kept from its mortal wound by a hair—a word!—I demand that dreadful word; though it be as a flash of lightning to destroy me, speak it."

At last, Mathilda's father gives in to her pleading. Although he does not make a clear statement of sexual desire, the reader and Mathilda understand his meaning:

> And then his manner changed, and fixing his eyes on me with an expression that convulsed every nerve and member of my frame—"... you are my light, my only one, my life.—My daughter, I love you!" The last words died away in a hoarse whisper, but I heard them and sunk on the ground, covering my face and almost dead with excess of sickness and fear: a cold perspiration covered my forehead and I shivered

Pluto abducts Proserpine while a group of nymphs cling to his chariot in *The Abduction of Proserpina*. This painting is from 1631. Mary Shelley based her drama *Proserpine* on this myth. *(Painting by Rembrandt van Rijn)*

in every limb—But he continued, clasping his hands with a frantic gesture.

Mathilda expresses her horror, then runs to the house and orders the servants to find her father where she left him. She escapes to her room.

Chapter 6

Chapter 6 focuses on Mathilda's distress over learning of her father's incestuous desire. At first she declares her father dead to her, but then she wonders if many years in the future, he might not be able again to act toward her as a father should. She places a curse upon him, silently commanding him to wander for another 16 years and then return as a parent to a child. The gothic style becomes clear in her thought that includes references to endless wandering, a ghost, and hell: "That he should be restless I understood; that he should wander as an unlaid ghost and find no quiet from the burning hell that consumed his heart." The last time that she catches sight of him, he is beneath a tree with a corpse-like appearance. The chapter closes as a servant delivers a letter to Mathilda from her father, explaining that he has departed and has left orders for the servants to care well for her.

Chapter 7
Chapter 7 begins with Mathilda reading her father's lengthy letter. He immediately declares his guilt and his intention:

> I have betrayed your confidence; I have endeavoured to pollute your mind, and have made your innocent heart acquainted with the looks and language of unlawful and monstrous passion. I must expiate these crimes, and must endeavour in some degree to proportionate my punishment to my guilt. You are I doubt not prepared for what I am about to announce; we must seperate [sic] and be divided for ever.

He compares himself to the devil and asks not for Mathilda's pity but for her pardon along with her abhorrence of him. He defends his request by recalling their first happy days together on Loch Lomond and recounts how often he had thought of her during her first 16 years, writing, "All delightful things, sublime scenery, soft breezes, exquisite music seemed to me associated with you and only through you to be pleasant to me." He compares her eyes to the "divine lights" of Beatrice that shone on Dante. He had believed himself able to overcome his unnatural love for her, but confesses that he could not. He adds,

> Yet I will not die; alas! how dare I go where I may meet Diana, when I have disobeyed her last request; her last words said in a faint voice when all feeling but love, which survives all things else was already dead, she then bade me make her child happy: that thought alone gives a double sting to death.

He makes clear that he carries several layers of guilt for his betrayal of the two women he should have best cherished. He notes that he plans never to see her again, advising, "You must forget me and all the evil that I have taught you. Cast off the only gift that I have bestowed upon you, your grief, and rise from under my blighting influence as no flower so sweet ever did rise from beneath so much evil." As Mathilda understands that death looms for her father, she thinks, "My blood froze at the thought: a sickening feeling of horror came over me that allowed not of tears." Where previously she had wished him dead, metaphorically if not physically, she withdraws that wish and prepares to pursue him. Such a pursuit of one character by another is a hallmark of the gothic tale.

Choked by emotions during the carriage ride, Mathilda notes the sympathy of the aged steward she has brought with her. She has a dream that her father has died in the sea, and for the remainder of her journey, she is filled with dread that her dream will become reality. When they reach an inn, they discover that her father left his horses and word that he was going out on foot but would be returning. Mathilda hires a guide to help her track him, although a tremendous storm has arisen. With the steward Gaspar still beside her as the thunder crashes around them, Mathilda says, "Mark, Gaspar, if the next flash of lightning rend not that oak my father will be alive." The next horrendous strike destroys the tree, and Mathilda fears she has prophesied her father's death. They discover he had reached a town and borrowed a horse, saying he was traveling another five miles to a small town close to the sea.

The pursuit continues, with Mathilda soaked and yet still burning with emotion. As they come closer to the ocean, Mathilda notes, "The sound is the same as that which I heard in my dream. It is the knell of my father which I hear." The chapter concludes on a highly emotional note as Mathilda and Gaspar enter a cottage by the sea:

> . . . we knocked at the door and it was opened: the bed within instantly caught my eye; some-

thing stiff and straight lay on it, covered by a sheet; the cottagers looked aghast. The first words that they uttered confirmed what I before knew. I did not feel shocked or overcome: I believe that I asked one or two questions and listened to the answers. I har[d]ly know, but in a few moments I sank lifeless to the ground; and so would that then all had been at an end!

Chapter 8

Mathilda begins chapter 8 ill and weak. She is cared for by strangers but feels little friendship, telling her audience:

> Yet sorrow only slept to revive more fierce, but love never woke again—its ghost, ever hovering over my father's grave, alone survived—since his death all the world was to me a blank except where woe had stampt its burning words telling me to smile no more—the living were not fit companions for me, and I was ever meditating by what means I might shake them all off, and never be heard of again.

She considers her future, deciding to return to isolation in nature, knowing that she could not participate in the pretense that living among others would require. She could not endure the false smiles, the secrets, the lies. However, due to her wealth and servants, she understands that disappearing from society will prove difficult. She concocts a plan to feign death. First, she must deal with various relatives who try to comfort her, their attentions resulting in Mathilda's increased guilt. She returns to London, which eventually becomes like a prison, and she feels on the verge of insanity, often imagining herself close to her father's grave. Only in nature can she feel at rest, as she explains: "While in London these and many other dreadful thoughts too harrowing for words were my portion: I lost all this suffering when I was free; when I saw the wild heath around me, and the evening star in the west, then I could weep, gently weep, and be at peace." She writes notes that give the impression that she will commit suicide and departs London. Instantaneously she feels relief, as she undergoes a metaphysical transformation under the attentions of a personified Nature:

> . . . methought I was an altered creature. Not the wild, raving & most miserable Mathilda but a youthful Hermitess dedicated to seclusion and whose bosom she must strive to keep free from all tumult and unholy despair—The fanciful nunlike dress that I had adopted; knowledge that my very existence was a secret known only to myself; the solitude to which I was for ever hereafter destined nursed gentle thoughts in my wounded heart. The breeze that played in my hair revived me, and I watched with quiet eyes the sunbeams that glittered on the waves, and the birds that coursed each other over the waters just brushing them with their plumes. I slept too undisturbed by dreams; and awoke refreshed to again enjoy my tranquil freedom.

Mathilda moves inland to a small, rudimentary shelter, employs a single servant part-time, and gives herself over to the love only available through nature and reading. At chapter 8's conclusion, she wishes herself dead; however, she is not moved to commit suicide.

Chapter 9

The reader learns in chapter 9 that two years pass. Mathilda grows weary of constant solitude, desiring not sympathy or wisdom but, rather, a "sweet and mutual affection" as one can enjoy only with those who share a past. She does find a friend, the son of a preacher, named Woodville. Shelley includes a long explanation regarding the character of Woodville and Mathilda's relationship with him, despite the fact that she began the novel with Mathilda addressing her story directly to Woodville, who would not require the information. Woodville is described in the most idealistic of terms:

> He was one of those very few whom fortune favours from their birth; on whom she bestows all gifts of intellect and person with a profusion that knew no bounds, and whom under her peculiar protection, no imperfection however slight, or disappointment however transitory has leave to touch. She seemed to have formed his mind of that excellence which no dross can tarnish, and his understanding was such that no error could pervert. His genius was tran-

scendant, and when it rose as a bright star in the east all eyes were turned towards it in admiration. He was a Poet.

Everyone loves Woodville, but his superior nature prevents his feeling any pride. Mathilda compares him to an angel and tells of his love for the wealthy and beautiful Elinor. They have to delay their wedding in order for Elinor to come of age and gain her inheritance. Mathilda lets the audience know that would not happen by saying,

> the earth would not be the earth it is covered with blight and sorrow if one such pair as these angelic creatures had been suffered to exist for one another: search through the world and you will not find the perfect happiness which their marriage would have caused them to enjoy; there must have been a revolution in the order of things as established among us miserable earth-dwellers to have admitted of such consummate joy.

While Woodville is away, he learns that Elinor is ill. His return is delayed by three days, and she is on her deathbed. He feels that surely if he kisses and warms her, she will recover. He watches over her for 12 hours, and then she dies.

Chapter 10

In the opening of chapter 10 Mathilda explains that Elinor's death had occurred six months previously. At first, Woodville was inconsolable and felt himself completely changed and with no hope of recovery. However, he eventually came to the country to heal. He seeks solitude and occasionally imagines that he sees Elinor. He rides past Mathilda one day in the woods, and when she rises to escape unseen, his startled horse rears and throws him to the ground, then runs away. Not seriously injured, Woodville is revived with some water. As they converse, Mathilda is for the most part quiet, while Woodville speaks optimistically of the good in the world. A philosopher as well as a poet, he muses that those creatures that are evil should not be destroyed but instead placed in isolation, as that is the greatest punishment for a living being. He describes Elinor as a "celestial creature," while Mathilda is careful not to reveal her torturous secret. Woodville notes that while he is recovering from his grief, Mathilda grows more pale and distant. He coaxes her to share her grief, and finding his is the gentle caring personality for which she had longed, Mathilda says,

> Like a refreshing shower on an arid soil they revived me, and although I still kept their cause secret he led me to pour forth my bitter complaints and to clothe my woe in words of gall and fire. With all the energy of desperate grief I told him how I had fallen at once from bliss to misery; how that for me there was no joy, no hope; that death however bitter would be the welcome seal to all my pangs; death the skeleton was to be beautiful as love.

In an outburst, Mathilda accuses Woodville of cruelty, explaining that she did not want his friendship and he forced it on her. As quickly as she makes that statement, she withdraws it, apologizing. He continues patiently to draw Mathilda out of her dark world, but as soon as he leaves, she again descends. She again blames him, her thoughts concluding the chapter:

> . . . if his gentle soul were more gentle, if his intense sympathy were more intense, he could drive the fiend from my soul and make me more human. I am, I thought, a tragedy; a character that he comes to see act: now and then he gives me my cue that I may make a speech more to his purpose: perhaps he is already planning a poem in which I am to figure. I am a farce and play to him, but to me this is all dreary reality: he takes all the profit and I bear all the burthen.

Chapter 11

In Chapter 11, Mathilda becomes angry when, during a rainstorm, Woodville does not return as he had promised to do. She concocts a double suicide plot and then determines to die in front of him if he refuses to join her. She prepares her room with flowers and imagines repeatedly the scene when she will ask him to join her in drinking poison, shame him if he will not, and then die alone. She delivers a long, dramatic monologue, describing how he will be reunited with Elinor if he joins her, that they will sleep a "sweet slumber" together and awake in a far better place. When Woodville arrives and learns her plan, he feels sympathetic but will not comply. The deeply sympathetic look that he extends to Mathilda counteracts her stern words and fills her with a "softened grief." He explains that he wanted death as well at first, but he conquered it, crushing its sting beneath his feet. He declares he will not concede defeat as long as any hope exists that he may bring any bit of happiness to the earth. He tries to convince Mathilda by reminding her that he has family who depend on him, and also by noting her own youth and beauty, worthy of life. While his words at first give Mathilda some relief, she regains her gloomy attitude. As the chapter concludes, she is thinking of how to avoid going insane if she continues to live.

Chapter 12
Chapter 12 begins with Woodville still trying to persuade Mathilda not to die, and with Mathilda wanting to accept his idealism. He must leave to care for his mother, but he asks her confidence in his love and friendship to sustain her. She can think only of dying and imagines herself as Dante entering Paradise, fantasizing the beauty that awaits her. She sleeps outside but chills and becomes ill, finding her way the following day to her house and spending some time in a fever. She remains ill through the winter, attended by a doctor, but weakens steadily and accepts that hers will be an "innocent death" after all—she will need no poison. In a long, final monologue, she bids nature and her life farewell and writes that she is glad Woodville is not there, as she does not want to sadden him. She notes that she has spent three months recording her "drama." She concludes that the only hope is that violets will bloom on her grave after she passes on, while Woodville's hopes are of the world.

COMMENTARY

Mathilda as Autobiography
Although critics warn readers against reading *Mathilda* solely in terms of Mary Shelley's own life, the temptation to do so is great. Following the deaths of her children, Mary blamed her husband and suffered severe depression. Her novel seems to incorporate the guilt she later felt over her behavior, while the rough draft is indicative of her feelings of loss for those who had died. As *Fields of Fancy*, the draft that would become *Mathilda*, opens, Shelley illustrates the use of the imagination as an escape mechanism when the fairy Fantasia tells the narrator,

> "You mourn for the loss of those you love. They are gone for ever & great as my power is I cannot recall them to you—if indeed I wave my wand over you you will fancy that you feel their gentle spirits in the soft air that steals over your cheeks & the distant sound of winds & waters may image to you their voices which will bid you rejoice for that they live."

Nevertheless, Shelley also remarks on the limits of the power of the imagination when her narrator tells Fantasia, "some times indeed I have called you & you have not come." The depth of the narrator's grief echoes Shelley's own when she tells her readers that she has lately been accustomed "to accuse the air the waters all—all the universe of my utter & irremediable misery." The narrator feels guilty about using fancy as an escape—"as to follow her [Fantasia] was to leave for a while the thought of those loved ones whose memories were my all although they were my torment I dared not go."

Anne K. Mellor notes as crucial the fact that Shelley had defined herself in terms of her relation to someone else for her entire life: as daughter, mistress, wife, and then widow. She faced a lifelong challenge in placing herself in the spotlight of family or the public, a challenge she was forced to meet, once a widow who had to support herself through writing. She wrote of that challenge in a letter in 1838, regretting that she could not be the political radical that her mother had been, due to her lack of that forceful personality:

> Alone and poor, I could only be something by joining a party; and there was much in me—the woman's love of looking up, and being guided, and being willing to do anything if any one supported and brought me forward—which would have made me a good partisan. But Shelley died, and I was alone . . . my being poor, my

horror of pushing, and inability to put myself forward unless led, cherished and supported,— all this has sunk me in a state of loneliness no other human being ever before, I believe, endured.

Many critics see the novel's conclusion, in which the Percy Shelley representative, Woodville, speaks to the dying Mathilda of the importance of nature and art, as Mary Shelley's rebuke against her husband. Woodville's physical description is a perfect match for Percy, and Woodville is a poet who shares much of Percy's philosophy. However, Mathilda is not a good match for Woodville. She desires to extend her romantic view of life to death, imagining a manner by which she and Woodville may die together as an expression of their love. Through Mathilda, Mary Shelley may rebel against the fact that she had no control over her husband's death. Critics suggest that it was likely she viewed his frequent sailing jaunts and the fact that he left her in a weakened state to visit a male friend, which led to his drowning, as a betrayal.

In the novel's first chapter, all attention is on the history of Mathilda's father, who meets and marries a young woman. She shares with him her interest in politics and philosophy, gives birth to Mathilda, and dies. Parallels to Mary Shelley's parents are clear. The parallels to Shelley's life continue as Mathilda matures with a romantic view: She is quite passionate and a lover of nature. She matures in Scotland, where Shelley herself had recognized her capacity for creativity while visiting family friends. Although Mathilda does write her story, she does not consider writing her talent. Mathilda's art is music—she plays a harp—but she shares Shelley's reading material—works by Milton and Shakespeare, among others.

Not only might Shelley's mind have been focused on tragedy following the deaths of two children, the suicide of a stepsister, and the suicide of her husband's first wife, other personal relationships might be seen in play in the writing of *Mathilda*, especially her relationship with GEORGE GORDON BYRON (Lord Byron). The popular rumor of incest between Byron and his half sister Augusta was further emphasized when Byron made public his enthusiasm for a privately printed drama by Matthew Lewis, discussed below, that featured an incestuous mother. Byron's drama *Manfred* (1817) hinted at incest, and Percy Bysshe Shelley's *The Revolt of Islam* (1818) in its first design featured incest between its main characters, Laon and Cythna. The Shelley-Byron circle was rumored to have engaged freely in, as critic Emily Sunstein writes, a "League of Incest," with Mary and her stepsister Claire sexually involved with various males. Certainly Godwin may have delayed *Mathilda*'s publication for fear that contemporaries might see autobiographical aspects in the story of death, isolation, and the illicit love of a father for his daughter.

The Gothic Tradition

However, there are many other ways of examining the novella. Many critics have pointed out that it depends heavily on the gothic tradition. Its style is verbose, its plot loosely formulated, and its characters sometimes stereotypical, but all of those elements would be expected in the gothic genre. Like many such subcategories of fiction, gothic follows a predictable formula, which is why its afficionados continually return to it. Shelley initially intended *Mathilda* to be a series of allegorical stories presented as Dante did his in the *Divine Comedy*. The original preface featured Mathilda's spirit describing the tale as one of "dark & phre[n]zied passions" the spirit felt forced to tell. The spirit describes struggling to find the proper language "to paint the tortures of the human heart." *Fields of Fancy* was structured as a dream sequence. The fairy Fantasia takes its author to the Elysian Fields, where she meets Mathilda and hears her story.

The title, the setting, and the fanciful narrative frame probably grew from *The Cave of Fancy*, another story that Shelley did not complete. While some believe the name Mathilda is based on Mary, others suspect it came from Dante's *Purgatori*; *Mathilda* contains several references to Dante. Additional explanations place the name firmly in the gothic tradition, as discussed below in the Characters section. As allegory, the tales would have featured passion as a mere path to wisdom. However, when Shelley revised the novel to become *Mathilda,* the story's passion became its driving force, its sensational nature perhaps helping to sell copies had it been published when written.

Mathilda resembles *Frankenstein* in its gothic character and its emphasis on isolation. As she did in many stories, including "Transformation," Shelley created a narrator who shares a story as a cautionary tale, so that others may escape a similar horrifying fate. When Mathilda compares herself to Oedipus at a time when he also faced death, she strongly foreshadows the situation in which Mathilda is discovered. Mathilda does not tell the story to an unidentified audience but relates it to her friend Woodville, a character who shares some traits with Victor Frankenstein's best friend, Henry Clerval, and is believed to be modeled after Percy Shelley. Mathilda labels herself a monster in the novel's final chapter and includes a self description that clearly echoes that of the monster in *Frankenstein:*

> Why when fate drove me to become this outcast from human feeling; this monster with whom none might mingle in converse and love; why had she not from that fatal and most accursed moment, shrouded me in thick mists and placed real darkness between me and my fellows so that I might never more be seen?, [sic] and as I passed, like a murky cloud loaded with blight, they might only perceive me by the cold chill I should cast upon them; telling them, how truly, that something unholy was near?

In addition to the gothic tradition, Shelley called upon the ideology of contemporary English society. As Anne K. Mellor points out, Shelley's sentimental novels, including *Lodore* (1835) and *Falkner* (1837), celebrated the idyllic relationships among members of English families, particularly those of fathers and daughters, as well as an egalitarian approach to family that held males should contribute to its strength equally with females. Individual ambitions, as well as desires, on the part of either parent must be subservient to the family's needs. However, her work also reveals conflict between the ideal and reality, particularly in *Mathilda.* Father-and-daughter relationships do not always prove equal, and in many cases they produce what Mellor terms *mutilated lives.* Shelley's novel reveals the costs to be paid by a daughter who relegates her own needs to those of a selfish, egoistic parent. Sacrifice was ever-existent for the individual who defined herself in terms of another, whether as daughter, sister, or mother.

The Incest Theme

Perhaps the most striking feature of the novel is its incest theme. Shelley's correspondence and journal entries show that she began to study incest literature in May 1818 while visiting Maria Gisborne, a family friend with whom she frequently corresponded. Gisborne gave Shelley a copy of the "Cenci manuscript," which recounted the true Renaissance tale of Count Francisco Cenci, who raped his daughter Beatrice, to be later murdered by her. Percy Shelley became interested in publishing a translation of the manuscript, a project on which Mary assisted. The two had, in their famous joint readings, read Sophocles' incest-themed *Oedipus.* Percy had also suggested that Mary translate Alfieri's tragedy *Myrrha* (1785), which features father/daughter incest. It was based on the Latin poet Ovid's tale of Myrrha and Cinyras from his *Metamorphosis* (before A.D. 8). Percy Shelley's *The Cenci* (1819) was not only Mary's favorite of his publications and his most gothic in nature, but it was also his most commercially successful, attesting to the popularity of the incest theme.

Percy and Mary Shelley were definitely not alone in utilizing the incest theme, which had begun in the 18th century. Incest tales generally followed a pattern of sibling separation at birth, followed by a later reunion. Horace Walpole, author of the prototypical gothic novel *The Castle of Otranto* (1764), followed his success with an incest drama entitled *The Mysterious Mother.* Conscious of its taboo subject matter, he printed the tragedy privately and withheld it from publication for years, calling it "revolting" in his correspondence. Critics suggest that he also probably took pride in the creation of a new character in the incestuous mother, the countess of Narbonne. Matthew Lewis's sole and extremely popular novel *The Monk* (1796) offered a scene depicting the rape and murder of his character Antonia, followed by the astounding revelation that she had been thus attacked by her brother. Its shock effect was calculated and escalated by the fact that Lewis served in Parliament.

Shelley also looked to Ann Radcliffe's villains in *The Italian* (1797), Montoni and Schedoni, to shape the character of Mathilda's father. E. J. Clery notes that the description of Mathilda's father as he describes his reaction to Diana's death is based on Radcliffe's villain characterizations, as well as on Joanna Baille's villain in her drama *De Monfort* (performed 1800). While many readers may envision Mathilda as a victim, or see her plight as symbolic of Shelley's own victimization, Mathilda's pursuit of her father following his illicit proposition shows agency and power. In addition, the themes of confession and then pursuit grow from a rich gothic literary heritage.

Mathilda does demand that her father speak the "word," more important to her as a creative agent than as philosophical consideration of the act. She notes that it may destroy her "as a flash of lightning," but in reality it destroys her father. The lightning imagery had already been employed several times in the novel in connection with Mathilda's father, so it may act as foreshadowing for the scene of his demise. Mathilda remains firmly in control, even as she searches for her father, assuming the letter he has left behind predicts suicide. An alert reader must question her motives, based on her comparison, earlier in the text, of herself to the Furies, the Eumenides, also known as the Erinyes. As goddesses of vengeance, they served traditionally to punish anyone breaking social rules by rendering them mad. They acted most often in cases of matricide or patricide. In a neat reversal of the traditional story element, Mathilda's father has symbolically killed his child by destroying her innocence. As a symbolic Fury, Mathilda hunts her father to seek revenge for that "murder."

Clery also cautions against projecting the theme of child abuse upon *Mathilda*. One should view incest as the gothic representation of "unnatural horror." Determination of responsibility and guilt should not be viewed traditionally. Mathilda claims "no crimes" in the story's opening, although later she does describe her guilt over feelings of complicity in her father's suicide. Mathilda also chooses herself to sacrifice the generous financial inheritance left by her father. She figuratively "kills" any relationship to him by feigning death and recreating the isolation of her childhood that she experienced prior to his reappearance in her life. She desires a "solitary house" where any chance of "molestation," even from the sight of another human, is diminished. She regresses to her childhood, again playing the harp, employing one servant, returning to reading, and even invoking her previous life of fancy. But where her early fantasies involved her playing a romantic lead in a self-fashioned drama, the new fantasy involves her portraying a nun. She assumes appropriate costuming, symbolic of a blatant attempt to regain her innocence. That aspect of the novel accommodates 21st-century sensibilities. Later readers would understand such concepts in an age where celebrities and commoners alike declared themselves virgins by voluntarily assuming a life of chastity following sexual activity, supported by groups including the Society for the Recapture of Virginity. Shelley's metaphorical approach fits well into the poetic fanciful framework within which Mathilda operates.

The works by Byron and Shelley mentioned above confirm the popularity of the incest theme as well as the use of such themes simply to promote sales through sensationalism. The preface to Percy Bysshe Shelley's original version of *The Revolt of Islam* stated openly that the relationship between Laon and Cythna was "intended to startle the reader from the trance of everyday life." Just as Godwin suppressed publication of *Mathilda*, Percy Shelley's publisher forced removal of the incest theme prior to publication of *The Revolt of Islam*. Juliet Byington notes that, especially for romantics, the theme of incest was "at the heart of writing about sibling relationships. The Romantics emphasized shared childhood experiences between brothers and sisters, basing the perfection of their union upon the mutual associations built during an idyllic childhood." Romantics viewed the bond of family as so strong that it would receive preference over feelings adult siblings might develop during involvements outside of the immediate family, even within marriage. Those writers viewed incest as the most extreme case of self-love, an overindulgence they would find attractive in their emphasis of the importance of the individual.

Sigmund Freud's later ideas regarding the strong role of incestuous desire in maturation also supported continued incest interest. All incest stories end in tragedy, a result Freud viewed as parallel to the earliest punishment for incest, which was death. The taboo would continue as a theme throughout the 19th century and into the future, with two notable Victorian novels, Charlotte Brontë's *Wuthering Heights* (1847) and George Eliot's *The Mill on the Floss* (1860) suggesting incest in their character relationships. In Clery's opinion, Mary Shelley should be credited for not anticipating challenges to her novel's publication, viewing it as extending her creativity and investigation of political and natural issues of morality.

The incest theme has always existed, with critics pointing to the story of Adam and Eve as its literal and figurative birth in Western literature. As to its taboo nature, historians are not sure how that taboo developed. Some suggest that rather than as a product of the development of moral codes, the taboo originated in a desire for humans to separate their behavior from that of the broader animal world where indiscriminate mating occurred. It may have represented an early aspect of efforts to retain domestic order. Because the family is the most basic representation of social order, a delineation of acceptable relationships within the family proved necessary to maintain civic order and to distinguish human endeavors from what was viewed by some as the more chaotic natural order. By 1500, laws against incest were in place. Later in that century, in England, Queen Elizabeth I created a court to address crimes associated with incest and instituted set punishments for incestuous activity.

Mathilda incorporates the most common of the incestuous relationships seen in literature, that between a father and daughter. Shelley follows the established pattern of death for those involved in incest, but she chooses for Mathilda's father to die, rather than for Mathilda to be punished with death. She will later die, but not from suicide. Her plotting contrasted with that of Ovid and Alfieri, in which the daughter figure feels passion toward her father and kills herself. Shelley's choice represents an interesting departure from the typical gothic approach and is a plot reversal important to feminist critics. Her simultaneous incorporation of many of the typical gothic elements reveals formulative skill buoyed by creativity.

Other Critical Approaches

The novel could also be analyzed by using well-known critical approaches. Formalist critics who study elements such as plot, character, setting, and style, along with stylistic elements including symbolism, irony, foreshadowing, detailed description, and imagery, would have much to discuss. The elements of the gothic plot are all present, as discussed above. The gothic subgenre also calls for hyperbole, or exaggeration, an aspect of style, and it is abundant, as in this passage from chapter 6:

> Yes it was despair I felt; for the first time that phantom seized me; the first and only time for it has never since left me—After the first moments of speechless agony I felt her fangs on my heart: I tore my hair; I raved aloud; at one moment in pity for his sufferings I would have clasped my father in my arms; and then starting back with horror I spurned him with my foot; I felt as if stung by a serpent, as if scourged by a whip of scorpions which drove me—Ah! Whither—Whither?

Also present in that passage is personification of despair, depicted as a fanged phantom.

Mathilda's declarations are fraught with emotion, and her descriptions filled with adjectives and adverbs, as well as sound elements such as alliteration, the repetition of consonants at the beginning of closely placed terms, and rhyming. All of those elements are evident in this passage from chapter 5:

> It is strange but even now I seem to see the spot—the slim and smooth trunks were many of them wound round by ivy whose shining leaves of the darkest green contrasted with the white bark and the light leaves of the young sprouts of beech that grew from their parent trunks—the short grass was mingled with moss and was partly covered by the dead leaves of the last autumn that driven by the winds had here and there collected in little hillocks—

there were a few moss grown stumps about— The leaves were gently moved by the breeze and through their green canopy you could see the bright blue sky—As evening came on the distant trunks were reddened by the sun and the wind died entirely away while a few birds flew past us to their evening rest.

Symbolism is also abundant. For example, chapter 6 begins, "My chamber was in a retired part of the house, and looked upon the garden." The garden is commonly suggestive of the Garden of Eden, a location of temptation where Eve succumbed to the serpent and Adam to Eve. However, the fact that Mathilda is in a distant portion of the house that only looks out onto the garden suggests that she has willfully separated herself from that temptation, although she is aware of its presence. In another instance from chapter 8, Mathilda states, "Mine was an idle, useless life; it was so; but say not to the lily laid prostrate by the storm arise, and bloom as before." In that sentence, the lily serves double duty. As a flower, it represents women, but it is a special type of flower. Generally, lilies are white, associated with innocence and naïveté, but they are also common flowers presented to those grieving the death of a loved one. In addition, as Mathilda notes, flowers may be quickly destroyed by a storm, never to rise again, as will happen to her.

Even the term *arise* proves symbolic, as it is a biblical command often issued to those ready to begin a new life. Thus, Shelley uses it ironically, where *irony* may simply be defined as a situation or statement in which things are not as they seem. Shelley's irony is not disguised but rather blatant, easily recognized on the surface of scenes and statements. The entire misunderstanding between Mathilda and her father is ironic. Mathilda believes he loves her as a daughter, and, desiring that love, she goads him to interact with her. All the while, her father regards her with incestuous desire, and her increased intentions simply heighten that desire. When her wish is granted, it destroys what she had hoped to preserve.

Shelley also employs various figures of speech, including the metaphor used in this passage from chapter 8: "I who had before clothed myself in the bright garb of sincerity must now borrow one of divers colours: it might sit awkwardly at first, but use would enable me to place it in elegant folds, to lie with grace." Mathilda's falsehoods are so thorough and complete that they cover her, as clothing would. Because a change in clothing typically signals a change in identity, the reference doubly indicates Mathilda's disguise.

In addition, Shelley develops strong imagery throughout, employing use of details, allusions, and comparisons. Here is an example from chapter 7: "[E]very moment my misery encreased [sic] and the fever of my blood became intolerable. The summer sun shone in an unclouded sky; the air was close but all was cool to me except my own scorching skin." The term *fever* suggests an illness, or unnatural and destructive condition, as well as heat, which is often connected to emotion. The summer sun unblocked by any clouds apparently does not produce as much heat, nor does the "close" or stifling air, as does Mathilda's own skin. The skin reference returns us to the image of her heated blood, flowing just under that skin. Heat is also used several times in conjunction with cold, a method employed since classic literature to indicate the capricious nature of emotion and passion.

Some elements that would interest psychoanalytic critics are obvious and more familiar, such as the incest theme, which suggests Freudian analysis based on theories that would appear later in the 19th century. Freud would propose the theory of the Oedipus complex, a son's sexual fixation on his mother, and Shelley compares Mathilda to Oedipus in her introduction. Shelley's inclusion of a number of dreams and visions would also interest psychoanalytic critics. Freud viewed literature as resulting from the artist's dreams, which represented repressed desires. The dream and vision sequences in Shelley's novel lend themselves to interpretation of repressed desires on the part of characters, as well as on the part of Shelley herself. Freud's student Carl Jung pointed to various literary archetypes, such as seasons, day, night, birth, and death, that help unify literature by adding specific meaning. All of those archetypes hold symbolic importance in *Mathilda*.

Northrup Frye's monomyth model, based on the four seasons, also works well when discussing *Mathilda*. For instance, when Mathilda pursues her father after discovering his romantic desire for her, Shelley takes great care to let readers know the season is summer. Frye's monomyth of summer is subtitled "Romance," and it includes elements of innocence, definitely present in Mathilda before her father clarifies his incestuous attraction to her. Additional psychoanalytic critical approaches would include analysis based on the theories of Jacques Lacan. Lacanian analysis emphasizes fragmentation of the individual's identity due to a failure to return to the childhood relationship with the mother. In addition, he stressed the term *jouissance* to refer to a character's experiencing condensed joy or horror. More often than not, *jouissance* suggests emotions in relation to sexual experiences. *Mathilda* contains abundant references and situations that allow a Lacanian analysis, such as the loss of Mathilda's mother and the condensed horror she feels following her father's declaration.

A reader could gain understanding from the novel through application of structuralism, which holds that a text is understood through investigating the relationships between various components that support a system. Literature supports its system through shared plot elements or shared character types. When an author of a story includes allusions to other works of literature, structuralists look at the relationships between those works. That relationship is known as intertextuality. *Mathilda* exhibits intertexuality through a number of references to other literary works. For example, in the introduction, Mathilda says of her surroundings, "It is as the wood of the Eumenides none but the dying may enter; and Oedipus is about to die." She thus signals readers that she is on the verge of death, as were those who entered the mythical wood of the Eumenides. *The Eumenides* is the third part of the Greek dramatist Aeschylus's trilogy titled *Oresteia*. In that play, the Eumenides act as the chorus, commenting for the audience on the happenings on stage. They are also Furies, monster goddesses who pursue Orestes to punish him for killing his mother, Clytemnestra, at the bidding of her spirit. Through this reference that appears early in the novel, the reader understands that Mathilda may envision herself as the cause of someone's death, or that she may believe she deserves to be punished.

In chapter 5, Mathilda's reference to Dante reminds the readers of the circles of hell, foreshadowing the descent into suffering that Mathilda and her father will soon suffer. Shelley closely follows that reference with one to Sir Guyon's descent into the halls of Avarice in Spenser's *The Faerie Queene*, again strongly predicting the subsequent action. In chapter 6, when Mathilda compares her grief to that felt by Boccaccio's Sigismunda over the heart of Guiscardo, the reader may take away several impressions. First, Shelley has read Boccaccio's *Decameron*, which suggests a sophisticated literacy, particularly in conjunction with additional references to the classics. Second, the scene to which Shelley refers perfectly suits her rising action: Sigismunda literally holds the heart of her husband in a golden chalice as she grieves his death. Shelley's use of the reference calls attention to the fact that Mathilda's father fantasy has died. However, it also suggests that perhaps Mathilda is complicit in incest, desiring to return the taboo love extended by her father in a wife-husband relationship. Finally, the fact that Shelley references classical literature helps place her novel within the tradition of incest literature, parental murder, and elevated emotional expression. She also references and alludes to the Bible on various occasions, such as in chapter 11, when Woodville says of death that he has "trampled the phantom under foot, and crushed his sting." His phrase alludes to I Corinthians 15:55—"Death where is thy victory? Death where is thy sting?" Such an allusion adds authority to Shelley's writing and allows readers familiar with the Bible to select either sacred or profane allusions as points of reference. These are a few of many references that help ground the knowing reader in traditions that support understanding of *Mathilda*.

Marxist critics—intent on identifying which party holds financial power over the other, material inequities, and themes of revolt—would find the servants and their relationships to Mathilda and others of interest. Her first caretaker replaces her mother but is apparently sent away without warning, signaling a lack of power. Mathilda specifically refers to her father's servants when she stays with him for a time in the home he had shared with her mother, and her father's steward accompanies her in an attempt to locate her father. She notes that when she reached the inn where he had left on foot, she hired a guide, and "the bribe was high" enough for him to agree to follow her father even in bad weather. In her position as an heiress, she is served by many servants, and even after her feigning of suicide and desiring to be completely alone, she has a single servant with her. That implies that a servant, of a different social class, is not considered a threat to her self-imposed exile. Servants become basic commodities in *Mathilda*, with their presence simply assumed, like that of various objects.

Finally, feminist critics—very much interested in gender power relationships, the woman as object, and the importance of the woman's body—view Mathilda as both a passive victim and an active agent of change. Anne Mellor explains that in Shelley's patriarchal culture, women were treated like daughters even by their husbands, so the conflation of roles has some basis in reality, as does the frustration caused to many women by confinement to that role. As Mellor notes, women lacked much of a social role outside of their fathers' houses. Women were encouraged to find and marry husbands who were like their fathers—mature, wise, more experienced, and financially secure, guaranteeing continued dependence of a younger woman on an older man. The child-bride syndrome blurred the lines between wives and daughters, which could promote the type of incestuous desire exhibited by Mathilda's father. In chapter 12, Mathilda makes clear that marriage for her will be equivalent to death, and that she desires an eternal union with her father. She will enter that union attired as a virgin bride:

> In truth I am in love with death; no maiden ever took more pleasure in the contemplation of her bridal attire than I in fancying my limbs already enwrapt in their shroud: is it not my marriage dress? Alone it will unite me to my father when in an eternal mental union we shall never part.

The shroud would probably be white, a symbol of female purity, youth, and naïveté, and a garment that presses the body into a cocoon-like state, much like swaddling used to confine infants. In using the comparison of bridal attire to a funeral shroud, Shelley suggests the confined life that all women anticipate during marriage, with little hope for intellectual or emotional metamorphosis. They may forever be suspended in a childlike state, an object awaiting actions performed upon it by the male.

Mathilda also exhibits a great deal of hostility toward her father, made clear in the dream in which she pursues him. While she has no real power over her father, she gains that power through her prophetic dream. As she pursues her father like the Eumenides, who were strong, terrifying female agents, she literally drives him to his death. She further aligns herself with those monster goddesses by continually referring to herself as a monster. She insists upon that characterization, despite Woodville's attempts to correct it to the more traditional view of the female as an object or treasure, valued for their beauty and support of men.

Mathilda's tale also allows her a great deal of power. Her story of death and terror trumps Woodville's story of self-forgiveness and redemption, giving her control over her destiny that many female gothic figures lack. Through Mathilda, Shelley may be seen as both supporting and countering a major tenet of Jean-Jacques Rousseau, who was an important influence on Shelley's mother, MARY WOLLSTONECRAFT, as stated in *Emile* (1762): In order to live, one must act, thus devaluing the passivity characteristic to gothic heroines. If one views Mathilda as a passive woman who has no control over her existence, then Rousseau's edict dooms her. However, more recent interpretations see Mathilda as taking control through verbalization. Not everyone is empowered to act in the manner that Rousseau and later liberal ethics valued. Mathilda represents a different type of agency, or manner of action. She speaks that which should never be spoken.

CHARACTERS

Mathilda Mathilda is clearly the heart and soul of the story and has been characterized in various fashions. One of the most popular is as Mary Shelley's alter ego, an approach that feminist critics find at once simplistic and uninformed. To relegate Mathilda to autobiography is to ignore the tradition of gothic writing, as discussed above, and the agency that some see as part of Mathilda's characterization. As part of that tradition, the heroine comes under threat, generally from mysterious and even metaphysical forces, to be rescued by a dark, mysterious hero, Byronic in nature (see BYRONIC HERO). Shelley does not write in the pure gothic mode but instead in the mode of the incest novel, casting Mathilda in a common role, as discussed above. She will have no salvation apart from a death that promises peace. Even her name, always crucial to a character's identity, raises reader expectations. It was also the name of the seducer of monk Ambrosio in Matthew Lewis's *The Monk* (1814), already noted as an influence on Shelley. Horace Walpole uses a character named Matilda as a pawn in an incest plot in *The Castle of Otranto* (1764). That Matilda character's father, the evil Manfred, promises his daughter to the father of his dead son's fiancée. Manfred will trade his daughter for the young woman who originally intended to marry his son, creating a double trade of daughters to fathers for sexual uses. In addition, Percy Shelley had named the female main character of his early gothic story *Zastozzi, A Romance* (1810) Matilda.

Shelley also uses Mathilda to illustrate her own role of storyteller, again within a tradition of such approaches. Mathilda relates what has happened as a cautionary tale to her audience; it is her dying statement. She warns against several things: pushing others to do something they do not wish to do, misplaced trust, irresponsible parents, and unrealistic expectations, among others.

Anne-Lise François and Daniel Mozes view Mathilda's communication as the major violence in the novel, using it to challenge the Enlightenment belief in the superiority of the rational. That rational audience is Woodville, who plays the role of late confidant in her tale, but who never knows the extent of her story. As a romantic turned cynic, Mathilda cannot accept his optimistic view. Mathilda is viewed as an Eve figure, one seduced by a desire for knowledge, as she begs her father to share his damning secret. She echoes Frankenstein's isolation and at one point labels herself Cain, alluding to the biblical story of Adam and Eve's son, who, in punishment for sinning by killing his brother, bore a mark on his head and was doomed to wander the earth. As Mathilda tells Woodville, "I belonged to another world; so he had seen that sign: and there it lay a gloomy mark to tell the world that there was that within my soul that no silence could render sufficiently obscure."

As a storyteller, Mathilda clashes with Woodville over his use of her "story," a commodity to which she clings ferociously. In his affection for her, he may want to characterize her as an innocent, something that Mathilda clearly resists. Her preferred characterization is that of a monster, cast off by society, as she tells Woodville that "unlawful and detestable passion had poured its poison into my ear" and "It must be an excess of madness that could make me imagine that I could ever by aught but one alone; struck off from humanity; bearing no affinity to man or woman; a wretch on whom Nature had set her ban." Again, echoes of traditional tales of sin followed by a physical marking, banishment, isolation, and wandering are notable.

Readers are also reminded that Victor Frankenstein's monster was made monstrous by his "father." Both Mathilda and the monster are treated as objects, judged by their appearances rather than their intelligence or personality.

The reader sees Mathilda mature through her exposure to her incestuous father. Where as a child she believed evil was an intentional act, she learns as a woman that "involuntary feeling," such as that which possesses her father, results in crime. She concludes in chapter 4 that "the worst fiend of all" is "Remorse" from actions and intents that cannot be undone. Critics believe that Mary Shelley may reflect in those lines on her own remorse and resultant guilt over her bitter final weeks with Percy Shelley, or over the loss of several children.

Mathilda's father Early critics view Mathilda's father as modeled on William Godwin. While later critics do not deny the biographical elements present in the novel, they do urge an expanded view. One method of expanding the view is to place the father within the tradition of the gothic villain. His moodiness, at first explained by guilt over the death of his wife, extends beyond reason. All of his movements are large and dramatic; he does nothing by halves. He could have permanently abandoned Mathilda, leaving her to forever love her fantasized version of a father, yet he selfishly returns. That inability to resist temptation is a hallmark of gothic fiction, in which young women are regularly placed in danger with need of rescue. However, for Mathilda there will be no rescue. Had she been threatened by ghosts or demons, as is the fate of many gothic heroines, she might have been saved. But her father's threat is all too real and impossible for a daughter to combat. He takes advantage of Mathilda's determination to create a relationship with him, even returning to the scene of his first love with Diana. In her role as promoter of the sanctity of the family, Shelley assures Mathilda's father's punishment for abandoning his traditional responsibilities and betraying his daughter. Some critics do point out that he at first wants to protect his daughter by withholding knowledge. However, he also gives in to her requests, despite the predictable results.

Woodville Like Henry Clerval in *Frankenstein* and like Percy Bysshe Shelley, Woodville is an artist, a poet, and a brilliant man loved by all. He is perfection, "like an angel with winged feet." He shares Mathilda's romantic tendency to retreat to nature with his grief, an action foreshadowed by his symbolic name. Unlike Mathilda, he recovers from the death of his love, Elinor, appropriating nature's power to heal himself. In his optimism, he might be expected to influence Mathilda's recovery as well, but she will not accept his attitude toward life. Each is a storyteller attempting to capture the other and symbolically make them a part of one another's story. Woodville applies logic in conversation with Mathilda to convince her of the value of her life and the optimistic nature of an unknown future, but Mathilda refuses to adopt his attitude. The final section of the novel leaves Mathilda firmly in charge as the story agent. She makes clear that she wants to shape Woodville's story, retelling what he must have already shared with her. She also must triumph in the competition between Mathilda and Woodville for possession of her story. Woodville discusses making her a romantic character in one of his poems, but she undercuts that view with her own self-fashioning as a monster.

Shelley's depiction of Woodville is not all positive. Mathilda views his desire to use her in his poetry as his metaphorically profiting from her pain. When Mathilda's plan for a double suicide fails, Shelley may suggest that, as so frequently happens in literature, someone must remain behind to tell the story—this is the poet's job. Woodville is to help others understand themselves by rising above his own torment, as Percy Bysshe Shelley wrote in his *Defence of Poetry*, to teach and delight.

Percy Shelley defined the imagination as the "mind acting upon . . . thoughts so as to color them with its own light, and composing from them, as from elements, other thoughts, each containing within itself the principle of its own integrity." Both Woodville and Percy Shelley have a strong, spoken, moral sense of responsibility to their families and to all they love. The last that Mathilda knows of Woodville, he has left to care for his sick mother. Yet some see Mathilda's clash with Woodville as emblematic of Mary's conflict with Percy Shelley. She may be angry that Percy died, which represented the ultimate abandonment of family, regardless of his declaration of love. Not only did he die, but he did so during a period when she did not feel well, had little energy to share any of his physical pursuits, and was again suffering guilt and perhaps blaming him for the loss of a child. As her journals and letters indicate, she would surely have crafted more affectionate and passionate final days with her husband had she realized that his absence when he went out sailing would become permanent. Woodville offers her a manner by which to discuss her grief with her absent husband.

Diana Although she does not have a large part in the novel, Diana's influence on both her husband and Mathilda prove crucial. Her name is symbolic, as Diana was the Roman goddess of the hunt and associated with the woods and nature, a strongly romantic trait. She is also associated with the moon, an important feminist symbol for woman. An emblem of chastity, Diana was also associated with Virbius, the Woodland god. Thus, Mathilda's mother may be seen as associated with Woodville, the character who represents Percy Bysshe Shelley. Mary's own mother, Mary Wollstonecraft, and Percy constituted Mary's strongest moral, ethical and creative inspirations and guides. They also probably caused her greatest frustrations. Critics suggest that the deaths of Diana and of Mathilda's aunt may reflect Shelley's hidden hostility toward abandonment by her mother. Mathilda's aunt is as cold as Diana was warm, also a probable reflection on the contrast between Mary Wollstonecraft Godwin and Mary Jane Godwin, Mary's stepmother.

Diana may be associated with Diotima, the character with whom the narrator of *Fields of Fancy* interacts while visiting the Elysian Fields. Diotima is described by the narrator as about 40 years old and emblematic of poetry: "[H]er eyes burned with a deep fire and every line of her face expressed enthusiasm & wisdom—Poetry seemed seated on her lips which were beautifully formed & every motion of her limbs although not youthful was inexpressibly graceful." Diana plays a crucial role in Plato's *Republic*, originating the idea of platonic love.

FURTHER READING

Castle, Terry. *The Female Thermometer: Eighteenth-Century Culture and the Invention of the Uncanny.* New York: Oxford University Press, 1995.

Clemit, Pamela. "From the *Fields of Fancy* to *Mathilda*: Mary Shelley's Changing Conception of her Novella." In *Mary Shelley in Her Times*, edited by Betty T. Bennet and Stuart Curran, 64–75. Baltimore: Johns Hopkins University Press, 2000.

Clery, E. J. *The Rise of Supernatural Fiction, 1762–1800.* Cambridge: Cambridge University Press, 1995.

———. *Women's Gothic: From Clara Reeve to Mary Shelley.* Tavistock, Devon, U.K.: Northcote House, 2000.

Delamotte, Eugenia. *Perils of the Night: A Feminist Study of Nineteenth-Century Gothic.* New York: Oxford University Press, 1990.

Fisher, Benjamin, F. *The Gothic's Gothic: Study Aids to the Tradition of the Tale of Terror.* New York: Garland, 1988.

Ford, Susan Allen. "'A Name More Dear': Daughters, Fathers, and Desire in *A Simple Story, The False Friend,* and *Mathilda.*" In *Re-Visiting Romanticism: British Women Writers, 1776–1837*, edited by Carol Shiner Wilson and Joel Haefner, 51–71. Philadelphia: University of Pennsylvania Press, 1994.

François, Anne-Lise, and Daniel Mozes. "Don't Say 'I Love You': Agency, Gender and Romanticism in Mary Shelley's *Matilda.*" In *Mary Shelley's Fictions: From* Frankenstein *to* Falkner, edited by Michael Eberle-Sinatra, 57–74. New York: St. Martin's Press, 2000.

Frank, Frederick S. *The First Gothics: A Critical Guide to the English Gothic Novel.* New York: Garland, 1987.

Hume, Robert D. "Gothic Versus Romantic: A Revaluation of the Gothic Novel." *PMLA* 84 (March 1969): 285.

"Incest in Victorian Literature—Introduction." In *Nineteenth-Century Literary Criticism*, vol. 92, edited by Juliet Byington. Gale Cengage, 2001. Available online. URL: http://www.enotes.com/nineteenth-century-criticism/incest-victorian-literature. Accessed June 29, 2009.

Johnson, Barbara. "My Monster/My Self." *Diacritics* 12 (Summer 1982): 2–10.

Mellor, Anne K. *Mary Shelley: Her Life, Her Fiction, Her Monsters.* London: Routledge, 1989.

Nitchie, Elizabeth. *Mary Shelley, Author of "Frankenstein."* New Brunswick, N.J.: Rutgers University Press, 1953.

———. "Mary Shelley's *Mathilda,* an Unpublished Story and its Biographical Significance." *Studies in Philology* 40 (1943): 447–452.

Rajan, Tilottama. "Mary Shelley's Mathilda: Melancholy and the Political Economy of Romanticism." *Studies in the Novel* 26 (1994): 43–68.

Robinson, Charles E. "Mathilda as Dramatic Actress." In *Mary Shelley in Her Times*, edited by Betty T. Bennet and Stuart Curran, 76–87. Baltimore: Johns Hopkins University Press, 2000.

Rousseau, Jean-Jacques. *Emile.* Translated by Barbara Foxley. New York: Dutton-Everyman's Library, 1963.

Shelley, Mary Wollstonecraft. *Mathilda.* Edited by Elizabeth Nitchie. Available online. URL: http://www.gutenberg.org/etext/15238. Accessed June 20, 2009.

Spatt, Hartley S. "Mary Shelley's Last Men: the Truth of Dreams." *Studies in the Novel* 7, no. 4 (Winter 1975): 526–537.
Sunstein, Emily W. *Mary Shelley: Romance and Reality*. Boston: Little, Brown, 1989.
Todd, Janet. Introduction to *Mary, Maria and Matilda*, edited by Janet Todd, vii–xxviii. New York: New York University Press, 1992.

"The Mortal Immortal" (1833)

Mary Shelley's short story "The Mortal Immortal" draws on a rich tradition of tales in which humans bargain with dark forces in order to gain wealth, power, or immortality. It continues to capture the reading public's imagination, as evidenced by its availability in electronic format at popular websites celebrating SCIENCE FICTION, such as those listed in the Further Reading section of this entry. It may also be found as hypertext at scholarly sites, such as http://www.rc.umd.edu/editions/mws/immortal/contents.html, which also supplies context for the story.

The story first appeared in THE KEEPSAKE for 1834, a publication whose readers would be familiar with the Faustian legend. That legend featured a German magician who agreed to sell his soul for immortal youth, great wealth, and other powers. Supposedly based on a wandering German scholar born in the 15th century with an evil nature who delved into black magic, the popular myth inspired many variations. Some of the most familiar retellings included Christopher Marlowe's play *Doctor Faustus* (1604); a two-part drama, *Faust* (1808 and 1832), by German poet Johann von Goethe; and the novel *Doctor Faustus* (1937), by the German writer Thomas Mann. It also inspired operas and numerous poems.

In 1798, Robert Southey published a poem based on the real-life German cabalist and alchemist Cornelius Agrippa, author of *De Occulta Philosphia Libri Tres* (1529) and an individual well known to the public. A cabalist is one who seeks power through intrigue, or who has a special knowledge or talent. *Cabalist* may also refer to a student of the Jewish Kabbalah. In *Frankenstein*, Shelley directly references Agrippa in Victor's explanation of his early reading and self-education:

> In this house I chanced to find a volume of the works of Cornelius Agrippa. I opened it with apathy; the theory which he attempts to demonstrate and the wonderful facts which he relates soon changed this feeling into enthusiasm. A new light seemed to dawn upon my mind, and bounding with joy, I communicated my discovery to my father. My father looked carelessly at the title page of my book and said, "Ah! Cornelius Agrippa! My dear Victor, do not waste your time upon this; it is sad trash."

Southey titled his poem "Cornelius Agrippa; A Ballad, of a Young Man that would Read Unlawful Books, and how he was Punished." In the poem, an assistant to Cornelius is punished by the devil for reading dark, forbidden secrets. Unknowingly, the assistant calls on the devil, who appears and demands to know what the young man wants. In the devil's presence, the assistant's bone marrow seems to melt, and he is struck dumb, unable even to pray. The horned devil, his tail "like a fiery serpent" tears out the young man's heart, grins "a horrible grin at his prey; / and in a clap of thunder vanish'd away." Shelley probably read Southey's work and may also have been influenced by Frances Sheridan's *The History of Nourjahad* (1767), another tale with a theme of immortality to which Shelley refers in her story. Shelley also refers to the figure of the Wandering Jew, joining a number of writers who do so. Those writers included Samuel Taylor Coleridge in his poem often quoted by Shelley in various works, *The Rime of the Ancient Mariner* (1798). The wandering theme may also have referred to the real-life figure who inspired the Faustian legend in Germany.

Other likely influences included Washington Irving's tale "Rip Van Winkle." Not only did its theme of an enchanted sleep affect her story, but Shelley also showed interest in developing a personal relationship with Irving, who had impressed her with his cordiality. She wrote of her interest

"The Mortal Immortal" 255

immortality from the beginning, the stories share more than just the Faustian plot. Winzy's vanity, as well as his interest in mirrors and his reflection, echo in Gray. In addition, Winzy admits that he wears a type of mask in disguising his age, as does Gray. Finally, Bertha's warnings to Winzy are ones that Gray might have taken to heart: "My youth was a disease, she said, and I ought at all times to prepare, if not for a sudden and awful death, at least to awake some morning white-headed and bowed down with all the marks of advanced years."

While the story opens with the date July 16, 1833, the reader learns that the narrator's story began in the 1500s. That information suggested to Shelley's contemporary readers that while the occult supposedly belonged to a distant, less well-informed culture, vestiges remained. She adds to the story's grotesque by offering her audience the idea that those from another era might walk among them.

SYNOPSIS

The story opens with a date: July 16, 1833. The unidentified narrator follows with the striking statement that on that date, he completes his 323rd year. He notes he is not to be confused with the "Wandering Jew," one of several allusions to other stories that will appear during the tale. Questions follow regarding the narrator's identity and his immortality. He remarks that he discovered one gray hair that day, but it may not signal aging, as it could have been there for three centuries. He desires to tell his story in order to gather the reader's opinion but also simply to pass the time, as he has so much of it. He has heard of those who sleep for hundreds of years and of the "fabled Nourjahad" who was tricked into believing himself immortal, causing him to sleep for years at a time. He next references Cornelius Agrippa, noting that everyone has heard of that scholar and his assistant, rumored to have been destroyed by Agrippa for interfering with an experiment. Rumors held that Agrippa's potion had successfully invoked the appearance of the devil. The narrator began as a young pupil of Agrippa, although he was not present during the rumored "accident." Although his friends urge him not to return to the laboratory, Agrippa offers him gold to stay, making him feel as if tempted by

Photograph of Washington Irving from 1861. Mary Shelley showed an interest in developing a personal relationship with Irving, whose work she admired. *(Photograph by M. B. Brady. Library of Congress)*

to her friend John Howard Payne, who shared her letters with Irving, despite her request that he not "repeat tales out of school." Although Shelley never expressed in writing anything other than friendship toward Irving, Payne presented her letters with introductory remarks noting that had Irving met Shelley casually, he "very possibly . . . would have fallen in love with her." Irving expressed no desire to meet Shelley, noting in his journal only that he read her letters "before going to bed."

As is true with much of Shelley's writing, her story influenced future works as it also looked to the past for some of its own influences. For instance, Oscar Wilde's novel *The Picture of Dorian Gray*, first published in *Lippincott's Monthly Magazine* in July 1890, comes to mind. Although Gray differs from Winzy in that he desires and seeks

Satan. His chattering teeth and hair standing on end cause him to run away to a spring where he commonly meets a childhood friend named Bertha. Bertha was born to the same low station as the narrator, but she became an orphan and was adopted by a wealthy aristocratic woman. Bertha now wears silk and lives in great luxury, and her patroness urges her to no longer associate with those beneath her station. Although she is forbidden to visit the narrator's cottage, they secretly meet in the woods.

Bertha is unhappy, growing angry and haughty over the fact that she is told not to spend time with the narrator. The two had always intended to marry. However, after they had been apart for a time, Bertha reproached the narrator for being poor. Remembering Agrippa's offer, he tells her that he can get money but is too frightened to do so. She reproaches him again for not considering her a goal worthy of taking a risk. In his shame, he decides to take the job.

The narrator works for a year and earns large sums of money. He never sees "a cloven foot" or hears "demoniac howls." He continues to secretly meet Bertha, describing her as a "coquette" and himself as "jealous as a Turk." She does many things the narrator feel slight him, and because she is surrounded by wealthy young men, he wonders how he has a chance to win her heart. Agrippa keeps him at work for a time, causing him not to be able to keep appointments with Bertha. Her "haughty spirit fired" at such "neglect." When the narrator escapes work for a few moments, hoping Bertha will console him, she instead dismisses him scornfully. She desires revenge and gains it later by spending time with Albert Hoffer, a wealthy young man her patroness favors. The narrator is again attacked by jealousy to the point that he wishes he had never met Bertha.

Agrippa has mixed a potion he has watched for three days without sleep. He asks the narrator to watch the potion and awaken him when it begins to change from its rose color to white, after which it will "emit golden flashes." He explains to the narrator, who is at last identified by name, "Winzy . . . do not touch the vessel," explaining that if the liquid is consumed, it will make its victim no longer capable of love. That is the state that Winzy desires, and he continues to feel maddened by jealousy, as if his heart contained "Serpents and adders." In a frenzied state, he is then mesmerized by the flashes of light and wonderful fragrance emitted by the potion as it matures. He drinks half of the liquid, seeking revenge on Bertha by killing his emotion. When Agrippa awakens and cries out, Winzy drops and breaks the container, wasting the remaining liquid. Agrippa does not realize that Winzy has drunk any of his potion; he believes it is all on the floor and that his assistant has "destroyed the labour" of his life. He eventually calms down and tells Winzy he may leave.

Winzy enjoys the most wonderful rest of his life; he "trod air" upon awakening, remembering the paradise of the night before. "Earth appeared heaven," and he celebrates being "cured of love." He returns to work, where Agrippa feels certain he can recreate his miracle and goes to work again. Winzy takes a holiday, dresses carefully, checking his appearance in a polished shield that substitutes for a mirror. He feels joyous, his heart light, as he sees Bertha from afar on the marble steps of her palace. She runs toward him, and Winzy notices her patroness watching them. The old woman tells Bertha to beware. Winzy hates the old woman but reminds himself that he is cured of love.

Winzy finds out that Bertha had been nearly forced to commit to marry Albert. When her pride made her refuse to do so, the old woman threatened to dismiss her from the household. Bertha begs Winzy to take her to his mother's poor dwelling and freedom. Without hesitation, Winzy clasps her in his arms and spirits her away with joy and tenderness. She is welcomed by his family, and Winzy, in the evidence of his strong feelings of love for Bertha, assumes the potion did not work. He marries Bertha and does not return to work for Agrippa. He is grateful to the philosopher for giving him a potion that he believes has filled him with courage. While the potion did not fulfill its design, "its effects were more potent and blissful than words" could express. Bertha does not understand Winzy's cheerfulness but enjoys it.

Five years later, Winzy is called to see Agrippa on his deathbed. There the philosopher refers to his potion, having mixed a new batch, as "the

Elixir of Immortality." He struggles to drink it, hoping to save himself, but he fails and dies, never having duplicated his potion. Winzy now knows the truth: He will never die. He gazes into a mirror and notes no change in his face over the past few years. Later, he laughs at his willingness to believe in his own immortality and that Agrippa could have summoned dark powers. He had simply created a wonderful drink with strong medicinal powers, which will surely wear off. Winzy enjoys longevity, not immortality.

Winzy soon discovers that he and Bertha will pay a price for his condition. As Bertha's beauty begins to fade, her jealousy over Winzy's youthful appearance grows. The couple have no children, so they become one another's world. Although Bertha becomes more peevish, Winzy continues to cherish her. When Bertha is 50 years old, Winzy is still only 20. He begins to fake the movements of the elderly, adopting "habits of a more advanced age." He stops dancing and joining the gaiety of local celebrations. Before long, the couple's age difference grows so marked that they have to move, as they are "universally shunned." Nobody will buy their farm's produce, and Winzy has to travel miles to be able to sell it and support them. Bertha demands to know the truth about Winzy, and she begins to make up fantasy situations, predicting that his youth is actually a disease and that one day he will awaken to his true appearance. She worries that he will be attacked and killed if people suspect his dabbling in black arts, and that she might be stoned. At one point, she demands that he share his secret with her, or she will reveal him as a sorcerer to the public and denounce him. He speaks of a long life, not immortality. He tells Bertha that he suffers from Agrippa's "accursed arts" and will leave her. Bertha immediately relents and calls him back, hugging and kissing him. She says they will go away together, and she hopes "the charm" will soon wear off.

The couple sell everything and have enough money to move to western France, although Bertha hates to leave the village and all with which she is familiar. Winzy feels sorry for her and tolerates her various "feminine arts," such as the liberal use of rouge and dressing in clothing inappropriate to her age in order to appear younger. Winzy asks, "Did I not myself wear a mask?" He cannot speak to another woman for fear of Bertha's jealousy, and he listens to Bertha constantly make remarks to her friends such as the one that "there was ruin at work within" his frame, despite his youthful appearance. She claims his "worst symptom" is what appears to be good health, as his youth is a disease. They live together for many years until her death, and her loss greatly saddens Winzy.

Winzy lives for centuries without pleasure. He comments that he will end his story at that point, philosophizing about death, "mysterious, ill-visaged friend of weak humanity." He continues to wonder whether he is truly immortal, hoping that he might die by elements, such as "strangling waters" or fire or sword. However, he does not want to participate in forcing his fellow man to kill him. He also contemplates suicide and concludes the story by noting that he will challenge the "powers of frost in their home—beset by famine, toil, and tempest" and hope for death. Whether he conquers nature and survives a hero or is killed in his efforts, he will become immortal through fame.

COMMENTARY

"The Mortal Immortal" focuses on the transgressive desire to alter the natural human state. While the narrator, Winzy, does not realize that the potion he drinks will lead to immortality, he does believe it will cause him to lose the will to love, a loss he greatly desires. He has been plunged into despair by jealousy over Bertha's feigned relationship with another man. He describes Bertha as "somewhat of a coquette," which leads him to feel "jealous as a Turk." Jealousy continues as a focus throughout the story, allowing Shelley to warn readers of its damaging potential. Winzy compares the destructive emotion to a snake and foreshadows temptation as a topic when he states, "Jealousy, with all its venom . . . entered my breast." A short time later, Winzy notes, "Serpents and adders were in my heart as the word 'Never!' half formed itself on my lips. False girl!—false and cruel!" After Winzy and Bertha marry, Bertha becomes jealous of Winzy's youthful appearance, and Winzy tells his audience, "Her jealousy never slept."

Shelley also takes on class structure through Bertha's elevation in social stature when she is adopted by a "rich, childless" aristocratic woman. However, where in other of Shelley's works she offers a critique of social structure and its exclusionary effect, in this story she instead emphasizes the importance of one's keeping to the proper social station in life. When Bertha realizes that she does love Winzy, and her patroness has forbidden her to see him, she asks Winzy to take her away from "the detested luxuries and wretchedness of this noble dwelling." She wants to stay instead with Winzy's mother, equating poverty with happiness. Once back within her originally appointed social station, she is a "fair fugitive, escaped from a gilt cage."

Those familiar with Shelley's other writings will recognize additional common themes, topics, and imagery. The desire for immortality through stories that will outlive the narrator is common to many of her characters. Winzy's plan at the story's conclusion to stage an exploration to a place where he will wage war with frost is reminiscent of the scenes of the frozen north and Walpole's exploration in *Frankenstein*.

The story appeals to several schools of criticism. Psychoanalytic critics would translate Winzy's various emotions into products of the id, ego, and superego, while feminist critics would see a gender role reversal in Winzy's interest in his appearance. They would also note Winzy's nonjudgmental attitude toward Bertha's concerns about appearing older than him and her use of deception to try to hide that appearance. The imagery of a bird in a cage and the use of mirrors to symbolize self-reflection is common to women's literature and often noted by feminist critics. Shelley compares Bertha to a bird in a cage, but she does the same with Winzy, who describes his body as "too tenacious a cage for a soul which thirsts for freedom." Interestingly, it is Winzy who twice indulges in gazing at his reflection, rather than Bertha. Thus, Shelley neatly inverts gender behavior expectations. Deconstruction critics might find interesting Shelley's inversion in privileging life over death. Winzy actually longs for death, calling it his beacon of hope. He compares his seeming immortality and inability to die to a sailor lost on a stormy sea with no guidance, declaring that his condition is even worse than that of the sailor. While a lost sailor might be rescued by another ship, Winzy will enjoy no rescue. He cries out, "Oh, for the peace of the grave! The deep silence of the iron-bound tomb!" Nothing will satisfy him except the cessation of his thought processes and the stilling of his heartbeat.

Critics might project autobiographical meaning on various aspects of the story. Knowledge of details from Shelley's life might make one believe that her protagonist's thoughts of suicide after he outlives the love of his life might come from her real-life experience. She had considered suicide following PERCY BYSSHE SHELLEY's death by drowning, expressed in her correspondence. However, unlike her protagonist, she had a child to live for, and the section of the story in which the narrator notes that because he and his wife Bertha lack children, they are one another's only friends may attest to the fact that she can imagine an even lonelier state than her own widowed condition. Other autobiographical echoes in the story may be heard when Winzy and Bertha have to emigrate from Bertha's home to France, due to the rejection by their neighbors and onetime friends. Mary and Percy Shelley had suffered the same type of rejection by their friends after running away together when Mary was 16 and Shelley a married family man in his 20s.

CHARACTERS

Winzy As the story's narrator and protagonist, Winzy must be viewed as trustworthy by the reader. Shelley achieves this characterization through his honest telling of the facts of his life and through his mixed emotions regarding his magical state. Readers must abandon realism to accept Winzy's immortal state; however, as is often true of fantasy and science fiction, reality in everyday details is required. He is naive, trusting, and desperately in love with Bertha. He does not work with Agrippa in order to discover how to practice black arts but, rather, to earn money that will allow him to keep company with Bertha. Readers can empathize with the jealousy Winzy feels in reaction to Bertha's wealthy lover, and it is that jealousy that tempts him to drink the magic potion. He expresses his emotions freely and honestly, remaining a good husband for Bertha, even when she ages as he does not. He is a positive character, able to accept Bertha's personal attacks against him with the understanding of how his youthful appearance and physical abilities contrast with her own diminishing beauty and physicality. Winzy can be seen as an everyman, tempted by powers he does not understand, desiring only to love and to escape painful emotions, and in the end wanting a normal end to life as others have. Also like his fellow humans, he desires to leave behind some influence on humanity, hoping for fame through his attempt to accomplish something that has never been accomplished. He desires immortality through the word, rather than the flesh.

Bertha Bertha is a flat character, never changing her basic personality and approach to life. She exists to advance Winzy's story, but she does so in an interesting way. At first, she appears to be a fairy tale character, a poor orphan plucked from poverty to be raised by a wealthy childless woman. Shelley uses her to help undercut reader expectations of a happy and prosperous union for Bertha and Winzy. When Bertha declares that poverty is better than wealth, positive expectations remain. However, while Bertha separates herself from outside influences that threaten the couple's relationship, Winzy does not. He does not overcome temptation and falls to the lure of magic and the black arts. Bertha's reaction to Winzy's ever-lasting youth is to be expected, and she allows introduction of the strange thought that youth and vigor might equate to disease.

FURTHER READING

Hofkosh, Sonia. "Disfiguring Economies: Mary Shelley's Short Stories." In *The Other Mary Shelley: Beyond* Frankenstein, edited by E. Audrey, A. Fisch, Anne K. Mellor, and Esther H. Schor, 204–219. New York: Oxford University Press, 1993.
Purinton, Marjean. "Mary Shelley's Science Fiction Short Stories and the Legacy of Wollstonecraft's Feminism." *Women's Studies* 30, no. 2 (April 2001): 147–174.
Shelley, Mary. "The Mortal Immortal." Hypertext edition, edited by Michael Eberle Sinatra. Available online. URL: http://www.rc.umd.edu/editions/mws/immortal/. Accessed June 7, 2010.
———. "The Mortal Immortal." In: *Viable Paradise: Fantasy and Science Fiction Writers'* Workshop. Available online. URL: http://www.sff.net/people/DoyleMacdonald/l_mortal.htm. Accessed June 7, 2010.
———. "The Mortal Immortal." With notes by Blake Linton Wilfong. Available online. URL: http://wondersmith.com/scifi/mortal.htm. Accessed June 7, 2010.
———. *Selected Letters of Mary Wollstonecraft Shelley.* Edited by Betty T. Bennett. Baltimore: Johns Hopkins University Press, 1995.

Proserpine and Midas (ca. 1820)

Mary Shelley wrote two verse dramas, both based on mythological stories. The dramas, which were never performed, are not widely read due to their perceived lack of distinction and sophistication. However, Shelley's poetry is well suited to its purpose, and while it may not reach PERCY BYSSHE SHELLEY's lyrical heights, it is an effective vehicle for a dramatic retelling of two popular myths. Both dramas are readily available online in electronic form, with an introduction by critic André Henri Koszul. Some critics believe that they were never meant to be staged but instead fall into the "closet drama" genre, a category for dramas written to be read aloud among friends. Others believe that Shelley's inclusion of stage directions in drafts do indicate her initial focus on the performance of both plays.

For these plays, Shelley selected two myths, each with the proven ability to hold audience interest over centuries. According to the Shelley critic Judith Pascoe, these particularly allowed Shelley "to attempt the theatrical evocation of transformation and loss," two of her favorite themes.

SYNOPSES OF THE PLAYS

Proserpine
The familiar Latin myth of Proserpine, or Proserpina, who is the equivalent of the Greek goddess Persephone, provides an explanation for the existence of the four seasons. *Proserpine* literally means

"to emerge" and thus is fitting for a celebration of the season of spring and new life. Proserpine was the daughter of Jupiter, king of the gods, and Ceres, goddess of the Earth. The story tells of Venus, the goddess of love, commanding her son Amor (Cupid) to shoot Pluto, god of the underworld, with an arrow to cause him to fall in love. As Proserpine played with nymphs and collected flowers by the Fountain of Aretusa near Enna in Sicily, Pluto emerged from the volcano Etna. Driving four black horses, Pluto, also Proserpine's uncle, was a terrifying sight. He kidnapped Proserpine and took her into the underworld, where he forced her to become its queen.

Ceres searched everywhere for her daughter, to no avail. She found only a belt floating on a lake, composed of the tears of the nymphs Proserpine had been with when abducted. Ceres became so angry over her daughter's disappearance that she vowed to bring famine to the earth and make it barren. As she stomped about, deserts were created in her footprints and the earth no longer produced any growing thing. Jupiter sent Mercury as a messenger to Pluto, commanding him to free Proserpine, so that fruits, vegetables and flowers would again bloom on the earth. Pluto released the girl to return to her mother, but only for six months out of the year. The other six months she had to return to help him rule the underworld. Those six months were represented by the six pomegranate seeds that Pluto made Proserpine eat before leaving him. The seeds symbolized fidelity in marriage and later were believed to be an aphrodisiac. Thus, the earth enjoys six months of "life" in spring and summer and six months of "death" in fall and winter, making Proserpine a life-and-death-cycle goddess.

Percy Shelley added lyric poetry to the drama, including that which opens the play, as the character Ino describes to Proserpine another earlier abduction, that of Proserpine's favorite nymph, Arethusa, by the river god Alpheus. Arethusa would later be freed to return to Proserpine's service. That poem acts as foreshadowing of Proserpine's fate. Percy Shelley's ability to capture the terror of Arethusa suited romantic era literature, which focused firmly on heightened emotions. That heightening leads to hyperbole that may impress today's readers as adding an unintended comic effect. An excerpt from his poem reads:

> Oh, save me! oh, guide me!
>   And bid the deep hide me,
> For he grasps me now by the hair!
>   The loud ocean heard,
>   To its blue depth stirred,
> And divided at her prayer[,]
>   And under the water
>   The Earth's white daughter
> Fled like a sunny beam,
>   Behind her descended
>   Her billows unblended
> With the brackish Dorian stream:—
>   Like a gloomy stain
>   On the Emerald main
> Alpheus rushed behind,

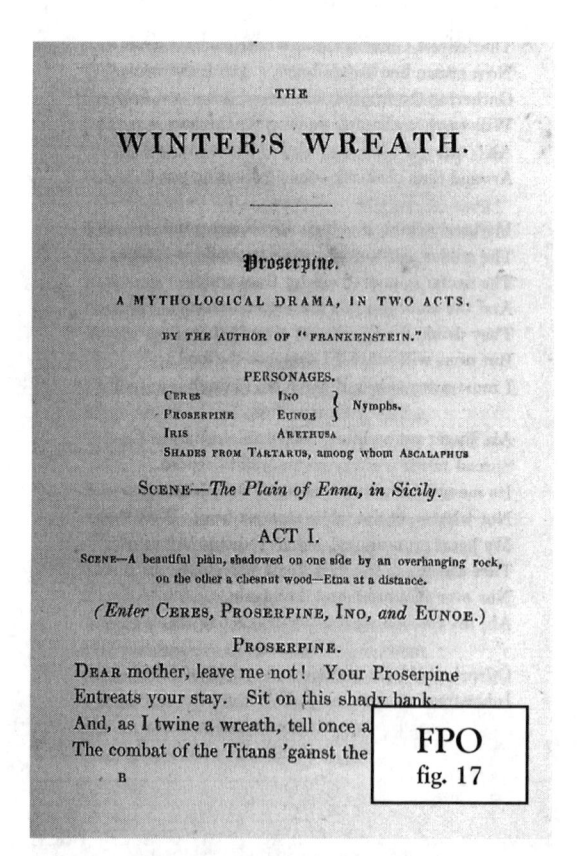

Title page of Mary and Percy Shelley's play *Proserpine* from *The Winter's Wreath for 1832*

As an eagle pursueing
A dove to its ruin,
Down the streams of the cloudy wind.

Later, when Proserpine disappears, Ceres orders a search for her daughter, but no evidence of her fate is discovered. Mary Shelley concludes the first act with the following lines, spoken by the bereft mother:

Eunoe does not return: in vain she seeks
Through the black woods and down the
   darksome glades,
And night is hiding all things from our view.
I will away, and on the highest top
Of snowy Etna, kindle two clear flames.
Night shall not hide her from my anxious search,
No moment will I rest, or sleep, or pause
Till she returns, until I clasp again
My only loved one, my lost Proserpine.

Shelley thus delays sharing with the audience the fact that Proserpine is indeed kidnapped and being held in the underworld until the second act. While most viewers/readers would know the tale and anticipate Proserpine's abduction, Shelley heightens dramatic effect. She uses the division into acts to break the action, having built momentum toward the revelation of Proserpine's fate.

In act 2, Ceres threatens Jove with the destruction of the earth's bounty. Should her daughter be forced to remain in the underworld, she will follow her, and the earth will fall barren. Shelley writes:

Is there no help, great Jove? If she depart
I will descend with her—the Earth shall lose
Its proud fertility, and Erebus
Shall bear my gifts throughout th' unchanging
   year.
Valued till now by thee, tyrant of Gods!
My harvests ripening by Tartarian fires
Shall feed the dead with Heaven's ambrosial
   food.
Wilt thou not then repent, brother unkind,
Viewing the barren earth with vain regret,
Thou didst not shew more mercy to my child?

Such lines echo the blank verse employed by Shakespeare with which Shelley was so familiar. She and Percy had read all of Shakespeare's works during 1818–19, and Percy recognized Mary's penchant for dramatic structure in *Frankenstein* (1818). Partly due to his urging, Mary later tutored herself in drama for two years by reading essays about the form, as well as English, French, Latin, and Italian drama.

Midas
The Greek myth that inspired Shelley's second drama, the story of King Midas, is considered a "lesser myth." It may teach a lesson, but it does not explain crucial natural phenomenon as the myth of Proserpine does. It remains a popular tale for children who know a portion of the story as "The Myth of the Golden Touch." A second part of the tale tells of Midas having been cursed with donkey ears after interfering with a poetry contest. Shelley reversed the two strands of the myth to present the story of the poetry contest first. In the opinion of the critic Judith Pascoe, Shelley did this for dramatic effect. As Pascoe explains, had the play been performed, the stage setting between the two acts would have been transformed from the drab earth tones of act 1's poetry contest to a glittering golden "tableau." In his first address, the actor portraying Midas says the word *gold* or *golden* more than 20 times in his 44 lines. Although no evidence exists that Shelley tried to find a theater manager to discuss production of this play, the effect on readers of the detailed stage descriptions would be strong, allowing them to envision the stage as Shelley intended. Even so, despite the contrast between acts, her effects would not have made much impression during the era in which she wrote, when theater managers desired spectacular visual effects, including horses galloping across stages. The proliferation of closet dramas supports the romantic period's emphasis on, according to Pascoe, "the exploration of human emotions," rather than bombastic visual effects.

As Shelley's drama unfolds, Midas, a wealthy king in the province of Phrygia in Asia Minor, is called upon to judge a music contest. According to myth, he must state which is the better musician of two contestants. The first is Pan, the goat-hoofed god of flocks and shepherds, and the second Apollo, son of Zeus and the official god of music. When Midas selects Pan, the annoyed Apollo transforms the king's ears into those of an ass. Shelley's verse captures the humor of the moment in Midas's interchange with his minister Zopyrion, who feigns sympathy for the egotistical monarch:

> Midas: What said he? is it true, Zopyrion?
> Yet if it be; you must not look on me,
> But shut your eyes, nor dare behold my shame.
> Ah! here they are! two long, smooth asses['] ears!
> They stick upright! Ah, I am sick with shame!
>
> Zopyr: I cannot tell your Majesty my grief,
> Or how my soul's oppressed with the sad change
> That has, alas! befallen your royal ears.

In the next stanza, Zopyrion suggests a solution for Midas, although secretly he finds the situation hilarious. He spends the remainder of the drama wanting to tell others about the king's ears, but Midas has sworn him to secrecy:

> Zopyr: You wear a little crown of carved gold,
> Which just appears to tell you are a king;
> If that were large and had a cowl of silk,
> Studded with gems, which none would dare gainsay,
> Then might you—
>
> Midas: Now you have it! friend,
> I will reward you with some princely gift.
> But, hark! Zopyrion, not a word of this;
> If to a single soul you tell my shame
> You die. I'll to the palace the back way
> And manufacture my new diadem,
> The which all other kings shall imitate
> As if they also had my asses['] ears.

Soon after the transformation, Pan's brother Silenus, known for always being drunk and riding an ass, appears in Midas's famous rose gardens, wandering about in a disoriented manner. Midas makes sure that Silenus safely returns to Bacchus, god of the vine and wine. To show his gratitude,

Bacchus grants Midas a wish for returning Silenus in this painting from the 17th century. Mary Shelley based her drama *Midas* on the myth of King Midas. *(Painting by Nicolas Poussin)*

Bacchus agrees to grant Midas one wish. The greedy Midas asks that all he touches be turned to gold. Zopyrion, standing nearby, softly wonders aloud why Midas did not instead wish away Apollo's curse in order to regain his own ears.

Midas quickly discovers the error in his wish when he is unable to eat, as all food transforms into solid gold, even at the touch of his lips. Regretting his wish, he requests that it be reversed, and Bacchus grants his request. By the drama's conclusion, though he apparently still retains the ass's ears, Midas rejoices, giving all his gold to the peasants and concluding the play by saying: "Rich, happy, free & great, that we have lost / Man's curse, heart-bartering, soul-enchaining gold."

COMMENTARY

In his introduction to the 1922 edition of *Proserpine & Midas*, André Koszul notes of Shelley's plays that they bridge a gap between "the pulse beating so wildly . . . in *Frankenstein*" and the "increasingly sluggish flow" of the rhythm in her later novels. In his opinion, the plays display "an artistic mood" informed by "the serene joy and clear warmth" of Shelley's surroundings in Italy where she created the pieces. They combine "youthful buoyancy" with a "quiet and unpretending philosophy." He writes that her dramas were every bit the equal in creativity and skill of some of her fiction. *Proserpine* was published in 1832, but *Midas* did not appear until 1922.

The composition of the plays followed a time of grief and loss for the Shelleys. While Mary's early days in Italy proved an energetic period of reading, discussion, and writing for her and for Percy, the loss of their daughter Clara in September 1818 and of their son William in June 1819 reduced Mary to despair. She wrote in her journal on June 27, 1819, that she had lost interest in everything. The Shelleys' friend Leigh Hunt suggested in July that she might turn to writing again, but by then she had even stopped writing in her journal.

The arrival in November of another son, Percy Florence Shelley, lifted Mary's depression. While she would still suffer "low spirits" from time to time, she began a period of intense study and writing, even learning Greek, that extended into 1820. She began a new novel, eventually published as *Valperga* (1823), and her dramas were probably both written in 1820 as well. Support for that date comes from the fact that the dramas contained some lyrics by Percy Shelley that Mary published after his death in *Posthumous Poems* (1824), noting that Percy wrote them in 1820. Percy had also translated canto 28 from Dante's *Purgatorio* in 1820, which suggests that *Proserpine* had perhaps served as an inspiration.

A stronger source for the dating of the plays comes from a note written by Thomas Medwin in the margin of his copy of *Life of Shelley* (1847), referencing the year 1820. He referred to "some little Dramas on classical subjects" that Mrs. Shelley had been working on. One was "The Rape of Proserpine . . . she also wrote one on Midas," and he refers to the inclusion of some of Percy's lyrics.

Koszul writes of the plays that they were "one of the earliest indications of the revival, in the heart of romanticism, of the old love of classical myths and classical beauty" (see ROMANTICISM). He explains that the Augustan Age regarded the myths as "pleasant fancies, artificial decorations," with no fresh or loving approach to the stories, despite their frequent mentions in poetry by Dryden, Pope, Swift, Gay, and others. For 18th-century English poets, mythology represented more of a "poetical curriculum" demanded by "Tradition and Propriety" to be reflected in their work. Shelley, along with members of her husband's romantic circle, helped "let free the classical sense" from "its antiquarian trammels."

Mary Shelley had studied the subject of mythology and wrote a brief essay comparing mythology to Christianity. She apparently believed that "the creed and proofs of mythology" could be found in poets' words. She wrote that the "power, wisdom, beauty & obedience" of the Greeks were greater and lasted longer than those of the Jews. She also found similarities in the interpretation of mythology by Virgil and of Christianity by John Milton. In Koszul's opinion, the dramas should be considered not only a literary but an intellectual exercise. In addition, they represent a touching example of the collaborative possibilities when Mary and Percy worked together. Like most prefeminist theory critics, Koszul sees the couple's relationship as one in which Percy mentored Mary, with Mary having little to no influence on Percy and not much original motivation to write.

On May 14, 1832, Shelley wrote to Alaric A. Watts, proposing *Midas* for publication in *Literary Souvenir*: "I do not know whether the enclosed drama will suit your Annual . . . I may mention that this drama has been seen & liked by two or three good judges whose opinion emboldens me to send it you." *Proserpine* would instead appear in *The Winter's Wreath* that same year. *Midas* first appeared in 1922 on the centenary of Percy Bysshe Shelley's death.

FURTHER READING

Pascoe, Judith. "*Proserpine* and *Midas*." In *The Cambridge Companion to Mary Shelley*, edited by Esther Schor, 180–192. Cambridge: Cambridge University Press, 2004.

Shelley, Mary Wollstonecraft. *Proserpine & Midas: Two Unpublished Mythological Dramas*. Edited by A. Koszul. London: H. Milford, 1922. Available online. URL: http://www.gutenberg.org/etext/6447. Accessed June 20, 2009.

"Roger Dodsworth: The Reanimated Englishman" (1821)

"Roger Dodsworth: The Reanimated Englishman" has been called SCIENCE FICTION by some critics, though others label it philosophy. Betty T. Bennett calls it a "delightfully witty essay." This philosophical and political work is not intended to inspire fear over the concept of a man brought back to life 160 years after being frozen in an avalanche, but rather to provoke thought. Shelley submitted it to Cyrus Redding, the working editor of the *New Monthly Magazine*, in 1826. However, it was not published until 37 years later, when Redding included it in his memoir *Yesterday and To-day*. He wrote that Shelley gave him the work "many years ago, and long before her decease. I did not use it for the purpose originally intended, and I therefore print it in another place than that in which it was originally intended to appear."

As explained by Bennett, Charles E. Robinson, and other critics, Shelley wrote the piece in response to a hoax that appeared in the *Journal du Commerce de Lyon* on June 28, 1826. The report claimed that one Mr. Dodsworth, reportedly the son of the real-life "antiquary Dodsworth, who perished in the reign of Charles I," had been discovered frozen beneath an avalanche by a Dr. Hotham of Northumberland. Shelley's piece describes Dodsworth as "a human being whose animation had been suspended by the action of the frost." Following the original article, she notes that when "the usual remedies" had been applied, "the patient was resuscitated." She based her opening statements on those made by the *Journal du Commerce de Lyon* that described the doctor placing the frozen body first into cold water, followed by lukewarm water, and then removal to a warm bed, with its faculties eventually restored by the treatment usually administered to suffocation victims. Although Dodsworth experienced "stiffness in all his joints," the account predicted that he would soon recover normal use of his faculties.

Between July 4 and July 9, 1826, six British newspapers carried the story, announcing the discovery of a frozen man who had been thawed and returned to life, some treating the event, according to Robinson, with "low forms of humor." Robinson explains that the editor of the Tory-supported publication *John Bull* reported Dodsworth was lodging in London, residing at St. James's Place. That report prompted one Joseph Jekyll to write in a letter to his sister-in-law that Samuel Rogers, who lived at St. James's Place, had better not stick his head out of his residence because he had been described in the *John Bull* as the person dug out from an avalanche. *John Bull*'s editor, Theodore Hook, had often satirized Rogers, a declared Whig, for his pallor and retiring personality. Later letters to the publication clarified that Dodsworth was actually residing with Rogers, as others picked up on the story and continued the joke. Hook received letters from someone who had adopted the persona of Dodsworth in order to write directly to the magazine. The first letter gave an account of Dodsworth's attempts to familiarize himself with present-day England, noting that "atte present I am reeding ye history of Englande, written by one Hume, and it is prettye to read of menne and things off which I had no knowledge." Hook printed the letters until he tired of the joke.

The poet Thomas More also participated in the hoax, contributing a poem to the mix that was entitled "Roger Dodsworth." More's intent is overtly political, as his satirical verse targets the Tories. It opened thus: "TO THE EDITOR OF THE TIMES. Sir—Having just heard of the wonderful resurrection of Mr. Roger Dodsworth from under an avalanche, where he had remained, bien frappe, it seems, for the last 166 years, I hasten to impart to you a few reflections on the subject.— Yours, etc." The poem reads, in part:

> Oh thaw Mr. Dodsworth and send him safe home—
> Let him learn nothing useful or new on the way;
> With his wisdom kept snug from the light let him come,
> And our Tories will hail him with "Hear!" and "Hurrah!"

What a God-send to them!—a good, obsolete man,
Who has never of Locke or Voltaire been a reader;—
Oh, thaw Mr. Dodsworth as fast as you can,
And the Lonsdales and Hertfords shall choose him as leader.

At the time when Shelley wrote *Frankenstein* (1818), public interest in galvanism and its suggested power to reanimate helped make her novel extremely popular. However, Shelley's essay does not dwell on the sensationalism of the act of reanimation. Rather, she focuses on Dodsworth's reaction to his situation and what his reaction and position as a traveler from the past to the present suggests for readers about their own legacies. Although the work bears a serious intent, she opens with a humorous description of the tendencies of human nature and of our fascination with history, describing the quick action of the antiquarian society. It had already discussed the awarding of various medals to Dodsworth and had begun "to consider what prices it could afford to offer for Mr. Dodsworth's old clothes, and to conjecture what treasures" his pockets might hold. Shelley calls attention to the commodity-centered society that immediately longs to place a monetary value on priceless antiquities, making this their primary concern. For later readers, the thought that such treasures might be auctioned off to the highest bidder would still ring true.

Shelley's piece next notes that poets, artists, antiquarians, and historians awaited the discoveries about the past that Dodsworth might reveal. She captures the importance of the event in announcing that it delayed all further recording of history, as writers waited for Dodsworth to bestow his firsthand account. She references her own father's work when she writes: "Poems from all quarters, of all kinds, elegiac, congratulatory, burlesque and allegoric, were half written. Mr. Godwin had suspended for the sake of such authentic information the history of the Commonwealthy he had just begun." She describes the reanimation, but without emphasis, as if it were an acknowledged scientific procedure:

Animation (I believe physiologists agree) can as easily be suspended for an hundred or two years, as for as many seconds. A body hermetically sealed up by the frost, is of necessity preserved in its pristine entireness. That which is totally secluded from the action of external agency, can neither have any thing added to nor taken away from it: no decay can take place, for something can never become nothing.

Shelley's unpublished writings reveal that she had previously employed the premise of a reanimated visitor from the past. The scholars Graham Allen and Elena Anastasaki view Shelley's fragment "Valerius: the Reanimated Roman" as anticipating "Roger Dodsworth." In the fragment, Valerius is a Roman consul who reflects on modern Italy and expresses his disillusionment over what he views as its deterioration. Shelley supplies no details regarding the manner by which the despondent Valerius reappears on the earth centuries after his death. His message holds greater importance than the metaphysics of his reappearance. Allen notes that "Valerius" focuses on "reversibility, a vision of history which sees the possibility for rebirth alongside that of decay and destruction." Readers understand that Valerius, who shares his thoughts with an Englishman, is hopeful that Rome can return to its previous glory.

Allen suggests that the same theme of hope is found in the report of Dodsworth, which, like "Valerius," contains a "clear political and historical point." Dodsworth also returns to his home country, England, a few centuries following his death; however, he does not speak. Instead, Shelley's narrator imagines how Dodsworth might react to modern England. At first, he mourns his life and loves lost forever. Then the narrator notes, "But we do not wish to be pathetic . . . necessity, tyrant of the world, in some degree reconciles Mr. Dodsworth to his fate." Dodsworth begins to admire the clothing of the day and dresses "in the modern style," looking "with admiration on a small Genevese watch." Shelley emphasizes the power of politics to evoke terror in a passage when Dodsworth sings a royalist song "against old Noll [Oliver Cromwell]." He then looks around fearfully to see whether he might have been discovered before realizing he need no longer fear persecution for his political beliefs.

The narrator continues to muse that Dodsworth may decide to "become whig or tory" or "content himself with turning contemplative philosopher, and find sufficient food for his mind in tracing the march of the human intellect." However, the narrator at last guesses that Dodsworth "will probably fall at once into the temporizing tone of mind now so much in vogue . . . he will still be the moderate, peaceful, unenthusiastic Mr. Dodsworth that he was in 1647." Shelley then gathers momentum to reach the point of her essay, writing that regardless of one's education or circumstance, the mind "cannot create, nor give intellect, noble aspiration, and energetic constancy where dullness, wavering of purpose, and groveling desires, are stamped by nature."

Shelley recalls the theories of Virgil and Pythagoras that individuals would die and then return to life "with the same sensibilities and capacities" as before. Remembering previous lives would clearly be useful for "kings and statesmen, and in fact for all human beings, called on as they are, to play their part on the stage of the world." Such an arrangement, Shelley holds, would allow us to "obtain a glimpse of heaven and of hell, as, the secret of our former identity confined to our own bosoms, we winced or exulted in the blame or praise bestowed on our former selves." She suggests that certain important characters would discover themselves to be hypocrites if their former existences were illuminated. For instance, a "judge as he passed sentence would suddenly become aware, that formerly he had condemned the saints of the early church to the torture, for not renouncing the religion he now upheld." The narrator suggests that "nothing but benevolent actions and real goodness would come pure out of the ordeal." Thus, Shelley asks readers to consider the benefits of our learning not only the lessons of world history but of our own history, and also to consider what heritage we leave to those who follow. Our firmest beliefs may be built on shifting sands. Shelley asks readers to consider the ephemeral nature of cultural values and to gauge the risks inherent to conformity.

One of Shelley's favored topics is that of personal isolation, and interested readers have discovered through her personal writings and the reports of others that she suffered from loneliness and rejection during a great deal of her life. "Roger Dodsworth" seems to reflect this concern. The emphasis on isolation, disorientation, and abandonment remains prominent in Dodsworth's feelings of having "no affinity between himself and the present state of things." It is also echoed in Valerius's description of "the feeling so dreadful to the human mind, the feeling of utter solitude." Interestingly, in the case of Dodsworth, the lack of affinity is not tragic. Shelley writes, "perhaps he opened his eyes only to shut them again more obstinately; perhaps his ancient clay could not thrive on the harvests of these latter days."

FURTHER READING

Allen, Graham. "Reanimation or Reversibility in 'Valerius: The Reanimated Roman': A Response to Elena Anastasaki." *Connotations* 19, nos. 1–3 (2009/2010): 21–33.

Anastasaki, Elena. "The Trials and Tribulations of the *revenants*: Narrative Techniques and the Fragmented Hero in Mary Shelley and Théophile Gautier." *Connotations* 16, nos. 1–3 (2006/2007): 26–46.

Ketterer, David. "Metaphoric Matrix: Magnetism in Frankenstein." In *Selected Proceedings of the 1978 Science Fiction Research Association National Conference*, edited by Thomas J. Remington, 55–67. Cedar Falls: University of Northern Iowa Press, 1979.

Redding, Cyrus. *Yesterday and To-day*. London: T. Cautley Newby, 1863.

Robinson, Charles E. "Mary Shelley and the Roger Dodsworth Hoax." *Keats-Shelley Journal* 24 (1975): 20–28.

Shelley, Mary. "Roger Dodsworth: The Reanimated Englishman." In *The Mary Shelley Reader*, edited by Betty T. Bennett and Charles E. Robinson, 274–281. New York: Oxford University Press, 1990.

———. "Valerius: The Reanimated Roman." In *Mary Shelley: Collected Tales and Stories*, edited by Charles E. Robinson, 332–344. Baltimore: Johns Hopkins University Press, 1976.

———."Valerius: The Reanimated Roman." Available online. URL: http://arthursclassicnovels.com/shelley/valrom10.html. Accessed February 7, 2011.

"Transformation" (1830)

First published in 1831 in THE KEEPSAKE, Mary Shelley's short story "Transformation" shares many traits with her other fiction. Most of her work makes clear her fascination with attempts by humans to remake themselves, either through self-transformation or creation of the perfect human through a kind of black science. Her more fortunate characters learn that attempts at a physical transformation more often than not prove futile. That self-education motivates them to undertake instead a more successful internal mental or spiritual transformation, the result of what later readers might term a *reality check*. "Transformation" is classified as gothic (see GOTHIC FICTION) or horror fiction, although supported by basic tenets found in romantic fiction. Romantic ideals greatly affected all of Shelley's works, influenced by her marriage to, and collaboration with, one of the best-known romantic poets, PERCY BYSSHE SHELLEY. Her father, WILLIAM GODWIN, was later credited for sparking the romantic movement through the ideals expressed in his *An Inquiry Concerning the Principles of Political Justice and Its Influence in General Virtue and Happiness* (1793). In addition, Shelley was privy to much conversation with other romantic poets, particularly GEORGE GORDON BYRON (Lord Byron).

Traditional critics focus on the theme of science versus nature in some of Shelley's fiction. An intellectual observer of a time during which the nascent field of science offered the possibility of horrendous future changes, Shelley seemed possessed by the goal of warning people away from adopting science to act against nature. That approach has been most widely discussed in reference to her most popular and best-known tale, *Frankenstein; or, The Modern Prometheus* (1818), although more recent criticism notes that approach to be a "misreading" of her fiction.

Others of Shelley's stories that did not include the temptations of science depended instead upon a tried-and-true plot line, that of an individual willing to trade his soul for the promise of great wealth or an equally attractive material goal. "Transformation" echoes the Faustian tale in which a protagonist trades his soul to Satan for the reward of immortality or other great powers. It strongly emphasizes the idea of a fall from grace followed by redemption, a nod to one of Shelley's greatest influences, John Milton's PARADISE LOST (1667). In addition, in her warning to turn to nature for answers, rather than science, Shelley embraced a key tenet of ROMANTICISM. While one should not turn to any single label in an attempt to categorize "Transformation," an examination of the dichotomy of science/faith remains valid as one method of analysis. Also important are theories that view "Transformation" as a tale that offers a critique not of science in general but rather of its masculine nature and its attitude toward the female body as "other." Science offered men power and control not available to women and was used to further objectify women's bodies. Finally, recent scholarship examines Shelley's characterization of the mostly silent female in "Transformation"—Juliet.

SYNOPSIS

"Transformation" features a traditional fall from grace and redemption plot line, emphasizing horror aspects of the fall. Guido Cortesi narrates his own story, as in other stories in which Shelley adopts a male voice. Born wealthy and privileged to a moral, ethical, aristocratic father, Guido has a rebellious streak as a child that grows into arrogance and resistance as he matures. While his father attempts to set an excellent example for his son, Guido only mimics his father's good acts, biding his time until he may begin to act on his evil tendencies. His father's friend, Marchese Torella, is ensnared in political turmoil that sends him into exile. He leaves behind his beautiful, angelic daughter, Juliet, in the care of Guido's father. Three years older than Juliet, Guido vows the two will marry, formalizing his vow in a chapel when Juliet is still a child. A few years later, Torella returns to Genoa, and Juliet returns to her home to be raised by her father, who agrees that Juliet may later marry Guido. Following his father's death, Guido is informally adopted by Torella.

At age 17, Guido sets out for Paris and begins living a debauched and profligate life. He attracts wild friends more than happy to help spend his fortune, which he goes through at an alarming rate. With the revolution of Charles VI of France, Guido must depart Paris. He has wasted almost all of his inheritance but assumes he will accumulate additional wealth upon his return home. In order to promote the guise of wealth, he sells his last estate for half of its value. The funds allow him to return home and continue the ruse of being wealthy for a short time. He sends Juliet an expensive gift but does not visit her father as protocol demands. When he finally travels to the Torellas' estate, producing the contract his father had written regarding his personal value, the fact that Guido no longer possesses his family fortune is revealed. Rather than refusing to give Guido his daughter in marriage, Torella proposes an alternate agreement. While financially generous, it establishes controls over Guido's actions, and the young man's pride will not allow him to accept the agreement. He departs and then attempts to institute a wild scheme to kidnap Torella and Juliet. When the scheme fails, Guido is isolated and penniless.

Guido wanders in poverty until reaching a beach, where he observes a floundering ship that eventually sinks, killing all aboard except for a dwarf. The dwarf floats to shore astride a large chest filled with treasure. Guido finds the dwarf repulsive and ugly and soon realizes that he is a demon sent to tempt Guido. The dwarf offers to trade his own misshapen form for Guido's handsome body for three days, after which he will reward Guido with the entire treasure. Guido hesitates but then agrees after learning that an antidote to the spell that traps him inside the dwarf's body and liberates the dwarf inside him is for the blood of the two to mix. While in torment awaiting the dwarf's return, Guido dreams that the dwarf, disguised as him, will claim Juliet. When the agreed-upon three days pass and the dwarf does not return, Guido sets out for the Torellas' estate. He must hide along the way in order to avoid humiliation and abuse at the hands of others against his hideous form.

When he arrives at the estate, his fears are realized. Everything is in a state of celebration, and Guido understands that the dwarf has convinced Torella and Juliet that he is a repentant Guido, now ready to change his life and marry Juliet. At last understanding that he must rescue Juliet from the fate created by his own misplaced hate and desire for revenge, Guido, in disguise as a dwarf, attacks the dwarf. Both are stabbed, and the dwarf dies, leaving Guido to reoccupy his rightful body when their blood runs together and the spell is broken. In the confusion, Juliet and others assume that Guido has saved the household from the insane dwarf, and no one ever learns about the spell or Guido's humiliation. Weakened by the physical encounter, Guido remains strong enough to marry Juliet and spend his remaining years with her, a much happier and wiser man.

COMMENTARY

"Transformation" begins with an explanation of its narrative design. The epigram—excerpted from the romantic poet Samuel Taylor Coleridge's *The Rime of the Ancient Mariner*—emphasizes the theme of confession, as its speaker states, "And till my ghastly tale is told / This heart within me burns." He also makes clear that only by sharing the story with others will he be set free from "a woeful agony." *Frankenstein* introduced this approach on Shelley's part, inviting its readers into the private world of letters and journals that act as a confessional not only for Victor Frankenstein but also for his audience of one, a ship's captain charged as chronicler of the scientist's mad tale. Based in the classic tradition that one may achieve immortality by becoming the subject of such tales, Shelley makes this wish for herself, mouthing it through her various protagonists.

The protagonist/narrator of "Transformation" introduces his tale to his audience as a confessional, explaining that a priest, now dead, had already heard his religious confession. As in others of Shelley's stories, this confessional remains a crucial aspect of a cautionary tale, prompted in this case by the narrator's experiencing an "intellectual earthquake" that moves him to "tell a tale of impious tempting of providence and soul-subduing humiliation." He shares that he has never told anyone his story but is convinced that in the telling, he may save others, so he will proceed. Shelley consistently warns of the human propensity to fall to such temptation, often injecting imagery and references to man's original Fall in the Garden of Eden. As Adam and Eve partook literally of the fruit of knowledge to which they should not have become privy, so do Shelley's heedless characters, some of whom pay the ultimate price for so doing.

The narrator first identifies his birthplace as Genoa, praising the natural environment in which he matured, as if to release it from any claims of guilt for his having been born with "the most imperious, haughty, tameless spirit." He also releases his aristocratic father from blame, noting the many attempts made to train him in proper behavior. The narrator confesses that he followed his father's precepts only for self-gain, not because he shared the good man's noble motivation. Shelley adopts multiple subplots from *Frankenstein* when the narrator explains that his father's only friend, Marchese Torella, was banished from Genoa due to "political tumult," leaving his daughter Juliet to mature in the narrator's household. Predictably, the narrator falls in love with Juliet but claims her more as an object, a treasure, than as an emotional mate. Juliet is shaped as what Virginia Woolf, the modernist feminist writer, termed the stereotypical angel of the house, a woman sweeter than a May rose, gentle, reliable, "loving, and pure," a "celestial tenement," all of this at the tender age of eight years. Juliet's more-than-human nature is confirmed by the narrator's first confessing his feeling to her in a chapel and declaring her his intended.

Feminist critics observe with interest the objectification of all female characters in Shelley's fiction. Early readings characterized the passive females as merely useful to the cautionary theme of the story, as they were in the traditional fairy tale. However, later feminist scholarship has offered somewhat more useful interpretations of their roles.

The narrator of "Transformation" does not have a name until well into the story, when he refers to himself in the third-person point of view as Guido.

He remains a ne'er-do-well, spending debauched, youthful years prospering from his father's wealth until his father dies when Guido is 17. By that time, Torella has returned and becomes Guido's new father figure. As in *Frankenstein*, where Victor and Elizabeth also matured as brother and adopted sister, the romantic involvement of Shelley's characters hints at incest, a fact that many psychoanalytic critics find of interest.

Guido departs Genoa to travel Europe, spending much time in Paris under the mad King Charles VI, allowing readers to date the story to the 1380–1422 reign of the French monarch known as "Charles the Foolish." Shelley adds much detail of the terror caused by political unrest, calling reader attention to the subject of political upheaval in France that led to revolution and regicide shortly before Shelley's birth in 1789. She reflects the interest of her parents, MARY WOLLSTONECRAFT and William Godwin, both of whom were extremely active in revolutionary movements but encountered conflict in trying to live their radical ideology. Her contemporaries would have known of the revolution and might have seen Shelley's focus on a bloody revolution sparked by the arrogance inherent to a class system as a part of the cautionary nature of her story.

Still "arrogant and self-willed," Guido throws away much of his fortune, wasting it on entertaining his entourage and learning the ways of love, in order to romance women. He returns to Genoa to claim Juliet, conducting various schemes to fool her and her father into believing he remains wealthy and presenting Juliet with an expensive horse. Unrealistically, Guido assumes that he will quickly rebuild his fortune, but instead he learns that will be impossible. Labeling himself for his reading audience a "beggar" surrounded by luxury, he nevertheless continues a debauched lifestyle in order to support the identity he desires. The shaking of that destructive self-identity constitutes the transformation referenced in the story's title.

Guido behaves badly toward Torella, failing to follow custom and call on the older man, haughtily believing that Torella should seek him out. When Guido does at last visit Torella in May, at a time when "heaven and earth wore a mantle of surpassing beauty," the older man cannot conceal his displeasure over Guido's reputation but soon forgives him, possessing a "good old man's heart." As for Juliet, Shelley follows the model of male writers, freezing Juliet's maturation process. She reduces Juliet to a child in order to emphasize her innocence, evident in her comparison to a cherub and the description of her mouth as possessing "infantine sweetness."

Guido's raw emotions leave him jealous and possessive, rather than grateful for the possibility of a promising future with Juliet. He cannot hide his basic character, and his wasteful lifestyle becomes clear when the contract drawn up by his father promising certain wealth to Juliet upon her agreeing to marry Guido is revealed as worthless. Torella still maintains Guido's honor, offering a new contract with Guido, but one that contains spending restrictions. Guido's greed drives him to reject that offer, as he states, "Roused pride became the tyrant of my thought." Shelley makes clear that human pride is a culprit certain to lead to disgrace and downfall.

As Guido continues to destroy his connections to this supportive adoptive family, he attempts to draw Juliet into his downward spiral. He urges her to leave her "cold-hearted, cold-blooded" father with the specious argument that if she does not, she will rob him, Guido, of his only treasure, her. Feminist critics would note Juliet's further objectification, undergoing a transformation herself into a material commodity, a detail also of interest to Marxist critics. Guido concludes his temptation of Juliet by inviting her to join him to "defy the world," their love for one another becoming "a refuge" from life's challenges. In this scene, Guido takes on the Satan role in the Garden of Eden, while Juliet represents Eve. Interestingly Juliet suddenly becomes more active, rejecting temptation in a way Eve could not.

New Historicist critics would look to Shelley's own stormy marital history and claim some autobiographical influence in this passage. She had run away with Percy Shelley as a teenager, while he was still married, and the two had lived as self-exiles from England, where Shelley's father and the wider community were outraged by their actions. Whether she projects her own past situation onto Juliet's ability to withstand Guido's invitation, instead urging Guido to obey her father, who had only the best intentions toward them, is doubtful. However, the story's message is clear: Following the rules will lead to a positive outcome, where rebellious activity likely will not. At this point, Guido refers to himself as a "Fiend," and a short time later, he categorizes his abandoning Juliet as possession by a fiend who has overtaken his soul. The reader understands that as an ironic quest character, Guido has begun his descent.

Consumed by rage, the product of his pride, Guido plots to kidnap Torella and Juliet with the assistance of his friends. The reader recognizes the insanity of such a plan and can predict its failure. Now a true outcast and abandoned by his one-time companions, who have returned to France, Guido wanders alone along a deserted beach. Shelley injects various archetypes to help ground readers in the tradition of the cautionary tale, with strong links to biblical mythology. The sea itself invokes visions of a failed HERO'S JOURNEY, or odyssey, while calling to mind the ebb and flow of emotions. Guido's seizure by the desire for revenge suggests the fatal flaw the Greeks labeled *hamartia*, which in classic drama led directly to the classical hero's demise. Shelley applies figurative language to characterize the revenge through personification as a serpent that stings Guido. The serpent, another archetype, evokes echoes once again of Eden, suggesting temptation but also the ending of what promised to be a joyful and carefree future. In his mental anguish, Guido understands that he cannot follow his companions to Paris without wealth, and he thinks of himself as "a new Coriolanus," separated from his previous glory by Torella. The reference to Coriolanus takes knowledgeable readers back to Shakespeare's play of the same name, an association that reader response and structuralist critics would term *intertexuality*. Coriolanus, once a hero of Rome, is eventually driven from the city by his former supporters, actions parallel to those of Shelley's tale. In addition, through that reference, Shelley calls attention to the topic of self identify. Born Caius Martius, the war hero is renamed Coriolanus for the Italian city he conquered, Corioles. Character names remain crucial in literature as symbolic of identity. For instance, Juliet's name links her inextricably with Shakespeare's heroine, but this Juliet will triumph over the spiritual death offered by her lover, Guido. At this point in the story, then, readers understand through the Coriolanus reference (or on their own) that Guido has lost his sense of identity.

The cautionary nature of the story becomes clear as Guido adopts another biblical allusion to intellectualize the fact that he has "reaped the harvest" of his actions. After much struggle with emotions such as hate, he recognizes that he has lost Juliet. She appears as a vision, with an "angel face and sylphlike form" to torment Guido. He continues his ironic quest, observing the destruction of a ship offshore that washes to the beach a human riding on a sea chest filled with treasure. The traditional quest hero would have been aboard the ship and completed a successful adventure, avoiding the destruction endured by the hands on this ship.

Shelley's rich imagery shapes the human figure and Guido's thoughts in such a way as to suggest that all that has happened may be a continuation of Guido's vision state. Psychoanalytic critics might analyze what happens next as part of a dream sequence, in which hidden desires suppressed by the libido rise to the surface, particularly when the human form is recognized as a dwarf. Followers of Carl Jung would suggest that the dwarf personifies Guido's libido in its purest emotional form. In selecting a dwarf as trickster/villain, Shelley contributes to a tradition seen in the fairy tale "Rumpelstiltskin." Edgar Allan Poe, America's first and best-known master of horror, would also adopt dwarf characters, such as Hop Frog, to suggest the terror of the not fully developed human. However, Poe humanizes the dwarf who takes revenge on those who mistreat him. Various critics point to Shelley's experience with miscarriages and the loss of almost all of her children as inspiration behind her undeveloped characters, including the woman monster Victor Frankenstein agrees to create as a companion for his monster. In the dwarf, Guido experiences a reflection of his lesser, debased self.

In his isolation, Guido's heart warms to another human, even as he describes him as "odious." However, when the dwarf declares, "By St. Beelzebub!" he clearly depicts himself a minion of Satan. Readers then recognize that Guido's temptation will continue, with the remorse he has experienced as a serpent's sting from transforming into another demonic figure. The dwarf takes credit for having conjured the storm that meant doom for the ship's occupants and left the treasure all to him. Treasure plays a significant part in the hero's journey as his reward for completing an honorable quest. Thus, Shelley again emphasizes the ironic nature of Guido's quest. She further extends that plot line as Guido labels the dwarf a magician and considers the seductive nature of "power, in all its shapes." Mystical occurrences and shape-shifters are stock elements of the quest plot sequence. The dwarf's ill-gotten treasure echoes the previous reference to Juliet, now lost, as treasure, further emphasizing Guido's fall.

Guido's deal with Lucifer is an exchange of physical form for three days, with that time period suggesting the three days required for Christ's transformation from death to a new existence. The dwarf's suggestion that they exchange their bodies sickens Guido, but his new companion's seductive language convinces him to agree. The dwarf embraces Guido as a cousin and verbalizes Guido's resistance to the attempts of Torella to rescue him as a courageous unwillingness to "submit to the tyranny of good." Shelley includes the figurative language of paradox in that phrase, supporting her message that Guido has wandered so far from his humanity as to confuse good with evil.

That the dwarf would see the self-control required for humans to act against their baser nature to achieve good confirms him as a demon. He tempts Guido not only with his promise of all the treasure in exchange for a body exchange, but also with his false sympathy. As the narrator Guido looks back on this scene, Shelley extends the serpent metaphor in his sharing with the reader that at that moment, "a thousand fanged thoughts" stung him. He acknowledges that to his audience, his agreeing to such an exchange appears to be madness. However, he reminds the audience that he was talking with someone who, although ugly, had a voice designed to "govern earth, air, and sea." Shelley once again warns her audience that control over natural elements remains outside mankind's realm, and any desire on man's part to exercise such control simply tempts disaster. Guido rationalizes his actions by referencing rules that govern the art of magic and restrain its practitioners from breaking "formulas and oaths" such as the one the dwarf agreed to. His thought process supports a common movement in fiction plotting from order to chaos, emphasizing how easily such a transformation can take place. Order demands rules and rituals, and *chaos* is generally defined as a lack of those rules. However, the demon seduces Guido into believing that the chaos he presently inhabits is also governed by rules. Milton did the same in his depiction of the newly formed hell following Satan's fall, when the various demons are controlled by hierarchical order.

Predictably, Guido agrees to exchange bodies with the dwarf, who promises to return in three days, leaving in Guido's care the treasure as a bond. Before the dwarf departs, he confesses that were his and Guido's blood allowed to mix, the spell would be broken. Guido's world within the dwarf's body is dark and troubled and may be compared to a nightmare world. Shelley's skill as a horror writer is made clear through the mental torment of her protagonist. He suddenly realizes through his dreams that the dwarf-in-disguise intends to possess Juliet. When he awakes, it is with an epiphany of sorts as he wonders whether his dream did not mirror the truth. Psychoanalytic critics would point out that Guido recognizes in his vision his own evil attempts to possess Juliet against her will. Again Shelley employs a traditional symbol with the mirror, representative of self-contemplation and self-identity. She also suggests that storytelling and literature hold a mirror to the world, allowing their audiences to view the truth such tales intend to teach. That symbol will reappear significantly in the story's conclusion.

When the dwarf fails to return following the three-day promised period, Guido leaves the treasure to travel to the Torella estate. His worse fears realized, he observes the celebration that precedes a wedding. The plot's action escalates to its climax in a bloody confrontation between Guido and the dwarf as they fight to the death. Briefly a confusion of identities between Guido-as-dwarf and dwarf-as-Guido occurs in the tradition of the quest, which often involves disguises. Psychoanalytic critics look to that scene as symbolic of Guido's struggle with his own alter ego, the pitting of his good essence against his evil essence. This interpretation is strengthened when Guido takes advantage of the antidote to the spell by assuring his blood mixes with that of the dwarf. Badly wounded, Guido is tended by Juliet as he recovers. He realizes that everyone assumed the dwarf, actually Guido, had invaded the estate intending harm to Juliet. Guido understands that by remaining silent regarding the true details of his situation, he may preserve his newfound positive reputation.

Thus, Guido experiences transformation and resurrection, the latter act clarified in his comment while ill, "Again I returned to life." Although not a BYRONIC HERO in the purest sense, he does suffer a permanent physical loss as a result of his redemption, typical of that type of character, remaining weakened and somewhat bent over for the remainder of his life. He assumes his responsibilities and lives a productive life, having rejected his "accursed pride" and turning no more to "demoniac violence and wicked self-idolatry." When he awakens from delirium, he requests a mirror. Juliet fears he will be upset by his wan and sickly appearance, but Guido seeks more than a view of his surface appearance. He tells readers, "I thought myself a right proper youth when I saw the dear reflection of my own well-known features." Indeed, he demands to be surrounded by mirrors, consulting them more often than any Venetian beauty. To perceived reader criticism of his vanity, he responds that "no one better knows than I the value of his own body; no one, probably, except myself, ever having had it stolen from him." Feminist critics look to both Guido's silence and his ongoing fixation on mirrors throughout his life as an interesting gender role change. In addition, his allusion to the theft (or exchange) of his body may be seen as a subtext describing the common situation of Juliet and the women she represents, most of whom had no say in the control of their own bodies.

The act of contrition that assures readers that Guido's change is genuine is his choosing to never return to the beach to claim the treasure chest, instead finding his reward with Juliet and the chance for a new life. He shares with readers a suggestion made by his confessor that the dwarf might actually have been a good spirit, sent to earth to help him recognize his faults. His transformation is complete when he assumes a new name, Guido il Cortese, Italian for Guido the kindhearted. On the surface, he exchanges material for spiritual reward, allowing Shelley to reemphasize that good behavior will be rewarded on a higher plane. However, later critics, feminist critics especially, are quick to point out that he will still inherit a fortune, all due to his selection of the correct bride, simply a different type of commodity.

CHARACTERS

Guido The main character, Guido represents the human tendency toward arrogance and self-interest that can only be tempered through self-discipline and dedication to all that is good in life. He is a storyteller of the type who hopes others will profit from his testimony about a secret shame. He makes a sound chronicler because he has gained sharp self-insight and clear vision following his temptation and suffering. Like Victor Frankenstein, he tells his tale to save others, but unlike Victor, he gains grace before his fate is sealed. Like a character in a Greek drama, Guido must be of aristocratic blood to make his fall meaningful. He must descend from a heady height to create terror in his audience. What happens to him must be horrifying to allow his audience to experience catharsis and gain knowledge without themselves suffering any harm. He shares some traits with the Byronic hero, including a passionate, moody personality and suffering a permanent physical loss due to his exploits, but he lacks the trademark mysterious background of that character type. Using such labels can be problematic, particularly when they are new at the point in history when a work is created. Ironically, Shelley knew the real Byron all too well, and whether she based her male characters on him remains unclear.

Guido rebels not so much against his father but, rather, what his father represents, which is control. This factor makes him realistic for readers who have possibly experienced similar tension with authority figures, particularly in matters of romance. It provides traditional man-versus-man conflict that is supported by man-versus-self conflict. His regard of Juliet as little more than a possession is a common depiction of 19th-century fiction, designed in part to fulfill female fantasies of nurture and care by a strong male, fantasies feminist critics would say had their source in a patriarchal culture.

Guido is definitely a man's man, carousing with male friends until his funds are depleted. His early immaturity, seen in displays of excess, would be indulged, but at a certain point, he is expected to step into his father's shoes, take a respectable wife, and lead a respectable life, represented by Torella. The fact that he feels shame over the loss of his fortune humanizes him, but his stubborn attitude and resistance to the chance for redemption offered by Torella quickly escalates into hate and jealousy, moving him closer to the inhuman. Thus, when the dwarf enters his life, Guido has already begun a transition that privileges his dark instincts. His descent into a destructive rage makes him a perfect victim for the demon's temptation.

Guido's better instincts win during the battle on the beach, and he becomes more sympathetic when his thoughts turn to the rescue of Juliet. Only when he understands that he may have sacrificed her life in addition to his can he begin his ascent back toward the light of humanity. His tone is properly repentant throughout the tale, and readers are pleased to see the epiphany that restores his life from chaos to the order that the properly formed family unit of Guido, Juliet, and Torella offers.

The Dwarf The dwarf, who is the antagonist and a minor character, makes an outstanding villain due not only to his amorality but also to his misshapen body. Shelley uses what her readers would view as his physical deformity to arouse horror and disgust. Echoes of the same logic Satan used in Eden to convince Eve of the virtue of his suggestion is plied by the dwarf. The dwarf makes no claim to be anything other than what he is, dropping abundant hints that he is a demon sent to earth to fulfill Satan's desire. In somewhat of a twist on the traditional Faustian tale, in which a human soul is offered in trade for immortality, Guido offers his body in trade for treasure. His soul remains intact, allowing him to then intercede in the dwarf's wicked plan to claim Juliet. Readers would be aghast at the idea of such a homely creature, although disguised in Guido's handsome form, marrying and lying with Juliet. In personifying all of Guido's evil passions, the dwarf may summarily be dispatched and Guido's dark personality with him. He is as important a symbolic figure as he is a "real" demon, for he represents the dark side that Shelley suggests all humans—or, more properly, all males—possess and must conquer in order to live productive and blessed lives. He also proves that a minor character may prove of major importance to a story's plot. In an additional critical analysis, Marjean D. Purinton sees Guido's transformation into the dwarf as Shelley inverting the commodification of women's bodies. That commodification provided the basis for "the exchange upon which the nineteenth-century marriage myth rests."

Juliet Most critics deem Juliet a stock figure, a caricature of the pure woman in need of rescue well represented in traditional literature. Shelley leaves Juliet a child for the most part, incapable of caring for herself or others. While her naïveté would be prized in Shelley's age, Juliet's banal, dull innocence is viewed as a liability by later readers. She is there as an object, a possession over which males may do battle. The first battle occurs between Guido and an unnamed young man who shows Juliet attention; Guido soundly trounces him. The second battle occurs between Guido and Torella, and the older man proves victorious. The final battle between Guido and the dwarf is far more serious, as it is for Juliet's virtue. Like the damsel of old, she can be rescued by a strong, active male who saves her from a fate over which she can have no control. She plays a critical part, however, as Guido would not have found grace had he not felt guilty for sacrificing Juliet to his pride and arrogance.

More recent scholarship asks readers to reconsider that characterization of Juliet. Some critics see her silence as the manner by which Shelley calls attention to the condition of women within her own era. Juliet's "lack of agency," or ability to participate, may be viewed in the opposite fashion, as her restraint that allows Guido to learn and speak his own realization. Marjean D. Purinton describes Juliet as emodying "the woman of [Mary] Wollstonecraft's gilded cage, imprisoned by societal limitations imposed on women." She views the transformation of Guido as "a critique of society structured on the privilege of patriarchy." Had Juliet moralized to and instructed Guido, she would be seen as a harpy or shrew by Shelley's readers. She maintains silence, providing an example for Guido through her own moral and ethical lifestyle. He understands that unless he literally transforms, he cannot share her life. He understands this when he views his dwarf self, repentant and kind to Juliet, benefitting from the promise of a new and rich life.

Torella Torella is another crucial minor character. His stepping in to take the place of Guido's father offers the same blended family that Shelley shaped in *Frankenstein*. As in her novel, the young lovers mature as brother and sister, although Guido declares his love to Juliet early on. Torella's part is to remain strong in the face of Guido's arrogance and aggression. His love and respect for Guido stand in stark contrast to Guido's attitude toward him, which allows Shelley to emphasize that Guido's youth is at least partly responsible for his false pride. With maturity and grace, Guido may evolve into a man of Torella's stature.

FURTHER READING

Burke, Edmund. *Reflections on the Revolution in France*. Edited by Conor Cruise O'Brien. Harmondsworth, U.K.: Penguin, 1968.

Cantor, Paul A. "Mary Shelley and the Taming of the Byronic Hero: 'Transformation' and the Deformed Transformed." In *The Other Mary Shelley; Beyond Frankenstein*, edited by Audrey A. Fisch, Anne K. Mellor, and Esther H. Schor, 89–106. New York: Oxford University Press, 1993.

Godwin, William. *Enquiry Concerning Political Justice*. Edited by Isaac Kramnick. Harmondsworth, U.K.: Penguin, 1985.

Hofkosh, Sonia. "Disfiguring Economies: Mary Shelley's Short Stories." In *The Other Mary Shelley:*

Beyond Frankenstein, edited by E. Audrey, A. Fisch, Anne K. Mellor, and Esther H. Schor, 204–219. New York: Oxford University Press, 1993.

Keller, Evelyn Fox. "Feminism and Science." *Signs* 7, no. 3 (1982): 589–602.

Purinton, Marjean D. "Mary Shelley's Science Fiction Short Stories and the Legacy of Wollstonecraft's Feminism." *Women's Studies* 30, no. 2 (April 2002): 147–175.

Simpkins, Scott. "They Do the Men in Different Voices: Narrative Cross Dressing in Sand and Shelley." *Literary Criticism* 26, no. 3 (Fall 1992): 400–418.

Valperga, or the Life and Adventures of Castruccio, Prince of Lucca (1823)

Originally titled *Castruccio, Prince of Luca,* Mary Shelley's novel was first submitted for publication by PERCY BYSSHE SHELLEY to his publisher, Charles Ollier, on July 21, 1821. In his letter, he requested that his wife not be identified by the phrase used in previous publications of her work, "by the author of *Frankenstein*," for fear some readers and critics might be "prejudiced by *Frankenstein*" against Mary's second work. He predicted correctly, as her second novel would challenge what the scholar Stuart Curran labeled "facile cultural assumptions" that were clear in conservative periodical reviews.

Published in 1823, *Valperga* represented Mary Shelley's departure from the GOTHIC FICTION genre, which had so strongly informed *Frankenstein* (1818) and *Mathilda* (written 1819; published 1959). While aspects of the gothic would continue to appear in her works, its presentation was tempered in *Valperga* by Shelley's incorporation of large amounts of historical detail, modeled after the newly devised subgenre of historical fiction by Sir Walter Scott. He had also written about the same historical figure, Castruccio. Influences also included Sophia Lee's *The Recess* and works by Joanna Baillie, who had explored the theme of political ambition in her drama *Ethwald*. While Shelley's character Euthanasia operates as the heroine, critics agree that Beatrice is the most vividly drawn character. In her conversion to the Paterin belief that evil will prevail, Beatrice was viewed by Shelley's father, WILLIAM GODWIN, as *Valperga*'s main asset in her embodiment of the grotesque.

Godwin had much input into this novel. After Shelley could not find a publisher for the book, she turned the project over to her father, telling him that if he could get it published, he could have any profits. Godwin enthusiastically took on the project, which echoed so much of his basic philosophy. It was published by the minor firm of G. and W. B. Whittaker.

Critics have viewed the novel in various ways. Some see it as simply romance, in the vein of Scott, with Shelley reenvisioning history to fit her romantic needs. Those who agree that politics are its central concern write of it as only an organizing principle for the plot and charge Shelley with philosophical inconsistency. More recent scholarship views the novel as a serious political project, informed by Shelley's intensive study of history and by her parents' and Percy's theories, especially those of her father. Through *Valperga*, she critiques the destructive nature of male ambition and egotism.

Readers catch a glimpse of Shelley's method of study in her preface, which contains citations of various historical sources for the life of Castruccio, a 14th-century citizen of Lucca, Italy. His biography was well known to readers, having been included in Niccolò Machiavelli's profiles of rulers and used as the subject of various works of literature that followed. Shelley includes among her sources "Macchiavelli's romance" *La vita di Castruccio Castracani da Lucca* (1532). As one of *Valperga*'s reviewers wrote, "the marvellous rise of such a man to sovereign and tyrannic power, his preservation of all his original manners in that high estate, his deep ambition, his fiery valour, his sportive wit, his searing ironies" had "long been familiar" to informed readers.

Castruccio supported the Ghibeline political faction, which in turn supported the (German) Holy Roman Empire. The Ghibelines constantly clashed with the Guelphs, who supported the pope and the independence of Italian cities. Many of Shelley's readers and those in later eras were familiar with the Ghibeline/Guelph conflict through knowledge of Dante Alighieri, author of the *Divina Commedia* and member of a prominent Florentine family who sided with the later White Guelphs, who opposed the papacy. His political views later caused Dante's exile from Florence, with exile emphasized as a fate shared by several characters in *Valperga*. The Florentine Guelphs play a prominent role in the novel as inhabitants of a republican city during the time period that Shelley features. Their historical conflict with the Ghibelines offered Shelley the perfect structure for a novel based on the clash caused by two ferociously different political ideologies. The real-life Castruccio earned promotion through a military career and eventually became prince of Lucca, earning a reputation as a cruel tyrant who would stop at nothing to advance his rule.

Various critics have found fault with Shelley's nonadherence to historical fact in *Valperga*. Countering such complaints, the scholar Betty T. Bennett points out that Shelley announces in the preface her deviation from historical fact when she writes: "The dates here given are somewhat different from those adopted in the following narrative." She undertakes historical revision in order to fabricate relationships for Castruccio with two fictional women: Euthanasia and Beatrice. Euthanasia represents a combination of Godwin rationality and Percy and Mary Shelley's emphasis on the necessity of love as a part of decision making. Beatrice represents the imagination, a positive element of the romantic ideal, but she demonstrates the dire consequences of imagination that is misguided by superstition, including that of religion. Through Euthanasia, Shelley demonstrates her view of history as an ongoing conflict between specific sets of forces, in this case between those that trust human rationality to institute a successful republic and those that desire centralized power for a few individuals. As Bennett notes, the conflict is set out in the novel's complete title. Valperga is Euthanasia's home and represents social equality, independence, and shared responsibility. In contrast, Castruccio represents a tyrannical governmental rule bent on its own "aggrandizement and perpetuation," unafraid to destroy its subjects to reach its goals. The two cannot coexist; therein lies the novel's tension. The ambitious desire for fame and power corrupt the young, idealistic Castruccio. However, it does not have the same effect on Euthanasia or on the other important female figure in the novel, Beatrice, who represents irrational loyalty in her devotion to, and eventual betrayal by, Castruccio.

Stuart Curran explains that in addition to providing "immersion in local Italian history and culture," the novel "reveals a deep ideological identification" with Jean Charles Léonard Simonde de Sismondi's *Histoire des républiques italiennes du moyen âge* (1809–18). In the preface, Shelley describes Sismondi's work as a "delightful publication." It provided a history of medieval Italian states that had not yet been translated when Shelley was at work on her novel, but she assimilated its ideas into *Valperga*. She used the second edition of Sismondi's history, published in Paris in 1818, in which he emphasized the parallels between Napoleon's heavy-handed rule and that of Castruccio. While she does not emphasize that comparison in

FPO fig. 19

Portrait of Dante Alighieri from 1530. Mary Shelley alludes to Dante's work in her novel *Valperga*. *(Painting by Florentinischer Meister)*

her novel, she does stress that what is at stake in Valperga, and by extension in human civilization, is republican liberty in perpetual conflict with the aristocratic government still practiced in England and most European countries. Sismondi characterized the Guelphs as emblematic for local and democratic values, in contrast to the imperialist values of autocracy.

Because Godwin edited the novel, some scholars have written of concerns that it should be credited to him, rather than to Shelley. So many of Godwin's ideas inhabit the plot and character shaping that some critics believe he might have heavily rewritten Shelley's text. Their belief is based in part on a letter Godwin sent to Shelley, stating about his work on the novel that he had "taken great liberties," but only through "taking away" elements that would "prevent its success." Comparison of the published novel to a 17-page surviving fragment of the original manuscript of *Valperga* presently housed in the Pierpont Morgan Library has helped lessen the concern about its authorship, although it cannot be strictly proven that Godwin did not apply a heavier hand. Bennett offers examples from the original manuscript in comparison to the final printed version to illustrate that Godwin did what most editors do. For instance, he altered punctuation, replacing an ampersand with the word *and*, and changed specific words here and there without loss of their original sense. Additional examples of editorial practice supplied by Bennett include replacing the word *join* with the *unite* and *among* with the term *upon*. Common sense suggests that Godwin would not have altered its political message and ideology because they matched his own.

Variations from Godwin's ideology also show that Shelley's voice strongly inhabited her novel. While many of Euthanasia's specific ideas regarding civic rule match Godwin's, she varies in her call for "content of mind, love and benevolent feeling" for everyone. As Bennett points out, Godwin did not go that far, instead noting, in Frederick L. Beaty's words, "the 'necessity of human affections as a concomitant of universal love.'" Curran adds the book's format as support for Shelley's authorship. In the three-volume format preferred by her era and its similar length to contemporary novels, *Valperga*'s individual volumes are comparable in length to one another and share notable "formal balances." This would have been the responsibility of Shelley, not Godwin. He also points out that Shelley mentioned a preference for her original title in her correspondence to her father, but she did not protest any changes he made. That lack of protest indicates there were few to no important alterations.

An original reviewer of *Valperga* wrote in *Blackwood's Edinburgh Magazine*: "We must confess, that in much of what we looked for, we have been disappointed; but yet, even here at the outset, we do not hesitate to say, that if we have not met with what we expected, we have met with other things almost as good." His main disappointment was in what he judged a weak characterization of Castruccio. He includes a gender-based judgment about that weakness, writing,

> We suspect, that . . . far too much reliance has been laid on thoughts and feelings, not only modern, but modern and feminine at once. Perhaps we might say more; nay, perhaps we should not be saying too much, if we plainly expressed the opinion, that a very great part of Mrs Shelley's book has no inspiration, but that of a certain *school*, which is certainly a very modern, as well as a very mischievous one, and which ought never, of all things, to have numbered ladies among its disciples.

He does add, before including a summary of the plot, "But, in spite even of this, we have closed the book with no feelings but those of perfect kindness—and we shall say no more of matters that will, perhaps, suggest themselves to our readers quite strongly enough, without our giving ourselves any trouble."

SYNOPSIS

Valperga was originally published in the three-volume format common in Shelley's day. Today it mainly appears without the volume divisions. In the following synopsis, the volume divisions are given along with the consecutive chapter numbering common today.

Volume 1: Chapters 1–5

Volume 1 is devoted to Castruccio's upbringing and training and to his early relationships with Euthanasia. The narrator opens by making clear that Italy differed from the rest of Europe, still "immersed in barbarism" when it emerged "from the darkness of the ruin of the Western Empire," alluding to the sack of Rome. She describes Lombardy and Tuscany as producing "astonishing specimens of human genius," but they were yet "torn to pieces by domestic faction." The narrator also describes the conflict between the Ghibelines, also called the Bianchi, friends of the emperor and believers in his "universality of . . . sway"; and the Guelphs, the Neri, who were "partizens of liberty." The Neri had been exiled from Pistoia, a town between Florence and Lucca and moved to Lucca. Among them was the family of Ruggieri Antelminelli, who had been loyal to emperors in the war. Castruccio Antelminelli is 11 years old at the time of the novel's opening, caught in a flare-up of the political quarrel.

Driven from the palazzo, the Ghibelines are in danger. Castruccio's mother, Madonna Dianora, is frightened by the sounds of trampling horses. Although Castruccio wants to stay with his parents and face their enemies, they decide that he and Dianora will escape to the castle of Valperga to stay with their friend the Countess. Castruccio tries to comfort his mother but begins sobbing. The two leave as Florence bursts into "a frightful state of civil discord" where "not a day passe[s] without brawls and bloodshed." Many flee the city, catching up to and telling Castruccio of the horrors, filling him "with rage and desire of vengeance." The narrator explains that is how the children assumed their parents' "hatred against their persecutors," their wounds never healing, and the "feelings of passion and anger which had given rise to the first blow" remain high. The exiles end up in Dianora's hometown of Ancona, where Ruggieri later joins them. Once a political leader, he now must adjust to a more pedestrian life. His joy is his son, described as "apt and sprightly . . . bold in action, careless of consequences, and governed only by his affection for his parents." He is an adventurous boy who enjoys sailing and horseback riding with no bridle or saddle, actions that worry his mother, although she does not try to stop him. She grows frail and dies, leaving her son and husband in grief. Castruccio remains "the sunbeam, solitary, but bright, which enlightened his [Ruggieri's] years of exile and infirmity."

At age 14, Castruccio leaves on a mysterious adventure and writes his father a note stating he will return. He has heard of "a strange and tremendous spectacle" that will occur in Florence, and all "who wished to have news from the other world" have been called to be at the bridge of Carraia in Florence on May 1. At the Arno, Castruccio sees what appears to be a scene from hell. The crowd on the bridge is too heavy, and it crashes into the river, with terrible results. The narrator notes that the horror of the ensuing confusion, with some people flying through the air, falling to their deaths, spectators trying to help the victims, and "all, as himself, seized with a superstitious dread, which rebuked them for having mimicked the dreadful mysteries of their religion." Castruccio flees in terror, runs into an empty church, and meets his father's former servant, Marco, who tells him that the Countess and Castellana of Valperga are in Florence with their daughter, Euthanasia dei Admirari, who is two years younger than Castruccio. The two had spent much time together as they matured, because their fathers were friends.

Euthanasia's father has gone blind, and she reads to him, educating herself in classic languages and studying the political situation so she can converse with her father. As she listens to men discussing the ongoing conflict, she does "not acquire that narrow idea of the present times, as if they and the world were the same, which characterizes the unlearned." Shelley makes clear her belief that change from the past would prove essential to the gaining of equality for all. As supporters of the Guelph party, Euthanasia and her family long for a free republic. Euthanasia listens to her father's impassioned support of independence and "her soul, adapted for the reception of all good, drained the cup of eloquent feeling that her father poured out before her." The stage is set for tension between Castruccio and Euthanasia, good friends but supporters of conflicting political ideologies.

Castruccio is fond of Euthanasia—"he could, he thought, feed for life on her sweet looks, in which deep sensibility and lively thought were pictured, and a judgment and reason beyond her years. Her eyes seemed to read his soul." He shares the story of his family's exile to Ancona with Euthanasia. The two friends understand that when he leaves the following day, they will not see each other again for a time, due to their differences. Euthanasia explains that they should cherish one another's memory and tells Castruccio that she knows he will always behave honorably, and that he can count on her friendship.

Castruccio returns home and prepares for his future through study and hard work. After his father dies when he is 17, Castruccio determines to travel to Este, Lombardy, with a letter of introduction his father wrote to a friend and fellow exile named Francesco de Guinigi. Although stricken for a time by the same fever that killed his father, Castruccio recovers and, determined to find fame, travels through the mountains to Este. Nature helps to revive him as the mountains' beauty "and the picturesque views for a while beguiled his thoughts." The reader glimpses his future personality as he pauses in solitude, apart from any "censuring eye" to

> throw his arms to the north, the south, the east, and the west, crying,—"There—there—there, and there, shall my fame reach!"—and then, in gay defiance, casting his eager glance towards heaven:—"and even there, if many may climb the slippery sides of the arched palace of eternal fame, there also will I be recorded."

At this point, Shelley has established Castruccio as the voice of passion, desiring self-aggrandizement, and Euthanasia as the voice of reason, desiring good for all.

When Castruccio arrives at Guinigi's home, he discovers his father's comrade is no longer a warrior but a farmer enjoying a simple life, taking sustenance from nature. He is shocked by the appearance of the soldier and knight's home, and Guinigi explains, "You come to the dwelling of a peasant who eats the bread his own hands have sown; this is a new scene for you, but you will not find it uninstructive." Although Castruccio is disappointed and cannot support Guinigi's motivations, he does not condemn them. When he finds the lifestyle becoming seductive, he forces himself to turn from nature's beauties and adjust his "fancy . . . to adorn with beauty vice, death, and misery, when disguised by a kingly rove, by the trappings of a victorious army, or the false halo of glory spread over the smoking ruins of a ravaged town." Guinigi thinks "only of the duty of man to man, laying aside the distinctions of society." This desire for equality is that of the Guelphs, and as one raised in the Ghibeline tradition, Castruccio finds the change in his father's comrade at arms unacceptable. He lives under Guinigi's teachings for a year but concludes he would rather be entombed alive than die never having achieved fame. He asks Guinigi, "Is it not fame that makes men gods?" Shelley extols the life of one who works in nature, like Guinigi, by supplying abundant imagery of "the most beautiful vegetation . . . the hedges were of myrtle, whose aromatic perfume weighed upon the sluggish air of noon, as the labourers reposed, sleeping under the trees, lulled by the rippling of the brooks."

Castruccio eventually rejects Guinigi's desire for equality among all and particularly his aversion to war and its results that "occasion such exultation to the privileged murderers of the earth." His background will not allow him to relinquish a moral code that directs rigid control of those who will not adhere to social edict handed down by a dictator. He does comply with Guinigi's plan to educate him in the ways of knighthood outside of Italy. Castruccio agrees to travel to England with Ethelbert Atawel, an embassy chief to the pope, where he will participate in the English court. He will also meet a wealthy relative in England named Alderigo, who will help relieve Castruccio's poverty. Before departing, the younger and the older man travel to Venice, where Castruccio is impressed by its wealth and meets various nobles as full of dreams of self-aggrandizement as he. Guinigi departs, leaving Castruccio with Atawel, who the boy judges to be not nearly the intellectual match of Guinigi; rather, he is more a man of the world. At age 18, Castruccio possesses "a manliness of thought and firmness of judgment beyond his years." The narrator identifies the year as 1309.

Castruccio is seduced by the power represented in the English court, where he is received by King Edward. He feels that he can identify with the king due to the many political challenges to his rule. Impressed by Alderigo's influence, Castruccio dazzles the lords in turn with his horsemanship and social abilities. The king takes him into his confidence, giving Castruccio a message to transmit to the royal favorite, Gaveston, in exile in Dublin. These interactions fill Castruccio with "pride, hope, and joy." Lying to Atawel and Alderigo about his destination, he travels to Dublin with the message for Gaveston and becomes his friend. Gaveston did not learn "modesty from adversity; his wealth and luxury was increased, and with these his vanity and insufferable presumption." Thus, he serves as a negative role model for Castruccio, still young and impressionable. The nobles clearly detest Gaveston, and when they learn that Castruccio is his confidant, they turn their hate against the boy. Castruccio takes the king's side in a heated argument during a court gathering and yells in Italian, "By blood, and not by words, are blows to be avenged!" while stabbing the king's adversary. He must be removed from England hastily, knowing that his visit has failed, and he departs in shame.

Volume 1: Chapters 5–9

Castruccio first travels to Ostend, a Belgian port, and sits beside the sea shedding "bitter tears of repentance and conscious guilt," mourning his "rashness and folly." However, his major concern is that his adversary "might not have died—and then what was he?" He longs for Italy and is joined by a rich merchant who knows Castruccio's cousin and is also a native of Italy; he, too, misses "the delights of that paradise." Castruccio learns all of the news from his native country and then travels to Flanders and joins a French camp, meeting with Scoto, to whom Alderigo had referred him. Castruccio learns to wear armor and performs with "bravery, enterprize and success" in various battles, coming to the attention of King Philip. He learns much from Scoto but must depart to join Henry of Luxemburgh [sic], an emperor of Germany and a Ghibeline, to fight for control of Italy.

Castruccio crosses the Alps, and he discovers a man who has fallen over the steep incline beside the trail and is desperately clinging to a cliff. Castruccio rescues him and tells him they would find a much easier path to Italy, and that there he "will find a paradise that will cure all your evils." They travel through a fearful night to arrive at the home of the stranger's friend, Messer Tadeo della Ventura, in a town called Susa. When the two men learn of Castruccio's identity, the traveler embraces him and explains to Tadeo that the boy is a "gallant soldier, whose name has been spread through France, as that of the bravest warrior and the ablest commander that fought in the Low Countries." Then the traveler reveals his name as Benedetto Pepi, a Cremonese returning to Italy after earning his own laurels and knighthood under Scoto. Castruccio learns more of conditions in Italy and debates with his new friends the impossibility of Guelphs and Ghibelines living together peacefully.

Pepi declares that any ruler wanting to establish peace in Italy will have to kill all members of one of the political parties. He adds passionately that Florence will never submit, although Bologna, Lucca, and Sienna may. When Castruccio asks him why he feels so strongly, as Cremona is a long distance from Florence, Pepi replies it is not because he has ever been harmed by a Florentine, but because he is a Ghibeline. He hates any people "that despise the emperor, and all lawful authority; that have as it were dug up the buried form of Liberty." Castruccio continues to learn from his various role models, ever strengthening his determination to gain fame, glory, and power. His travels continue to Milan, where the city's wealth astounds him. He meets Guigini's son, Arrigo, and learns of Guigini's death. The Germans invade, overcome Milan, and push on to other Guelph towns. Castruccio rides with the Germans and eventually takes charge over a small band, routing and killing innocent families without compassion.

Castruccio travels to Genoa with a new friend, Galeazzo Visconti. The emperor is crowned at the Vatican and returns to Tuscany, unsuccessfully attacking Florence and dying there in August 1313. The narrator makes the point that after all of the destruction and havoc that the emperor wreaked, political conditions are little changed as a result. Castruccio enacts a treaty with a man named Uguccione, hated by the Ghibelines, in order to overthrow the Guelphs of Lucca, an agreement that causes his countrymen to view him as a traitor; many later forgive him. However, those at a distance who do not know Castruccio continue to hate him, particularly when the Ghibeline exiles enter Lucca and it is captured by Uguccione, the "hated Pisan Tyrant." Three years have passed as Castruccio gains experience in war.

One person in Florence feels a special kindness toward Castruccio—Euthanasia, now an orphan. Sole heiress to her family's fortune, she is "a queen in Valperga . . . at Florence she was considered one of its first citizens; and, if power, wealth, and respect could have satisfied her, she must have been happy . . . villages under her jurisdiction became prosperous; and the peasantry were proud that their countess preferred her residence among them to the gaieties of Florence." There are rumors that while she admires men of Florence and is gracious to all, at the age of 22, she has never loved.

The narrator forewarns both Euthanasia and the reader of disaster to come:

> Is there not a principle in the human mind that foresees the change about to occur to it? Is there not a feeling which would warn the soul of peril, were it not at the same time a sure prophecy that that peril is not to be avoided? So felt Euthanasia: and during her evening meditations she often enquired from her own heart, why the name of Castruccio made her cheeks glow; and why praise or dispraise of him seemed to electrify her frame.

When Castruccio hears that Euthanasia is now the countess of Valperga, beautiful and wise but resisting the courtship of men, he sends Arrigo to spy on her and report back to him to confirm what he hears. Arrigo does so, and despite Euthanasia's political leanings, Castruccio decides to visit her at Valperga.

Volume 1: Chapters 10–14

Euthanasia explains to Castruccio that she has lived as a solitary hermit and says, "Love, and hope, and delight, or sorrow and tears; these are our lives, our realities, to which we give the names of power, possession, misfortune, and death." She goes on to praise liberty and equality and the virtues of Florence for representing those ideals. Many pages are devoted to her history and explaining her attachment to her homeland.

Castruccio departs to participate in the overthrow of Florence, where he is wounded. When Euthanasia sees him again, he tells her that "all my laurels are spoils for you. Nay, turn not away as if you disdained them; they are the assurance of the peace that you desire. Do not doubt me; do not for a moment suffer a cloud of suspicion to darken your animated countenance." He is later captured by a traitor and imprisoned, but he is freed by his followers and takes over Uggucione's palace in Lucca. He reunites with Euthanasia, and she recognizes that she loves Castruccio. He greets her with the cry "Victory!"; to which she replies, "Victory and security!" Castruccio remains hopeful that she will yield to his principles, and she spends a happy year watching him construct a treaty between Florence and Lucca. Valperga, situated precisely between the two cities, is dependent on the treaty to retain its own peaceful neutrality. Euthanasia is never happier than when her dependents are happy, and they all love her for her efforts to ease the strains of their lives. Castruccio respects her ministrations to the ill but often finds her focus on peace amusing. His nature leans toward practicality and the completion of his plans.

Euthanasia prepares her castle to host a festival beginning on May 1. The gathering attracts varied entertainment and people—"nobility, wealth and beauty"—from across the country. Shelley spends pages describing the intricately decorated scene and the storytellers, musicians, and dancers who participate. Then Pepi arrives and persuades Castruccio to join him in plans for military action that Castruccio does not quite understand but to which he agrees, concluding the first volume.

Volume 2: Chapters 15–20

In the second volume, Castruccio meets Beatrice after lovingly leaving Euthanasia in Florence to travel to Rovigo, where he has promised to meet Galeazzo Visconti, tyrant of Milan, who wants

Castruccio to join his Ghibeline forces. Castruccio argues with Galeazzo's plans, but Galeazzo taunts him by diminishing the importance of his accomplishments, including the peace he has managed to enforce: "That is well—at present you are at peace with them; but it must be a peace to crush, and not to invigorate them." The narrator states, "These were the lessons with which Galeazzo awakened the latent flame in the soul of Castruccio." Castruccio plans to sneak into Este in disguise, helped by the marquess of Este and her beautiful, virginal companion, Beatrice, who is considered a prophetess.

Beatrice counsels Castruccio on how to speak to the bishop, the marquess's brother, in order to gain what he needs. Castruccio hears from the bishop the story of his finding Beatrice with the fabled Magfreda, companion to Wilhelmina of Bohemia, who had believed herself the incarnation of the Holy Spirit. He had raised Beatrice, and her prophetic talents are revered. Castruccio is fascinated by her virginal innocence and eventually seduces her. Fiercely supportive of Castruccio, she believes him to represent a spiritual cause as Ferraro is invaded and then peace restored. She does not know he wants to return to Lucca and promises that she "with prophetic words, and signs from heaven that lead the multitude, will conduct you to greater glory and greater power than you before possessed." Dumbfounded by his plans to leave her, Beatrice refuses to believe that he will return. When he tells her about Euthanasia, she promises to pray for her and tells Castruccio: "It will kill me: but I swear by all my hopes never to see you more."

Castruccio meets Pepi as promised and is startled by his plan to hand over Cremona to Cane, the lord of Verona. Castruccio feels contempt for Pepi and his common background. Then he learns that Pepi has managed to hold all debts of every local nobleman, buying their bonds after selling his entire estate for funds to carry out his plan. Filled with disdain, Castruccio calls Pepi a vile Jew, "a usurer, a bloodsucker!" Pepi leads Castruccio deep into the earth through a maze of tunnels. On the verge of insanity, Pepi shows Castruccio his collection of parchments hidden in the cavern; they represent his control over the noblemen. Castruccio departs, leaving his cloak behind. He tells Pepi it will serve as a wrap for his limbs when he again descends to his tomb. After he leaves, Pepi puts his plan into action, telling the local Guelphs that he can persuade the Ghibelines not to exile them. Many agree to join Pepi, although they hate him. He later dies when Cane leads the Ghibelines to victory over Cremona. The narrator notes that "all the boasted possessions of Pepi were, as himself, a loathsome and useless ruin."

Castruccio travels to meets Euthanasia. She has been approached by Galeazzo as a friend of Castruccio, and one who intends to extend his dominance throughout Italy with Castruccio's help. She goes silent, having "believed in Castruccio's promises of peace; and the foundations of her very life seemed to give way, when his faith appeared tainted with falsehood." She feels that Galeazzo has misunderstood Castruccio's intentions, but as she hears more from him, she understands that Castruccio's desire for fame and power have superseded his desire for peace and to be with her. She becomes "sorrowful and disturbed." During a violent storm, the two reunite in Valperga after two years of separation. He makes clear that he loves and wants to marry her, at which point the narrator states, "it is difficult to answer the language of passion with that of reason." Euthanasia infuriates Castruccio by rejecting him, stating that she cannot be a traitor to Florence. He replies, "You sacrifice me to a bubble," devaluing her ideals. The narrator notes that he leaves her "to doubt, suspense, and grief."

Volume 2: Chapters 21–25

Castruccio exiles 300 families from Lucca, returns to Valperga, and again is rejected by Euthanasia. The narrator notes that he is changed, "full of thought,—with a bent brow, a cruel eye, and a heart not to be moved from its purpose by weakness or humanity." Euthanasia is visited by a beautiful pilgrim who is startled to learn that Castruccio is still alive; the reader understands that it is Beatrice. She abruptly departs, saying she is traveling to Rome. When Castruccio visits Euthanasia, he tells her the entire story of Beatrice, whom they then try to find, but she has vanished. Euthanasia considers how totally she has loved Castruccio, thinking them meant only for one another, but

> the story of Beatrice dissolved the charm; she looked on him now in the common light of day; the illusion and exaltation of love was dispelled for ever: and, although disappointment, and the bitterness of destroyed hope, robbed her of every sensation of enjoyment, it was no longer that mad despair, that clinging to the very sword that cut her, which before had tainted her cheek with the hues of death.

She determines to return to duty and to care for her friends and those who depend on her. Her ideas clearly conflict with Castruccio's when she states that "the essence of freedom is that clash and struggle which awaken the energies of our nature, and that operation of the elements of our mind, which as it were gives us the force and power that hinder us from degenerating, as they say all things earthly do when not regenerated by change."

Volume 3: Chapters 26–30

In the third volume, Euthanasia is thoroughly disillusioned with Castruccio, who becomes more and more cruel and conniving in his desire for power. She tries not to think of him, but "every moment of every day, was as a broken mirror, a multiplied reflection of his form alone." He wants her to join his military ventures, but she continues to refuse, vowing to retain the neutrality of Valperga. Despite his feelings for her, Castruccio takes her prisoner when he captures Valperga.

In chapter 26, Euthanasia departs her castle with dignity, blessing the peasants who have been routed from their homes and who lost many members of their families. She cannot look closely at either side of the path she walks with her escort, for fear she will see a dead body left from the recent battles. She meets with Arrigo, who tries to comfort her with the assurance that she will live at Florence surrounded by friends in luxury and that "the prince has promised, and intends to keep his promise, that your revenues shall not be injured by the loss of your castle."

Castruccio meets with her, urging her to remain in Lucca and treating her respectfully. She tells him, "We are divided; there is an eternal barrier between us now, sealed by the blood of those miserable people who fell for me. I cannot, I do not love you." She tells him that if the blood and tears of her people represent his "acts of courtship," she must state that she would rather take a lion in his den as her husband "than become the bride of a conqueror." He declares that he will still cherish her and will act as her protector should she need him. Euthanasia cries, "could you not have spared me this? Leave me; farewell for ever," after which he kisses her hand and departs. Euthanasia suffers a fever and delirium, but then nature heals her, her youth and strong constitution contributing to her recovery. Chapter 26 concludes with the question, "Where during this time was the prophetess of Ferrara?"—referring to Beatrice.

Euthanasia understands that her loss is double, as her home is taken away, along with her love for Castruccio and desire for a peaceful family life with him. She remains in Lucca in order to recover from her illness and thinks often of Castruccio. The narrator explains of Euthanasia:

> Sometimes she thanked Providence that she had not become the wife of this man: but it was a bitter thankfulness. She had not been wedded to him by the church's rites; but her soul, her thoughts, her fate, had been married to his; she tried to loosen the chain that bound them eternally together, and felt that the effort was fruitless: If he were evil, she must weep; if his light-hearted selfishness allowed no room for remorse in his own breast, humiliation and sorrow was doubly her potion, and this was her destiny for ever.

The narrator also clarifies changes in Castruccio. Although he had become a tyrant, "He did not slay his thousands . . . but he had received the graft of vainglory into his soul, and he now bore the fruits. He put to death remorselessly those whom he suspected, and would even use torture, either to discover other victims, or to satisfy his desire of revenge." Drought sets in, followed by a cold and early winter, the worst cold in many years, causing a loss of fruit trees. Euthanasia thinks of the country as a once young mother nursing her baby that had become "as forlorn as that mother if she be ruthlessly bereft of her infant."

Just as Euthanasia decides to depart for Lucca, a messenger tells her of a woman heretic imprisoned in the dungeon who wants to see her. It is Beatrice, sent to prison by inquisitors. Euthanasia volunteers to speak to Castruccio on her behalf but feels it will be better for her to try to intercede with the inquisitors. Beatrice urges her to see Castruccio but, when the time allowed for her visit has ended, begs her to stay. Euthanasia determines to see Castruccio and tries to imagine Valperga restored and all that has happened merely a dream that will vanish when she speaks with him.

Castruccio at first does not concede to Euthanasia's request for the "heretic's" release, but when he learns her identity, he is astounded. He immediately tells Euthanasia to take "poor, poor Beatrice" and care for her. Once again, he begs Euthanasia to join him. When she refuses, he at first appears humiliated but quickly recovers his pride. Euthanasia frees Beatrice, who is near madness due to her conversion to the Paterin persuasion, a religion that believes in the power of evil to conquer good. Castruccio writes to Euthanasia, asking her again to save Beatrice. Beatrice begins a diatribe regarding "the spirit of evil" that Shelley carries over several pages. Euthanasia is determined to convert Beatrice, saying to the sleeping girl: "I will endeavour to teach you the lessons of true religion; and, in reducing the wandering thoughts of one so lovely and so good, I shall be in part fulfilling my task on the earth." When they later discuss her youth, a time when she had felt so confident of her abilities, Beatrice tells Euthanasia that she will not become "a dupe, a maniac" and fall again; "Cease, cease, in mercy cease, to talk of my childhood; days of error, vanity and paradise! My lessons must all be new; all retold in words signifying other ideas than what they signified during my mad, brief dream of youth. Then faith was not a shadow: it was what these eyes saw; I clutched hope, and found it certainty." Euthanasia responds whenever Castruccio writes to enquire as to Beatrice's condition.

Beatrice slips away one day and returns to tell Euthanasia that she has seen Castruccio. Still under his spell, she describes him with passion: His eyes, which, like the eagle's, could outrace the sun, yet melt in the sweetest love, as a cloud, shining, yet soft; his brow, manly and expansive, on which his raven curls rest; his upturned lips, where pride and joy, and love, and wisdom, and triumph live, small spirits, ready to obey his smallest will; and his head, cinctured by a slight diadem, looks carved out by the intensest knowledge of beauty! How graceful his slightest motion!

Euthanasia admits that she once loved Castruccio as well, but "he cast off humanity, honesty, honourable feeling, all that I prize. . . . Glory and conquest are his mistresses, and he is a successful lover."

Beatrice continues the story of her past, confessing that she had asked help of her adoptive father in seeking forgiveness for allowing herself to have been deceived by earthly pleasures. She continued to love Castruccio, seeing him in her dreams. She could no longer go to public places or visit with her followers. She set out on a pilgrimage, deserting everything that had made life tolerable, as penance experiencing an isolation she had never known. She spent the summer traveling across Europe and had seen Euthanasia in September. She then recalled fainting and awakening "the slave of incarnate Evil," in a house of women in which a man was in charge. She lived there for three years, witnessing and enduring unspeakable things, "a tale for infidels"; she became a Paterin. Suffering agonies while under control of the heretic in charge, she eventually escaped and was returned to mental health by a healer. After listening to Beatrice's terrifying tale, Euthanasia writes it down in case Castruccio wants to have the explanation.

Volume 3: Chapters 31–38

Euthanasia works with Beatrice to regulate the powers of her mind. As Euthanasia explains, "The human soul . . . is a vast cave, in which many powers sit and live. First, Consciousness is as a centinel at the entrance; and near him wait Joy and Sorrow, Love and Hate, and all the quick sensations that through his means gain entrance into our hearts." She continues her extended comparison of the mind to a cave, adding that in the inner cave live Poetry and Imagination, Heroism, and Self-sacrifice, and "the highest virtues." Beatrice cannot absorb the lessons. She converses with a priest, and a witch places her under a spell, causing her mental condition to deteriorate. She sees Castruccio one last time before dying, "peacefully, and calmly as a child" once the witch's spell is removed.

Castruccio continues his destruction, driving toward Florence. The narrator states that "he was quick to distrust, and cold looks and averted favour followed suspicion . . . hatred quickly came, and that never failed to destroy its object." Euthanasia meets friends there and engages in a plot against Castruccio, proposed by her cousin, Francesco Bondelmonti, although she does not like some of the other individuals involved, particularly Battista Tripalda. Part of her understanding is that Castruccio's life will be spared. The narrator explains:

> She felt deeply the danger of the project in which she had embarked; . . . [S]he approached the foundations of [Castruccio's] power by a path encompassed with danger; she groped through the murky air of night, and owls and bats flitted before her, and flapped their wings in her eyes; her footing was unsteady;—a precipice yawned on each side, and the probable result of her undertaking was ignominy and death.

Tripalda turns informer, and Castruccio stops the plot. When his compatriot Vanni Mordecastelli asks what to do with the traitors, Castruccio replies they must all die, and "not by an easy death. That were a poor revenge. They shall die, as they have lived, like traitors; and on their living tombs shall be written, 'Thus Castruccio punishes his rebel subjects.'" Euthanasia will not be executed; he will deal with her himself. He tells Mordecastelli, "Leave her to me. I will be her judge and executioner." His revenge is to exile Euthanasia, knowing the isolation from all she has loved will be punishment enough. He also states that he never wants to hear her name again. When he goes to the dungeon to tell her of his decision, she protests: "And yet I will not yield; I will not most unworthily attend to my own safety, while my associates die. No, my lord, if they are to be sacrificed, the addition of one poor woman will add little to the number of your victims; and I cannot consent to desert them." By the end of their interview, Castruccio weeps. He rides with her to the Lago di Macciucoli, kisses her hand and departs. Her vessel sets sail for Sicily and is destroyed in a storm. According to the narrator,

> She was never heard of more; even her name perished. She slept in the oozy cavern of the ocean; the sea-weed was tangled with her shining hair; and the spirits of the deep wondered that the earth had trusted so lovely a creature to the barren bosom of the sea . . . she quitted a life, which for her had been replete with change and sorrow.

CONCLUSION

The novel's conclusion begins with the statement, "The private chronicles, from which the foregoing relation has been collected, end with the death of Euthanasia. It is therefore in public histories alone that we find an account of the last years of the life of Castruccio." Shelley chronicles the political actions across Italy when Castruccio joined Louis of Bavaria, crowned at Milan. He managed to release Galeazzo Visconti from prison, and the two enjoyed an enthusiastic reunion. But "Galeazzo found, that, if he had lost sovereignty and power, Castruccio had lost that which might be considered far more valuable; he had lost his dearest friends . . . although he disdained to acknowledge the power of fortune, she had made him feel in his heart's core her poisoned shafts." After executing more military campaigns, the two men died on the same day, Visconti at Pescia and Castruccio at Lucca on September 3, 1328.

COMMENTARY

Much critical effort has focused on the biographical elements in *Valperga*, particularly the political and philosophical models provided for Shelley by the beliefs of her husband and parents. For example, when Castruccio meets Guinigi, he ignores his father's edict to "be guided by his advice," instead choosing violence to enforce class structure. Shelley's use of the phrase *privileged murderers* to label those who participate in that violence was inspired by her husband's phrase *legal murderers* in the *Esdaile Notebook*. Castruccio's ignoring of Guinigi's advice and his ambition become a illustration of vivid political ideology that supported suppression, partially through lack of education, and the killing of a populace by a tyrannic force for the purpose of promoting order. That ideology ran counter to Godwin's and the Shelleys' beliefs that humans should be allowed to exercise their innate rational nature to govern themselves, resulting in social equality for all. Euthanasia's support of education and equality represent the romantic ideal and challenge the aristocratic order. Mary Shelley grounds that ideology in the respected history of Florence. She also draws directly from her parents' ideas, as Euthanasia often repeats Godwin's philosophy. Godwin and MARY WOLLSTONECRAFT both supported education and social equality, with Godwin writing that "all private considerations must yield to the general good."

Euthanasia's declaration that society should encourage change echoes Godwin's assertion that a healthy society must constantly evolve, selecting change rather than stasis. Her comparison of society to nature in urging that humans use their minds to prevent degeneration echoes the romantic ideal of nature as a healing and nurturing force. As a highly educated woman who can both love and lead, whose appreciation of literature and history translates into political activism, Euthanasia represents Mary Shelley's perfect woman. However, like Fanny Derham in *Lodore*, Euthanasia, as an intelligent, educated, and independent woman, has no place in society. Such a woman will always become a social outcast, like Fanny, or a literal outcast/exile, like Euthanasia. Shelley does not allow *Lodore*'s narrator to predict Fanny's fate, and she sends Euthanasia to her death rather than live each day in isolation as a disillusioned idealist. Neither of these examples of a strong female character benefits from her strength. Simultaneously, Beatrice's moral self-sacrifice leads to literal death following her imprisonment for heresy.

Betty T. Bennett explains that Castruccio's exile of Euthanasia for political activism echoes Wollstonecraft's demand for political responsibility among women; as Euthanasia attacks the remorseless nature of autocratic rule, she supports both Godwin's and Wollstonecraft's ideology. Castruccio admires and loves Euthanasia, but her ideology so directly contradicts his own that he recognizes both cannot simultaneously exist within their relationship. As the heartless, ruthless autocrat, Castruccio chooses power over affection. Shelley probably alludes to Percy's death at sea when her narrator notes of Euthanasia's death, "Is not the catastrophe strangely prophetic." Bennett points out that it is prophetic because Euthanasia's ideology is based on aspects of Percy Shelley's ideology.

Various scholars have countered criticism that Shelley compromised her own beliefs in order to sell books by avoiding extreme political declarations in her personal life. Anne K. Mellor explains that Shelley well understood that society would not look favorably on any woman seen to openly advocate Mary Wollstonecraft's often-demonized political positions. Such advocacy would be socially unacceptable due to the public denunciation of Wollstonecraft on moral and spiritual grounds. Shelley also clearly recognized that her mother did not offer a viable role model for a woman of her era; such models remained in the realm of fantasy in the early 19th century. Thus, she adopted that fantasy approach through fiction to offer models to her readers, such as Euthanasia. However, she also realistically demonstrated to women the dangers in openly practicing or supporting beliefs that countered cultural mores. Besides, Shelley had always been a conservative who had no qualms about operating within the confines of the orderly bourgeois family design. That family would keep her son safe and allow her to find a fulfilling role as his educator and "moral guardian." If men could operate as did women by a commitment to preserve and nurture life rather than end it for personal interests, society would benefit tremendously. That is the message she seeks to impart through her fiction.

Formalists would examine the traditional elements of fiction to find meaning in the novel. Among those elements, symbolism plays an important role. Shelley repeats the use of some familiar symbols, such as that of the moon, generally symbolic of woman. In chapter 5 of the first volume, the moon is the enemy of Castruccio and the traveler he saves in the mountains as they try to negotiate treacherous paths at night. This environment of danger serves to challenge the men's purpose, thus symbolically supporting a traditional male/female dichotomy. The traveler tells Castruccio, "Do not trust to the moon . . . its shadows are deep and fearful, and its light not less dangerous; sometimes a shadow cast from among trees across the road, will look like a running stream." His warning may also be seen as a warning against women in anticipation of Castruccio's interaction with Euthanasia and Beatrice. However, in chapter 5 of volume 3, the narrator notes that "'the mother of the months' had many times waned, and again refilled her horn; and summer, and its treasure of blue skies, odorous flowers, merry insects, and sweet-voiced birds, again bade the world be happy." Here the moon is a positive symbol of nurturing, labeled a "mother" and associated with the many joys of summer, as well as the horn of plenty. This scene also offers an example of Shelley's trademark imagery, emphasizing abundant detail to create a scene and also set a mood for the reader.

As an aspect of style, hyperbolic description is always found in Shelley's writing. An example may be seen when the narrator describes Castruccio following his betrayal of ideals that Euthanasia believed they shared: "Once indeed he had loved, and he had drank life and joy from the eyes of Euthanasia." Shelley also uses the traditional symbolic meaning of the seasons to great advantage. During the time that Euthanasia grieves for her loss of respect and love for Castruccio, winter, with its symbolism of death, provides the setting. When Euthanasia holds her festival in May, which as a month of spring symbolizes the promise of new life, the reader anticipates it will be a happy affair. But Shelley uses this expectation in an ironic manner, inverting the traditional symbolic value of May. Irony is an aspect of style, or word choice on the part of a writer, that basically means that conditions are not as they seem. Therefore, she warns readers that while the celebration should herald new life, it actually represents the end of an era and will be the last to be held at Valperga. This underlying message is emphasized by the appearance of Pepi, who represents a militant challenge to the present peaceful order.

Euthanasia's name is stronger than the ordinary symbol, closer to allegory, as it literally means a merciful death. That definition proves ironic, because her death as designed by Castruccio—a natural one but to be preceded by the tortures of isolation—will not be merciful. On the other hand, Shelley actually designs a merciful death by having Euthanasia die at sea in order to avoid the fate Castruccio intends her to suffer. In this example and others, the reader can see Shelley's skill in transmitting multiple messages to her audience.

Intertexuality, an approach to analysis in both reader response and structuralist criticism, could be applied to *Valperga*. Intertexuality refers to the allusion to, or mention of, works and authors within a work that allow readers to better understand the ideas of one work in consideration of another. Shelley alludes often to Dante in *Valperga*, both specifically by name and in her multiple references to hell and paradise, the latter also reminding educated readers of Milton's PARADISE LOST (1667). In addition, Dante was a well-known member of the Guelph political faction, which directly related to Shelley's topic. In another example, the narrator notes that William Borsiere was among the entertainers at Euthanasia's May festivities. Boccaccio had referred to Borsiere in the eighth story of the first day of his *Decameron* (ca. A.D. 400). Although he could not have been alive during the time that provides the setting for *Valperga*, the reference adds some authority and familiarity to the novel.

Shelley also includes much praise for Italy, referring to it as a "paradise" on multiple occasions, and supplying imagery of abundance and beauty prior to full military action. She also praises the Italian imagination in describing their methods of communication: "No nation can excel the Italians in the expression of passion by the language of gesture alone, or in the talent of extemporarily giving words to a series of action which they intend to represent." Having resided in Italy and made many permanent friendships there, Shelley could speak with some authority. Her selection of Castruccio's biography to make her point regarding the importance of independence and human free agency was surely related to the fact that informed readers would recognize Florence as a seat of republicanism.

CHARACTERS

Castruccio As noted above, Castruccio is based on a real-life character as part of Shelley's approach to historical fiction. Readers who do not understand that subgenre may hold Shelley accountable for not sticking to the facts of history as recorded. Because she clearly states not only that she is writing fiction but that she has taken liberties with dates and *based* her story on fact, that reader charge would not be a legitimate one. Shelley takes great care in shaping Castruccio's personality, demonstrating his brilliance and showing that he possessed the same malleable character that all healthy young people possess. The forces that first shaped that character were the political beliefs adhered to by his family and his culture, which became the largest portion of his inheritance. Although, in his uncorrupted state, he appears rational enough to participate in some debate regarding the pros and cons of the Ghibeline stance, he will give in to the irrationality of passion, made clear by Shelley. Most critics agree that he represents the destructive force of what some label the "masculine sublime," which has as a crucial ingredient unrestricted male desire for power. Shelley wants to showcase that overweening ambition as in conflict with the feminine alternative, as discussed by Daniel E. White, that is associated with beauty and the individual freedom offered by democracy. As representative of a totally ego-driven force, the masculine sublime threatens the peaceful coexistence that should exist between man and wife, father and children.

Readers should be dismayed by Castruccio's growing loss of control over the emotion that feeds his ambition. Not only does he sacrifice the lives of many to his desire for power, he also sacrifices a rich, productive relationship with Euthanasia. Obviously, Shelley's readers would not operate within the aristocratic circles of these characters, but she attempts to demonstrate that her characters' fictional conflicts can be applied to the everyday relationships of males and females, regardless of their social class. One need not be a public power broker; brokering takes place daily within the family unit. Shelley demonstrates the manner by which males are trained to desire control of others and instructed in the desirability of ambition. Much of that training involves the input of minions, also male, who encourage a leader in order to benefit from that leader's accomplishments themselves. However, she includes the model of Guinigi, a man who rejects his warrior role to take up the more intrinsically satisfying life of the farmer peasant. The poor have been traditionally depicted as a happier lot, based on their lack of responsibility. But Shelley demonstrates this depiction as a false characterization in *Valperga* and also in *Frankenstein*, supporting both of her parents' belief in the evils of social hierarchy. Instead, she demonstrates that Guinigi benefits from constructive activities in which he nurtures life from the natural elements, rather than killing humans.

Shelley hints in the novel's title that Castruccio will not be its main topic. By privileging Valperga, Euthanasia's estate and symbol of neutrality, Shelley indicates that the fictional portion of her story holds the greatest interest for her. To the end of the novel, Castruccio has affection for Euthanasia but is limited by his desire for constantly increasing power, which conflicts with her desires.

Euthanasia As stressed above, Shelley combines the characteristics of several real people in fashioning Euthanasia: Godwin, Wollstonecraft, Percy Shelley, and herself. Euthanasia represents Mary Shelley's feminine ideal in contrast with the romantic vision of the masculine sublime. She believes in the application of rationality coupled with love as the best manner by which to solve conflict. That belief demands self-sacrifice, a typical female attribute. However, it also incorporates the male characteristic of rationality and logic, supported by education. Like Castruccio, Euthanasia is a flat character: She experiences no change from the beginning to the conclusion of the novel, unless one allows as an epiphany her realization that she cannot change Castruccio. She must remain flat in order to reflect her dogged determination to uphold her ideals of peace based on civic equality.

Shelley tempers Euthanasia's characterization so as not to insult male readers. She is respectful and polite to males, discussing rather than attacking their errant ideas. She is also referred to as "Madonna," which readers would translate as mother, making more acceptable to readers her satisfaction with her unmarried state. She is mother to her people, those who work her lands and thus depend on her for nurture and existence. She also shows strong motherly instincts toward Beatrice, never giving up on rehabilitating the young woman. Euthanasia never allows passions such as jealousy or anger to cloud her vision in respect to Beatrice. She shows the positive results that a mother without prejudice, who sacrifices her individuality to the group, can accomplish. The cause of her ultimate failure is Castruccio, her intellectual equal but one who depends on motives other than the good of the people under his care or rule. He exults in violence by the novel's conclusion, wreaking misplaced vengeance on the innocent. His order to exile Euthanasia is also a selfish one. He does not want to be haunted by the killing of one he so loved and valued, but who rejected him. He sends her away so that no other male may have her, nor will her "children" be able to depend upon her responsible attitude to care for them. The fact that separation from her "family" kills her demonstrates Shelley's support of a strong, intelligent responsible woman as a mother, the socially acceptable role for her. However, she also seeks to demonstrate that the woman cannot raise a family alone. Men must also take responsibility for their roles as fathers, something Castruccio refuses to do.

Beatrice Like Euthanasia, Beatrice also represents the feminine ideal of self-sacrifice, but because her sacrifice is to a faulty blind passion, it does not have the worth of that of Euthanasia. She is fully devoted to Castruccio the man, which blinds her to the existence of Castruccio the tyrant. Even as she is tyrannized by his rejection of her, she cannot recognize his faults. Until she dies, she characterizes him as an ideal, making him her religion. She helps Euthanasia understand that she must throw off her love for Castruccio. As Euthanasia struggles with her decision, the narrator explains, "She considered Castruccio as bound to Beatrice; bound by the deep love and anguish of the fallen prophetess . . . bound by his falsehood to her who was then his betrothed, and whom he carelessly wronged" proving "how little capable he was of participating in her own exalted feelings." Euthanasia attempts to teach Beatrice about true faith that does not place the demands on humans that Castruccio has placed on Beatrice, but she does not understand. She is willing even to place her well-being in the hands of a witch if it will result in Castruccio's return. As the narrator states: "She would risk her soul, to gain a moment's power over Castruccio." Later, as Beatrice rants, Euthanasia attempts to discern whether Beatrice's strange words "proceeded from the heated imagination of the prophetess, or from some real event of which Euthanasia was ignorant."

Shelley's message is clear: The romantic imagination must have boundaries of rationality in order to be a positive force. She foreshadows this message in a previous passage: "'Poor Beatrice! . . . She had inherited from her mother the most ardent imagination that ever animated a human soul." Shelley also suggests the strong influence of mothers, even when absent early in a daughter's life, just as Wollstonecraft had influenced her.

FURTHER READING

Beaty, Frederick L. *Light from Heaven.* DeKalb: Northern Illinois University Press, 1971.

Bennett, Betty T. "The Political Philosophy of Mary Shelley's Historical Novels: *Valperga* and *Perkin Warbeck.*" In *The Evidence of the Imagination,* edited by Donald H. Reiman, Michael C. Jaye, and Betty T. Bennett, 354–371. New York: New York University Press, 1978.

Brewer, William D. "Mary Shelley on the Therapeutic Value of Language." *Papers on Language and Literature* 30 (1994): 387–407.

Clery, E. J. *Women's Gothic: from Clara Reeve to Mary Shelley.* Tavistock, Devon, U.K.: Northcote House, 2000.

Curran, Stuart. Introduction to *Valperga: or, The Life and Adventures of Castruccio, Prince of Lucca,* by Mary Shelley, xii–xxvi. New York: Oxford University Press, 1997.

———. "Valperga." In *The Cambridge Companion to Mary Shelley*, edited by Esther Schor, 103–115. Cambridge: Cambridge University Press, 2004.

Lew, Joseph W. "God's Sister: History and Ideology in *Valperga*." In *The Other Mary Shelley: Beyond Frankenstein*, edited by Audrey A. Fisch, Anne K. Mellor, and Esther H. Schor, 159–181. New York: Oxford University Press, 1993.

Lockhart, John Gibson. "*Valperga; or the Life and Adventures of Castruccio, Prince of Lucca.* By the Author of 'Frankenstein.'" (Review) *Blackwood's Edinburgh Magazine* 13 (March, 1823): 283–293. Available online. URL: http://www.rc.umd.edu/reference/chronologies/mschronology/reviews/valpbw.html. Accessed July 26, 2009.

O'Sullivan, Jane. "Beatrice in Valperga: A New Cassandra." In *The Other Mary Shelley: Beyond Frankenstein*, edited by Audrey A. Fisch, Anne K. Mellor, and Esther H. Schor, 140–158. New York: Oxford University Press, 1993.

Powers, Katherine Richardson. *The Influence of William Godwin on the Novels of Mary Shelley.* New York: Arno Press, 1980.

Rajan, Tilottama. "Between Romance and History: Possibility and Contingency in Godwin, Leibniz, and Mary Shelley's *Valperga*." In *Mary Shelley in Her Times*, edited by Betty T. Bennett and Stuart Curran, 88–102. Baltimore: Johns Hopkins University Press, 2000.

———. Introduction to *Valperga*, by Mary Shelley. Peterborough, Ontario, Canada: Broadview Press, 1998. 1–2.

Rossington, Michael. "Truth Uncertain: The Republican Tradition and Its Destiny in Valperga." In *Mary Shelley in Her Times*, edited by Betty T. Bennett and Stuart Curran, 103–118. Baltimore: Johns Hopkins University Press, 2000.

Shelley, Mary. *The Journals of Mary Shelley, 1814–1844.* 2 vols. Edited by Paula R. Feldman and Diana Scott-Kilvert. Oxford, U.K.: Clarendon Press, 1987.

———. *Valperga: or, The Life and Adventures of Castruccio, Prince of Lucca.* New York: Oxford University Press, 1997.

Sunstein, Emily W. *Mary Shelley: Romance and Reality.* Boston: Little, Brown, 1989.

Ty, Eleanor. "Mary Wollstonecraft Shelley." In *British Romantic Novelists, 1789–1832.* Vol. 116 of *Dictionary of Literary Biography*, edited by Bradford K. Mudge, 311–325. New York: Gale Research, 1992. Available online. URL: http://people.brandeis.edu/~teuber/shelleybio.html#MainEssaySection. Accessed June 2, 2009.

Part III

Related People and Topics

Byron, George Gordon (Lord Byron) (1788–1824) Of all the great romantic poets, George Gordon Byron, Lord Byron, could be described as the one most vividly "of the world"—or the one least focused on the poet's task. The scholar Jerome J. McGann describes Byron's writing as establishing "explicit filiations" with the cultures in which he worked and thrived. According to McGann, Byron wanted to "represent the historical patterns and continuities which connected the present to the recent and distant past"; through his work, which is, in effect, "a poetry of experience." Byron included himself in all of his works, making clear his relationship to history and culture and emphasizing his own life as of "world-historical dimensions." His elevated style challenged convention while simultaneously reflecting classical traditions. Byron molded his poetry to fit the chaos inherent to the cultural and political revolutions of his age, resulting in a vibrant and forceful social reflection that informed not just Mary Shelley's life but also her work. It is likely she learned from Byron to train her artistic lens on society, as his poetry had done. As a result, he elicited great passion from his reading public, who at first adored and later despised him.

Born in London on January 20, 1788, Byron had a mixed heritage. His mother was Scottish of French extraction, while his father's ancestors had arrived in England along with William the Conqueror. The family took pride in tracing the origin of its wealth to King Henry VIII and its lineage to England's own history. A sensitive child, Byron adored his emotionally unstable mother. Although he would be regarded as flamboyant later in life, he was shy when young due to his being born with a clubfoot. Byron spent his early years in Scotland, where a nurse supposedly made sexual advances when he was only nine. Such rumors pepper Byron's biography, a life whose details for some overshadowed the importance of his art. This would also prove the case later for Mary Shelley.

At the age of 10, Byron received his title when his grandfather died. Although other heirs were in line before young George Gordon to inherit the title from the fifth Baron Byron of Rochdale, those relatives defaulted for various reasons. The inheritance fell to Byron, a mere child, who gained the family estate and privileges in Parliament. He moved with his mother to the family's decaying Newstead Abbey in England and reveled in its ancient and mysterious halls. The close attention that Byron would devote to details of place in his later works probably began with his love for the Abbey.

Byron eventually wore a brace on his leg that helped diminish the problems caused by his clubfoot. By the time he began school in 1799, he had learned to accept his leg's deformity and even to joke about it. He moved on to Harrow School in 1801, another place for which he formed a strong attachment and where he may have experimented sexually with other males. He returned to Newstead in 1803 and fell in love with his cousin; her rejection prompted him to write his first melancholy verse. Next, Byron spent time at Trinity College, Cambridge University, where he engaged in a bohemian lifestyle that burdened him with debt and a reputation for promiscuity. At Trinity, he

fig. 20

Portrait of a young Lord Byron from his collected works, published by John Murray in 1902

also formed a lifelong friendship with John Cam Hobhouse, who piqued Byron's interest in liberal politics.

Byron's later works would show the effect of his having matured at a time when France was in conflict with most of Europe. However, that effect was not reflected in his first published collection, *Fugitive Pieces* (1806), described as "wretched verse." He revised that work three times, retaining its autobiographical focus. In its third incarnation as *Hours of Idleness* (1807), the collection was scathingly reviewed in the *Edinburgh Review* (January 1808). The review, written by the reformist Henry Brougham, focused more on Byron than on the writing itself, criticizing the poet's self-conscious, personal approach. That review prompted Byron to publish a major satirical poem, *English Bards and Scotch Reviewers* (1809), a pretentious title for one of his youth and lack of experience.

England's political actions continued to dismay Byron, who became especially angered by Great Britain's actions against the Danish in 1808. The British seized Denmark's fleet and then signed a treaty, which they promptly broke, supporting a Swedish invasion of Denmark. That same year, Byron took his seat in Parliament and later engaged in a tour of Spain and Greece, accompanied by Hobhouse. In Malta, he became enamored of a married woman, an attachment that nearly resulted in a duel. As he continued to travel, he enjoyed additional relationships with women and greatly admired his landlady's daughter, Theresa Marci. She was the subject of his 1810 poem "Maid of Athens," although in a letter he admitted to also loving her two sisters, "these divinities, all of them under [the age of] fifteen." Byron became enthralled with Greece and would return and eventually die there while supporting its independence fighters.

Returning to London in July 1811, Byron was crushed by news of his mother's death at Newstead. The following year, he attracted attention by making his first speech in Parliament. Sickened by what he viewed as his native country's hypocrisy, he wrote the satirical poem "The Curse of Minerva" (1812), renouncing Britain's foreign policies in a supposed attack on Lord Elgin's efforts to save Greek culture through the famous Elgin Marbles. When he published the first two cantos of the autobiographical *Childe Harold's Pilgrimage: A Romance* a month later, Byron created a sensation that transformed him into a celebrity on the Continent as well as in England. The political and social commentary in the poem clarified the conflict between romantic idealism and a reality that included a strict social structure and the suffering of the poor.

McGann writes that *Childe Harold* revealed "the spectacle of political ruin was no more than an expression of what was truly to be lamented: the suffering which it brought to the lives of individual persons." The voice of Childe Harold was also that of Byron, and both character and poet make clear their feelings of disenfranchisement from society. The topic of alienation was nothing new; however, the fact that the individual disenfranchised in this poem belonged to the upper class was unusual. Childe Harold told of desperation despite being of the elite. Social stature could not protect any individual against despicable actions executed in the name of nationalism. It also featured the literary landscape that enthralled his readers, including Mary Shelley.

The next few years transformed Byron's fame for literary and political accomplishments into notoriety. The public watched and tongues wagged as he charged through high society events and created the works later known as his "Byronic Tales." His works sold at an amazing rate, and he became adored throughout Europe, birthing the dark, brooding, egotistical character labeled the BYRONIC HERO.

Byron's fame brought additional romantic relationships, most notably with Lady Caroline Lamb, and he was rumored to have had an affair with his half sister, Aurora Leigh. He attempted to form a traditional relationship when he married Anne Isabella Milbanke in January 1815. They settled in London, where Byron was plagued by debt collectors for money owed on his estate, causing him to hide at his publisher's house. Aurora Leigh visited Byron, and rumors circulated regarding the nature of their relationship. Approximately one year following Byron's wedding and after the birth of his and Isabella's daughter, Augusta Ada, Byron's wife returned to her parents' house. Although facts never surfaced, many believed Byron had committed incest with Aurora Leigh, perhaps fathering her first child. Disgusted and frustrated, he signed a marriage separation agreement and left England permanently. His self-exile allowed him to demonstrate his belief that Britain had begun to desert its ideals in favor of alliances abroad while at home supporting the needs of the traditional upper class against the poor.

After traveling for a time, Byron settled at Villa Diodati near Geneva, where he became friendly with the Shelleys. PERCY BYSSHE SHELLEY shared the attraction of many to Byron and judged him an old soul, labeling him the "Pilgrim of Eternity." Accompanied by his physician and friend, JOHN POLIDORI, Byron spent much time with his new friends. Mary's half sister, Claire Claremont, had an affair with Byron while in London and hoped to renew their relationship while in Geneva, but he had little interest in doing so. Her presence almost ended the friendship with the Shelleys before it had begun. The first awkward meeting with the Shelleys was recorded in Polidori's diary entry: "M Wollstonecraft Godwin . . . called here Mrs. Shelley" arrived with her lover, Percy, who was married, as well as her sister, Byron's mistress.

However, the group overcame the rocky first meeting, and Byron rented a house on the opposite shore from the Shelleys at Cologny. Both moved again, this time settling even closer together. According to Emily W. Sunstein, Byron and Claire again became lovers, Claire knowing that she was pregnant. She convinced the Shelleys that she was Byron's true mistress, although he never formalized their relationship. Mary enjoyed the daily boating activities and took their son William along. While boating with Shelley, Byron was inspired to write his narrative poem *The Prisoner of Chillon*. He also continued *Childe Harold*, his narrator searching for true heroism in a time of moral default. The verses expressed the revulsion that Byron sometimes felt over the public's reaction to him. According to Sunstein, that summer, rumors flew "that Byron, the incestuous lover of his sister, Shelley, Mary Godwin, and her 'sister' had formed a League of Incest in which Godwin's daughters slept with both men."

Mary commented in her journals on how much she learned by sitting quietly and listening to Percy and Byron discuss history, politics, and world affairs. She would later quote from Byron in her historical fiction *The Fortunes of Perkin Warbeck* (1830). Her personal writing emphasized the inspiration gained during the summer of 1818. She thought of her group, according to Sunstein, "as a modern Promethean cadre, she carrying forward her mother's torch of female liberation." Although her artistic gains through exposure to Byron's genius proved enormous, Shelley also paid a high price in her association with his notoriety, an association in the public's mind that would be lifelong.

The Shelley party returned to London, and on January 12, 1817, Claire gave birth to Byron's daughter, whom she named Alba, while Byron named the infant Allegra. The baby lived with the Shelleys for a time, and Claire continued to be a distraction to their relationship. She so came to hate Bryon that she would later write of him and Percy Shelley, "I saw the two first poets of England . . . become monsters of lying, meanness, cruelty and treachery—under the influence of free love Lord B became a human tyger slaking his thirst for inflicting pain upon defenceless women."

Byron visited the Bernese Oberland with his old friend Hobhouse and gained the scenic inspiration for the Faustian *Manfred* (1817). That play expressed his feelings of remorse and his continued struggle with the conflict between ROMANTICISM and reality. In autumn 1814, he visited Italy and studied Armenian, also falling in love with the wife of his landlord, despite intermittent pleas from Claire to rejoin her. He met up with Hobhouse in Rome the following spring. The Roman ruins moved him to write a fourth canto for *Childe Harold* (1818), which he followed with a satire, *Beppo* (1818).

Byron's next romantic interest was Margarita Cogni, but, never distracted long from his writing, he began work on *Don Juan* (1819), another verse satire. In 1818, the year that Mary Shelley published *Frankenstein*, the Shelleys brought Alba/Allegra to Byron, some sources say due to Mary's fears that others would suspect the child belonged to Percy Shelley. During that same year, Byron at last sold much of the family estate and escaped debt. Before long, Claire began to plead with him to return custody of Alba to her, calling on the Shelleys to intercede with Byron, which they were reluctant to do.

A new romance with the married 19-year-old Countess Teresa Guiccioli rescued Byron from the over-indulgent state in which he had gained much weight. McGann describes 1820 as a "watershed year" for Byron. La Guiccioli afforded him a sense of "emotional stability" that helped him shake his self-absorption, permitting him to again interact with his political environment. After he and the countess followed one another about Italy for a time, he became her man-in-waiting, and they returned to Ravenna. There, thanks to connections on the part of the countess's father and brother, Byron became a part of the revolutionary secret police squad, the Carbonari. He unabashedly fell in love with the Italian people and their culture and, with full enthusiasm, devoted himself to support of the causes of the countess's family.

Again engaged with the world and his surroundings, Byron began a prolific writing period. Among his major works completed at that time were the first three cantos of *Don Juan*, his play *The Two Foscari*, and the closet drama *Cain*, all published in 1821. Late that year, Byron decided to leave Allegra at a convent in Ravenna. He loved his daughter and at first enjoyed showing her off to others, but eventually he came to feel that she had become too headstrong. Tragically, she died on April 20, 1822, devastating Claire. Claire would later blast Mary Shelley for modeling the title character of her novel *Lodore* (1835) after Byron, in part because Lord Lodore kidnaps his daughter, removing her from her mother to take her to America.

Just before Allegra's death, Byron's social and political activism caused his publisher, John Murray, to reject his work due to its controversial nature. Consequently, John Hunt, a man of far more liberal opinions than Murray, became Byron's publisher. Teresa had to leave Byron when her father and brother were exiled for participation in an attempted uprising, and Byron followed them to Pisa, reluctantly leaving Ravenna and his causes behind. The relocation allowed him to see Teresa often, as her father and brother were able to settle near Pisa.

In 1822, the whole group moved to Leghorn, near the Shelleys, and Byron and the poet Leigh Hunt joined Shelley in planning to publish a new journal. EDWARD TRELAWNY, an adventurer who greatly admired the romantics, joined the entourage and became attached to Byron in particular. Mary took advantage of the opportunity to become friends with Teresa, to whom she would continue to write in the Italian language, long after Byron's death.

Following Percy's Shelley's drowning in July, the plans for the journal fell apart, and Hunt was left with no employment. Byron found himself suddenly responsible for Hunt, Hunt's disagreeable wife, and their six children. When Hunt's brother published a new periodical, *The Liberal*, Byron supported the effort; its first edition contained his "The Vision of Judgment" (1822). "Vision" was a satire written in response to an elegiac poem by England's poet laureate, Robert Southey. Southey's poem, entitled *A Vision of Judgment* (1820), celebrated King George III after his death. Southey referred to Byron's "Satanic School," while Byron accused of Southey of writing "the gross flattery, the dull impudence, the renegado intolerance, and impious cant" that amounted to "the sublime of himself." Byron's "Judgment," considered profane and an attack on the monarchy, led to Hunt's imprisonment.

At the end of the summer of Percy Shelley's death, Byron moved Teresa, her brother, and her father to Genoa and was followed by Mary, who rented a house for herself and the Hunts. Byron contributed more work to *The Liberal*, including the latest additions to *Don Juan*. Boredom and restlessness soon drove him to search for a new activity. Meanwhile, he had promised to lend Mary enough money to pay for the trip back to London for her and her son, Percy Florence Shelley, but he did not fulfill his promise. She had to find an alternative source of funds.

Always with an eye to his place in history, Byron responded eagerly in 1823 when the London Greek Committee asked him to act on their behalf to support the Greeks who were fighting for independence from the Turks. He arrived at Cephalonia in August, settling at Metaxata, where he became enamored with a Greek boy to whom he would dedicate some of his last poetry. Trelawny joined Byron, also claiming to support the cause of Greek independence. Fully committed to his charge, Byron donated a large sum of money toward preparation for battle by the freedom fighters. He moved to Missolonghi and helped prepare men for battle until he became ill in February 1824. He grew weaker following bleeding treatments, with Trelawny remaining close at hand. While Byron was ill, some of the Greeks revolted against their own forces, forcing Byron to face the reality that he was more dedicated to the Greek cause than many of the nationals.

In spring 1824, just as he had seemed to be recovering, he worsened after being caught in a storm. Byron died on April 19, never having participated in a true battle. The Greeks celebrated him as a national hero and removed his heart from his body to bury at Missolonghi. When it was refused burial in Westminster Abbey, Byron's body was interred with ancestors near Newstead. Repeated attempts to honor Byron in Westminster were denied until 1969, when, due to the efforts of the dean of Westminster, a plaque in Byron's honor was hung in the Abbey.

A great writer of Oriental tales, Byron actually experienced the exotic East that so fascinated the reading English public, including Mary Shelley. Like her contemporaries, she was enthralled with an area of the world about which she knew little, her fascination obvious in the character of Safie in *Frankenstein*, as well as in the setting and characters of her short story "The Evil Eye" (1830). Much of the story she based on the experiences of Lord Byron while in Greece, and she drew directly from Byron's "The Giaour." Trelawny would later take advantage of his short relationship with Byron to write a book that included experiences that could not be documented.

With the development in later centuries of a consciousness of "politically incorrect" subject matter, Byron's eastern tales and those of his contemporaries would fall out of favor. Later postcolonial literary critics such as Edward Said believed that no modern reader should enjoy those stories. According to Thomas M. Disch in a 2010 review of a book about Byron, Said believed such tales "trivialize cultures and fail to do justice to their diversity."

Byron's effects were far-reaching, and his work remains an important part of the English literary canon. In addition, his romantic activities continue to fascinate readers and authors of both nonfiction and fiction. Examples from the many novels based on Byron's exploits include Amanda Prantera's *Conversations with Lord Byron on Perversion, 163 Years after His Lordship's Death* (1987); John Crowley's *Lord Byron's Novel: The Evening Land* (2005); and Daisy Hay's *Young Romantics: The Tangled Lives of English Poetry's Greatest Generation* (2010).

FURTHER READING

"The Byron Chronology." *Romantic Circles: Scholarly Resources*. Available online. URL: http://www.rc.umd.edu/reference/chronologies/byronchronology/index.html. Accessed June 20, 2009.

Byron, George Gordon Byron, Lord. *Byron's Letters and Journals*. Edited by Leslie A. Marchand. Cambridge, Mass.: Harvard University Press, 1973.

———. *The Complete Poetical Works of Lord Byron*. Edited by Jerome J. McGann. Oxford: Clarendon Press, 1980.

———. "An Unpublished Letter Written by Lord Byron from Athens." *Annual of the British School at Athens* 22 (1916/1917–1917/1918): 107–109.

———. *Works of Lord Byron*. Mobile Reference: Amazon Digital Services, 2009.

Christensen, Jerome. "Byron's Career: The Speculative Stage." *English Literary History* 52, no. 1 (Spring 1985): 59–84.

Colligan, Collette. "The Unruly Copies of Byron's *Don Juan*: Harems, Underground Print Culture, and the Age of Mechanical Reproduction." *Nineteenth-Century Literature* 59, no. 4 (March 2005): 433–462.

Disch, Thomas M. "My Roommate, Lord Byron." *Hudson Review* 54, no. 4 (Winter 2002): 590–594.

Douglas, Paul. "An Unpublished Letter from Byron to Lady Caroline Lamb." *Notes & Queries* 53, no. 3 (September 2006): 322–323.

Dyer, Gary. "Thieves, Boxers, Sodomites, Poets: Being Flash to Byron's *Don Juan*." *PMLA*. 116, no. 3 (May 2001): 562–78.

Eisler, Benita. *Byron: Child of Passion, Fool of Fame*. New York: Vintage, 2000.

Elledge, Paul. *Lord Byron at Harrow School: Speaking Out, Talking Back, Acting Up, Bowing Out*. Baltimore: Johns Hopkins Press, 2000.

Giraldi, William. "Pilgrim of Eternity: The Loves and Legends of Lord Byron." *American Scholar* 78, no. 3 (Summer 2009): 112–114.

Hawley, Michelle. "Harriett Beecher Stowe and Lord Byron: A Case of Celebrity Justice in the Victorian Public Sphere." *Journal of Victorian Culture* 10, no. 2 (Winter 2005): 229–256.

Heinzelman, Kurt. "Lord Byron and the Invention of Celebrity." *Southwest Review* 93, no. 4 (2008): 489–501.

Knox-Shaw, Peter. "Persuasion, Byron, and the Turkish Tale." *Review of English Studies*, New Series 44, no. 173 (February 1993): 47–69.

The Life and Work of Lord Byron, 1788–1824. Available online. URL: http://englishhistory.net/byron.html. Accessed August 5, 2010.

Lipman, Samuel. "Lord Byron Undone." *Grand Street* 5, no. 3 (Spring 1986): 180–193.

Lowenstein, Jerold. "Lord Byron on Love and Water." *Oceans* 17, no. 2 (March/April 1984): 72.

Marandi, Seyed Mohammad. "The Oriental World of Lord Byron and the Orientalism of Literary Scholars." *Critique: Critical Middle Eastern Studies* 15, no. 3 (Fall 2006): 317–337.

Markovits, Benjamin. *A Quiet Adjustment*. New York: W.W. Norton, 2008.

———. *Imposture*. New York: W. W. Norton, 2007.

McGann, Jerome J. Introduction to *Lord Byron*, edited by Alice Levine and Jerome J. McGann, xi–xxiii. New York: Oxford University Press, 1986.

Mekler, L. Adam. "Broken Mirrors and Multiplied Reflections in Lord Byron and Mary Shelley." *Studies in Romanticism* 46, no. 4 (Winter 2007): 461–480.

Mole, Tom. "Lord Bryon and the End of Fame." *International Journal of Cultural Studies* 11, no. 3 (September 2008): 343–361.

Moore, Thomas. *Life of Lord Byron, Vol. 1, with His Letters and Journals*. 1854. Reprint, Memphis, Tenn.: General Books, LLC, 2010.

Murray, John. *The Letters of John Murray to Lord Byron*. Edited by Andrew Nicholson. Liverpool, U.K.: Liverpool University Press, 2007.

Nemerov, Howard. "Poetry and Life: Lord Byron." *Hudson Review* 7, no. 2 (Summer 1954): 285–291.

O'Brien, Edna. *Byron in Love: A Short Daring Life*. New York: W. W. Norton, 2009.

Oliver, Susan. "Crossing 'Dark Barriers': Intertextuality and Dialogue between Lord Byron and Sir Walter Scott. *Studies in Romanticism* 47, no. 1 (Spring 2008): 15–35.

Phillipson, Mark. "Alteration in Exile: Byron's 'Mazeppa.'" *Nineteenth-Century Literature* 58, no. 3 (December 2003): 291–325.

Polidori, John. *The Diary of Dr. John William Polidori, Relating to Byron, Shelley, etc*. Edited by William Michael Rossetti. London: Elkin Mathews, 1911.

Pollitt, Katha. "Lord Byron's Great Insight: Mad, Bad, and Dangerous, He Understood What Women Wanted." *Slate* (July 13, 2009). Available online. URL: http://www.slate.com/id/2222669. Accessed July 18, 2009.

Rollin, H. R. "Childe Harolde: Father to Lord Byron?" *British Medical Journal* 2, no. 5921 (June 29, 1974): 714–716.

Sunstein, Emily W. *Mary Shelley: Romance and Reality*. Baltimore: Johns Hopkins University Press, 1991.

Tannenbaum, Leslie. "Lord Byron in the Wilderness: Biblical Tradition in Byron's 'Cain' and Blake's 'The Ghost of Abel.'" *Modern Philology* 72, no. 4 (May, 1975): 350–364.

Vail, Jeffery W. *The Literary Relationship of Lord Byron and Thomas Moore*. Baltimore: Johns Hopkins University Press, 2001.

Woolfson, Susan J. "Byron's Ghosting Authority." *English Literary History* 76, no. 3 (Fall 2009): 763–792.

Byronic hero The Byronic hero character, named for the romantic poet GEORGE GORDON BYRON (1788–1824), Lord Byron, became a favorite of gothic novel authors (see GOTHIC FICTION), including Mary Shelley and also Emily and Charlotte Brontë, among many others. The Byronic hero has been described by the scholar Edward Quinn as "dark, brooding, rebellious and defiant." While critics agree the term grew from characters in Byron's work, the poet himself also seems to fit

battles, he inevitably gains the admiration of readers, who appreciate his loyalty to a personal code. Dark, brooding, often with a mysterious background and a physicality bordering on the brute, the Byronic hero is a highly passionate and intelligent character.

Familiar Byronic heroes include Mr. Rochester from Charlotte Brontë's *Jane Eyre* (1847) and Heathcliff from Emily Brontë's *Wuthering Heights* (1847). In many plots, the Byronic hero must metaphorically die in order to enjoy symbolic "rebirth," often suffering a physical maiming, such as through baptism by fire in *Jane Eyre*; or a literal death and rebirth as a spirit being, such as that suffered by Heathcliff. Shelley's short story "Transformation" (1831) features Guido, a character with some Byronic tendencies who suffers a permanent disability following confrontation with an evil dwarf. Some 20th- and 21st-century readers and critics of John Milton's PARADISE LOST, a work that had a tremendous influence on Shelley, characterized Satan as a Byronic hero, seen through the lens of ROMANTICISM. The term is still used as a reference in psychological and sociologic studies of the aggressive male.

FPO
fig. 21

Portrait of George Gordon Byron (Lord Byron), friend of Mary and Percy Shelley, from 1813 *(Painting by Richard Westall)*

the description. With her personal knowledge and understanding of Byron, Mary Shelley would appear to have been primed for utilizing such a character. However, critics continue to debate whether any of Shelley's heroes can firmly be labeled Byronic, although many possess various aspects of that character type.

The Byronic hero was often a womanizer and adventurer who sought revenge for what he perceived as wrongful treatment. He could soften for those he loved, revealing a tender side, but for the most part, he remained an unpleasant force. Fellow characters found themselves both attracted to and repelled by the Byronic hero's enigmatic nature. Surprisingly, the reader usually forgives the hero's faults, tending to focus instead on his strength of character as he bravely deals with conflict, both internal and external. While the hero does not always achieve victory over the forces he

FURTHER READING

Bogg, Richard A., and Janet M. Ray. "The Heterosexual Appeal of Socially Marginal Men." *Deviant Behavior* 27, no. 4 (July/August 2006): 457–477.

Ernest, James Lovell. *Byron and the Byronic Hero in the Novels of Mary Shelley*. Dallas: University of Texas Press, 1951.

Hishmeh, Richard. "Byron: Romantic Posturing In the Age of Modernism." *Hemingway Review* 29, no. 2 (Spring 2010): 89–104.

Holland, Meridel. "Lord Byron's 'The Dream' and *Wuthering Heights*." *Brontë Studies* 34, no. 1 (March 2009): 31–46.

Janssen, David A. "The Byronic Hero in Film, Fiction, and Television." *Gothic Studies* 7, no. 2 (November 2005): 219–221.

Mellor, Anne K. *Romanticism and Gender*. London: Routledge, 1992.

Wootton, Sarah. "The Byronic in Jane Austen's *Persuasion* and *Pride and Prejudice*." *Modern Language Review* 102, no. 1 (January 2007): 26–39.

———. "The Changing Faces of the Byronic Hero in *Middlemarch* and *North and South*." *Romanticism* 14, no. 1 (2008): 25–35.

feminist criticism Born of a political and social movement that claimed material, social, and civic rights for women, feminist criticism became important in the mid-20th century. The feminist agenda is basically fourfold: (1) to recover works written by women but not originally credited to them, and to include known women writers in the literary canon; (2) to revise the approach to reading female-written works, searching for a subtext that works against stereotypes of women in literature; (3) to investigate whether naturally engendered differences exist between writing by women and writing by men; (4) to study stereotypes of women created in literature by male writers and observe how such characterizations change over time, as well as how women read about women. All of these approaches apply to fiction by Mary Shelley.

Like all literary critics, feminist critics examine formal elements of literature to arrive at meaning in works of literature. Those elements in fiction include plot, character, theme, setting, style, and point of view. They also include format, figurative language, sound, imagery, and rhythm. However, feminist critics consider additional elements in their analysis and interpretation. Those additional elements draw on the historical era in which authors write and how literature depicts that era and its social mores, particularly those pertaining to women's rights. Such critics also regard details about the author's life as crucial, especially if the author's background seems to be responsible for her inclusion of certain subjects and themes. For instance, the prominent focus on the study of natural science during Shelley's era would be crucial to themes of her fiction, as would beliefs inherent to ROMANTICISM and its literature, including the privileging of the individual above the group, the importance of interaction with nature, and the focus on transcendentalism.

Power relationships in literature are particularly important to feminist critics. In Shelley's fiction, males always hold power while few female characters rise above flat stereotypes. However, while the male traditionally holds material power over the female, especially in works before the mid-20th century, she may succeed in subverting that power by turning what may at first be a disadvantage to her advantage. For example, males might demand silence of females as a culturally approved point of control, but the female character might, by failing to reveal crucial knowledge, use her silence to her benefit. An example is Constance in Shelley's story "The Dream" (1832), who takes her silence and feelings of isolation so far as to plan a move into a convent, a female bastion free of male sexual and material demands.

Women characters may also claim power bestowed by their particular talents, such as the title heroine of Charlotte Brontë's *Jane Eyre* (1847), whose art fills her with an unfeminine passion, which she freely expresses in her narration. In a few cases, female characters claim male power, such as Jane Austen's title character of *Emma* (1816), who, secure in her inheritance of her father's fortune, states that she will not marry as she wields her considerable social power in an attempt at love matches. In still other cases, the female protagonist may meet tragedy as punishment for her independence, a characteristic that would have been admired and rewarded in a male. Feminist critics see this in Shelley's character Fanny from *Lodore* (1835). Although Fanny does not die or suffer physical damage, she remains isolated due to her intellectual abilities. The novel closes as the reader learns that Fanny's fate is unknown. Another example, Bertha Rochester, Rochester's spirited first wife in *Jane Eyre*, goes mad and eventually dies due to her independent actions. Her figure is used as a metaphor for the marginalized woman in Sandra M. Gilbert and Susan Gubar's seminal feminist work *The Madwoman in the Attic: The Woman Writer and the Nineteenth-Century Literary Imagination* (1979).

Feminist critics also focus on the importance of traditional symbols in fiction, such as the caged bird, long symbolic of a woman admired for her appearance and her talent, yet restrained and imprisoned, physically, emotionally, or spiritually. In Shelley's *Lodore*, Edward Villiers compares Ethel to a bird, and in *Falkner* (1837), Alithea is compared to a bird on multiple occasions. Other traditional symbols include all types of flowers, but especially the rose. A rosebud generally represents a young, virginal woman, while a fully bloomed rose symbolizes a woman of sexual maturity. The heroine of Shelley's "Transformation" (1831), Juliet, is introduced early on through comparison to an opening rose in May. Shelley incorporated various flowers and plants throughout her fiction, not surprising in light of her dedication to romanticism, which had as a major tenet the importance of nature to spiritual health.

Certain colors relate symbolically to women, such as white, which in the Western tradition represents purity or naïveté. Thus, women who wear white may be innocent young girls, or white may be used ironically to indicate women who have lost their innocence. Shelley repeatedly employs the color white in *Frankenstein* (1818); Mont Blanc, which means "White Mountain," towers over much of the novel's action, symbolizing the removal of purity from Victor's and the monster's evil activities. The moon traditionally represents woman who lacks her own importance and thus reflects the light of the sun, symbolic of man. Most of the monster's significant activity occurs during night, and the moon is often referenced as if it nurtures the creature born without a mother.

Mirrors are symbolic of self-reflection and indicate questions of self-identity for both male and female characters, but they are even more important for females, who traditionally had to worry about their appearance constantly. In writing about literature, feminist critics have also noted how women themselves have been used as mirrors for men, who desired their praise and support in such a way that the women served as reflections for the men themselves. Shelley's fiction takes this traditional approach in several instances. However, in "Transformation," it is the male protagonist/narrator who refers to a vision as mirroring truth. Because the narrator makes clear in the story's beginning the importance of passing along his tale to others, Shelley may suggest literature's value in portraying truth about human nature. In literature, women of great beauty may also be compared to statuary or other collectible works of art, often important to men only for their material value, another approach taken in "Transformation" and other of Shelley's stories.

Also important to feminist critics is the presence of any type of domestic creative endeavor on the part of women characters, as for centuries women had to suppress their artistic bent; painting, writing, and sculpting were viewed as imprudent and impractical for them. They engaged instead in "approved" activities, such as any type of needlework, cooking, and gardening, to express their artistic talents. Even at such traditional activities, female subjects could prove subversive, as does Madame Lafarge in Charles Dickens's *A Tale of Two Cities* (1859): She used purled and dropped stitches to fashion a death list for the Parisian death squads into her knitting.

Feminist critics find interesting three traditional roles for women in early fiction, including that of the "angel in the house," an idea especially associated with Victorian women. In the late 1850s, the British poet Coventry Patmore wrote a series of poems entitled *The Angel in the House,* which praised women who could manage large families, serve others, and remain pure and "angelic." This image led the modernist writer Virginia Woolf to later declare that she had to kill the angel in the house in order to liberate her imagination to write as she should. Stories such as "Transformation" supported that categorization of woman as angelic, innocent, and childlike.

A second stereotype, also promoted by early Victorian fiction, was the invalid. Many women suffered physical disability following multiple unplanned childbirths, and the prone position was quite an acceptable one for a wife and mother. Shelley characterizes several mother figures in this manner, and some, such as Mrs. Frankenstein, die due to their selfless care of others. Feminist critics see a subtext in Shelley's work that undercuts the stereotype of the perfect Victorian family and its angelic mother in her criticism of irresponsible males who abandon their responsibility to their families.

The third stereotype of the whore appeared in various versions. The whore might appear as a temptress, stealing an unwitting male from his wife and family. In another version, she might possess "a heart of gold" and sacrifice not only her body, to financially support herself, but also her emotional and spiritual needs. She falls in love with men who, lacking the stigma attached to the women whose sexual services they used, reject whores as potential wives or serious lovers. Belle Watling in *Gone With the Wind* (1936) represents such a character in her relationship with Rhett Butler. Shelley does not include this stereotype, possibly because of the attitudes toward free and open sexual affair espoused by her romantic associates, including her husband.

By the time that feminist criticism arrived in the mid-20th century, critics also focused on changing the traditional literary canon studied in education. Long filled mainly with white male writers, the canon slowly altered over several decades to include not only white women writers but also women of color and of various ethnic backgrounds. Mary Shelley, along with Jane Austen and the Brontë sisters, had been included for some time. However, only her first novel, *Frankenstein*, was much read, and it was categorized as gothic or horror fiction (see GOTHIC FICTION), genres often considered something less than high literary fiction. Critics such as Hartley Spatt later disputed the claim that gothic fiction takes a secondary position to that of romantic fiction. In addition, Shelley's importance to fiction is now supported through consideration of her entire body of work, not just *Frankenstein*.

FURTHER READING

Behrendt, Stephen. "Mary Shelley, *Frankenstein*, and the Woman Writer's Fate." In *Romantic Women Writers: Voices and Countervoices*, edited by Paula R. Feldman and Theresa Kelly, 69–87. Hanover, N.H.: University Press of New England, 1995.

Buikema, Rosemarie, and Anneke Smelik, eds. *Women's Studies and Culture: A Feminist Introduction*. Atlantic Highlands, N.J.: Zed Books, 1995.

Dunker, Patricia. "Mary Shelley's Afterlives: Biography and Invention." *Women* 15, no. 2 (summer 2004): 230–249.

Ellis, Kate. "Fatal Attraction or the Post-Modern Prometheus." *Journal of Sex Research* 27, no. 1 (February 1990): 111–122.

Felski, Rita. *Literature after Feminism*. Chicago: University of Chicago Press, 2003.

Gilbert, Sandra M., and Susan Gubar. *The Madwoman in the Attic: The Woman Writer and the Nineteenth-Century Literary Imagination*. 2nd ed. New Haven, Conn.: Yale University Press, 2000.

Heilbrun, Carolyn G. *Writing a Woman's Life*. New York: Ballantine, 1988.

Poovey, Mary. *The Proper Lady & the Woman Writer: Ideology as Style in the Works of Mary Wollstonecraft, Mary Shelley, & Jane Austen*. Chicago: University of Chicago Press, 1983.

Rose, Ellen Cronan. "Custody Battles: Reproducing Knowledge about *Frankenstein*." *New Literary History* 26, no. 4 (Autumn 1995): 809–823.

Spatt, Hartley. "Mary Shelley's Last Men: the Truth of Dreams." *Studies in the Novel* 7, no. 4 (Winter 1975): 526–537.

Todd, Janet. *Death and the Maidens: Fanny Wollstonecraft and the Shelley Circle*. Berkeley, Calif.: Counterpoint, 2007.

Yousef, Nancy. "The Monster in a Dark Room: *Frankenstein*, Feminism and Philosophy." *Modern Language Quarterly* 63, no. 2 (June 2002): 197–226.

Godwin, William (1756–1836) Born into a very religious family on March 3, 1756, William Godwin, Mary Shelley's father, later studied philosophy that would undermine his Calvinistic background. He became a minister in 1778 but almost immediately caused uproar by publicly questioning church doctrine. He left his first appointment after two years, hoping to eventually return to the ministry after regaining his confidence in the church and his own opinions. He spent 10 years in turmoil over the conflict between new and old ideas, finally turning to atheism in 1783. He based his decision, in part, on his study of French philosophers such as Jean-Jacques Rousseau (1712–78); Paul-Henri Thiri, Baron d'Holbach (1723–89); and Claude Adreine Helvétius (1715–75), whose work, along with that of John Locke (1632–1704), led Godwin to conclude that the doctrine of original sin was false. Children were born without guilt and could be educated in the best aspects of human nature by studying history and languages. Following his shift in philosophy, Godwin moved to London, where

Portrait of William Godwin from 1830 *(Painting by Henry William Pickersgill)*

he first sought writing assignments and considered becoming a teacher.

Although he left the church, Godwin did not change his desire to institute social reform. Living mostly in London, he wrote to support his views, publishing multiple essays in various journals as he began to develop his philosophy, making clear early on that he believed man need turn to no higher authority, whether civil or spiritual, but could depend on his individual judgment to guide his decisions and actions. He learned that writers could earn money, but they did not enjoy any profits from sales of their materials.

Godwin became expert in the political affairs of India and Ireland. Challenged by his own honesty, which tended to offend people, he spent nine years learning to write for public consumption, producing three novels and a number of reviews and commentaries. He was active in radical political groups prior to the outbreak of the French Revolution and was in the crowd that heard the Dissenting minister Richard Price deliver his famous prorevolutionary sermon on November 4, 1789.

During this period, Godwin met MARY WOLLSTONECRAFT, his future wife and a reformist writer. She had written the anonymous *A Vindication of the Rights of Man* in response to Sir Edmund Burke's 1790 treatise *Reflections on the Revolution in France*. She then raised the ire of many by suggesting that women deserved education in her seminal feminist publication *A Vindication of the Rights of Woman* (1792). In that work, she applied the ideals of liberty and equality to support her claims. Godwin also responded to Burke with his most famous work, *An Inquiry Concerning the Principles of Political Justice and its Influence in General Virtue and Happiness* (1793). Godwin's condemnation of all organized control over humans—including, in part, taxation, marriage, and all contractual agreement, as well as legal punishment of crimes—brought him instant fame. While they moved in the same circles, Godwin and Wollstonecraft did not know one another well. Before they finally met and fell in love, Wollstonecraft moved to Paris in order to observe the aftermath of the French Revolution.

The following year, 1794, Godwin published a novel entitled *Caleb Williams*, which equaled the popularity of his *Inquiry*. Departing from the traditional approach of offering a murder mystery for readers to solve, Godwin instead wrote an analysis of the murderer and the detective who pursued him, suggesting that the social conventions of pride and honor led to the crime. His fiction allowed him to appeal to a new audience, one not adept at following the abstract reasoning of his nonfiction. The novel's preface reflects its similarity to political tracts written by Godwin. It read, in part:

> It is but of late that the inestimable importance of political principles has been adequately apprehended. It is now known to philosophers that the spirit and character of the Government intrudes itself into every rank of society. But this is a truth highly worthy to be communicated to persons whom books of philosophy and science are never likely to reach. Accordingly, it was proposed, in the invention of the following work, to comprehend, as far as the

progressive nature of a single story would allow, a general review of the modes of domestic and unrecorded despotism by which man becomes the destroyer of man.

The statement was so strong that Godwin's publishers feared accusations of treason and withheld the preface until later editions. Critics consider *Caleb Williams*, subtitled *or Things as They Are*, the best-written "doctrine novel"—one designed to teach a lesson about social concerns—of the 18th century. Godwin's method was to determine his climax, then plan the plot backwards, resulting in a tightly knit series of events. Critics later noted a weakness in Godwin's novel shared with other writings of its type and time: Characters were simply mouthpieces for the author to state his personal political and social opinions; they modeled stereotypical attitudes and reactions.

A major anarchist of the Age of Reason, Godwin opposed what he saw as the tyranny of institutions as well as organized resistance to them, insisting men could settle their differences only through one-on-one interaction and negotiations. Some described his ideas as simplistic and overly optimistic, contradicting Godwin's own rational approach. Although his activism did not carry so far as to outwardly support the statement by the London Corresponding Society that social agitation was the *best* choice to promote social change, Godwin did believe that change was imperative. For instance, he wrote in *Social Justice*, "Man is in a state of perpetual progress. He must grow either better or worse, either correct his habits or confirm them. The government proposed must either increase our passions and prejudices by fanning the flame, or by gradually discouraging tend to extirpate them." In 1794, Godwin acted on his belief to publish *Cursory Strictures on the Charge Delivered by Lord Chief Justice Eyre to the Grand Jury*, although he did publish it anonymously. His well-reasoned argument helped convince a jury to declare several citizens on trial for treason innocent.

In 1796, Wollstonecraft returned to London with her illegitimate daughter, Fanny Imlay, the result of an affair while in Paris with the American Gilbert Imlay. Wollstonecraft had pursued Imlay as he traveled about Europe having multiple sexual relationships. He refused to commit to a formal relationship with her and Fanny, prompting Wollstonecraft's suicide attempt. Scholars note such desperate behavior as evidence of the difficulty in Wollstonecraft living her ideal of the independent woman. In other areas of her life, she exceeded expectations, lifting herself from abject childhood poverty and a difficult upbringing to become one of the first female professional writers of her era.

The 40-year-old Godwin admired Wollstonecraft and all that she had accomplished and was not at all concerned over the fact that she had an illegitimate child. He knew of Fanny's status, although some official records showed that Imlay and Wollstonecraft had married. Godwin and Wollstonecraft agreed on many topics, including the lack of need for marriage, which they judged a limiting social institution. They became lovers but decided to live apart and unmarried, until Wollstonecraft became pregnant. After considering the civil repercussions against a child born without a father, they wed but continued to live apart. By all accounts, their brief relationship burned brightly, bringing Wollstonecraft a modicum of stability and support for the first time in her life and Godwin the satisfaction of a partner more than his intellectual equal. They would give birth to one of the great novelists of the 19th century, Mary Wollstonecraft Godwin, later Mary Shelley.

When Wollstonecraft died of puerperal fever 10 days following Mary's birth in August 1797, Godwin was devastated. In the hope of redeeming Wollstonecraft's reputation and to ease his grief, he published her incomplete novel, *Maria, or the Wrongs of Women*, in 1798 as part of *Memoirs of the Author of a Vindication of the Rights of Woman*. Unfortunately, the public did not react positively when they learned even more personal scandalous details of Wollstonecraft's life than had previously been revealed, and she was labeled "an unsex'd female," rather than receiving the status for which Godwin had hoped.

Despite the public opinion of his wife, Godwin determined to raise his two daughters as Wollstonecraft would have liked, which included an education reflecting many aspects of the philosophy of Rousseau. He struggled to do so with the help of a housekeeper and nurse who helped the girls learn to read. When the servant ran away with a lover, Godwin decided he badly needed a wife to help him with his increasingly demanding daughters. After rejection by two women, his proposal was accepted by a neighbor, Mary Jane Clairmont. They wed when Mary Godwin was four years old, with Mary Jane bringing two children—Jane, later called Claire, and Charles—into the Godwin household. Their family expanded with the 1803 birth of their son, William. With Mary Jane's help, Godwin founded a publishing company, producing books mainly for children.

Mary Godwin matured learning from both Godwin's mind and his library. A moody child who never seemed satisfied with the amount of attention her sometimes aloof father gave to her, Mary was a voracious reader. Like her formidably intelligent parents, she was driven from a young age to express herself and greatly benefitted from exposure to the endless stream of visitors who came to the house to speak with Godwin. She listened to the conversation some of her culture's finest thinkers and creators, including Charles Lamb, William Wordsworth, William Hazlitt, and one of Mary's later favorite poets, Samuel Taylor Coleridge. She also read her mother's works and knew of her public reputation.

Godwin noticed Mary's strained relationship with her stepmother and sent her away for a time to school and, more important, to visit his friends the Baxters in Scotland. That visit had a permanent effect on her writing, the inspiration of its scenery and sense of history later apparent. It also allowed her a view of a more traditional family, something that Godwin could not offer, nor did he care to. Mary's desire for the familial relationships she witnessed when spending time with the Baxters would inhabit much of her fiction. Most critics agree that the unusual background of her parentage had an enormous effect on her emotional development and her creative output. Godwin's influence on the shaping of Mary's fictional daughter characters and their interactions with their father characters was obvious, resulting in many unflattering and unfortunate profiles of irresponsible men.

Godwin first met Mary's future husband, the poet PERCY BYSSHE SHELLEY, when Mary was a young teen. Shelley visited Godwin often and became his pupil, greatly benefitting from the intellectual discussions about the social ideals they shared. In turn, Godwin took advantage of Shelley's financial patronage. However, he became alarmed when he noticed a romantic relationship developing between the older, married Shelley and his daughter. He forbade Mary to see Shelley, an act that directly contradicted the philosophy of free will he had staunchly defended earlier in his life. He was so shocked and angry with Mary when she ran away with Shelley and her stepsister Claire that he refused to see her upon her return three months later. Mary was hurt and confused by his rejection, assuming his anger would diminish over time; it did not. He staunchly upheld his edict against seeing Mary until she at last married Shelley, following the drowning death of the poet's estranged wife. A short time later, Fanny Imlay committed suicide, unable to deal with the depression that would also haunt Mary throughout her life.

Godwin did adjust to Mary's marriage, and before long, he began repeated requests for continued financial support from Percy, even though Shelley's financial condition was not secure. A generous man, Percy sent money to Godwin as often as possible, believing that as an intellectual who benefitted society, his request of Percy, a man from an aristocratic background, was legitimate. Unfortunately, Shelley lacked the title and the wealth of his family, and neither his titled grandfather nor his father was pleased with his desertion of his original family in favor of Mary. Thus, his allowance was not as generous as his lifestyle required, and funding Godwin proved a financial hardship to the new Shelley family.

Godwin worked to keep Wollstonecraft's memory alive and loved Mary, but his actions and attitudes had mixed effects on her life. While he obviously inspired the thought and writing of both Mary and Percy Shelley, he also antagonized them on occasion. In addition to serving as a financial drain to their resources, Godwin was frequently insensitive to Mary's emotional state and attempted to manipulate her. In a letter to his friend Leigh

Hunt dated August 15, 1819, Percy reacted to two letters that Godwin sent to Mary shortly after his grandson, William Shelley's, death. Percy Shelley tells Hunt that they cannot yet return home as Mary is "dreadfully depressed" and he "cannot expose her to Godwin" in her present state. He explains that he "wrote to this hard-hearted person . . . on account of the terrible estate of her mind," noting that he had not written to Godwin in a year. He had urged Godwin to send his daughter comforting words in which she might find solace. The next letter the Shelleys received from Godwin referred to Percy as "a disgraceful and flagrant person," claiming that Percy was "under great engagements" to augment his most recent contribution of £4,700 to Godwin's support with additional funds. He threatened to cease communicating with Mary if she did not "force" Percy to send him money. Percy closes the letter to his friend by writing, "He cannot persuade her that I am what I am not, nor place a shade of enmity between her and me—but he heaps on her misery, still misery.—I have not yet shewn her the letter—but I must."

Godwin followed with another letter written on September 9, harshly criticizing Mary for "lowering your character in a memorable degree," placing herself "among the commonality and mob of your sex," rather than showing "noble spirits that do honour to our nature" in the face of the loss of her child. He excoriates her for ignoring "all that is beautiful, and all that has a claim upon your kindness . . . because a child of three years old is dead!" Mary confessed to at times feeling like a child again when interacting with her father, weeping at the "idea of his silent quiet disapprobation." However, Godwin's methods worked: She constantly pleaded with Shelley to send her father money. His relationship with Percy Shelley remained strained throughout Shelley's short life.

As pointed out by the scholar Betty T. Bennett, Godwin did influence Percy Shelley's thought and works, as evident in Shelley's "A Retrospect of Times of Old." He indicts as "legal murderers" the Egyptian king Sesostris, Caesar, Pizzaro, Moses, and Mohammed, and in a footnote he includes contemporary murderers of his own era: Frederick of Prussia, Napoleon Bonaparte, the 18th-century Russian general Alexander Suwarroff, Wellington, and Nelson. When Godwin discussed a "History of Political Society" in *An Enquiry Concerning Political Justice*, he had accused Sesostris, Caesar, Mahomet (Mohammed), and "the Spaniards in the new world" of creating wars as a means to personal political ends. Shelley's echoing of Godwin's earlier indictment demonstrates a major theme that he and Mary both carried forward: Those in the present must learn from the past. However, the fact that Percy Shelley could add to the list from his own era demonstrated that the opposite too often proved true: People did not learn from the past. That fact became important to Mary's historical novels written and published after Shelley's 1822 death by drowning.

As Mary began to write and publish, Godwin often acted as her editor and adviser. He made the decision not to publish her second work of fiction, the novella *Mathilda*, written in 1820, even though Mary had decreed that the profits would have gone to him. Its topic of incestuous desire on the part of a father for his daughter so disturbed Godwin that he withheld the manuscript, which would not be published until 1959. He would play an even greater part in her writing life following Percy's death, serving as her main adviser. Mary moved in with him from time to time, having developed a tolerance for Mary Jane Godwin.

Godwin's specific influence on Mary Shelley's work is most clear in her two historical novels, *Valperga, or the Life and Adventures of Castruccio, Prince of Lucca* (1823); and *Perkin Warbeck* (1830). A devoted student of history at her father's and her husband's insistence, Mary had studied all of Godwin's writings and had a thorough understanding of his focus on the use of reason in his first edition of *Political Justice*. She also noted his adding to the second edition the importance of the application of "private affections" to decision making, a change he made following Wollstonecraft's death. Mary would use that dual approach—the application of reason versus that of affection—to help shape the conflict between her characters in her historical novels.

Shelley's historical fiction reveals other philosophical influences on her introduced by both of her parents. Godwin's *Political Justice* discusses the destruction wreaked by egotistical monarchs and tyrants on their cultures, along with the necessity in a civilized society for encouragement of change. Wollstonecraft had acted as an agent of that change in writing about the British system that it sacrificed the poor to advance the wealthy and historically supported the destruction of all social class systems in the name of equality. All of these ideas are represented in Mary's historical novels. As for Godwin's discussion of the conflict an individual naturally suffers when he or she desires freedom from oppression, it is one repeated by Mary's character Euthanasia in *Valperga*. Not only does Euthanasia stress the necessity of struggle to produce independence, but she also precedes her discussion with praise for a study of history. Although Godwin may have actually suggested the topic for his daughter's novel *Perkin Warbeck*, his influence is by far the greatest on *Valperga*, with later scholars noting that Euthanasia could almost serve as his mouthpiece.

After completing *Valperga*, Mary could not come to terms with a publisher and sent the manuscript to Godwin. She told him that if he could find a publisher, he could keep any income the novel generated. Godwin accepted the challenge and also edited the manuscript, a fact that later Mary Shelley scholars found pertinent to assessing the extent of her knowledge of history and her political views. Concern existed that Godwin had radically altered the manuscript, raising the question of how much of the novel is actually written by Mary. However, as Bennett explains, comparison of an existing 17 pages of Mary's manuscript with the published novel clearly demonstrates that Godwin's changes were of a minor editorial nature; they in no way affected the story's plot, theme, or characterizations.

Godwin would later repudiate many of his most famous early ideas, at least their radical aspects. In the 1820s, he spoke against the suffrage movement after having supported Wollstonecraft's cry for female independence. He also produced an important work in reply to Thomas Robert Malthus's *Essay on the Principle of Population*, titled *Of Population* (1820); it seemed to contradict his previous writing about rationality and its application to the benefit of the individual. He proposed that rational humans would limit procreation through voluntary restraint of sexual desire for the good of the race. His prolific work also includes *Thoughts on Man* (1831); a life of Chaucer (1803–04); and the novels *Fleetwood* (1805), *Mandeville* (1817), *Cloudesly* (1830), and *Doloraine* (1833).

Despite their differences, Godwin and Mary remained close in the last years of his life. Shelley wrote to Frances Wright on September 12, 1827, regarding the influence of her parents, saying that Wollstonecraft's "greatness of soul & my father [sic] high talents have perpetually reminded me that I ought to degenerate as little as I could from those from whom I derived my being." Shortly after, in October, Godwin wrote to Mary of their differences that at age 72, "I am all cheerfulness, and never anticipate the evil day with distressing feelings till to do so is absolutely unavoidable . . . But I am afraid you are a Wollstonecraft. We are so curiously made that one atom put in the wrong place in our original structure will often make us unhappy for life."

Godwin's contributions to his culture were rewarded when he was named Usher of the Exchequer, with a pension, in 1833, an act that greatly pleased Mary. He died three years later at age 80, on April 7, 1836. Mary made sure that her stepmother, Mary Jane, received the portion of the pension due to her and took care of her father's burial arrangements. He had requested to be buried with Mary Wollstonecraft in St. Pancras; Mary Jane Godwin would also be buried there in 1840. Following Mary Shelley's death in 1851, her parents were moved and buried with her in Bournemouth.

FURTHER READING

Bennett, Betty T. "The Political Philosophy of Mary Shelley's Historical Novels: *Valperga* and *Perkin Warbek*." In *The Evidence of Imagination: Studies of Interactions between Life and Art in English Romantic Literature*, edited by Donald H. Reiman, et. al., 354–371. New York: New York University Press, 1978.

Carlson, Julie A. *England's First Family of Writers: Mary Wollstonecraft, William Godwin, Mary Shelley*. Baltimore: Johns Hopkins University Press, 2007.

Clemit, Pamela. *The Godwinian Novel: The Rational Fictions of Godwin, Brockden Brown, Mary Shelley.* New York: Oxford University Press, 1993.

Clemit, Pamela, Harriet Jump, and Betty T. Bennett, eds. *Lives of the Great Romantics III: Godwin, Wollstonecraft & Mary Shelley by their Contemporaries.* London: Pickering & Chatto, 1999.

Godwin, William. *The Collected Novels and Memoirs of William Godwin.* 8 vols. Edited by Mark Philip. London: Pickering & Chatto, 1992.

———. *The Political and Philosophical Writings of William Godwin.* 7 vols. Edited by Martin Fitzpatrick. London: Pickering & Chatto, 1993.

Marshall, Peter H. *William Godwin.* New Haven, Conn.: Yale University Press, 1984.

Mellor, Anne K. *Mary Shelley: Her Life, Her Fiction, Her Monsters.* London: Routledge, 1989.

Paul, C. Kegan. *William Godwin, His Friends and Contemporaries.* 1876. Reprint, New York: AMS Press, 1970.

gothic fiction The term *gothic* derives literally from the word *Goth*, referencing Germanic people who invaded the Roman Empire early during the Christian era. The term *Gothic* became associated with medieval art and all that was uncultured and barbaric. Gothic fiction became popular during the 18th and 19th centuries, emphasizing the grotesque and depending on mystery, mysticism, coincidence, and secret identity as plot aspects. Gothic novels were generally set in a past era, and their characters inhabited ancient, mysterious structures, often with secret passages and unexplained noises and movement.

Writers appropriated the association of the term *gothic* with often crude elements in order to produce fiction in reaction against the 18th century's cultivated neoclassicism. In much early gothic fiction, evil men with dark, secretive pasts wreaked havoc on communities until a younger warrior/knight figure, whose true identity remained disguised, either by accident or purposefully, came to the rescue. An early example was Tobias Smollett's *Ferdinand, Count Fathom* (1753), but the novel recognized as the first true gothic work is Horace Walpole's *The Castle of Otranto* (1764). In Walpole's novel, a helmet comes down from atop a statue and becomes enormous, as does the statue itself, eventually filling and overwhelming the castle, shattering its walls.

Ann Radcliffe made the gothic form famous and introduced persecuted, helpless heroines in imminent danger of death. The most widely read of her novels was *The Mysteries of Udolpho* (1794), which Jane Austen parodied, along with the gothic form in general, in her posthumously published *Northanger Abbey* (1818). By that time, the gothic had lost favor with readers. However, that same year, Mary Shelley single-handedly resuscitated the gothic with *Frankenstein*. Shelly used murder and a monster, supported by her romantic ideals, to frame questions of her day regarding the value of science and the worth of the individual imagination. She also incorporated the gothic into some of her shorter fiction.

Shelley greatly admired the writing of Sir Walter Scott, who did not write gothic novels in a pure sense, but many of his works contained gothic elements, including ghosts. Both Charlotte and Emily Brontë employed the gothic in their mid-19th century novels. In *Jane Eyre* (1847), Charlotte Brontë set her diminutive protagonist in a mysterious estate mansion, complete with ghostly attic forms, fires, a brooding BYRONIC HERO, and extrasensory contact, and aligned Jane's creativity with her animal passions, revolting the more conservative of her readers. Emily Brontë chose the wild surroundings of the British moors for her ghostly tale of revenge and love beyond the grave, *Wuthering Heights* (1847). Gothic romances continued their popularity into the 21st century, both through the continued reading of classic gothic tales and the productions of new novels that adopt old formats but may add new emphases, including sexual relations and the occult.

FURTHER READING

Botting, Fred, *Gothic.* London: Routledge, 1996.

Hogle, Jerrold E. *The Cambridge Companion to Gothic Fiction.* New York: Cambridge University Press, 2002.

———. "*Frankenstein* as neo-Gothic: From the Ghost of the Counterfeit to the Monster of Abjection." In *Romanticism, History, and the Possibilities of Genre:*

Re-forming Literature, 1789–1837, edited by Tilottama Rajan and Julia M. Wright, 176–212. New York: Cambridge University Press, 1998.

Le Tellier, Robert Ignatius. *Sir Walter Scott and the Gothic Novel.* Lewiston, N.Y.: E. Mellon Press, 1995.

Spatt, Hartley. "Mary Shelley's Last Men: the Truth of Dreams." *Studies in the Novel* 7, no. 4 (Winter 1975): 526–537.

Wallace, Diana. "Uncanny Stories: The Ghost Story as Female Gothic." *Gothic Studies* 6, no. 1 (May 2004): 57–68.

Whatley, John. "Romantic and Enlightened Eyes in the *Gothic Novels* of Percy Bysshe Shelley." *Gothic Studies* 1, no. 2 (December 1999): 201–222.

hero's journey (quest) The story of the hero's journey, or quest, has existed for centuries, with Homer's *The Odyssey* serving as the prototypical example. Plot aspects of the quest often appear in the modern English language romance novel and may be identified in international literature. In a classical quest, the male hero completes a journey focused on winning a prize through the application of wits and daring. As the plot developed, females also became hero figures, and, beginning in the latter half of the 19th century, the quest could focus on an internal, or psychological, journey toward self-realization or actualization, generally signaled by an epiphany on part of the protagonist. In later versions, the quest might prove ironic, the main character never achieving the goal or prize, perhaps due to pride that the traditional hero learns to overcome. Shelley's Victor Frankenstein is such an ironic hero, and his story may be understood by analyzing how the steps of his journey differ from those of the traditional quest.

The journey's steps have been labeled and analyzed by critics and philosophers, most popularly by the 20th-century's American expert on mythology, Joseph Campbell (1904–87). His *The Hero with a Thousand Faces* (1949) and *The Power of Myth* (1988) use an approach based on the psychoanalytic theories of Carl Gustav Jung (1875–1961), who used the theory of the collective unconscious to explain the similarities in the hero story across cultures. Jung believed that such an unconscious dwells in the depths of the psyche, housing the cumulative knowledge, experience, and image of the entire human race. From that accumulation emerged, in literature, recurrent plot patterns, images, and characters, referred to as archetypes that can arouse emotions, due to each individual's collective unconscious. Jung's archetype theory can be applied to an understanding of traditional symbols, such as the seasons, colors, water, and other objects representing human ideas and emotions, many of which occur in the quest. The Canadian critic Northrup Frye (1912–91) gained fame for using archetypes to develop a codification of symbols, seen in his famous work *The Secular Scripture: A Study of the Structure of Romance* (1976).

The initial stage of the hero's journey may be referred to as "Of the Ordinary World," featuring the man or woman who acts as the story's protagonist, tending to everyday matters. Victor Frankenstein may be seen enjoying family life as a child, learning lessons from his family and nature. The second stage, called "Departure," depicts substages such as "A Call to Adventure," when a particular occurrence stirs conflict in the hero over whether to depart from a comfortable routine to accept a challenge to seek a reward outside his normal sphere. Frankenstein's call to adventure comes when he is to leave home to attend university, something he at first resists, as he does not want to leave his family. That call may be met with "Refusal," when the protagonist for a time declares that he will not embark on the journey.

After experiencing refusal but then agreeing to make the journey, the hero is observed "Crossing the Threshold," indicating that he physically departs his familiar world to enter a new one. Frankenstein leaves his home and enters the completely new world of the university and learning. The journey from home undertaken by countless young male protagonists in countless novels who leave to "seek their fortunes" represents this stage, and Victor Frankenstein is no exception. However, he will give in to temptation to betray nature and God, seeking his fortune in fame and glory. Because he is so self-centered and does not act with humility on behalf of others, he is doomed to fail. While Odysseus traveled over water, the journey may be cross-country, as with Victor; through outer space; or through the subconscious.

In the "Initiation" stage, the hero must prove his valor or intelligence by meeting a number of challenges, which may be physical, spiritual, or psychological. He may have help from a guide figure, as Athena helped Odysseus, or Obi-Wan Kenobi and Yoda help Luke Skywalker in the popular *Star Wars* movie trilogy. With this guidance, the hero may fight monsters; deal with shape-shifters, witches, or other enchanted beings; see and interpret visions; be caught up in disorienting magical spells; and learn new skills affording him new powers. Victor's initiation is his creation of the monster. However, he lacks the traditional guidance of the hero and deserts his creature for selfish reasons. The monsters he deals with are his own psychological challenges.

The hero will also suffer a loss during the journey, often of the guide, which may plunge him into depression or cause him to feel he cannot complete the journey. Victor's loss of Clerval may represent his loss of a guide, as Clerval embodies the moral conscience that appears absent in Victor. Victor's losses mount with the death of his wife Elizabeth, following that of a dear family servant and his baby brother, who are sacrificed to settle his debt to the monster and to humanity for having created the monster. His father will also die, unable to survive the loss of Elizabeth coming on the heels of the many additional family deaths.

In the traditional tale, loss necessitates a renewal of purpose, moving the hero into the next stage, labeled "Descent." He may undertake a literal descent, as Odysseus did when he visited Hades to consult with past heroes, collecting their wisdom. Hades may be represented by any number of dark locations, generally reached by a movement downward, whether into a cave, a tunnel, dark woods at the bottom of a hill, or a concrete bunker. An example of these stages may be clearly identified in the biblical story of Jonah and the whale. When Jonah is ordered to make a journey, he refuses, attempts to hide, and loses his independence when he is swallowed by a whale. The belly of the whale represents an archetypical symbol, a dark, forbidden, frightening, sometimes deadly location, into which the hero descends. The phrase "in the belly of the whale" or "in the belly of the fish" applied colloquially indicates a threatening retreat from the real world where a person may be tested. Victor's descent may be observed in reverse, when he first returns home and climbs the mountains. However, there he confronts the truth in the shape of the monster. Rather than gaining wisdom to take responsibility for his actions, Victor further descends into the psychological and emotional darkness of hatred and the desire for revenge. His later descent into madness in his desire for revenge may be represented by his journey into a world of ice and snow and complete isolation as he seeks to kill the monster.

Reinvigorated by newfound wisdom, the traditional hero emerges from the depths, traveling literally upward or outward from the low ground, reemerging with renewed strength and confidence. While he may be further challenged, he will successfully reach his goal, procure his treasure, and begin the final stage, "The Return Home." The hero may initially refuse or resist, necessitating an event to convince him, or the return may become in itself a lengthy quest, as was that of Odysseus; it may also be completed quickly and without event. Victor's pursuit of the monster becomes his pursuit of a goal, although he will never achieve his goal. He suffers loss after loss, until his entire family, except for one brother, has been murdered by the monster that he has created. Each time he returns home, another death occurs.

An additional stage might involve a responsibility on the hero's part to share what has been learned, through storytelling and writing, as in the German version of an initiation story that traces the development of a writer, called a *kunstleroman*. The bildungsroman, which features the development of a young person into maturity, may feature many aspects of the quest. Many examples of the bildungsroman have been written, including romance genre novels by Sir Walter Scott, known to have influenced Shelley, who corresponded with him. Modern, darker versions of the quest may be designed to question what constitutes success, or they may exist as ironic quests, like that in *Frankenstein*, in which no reward is gained by the protagonist, or the protagonist even loses his or her life or a grasp on the meaning of life or self-identity. *Frankenstein* also incorporates storytelling through the character of the explorer Walton, who relates Victor's tale in letters to his sister. Shelley's novel *The Last Man* (1826) also represents an ironic quest and incorporates the idea of storytelling by the narrator who leaves his story behind, even though he is supposedly the last human.

FURTHER READING

Brackett, Virginia. "Quest." In *Classic Love and Romance Literature: An Encyclopedia of Works, Characters, Authors, and Themes.* Santa Barbara, Calif.: ABC-Clio, 1999, 275–276.

Campbell, Joseph. *The Hero with a Thousand Faces.* 1949. Reprint, Princeton, N.J.: Princeton University Press, 1968.

———. *The Power of Myth.* Edited by Betty Sue Flowers. New York: Doubleday, 1988.

Fraser, Robert. *Victorian Quest Romance: Stevenson, Haggard, Kipling and Conan Doyle.* Jackson: University Press of Mississippi, 1998.

Frye, Northrup. *The Secular Scripture: A Study of the Structure of Romance.* Cambridge, Mass.: Harvard University Press, 1976.

Luttrell, Claude. *The Creation of the First Arthurian Romance: A Quest.* Chicago: Northwestern University Press, 1974.

Schechter, Harold, and Jonna Gormely Semeiks, eds. *Discoveries: 50 Stories of the Quest.* Indianapolis: Bobbs-Merrill Educational Publishers, 1983.

The Keepsake Mary Shelley published often in *The Keepsake*, one of a number of "ladies' annuals" that proved popular in the early 19th century. During the 10 years from 1828 to 1838, *The Keepsake* became an annual collectible, beautifully bound and artfully illustrated, a perfect holiday gift to be found in many British middle-class homes. First published by Charles Heath and edited by Frederick Mansel Reynolds, *The Keepsake* published pieces by well-known male figures, including Sir Walter Scott, William Wordsworth, and Robert Southey. But the high fees commanded by these well-known male writers soon caused a change in marketing strategy by Heath and Reynolds. They decided to market exclusively to women who were becoming an impressive force in the economic arena. Others followed suit, and *The Keepsake* became the most successful journal of its type. Feminine in styling, it sported a watered-silk crimson binding and gilt-edged pages and was available in two sizes at two prices. The smaller size cost 13 shillings, and the larger cost two pounds 12 shillings and six pence. The beautiful illustrations could also be purchased separately and proved so popular that authors were sometimes asked to compose stories to accompany the steel-plate engravings. In all, Shelley published 21 stories for the gift books during the years 1823 to 1839, 16 of those for *The Keepsake*.

The financial success of annuals like *The Keepsake* sparked ridicule by "serious" writers, including William Makepeace Thackeray, who labeled them "a little sham sentiment . . . employed to illustrate a little sham art." Devalued as "sham art," the annuals' stories and poems were labeled hack writing. Thus, Shelley later gained a reputation with literary critics as a "hack writer" based on the commercial appeal of one of her favorite publishing venues and on her discussion of money in her correspondence with the annuals' publishers. However, as the scholar Charlotte Sussman makes clear, Shelley never offered any pretense for publishing in the annuals other than for income. In addition, she also discussed income with her book publishers, making clear that her discussion of money did not distinguish any particular material that she composed. She desperately needed income to support herself and her son until he received an inheritance upon his grandfather's death in 1844, and *The Keepsake* offered a ready source of income. In addition, it allowed her to be a self-sustaining author. She also used *The Keepsake* to keep alive awareness of PERCY BYSSHE SHELLEY's work, publishing three of his previously unpublished poems and his fragment entitled "On Love" in the annual. Finally, criticism of Shelley falls short because her short stories appeared in venues in addition to ladies' magazines. Examples include "The Bride of Italy," published in *London Magazine* (1824).

The annuals were later considered important for their change in the manner by which literature could be consumed. For the first time, it was available in a venue fashioned for a specific audience and primarily as a product. The *Forget Me Not* was the first ladies' annual, published in 1822. Others soon followed, all produced as lavish volumes that one critic compared to flowers, noting that any critique of the annuals should be written in "a lady's boudoir." Sussman points out that the comparison to flowers suggests not only the books' ornamental appearance but also their assumed impermanence, based on the lack of literary value attributed to their contents. They were designed to match fashionable trends each year, suggesting the purchasing power of the middle-class fashion-conscious woman. Sussman describes the contents as spreading "middle-class ideas of propriety and . . . financial responsibility" while also offering readers the opportunity to "see" exotic locations where they probably would never travel. Shelley offered such exotic locations in "The Evil Eye" (*The Keepsake*, 1830) and "The Dream" (*The Keepsake*, 1832), both discussed in this volume.

By never leaving their socially inscribed domestic spheres, proper ladies could enjoy the sometimes dangerous and mystical actions of the stories' characters in a socially acceptable format. The plots often contained "volatile" contents, such as discussions of divorce, illicit love, dangerous and violent jealousy, factual depictions of the depressed conditions of orphans and unmarried women, all of which related to a defining class structure. Critics such as Sussman point out a tension between the physical, commodified beauty of the volumes and the subversive nature of their contents. As she writes, "the stability of the book is meant to compensate for the instability of experience."

Shelley's stories also offered examples of women measured by their financial worth, combined with their physical beauty and an unshakeable moral virtue. Examples published in *The Keepsake* included "The Mourner" (1830), "The False Rhyme" (1830), "Transformation" (1830), and "The Parvenue" (1836). Entries for "The False Rhyme" and "Transformation," probably Shelley's most widely read story today, are included in this volume. Shelley also considered the challenges of marriage, which commonly result in negative results for women in stories such as "The Invisible Girl" (*The Keepsake*, 1833), "The Mourner," "The Parvenue," and "The Mortal Immortal" (*The Keepsake*, 1833), the latter also discussed in this volume. For a complete list of Shelley's publications in the annuals, please see Sharon Lawson's chronology, cited below.

FURTHER READING

Lawson, Sharon. "A Chronology of the Life of Mary Shelley." Available online. URL: http://www.rc.umd.edu/reference/chronologies/mschronology/chrono.html. Accessed June 24, 2010.

O'Dea, Gregory. "'Perhaps a Tale You'll Make it': Mary Shelley's Tales for *The Keepsake*." In *Iconoclastic Departures: Mary Shelley after Frankenstein: Essays in Honor of the Bicentenary of Mary Shelley's Birth*, edited by Syndy M. Conger, Frederick S. Frank, and Gregory O'Dea, 62. Madison, N.J.: Fairleigh Dickinson University Press, 1997.

Pascoe, Judith. "Poetry as Souvenir: Mary Shelley in the Annuals." In *Mary Shelley in Her Times*, edited by Betty T. Bennet and Stuart Curran, 173–184. Baltimore: Johns Hopkins University Press, 2000.

Sunstein, Emily. Mary Shelley: *Romance and Reality*. Boston: Little, Brown, 1989.

Sussman, Charlotte. "Stories for *The Keepsake*." In *The Cambridge Companion to Mary Shelley*, edited by Esther Schor, 163–179. Princeton, N.J.: Cambridge University Press, 2003.

Milton, John (1608–1674)   See Paradise Lost.

Paradise Lost (1667 and 1674) John Milton's *Paradise Lost* is one of the great poems in the English language. An influence on countless later literary works, it had an enormous effect on Mary Shelley's *Frankenstein* (1818). Shelley reflects on the epic's biblical topics of man's creation by God, the temptation of man by Satan to gain more knowledge than God granted, and God's eventual bestowal of grace upon humans. Such reflection allowed Shelley to reveal just how at odds with God and nature Victor Frankenstein's actions place him. Frankenstein's perversion of God's act of creation leads to damnation and doom, a point that Shelley relentlessly drives home to her readers. That she chose to directly reference Milton's work to support her cause, rather than the Bible itself, is telling. Perhaps she could better relate to a poetic, literary presentation of the story, once removed from its original religious document. In her original preface to the novel, Shelley wrote:

> I have thus endeavoured to preserve the truth of the elementary principles of human nature, while I have not scrupled to innovate upon their combinations. The *Iliad*, the tragic poetry of Greece—Shakespeare, in the *Tempest* and *Midsummer Night's Dream*—and most especially Milton, in *Paradise Lost,* conform to this rule; and the most humble novelist, who seeks to confer or receive amusement from his labours, may, without presumption, apply to prose fiction a licence, or rather a rule, from the adoption of which so many exquisite combinations of human feeling have resulted in the highest specimens of poetry.

Milton (1608–74) first published *Paradise Lost* in 10 books. After revision, he reissued the work in 1674, reorganized into 12 books. He had a lofty goal, explained in the opening lines of book 1, where he references his own blindness as well as his objective in his appeal for help to the "Heav'nly Muse" (6):

> . . . What in me is dark
> Illumine, what is low raise and support;
> That to the highth of this great Argument
> I may assert Eternal Providence,
> And justify the ways of God to men. (ll. 22–26)

Milton's work strikes most readers as a drama, but one too massive for a stage to hold. It spawned an industry of criticism focusing on aspects including the architecture of Milton's cosmos; his debt to Virgil, Plato, and other classicists; his focus on the heroics of Christianity and Christian doctrine; his application of the tradition of nature and the garden; the heroic nature of Satan; his relation to Catholic Neoplatonism; and the baroque aspects of his style, to mention only a few. Shelley drew on almost all of those elements. For instance, Victor is caught up in the era's new scientific views, which challenged the traditional view of the cosmos and man's relation to other living

Cameo portrait of John Milton. Mary Shelley greatly admired Milton's work and considered him to be one of the three poets worthy of imitation. This portrait was published in the *New International Encyclopedia* in 1905. *(Engraving by George Vertue)*

things. While Henry Clerval constantly reminds him of poetry, the classics, and the new romantic challenge to the classics, Victor is obsessed with moving beyond the garden's natural metaphor for creation. Shelley clearly shows his divorce from nature as he so closely focuses on the elements in his home in the Alps but later rejects the blessings of the outdoors for the temptation of the laboratory. Victor will call his monster a demon, suggesting his relationship to Satan and all things evil, and Shelley offers little by way of traditional religion and spirituality to rescue Victor or his family. Finally, Victor's hyperbolic thoughts and emotional reactions move beyond the baroque to embrace the grotesque.

Through the ages, critics tended to see Milton in two different ways. One group viewed him as sympathetic to Satan, in the tradition of 19th-century romantic poets with whom Shelley remained intimately involved. Others viewed him as firmly in God's camp, like later writers including C. S. Lewis

(1898–1963). In 1967, in *Surprised by Sin*, the premiere Milton scholar Stanley Fish forever changed the public view of Milton by approaching *Paradise Lost* from the view of reader response criticism. He declared that the poem is simply about readers and their fallen natures, proven each time they felt sympathy with Satan or bristled at something that God said. Shelley clearly focuses on human nature, represented by Victor's fall from grace when he separates himself from the natural order by trying and predictably failing to assume nature's creative guise. It is not that Victor ever felt sympathy with Satan, but Shelley's later readers would sympathize with Victor's monster, viewing Victor as more properly the monstrous being when he abandoned his responsibility owed his offspring.

Milton organizes his book according to the Bible's story of the world's creation, including the creation of the Garden of Eden, Satan's eviction from heaven to hell, the creation of Adam and Eve, and their temptation and eventual eviction from the garden. He adds much original detail, particularly with the subject of Satan, a figure drawn so clearly and dramatically that many post-ROMANTICISM readers viewed him as a heroic figure, a BYRONIC HERO of sorts. This view remains easily understood, particularly as Satan proudly declares his preference for the position of ruler of Hell to servant in Heaven. At that moment, he seems to seek the independence and self-identity for which human nature longs. Graced with slick wit, he unfortunately lacks the imagination to see any possibilities outside of himself, perhaps the ultimate sin in a poet's view and an attitude Shelley can reproduce in her protagonist. Victor embraces the same sin of egotism, as evidenced by the series of self-references in this passage from Shelley's novel:

> My attention was fixed upon every object the most insupportable to the delicacy of the human feelings. I saw how the fine form of man was degraded and wasted; I beheld the corruption of death succeed to the blooming cheek of life; I saw how the worm inherited the wonders of the eye and brain. I paused, examining and analysing all the minutiae of causation, as exemplified in the change from life to death, and death to life, until from the midst of this darkness a sudden light broke in upon me—a light so brilliant and wondrous, yet so simple, that while I became dizzy with the immensity of the prospect which it illustrated, I was surprised that among so many men of genius who had directed their inquiries towards the same science, that I alone should be reserved to discover so astonishing a secret.

While Victor does imagine the power he may possess, he lacks the ability to comprehend nature's perfectly balanced plan of degeneration and death as inherent to its life rhythm.

Book 1 of *Paradise Lost* opens with an argument focusing on man's fall, particularly on the reason why he disobeyed God, with Milton laying the blame at Satan's feet. Platonic argument and reason play a large role in additional books within the poem. However, they are particularly acute in the first book as Satan argues against his fallen position and in favor of reigning in Hell and on earth, should Heaven remain out of his reach. Victor's thoughts detailed above echo Satan's rejection of Heaven's, or in his case, nature's, supremacy as he plans to rule science and ultimately defeat death on earth.

Milton sets the scene, describing Satan and his angel minions "lying on the burning Lake, thunderstruck and astonisht." They will later hold counsel, in which various devils are identified by name. They gather in the tradition of a procession of heroes, coming "like a Deluge" (1:353), their leaders appearing as "Godlike shapes and forms / Excelling human, Princely Dignities, / And Powers that erst in Heaven sat on Thrones" (1:357–359). The long list of supernatural beings will include Moloch, who best conveyed power and lust in his Old Testament characterization; Chemos, described as "th' obscene dread of Moab's Sons" (1:406); Astoreth, called by the Phoenicians "Queen of Heav'n, with crescent Horns" (1:439); the fish-deity Dagon, whose image supposedly fell before the Ark of the Covenant, losing its head and palms; and Belial marching in the rear position, "than whom a Spirit more lewd / Fell not from Heaven" (1:490–491).

These fallen angels lead their troops across scalding terrain that burns their feet, lacking "anguish and doubt and fear and sorrow and pain" (1:558) that haunt humans, freeing them to breathe as one force with a single thought. Milton redefines traditional heroism and offers a chilling description of Satan, their "dread commander" (1:589) who stands "In shape and gesture proudly eminent," a tower, having not yet lost its "Original brightness, nor appear'd / Less than Arch-Angel" (1:592–593). Satan rallies his troops, explaining that he has heard of a new kingdom called Earth, and he declares they will all either return to heaven or investigate the new kingdom.

Satan's attractive persona and golden tongue have long been blamed for his ability to tempt Eve to claim the knowledge that God forbids. Victor Frankenstein finds his temptation in science, actually a pseudoscience that his father and some of his professors warn him to avoid. Shelley does not go so far as to claim science is evil; rather, she cautions against the desire for destructive power that it breeds. Frankenstein is seduced by the idea that he can challenge God's natural plan, a challenge made possible through knowledge that has been forbidden and is connected to the black arts of Hell. Satan and all of his minions, with all of their combined powers, try the same and fail, but Victor takes no heed of biblical or human warnings, through advice, religious creed, or Clerval's attempts to fix his attention on the supremacy of nature and its life-and-death cycle.

Book 2 begins with Satan's debate over the wisdom of launching another attack against Heaven, as he describes its wealth and beauty. Moloch, characterized by Milton as "the fiercest Spirit . . . now fiercer by despair" (2:44–45), stands and urges "open War" (2:51), and Belial will follow. Milton employs the tradition of the Homeric counsel in this scene. Likewise, *Frankenstein* incorporates many traditions of the Homeric HERO'S JOURNEY, but in an ironic manner. Victor makes his own descent, although his is psychological, and he seeks no counsel when it might best serve him. However, after the murder and mayhem Frankenstein releases, Shelley does insert a scene that suggests Homeric counsel. Victor visits the graveyard where his family members are buried, suggesting Ulysses' descent into Hades where he sought wisdom from the shades representing dead warriors:

> The spirits of the departed seemed to flit around and to cast a shadow, which was felt but not seen, around the head of the mourner. . . . "And I call on you, spirits of the dead, and on you, wandering ministers of vengeance, to aid and conduct me in my work. Let the cursed and hellish monster drink deep of agony; let him feel the despair that now torments me." I had begun my adjuration with solemnity and an awe which almost assured me that the shades of my murdered friends heard and approved my devotion; . . .

Unfortunately, Victor never sought the counsel that might have saved him and his loved ones from their fate. In this scene, he merely seeks support from the departed for his plan of revenge against the monster.

As *Paradise Lost* continues, Satan urges the company to look to the future and learn to accept Hell, because "This horror will grow mild, this darkness light" (2:220), a line in which Milton employs paradox to make clear the futility and false logic of Satan's argument. Mammon adds his idea that the group can be sufficient unto itself, not requiring God for existence, proposing they will eventually be able to imitate God's Light, as their "torments" will "Become our Elements" (2:274–275). One hears echoes of that speech in Victor's thoughts and ideas as he believes that he, empowered by man's rationality and scientific discoveries, can obtain God's/nature's creative powers: "The sun does not more certainly shine in the heavens than that which I now affirm is true. Some miracle might have produced it, yet the stages of the discovery were distinct and probable." Toward the conclusion of the novel, Victor finds his suffering bearable at times, recalling Satan's statement that horror will grow mild and "darkness light." Victor is able to escape his own torment in dreams of his family, his impulses becoming "mechanical." He becomes so confused that he believes God supports his plan to murder the monster. He tells Walton, "At such moments vengeance, that burned within me, died in my heart, and I pursued my path towards the destruction of the daemon more as a task enjoined by heaven, as the mechanical impulse of some power of which I was unconscious, than as the ardent desire of my soul."

Victor later draws a direct parallel to Homer's *Odyssey* and also can be heard to echo Satan's idea that hell will eventually become acceptable as he grows accustomed to his isolation in the frozen north during his pursuit of the monster. Victor muses that

> The Greeks wept for joy when they beheld the Mediterranean from the hills of Asia, and hailed with rapture the boundary of their toils. I did not weep, but I knelt down and with a full heart thanked my guiding spirit for conducting me in safety to the place where I hoped, notwithstanding my adversary's gibe, to meet and grapple with him.

Shelley's substitution of the imagery of ice for the fire of hell is a common trope, explained in more detail below.

Following the speech-making in book 2 of *Paradise Lost*, the demons applaud Mammon's logic, and then Beelzebub, second only to Satan, speaks. Beginning rationally, he counters the previous arguments with the opinion that the company's ejection into hell was their doom, not their rescue, pointing out that God will rule Hell as well as Heaven. He thus proposes a third suggestion, which is that the group attempt to discover and conquer God's newest creation:

> . . . There is a place
> (If ancient and prophetic fame in Heav'n
> Err not) another World, the happy seat
> Of some new Race call'd Man, about this time
> To be created like to us . . . (2:349)

The group accepts Mammon's plan as a way to "surpass / Common revenge" (2:370–371). Satan agrees to make the journey to the "unknown Region" (2:443) alone, after which the group praises Satan for volunteering and disregarding his own safety.

One could draw parallels between Satan's journey to discover the "new Race call'd Man" to Victor's own consideration of creating a new race of man. Victor will also journey emotionally and physically to an "unknown Region," as his once accommodating and nurturing surroundings turn hostile and unfamiliar. Man's creation in the Bible is described simply and emphasizes one important detail: God has shaped this creature in his own image. Thus, the "new Race" holds a particular threat for the powers of darkness. Shelley's description of Victor's creation of his personally designed new Race holds up a mirror to the biblical story, revealing in a reverse image the shortcomings of man's vision as compared to that of God:

> How can I describe my emotions at this catastrophe, or how delineate the wretch whom with such infinite pains and care I had endeavoured to form? His limbs were in proportion, and I had selected his features as beautiful. Beautiful! Great God! His yellow skin scarcely covered the work of muscles and arteries beneath; his hair was of a lustrous black, and flowing; his teeth of a pearly whiteness; but these luxuriances only formed a more horrid contrast with his watery eyes, that seemed almost of the same colour as the dun-white sockets in which they were set, his shrivelled complexion and straight black lips.

Victor's journey fails, and he does not bring light into the world of human misery, but rather increases it after rejecting the natural order.

In addition, Victor becomes so consumed with desire for revenge against the monster for killing his friends and family that what little rational capability had been left to him is overcome by emotion. That satanic desire for vengeance eats away at his humanity, rendering him equal to the monster that had killed for revenge. Victor first employs the term in chapter 9 of *Frankenstein*. He begins by seeming to accept blame and responsibility for the death of his brother and the execution of the family's servant, Justine. However, he quickly shifts focus to revenging those deaths as he considers the monster's actions: "When I reflected on his crimes and malice, my hatred and revenge burst all bounds of moderation. . . . I wished to see him again, that I might wreak the utmost extent of abhorrence on his head and avenge the deaths of William and Justine."

Milton's story unfolds as Satan makes his journey through a brilliantly described landscape "of fierce extremes, extremes by change more fierce" moving "From Beds of raging Fire to starve in Ice" (2:599–600). Again, one can see Milton's influence and that of others, including Dante (1265–1321), in Shelley's use of the popular imagery of fire and ice to represent death or man's shifting emotions. Shelley's readers frequently find her protagonists facing ice and fire symbolic not only of shifting passions but also of death. *Frankenstein*'s Robert Walton writes to his sister in the novel's opening letter of the temptation to view the land of ice as a heavenly landscape, inspirational and with powerful allure:

> This breeze, which has travelled from the regions towards which I am advancing, gives me a foretaste of those icy climes. Inspirited by this wind of promise, my daydreams become more fervent and vivid. I try in vain to be persuaded that the pole is the seat of frost and desolation; it ever presents itself to my imagination as the region of beauty and delight.

However, Walton's daydreams dissolve into hellish nightmares when he finds himself and his crew trapped in ice. Where he had first imagined gaining fame as an adventurer who conquered new worlds, in reality he faces the threat of bearing the legacy of multiple deaths, in place of the honor and glory he had sought. Victor dies literally trapped in ice on Walton's boat and is described by the monster as lying "white and cold" in death. Alternatively, the monster vows to die by fire: "I shall collect my funeral pile and consume to ashes this miserable frame."

Critic Richard Hardin writes of books 1 and 2 in *Paradise Lost* that they contain "Fear [as] the dominant chord," with imagery of "fire and darkness, hugeness, heights and depths, wandering, dislocation, dissonance—all the terrors of the night." The result is an emphasis on dread, terror, all that is terrible and "horrid." Shelley's *Frankenstein* includes similar imagery inspiring identical emotions of fear, dread, and horror, both in her characters and, by extension, her readers.

For instance, Mont Blanc serves as a crucial symbol for Shelley, looming high above the haunts of man, both inspiring and terrifying in its representation of nature's supremacy, against which Victor will transgress. Its pristine height emphasizes Victor's lower position in relation to nature's high status in the romantic view. While Victor begins the novel and his education aligned with nature and the mountains, he must descend to a lower physical position in order to attend university and gain human knowledge. Later, he must again climb upward into the Alps to first confront the monster and the terror that such confrontation brings. He will once more descend to complete most of the plot's action on a lower plane where base emotions rule.

As for wandering and feelings of dislocation, just before Clerval is killed, Victor notes his deep feelings of isolation that align him with a walking corpse: "I walked about the isle like a restless spectre, separated from all it loved and miserable in the separation." After Clerval's murder, Victor sinks into dissonance and suffers constant night terrors, stating, "But sleep did not afford me respite from thought and misery; my dreams presented a thousand objects that scared me. Towards morning I was possessed by a kind of nightmare; I felt the fiend's grasp in my neck and could not free myself from it; groans and cries rang in my ears." Following Elizabeth's death, he feels a further separation from other humans and all that was once familiar as his own emotions are exacerbated, telling Walton, "When I recovered I found myself surrounded by the people of the inn; their countenances expressed a breathless terror, but the horror of others appeared only as a mockery, a shadow of the feelings that oppressed me." Victor grows more isolated from the fellow humans he at first had thought to benefit through his unnatural act, ending up a homeless wanderer haunted by the horror of his existence.

This close account of the first two books of *Paradise Lost* offers a sampling of Milton's style and format and Shelley's use of his patterns, some inherited from his own poetic models, in her writing. In summary of the remainder of Milton's rendition of the creation and temptation story, his tale continues in book 3 with God's observation of Satan and his prediction of man's fall. Book 3 includes a description of how God plans to punish the betrayal, but also of his accepting of man's need for grace, which God will offer in the future. Victor Frankenstein admits his need for grace but never attains the proper humility to accept responsibility for his miscreant. While he may intellectualize that multiple deaths result from his actions, he always blames those deaths on the monster.

In Milton's book 4, Satan discovers the Garden of Eden and observes the humans, eavesdropping on their discussion of the Tree of Knowledge. He selects Eve to receive his attention. The angel Uriel hears that a devil has escaped Hell and warns the archangel Gabriel, who finds Satan tempting Eve in a dream. Although she rejects that first temptation, Satan will not give up. Victor soon begins referring to his creation as a "daemon," ostensibly to align him with evil. However, Shelley more broadly suggests the temptation theme with that label, and her readers will acknowledge the monster as a result of Victor's own temptation to overstep his proper place in nature's plan.

In book 5, Eve shares her troubled dream with Adam, who then is counseled by the archangel Raphael about Satan's evil nature and the necessity of man's obedience to God. As Victor falls to the temptation to create the monster, he describes himself as in a trance, working at night in a dreamlike state to hide from the world what he understands are unacceptable actions, such as grave robbing. Like Eve, Victor is unable to resist his desire to possess all knowledge, despite the fact that his instincts tell him he is wrong. An unnatural impulse possesses him, as it did Eve, and he acts on the forbidden knowledge to promote his unholy preoccupation:

> One secret which I alone possessed was the hope to which I had dedicated myself; and the moon gazed on my midnight labours, while, with unrelaxed and breathless eagerness, I pursued nature to her hiding-places. Who shall conceive the horrors of my secret toil as I dabbled among the unhallowed damps of the grave or tortured the living animal to animate the lifeless clay? My limbs now tremble, and my eyes swim with the remembrance; but then a resistless and almost frantic impulse urged me forward; I seemed to have lost all soul or sensation but for this one pursuit. It was indeed but a passing trance, that only made me feel with renewed acuteness so soon as, the unnatural stimulus ceasing to operate, I had returned to my old habits.

Adam hears of Satan's revolt, and in book 6, Raphael describes in detail the war in Heaven. God's son attacks and triumphs over Satan and over his devils at the poem's exact midpoint. Book 7 contains Raphael's explanation to Adam about God's creation of the earth and of humans, who may aspire to join him in Heaven. Adam also learns of the creation of the world in six days. In Book 8, Adam requests more knowledge, particularly of the universe, but Raphael explains he should only desire knowledge of his own world. Again, Shelley echoes this idea as Victor does not heed similar warnings from his father and his teachers. Adam shares with Raphael the passion he feels for Eve, causing Raphael to warn Adam before he departs to tend to higher instincts, as well as the base ones. Many of these topics are reflected by Shelley, including the temptation to gain destructive knowledge, a temptation to which Victor will fall, and the warning to humans to react as strongly to the best in them as they do to the worst. In addition, the monster's request for a woman as a partner reminds readers of God's bestowing such a partner on Adam. When Victor refuses to do the same for his own Adam, he further removes himself from nature's intentions, robbing his "son" of the satisfaction of a mate and dooming him to complete isolation.

As Adam and Raphael talk, Satan has returned in the form of a mist that slips under a barrier to again tempt Eve in book 9 of *Paradise Lost*. He enters the form of a sleeping serpent, arousing Eve's curiosity that a creature can speak when he later praises her beauty. Applying false logic, he persuades Eve to eat food from the Tree of Knowledge, which she carries to Adam after Satan slips from the garden. Victor practices similar false logic as he convinces himself to follow through on an experiment that rational humans, including his father and at least one of his professors, would never support. Shelley also incorporates multiple references to serpents in connection with the monster and to suggest temptation. Victor warns Walton, "You seek for knowledge and wisdom, as I once did; and I ardently hope that the gratification of your wishes may not be a serpent to sting you, as mine has been." The monster later tells Victor, "I will watch with the wiliness of a snake, that I may sting with its venom. Man, you shall repent of the injuries you inflict."

Adam discerns that Eve is already lost, and he eats in order to share her sin, so they will fall together. No longer innocent, they become concerned with their nakedness. The angels who had guarded the humans return to Heaven in book 10, as the Son of God comes into the garden to tell the humans of their fate. He takes pity on them and gives them clothing. The narrator tells of Satan's triumphant return to Hell and the opening of a direct path for sin and death to travel into the human world. Doom will be the future of Adam and Eve's children, and they beg God's son for mercy. This causes the Son to agree in book 11 to serve as an intercessor with God. However, the couple must still leave the garden, and the archangel Michael returns to evict them. As Eve sleeps, the angel tells Adam of man's future on earth, describing the later great flood that will rid the earth temporarily of sinful humans. Book 12 extends Michael's description, encompassing the arrival of God's son to sacrifice himself for man's redemption. The book concludes with Adam somewhat comforted by knowing of his progeny's redemption. He awakens Eve, and they leave the garden. However, Victor Frankenstein and his progeny receive no such redemption, as he never recognizes that he must ask for it after rejecting nature and its protective order.

The fact that Milton scholars have continued to study *Paradise Lost* for centuries proves it has lost none of its allure. In *How Milton Works* (2001), Stanley Fish holds that Milton believed a poem's value was grounded in the poet himself, not in any external evaluation of his writing. Milton never prioritized narrative, style, or plot above what he considered divine inspiration. According to Fish, Milton's tenacious belief energized his writing: By placing his faith first, he resisted the temptation to experiment with the aesthetics that other poets highly valued. Shelley would be one of those later writers to value Milton's themes, topics, and expression, as evidenced in her fiction.

FURTHER READING

Beck, Rudolph. "'The Region of Beauty and Delight': Walton's Polar Fantasies in Mary Shelley's *Frankenstein*." *Keats/Shelley Journal* 49 (2000): 29–49.

Bennett, Joan S. *Reviving Liberty: Radical Christian Humanism in Milton's Great Poems.* Cambridge, Mass.: Harvard University Press, 1989.

Blessington, Francis C. *Paradise Lost and the Classical Epic.* Boston: Routledge & Kegan Paul, 1979.

Bowra, C. M. *From Virgil to Milton.* New York: St. Martin's Press, 1967.

Curry, Walter Clyde. *Milton's Ontology, Cosmogony and Physics.* Lexington: University of Kentucky Press, 1957.

Daiches, David. *Milton.* London: Hutchinson University Library, 1966.

Fish, Stanley. *How Milton Works.* Cambridge, Mass.: Belknap Press of Harvard University Press, 2001.

———. *Surprised by Sin: the Reader in Paradise Lost.* New York: St. Martin's Press, 1969.

Frye, Roland Mushat. *God, Man, and Satan: Patterns of Christian Thought and Life in Paradise Lost, Pilgrim's Progress, and the Great Theologians.* Princeton, N.J.: Princeton University Press, 1960.

———. *Milton's Imagery and the Visual Arts: Iconographic Tradition in the Epic Poems.* Princeton, N.J.: Princeton University Press, 1978.

Gray, Erich. "Faithful Likenesses: Lists of Similes in Milton, Shelley and Rossetti." *Texas Studies in Literature & Language* 48, no. 4 (Winter 2006): 291–311.

Green, Andrew. "Intertextuality in Frankenstein." *English Review* 16, no. 1 (September 2005): 24–27.

Hardin, Richard. *Civil Idolatry.* Newark: University of Delaware Press, 1992.

Lamb, John B. "Mary Shelley's *Frankenstein* and Milton's Monstrous Myth." *Nineteenth-Century Literature* 47, no. 3 (December 1992): 303–319.

Lewalski, Barbara K. *Paradise Lost and the Rhetoric of Literary Forms*. Princeton, N.J.: Princeton University Press, 1985.

Steadman, John M. *Milton and the Renaissance Hero*. Oxford, U.K.: Clarendon Press, 1967.

Polidori, John William (1795–1821) John William Polidori was present during the famous session that proved the impetus for Mary Shelley's writing of *Frankenstein* (1818). Born in London on September 7, 1795, to a father who had served as a secretary to the poet/dramatist Alfieri, Polidori studied medicine and became a physician by age 20. A budding writer himself, Polidori was hired by GEORGE GORDON BYRON (Lord Byron) as his personal physician and traveling companion. Polidori was an uncle to the famous Rossetti family, including Dante, William, and Christina Rossetti; William Rossetti later served as his biographer.

In the 1831 revised edition of *Frankenstein*, Shelley describes the June 1816 evening in rainy Geneva when, along with PERCY BYSSHE SHELLEY, Lord Byron, Claire Claremont, and Polidori, she began the quest for a horror story in response to a dare. Whether Polidori contributed to the exchange of ghost stories during that dark and stormy night remains unknown, but critics including John Reiger discredit Shelley's time line, noting discrepancies with Polidori's diary entries. According to some sources, in addition to *Frankenstein*, Polidori's story "The Vampyre," perhaps the first vampire story in English, resulted from the competition. Percy Shelley and Claremont wrote nothing, and Byron may have produced a fragment that he chose not to complete. Some critics, citing an unsubstantiated claim in William Rosetti's journal, believe that Byron became jealous over the fact that Polidori had produced a story when he had not, and that shattered their relationship. In September 1816, Polidori returned to London and began studies to become a lawyer. He would die a few years later, by some reports from drinking acid following despair over his disappointing literary career.

As the story goes, Polidori showed his story to an acquaintance who passed it to another and another, until Henry Colburn published "The Vampyre" in *New Monthly Magazine* in April 1819. ("The Vampyre" is available today in print and electronic format.) Colburn attributed the story to Byron, due to its similarity to "A Fragment." Byron later denied authorship, and Polidori admitted that he had taken the plot from Byron, but that the actual production of the story was his own. The similarity of Polidori's protagonist, the egotistical and ruthless Lord Ruthven, to Byron was obvious to readers. Polidori's story was transformed into a spectacularly successful French melodrama on June 13, 1820. Some claim that "The Vampyre" inspired Christina Rossetti's "Goblin Market"; influenced the development of the French vampire novel; and helped birth the entire vampire genre, including Bram Stoker's *Dracula* (1897).

Polidori has appeared as a fictional character in some recent works. He was the narrator of Paul West's novels *Rat Man of Paris* (1986) and *Lord Byron's Doctor* (1989). In the latter work, Polidori serves as a Boswell-style chronicler, with his difficult charge, Byron, acting also as his subject. West imagines Polidori as a long-suffering figure, ill fated in life and love, who nurtures a love/hate relationship with Byron. In Benjamin Markovits' novel *Imposture* (2007), Polidori pretends to be Byron, partly to advance a romance with a woman who mistakes Polidori for the novelist (the two did resemble one another).

FURTHER READING

Byron, George Gordon, Lord Byron. *The Works of Lord Byron: Journals and Letters*. Edited by Roland E. Prothero, III. 1899. Reprint, London: John Murray, 1922.

Markovits, Benjamin. *Imposture*. New York: W. W. Norton, 2007.

Morrill, David. "'Twilight is Not Good for Maidens': Uncle Polidori and the Psychodynamics of Vampirism in 'Goblin Market.'" *Victorian Poetry* 28, no. 1 (Spring 1990): 1–16.

Polidori, John William. *The Diary of Dr. John William Polidori*. Edited by William Michael Rossetti. London: Elkin Mathews, 1911.

———. "The Vampyre." Available online. URL: http://www.sff.net/people/Doylemacdonald/l_vampyr.htm. Accessed February 19, 2009.

Rieger, James. "Dr. Polidori and the Genesis of *Frankenstein.*" *Studies in English Literature, 1500–1900* 3, no. 4 (Autumn 1963): 461–472.

Switzer, Richard. "Lord Ruthwen and the Vampires." *French Review* 29, no. 2 (December 1955): 107–112.

West, Paul. *Lord Byron's Doctor.* New York: Doubleday, 1989.

Prometheus The mythical character Prometheus proved crucial to the imaginations of both Mary and PERCY BYSSHE SHELLEY. One of Percy's most famous and enduring works, the drama *Prometheus Unbound,* was based on the myth made famous in the Greek classical drama *Prometheus Bound* by the ancient Greek playwright Aeschylus. Mary also made use of the Promethean myth; the subtitle of *Frankenstein* is *The Modern Prometheus.* She also made frequent reference to Prometheus in her other writing. For instance, in her final novel, *Falkner* (1837), she compares the suffering of her protagonist to that of Prometheus. The comparison is appropriate, as Falkland considers himself to have died on multiple occasions, to be brought back to life by Elizabeth, at which time his suffering the torment of guilt begins again.

According to mythology, Prometheus was born to Iapetus, a brother to Cronus, the titan son of Earth. Prometheus's mother, Clymene, a daughter of Ocean, also gave birth to Atlas, whose job it would become to support Earth on his shoulders. Like his uncle Cronus, Prometheus was known to be quite wily.

Zeus, son of Cronus and Rhea, had defeated his father, Cronus, when young and eventually became leader of the gods. As an all-powerful creator and destroyer, Zeus created man for his pleasure. During a gathering of immortals and the humans at Mecone, the Field of Poppies, Prometheus tried to trick his cousin Zeus. He cut up an ox and announced it would be shared with all, but he hid the meat and entrails in the stomach and wrapped the bones in fat. He asked Zeus as king to first choose what he wanted from the ox meat. Zeus was wise enough to recognize trickery, but he chose the fat knowing full well that it contained an inferior offering of only bones. Angry with Prometheus for trying to trick him, Zeus decided to punish men, loved by Prometheus. He ordered that man should never have access to fire. Prometheus betrayed Zeus by stealing fire and presenting it to man in a giant fennel stalk. Zeus, enraged, bound Prometheus to a rock where, each day, an eagle would eat his liver. The liver regenerated during the night, and the eagle returned to torture Prometheus again, each day devouring his liver. The repeated torture ended later when the demigod Heracles (or Hercules) was allowed by Zeus, who was his father, to release Prometheus.

The myth of Prometheus may be categorized as aetiological, meaning it was invented to explain a phenomenon, a ritual whose origin has been forgotten. When later Greeks made ritual offerings of slaughtered animals to the gods, they always kept the larger and better portion to meet their own physical needs. Some view the story of Zeus choosing Prometheus's inferior offering as an explanation for that ritual. The myth thus satisfied the human need to understand an early example of an action similar to their own that helped them to justify their actions.

Prometheus was not officially worshipped by the Greeks, and they built no temples to honor him. However, he was a popular immortal, an immoral trickster who came to be seen as a champion of the proletariat, the common man. Stories of the source of the fire that he gave to man vary. Some say he stole it by touching the sun's wheel with a torch, while others say it came from the forge of Hephaestus, patron of craftsmen, particularly those who forged and shaped metal. The giant fennel is a stalk about five feet in height with a white pithy center resembling a wick, and it may still be used in Greece as a torch.

FURTHER READING

Grant, Michael. *Myths of the Greeks and Romans.* New York: Penguin/Plume, 1995.

Aeschylus. *Prometheus Bound.* Available online. URL: http://www.theoi.com/Text/AeschylusPrometheus.html. Accessed June 10, 2010.

Shelley, Percy. *Prometheus Unbound: A Lyrical Drama in Four Acts.* Available online. URL: http://www.english.upenn.edu/Projects/knarf/PShelley/promtp.html. Accessed June 10, 2010.

psychoanalytic criticism Originally, psychoanalytic criticism utilized 19th-century psychoanalysis techniques developed by Sigmund Freud (1856–1939) to analyze literature, an approach labeled *Freudism*. However, as the legitimacy of Freud's theories was questioned, particularly those theories that applied to women, additional schools of psychoanalysis developed, and the approach became more commonly known as psychoanalytic criticism. This approach has no pure aesthetic theory of its own. Because its theories are based on models of the mind and human behavior rather than aesthetics, they are adopted by various critical approaches, including FEMINIST CRITICISM and deconstruction, among others.

Freud believed that all artists are neurotic and that they avoid mental illness through their creativity. He also believed that literature results from a writer's dream and can be interpreted like dreams, which he noted represent secret desires. Dream analysis applies well to Mary Shelley's stories, which include multiple references to dreams and visions. Biographical analysis also reveals many aspects of Shelley's own existence incorporated into her fiction; thus, the dreams of her fiction may well have been her own, masking hidden beliefs and longings. In addition, critics find Freud's theories regarding human sexuality and parent/child interactions useful in application to Shelley's work, particularly those with blatant or suggested incest themes. Freud proposed the theory of the Oedipus complex, a son's sexual fixation on his mother, based on the protagonist of Sophocles' play, *Oedipus the King*, who unknowingly slept with his own mother. In the introduction to Shelley's novel *Mathilda* (1959), the title character compares herself to Oedipus, clearly foreshadowing an incest theme.

Carl Jung (1875–1961), Freud's student, departed from Freud's theories to emphasize the interpretation of dreams as most important to understanding the human psyche. Whereas Freud believed most dreams were sexually driven, Jung looked to mythological images, labeled *archetypes*, in those dreams. Archetypes are recognizable in all cultures regardless of the culture's geographical location or developmental background. Jung also introduced the idea of the collective unconscious, a universal aspect of the psyche that stores memories common to all of humanity's past. It plays a key role in understanding the importance of ancient archetypes, which deeply affect the reader, awakening images in the collective unconscious. Cultures that developed unrelated to one another may share mythology with similar themes, such as a flood that covered the earth, destroyed most of its inhabitants, and allowed for a new beginning; thus, we can share a consciousness.

Archetypes include the four seasons, Earth's revolution around the sun, traditional familial roles such as motherhood and fatherhood, and colors, to name only a few examples. The psyche stores archetypes, and we react to them as recurring patterns in stories that unify all literature. A familiar archetype is that of the HERO'S JOURNEY, further elaborated on by the 20th-century philosopher Joseph Campbell (1904–87). The filmmaker George Lucas (1944–) adopted many of Campbell's ideas to make the iconic 20th-century movie *Star Wars* (1977). Its plot substitutes the setting of outer space for that of the ocean, generally crossed by the classical hero, and a starship for a sailing ship. However, it retains many of the elements of the hero's journey, such as the importance of a guide figure and especially the son/father identity emphasis. Shelley employed an ironic version of the hero's story when she wrote of Victor Frankenstein's failure to succeed in his efforts to create a human and to come to terms with his own "son," the monster.

The Canadian literary critic Northrop Frye (1912–91) advanced the theory of the collective unconscious in order to identify specific recurring symbols in stories that repeatedly signal the same meanings. Examples would be winter as a symbol of death, spring as a symbol of rebirth, or the lamb as a symbol of innocence. Frye placed all literature within what he called a monomyth, represented by a circle divided into the four seasons. Frye saw mythology as the driving force behind literature in all societies, as explored in his most famous work, *Anatomy of Criticism* (1957).

For example, the summer story appears at the top of the monomyth circle and is identified as

"Summer: Romance." Summer's six phases include complete innocence, youthful innocence of inexperience, completion of an ideal, happy society resists change, reflective and idyllic view, and society ceases to exist beyond contemplation. Symbols that correspond to summer include butterflies and flowers. At the opposite pole of the monomyth circle is "Winter: Irony and Satire." Three of its elements that most strongly apply to Shelley's stories are individual's faults, natural law, and world of shock and horror. The romantics emphasized the importance of the individual and the importance of nature as a source of inspiration and wisdom, and Shelley often focused on those ideals. This fact, in addition to her repeated emphasis on horror, recommends the monomyth for use in analysis of her fiction.

Theories by the French psychoanalyst Jacques Lacan (1901–81) emphasize the importance of "lack" and "fragmentation." Lacanian theory holds that we all suffer from "lack" because nothing can ever satisfy the desire one holds to return to what he terms "the imaginary order" represented by the mother. Only through the (impossible) return to the imaginary order with one's mother can wholeness be achieved. In Shelley's *Mathilda*, because Mathilda has lost her mother, she is doubly cursed with the inability to return to an order she never experienced. This is also true for the monster in *Frankenstein* (1818), who never had a mother.

Fragmentation of one's sense of self is also of concern. This aspect of the theory applies to Guido in Shelley's short story "Transformation" (1830). Guido loses his mother early on and experiences a literal fragmentation into two different beings—himself and the dwarf. In the case of the *Frankenstein* monster, his is a literal as well as a figurative fragmentation, as his body is made up of pieces of other people, increasing the challenge to his developing a discrete identity. In addition, for Lacan, literature could capture *jouissance*, a term meaning a moment of joy or terror, seen in many of Shelley's stories. It comes from our unconscious psyche and reminds us of a time when perfect order existed; during that time we were completely whole, unable to differentiate various images from the real order.

In addition to these traditional theories, many additional psychoanalytic theories that may be applied to literature continue to develop. Critics Karen Horney, Melanie Klein, and Nancy Chodorow have all revised theories relating to gender differences in reaction to, or as extensions of, Freud's Oedipus complex theory. Horney's and Klein's theories are especially applicable to Shelley's work.

As one of the earliest specialists in feminine psychiatry, Karen Horney held that women hold value only in relationship to their husbands and children; she compared the relationship of husband to wife to that of parent to child, a relationship that proves fraught with neurosis and misunderstanding. Horney's theories may be applied to literature that focuses on power relationships between family members, such as that between Mathilda and her father.

Klein worked during the same era as Freud, and the two discussed shared interests. She worked directly with children to propose developmental theories that in part focused on aggression and what she viewed as the human natural drive toward death. In light of Mathilda's focus on her own death and the aggressive love that she felt for her father, Klein's theories could also be applied to *Mathilda*.

Chodorow proposes that in Western culture, a boy has little conflict in developing self-identity, as he identifies with his father's independence and his father's "possession" of his mother. However, a girl may find development of identity challenged by her close relationship to her mother that prevents her bonding with her father.

FURTHER READING

Belcher, R. "Psychoanalytic Criticism: Sigmund Freud's ideas." Available online. URL: http://web.olivet.edu/english/rbelcher/lit310/310psy.htm. Accessed July 21, 2009.

Bressler, Charles E. *Literary Criticism: An Introduction to Theory and Practice*. Englewood Cliffs, N.J.: Prentice Hall, 1994.

Chodorow, Nancy. *The Reproduction of Mothering—Psychoanalysis and the Sociology of Gender*. Berkeley: University of California Press, 1978.

Emmett, Paul J., and William Veeder. "Freud in Time: Psychoanalysis and Literary Criticism in the New Century." *Annual of Psychoanalysis* 29 (2001): 201–235.

Frye, Northrop. *Anatomy of Criticism*. Princeton, N.J.: Princeton University Press, 1957.

Herring, David. "Northrop Frye's Theory of Archetypes." Available online. URL: http://edweb.tusd.k12.az.us/dherring/ap/consider/frye/indexfryeov.htm Accessed July 19, 2009.

Jacobus, Mary. The *Poetics of Psychoanalysis: In the Wake of Klein*. New York: Oxford University Press, 2006.

Jung, Carl. *The Archetypes and the Collective Unconscious*. Vol. 9, Part 1, *Collected Works*. 2nd ed. Edited by Gerhard Adler. Princeton, N.J.: Princeton University Press, 1980.

Klein, George. *Psychoanalytic Theory: An Exploration of Essentials*. New York: International Universities Press, 1976.

Wright, Elizabeth. *Psychoanalytic Criticism: A Reappraisal*. 2nd ed. New York: Taylor and Francis, 1998.

———. *Psychoanalytic Criticism: Theory in Practice*. London: Methuen, 1984.

quest   See HERO'S JOURNEY.

romanticism   Information about the artistic movement known as romanticism and those who practiced it could fill entire libraries, and a thorough investigation of the topic is well beyond the scope of this entry. Readers are encouraged to further research the crucial ideas summarized here that informed the work of PERCY BYSSHE SHELLEY and others who served as literary models for Mary Shelley. According to the scholar Marilyn Gaull, the English romantic period is generally represented by the reign of two kings—George III (1760–1815) and George IV (1821–30); two wars—the American War of Independence (1775–83) and the war against France (1793–1815); one of several French political revolutions (1789–93); England's Industrial Revolution (1780–1830); and a plethora of advances in science and changes in culture. Writers crucial to romanticism include William Blake (1757–1827), Samuel Taylor Coleridge (1772–1834), William Wordsworth (1770–1850), Sir Walter Scott (1771–1832; a reviewer of Shelley's *Frankenstein*), Robert Southey (1774–1843), William Hazlitt (1778–1830), Thomas De Quincey (1785–1859), Charles Lamb (1775–1834), GEORGE GORDON BYRON (Lord Byron), Percy Shelley, John Keats (1795–1821), Jane Austen (1775–1817), Thomas Carlyle (1795–1881), George Crabbe (1754–1832), WILLIAM GODWIN (Mary Shelley's father), and Leigh Hunt (Shelley's and Lord Byron's friend) (1784–1859). Due to Godwin's standing in literary circles, he knew and interacted with many of the writers, including Coleridge, whom Mary met when he visited the Godwin home while she was a child.

The movement later labeled *romanticism* emerged at the end of the 18th century in reaction to that century's focus on logic and the rational. Named the "Age of Reason," the 18th century produced literature that promoted ideas of order, the importance of the group over the individual, and the function of the poet to inform and of art to reflect the world around it. The revolution against such thought was formalized in the publication of *Lyrical Ballads* (1798), written by Wordsworth and Coleridge. Coleridge, especially, would provide inspiration for Mary Shelley's later writings. He adopted certain symbols, such as Mont Blanc, to represent the destruction of tradition, and Shelley imitated him, incorporating Mont Blanc into her first novel, *Frankenstein; or, the Modern Prometheus* (1818). Although not many readers contemporary to the romantics would take an interest in, or have access to, their work—Scott and Byron being exceptions—periodicals and papers gained a wide readership. Male poets could support themselves working as journalists or reviewers and produce their art on the side, so to speak. With the rising popularity of ladies' magazines later in the century, Mary Shelley joined other women and men to publish her short fiction and poetry in that venue.

The romantics believed in the superiority of the individual imagination over group logic and of the spirituality found in nature over that of organized religion. Through the romantics, the imagination, once equated with fantasy and even madness,

of the demigod PROMETHEUS. A renewed respect for the works of the Renaissance emerged, seen in Mary Shelley's frequent references to Shakespeare and to John Milton's PARADISE LOST (1667).

Romantic writers wanted their work to be accessible to the common reader and to reflect local tradition. After first imitating writers of other cultures, most notably the German romantics, English writers developed their own tales and used local phrasing, promoting a sense of national identity as well as individual identity. At the same time, they often included references to exotic lands and cultures, provoking the reader's imagination.

As Gaull notes, the romantics believed that despite developments in science and technology, an individual human would always be required to identify problems to be solved and to interpret all information collected through scientific or other means. The human imagination remained necessary to true perception. Percy Shelley wrote in A Defence of Poetry, published in 1840, 18 years after his death: "Reason is to imagination as the instrument to the agent, as the body to the spirit, as the shadow to the substance." His point regarding the crucial nature of imagination to romanticism is clear. And of the poets of his era, he noted, "They measure the circumference and sound the depths of human nature with a comprehensive and all-penetrating spirit, and they are themselves perhaps the most sincerely astonished at its manifestations; for it is less their spirit than the spirit of the age."

Portrait of Samuel Taylor Coleridge, family friend of the Godwins *(Painting by Washington Allston; engraving by Samuel Cousins. Library of Congress)*

proved able, according to Gaull, to "overcome the limits of observation and intellect." The artist proved central to his art, the inspiration for which came from within rather than from without. Emotions proved all-important, as expressed by Wordsworth's famous statement that "poetry is the spontaneous overflow of powerful feelings." Imagination and emotion trumped logic, and a search for self-identity on the part of the poet, often by interacting with nature, became an important theme. References to self in poetry became the norm, when previously such references were believed vulgar, unsuitable for poetry's high-culture aesthetics.

Although intent on change, the romantics did not overtly reject everything from the past. Rather, as explained by Gaull, they assimilated many classical topics and images considered too vulgar by those writing during the Age of Enlightenment. Examples are various stories from mythology reflected in writing by both Percy Bysshe and Mary Shelley's use

FURTHER READING

Beer, Gillian. "Darwin and Romanticism." *Wordsworth Circle* 41, no. 1 (Winter 2010): 3–9.

Bruhn, Mark J. "Romanticism and the Cognitive Science of Imagination." *Studies in Romanticism* 48, no. 4 (Winter 2009): 543–564.

Esterhammer, Angela. *Romanticism and Improvisation, 1750–1850*. Cambridge: Cambridge University Press, 2008.

Gaull, Marilyn. *English Romanticism: The Human Context*. New York: W. W. Norton, 1988.

Hubbell, J. Andrew. "A Question of Nature: Byron and Wordsworth." *Wordsworth Circle* 41, no. 1 (Winter 2010): 14–18.

Leadbetter, Gregory. *The Lake Poets and Professional Identity*. New York: Cambridge University Press, 2007.
Martin, Michael. "The Romantics." *Midwest Quarterly* 51, no. 3 (Spring 2010): 285–299.
Mole, Tom. *Romanticism and Celebrity Culture, 1750–1859*. Cambridge: Cambridge University Press, 2009.
Pfau, Thomas, and Robert Mitchell. "Romanticism and Modernity." *European Romantic Review* 21, no. 3 (Jun 2010): 267–273.
Potkay, Adam. *The Story of Joy: From the Bible to Late Romanticism*. Cambridge: Cambridge University Press, 2010.
Ruston, Sharon. *Shelley and Vitality*. New York and Basingstoke, U.K.: Palgrave, 2005.
Sha, Richard C. *Perverse Romanticism: Aesthetics & Sexuality in Great Britain 1750–1832*. Baltimore: The Johns Hopkins University Press, 2008.
Shears, Jonathon. *The Romantic Legacy of 'Paradise Lost': Reading against the Grain*. Farnham, U.K.: Ashgate, 2009.
Shelley, Percy Bysshe. *A Defence of Poetry*. Boston: Ginn & Co., 1891.
Singer, Katherine. "Stoned Shelley: Revolutionary Tactics and Women Under the Influence." *Studies in Romanticism* 48, no. 4 (Winter 2009): 687–707.
Wagenknecht, David, ed. "Romanticism and Its Public (a Symposium)." *Studies in Romanticism* 33 (1994): 523–588.
Wang, Orrin N. C. "Romanticism and the Rise of the Mass Public." *Modern Philology* 107, no. 2 (November 2009): 270–274.

science fiction Science fiction incorporates elements of other genres and subgenres, including fantasy, romance, and horror. Plots turn on logical developments that might occur in technology beyond those available in the author's era, as seen in Mary Shelley's *Frankenstein* (1818), "Roger Dodsworth" (1821), and *The Last Man* (1826). Such technology could include the use of inanimate figures, such as robots powered by technology to serve man, or the use of electric power to animate (from the term *anima*—literally, breath or soul) the dead, the latter forming the basis for Victor Frankenstein's experiments. Developments might also include advances allowing humans to ignore natural laws such as gravity or the confinements of time or space. Humans might also discover a way to assume animal powers, such as flight, speed, or strength, by ingesting potions or through the discovery of an unknown source of energy. Shelley's short story "The Mortal Immortal" (1833) provides a magical potion brewed in an alchemist's laboratory for its narrator, who, after drinking it, lives for more than three centuries.

Science fiction generally warns readers against what may at first seem a promising development, such as electricity and the resulting galvanism in *Frankenstein*, but in the end must be avoided due to negative effects. It also often emphasizes the corrupting nature of the power made available through unnatural advances, even to individuals whose intentions are positive. This is true for Victor Frankenstein, who hopes to offer humans a way to defeat disease and death but instead develops a monster that destroys several people. Victor's weak character contributes to the monster's destructive nature, and his unwillingness to accept responsibility for his errors causes the death of a number of his friends and family members. Developments at first thought to advance and improve the plight of mankind may become its scourge instead, resulting in disease, famine, war, pollution, chaos, or other aspects of doom, cautioning readers against unbridled enthusiasm over new concepts. Shelley's *The Last Man*, in which humans are wiped out by disease, might also be considered science fiction, but it would be more properly considered to be based on a futuristic disaster plot.

A few representatives of science fiction in its purest sense appeared during the 18th century. However, advancements in science and technology in the 19th century spurred its rapid growth. After *Frankenstein*, the new genre included Robert Louis Stevenson's *The Strange Case of Dr. Jekyll and Mr. Hyde* (1886), Edward Bulwer-Lytton's *The Coming Race or the New Utopia* (1871), Samuel Butler's *Erewhon* (1872), and H. G. Well's *The Time Machine* (1895), along with a myriad of short stories.

FURTHER READING

Bainbridge, William Sims. *Dimensions of Science Fiction*. Cambridge, Mass.: Harvard University Press, 1986.

Bleiler, Everett F. *Science-Fiction: The Early Years. A Full Description of More Than 3,000 Science-Fiction Stories from Earliest Times to the Appearance of the Genre Magazines in 1930.* Kent, Ohio: Kent State University Press, 1990.

Clute, John, and Peter Nichols, ed. *The Encyclopedia of Science Fiction.* London: Orbit, 1993.

Golden, Kenneth L. *Science Fiction, Myth, and Jungian Psychology.* Lewiston, N.Y.: Edwin Mellen Press, 1995.

Snodgrass, Mary Ellen. *Encyclopedia of Utopian Literature.* Santa Barbara, Calif.: ABC-Clio, 1995.

Shelley, Percy Bysshe (1792–1822) For the most part, Mary Shelley enthusiasts have a love/hate relationship with her husband, Percy Bysshe Shelley. Little doubt exists regarding his positive influence on Mary in continuing her literary education and influencing her reading selections. He was an enormously important poet and critic and trained Mary to help him with his work, her intimacy with his writings influencing later topics and themes in her own writing. He also tempered the activist attitudes of Mary's parents with his own romantic ideals that proved liberating for a young, starry-eyed woman. However, he could be overpowering, leading her to complain about him in letters and journal entries. Worse, his controlling approach to Mary caused generations of scholars to wonder whether some of what she claimed to be her own work might have actually been written by Percy. Such speculation began in the very first stages of her work when Sir Walter Scott attributed the authorship of *Frankenstein* (1818) to a man. From the beginning, Mary Shelley bore the suspicion that she might be only a ghost figure, a shade of her much more famous and celebrated husband.

Born the first of six children into an aristocratic family on August 4, 1792, Percy Bysshe Shelley was the son of Sir Timothy Shelley, a member of Parliament, and Elizabeth Shelley. His grandfather, Bysshe Shelley, had been a landowner made baronet in 1806, and his parents expected Percy to follow in his father's footsteps, inheriting the family's considerable fortune along with a seat in Parliament. He lived the childhood of the privileged, but from the beginning he seemed to rebel against the expectations of his class. Percy matured with a generous nature that belied the class consciousness of his parents and would lead to his lifelong habit of giving away money, even when he had little. He studied as a child with the clergyman Reverend Evan Edwards and later attended Syon House Academy, to be followed by six years of study at Eton College. While there, he corresponded with a cousin named Harriet Grove and arranged an informal engagement that ended in 1810.

By 1810, Shelley had published his first novel, *Zastrozzi*, in the popular GOTHIC FICTION genre, and he entered Oxford University that same year. He met a classmate who would remain his lifelong friend, Thomas Jefferson Hogg (1792–1862), and the two published a collection of poetry, *Posthumous Fragments of Margaret Nicholson* (1810). Described as bawdy, the collection dismayed university officials. His collaborations were not all of questionable nature; he also published a collection of poetry with his sister Elizabeth titled *Original Poetry; by Victor and Cazire* (1810).

fig. 25

Portrait of the poet Percy Bysshe Shelley, Mary Shelley's husband, from 1819 *(Painting by Alfred Clint)*

In 1811, Shelley published his second gothic novel, *St. Irvyne,* and also met his future first wife, Harriet Westbrook. His literary pursuits again perturbed the Oxford community, and on March 25, Shelley and Hogg were expelled from Oxford for writing a pamphlet, "The Necessity of Atheism." The publication and subsequent dismissal from university caused a rift with his father. While Shelley could have returned to his family's good graces and remained in line for his grand inheritance by renouncing the publication, he refused to do so. On August 29, at age 19, he eloped with the 16-year-old Harriet. Hogg attempted to seduce her shortly after the wedding, beginning a long series of sexual interrelationships between Shelley, the women in his life, and his male companions. Unwelcome at home, he left the country for a time.

In 1812, while living in Dublin, Shelley became involved in political activities and published two political pamphlets, then moved on to Wales. Returning to England in October, he met WILLIAM GODWIN, whose writings he much favored. He again left for Wales, returned to Ireland briefly, and then returned to London to publish his first serious piece, *Queen Mab: A Philosophical Poem* (1813). The poem paid homage to Godwin's social idealism. The Shelleys' daughter Ianthe was born on June 23, 1813, but his marriage was not thriving. He would later write to Hogg, describing his marriage as a "calamity," adding, "I felt as if a dead and living body had been linked together in loathsome and horrible communion."

In early 1814, Shelley published *A Refutation of Deism* and continued to nurture his relationship with Godwin, giving him money that his own family could not afford to lose and bringing his wife to the Godwin house for meals. He became infatuated with Mary, Godwin's daughter with MARY WOLLSTONECRAFT and reportedly visited her to court her as she read at her mother's grave. When Godwin interceded, suggesting that the two not see each other, Shelley threatened suicide before the entire Godwin family. As Percy took over from her father the role of major male influence in her life, he convinced Mary to run away with him, despite the fact that he was already married with a daughter and his wife pregnant. The two "eloped" on July 27, 1814, taking Mary's stepsister Jane, later called Claire, Clairmont with them.

The trio toured Europe, leaving behind an incensed Godwin and the reputation for living outside the boundary of social decorum that was to haunt Mary Shelley forever. Further complicating the runaways' lives, Harriet gave birth to Charles Shelley on November 30. In January 1815, Shelley's grandfather died, and in February, his first child with Mary was born prematurely and died. That summer, he received the first annual payment of £1,000 from his grandfather's estate, of which he paid £200 to Harriet. Shelley and Mary moved near Windsor Great Park in August, but Godwin spoke with neither Shelley nor his daughter in consequence of their actions. The strong reaction of their friends against their actions hurt and surprised Percy and Mary, who had to lead a rather isolated existence.

The couple had another baby in January 1816, a boy whom they named William. Shelley's next publication was *Alastor,* after which he visited Switzerland, where he decided to settle close to GEORGE GORDON BYRON (Lord Byron) with his family, which still included Claire. Some accounts note that Claire persuaded the Shelleys to live for a time close to Byron's home at Villa Diodati by Lake Geneva, following an affair she had with him. Byron lived as an informal exile from England due to accusations of incest with his half sister, Augusta Leigh; some believe that he fathered her only child. The two poets became close friends, and Shelley wrote two of his well-known poems, "Hymn to Intellectual Beauty" and "Mont Blanc," before returning to England with Mary in September. A year later, during bad weather, the group consisting of Shelley, Mary, Byron, and Byron's physician, JOHN WILLIAM POLIDORI, engaged in the famous writing contest that would result in Mary Shelley's writing *Frankenstein.* While Percy did not contribute to the writing, Byron produced a later-published "fragment," and Polidori published a horror story that many believe he stole from Byron's draft.

In late 1816, tragedy again struck the Shelleys when Mary's half sister Fanny committed suicide and, within about one month, Harriet Shelley drowned herself. The date of her death was established as November 9, although her body was not discovered for some time. Shelley and Mary learned of Harriet's death on December 15 and married on December 30. Following the couple's wedding, Godwin renewed his relationship with the Shelleys, remaining always on the outlook for financial support from his son-in-law, despite his earlier rejection of Mary. His constant expectations of money created a strain on the new marriage.

In 1817, Shelley became friends with the poet and editor Leigh Hunt. Claire Claremont gave birth to her daughter with Byron, initially named Alba, and later called Allegra, and Shelley petitioned for custody of his two children with Harriet. Based on his lifestyle, his petition was denied, and he despaired that he would never gain custody. The Shelley family moved to Marlow, living close to another poet friend of Shelley's, Thomas Love Peacock. In March, Shelley published *Proposal for Putting Reform to the Vote* and finished *Laon and Cythna*. Claire continued to cause friction for the couple. At first, her baby lived with the Hunts but later returned to the Shelleys, as Byron wanted no relationship with Claire or the baby.

During these years, Percy was guiding Mary in her reading and study and supporting her interest in languages. As the critic Julie Carson notes, while Mary Shelley biographers may "disagree over the intensity, persistence, longevity, and exclusivity" of Mary and Percy's romantic relationship, "all are united on the comparative harmony and consistency that characterized their reading and writing lives as a couple." The two began their relationship writing journals together, although Percy quickly lost interest. Mary continued the journals, which would become priceless sources of information for those later interested in the couple's activities. Mary took over the journal duties, the warm and passionate nature of some of her entries later countering charges that she was dispassionate or "cold," although, as Carson emphasizes, editors of her entries never characterize them as "revealing" or improper. Mary faithfully recorded, for instance, all of the books that she and Percy read. Her act of documenting her reading along with her passions and reactions to the couple's activities and friendships does not surprise those who understand the importance of reading to writers. Mary had an unequaled view of that importance in her relationships with members of Shelleys' circle. They all shared interest in German romances and horror tales, which influenced some of their writing, most importantly and famously that of Mary's *Frankenstein* (1818). Claire was known to have night terrors after reading the German tales, testimony to their effect.

Mary and Percy enjoyed translating, and he began work on *Rosalind and Helen* as they awaited the birth of another child. A daughter, Clara, was born in September 1817, and *History of a Six Weeks' Tour* was published that some year. Mary continued to assist Percy in his work, researching for him and reading and commenting on his manuscripts. Later that year, Shelley wrote *An Address to the People on the death of the Princess Charlotte*. He also published his lengthy poem *Laon and Cythna*. However, it had to be withdrawn due to public reaction to its references to incest and antireligious tone. Shelley republished it under the title *The Revolt of Islam* in 1818.

In March 1818, Shelley sailed to the Continent and sent Allegra Byron to live with her father. Although the Shelleys loved Allegra, Mary feared that others would suspect she was Claire's daughter with Percy. At first enthralled with his toddler daughter, Byron later found her tiresome and sent her away to be raised by nuns in a convent at Bagnacavallo. Alarmed by that development, Claire would later badger the Shelleys to help her regain custody of her daughter.

Shelley met John and Maria Gisborne at Leghorn in 1818 and, while visiting the Baths of Lucca, completed *Rosalind and Helen*, which would be published the following year. He traveled to Venice with Claire, and rumors spread of the two's sexual relationship. Mary brought the children to join their father, but Clara died in September. If Shelley shared Mary's grief, he may have dealt with it by beginning work on several pieces, the most important being act 1 of *Prometheus Unbound*. The demigod PROMETHEUS who so fascinated Percy as a symbol of life's duality became the subtitle of Mary's *Frankenstein; or, The Modern Prometheus*.

The couple next visited Rome, settling in Naples, which they left in February 1819. Shelley completed *Prometheus* in Rome, where his son William Shelley died, reportedly of malaria. Mary Shelley suffered a deep depression, and friends would later claim that she became cold to Shelley and no longer supported his creative activity. Some believe that she blamed Percy's desire to be constantly on the move for the deaths of Clara and William.

After moving to Leghorn in 1819, Shelley wrote *The Cenci* and "Mask of Anarchy," then moved to Florence, where the couple had their only child who would survive, Percy Florence Shelley, born on November 12, 1819. Shelley entered an extremely prolific period, writing *Peter Bell the Third*, "West Wind" and *Philosophical View of Reform*, while completing *Julian and Maddalo*. In 1820, the Shelleys moved to Pisa where he wrote "The Sensitive Plant." When the family returned to Leghorn, he wrote "Ode to Liberty," "To a Skylark," and "Letter to Maria Gisborne," and at the Baths of San Giuliano, he wrote "Witch of Atlas," "Ode to Naples," and *Swellfoot the Tyrant*. Claire continued to live with the Shelleys off and on, again stirring rumors about sexual liaisons. She contributed to the strain experienced by the couple, who were always in need of money and still sending funds to Godwin. In August 1820, Shelley published *Prometheus Unbound*.

In 1821, Percy became enamored of the mayor of Venice's daughter, Emilia Viviani, for whom he wrote *Epipsychidion*, described as a tale emphasizing the positive relationship between sexual desire, imagination, and spirituality. Early that year, he met the couple Edward and Jane Williams, with whom Mary became close friends. Mary reportedly became increasingly unhappy with Percy's various liaisons, but she continued to support his writing endeavors, which included *A Defence of Poetry* and *Adonais*. Shelley visited Byron, who was living at Ravenna, and persuaded him to move to Pisa to join their group.

Shelley's final works included "Charles the First" and poems that he dedicated to Jane Williams. His friend who had once tried to seduce Mary, EDWARD JOHN TRELAWNY, arrived in 1822. That year in April, Byron and Claire's daughter died at the convent where Byron had sent her, and Claire went into an emotional frenzy. Although she may have partially blamed Percy and Mary for her daughter's death, she continued to live with them from time to time.

When Allegra died, the Shelleys and the Williamses moved to San Terenzo. Percy began writing poems to Jane, who believed that had they not already been married to others, Percy would have proposed to her. Mary, again pregnant, seemed nervous and fearful. She did not know that her father and stepmother had been evicted from their home, because Percy hid their letters asking for more money. He wrote that he did so due to her "distressing, & sometimes alarming" condition. Eventually he did tell Mary, who took the news in stride, noting that it took its place in their disorderly lives.

Percy became fascinated with sailing, and Trelawny helped him design his own boat, the *Don Juan*, named after Byron's character from his famous poem. Byron had annoyed Shelley by painting the name on the sail. Mary wrote that for 21 days, he and Trelawny tried to wash out "the primeval stain" trying "turpentine, spirits of wine, buccata," none of which removed the lettering but instead "dappled" the sail. She wondered "what Ld B—would say, but Lord and poet as he is, he could not be allowed to make a coal-barge of our boat."

Shelley wrote "Triumph of Life" that spring and saved Mary's life on June 16, 1822, when she suffered another miscarriage: He stopped her hemorrhaging by by immersing her in ice to stop her bleeding. She again became depressed after the loss of yet another child, and Percy described Mary to others as being difficult and withdrawn. He spent more time away from her, much of it sailing and visiting friends. According to the biographer Emily Sunstein, Mary feared that Percy would die and begged him to take the family to the Baths of Pisa. On July 1, when Percy and Williams decided to sail to Leghorn to meet Leigh Hunt, with whom Shelley and Byron had plans to publish a literary journal, Mary reportedly dragged herself from the bed and yelled from the terrace, calling to him to return. Shelley and Williams both drowned in the Gulf of Spezia in a storm as they returned to San Terenzo on July 8, 1822, just before Shelley's 30th birthday. Trelawny found Shelley's body a few days later. Shelley had to be cremated by Italian law, but Trelawny rescued the poet's heart, grabbing it from the flames, which Mary kept until she died. Mary's daughter-in-law would later commission a statue of a dead, nude, reclining Shelley, as he might have appeared when his body was found at Viareggio, carved in marble by Edward Onslow Ford. Originally planned for location at Shelley's grave in Rome to appear beside Trelawny's memorial, it was deemed too large. It found a home in University College, Oxford, formally dedicated in 1893.

After Percy's death, Mary attempted to keep up many of their friendships, but most of their friends, particularly the Williamses and Hogg, turned against her, publicly accusing her of emotionally abandoning Shelley months before his death.

Percy Bysshe Shelley's gravestone in Rome *(Photograph by Massimo Consoli)*

Byron promised to lend her money following Shelley's death but then reneged on his offer. Mary had to suffer through the indignity of Sir Timothy Shelley offering to give her son to Byron to raise. However, she later took great interest in what was happening in Greece, where Byron and Trelawny had joined the revolutionaries, and she attended Byron's funeral in 1824. She would continue to correspond with his Italian lover, Teresa Guiccioli.

Trelawny proposed marriage to Mary, and then tried to persuade her to help him write a biography of Byron in order to support his own flagging celebrity. She refused, having promised never to make a profit from Byron's life. Due to the reputation of the romantic circle for their loose morals and her association with them, she would remain shy of publicity throughout her life, always avoiding any exposure that might affect her son, Percy. However, she remained devoted to Percy Bysshe Shelley's memory. She at first considered suicide after his death and later described feeling guilty for any coldness that she might have shown to him in their final days together.

On September 12, 1827, Mary wrote to Frances Wright, a Scot who had relocated to America to work in slavery reform movements, of Percy Bysshe's philanthropic nature: "For several years with Mr. Shelley I was blessed with the companionship of one, who fostered this ambition & inspired that of being worthy of him. He was was single among men for Philanthrophy—devoted generosity—talent & goodness." However, critics believe that the character development of many of her male characters as men who do not properly contribute to support of their families was based on Percy Shelley. At the same time, her more romantic and imaginative characters were also said to have been modeled on her husband.

Mary reflected on the general nature of men in her November 9, 1827, letter offering romantic advice to Robert Dale Owen: "[A] woman must very highly esteem & love a man before she can tell any of her heart's secrets to him. We—have no very excessive opinion of men's sympathetic and self sacrificing qualities—make yourself an exception." It seems likely that her comments resulted directly from Percy Shelley's influence on her life.

Whatever his personal challenges, Percy Bysshe Shelley remains a seminal force in English poetry and the development of the romantic movement. He helped revitalize the importance of the classics in a Hellenic revival, writing in his introduction to *Hellas* that "our laws, our literature, our religion, our arts have their roots in Greece." Despite the seeming contradiction between the lofty ideals of ROMANTICISM and the at-times melodramatic reality of his life, his celebration of the visionary life continues to inspire writers. Some believe that his death allowed him to escape the results of the realization expressed in his unfinished work *The Triumph of Life* of the corrosive effects of the "worldly life" upon the visionary.

FURTHER READING

Bande, Usha. "Rebellion, Reform and Regeneration in Shelley's Poetry." *Aligarh Journal of English Studies* 16 (1994): 105–113.

Cameron, Kenneth Neill. *Shelley: The Golden Years.* Cambridge, Mass.: Harvard University Press, 1974.

Cameron, Kenneth Neill, Donald E. Reiman, and Doucet Devin Fischer, eds. *Shelley and His Circle, 1773–1822.* 10 vols. to date. Cambridge, Mass.: Harvard University Press, 1961–2002.

Dowden, Edward. *The Life of Percy Bysshe Shelley.* London: Kegan Paul, Trench & Co., 1886.

Dunbar, Clement. *A Bibliography of Shelley Studies: 1823–1950.* New York: Garland, 1976.

Ferber, Michael. *The Poetry of Shelley.* London: Viking Press, 1994.

Fraistat, Neil. "Illegitimate Shelley: Radical Piracy and the Textual Edition as Cultural Performance." *PMLA* 109 (1994): 409–423.

Gisborne, Maria, and Edward E. Williams. *Maria Gisborne & Edward E. Williams, Shelley's Friends: Their Journals and Letters.* Edited by Frederick L. Jones. Norman: University of Oklahoma Press, 1951.

Hasan, Seemin. "The Mythic Mode in Shelley's Lyrics of 1820." *Aligarh Journal of English Studies* 16 (1994), 125–32.

Holmes, Richard. *Shelley: The Pursuit.* London: Weidenfeld & Nicolson, 1974.

Ingpen, Roger. *Shelley in England: New Facts and Letters from the Shelley-Whitton Papers.* 2 vols. Boston: Houghton Mifflin, 1917.

Murray, E. B. "Shelley's Contribution to Mary's *Frankenstein.*" *Keats-Shelley Memorial Bulletin* 29 (1978): 50–68.

Nair, Sharada. "Poetic Constitutions of History: The Case of Shelley." *Textual Practice* 8 (1994): 10–14.

O'Neill, Michael. *The Bodleian Shelley Manuscripts: A Facsimile Edition with Full Transcriptions and Scholarly Apparatus.* New York: Garland, 1994.

———. "'Trying to Make it as good as I can': Mary Shelley's editing of P. B. Shelley's Poetry and Prose." In *Mary Shelley in Her Times,* edited by Betty T. Bennet and Stuart Curran, 185–197. Baltimore: Johns Hopkins University Press, 2000.

Porter, Peter. *Percy Bysshe Shelley.* New York: Crown Press Group, 1994.

Purinton, Marjean D. *Romantic Ideology Unmasked: The Mentally Constructed Tyrannies in Dramas of William Wordsworth, Lord Byron, Percy Shelley, and Joanna Baillie.* Newark: University of Delaware Press, 1994.

Quinn, Mary A. Review of *The Prose Works of Percy Bysshe Shelley, Volume I* by E. B. Murray. *Wordsworth Circle* 25 (1994): 253–256.

Raisada, Harish. "Shelley's Radical Humanism." *Aligarh Journal of English Studies* 16 (1994): 64–87.

Shelley, Bryan. *Shelley and Scripture: The Interpreting Angel.* Oxford, U.K.: Clarendon Press, 1994.

"The Shelley Chronology." *Romantic Circles: Scholarly Resources.* Available online. URL: http://www.rc.umd.edu/reference/chronologies/shelcron/. Accessed June 20, 2009.

Shelley, Mary. *Selected Letters of Mary Wollstonecraft Shelley.* Edited by Betty T. Bennett. Baltimore: Johns Hopkins University Press, 1995.

Shelley, Percy Bysshe. *The Complete Works of Percy Bysshe Shelley.* 10 vols. Edited by Roger Ingpen and Walter E. Peck. London: E. Benn, 1926–30.

———. *The Defence of Poetry Fair Copies: A Facsimile of Bodleian Manuscripts. Shelley e.6 and adds.d.8.* Vol. 20 of the Bodleian Shelley Manuscripts. Edited by Michael O'Neill. New York: Garland, 1994.

———. *Drafts for Laon & Cythna, Cantos V–XII: Bodleian Manuscripts Shelley adds.e.10.* Vol. 17 of the The Bodleian Shelley Manuscripts. Edited by Stephen E. Jones. New York: Garland, 1994.

———. *The Hellas Notebook: Bodleian Manuscript Shelley adds. e.7.* Vol. 17 of the Bodleian Shelley

Manuscripts. Edited by Donald H. Reiman and Michael Neth. New York: Garland, 1994.

———. *The Major Works.* Edited by Zachary Leader, and Michael O'Neill. New York: Oxford University Press, 2009.

———. *Percy Bysshe Shelley: Selected Poems.* London: Bloomsbury Classics, 1994.

———. *Percy Bysshe Shelley: Selected Poems.* New York: Gramercy Books, 1994.

———. *Shelley's 1819–1821 Huntington Notebook.* Edited by Mary A. Quinn. Vol. 6 of Manuscripts of the Younger Romantics & the Bodleian Shelley Manuscripts. New York: Garland, 1994.

———. *Treasury of Percy Bysshe Shelley.* Read by Robert Eddison and Robert Speaight. Audiocassette. Musical Heritage Society, 1994.

Sunstein, Emily W. *Mary Shelley: Romance and Reality.* Baltimore: Johns Hopkins University Press, 1991.

Weinberg, Alan M. *Shelley's Italian Experience.* New York: Palgrave McMillan, 1993.

Weisman, Karen A. *Imageless Truths: Shelley's Poetic Fiction.* Philadelphia: University of Pennsylvania Press, 1994.

Trelawny, Edward John (1792–1881) Edward John Trelawny was born in London on November 13, 1792, his father a poor Guards officer and his mother a dark-skinned, possibly Arab, heiress described as having a masculine appearance. Trelawny hated his father, which he demonstrated as a child by killing his father's pet raven in a "duel." He joined the Royal Navy and retired at age 20 to become a self-described adventurer. Married to a wealthy woman by 23, he had multiple affairs. He met PERCY BYSSHE SHELLEY and Mary Shelley in Pisa in 1822 through their mutual friend, Edward Williams. Trelawny became infatuated with the Shelleys and GEORGE GORDON BYRON, Lord Byron, and would maintain contact with Mary during her entire life.

Mary Shelley spent her life in and out of love with Trelawny. Upon first meeting him, she described him in her diaries as a "half Arab Englishman . . . clever . . . but with the possibility of evil." Trelawny attempted unsuccessfully to romance Mary with Percy's approval, taking advantage of the Shelleys' open relationship. A large,

Portrait of Edward John Trelawny, friend of the Shelleys. Trelawny helped finance Mary Shelley's trip back to London after Percy Shelley's death. *(Painting by W. E. West)*

strong man with a booming voice and a piercing, commanding gaze, Trelawny would retain a stunning presence throughout his life, an appearance that contrasted with his mediocre social and intellectual talents. Mary wrote to her friend Maria Gisborne about Trelawny that "for his moral qualities I am yet in the dark he [sic] is a strange web which I am endeavouring to unravel."

While he enjoyed the income due to a younger son from an aristocratic family, Trelawny resented the fact that his older brother received more money. He seemed to have no particular goal other than attaching himself to the famous and daring, such as members of the Shelley circle. Byron possessed the "bad boy" reputation Trelawny wanted for himself, while Mary's "pedigree of genius" proved desirable, and Trelawny coveted Percy Shelley's learned manner and ethereal nature.

Trelawny took pride in telling his friends that he divorced his wife after a few years, accusing her of adultery. He also felt no regret at having left his two daughters in England, wandering about on his income and leaving bastards behind in each port he visited. According to Emily Sunstein, Byron observed that Trelawny was a solid example of "life following art, specifically Byron's Giaour, Corsair, and Lara." For all his faults, Trelawny gained the group's admiration. They considered him courageous, loyal, and a talented teller of tales. His belief in rumors of Mary's reputation for heightened sexual activity prompted him to offer himself to her, but he graciously accepted her refusal. She appreciated him in part for his lack of fixation on the feminine ideal and for his appreciation of her lack of meekness and humility, a part of that ideal. Mary would later write to Trelawny that when they first met, she felt "full of spirits & life" and mused that he must have thought her "a little wild."

Some sources credit Trelawny with indirectly causing the deaths of both Percy Shelley and Lord Byron. As the only person in the Pisa group with any naval experience, he was the obvious person to consult in the designing of Shelley's boat. The design apparently had flaws, a fear about which Mary wrote in her diary. When Percy Shelley and his friend Edward Williams were caught in a storm, the boat capsized, and the men drowned. Several days later, Trelawny found Percy Shelley's body on the beach, ravaged by fish. Supposedly, the fully clothed corpse still had a pocket of poems by Keats in the trouser pocket. Shelley's body had to be cremated due to Italian cholera regulations, and Trelawny famously snatched the poet's heart from the flames. Some accounts testify that he preserved the heart and bits of Shelley's bones in wine. In truth, Mary kept the heart, which would eventually be buried in a silver urn with her son Percy Florence Shelley in 1889.

With an unquenchable thirst for adventure, Trelawny accompanied Byron to Greece and enthusiastically engaged in the revolutionary fighting; however, reports of his success were mixed. He survived an attempted assassination that left a bullet lodged in his back, lived in a cave for a time, and married a 13-year-old girl. His experiences in Greece probably best defined him as an adventurer, although he would later exaggerate their importance.

Trelawny may have misadvised the doctors treating Byron in such a way as to speed his death from illness. Whether he did play such an unfortunate part in the deaths of the two men he reportedly most admired, he remained staunchly loyal to Mary for years after her husband's and Byron's deaths. Prior to their occasional reunions, she often remarked on looking forward to seeing him.

Not long after Percy's death, Trelawny defended Mary more than once against unfair and false accusations. For instance, he sternly corrected the author and critic Leigh Hunt, Percy Shelley's friend, for verbally attacking Mary. To Mary's embarrassment, she learned that Percy had shared with Hunt his belief that his wife had treated him coldly during their final weeks together. According to the critic Emily Sunstein, Hunt had peevishly written to Mary that she should have felt remorse over such neglect of Percy. He also accused her of being "willful, impatient, bad-tempered, imperious, critical and cold-hearted." Trelawny stepped in to tell Hunt that none of them should judge Mary, who, according to Percy, had suffered from problems unknown to anyone else except for him. That statement, along with Mary's passionate admission to suffering months of agony over thoughts that she might have not been as supportive of Percy as she should have been during their final weeks together, caused Hunt to apologize to her.

Despite his displaying such loyalty and devotion, Trelawny could also become surly. In anticipation of seeing him again in November 1829, Mary so praised him to friends that they believed the two would marry. But when Trelawny arrived in England for their reunion, he treated Mary unkindly, as he did others who served as the only remaining links to his time spent in Greece. He had enjoyed little public attention since that time, which represented the pinnacle of his career as an adventurer. To compensate for the lack of fame, he had begun to exaggerate his close relationship with Byron. Accused of lying by others who better knew the facts, he blustered all the more and seemed to convince himself that he was telling the truth.

When Trelawny learned Mary was acting as a consultant for the author and critic Thomas Moore as he wrote a biography of Byron, Trelawny insisted on contributing a completely inappropriate anecdote about Byron's sodomy with a Greek boy. He also expressed disappointment that Mary no longer lived up to his hyperbolic expectations. He anticipated finding her as in earlier days, railing against her father-in-law's, Sir Timothy Shelley's, stinginess and against the accusations of indecency brought by society against her. Instead, he found her accepting her lot in life, although still campaigning for its improvement. He became especially angry when Mary told him she was not going to write a biography of Percy Shelley. Upon learning that she feared the loss of income needed for support from Percy's father, Sir Timothy, who had forbidden her to write of his son, Trelawny dismissed her concerns. In his view, Mary's capitulation was an example of conforming to convention, something the Shelley group would never have done as a matter of principle.

Trelawny next attempted to rejuvenate his social reputation by entering London's high society. He quickly discovered that his insulting behavior and loutish comments were unwelcome. After dismally failing to gain the admiration of London's social scene, Trelawny continued to argue with Mary. When she attempted to explain that she no longer wanted to live for the past but preferred to look forward, he accused her of worldliness. Although she tried to help him understand her position, Trelawny ignored her explanation and departed for Florence without telling Mary goodbye. As Sunstein explains, his actions confirmed Mary's feeling that her former life, which he represented, had concluded.

Trelawny next became a self-proclaimed expert about Percy Shelley's life and writings, although they had known each other for only six months. He announced from Florence that he intended to write a biography of Shelley because Mary would not do so, insisting that she send him certain materials to support his efforts. Mary refused to cooperate, explaining that she would eventually write of her husband's life, but that she would not publish such a work during her or her son's lifetime. She continued to fear retribution from a society that still had not forgiven the romantic circle for their sexual indiscretions and outrageous lifestyles.

Trelawny was incensed that Mary would support Edward Moore's authorship of a Byron biography while refusing to help him in writing a biography of Shelley. He threatened to tell Sir Timothy of her assistance of Moore, knowing that the old man would cut off her allowance because details about Percy Shelley were certain to appear in any work about Lord Byron. Mary begged Trelawny to have mercy on her and not take advantage of her situation. She finally agreed to help Trelawny only if he would cut her out of the story. Trelawny continued to try to make his own tarnished star shine more brightly by claiming false ties to Shelley and Byron, fashioning himself a "rugged individualist," according to Sunstein. From that time on, he never hesitated to write negatively about Mary if so doing would somehow advance his own interests.

Trelawny wrote of his youth in *Adventures of a Younger Son,* ending the account at 1812. When Percy Florence Shelley and his wife considered who should write their "authorized" biography of Percy Bysshe Shelley six years after following Mary's death, they invited several writers who they believed had known the couple well to a discussion, including Trelawny. He refused to attend the meeting and issued his own account, *Recollections of the Last Days of Byron and Shelley* (1858), in which he fashioned Mary as gifted, attractive, and a devoted mate to an eccentric husband. However, in 1878, after being reduced to a reclusive, bitter man, he published an appalling account of Mary in *Records of Shelley, Byron, and the Author.* Because everyone else who might have been considered an authority on the Shelleys and Byron had died, Trelawny was viewed as an authority, and he severely harmed Mary's reputation in his book. Unfortunately, biographers who followed Trelawny often referred to his writings, until more reputable sources became available.

Richard Edmonds reviewed David Crane's 1998 biography of Trelawny, entitled *Lord Byron's Jackal—A Life of Edward John Trelawny* for the *Birmingham Post* in England. Edmonds described Trelawny as follows:

> A master of self promotion and an accomplished liar, Trelawny left a trail of spurious "facts" which the author has been at pains to pry loose

in order to get at the real facts. For example, Trelawny claimed friendship with Keats, whom he never met. He called himself one thing but the parish register gives another. He railed at poverty although being possessed of a very nice private income, and boasted to anyone who cared to listen of having been a pirate, when he was actually no more than a failed midshipman trailing a musket ball in his knee and a tacky divorce picked up somewhere along the line.

Trelawney died on August 13, 1881, age 89, in Sussex, England. At his request, he was buried in Rome next to Percy Bysshe Shelley.

FURTHER READING

Crane, David. *Lord Byron's Jackal—A Life of Edward John Trelawny.* New York: Harper Collins, 1998.

Edmonds, Richard. "Trelawney: the lay of the jackal; *Lord Byron's Jackal—A Life of Edward John Trelawny.*" *Birmingham Post*, 25 July 1998. Available online. URL: http://bit.lyhiOM39E.60774111.html. Accessed June 27, 2010.

Gerson, Noel. *A Biography of Edward John Trelawny.* New York: Doubleday, 1977.

St. Clair, William. *Trelawny: The Incurable Romancer.* New York: Vanguard, 1977.

Sunstein, Emily W. *Mary Shelley: Romance and Reality.* Boston: Little, Brown and Company, 1989.

Wollstonecraft, Mary (1759–1797) Mary Wollstonecraft has inspired many biographical accounts of her life and much criticism based on her writings. She is without dispute one of the most important, and perhaps the most important, English contributor to what would later be known as the feminist movement. Her seminal work, *A Vindication of the Rights of Woman* (1790), set in motion a movement supporting civil rights for women and, by extension, for all marginalized people. That she should also be mother to Mary Shelley and, even in death, exert an inestimable effect on Shelley's writing makes her an astounding woman indeed. Readers are urged to investigate criticism of Wollstonecraft's works to augment their understanding of the ideas and ideals that both inspired and at times inhibited Mary Shelley's creative output.

Mary Wollstonecraft was born on April 27, 1759, the second of five children born to Edward John Wollstonecraft, a brutal alcoholic, and his abused wife. Her grandfather had made a solid living as a weaver and left a fortune to his son, but Edward Wollstonecraft lost it through various poor investments. He moved the family from London around the country and back to London again. Mary supposedly slept on the landing outside her mother's room in an attempt to protect her from attacks by her father. She found approval and affection outside the family in a series of friendships with various girls, most famously Fanny Blood. She left home at 19 to work as a companion to a widow who lived in Bath, later opening a school that ultimately failed. Wollstonecraft next attempted to support herself as a governess for the children of Lord Kingsborough in Ireland. She taught herself languages and was able to enjoy some schooling at Newington Green, where she was inspired by the liberal views of one of her teachers, also a writer, Richard Price.

When Mary was 23, her mother died, and Mary joined the Blood family, sewing with Fanny and her mother to earn a living. Fanny helped her rescue Mary's younger sister Eliza from an abusive husband when Eliza had a mental breakdown. The baby that Eliza Wollstonecraft Bishop left behind died within the year, and Eliza had few choices for her future, as divorce was not acceptable. Still, Wollstonecraft displayed a sense of social justice in her attempt to help her friend that would guide all of her life's actions. When, in 1785, Fanny became pregnant while living in Lisbon, Mary left England to be with her during the baby's birth. After Fanny's death, Mary mourned her for the remainder of her life and continued to send money to the Blood family.

After her return to London, Wollstonecraft began her writing career with *Thoughts on the Education of Daughters* (1787). She caught the eye of a publisher named Joseph Johnson, who was interested in the political unrest in France and America. Wollstonecraft began to publish essays in Johnson's magazine, *Analytic Review*, that focused on the French and American revolutionary movements while also acting as a translator and political adviser for Johnson. Her publications moved her into a circle of intellectuals and activists.

Wollstonecraft published her first novel, *Mary, a Fiction*, in 1788, followed by a children's book, *Original Stories from Real Life* (1788), and an anthology, *The Female Reader* (1789). In reaction to Edmund Burke's conservative *Reflections on the Revolution in France* (1790), Wollstonecraft published *A Vindication of the Rights of Men* (1790), rebutting Burke's attack against the ideals that supported the French Revolution. Her analysis of class structure leading to exploitation of the working class and the possession of a disproportionate amount of wealth by the upper class made her a celebrity. One of her arguments supporting the French statesman Talleyrand was that women should be allowed to benefit from social reform because they would strengthen the movement for equality.

Wollstonecraft enjoyed and flourished intellectually in the company of Johnson; the poet William Blake; the revolutionary theorist Thomas Paine; and the artist Henry Fuseli, with whom she became romantically involved. Johnson's circle included the philosopher and novelist WILLIAM GODWIN, who had also written in response to Burke. While he and Wollstonecraft knew one another, they did not form a relationship at that time. Wollstonecraft supported herself by writing and clarified relationships between ROMANTICISM, feminism, and radicalism that would have an impact on her culture and on her daughter, Mary Shelley.

After publishing *A Vindication of the Rights of Woman* to acclaim in 1792, Wollstonecraft left England in part to separate from Fuseli, a man already in a traditional marriage that had no room for Wollstonecraft. She wanted to see the French Revolution for herself and lived in Paris, where she met the 41-year-old American adventurer and veteran of the American Revolution, Gilbert Imlay. She fell passionately in love with him and had a daughter named Fanny in 1794. In Paris, she became a member of a group of exiles that included Thomas Paine, who wanted, according to the biographer William St. Clair, "to witness and report the birth of the new order." The same year that Fanny was born, Wollstonecraft published *A Historical and Moral View of the Origins and Progress of the French Revolution*.

Although Imlay, who identified himself as a captain, officially recorded Wollstonecraft as his wife, she refused to marry him, believing that civil institutions such as marriage robbed individuals of their independence. In reality a European agent of the Scioto Land Company of Ohio, Imlay became involved in various schemes about which Wollstonecraft remained ignorant, and during the Reign of Terror, he deserted her, leaving her to care for Fanny on her own. Wollstonecraft saw many of her expatriate friends go to the guillotine and to prison, including Paine and Helen Maria Williams, another writer whose letters were published in William Godwin's *New Annual Register* accounts.

After hiding for a time in Paris, Wollstonecraft left to seek out Imlay, all the while having written a series of letters to him, pleading for the renewal of their relationship. He traveled around Europe and made little effort to spend time with Mary and Fanny. She decided to take the baby and travel with a servant to Scandinavia to assist him in business matters. When they relocated to London, Imlay would hardly speak with Wollstonecraft. She had been deeply hurt by not only his rejection but that of former acquaintances who did not want to associate with an unwed mother. Depressed and despondent, she wrote a note instructing her friend Mary Hays to care for Fanny. Then she walked into the rain until her clothes became heavy enough to cause her to sink under water and attempted suicide by leaping from Putney Bridge into the Thames. Boatmen rescued her.

In 1796, Wollstonecraft again met William Godwin, and an immediate attraction formed between the two. The writer Mary Hays had urged Godwin to see Wollstonecraft again and had scheduled a visit by him to her house, where Mary would be present. He saw her again at a dinner party a few days later, but a month passed before he paid her a social call. Unfortunately, as his journal notes, he found her "nah," or "not at home." According to St. Clair, he noted she was no longer "the strident feminist radical who had hogged the conversation at Godwin's meeting with Tom Paine on 13 November 1791 when they had first met."

Upon her return from the country, where she had hoped to rest and regain her health,

Wollstonecraft met Imlay in London. During that final meeting with her former lover, she controlled her emotions. Discovering that she had missed a call from Godwin, she brazenly made an unchaperoned visit to him on April 14. He visited her the following day, and they were soon seeing each other on a regular basis. Based on her experiences in Scandinavia, she wrote the book *Letters Written during a Short Residence in Sweden, Norway, and Denmark*, and Godwin was the first to read it before it was published in 1795.

By 1796, Godwin had recognized that he loved Wollstonecraft. She came to depend on his mental and emotional strength and selected a permanent apartment close to him. Despite their obvious recognition of their importance in one another's lives, Godwin was at a loss as to how he might express his passion or return hers. When Wollstonecraft wanted to become intimate, Godwin rejected her, hurting her feelings. She sent him a letter stating that she intended to make a life on her own, which prompted a quick response from Godwin. He wrote in part, that for the previous 36 hours, "I longed inexpressibly to have you in my arms. Why did not I come to you? I am a fool. I feared still that I might be deceiving myself as to your feelings. . . . Send me word that I may call on you in a day or two. Do you not see, while I exhort you to be a philosopher, how painfully acute are my own feelings?" For a time, the two found letters the best way to communicate. As Godwin became more comfortable with the situation, their relationship became permanent.

Like Wollstonecraft, Godwin opposed the oppression of marriage, but when she became pregnant, they knew they needed to formalize their relationship. Marriage would allow their child certain civil rights for which she would not be eligible if born out of wedlock. As St. Clair states, when they decided "to submit to the icy chains of custom, they underestimated their complexity." If she married Godwin, Wollstonecraft could no longer pretend that she and Imlay had been married, making Fanny openly illegitimate. While Wollstonecraft's relationships with other men did not disturb the liberal Godwin, society judged her harshly. The couple lost more friends who valued traditional relationships above a couple who transgressed against society's mores.

After marriage, Godwin began to revise his view of the bonds that he had previously judged oppressive. Wollstonecraft so affected him that he made substantive changes in the second edition of his famous *An Inquiry Concerning the Principles of Political Justice and its Influence in General Virtue and Happiness* (1793). In the first edition, he had made clear that women should be valued less than men by presenting the reader with a riddle: In a fire, whom would you rescue—the revered French theologian and writer François Fénelon or a chambermaid, even if she were your mother? Originally, he had written that no one should select their mother, whose low value to society as a woman was further reduced by her station as a servant. In the second edition, he changed the chambermaid to a valet to remove the automatic assumption that a woman proved of less value than a man. Wollstonecraft earned his complete love and devotion.

Portrait of Mary Wollstonecraft, mother of Mary Shelley *(Painting by John Opie)*

On August 25, 1797, Wollstonecraft went into labor, and a midwife attended the delivery of a baby girl. Godwin was delighted with his first child, but three hours later, the midwife warned him that his wife was still in danger, a result, as it turned out, of the midwife's failure to remove the placenta. St. Clair writes that Godwin later experienced intense guilt over not having insisted on a physician to attend Mary Wollstonecraft Shelley's birth. He called in a physician, who removed the placenta in pieces with unwashed hands, as was common for the era. The physician thus introduced the infection that killed Wollstonecraft 10 days later. He also forced Wollstonecraft to drink as much wine as possible and treated her with quinine. She received the best treatment available, but no cure for infection existed.

Some religious writers later claimed Wollstonecraft's death was "appropriate" based on her challenge to "the ordained place of women in society." St. Clair writes that Godwin made entries in his journal as he spoke with his wife in her last days: "Idea of death: solemn conversation" and "Talk to her of Fanny and Mary." On September 10, 1797, he simply recorded the time of her death, "20 minutes before 8." She was buried in St. Pancras Churchyard under the name Mary Wollstonecraft Godwin.

Godwin struggled to adjust to the loss that left him consumed by grief. He had not discovered serious passion until age 40, and a mere 13 months later, his wife was gone. In an attempt to celebrate his wife's work and passion for gender equity, he prepared two manuscripts for publication: *Posthumous Works of the Author of a Vindication of the Rights of Woman* and *Memoirs of the Author of a Vindication of the Rights of Woman*. He included all of Wollstonecraft's writings, along with her letters to Gilbert Imlay, information regarding her attempted suicides, her love affairs, and her apparent lack of religious faith.

Public moral judgment against Wollstonecraft's personal life was immediate and harsh, the quality and social value of her writing basically ignored. Where Godwin had sought to celebrate his wife's intellectual achievements, his actions resulted in her public vilification and the rejection of her works for some time. In 1798, the Reverend Richard Polwhele referred to Wollstonecraft and others who were "unnatural" due to their expression of opinions in his "The Unsex'd Females: A Poem." Horace Walpole labeled her a "hyena in petticoats" when responding to Wollstonecraft's perceived attack on Marie Antoinette in her *A Vindication of the Rights of Men*, but most of all due to her republican politics. The public's continued focus on Wollstonecraft's sexual activity and rejection of religion undermined her support of women's rights and Godwin's purpose in publishing her body of work. Decades would pass before her work would again be seen as a serious treatise and a crucial feminist work. As the scholar Anne K. Mellor explains, Godwin's sensational revelations made the work anathema to women who wanted to be taken seriously for their views. By the next century, however, Wollstonecraft's *Vindication* would be praised by female intellectuals, and in the 20th century, she was wholeheartedly embraced, at first by feminist scholars, and later by all scholars.

Wollstonecraft's effect remained strong in the Godwin household. Her portrait hung in the library, where Mary read everything that her mother had written or about her, including the negative public reaction to her mother's life. The image of her reading while sitting on her mother's grave remains popular with most Shelley aficionados, and Wollstonecraft's grave is also said to have been the location where the teenage Mary Godwin's relationship with PERCY BYSSHE SHELLEY was nurtured. When William Godwin felt unequal to the task of raising two daughters on his own and remarried, Mary nursed her feelings of perceived rejection by her father by trying to grow close to a mother she could never know on a personal level. The way she accomplished that was by familiarizing herself with her mother's voice in the only way she would ever hear it—through her printed words.

Mellor believes that much of Mary Shelley's fiction seeks to redeem her mother's reputation by softening its scholarly aspects and emphasizing her motherly tendencies. According to Mellor, she accomplished that redemption through depictions of children devoted to their parents, mimicking her own devotion. In reality, Shelley may have suffered a lifelong insatiable desire for the unconditional love for which mothers are commonly celebrated, having never been able to enjoy that love. For most of her life, Shelley celebrated an idealistic vision of family first formulated in her mother's *A Vindication of the Rights of Woman*, in which Wollstonecraft described an educated woman as an equal companion to her husband. However, Shelley would use her mother's influence in a subversive manner, celebrating Wollstonecraft's vision of the egalitarian family relationship while demonstrating that it did not and could not exist.

Mary wrote to Frances Wright on September 12, 1827, regarding the influence of Wollstonecraft: "The memory of my Mother has been always been the pride & delight of my life; & the admiration of others for her, has been the cause of most of the happiness [of my life]. Her greatness of soul & my father [sic] high talents have perpetually reminded me that I ought to degenerate as little as I could from those from whom I derived my being." Mellor theorizes that in *Frankenstein* (1818), Shelley attempted to demonstrate the results of the focus on her mother's revolutionary ideology—man's power over woman and the disastrous results of such hierarchical relationships. Victor Frankenstein would confine man to the public sphere, woman to the private. When Shelley constructed the DeLacey family, she had in mind Wollstonecraft's ideal of the family, a contrast to that of Frankenstein's patriarchal family unit.

Shelley stated that she lacked her parents' revolutionary fervor. However, Julie Carlson theorizes that Mary Wollstonecraft Shelley engaged in revolution through her fiction by continuing her parents' efforts to "rewrite the sentiments and literary conventions associated with family life," not through her outward promotion of social causes. Her revolution was staged through "literary reform." Shelley undoubtedly learned from her mother's engagement with her environment, an engagement that leads Tillottama Rajan to claim that Wollstonecraft "lived fiction and ideas as life, while rethinking life through fiction."

Those who study Wollstonecraft's biography and her writings are struck by the contrast between her ideals and principles and the tragic reality of her life. Despite the temptation to make her life more important than her work, a temptation they also face with Mary Shelley, scholars agree that Wollstonecraft's contribution to women's independence remains vital. Carlson writes that Wollstonecraft "altered women's position within family by vindicating the rights of women within and outside of marriage." In addition, and equally importantly for her daughter, she asserted "women's right to write about women." Both of her actions "associated women with rationality, public service, and inquiring minds."

FURTHER READING

Bahar, Saba. *Mary Wollstonecraft's Social and Aesthetic Philosophy: An Eve to Please Me*. Basingstoke, U.K.: Palgrave Macmillan, 2002.

Carlson, Julie A. *England's First Family of Writers: Mary Wollstonecraft, William Godwin, Mary Shelley*. Baltimore: Johns Hopkins University Press, 2007.

Clemit, Pamela. "*Frankenstein, Matilda,* and the Legacies of Godwin and Wollstonecraft." In *The Cambridge Companion to Mary Shelley*, edited by Esther Schor, 26–44. Cambridge: Cambridge University Press, 2004.

Kelly, Gary. "Politicizing the Personal: Mary Wollstonecraft, Mary Shelley, and the Coterie Novel." In *Mary Shelley in Her Times*, edited by Betty T. Bennet and Stuart Curran, 147–159. Baltimore: Johns Hopkins University Press, 2000.

Mulvey-Roberts, Marie. "The Corpse in the Corpus: *Frankenstein*, Rewriting Wollstonecraft and the Abject." In *Mary Shelley's Fictions: From Frankenstein to Falkner*, edited by Michael Eberle-Sinatra, 197–210. New York: St. Martin's Press, 2000.

Polwhele, Richard. *The Unsex'd Females: A Poem*. London: Cadell & Davies, 1798.

Rajan, Tilottama. "Framing the Corpus: Godwin's 'Editing' of Wollstonecraft in 1798." *Studies in Romanticism* 39, no. 4 (Winter 2000): 511–531.

Sapiro, Virginia. *A Vindication of Political Virtue: The Political Theory of Mary Wollstonecraft*. Chicago: University of Chicago Press, 1992.

Shelley, Mary. *Selected Letters of Mary Wollstonecraft Shelley*. Edited by Betty T. Bennett. Baltimore: Johns Hopkins University Press, 1995.

St. Clair, William. *The Godwins and the Shelleys: A Biography of a Family.* Baltimore: Johns Hopkins University Press, 1989.

Todd, Janet. Introduction to *Mary, Maria and Matilda*, edited by Janet Todd, vii–xxviii. New York: New York University Press, 1992.

Tomalin, Claire. *The Life and Death of Mary Wollstonecraft.* Rev. ed. London: Penguin, 1992.

Walpole, Horace. *Letters of Horace Walpole.* Vol. 15. Edited by Mrs. Paget Tonybee. Oxford: Oxford University Press, 1905.

Wolfson, Susan J. Review of *Romantic Corresponding; Women, Politics, and the Fiction of Letters. Tulsa Studies in Women's Literature.* 13 (1994): 387–407.

Wollstonecraft, Mary. *Letters to Imlay with Prefatory Memoir by C. Kegan Paul.* 1798. Reprint, New York: Haskell House, 1971.

———. *Letters Written during a Short Residence in Sweden, Norway, and Denmark.* Edited by Carol H. Poston. Lincoln: University of Nebraska Press, 1976.

———. *Maria, or The Wrongs of Woman.* New York: Norton, 1994.

———. *Mary, A Fiction.* Edited by Gary Kelly. London: Oxford University Press, 1976.

———. *A Vindication of the Rights of Men.* Delmar, N.Y.: Scholars' Facsimiles & Reprints, 1975.

———. *A Vindication of the Rights of Woman.* 2nd ed. Edited by Carol H. Poston. New York: Norton, 1988.

Part IV

Appendixes

MARY SHELLEY CHRONOLOGY

1756
March 3: William Godwin is born.

1759
April 27: Mary Wollstonecraft is born.

1768
Mary Jane Vial (Clairmont) is born.

1792
August 4: Percy Bysshe Shelley is born.

1794
May 14: Fanny Imlay (later to became Fanny Godwin) is born.

1795
June 4: Charles Gaulis Clairmont is born.

1797
March 29: Godwin and Wollstonecraft marry, Old St. Pancras Church, London; Fanny joins the family.
April 6: Godwins rent apartment at 29 The Polygon; Godwin lives at 17 Evesham Building, Chalton Street.
August 30: Mary Wollstonecraft Godwin is born; Godwin's journal entry: "Birth of Mary, 20 minutes after 11 at night."
September 10: Mary Wollstonecraft dies of puerperal fever; Godwin's journal entry: "20 minutes before 8."
September 15: Mary Wollstonecraft is buried, Old St. Pancras Church graveyard.

1798
April 27: Clara Mary Jane (Claire) Clairmont is born.

1801
May 5: Godwin and Mary Jane Clairmont meet.
December 21: Godwin and Clairmont wed; her children, Charles and Clara Mary Jane (later called "Claire"), join the Godwin family.

1803
March 28: William Godwin is born.

1805
The Godwins found children's publishing house, M. J. Godwin & Co.

1807
November 13: The Godwins relocate their residence and business to 41 Skinner Street.

1808
January: Mary publishes her first story as draft in "Mounseer Nongtongpaw, or the Discoveries of John Bull on a Trip to Paris" (reworking of Charles Dibdin's popular song).

1811
May 17–December 19: Mary Godwin takes "ocean cure" at Ramsgate for arm.

1812
June 7: Mary Godwin travels to Dundee to live with Godwin's friend William Baxter, forms friendship with Christina, Isabel, Christy Baxter.

November 10: Mary returns to London with Christy Baxter.
November 11: Mary meets Percy Bysshe Shelley and his wife, Harriet Shelley, at Skinner Street.

1813
June 3: Mary Godwin and Christy Baxter return to Dundee.
June 23: Percy and Harriet Shelley's daughter, Eliza Ianthe is born.

1814
March 30: Mary returns to London from Scotland.
May 13: Mary again meets Percy Shelley.
June: Shelley realizes "the full extent of the calamity" of his marriage.
July 28: Mary and Percy Shelley elope to the Continent with her stepsister Claire.
July–August: Mary, Percy, and Claire travel through Europe—the source of Mary's *History of a Six Week's Tour*; study horror literature.
September 13: Mary, Percy, and Claire return to London; Godwin refuses to see them.
October: Isabel Baxter Booth will not see Mary, possibly due to husband.
October–November: Percy Shelley evades creditors.
November 14: Percy introduces Thomas Jefferson Hogg to Mary.
November 30: Percy and Harriet Shelley's son Charles Shelley is born.

1815
January 5: Percy Shelley's grandfather, Sir Bysshe Shelley, dies.
February 22: Percy Shelley and Mary Godwin's first daughter is born prematurely.
March 6: Percy and Mary's first daughter dies; Mary dreams her baby is brought back to life when warmed by fire.
April: Percy's father Sir Timothy brings suit for control of his father's estate.
May 13: Percy provisionally to receive £1,000 per annum; he bestows 200 pounds per annum on Harriet Shelley.
June: Mary and Percy travel along the southern coast of England and Devon.
August: Mary and Percy live at Bishopsgate.

1816
January 24: William Shelley, son of Percy Bysshe Shelley and Mary Godwin is born.
April: Claire Claremont and Byron are lovers; Mary meets Byron.
May 3: Mary, Percy, son William, and Claire Clairmont travel to Switzerland; Claire is pregnant.
May 17: Travel party settles close to Byron's home, Villa Diodati, in Switzerland.
ca. June 16: Mary begins writing *Frankenstein*; Shelley travels around the lake with Byron.
July 21: Mary, Percy, and Claire move to Chamonix.
July 24: Mary's journal refers to "her story," *Frankenstein*, for the first time.
September 8: Mary, Percy, William Shelley, and Claire return to England, go to live at Bath.
October 9: Fanny (Imlay) Godwin, depressed, commits suicide.
ca. December 10: Harriet Shelley commits suicide; her body is discovered in the Serpentine River.
December 15: Mary Godwin and Percy Shelley learn of Harriet's death.
December 30: Mary Godwin and Percy Shelley marry at St. Mildred's, Bread Street, London; William Godwin agrees to see Mary again; the Shelleys live with the Godwins and Hunts for one month.

1817
January 12: Claire Clairmont and Byron's daughter, Allegra, born; the birth remains secret.
January: The Shelleys relocate to London.
March: The Shelleys relocate to Albion House, Marlow.
Mary writes to Leigh Hunt, "Our house is very political as well as poetical and I hope you will acquire a fresh spirit for both when you come here."
January–July 1818: Shelley sues for custody of his children.
April–December: Mary finishes *Frankenstein*, begins *History of a Six Weeks' Tour*.
May: Percy Shelley writes *Laon and Cythna*.
September 2: Mary and Percy's daughter Clara Everina Shelley is born.
December–January 1818: Mary publishes *History of a Six Weeks' Tour* (anonymously); Percy publishes *The Revolt of Islam*.

1818

January 1: *Frankenstein* is published anonymously in three volumes; Percy's publisher, Charles Ollier, and Byron's publisher, John Murray, refuse to publish it.

January–February: The Shelleys and Claire move to London.

March 11: The Shelleys, Claire, and Allegra travel to Italy.

April 4: The group arrives in Milan.

May: The group travels to Pisa and Leghorn.

June 11: The group moves to Casa Bertinin, Bagni di Lucca.

June 14: Mary writes to Sir Walter Scott to thank him for his positive review of *Frankenstein*, which was credited to Percy Shelley: "I am anxious to prevent your continuing in the mistake of supposing Mr. Shelley guilty of a juvenile attempt of mine."

August 17: Percy and Claire travel to Venice and Este.

September 5: Mary and children join Percy and Claire at Este; Percy begins *Prometheus Unbound*.

September 24: Clara Shelley dies of dysentery in Venice.

September–October: The Shelleys visit Byron's villa in Este.

October 29: Allegra travels to Venice to live with Byron; Claire can visit only in company of the Shelleys.

November 5: The Shelleys and Claire go to Rome until November, then depart for Naples; Mary writes to her friend Maria Gisborne of Clara's illness "and the dreadful state of weakness that succeeded to it—In this state she began to cut all her teeth at once—pined a few weeks, and died—."

December 27: The birth of "Elena Adelaide" is registered in Naples with Percy Bysshe Shelley and Marina Padurin first listed as parents; the child's identity is undetermined—the illegitimate child of Percy or one he planned to adopt to replace Clara.

1819

March: The Shelleys relocate to Palazzo Verospi, Rome.

May: Percy begins *The Cenci* as Mary translates a manuscript for his use.

June 7: William dies of malaria in Rome; the Shelleys move to Leghorn, then Villa Valsovano, near Montenero.

August: Mary begins *Mathilda*.

October: The Shelleys and Claire relocate to 4395 Via Valfonda, Florence.

November 10: Claire leaves for Vienna.

November 12: The Shelleys' son Percy Florence is born; Mary writes to Marianne Hunt of the baby, "it is a bitter thought that all should be risked on one yet how much sweeter than to be childless as I was for 5 hateful months."

1820

January: The Shelleys move to Casa Frasi, Pisa.

March–April: Mary begins *Castruccio, Prince of Lucca*, which will be renamed *Valperga*; Percy publishes *The Cenci*.

April: Mary writes the drama *Proserpine*.

ca. May: Mary writes the drama *Midas*.

June: A former servant attempts blackmail with information regarding the mysterious infant Elena Adelaide.

June 10: Elena Adelaide dies.

June 15: The Shelleys move to Leghorn.

June 20: Mary writes to a friend in Rome requesting that for William, "a plain stone . . . be erected to mark the spot with merely his name & dates"; she later writes she "ought to have died on June 7 last."

August: The Shelleys move to Casa Prinni, Bagni San Giuliano; Percy publishes *Prometheus Unbound*.

October: The Shelleys reside at Palazzo Galetti, Pisa.

October 21: Percy's cousin Thomas Medwin visits.

November: The Shelleys meet Emilia Viviani, daughter of Pisa's governor and later Percy's love interest/infatuation.

1821

January 19: Medwin introduces the Shelleys to Edward and common-law wife Jane Williams.

February–March: Shelleys move to Casa Aulla, Pisa; Percy writes *Epipsychidion* for Emilia Viviani.

May: The Shelleys return to Bagni San Giuliano; Percy publishes *Epipsychidion*.

July: The first translation of *Frankenstein* is published in French.

August 10: Mary writes to Isabella Hoppner, "I am perfectly convinced, in my own mind that Shelley never had an improper connexion with Claire. . . . I swear by the life of . . . my blessed and beloved child, that I know these accusations to be false—."
August: Mary finishes *Valperga*.
October: The Shelleys return to Pisa.
November: Byron visits the Shelleys with his lover Teresa Guiciolli.

1822

January: Edward John Trelawny visits Pisa.
January 31: Mary offers to publish *Castruccio* to benefit Godwin; he accepts and the book will appear in 1823.
March: Mary writes to Claire of Byron, "No one can more entirely agree with you than I in thinking that . . . A [Allegra] ought to be taken out of the hands of one as remorseless as he is unprincipled."
April 19: Allegra Byron, Claire and Byron's daughter, dies.
April 30: The Shelleys relocate with the Williamses to Casa Magni, San Terenzo.
June 16: Mary miscarries; Percy saves her, stopping a hemorrhage by ice immersion.
July 1: Percy and Edward Williams set sail in Shelley's boat *Don Juan* to Leghorn to meet Leigh Hunt's family.
July 8: Percy and Williams drown in the Gulf of Spezia during their return.
July 15: Percy's and Williams's bodies wash to shore.
July 20: Mary and Jane Williams relocate to Pisa.
August 14 or 16: Percy's body is cremated at Viareggio.
August 21: Mary writes to an envoy in Tuscany, "It is my intention to forward the remains of him I have lost to Rome, to be buried there beside a darling boy whom we lost three years ago."
August 22: Mary writes to Maria Gisborne, "And so here I am! I continue to exist—to see one day succeed the other; to dread night; but more to dread morning & hail another cheerless day."
September 11: Mary relocates to Genoa and rents Casa Negroto.
September 17: Jane Williams leaves Mary to move to London with a letter of introduction to Thomas Jefferson Hogg.
September 20: Claire moves to Venice.
October 3: Byron moves to Genoa, lives in Casa Saluzzo.
October 4: The Hunt family relocates to Casa Negroto to be close to Mary.
October 15: Mary writes to Jane Williams, "write often my dear Jane. I would not that the chain that binds us should be snapped."

1823

January 21: Percy Bysshe Shelley's ashes are interred at Protestant Cemetery, Rome.
February 6: Sir Timothy Shelley refuses to support Mary and offers Byron the guardianship of Percy Florence if Mary will give up custody.
February 19: Mary publishes *Valperga*.
February 25: Mary officially refuses Sir Timothy's suggestion that she relinquish custody of Percy to Byron; she wrote to Byron on February 23 of the "insolent & hardhearted proposition about my poor boy" that it did "a little overcome my philosophy."
July: Mary writes the poem "The Choice," reflecting thoughts on suicide.
July 24: Byron and Edward Trelawny depart for Greece.
July 25: Mary and Percy Florence depart for England.
July 28: Drama by Richard Brinsley Peake, *Presumption; or the Fate of Frankenstein*, is staged for 37 performances.
August 12–20: Mary and Percy Florence visit Paris.
August 18: Drama by Henry M. Milner, *Frankenstein; or, the Demon of Switzerland*, is staged for eight performances.
August 25: Mary and Percy Florence arrive in London, live with the Godwins.
August 29: Mary watches a dramatic presentation of *Frankenstein*.
September 1: Drama, *Humgumption; or, Dr. Frankenstein and the Hobgoblin of Hoxton*, is staged for six performances.
   Drama, *Presumption and the Blue Demon*, is staged for two performances.
September 3: Mary receives a £100 advance for a new edition of *Frankenstein*.

September 8: Mary and Percy move to Brunswick Square.
September 11: Mary writes to Leigh Hunt of Isabel Baxter Booth, "I have now renewed my acquaintance with the friend of my girlish days.... The great affection she displays for me endears her to me & the memory of early days—."
October 20: Drama by Richard Brinsley Peake, *Another Piece of Presumption,* is staged for nine performances.
November 27: Mary receives an allowance from Sir Timothy for Percy, to be repaid.
Winter: Mary begins *The Last Man;* six characters resemble those in Shelley circle.

1824

January: Mary publishes "Recollections of Italy" in *London Magazine* (9: 21–26).
March 24: Mary publishes "On Ghosts" in the *London Magazine* (9: 253–256).
April: Mary publishes "The Bride of Modern Italy" in the *London Magazine* (9: 351–363).
April 19: Bryon dies in Greece.
April: Mary submits a tribute to Byron to *London Magazine*—it is not published.
May 16: Mary writes to Byron's lover Teresa Guiccioli, "Come dirvi che la pace vi attendera quando il tempo abbia guarito le piaghe del dolore, e provo che queste piaghe sono immediablile dal tempo?"
  [*translation*] "How can I tell you that peace awaits you when time has healed the wounds of pain, when I know that these wounds are incurable by time?"
June: Mary publishes *Posthumous Poems of Percy Bysshe Shelley;* Sir Timothy objects, threatens to cut allowance if more copies are sold.
June 21: The Shelleys move to 5 Bartholomew Place, Kentish Town, close to Jane Williams.
July 9: Mary attends Lord Byron's burial.
August: Sir Timothy offers £200 per annum allowance.
December 13: Drama, *Frank-in-Steam; or, The Modern Promise to Pay,* is staged for four performances.

1825

February 19: Mary requests of John Cam Hobhouse, a member of Parliament, to view a session to gain details for debate scenes in *The Last Man:* "I am engaged in a tale which will certainly be more defective than it would otherwise be, if I am not permitted to be present at a debate."
June 25: Actor, playwright, and composer John Howard Payne proposes marriage to Mary.
October: Trelawny is falsely accused in Greece as a traitor to the Greek cause and suffers a nonfatal pistol wound; Mary writes to the Honorary Secretary to the Greek Committee that "my sorrow for his pain will be diminished if . . . it will . . . [bring] him back to his English friends."

1826

January 23: Mary publishes *The Last Man.*
June 10: The Parisian drama *Le Monstre et le magician* is presented by Jean Toussaint Merle and Antoine Nicolas Beraud; there are 96 performances.
August: Mary spends time with Jane Williams.
September 14: Percy Florence inherits the baronetcy upon the death of Percy Bysshe and Harriett Shelley's son, Charles.
October 9: A translation by James Kerr of the drama *Le Monstre et le magicien,* by Jean Toussaint Merle and Antoine Nicolas Beraud, runs in London, for four performances.
October 30: Mary sends thanks to the editor and proprietor of *The Literary Souvenir* for an "elegant little volume" he has sent her, then adds "in consequence [of] my habit of withdrawing my name from public notice, I should be glad that my signature were not added to your interesting autographs."
December: Mary publishes "A Visit to Brighton" in *London Magazine.*

1827

Spring: Jane Williams labels herself Hogg's wife, although she is still married to her first husband.
May: Mary's allowance is now £250 per annum.
July: Jane Williams betrays Mary with false accusations as Mary writes to her, "It is a pleasant thing to turn in one's mind's eye to a friend's sweet home & know that there is tranquillity there."
July 13: Isabel Robinson informs Mary of Jane's stories characterizing Mary as cold and distant

from Percy just before death; Mary delays a confrontation with Jane until the following year.
July–October: Mary accompanies Isabel Robinson and Mary Diana Dods ("Mr. and Mrs. Walter Sholto Douglas") to Sompting, Arundle; she writes to Payne on September 25 requesting help in obtaining passports, describing the two women in comparison to herself.
September: Percy Florence begins school.

1828

February 11: Mary confronts Jane Williams, writing to her, "I have committed many faults . . . but for four years I committed not one fault towards you."
March 25 or 26: Percy Florence begins attending Edward Slater's Gentlemen's Academy in Kensington.
April 11: Mary visits Paris, contracts smallpox, meets Prosper Mérimée and General Lafayette.
May 16: Mary writes to Jane Williams, "I shall hide myself until the mask that disguises me disappears from before me" and adds, "pray come to me if you can."
June–August: Mary convalesces at Dover and Hastings.
August: Mary lives with Robinsons in Paddington.
October: Claire Claremont moves to London.
November 15: Mary meets with Trelawny.
December: Mary moves to her own residence
November/December: Mary publishes "The Sisters of Albano" and "Ferdinando Eboli: A Tale" in *The Keepsake*.

1829

May–January: Mary clandestinely helps Cyrus Redding to publish in Paris the Galignanis' edition of Percy Bysshe Shelley's poems; Redding requests to include excerpts from Shelley's letters to Horace Smith, she declines, labeling the letters "too confidential" and full of "such heterodox notions as might horrify many good folks."
June: Mary's allowance is increased to £300 per annum for Percy's support.
July: Mary publishes review, "Modern Italy," in the *Westminster Review* (2: 127–140).
September: Claire Claremont relocates to Dresden.

October: Mary publishes review, "Loves of the Poets," in the *Westminster Review*, (11: 472–477).
November: Mary publishes "The Mourner," "The Evil Eye," and "The False Rhyme" in *The Keepsake*.
December: Cyrus Redding edits and publishes a pirated Paris Galignani edition of *The Poetical Works of Coleridge, Shelley, and Keats*.

1830

January 19: Mary writes to John Murray of a Byron biography, "The great charm of the work to me . . . is that the Lord Byron I find there is our Lord Byron . . . I live with him again in these pages."
February: William Godwin, Jr., marries Emily Eldred.
May: Mary reviews William Godwin's *Cloudesley* in *Blackwood's Edinburgh Magazine* (28: 711–716).
May 13: Mary publishes *The Fortunes of Perkin Warbeck*.
November & December: Mary publishes two stories described as being by "The Author of Frankenstein" in *The Keepsake*: "Transformation" (18–39) and "The Swiss Peasant" (121–146); three poems also attributed to her: "Absence" (22), "Dirge" (85), and "A Night Scene" (147–148); she would include "Dirge" in a June 1835 letter to Maria Gisborne.

1831

Mary anonymously edits Trelawny's memoirs and assists in arranging for publication.
March: Mary teases Trelawny in a letter regarding possible marriage by her or Claire that would leave him alone; he replies that she should not "abandon me by following the evil examples of my other ladies. I should not wonder if fate, without our choice, united us."
November: Mary publishes the revised edition of *Frankenstein*.
November/December: Mary publishes "The Dream" in *The Keepsake* (22–38).
Mary publishes drama *Proserpine* in *The Winter's Wreath for 1832* (1–20).

1832

January: Mary ends her relationship with *Westminster Review* when publication of her review of Edward Bulwer-Lytton's *Eugene Aram* is refused.

June–September: Mary lives at Sandgate.
July 21–August 25: Thomas Medwin publishes "Memoirs of Shelley" in the *Athenæum*.
August 1: The Trelawnys visit Mary.
August: Percy Florence attends school at Harrow; Mary writes to Maria Gisborne, "Mr. Percy is gone back to school—I love the dear fellow more & more every day—he is my sole delight & comfort."
September 8: Mary's half brother William Godwin, Jr., dies of cholera.
November/December: Mary publishes a poem in *The Keepsake*: "Stanzas" (52); the issue contains two stories attributed to "The Author of Frankenstein": "The Brother and Sister: An Italian Story" (105–141) and "The Invisible Girl" (210–227).

1833

Mary publishes "The Smuggler and his Family" in *Original Compositions in Prose and Verse*.
May: Mary moves to Harrow.
May 4: William Godwin receives a sinecure position as Yeoman Usher of the Exchequer and moves to 15 New Palace Yard; Mary writes to John Murray that she feels "particularly kindly toward the Conservatives also just now as they have behaved with the greatest consideration towards my father—preserving him in his place, which was about to be abolished by the Whigs."
November/December: Mary publishes "The Mortal Immortal" in *The Keepsake*.

1834

April: The printer misplaces 36 pages from volume 3 of *Lodore*; Mary writes to the publisher Charles Ollier, "I am totally at a loss what to do—I cannot be mistaken as to the package I sent . . . I have no copy at all . . . the servants remember the fact perfectly"; she rewrites the pages by June.
November/December: Mary publishes "The Trial of Love," attributed to "The Author of Frankenstein," in *The Keepsake* (70–86).
Mary publishes "The Elder Son," in *Heath's Book of Beauty. 1835* (83–123).

1835

February: Mary publishes volume 1 of *Lives of the Most Eminent Literary and Scientific Men of Italy, Spain and Portugal*.

April 7: Mary publishes *Lodore*.
June 11: Mary writes to Maria Gisborne of her life's "sorrows and disappointments," adding that "every feeling I have is blighted—I have no ambition—no care for fame—Loneliness has made a wreck of me . . . I am left to myself—crushed by fortune—And I am nothing."
October: Mary publishes volume 2 of *Lives of the Most Eminent Literary and Scientific Men of Italy, Spain and Portugal*.

1836

February 4: Jane Williams Hogg gives birth to Prudentia Sarah Hogg; Mary will be her godmother.
April 7: William Godwin dies of catarrhal fever with Mary and Mary Jane Godwin at his side.
April 8: Mary writes to Mary Hays of her father's direction in his will to bury him as close to Mary Wollstonecraft as possible: "Her tomb in St. Pancras Church Yard was accordingly opened—at the depth of twelve feet her coffin was found uninjured—the cloth still over it—& the plate tarnished but legible."
April: Mary writes to gain her father's annuity for his widow and also plans for all income from publication of his papers to support Mary Jane Godwin
Mary relocates to Regents Park, London.
November/December: Mary publishes "The Parvenue" by "Mrs. Shelley" in *The Keepsake* (209–211).

1837

January: Mary delays publication of Godwin's memoirs to protect Percy Florence against the inevitable "cry . . . raised against his Mother."
January 26: Mary writes to Trelawney and concludes, "If you are still rich & can lend me 20 pounds till my quarter I shall be glad."
February: Mary publishes *Falkner* in 3 volumes.
October: Percy Florence begins study at Trinity College, Cambridge University.
November: Mary relocates to Grosvenor Square.
November/December: Mary publishes "The Pilgrims" in *The Keepsake* (128–155).

1838

ca. August: Sir Timothy Shelley relents regarding publication of Percy Bysshe Shelley's work.

August: Mary publishes volume 1 of *Lives of the Most Eminent Literary and Scientific Men of France.*

November/December: Mary publishes two poems in *The Keepsake:* "Stanzas" ("How like a star you rose upon my life") (179) and "Stanzas" ("O come to me in dreams, my love!") (201), as well as a story: "Euphrasia: A Tale of Greece" (135–152).

December 7: Mary writes to Edward Moxon, "It gives me great pleasure to publish Shelley's poems with you . . . as I believe the publication will have justice at your hands."

1839

January: Mary falls into a lingering illness.

January–May: *Poetical Works of Percy Bysshe Shelley* is published in four volumes.

Hogg criticizes lack of dedication to Harriett Shelley of *Queen Mab,* causing Mary to thank him for his "kindly expressed insinuations" and labels his criticism "poison," which "almost killed me at first—now I am used to it."

March: Mary lives in Putney.

August: Mary publishes volume 2 of *Lives of the Most Eminent Literary and Scientific Men of France.*

November: Mary publishes volume 1 of *Poetical Works of Percy Bysshe Shelley.*

December: Mary publishes Percy Bysshe Shelley's *Essays, Letters from Abroad, Translations and Fragments.*

1840

June–early January: Mary tours the Continent with Percy Florence and friends.

July 20: Mary writes to her Aunt Everina Wollstonecraft, describing the beauties of her journeys and of Lake Como, adding, "The mornings are devoted to study. The afternoons to boating etc.—I often suffer from the terror I have of any accident happening to Percy on the water. . . . There is something strange & dreamlike in returning to Italy after so many many years." She helps provide for her aunt until her death in 1843.

1841

January: Mary lives at 84 Park Street, London; Percy Florence graduates from Trinity College, upon which Sir Timothy gives him £1,400 per annum.

June 17: Death of Mary Jane Clairmont, who is buried with her husband and Mary Wollstonecraft in St. Pancras Graveyard; they will later be moved to Bournemouth, a marker referencing all three remains at Clairmont's grave.

1842

June–August 1843: Mary tours the Continent again with Percy Florence and friends.

October 2: Mary writes to Claire, "Charles Dickens has come home in a state of violent dislike of the Americans—& means to devour them in his next work—he says they are so frightfully dishonest." Mary regrets this, explaining that she does not particularly like the Germans, but she would never put that in print.

1843

September: Mary resides at White Cottage, Putney.

1844

April 24: Sir Timothy Shelley dies; Mary and Percy Florence inherit the estate, and Percy Florence inherits the title.

July: Mary publishes *Rambles in Germany and Italy.*

1845

September: Ferdinand Gatteschi attempts blackmail of Mary.

October: A man claiming to be George "Byron," son of the poet, attempts blackmail with forged letters and original letters, some of which Mary and Percy, John Moxon, and John Murray bought from him at auction. Mary dissuades him from publishing by threatening an injunction against him.

1846

ca. February 27: Mary writes to Thomas Hookham of George "Byron," "the Rascal's notes make me sick . . . Peacock says I did wrong to give any money—I am sure I did so in offering so much so readily."

ca. March: Mary relocates to Chester Square.

May: Mary writes to Thomas Medwin, "Your letter has surprised and pained me—I had no idea that you contemplated the work you mention . . . the time has not yet come to recount the events of my husband's life."

1847
July 11: Mary writes to Leigh Hunt, "I see Medwins [sic] "Life" advertized as about to be published . . . Of course it will be a most blackguard Publication—tho' I do not think he will make it as scandalous as he threatened . . . I had a letter from him in which he says he expects it 'to make a great hubbub.'"

1848
June 22: Sir Percy Florence Shelley marries Jane St. John.
August: The Shelleys relocate to Field Place.

1849
September: Mary travels to the Continent with the Shelleys.

1851
February 1: Mary Shelley dies at age 53 at Chester Square and is buried at St. Peter's, Bournemouth, near Percy and Jane Shelley's home; the remains of Mary's parents are removed to St. Peter's to satisfy Mary's wish to be buried with them.

1859
August 28: Leigh Hunt dies.

1862
August 21: Thomas Jefferson Hogg dies.

1879
March 19: Claire Clairmont dies.

1881
August 13: Edward John Trelawny dies.

1884
November: Jane Williams Hogg dies.

1886
The Life of Percy Bysshe Shelley is first published (Edward Downde, Kegan, Paul, Trench & Co.).

1889
December 5: Percy Florence Shelley dies; he is buried with Mary and her parents.

1899
June 24: Jane Shelley dies; she is buried with Percy Florence and other family members.

1922
Mary's drama *Midas* is first published, edited by André Henri Koszul; Koszul will write in his introduction to *Proserpine and Midas,* "as the great Shelley centenary year has come, perhaps this little monument of his wife's collaboration may take its modest place among the tributes which will be paid to his memory."

1959
Mathilda is first published (University of North Carolina Press).

1968
The Journals of Claire Clairmont is first published (edited by Marion Kingston Stocking with David Mackenzie Stocking; Harvard University Press).

1995
Selected Letters of Mary Wollstonecraft Shelley is first published (edited by Betty T. Bennett—Johns Hopkins University Press).

1996
First large collection of Mary's writings is published: *The Novels and Selected Works of Mary Shelley* in 8 volumes (Pickering and Chatto, 1996).

1997
Celebration of the bicentennial of Mary Shelley's birth.

Bibliography of Works by Mary Shelley

The following list does not include all writings by Mary Shelley—only those published works most often discussed by critics and available to readers and students. Not listed here are a few poems and fictional fragments never published on their own but incorporated into her novels or personal writings, as well as some relatively unimportant nonfictional works, including reviews of works published in her era. Some of these pieces are mentioned in scholarly studies, such as her short story for young readers, "Cecil," Shelley's only work to seriously consider a mother/son relationship. That original manuscript is part of the Abinger Collection at the Bodleian Library. More of Shelley's works continue to be uncovered, as discussed by Betty Bennett in "Newly Uncovered Letters and Poems by Mary Wollstonecraft Shelley" in the *Keats-Shelley Journal* in 1997. One example of a newly discovered work is *Maurice, or the Fisher's Cot*, a 39-page children's story written for the daughter of friends, discovered in 1997 by that family's descendant. Shelley's edited collections of Percy Shelley's works are included in this list because critics agree that their publication proved crucial in establishing him as a major English poet. The eight-volume *The Novels and Selected Works of Mary Shelley*, edited by Nora Crook (general editor) and Betty T. Bennett (consulting editor) offers an in-depth consideration of most of Shelley's works.

Shelley also contributed a biographical sketch of her father, William Godwin, to the 1831 reprint of Godwin's novel *Caleb Williams*. While she began work on a *Life of William Godwin*, it was not completed.

"Absence" (poem, 1830)
"Bride of Modern Italy, The" (short story, 1824)
"Brother and Sister: an Italian Story, The" (short story, 1832)
"Choice, A Poem on Shelley's Death, The" (poem, private printing, 1876)
Complete Poetical Works of Bysshe Shelley, The (edited collection, 1824)
"Dirge" (poem, 1830)
"Dream, The" (poem, 1831)
"Elder Son, The" (short story, 1834)
"English in Italy, The" (review, 1826)
Essays, Letters from Abroad, Translations and Fragments by Percy B. Shelley (edited collection, 1839)
"Euphrasia: A Tale of Greece" (short story, 1838)
"Evil Eye, The" (short story, 1829)
"False Rhyme, The" (short story, 1829)
Falkner (novel, 1837)
"Ferdinando Eboli: A Tale" (short story, 1828)
Fortunes of Perkin Warbeck, The (novel, 1830)
Frankenstein; or the Modern Prometheus (novel, 1818)
"Giovanni Villani" (essay, 1823)
History of Six Weeks Tour (with Percy Bysshe) (travelogue, 1817)
"How Like a Star" (poem, 1838)
"I must forget thy dark eyes" (poem, 1832)
"Invisible Girl, The" (short story, 1832)
Last Man, The (novel, 1826)
Lodore (novel, 1835)
Lives of the Most Eminent Literary and Scientific Men of France, Volume 1 (biography, 1838)

Lives of the Most Eminent Literary and Scientific Men of France, Volume 2 (biography, 1839)

Lives of the Most Eminent Literary and Scientific Men of Italy, Spain and Portugal, Volumes 1 and 2 (biography, 1835)

"Loves of the Poets" (review, 1829)

Mathilda (novella, written 1819, published 1959)

Midas (drama, written 1820, published 1922)

"Modern Italy" (review, 1829)

"Mortal Immortal, The" (short story, 1833)

"Mounseer Nongtongpaw" (juvenile poem, 1808)

"Mourner, The" (short story, 1829)

"Night Scene, A" (poem, 1830)

"O come to me in dreams, my love!" (poem, 1838)

"On Ghosts" (essay, 1824)

"On Reading Wordsworth's Lines on Peele Castle" (poem, 1825 journal entry, first printed, 1938)

"Parvenue, The" (short story, 1836)

"Pilgrims, The" (short story, 1837)

Poetical Works of Percy Bysshe Shelley, four volumes (edited collection, 1839)

Posthumous Poems of Percy Bysshe Shelley (edited collection, 1824)

Proserpine (drama, written 1820, published 1832)

Rambles in Germany and Italy (travelogue, 1844)

"Recollections of Italy" (essay, 1824)

"Review of William Godwin's Cloudesley, A" (review, 1830)

"Sisters of Albano, The" (short story, 1828)

"Smuggler and his Family, The" (short story, 1833)

"Stanzas" (poem, 1832)

"Swiss Peasant, The" (short story, 1830)

"Visit to Brighton, A" (essay, 1826)

"Transformation" (short story, 1830)

"Trial of Love, The" (short story, 1834)

Valperga (novel, 1823)

Selected Bibliography of Secondary Sources

Alkon, Paul K. *Science Fiction Before 1900: Imagination Discovers Technology*. New York: Twayne, 1994.

Backes, Anthony. "Revisiting *Frankenstein*: A Study in Reading and Education." *English Journal* 83, no. 4 (1994): 33–36.

Barker-Benefield, G. J. *The Culture of Sensibility: Sex and Society in Eighteenth-Century Britain*. Chicago: University of Chicago Press, 1992.

Batchelor, Rhonda. "The Rise and Fall of Eighteenth Century's Authentic Feminine Voice." *Eighteenth-Century Fiction*. 4 (1994): 347–368.

Bennett, Betty T., and Charles E. Robinson, ed. *The Mary Shelley Reader*. New York: Oxford University Press, 1990.

Bleiler, Everett F. *Science-Fiction: The Early Years. A Full Description of More Than 3,000 Science-Fiction Stories from Earliest Times to the Appearance of the Genre Magazines in 1930*. Kent, Ohio: Kent State University Press, 1990.

Bloom, Harold, ed. *Mary Shelley: Modern Critical Views*. New York: Chelsea House, 1985.

Bowerbank, Sylvia. "The Social Order vs. The Wretch: Mary Shelley's Contradictory-Mindedness in *Frankenstein*." *ELH: English Literary History* 46 (Fall 1979): 418–431.

Copley, Stephen, and John Whale, eds. *Beyond Romanticism: New Approach to Texts and Contexts, 1780–1832*. London: Routledge, 1992.

Cronin, Richard. *The Politics of Romantic Poetry: In Search of the Pure Commonwealth*. New York: Palgrave McMillan, 2000.

Cunningham, Andrew, and Nicholas Jardine, eds. *Romanticism and the Sciences*. Cambridge: Cambridge University Press, 1990.

Dunn, Jane. *Moon in Eclipse—A Life of Mary Shelley*. London: Weidenfeld & Nicolson, 1978.

Eagleton, Terry. *Literary Theory: An Introduction*. Minneapolis: University of Minnesota Press, 1983.

Eichner, Hans. "The Rise of Modern Science and the Genesis of Romanticism." *PMLA* 97 (1982): 18–30.

Forbes, Joan. "Anti-romantic Discourse as Resistance: Women's Fiction 1775–1820." In *Romance Revisited*, edited by Lynne Pearce and Jackie Stacey, 293–305. New York: New York University Press, 1995.

Frank, Frederick S. "Mary Shelley's *Frankenstein*: A Register of Research." *Bulletin of Bibliography* 40 (September 1983): 163–188.

Gaull, Marilyn. *English Romanticism: The Human Context*. New York: Norton, 1988.

Gerson, Noel B. *Daughter of Earth and Water: A Biography of Mary Wollstonecraft Shelley*. New York: Morrow, 1973.

Gilbert, Sandra. "Horror's Twin: Mary Shelley's Monstrous Eve." *Feminist Studies* 4, no. 2 (June 1978): 48–73.

Gilbert, Sandra, and Susan Gubar. *The Madwoman in the Attic*. New Haven, Conn.: Yale University Press, 1979.

Grylls, Rosalie Glynn. *Mary Shelley*. New York: Oxford University Press, 1938.

Haskell, Francis. "The Shelley Memorial." *Oxford Art Journal* 1 (1978): 3–6.

Helene-Huet, Marie. *Monstrous Imagination*. Cambridge, Mass.: Harvard University Press, 1993.

Hitchcock, Susan Tyler. *A Cultural History of Frankenstein*. New York: W. W. Norton, 2007.

Hodges, Devon. "*Frankenstein* and the Feminine Subversion of the Novel." *Tulsa Studies in Women's Literature* 2 (Autumn 1983): 155–164.

Homans, Margaret. *Bearing the Word: Language and Female Experience in Nineteenth Century Women's Writing.* Chicago: University of Chicago Press, 1986.

Hustis, Harriett. "Responsible Creativity and the 'Modernity' of Mary Shelley's Prometheus." *Studies in English Literature, 1500–1900.* 43, no. 4 (Autumn 2003): 845–858.

Jacobus, Mary, Evelyn Fox Keller, and Sally Shuttleworth. Introduction to *Body Politics: Women and the Discourse of Science*, edited by Mary Jacobus, Evelyn Fox Keller, and Sally Shuttleworth, 1–10. New York: Routledge, 1990.

Jacobus, Mary. "Is There a Woman in This Text?" *New Literary History* 14 (Autumn 1982): 117–141. Republished in Jacobus, *Reading Woman.* New York: Columbia University Press, 1986.

Johnson, Barbara. "My Monster/My Self." *Diacritics* 12 (Summer 1982): 2–10.

Jones, Frederick. "The Letters of Mary Shelley in the Bodleian Library." *Bodleian Quarterly* 8 (Spring, Summer, Autumn 1937): 29–310, 360–371, 412–420.

———, ed. *Mary Shelley's Journal.* Norman: University of Oklahoma Press, 1947.

Keller, Evelyn Fox. "Feminism and Science." *Signs* 7, no. 3 (1982): 598–602.

———. *Reflections on Gender and Science.* New Haven, Conn.: Yale University Press, 1985.

Kiely, Robert. *The Romantic Novel in England.* Cambridge, Mass.: Harvard University Press, 1972.

Lederer, Susan E. *Frankenstein: Penetrating the Secrets of Nature.* Newark, N.J.: Rutgers University Press, 2002.

Lefanu, Sarah. *Feminism and Science Fiction.* Bloomington: Indiana University Press, 1989.

Levine, George, and U. C. Knopeflmacher, eds. *The Endurance of Frankenstein.* Berkeley & Los Angeles: University of California Press, 1979.

Lyles, W. H. *Mary Shelley: An Annotated Bibliography.* New York: Garland, 1975.

Marshall, Florence A. *The Life and Letters of Mary Wollstonecraft Shelley.* 2 vols. London: Bentley, 1889.

Martin, Philip W., and Robin Jarvis, eds. *Reviewing Romanticism.* New York: Palgrave McMillan, 1992.

McInerny, Peter. "*Frankenstein* and the Godlike Science of Letters." *Genre* 13 (Winter 1980): 455–475.

Mellor, Anne K. "A Novel of Their Own: Romantic Women's Fiction, 1790–1830." In *The Columbia History of the British Novel*, edited by John Richetti, 327–351. New York: Columbia University Press, 1994.

———. *Romanticism and Gender.* London: Routledge, 1992.

Mishra, Vijay. *The Gothic Sublime.* Albany: State University of New York Press, 1994.

Moore, Helen. *Mary Wollstonecraft Shelley.* Philadelphia: Lippincott, 1886.

Nitchey, Elizabeth. *Mary Shelley—Author of Frankenstein.* New Brunswick, N.J.: Rutgers University Press, 1953.

Poovey, Mary. "'My Hideous Progeny': Mary Shelley and the Feminization of Romanticism." *PMLA* 95, no. 3 (May 1980): 332–347.

———. "The Proper Lady and the Woman Writer: Ideology as Style in the Works of Mary Wollstonecraft, Mary Shelley, and Jane Austen." *Modern Philology* 83, no. 4 (May 1986): 434–437.

Randel, Fred V. "*Frankenstein*, Feminism and the Intertextuality of Mountains." *Studies in Romanticism.* 23 (Winter 1984): 515–533.

———. "'The Political Geography of Horror in Mary Shelley's 'Frankenstein.'" *ELH: English Literary History* 70, no. 2 (Summer 2003): 465–491.

Rubenstein, Marc A. "My Accursed Origin: The Search for the Mother in *Frankenstein.*" *Studies in Romanticism* 15 (Spring 1976): 165–194.

Ryan, Robert M. *The Romantic Reformation: Religious Politics in English Literature, 1789–1824.* Cambridge: Cambridge University Press, 1997.

Schor, Esther, ed. *The Cambridge Companion to Mary Shelley.* Cambridge: Cambridge University Press, 2004.

Selden, Raman, Peter Widdowson, and Peter Brooker. *A Reader's Guide to Contemporary Literary Theory.* 5th ed. New York: Prentice Hall/Harvester Wheatsheaf, 2005.

Shelley, Jane Gibson, Lady. *Shelley Memorials.* Boston: Ticknor and Fields, 1859.

Shelley, Mary. *Frankenstein: The 1818 Text, Contexts, Nineteenth-Century Response, Modern Criticism.* Edited by Paul J. Hunter. New York: W. W. Norton, 1995.

———. *Frankenstein: Complete, Authoritative Text with Biographical, Historical, and Cultural Contexts, Critical History, and Essays from Contemporary Critical Perspectives.* 2nd ed. Edited by Johanna M. Smith. Boston: Bedford/St. Martin's, 2000.

———. *Mary Shelley: Collected Tales and Stories with Original Engravings.* Edited by Charles E. Robinson. Baltimore: Johns Hopkins University Press, 1990.

Spark, Muriel. *Child of Light—A Reassessment of Mary Wollstonecraft Shelley.* Hadleigh, Essex, U.K.: Tower Bridge Publications, 1951. Revised as *Mary Shelley—A Biography.* New York: Dutton, 1987.

Spector, Judith A. "Science Fiction and the Sex War: A Womb of One's Own." *Literature and Psychology* 31 (1981): 21–32.

Sterrenburg, Lee. "*The Last Man*: Anatomy of Failed Revolutions." *Nineteenth-Century Fiction* 33 (December 1978): 324–347.

Stone, Lawrence. *The Family, Sex and Marriage in England 1500–1800.* London: Weidenfeld and Nicolson, 1977.

Sunstein, Emily W. *Mary Shelley: Romance and Reality.* Baltimore: Johns Hopkins University Press, 1991.

Thompson, E. P. *The Making of the English Working Class.* New York: Vintage, 1963.

Tillotson, Kathleen. *Novels of the Eighteen-Forties.* Oxford, U.K.: Clarendon Press, 1954.

Tropp, Martin. *Mary Shelley's Monster.* Boston: Houghton Mifflin, 1976.

Ty, Eleanor. "Mary Wollstonecraft Shelley." Available online. URL: http://people.brandeis.edu/~teuber/shelleybio.html#MainEssaySection. Accessed November 30, 2008.

Veeder, William. *Mary Shelley & Frankenstein: The Fate of Androgyny.* Chicago: University of Chicago Press, 1986.

Vincent, E. R. P. "Two Letters from Mary Shelley to Gabriele Rossetti." *Modern Language Review* 27, no. 4 (October 1932): 459–461.

Walling, William. *Mary Shelley.* New York: Twayne, 1972.

Ward, Geoff, ed. *A Guide to Romantic Literature, 1780–1830.* London: Bloomsbury, 1994.

Weiskel, Thomas. *The Romantic Sublime.* Baltimore: Johns Hopkins University Press, 1976.

Wilson, Carol Shiner, and Joel Haefner, eds. *Revisioning Romanticism: British Women Writers, 1776–1837.* Philadelphia: University of Pennsylvania Press, 1994.

Sources

Bennett, Betty T. *Mary Wollstonecraft Shelley: An Introduction.* Baltimore: Johns Hopkins University Press, 1995.

Lawson, Shannon. "A Chronology of the Life of Mary Shelley." *Romantic Circles.* Available online. URL: http://www.rc.umd.edu/reference/chronologies/mschronology/chrono.html Accessed June 24, 2009.

Shelley, Mary Wollstonecraft. *Selected Letters of Mary Wollstonecraft Shelley.* Edited by Betty T. Bennett. Baltimore: Johns Hopkins University Press, 1995.